Estimating Software Costs

Estimating Software Costs

T. Capers Jones

McGraw-Hill

New York   San Francisco   Washington, D.C.   Auckland   Bogotá
Caracas   Lisbon   London   Madrid   Mexico City   Milan
Montreal   New Delhi   San Juan   Singapore
Sydney   Tokyo   Toronto

Library of Congress Cataloging-in-Publication Data

Jones, T. Capers.
    Estimating software costs / Capers Jones.
       p.   cm.
    Includes index.
    ISBN 0-07-913094-1
    1. Computer software—Costs.   I. Title.
QA76.76.C73J66   1998
005.3'068'1—dc21   98-16287
                                    CIP

McGraw-Hill

A Division of The McGraw-Hill Companies

1 2 3 4 5 6 7 8 9 0   DOC/DOC   9 0 3 2 1 0 9 8

ISBN 0-07-9130941

The sponsoring editor for this book was Simon Yates, the editing supervisor was Bernard Onken, and the production supervisor was Sherri Souffrance. It was set in Century Schoolbook by Victoria Khavkina of McGraw-Hill's Professional Book Group composition unit.

Printed and bound by R. R. Donnelley & Sons Company.

McGraw-Hill books are available at special quantity discounts to use as premiums and sales promotions, or for use in corporate training programs. For more information, please write to the Director of Special Sales, McGraw-Hill, 11 West 19th Street, New York, NY 10011. Or contact your local bookstore.

 This book is printed on recycled, acid-free paper containing a minimum of 50% recycled, de-inked fiber.

Contents

Preface   xiii
Acknowledgments   xvii

Section 1   Introduction to Software Cost Estimation

Chapter 1. Introduction   3

How Software Cost-Estimating Tools Work   4
Cautions About Accidental Omissions from Estimates   15
Software Cost Estimating and Other Development Activities   17
Literature on Software Cost Estimating   20
References   22

Chapter 2. The Origins of Software Cost Estimation   25

References   35

Chapter 3. Features of Commercial Software Cost Estimating Tools   37

References   48

Chapter 4. Six Forms of Software Cost Estimation   49

Manual Software-Estimating Methods   49
Automated Software-Estimating Methods   49
Overview of Manual Software-Estimating Methods   50
Overview of Automated Software-Estimating Methods   52
References   66

Chapter 5. Software Cost Estimating and Other Project Management Tools   69

Available Software Management Tools   73
Emerging Software Management Tools   88

Summary and Conclusions   90
References   91

Chapter 6. Patterns of Project Management Tool Usage by Industry and Project Size   **93**

Management Information System (MIS) Projects   93
Outsourced or Contracted Projects   95
End-User Software Applications   96
Commercial Software Projects   96
Systems Software Projects   97
Military Software Projects   99
Overall Project Management Tool Usage Patterns   100
Software-Estimating and Project Management Tool Usage by
Application Size   101
Software Management Tools and Software Project Size   104
References   111

Chapter 7. Software Cost Estimating Tools and Project Success and Failure Rates   **113**

Predictive Estimation Methods Correlating with Successful
Software Projects   114
Measurement Methods Correlating with Successful Software Projects   115
Probabilities of Software Project Success or Failure   116
References   120

Chapter 8. Investment Costs and Return on Investment (ROI) for Software Project Management Tools   **121**

References   127

Chapter 9. Sources of Error in Software Cost Estimation   **129**

Judging the Accuracy of Software Cost Estimates   134
Classes of Software Estimation Errors   137
Range of Impact of Estimating Errors   152
References   156

Chapter 10. Software Project Management in the Twenty-First Century **157**

Integration of Project Management Tool Suites   157
Internet-Enabled Estimation and Benchmarking Services   158
Data Metrics, Data Estimation, and Data Quality   159
Estimation and Planning of Mixed Hardware, Software, and
Microcode Projects   161
Enterprise Estimation   162
Process-Improvement Estimation   164
Outsource Estimation   165
Management War Game Tools   166

Estimation on Handheld Computers   166
Summary and Conclusions   167
Suggested Readings   167

Section 2   Preliminary Estimation Methods

Chapter 11. Manual Software Estimating Methods   173

Rules of Thumb Based on Lines-of-Code (LOC) Metrics   174
Rules of Thumb Based on Ratios and Percentages   177
Rules of Thumb Based on Function Point Metrics   181
Design Goals of Function Point Metrics   182
Function Point Sizing Rules of Thumb   184
Rules of Thumb for Schedules, Resources, and Costs   199
Rules of Thumb Using Activity-Based Cost Analysis   204
Rules of Thumb for Year-2000 Repair Estimation   210
Rules of Thumb for Eurocurrency Conversion   212
Summary and Conclusions   213
References   215

Chapter 12. Automated Estimates from Minimal Data   217

Stage 1: Recording Administrative and Project Information   218
Stage 2: Preliminary Sizing of Key Deliverables   234
Stage 3: Producing a Preliminary Cost Estimate   257
Summary and Conclusions   262
References   263

Section 3   Sizing Software Deliverables

Chapter 13. Sizing Software Deliverables   267

General Sizing Logic for Key Deliverables   269
Sizing Based on Function Point Analysis of Software Applications   270
Volume of Function Point Data Available   280
Backfiring—Direct Conversion from Lines of Code to Function Points 283
The International Organization of Standards (ISO) Functional Size Standard   287
Software Complexity Analysis   288
Software Sizing with Reusable Components   300
Overview of the Basic Principles of Function Point Metrics   302
Function Point Complexity Adjustments   310
SPR Function Point Complexity Adjustment Factors   314
Source Code Sizing   317
Sizing Object-Oriented Software Projects   323
Sizing Text-Based Paper Documents   325
Sizing Graphics and Illustrations   331
Sizing Bugs or Defects   334
Sizing Test Cases   342

The Event Horizon for Sizing Software Artifacts   344
What Is Known as a Result of Sizing Software Projects   346
Strengths and Weaknesses of Software Size Metrics   347
Summary and Conclusions   351
References   351

Section 4   Cost Estimating Adjustment Factors

Chapter 14. Compensation and Work Pattern Adjustments   357

Setting Up the Initial Conditions for a Cost Estimate   364
Variations in Burden Rates or Overhead Costs   370
Variations in Work Habits and Unpaid Overtime   373
References   379

Chapter 15. Activity Pattern Adjustment Factors   381

References   388

Chapter 16. Software Technology Adjustment Factors   391

Adjustment Factors and Macroestimation Tools   392
Factors That Influence Software Development Productivity   397
Factors That Influence Software Maintenance Productivity   400
Patterns of Positive and Negative Factors   403
Adjustment Factors and Microestimation Tools   406
References   419

Section 5   Activity-Based Software Cost Estimating

Chapter 17. Estimating Software Requirements   423

Function Points and Software Requirements   430
Primary Topics for Software Requirements   436
Secondary Topics for Software Requirements   437
Positive and Negative Requirements Adjustment Factors   438
Requirements and End-User Software   441
Requirements and Management Information Systems (MIS) Projects   441
Requirements and Outsourced Projects   442
Requirements and Systems Software   442
Requirements and Commercial Software   443
Requirements and Military Software Projects   444
Evaluating Combinations of Requirements Factors   445
References   448

Chapter 18. Estimating Software Prototypes   449

Disposable Prototypes   452
Time-Box Prototypes   453

Evolutionary Prototypes   454
Default Values for Estimating Disposable Prototypes   456
Positive and Negative Factors That Influence Software Prototypes   459
References   462

Chapter 19. Estimating Software Specifications and Design   463

Positive Design Adjustment Factors   468
Negative Design Adjustment Factors   469
References   472

Chapter 20. Estimating Design Inspections   475

References   486

Chapter 21. Estimating Programming or Coding   487

The Impact of Reusability on Programming   494
The Impact of Experience on Programming   496
The Impact of Bugs or Errors on Programming   496
The Impact of Unpaid Overtime on Programming   498
The Impact of Creeping Requirements on Programming   500
The Impact of Code Structure and Complexity on Programming   501
The Impact of Unplanned Interruptions on Programming   502
The Impact of Application Size on Programming   503
The Impact of Office Space and Ergonomics on Programming   504
The Impact of Tools on Programming   505
The Impact of Programming Languages on Programming   506
The Impact of Schedule Pressure on Programming   509
References   509

Chapter 22. Estimating Code Inspections   511

References   519

Chapter 23. Estimating Software Configuration Control and
Change Management   521

Changes in User Requirements   527
Changes in Specifications and Design   529
Changes Due to Bugs or Defect Reports   530
Summary and Conclusions   531
References   531

Chapter 24. Estimating Software Testing   533

General Forms of Software Testing   537
Specialized Forms of Software Testing   540
Forms of Testing Involving Users or Clients   543

Number of Testing Stages   545
Testing Pattern Variations by Industry and Type of Software   546
Testing Pattern Variations by Size of Application   548
Testing Stages Noted in Lawsuits Alleging Poor Quality   549
Using Function Points to Estimate Test-Case Volumes   550
Using Function Points to Estimate the Numbers of Test Personnel   552
Testing and Defect-Removal Efficiency Levels   554
Using Function Points to Estimate Testing Effort and Costs   555
Testing by Developers or by Professional Test Personnel   557
Factors That Affect Testing Performance   559
References   560

Chapter 25. Estimating User and Project Documentation   563

References   570

Chapter 26. Estimating Software Project Management   573

The Roles of Software Project Management   576
Project Managers Who Are Also Technical Contributors   579
Project Management for Hybrid Projects Involving Hardware and Software   579
Project Management and External Schedule Pressures   580
Project Management Tools   581
Project Management on Large Systems with Many Managers   582
Time-Splitting, or Managing Several Projects Simultaneously   584
The Span of Control, or Number of Staff Members per Manager   585
Managing Multiple Occupation Groups   586
The Presence or Absence of Project Offices for Large Systems   589
Experience Levels of Software Project Managers   589
Quality-Control Methods Selected by Project Managers   589
References   590

Section 6   Maintenance and Enhancement Cost Estimating

Chapter 27. Maintenance and Enhancement Estimating   595

Nominal Default Values for Maintenance and Enhancement Activities   599
Major Enhancements   600
Minor Enhancements   602
Maintenance (Defect Repairs)   603
Warranty Repairs   607
Customer Support   608
Error-Prone Module Removal   609
Mandatory Changes   611
Complexity Analysis   611
Code Restructuring   613
Performance Optimization   614
Migration Across Platforms   614

Conversion to New Architectures   615
Reverse Engineering   615
Reengineering   616
Restructuring   616
Dead Code Removal   617
Dormant Application Removal   617
Nationalization   618
Year-2000 Repairs   618
Eurocurrency Conversion   624
Retirement or Withdrawal of Applications   627
Field Service   627
Combinations and Concurrent Maintenance Operations   628
References   635

Appendix A. Biographies of Software Estimation Pioneers   637

Barry Boehm's Interest in Software Cost Estimating   638
T. Capers Jones's Interest in Software Cost Estimating   643
Larry Putnam's Interest in Software Cost Estimating   656

Appendix B. Software Cost Estimating Vendors and Associations   679

Software Cost Estimating Associations   679
Software Cost Estimating Vendors   681

Appendix C. Annotated Bibliography of Software Estimation   701

Index   711

Preface

Readers should be aware that this is a book about software cost estimating written by someone who is in the software cost estimating business. Since my company builds and sells software-estimating tools, I have an obvious interest in the topic. But this is not just a book about how my company's estimating tools work. The domain of software cost estimating is an important one, and this book attempts to include the general principles under which all commercial software cost estimating tools operate.

Collecting historical data and designing and building software cost estimating tools have been my main occupations since 1971. My estimation work started at IBM when a colleague and I were asked to collect data about the factors that affected software costs.

After spending a year on collecting cost data within IBM and reviewing the external literature on software costs, it seemed possible to construct a rule-based automated estimating tool that could predict software effort, schedules, and costs for the main activities of IBM's systems software development projects; that is, requirements, design, design reviews, coding, code inspections, testing, user documentation, and project management.

A proposal was given to IBM senior management to fund the development of a software cost estimating tool. The proposal was accepted, and work commenced in 1972. From that point on I've designed and built a dozen software cost estimating tools for individual companies or for the commercial estimating market. The purpose of this book is to show some of the kinds of information needed to build software cost models, and to present an insider's view of the cost-estimating business.

This book is not a sales or marketing treatise. The book tries to cover the fundamental issues involved with software cost estimating. Indeed, a number of other estimating and metrics specialists have contributed ideas and information and are cited many times. The work of such other estimating specialists as Allan Albrecht, Dr. Barry Boehm, Frank Freiman, Dr. Randall Jensen, Larry Putnam, Dr. Howard

Rubin, and Charles Symons are discussed, although as competitors we do not often share proprietary information with each other.

In my view and also in the view of my competitors, accurate software cost estimating is important to the global economy. Every software project manager, every software quality assurance specialist, and many software engineers, systems analysts, and programmers should understand the basic concepts of software cost estimation— but comparatively few do. This is a view shared by all of the commercial software cost estimating vendors.

All of us in the commercial software cost estimating business know dozens of manual estimating algorithms. All of us in the cost-estimating business use manual estimating methods from time to time on small projects, but not one of us regards manual estimation methods as being sufficient for handling the full life-cycle estimates of major software projects. If manual methods sufficed, there would be no commercial software-estimating tools.

The software industry has achieved a notorious reputation as being out of control in terms of schedule accuracy, cost accuracy, and quality control. Estimating, planning, and quality control are so bad that a majority of large systems run late and exceed their budgets, and many are canceled without ever reaching completion.

It is an interesting phenomenon that most of the major overruns and software disasters are built upon careless and grossly optimistic cost estimates, usually done manually. Projects that use formal estimating tools, such as the competitive tools COCOMO, GECOMO, REVIC, SLIM, PRICE-S, ProQMS, SoftCost, or my company's tools (SPQR/20, CHECKPOINT, or KnowledgePlan), have much better track records of staying within their budgets and actually finishing the project without serious mishap.

Of course, readers need to be aware that this statement is being made by an author who is also an estimating-tool vendor; and therefore, they should seek independent confirmation that automated estimation is superior to manual estimation for large software projects.

The reason that manual estimating methods fail for large systems can be expressed in a single word: *complexity*. There are hundreds of factors that determine the outcome of a software project, and it is not possible to deal with the combinations of these factors using simple algorithms and manual methods.

This book illustrates the kinds of complex estimating problems that triggered the creation of the cost-estimating and software project management tool subindustries. The problems of large-system estimation are the main topic of concern, although estimating methods for small projects are discussed, too.

Estimation is not the only project management function that now has automated support. The book also attempts to place the subject of estimation tools in context with other kinds of project management tools, and to point out gaps where additional kinds of tools are needed.

As the century ends, software cost estimating tools are now part of a suite of software project management tools that includes cost estimating, quality estimating, schedule planning (often termed *project management*), methodology or process management, risk analysis, departmental budgeting, milestone tracking, cost reporting, and variance analysis.

These disparate tools have not yet reached the level of sophisticated and seamless integration that has been achieved in the domain of word processing coupled with spreadsheets, databases, and graphical tools, but that level of integration is on the horizon.

Because software cost estimating is a very complex activity involving scores of factors and hundreds of adjustments, this book has a fairly complex structure. It is divided into 6 main sections and 27 individual chapters plus 3 appendixes.

Section 1 includes an introduction to the topic of software cost estimation, and a survey of the features of software cost estimating tools. Section 1 also covers the business aspects of software project management, such as how much tools are likely to cost and what kind of value they create. Section 1 assumes no prior knowledge on the part of the reader.

Section 2 deals with several methods for creating early estimates, long before a project's requirements are completely understood. Early estimation from partial knowledge is one of the most difficult forms of estimation, and yet one of the most important. Far too often, early estimates end up being "engraved in stone" or becoming the official estimate for a software project.

This section discusses both manual estimating methods using rules of thumb and the somewhat more sophisticated preliminary estimating methods offered by commercial software-estimating tools.

Section 3 deals with the methods of sizing various software artifacts. All commercial software-estimating tools need some form of size information in order to operate, and there are a surprisingly large number of ways for dealing with size.

As this book is being written, sizing based on function point metrics is dominant in the software estimating world, but sizing based on lines of code, and on less tangible materials, also occurs.

Section 4 deals with how software cost estimating tools handle adjustment factors. There are more than 100 known factors that can influence the outcomes of software projects, including the capabilities of the team, the presence or absence of overtime, the methodologies and tools used, and even office space and ergonomics.

Although commercial software cost estimating tools offer default values for many important topics, the ranges of uncertainty are so great that users are well advised to replace generic "industry averages" with specific values from their own enterprises for key parameters, such as average salary levels, burden rates, staff experience levels, and other factors which can exert a major impact on final results.

Section 5 deals with the principles of activity-based cost estimation for 10 activities which occur with high frequency on many software projects:

1. Requirements gathering and analysis
2. Prototyping
3. Specifications and design
4. Formal design inspections
5. Coding
6. Formal code inspections
7. Change management, or configuration control
8. User documentation
9. Testing
10. Project management

There are, of course many more than 10 activities, but these 10 were selected because they occur with high frequency on a great many software projects. Unless the estimates for these 10 activities are accurate, there is little hope for accuracy at the gross project level.

Section 6 deals with the principles of activity-based cost estimating for 21 kinds of maintenance and enhancement activities. Maintenance estimating is far more complex than development estimating, since the age and structure of the base application has a severe impact.

There are also a number of very specialized kinds of maintenance estimating that can be quite expensive when they occur, but do not occur with high frequency—error-prone module removal, field service, and dealing with *abeyant* defects, which occur when a user runs an application but cannot be replicated at the maintenance repair facility. Section 6 also deals with several new forms of maintenance that are extremely costly—year-2000 repairs and Euro-currency conversion.

Appendix A provides biographical information for some of the software cost estimating pioneers. Although all pioneers who had built estimating tools prior to 1985 were invited to participate, only Dr. Barry Boehm and Larry Putnam were able to do so, in addition to the author of this book.

Appendix B contains information on how to contact the major vendors of software cost estimation tools.

Appendix C contains an annotated bibliography of works on software estimation.

T. Capers Jones

Acknowledgments

As always many thanks to my wife, Eileen Jones, for making this book possible in many ways. She handles all of our publishing contracts, and by now knows the details of these contracts as well as some attorneys. Thanks also for her patience when I get involved in writing and disappear into our computer room. Also thanks for her patience on holidays and vacations when I take my portable computer.

Appreciation is due to Dave Shough, a colleague at IBM who helped me collect data for my first estimating tool. Thanks, too, to Dr. Charles Turk, another IBM colleague and a world-class APL expert, who built the first estimating tool that I designed. Appreciation is due to the late Ted Climis of IBM, who sponsored much of my research on software costs.

Special appreciation is due to Jim Frame, who passed away in October 1997 just as this manuscript was being finished. Jim was the Director of IBM's Languages and Data Facilities laboratories, and the immediate sponsor of my first studies on software cost estimation. Jim was later ITT's vice president of programming, where he also supported software cost estimation research. The software industry lost a leading figure with his passing. Jim's vision of the important role software plays in modern business inspired all who knew him.

Great appreciation is due to all of my colleagues at Software Productivity Research for their aid in gathering the data, assisting our clients, building the tools that we use, and for making SPR an enjoyable environment. Special thanks to the families and friends of the SPR staff, who have had to put up with lots of travel and far too much overtime. Thanks to Mark Beckley, Ed Begley, Chuck Berlin, Barbara Bloom, Julie Bonaiuto, William Bowen, Michael Bragen, Doug Brindley, Kristin Brooks, Tom Cagley, Sudip Charkraboty, Craig Chamberlin, Michael Cunnane, Chas Douglis, Charlie Duczakowski, Gail Flaherty, Richard Gazoorian, James Glorie, David Gustafson, Bill Harmon, Bob Haven, Steve Hone, Jan Huffman, Peter Katsoulas,

Richard Kauffold, John Mulcahy, Phyllis Nissen, Jacob Okyne, Donna O'Donnel, Mark Pinis, Tom Riesmeyer, Janet Russac, Cres Smith, John Smith, Judy Sommers, Bill Walsh, and John Zimmerman. Thanks also to Ajit Maira and Dick Spann for their service on SPR's board of directors.

Thanks also to former long-time colleagues who have now retired or changed jobs: Lynne Caramanica, Debbie Chapman, Carol Chiungos, Jane Greene, Wayne Hadlock, Shane Hartman, Heather McPhee, Scott Moody, and Richard Ward. Thanks for both the years of help and the many long hours. Scott, Richard, and later Shane put in far too much overtime in building our first estimating tools.

Many other colleagues work with us at SPR on special projects or as consultants. Special thanks to Allan Albrecht, the inventor of function points, for his invaluable contribution to the industry and for his outstanding work with SPR. Without Allan's pioneering work in function points, the ability to create accurate baselines and benchmarks would probably not exist.

Many thanks to Hisashi Tomino and his colleagues at Kozo Keikaku Engineering in Japan. Kozo has translated several of my prior books into Japanese. In addition, Kozo has been instrumental in the introduction of function point metrics into Japan by translating some of the relevant function point documents.

Much appreciation is due to the client organizations whose interest in software assessments, benchmarks and baselines, measurement, and process improvements have let us work together. These are the organizations whose data make estimation tools possible.

There are too many groups to name them all, but many thanks to our colleagues and clients at Andersen Consulting, AT&T, Bachman, Bellcore, Bell Northern Research, Bell Sygma, Bendix, British Air, CBIS, Charles Schwab, Church of the Latter Day Saints, Cincinnati Bell, CODEX, Credit Suisse, DEC, Dunn & Bradstreet, Du Pont, EDS, Finsiel, Ford Motors, Fortis Group, General Electric, General Motors, GTE, Hartford Insurance, Hewlett-Packard, IBM, Informix, Inland Steel, Internal Revenue Service, ISSC, JC Penney, JP Morgan, Kozo Keikaku, Language Technology, Litton, Lotus, Mead Data Central, McKinsey Consulting, Microsoft, Motorola, Nippon Telegraph, NCR, Northern Telecom, Nynex, Pacific Bell, Ralston Purina, Sapiens, Sears Roebuck, Siemens-Nixdorf, Software Publishing Corporation, SOGEI, Sun Life, Tandem, TRW, UNISYS, U.S. Air Force, U.S. Navy Surface Weapons groups, US West, Wang, Westinghouse, and many others.

Thanks also to my colleagues in software estimation: Allan Albrecht, Barry Boehm, Tom DeMarco, Larry Putnam, Howard Rubin, Frank Freiman, Charles Symons, and Randall Jensen. While these researchers into software cost estimating may be competitors, they are also software cost estimating pioneers and leading experts. Without their research, there would be no software cost estimation industry. The software industry is fortunate to have researchers and authors such as these.

Appreciation is also due to those who teach software cost estimating and introduce this important topic to their students. Dr. Victor Basili and Professor Daniel Ferens have both done a great deal to bridge the gap between academia and the business world by introducing real-world estimation tools into the academic domain.

T. Capers Jones

Introduction to Software Cost Estimation

Software cost estimation is a complex activity that requires knowledge of a number of key attributes about the project for which the estimate is being constructed. Cost estimating is sometimes termed parametric estimating *because accuracy demands understanding the relationships among scores of discrete parameters that can affect the outcomes of software projects both individually and in concert. Creating accurate software cost estimates requires knowledge of the following parameters:*

- *The sizes of major deliverables, such as specifications, source code, and manuals*

- *The rate at which requirements are likely to change during development*

- *The probable number of bugs or defects that are likely to be encountered*

- *The capabilities of the development team*

- *The salaries and overhead costs associated with the development team*

- *The formal methodologies that are going to be utilized (if any)*

- *The tools that are going to be utilized on the project*

- *The set of development activities that are going to be carried out*

Although the factors that influence the outcomes of software projects are numerous and some are complex, modern commercial software cost-estimation tools can ease the burden of project managers by providing default values for all of the key parameters, using industry values derived from the integral knowledge base supplied with the estimation tools.

In addition, software cost estimation tools allow the construction of customized estimating templates that are derived from actual projects and that can be utilized for estimating projects of similar sizes and kinds.

This section discusses the origins and evolution of software cost estimation tools and how software cost estimation fits within the broader category of software project management.

In addition, this section discusses the impact of software cost estimation tools on the success rates of software projects and uses this data to illustrate the approximate return on investment (ROI) from software cost estimating and project management tools.

Introduction

Software cost estimating has been an important but difficult task since the beginning of the computer era in the 1940s. As software applications have grown in size and importance, the need for accuracy in software cost estimating has grown, too. As the end of the century approaches, software cost estimating is now a major business topic as businesses and government agencies try to meld the enormous costs of the onrushing year-2000 problem with the costs of normal development and maintenance work.

In the early days of software, computer programs were typically less than 1000 machine instructions in size (or less than 30 function points), required only one programmer to write, and seldom took more than a month to complete. The entire development costs were often less than $5000. Although cost estimating was difficult, the economic consequences of cost-estimating errors were not very serious.

As the twentieth century draws to a close, some large software systems exceed 25 million source code statements (or more than 300,000 function points), may require technical staffs of 1000 personnel or more, and may take more than 5 calendar years to complete. The development costs for such large software systems can exceed $500 million; therefore, errors in cost estimation can be very serious indeed.

Even more serious, a significant percentage of large software systems run late, exceed their budgets, or are canceled outright due to severe underestimating during the requirements phase. In fact, excessive optimism in software cost estimation is a major source of overruns, failures, and litigation.

Software is now the driving force of modern business, government, and military operations. This means that a typical Fortune 500 corporation or a state government may produce hundreds of new applications and modify hundreds of existing applications every year. As a result of the host of software projects in the modern world, software cost estimating is now a mainstream activity for every company that builds software.

In addition to the need for accurate software cost estimates for day-to-day business operations, software cost estimates are becoming a significant aspect in litigation. Over the past five years the author and his colleagues have observed dozens of lawsuits where software cost estimates were produced by the plaintiffs, the defendants, or both. For example, software cost estimation now plays a key part in lawsuits involving the following disputes:

- Breach of contract suits between clients and contractors

- Suits involving the taxable value of software assets

- Suits involving recovering excess costs for defense software due to scope expansion

- Suits involving favoritism in issuance of software contracts

- Suits involving wrongful termination of software personnel

And although the lawsuits are still in the future, it is becoming painfully obvious that cost estimating will also be part of the lawsuits that will involve the dreaded *year-2000 problem*. Indeed, the year-2000 problem will probably generate more litigation than any other problem in human history, and many kinds of software cost factors will be part of these lawsuits.

From many viewpoints, software cost estimating has become a critical technology of the twentieth century, and it should become an even more critical mainstream technology in the twenty-first century because software is now so pervasive.

How Software Cost-Estimating Tools Work

There are many kinds of automated tools that experienced project managers can use to create cost, schedule, and resource estimates for software projects. For example, an experienced software project manager can create a cost-estimate and schedule plan using any of the following:

- Spreadsheets
- Project management tools
- Methodology or process management tools
- Software cost estimating tools

A frequently asked question for software cost estimating tool vendors is "Why do we need your tool when we already have spreadsheets, project management tools, and methodology management tools?"

The commercial software-estimating tools are differentiated from all other kinds of software project management tools and general-purpose tools, such as spreadsheets, in these key attributes:

1. They contain knowledge bases of hundreds or thousands of software projects.

2. They can perform size predictions, which general-purpose tools cannot.

3. They can automatically adjust estimates based on tools, languages, and processes.

4. They can predict quality and reliability, which general-purpose tools cannot.

5. They can predict maintenance and support costs after deployment.

6. They can predict (and prevent) problems long before the problems actually occur.

Unlike other kinds of project management tools, the commercial software cost estimating tools do not depend upon the expertise of the user or project manager, although experienced managers can refine the estimates produced. The commercial cost-estimating tools contain the accumulated experience of many hundreds or thousands of software projects.

Because of the attached knowledge bases associated with commercial cost-estimating tools, novice managers or managers faced with unfamiliar kinds of projects can describe the kind of project being dealt with, and the estimating tool will construct an estimate based on similar projects derived from information contained in its associated knowledge base.

Figure 1.1 illustrates the basic principles of modern commercial software cost estimating tools.

The starting point of software estimation is the size of the project in terms of either logical source code statements, physical lines of code, function points, or, sometimes, all three metrics. The project's size can

Figure 1.1   Software-estimating principles.

be derived from the estimating tool's own sizing logic, can be supplied by users as an explicit input, or can be derived from analogy with similar projects stored in the estimating tool's knowledge base.

Once the basic size of the project has been determined, then the estimate can be produced based on the specific attributes of the project in question. Examples of the attributes that can affect the outcome of the estimate include the following:

1. The rate at which project requirements may change

2. The experience of the development team with this kind of project

3. The process or methods used to develop the project

4. The specific activities that will be performed during development

5. The programming language or languages utilized

6. The presence or absence of reusable artifacts

7. The development tool suites used to develop the project

8. The environment or ergonomics of the office work space

9. The geographic separation of the team across multiple locations

10. The schedule pressure put on the team by clients or executives

Using commercial estimating tools, these project attributes can either be supplied by the user or be inherited from similar projects already stored in the estimating tool's knowledge base. In a sense estimating tools share some of the characteristics of the object-oriented paradigm, in that they allow inheritance of shared attributes from project to project.

In software-estimating terminology, these shared attributes are termed *templates*, and they can be built in a number of ways. For example, estimating-tool users can point to an existing completed project and select any or all of the features of that project as the basis of the template. Thus, if the project selected as the basis of a template were a systems software project, used the C programming language, and utilized formal design and code inspections, these attributes could be inherited as part of the development cycle and could become part of an estimating template for other projects.

Many other attributes from historical projects can also be inherited and can become aspects of software-estimating templates. For example, a full estimating template can contain inherited attribute data on such topics as the following:

- The experience of the development team in similar applications
- The process or methodology used to develop the application
- The SEI capability maturity level of the organization
- The standards that will be adhered to, such as ISO, DoD, IEEE, and so forth
- The tools used during design, coding, testing, and so forth
- The programming language or languages utilized
- The volumes of reusable artifacts available
- The ergonomics of the programming office environment

Since software projects are not identical, any of these inherited attributes can be modified as the need arises. However, the availability of templates makes the estimation process quicker, more convenient, and more reliable because templates substitute specific knowledge from local projects for generic industry default values.

Templates can also be derived from sets of projects rather than from one specific project, or can even be custom-built by the users, using artificial factors. However, the most common method of template development is to use the automatic template construction ability of the estimating tool, and simply select relevant historical projects to be used as the basis for the template.

As a general rule, software-estimating templates are concerned with four key kinds of inherited attributes: (1) *personnel,* (2) *technologies,* (3) *tools,* and (4) the *programming environment,* as can be illustrated by Fig. 1.2.

Three of these four factors—the experience of the personnel, the development process, and the technology (programming languages and support tools)—are fairly obvious in their impact. What is not obvious, but is equally important, is the impact of the fourth factor—*environment.*

The environment factor covers individual office space and the communication channels among geographically dispersed development teams. Surprisingly, access to a quiet, noise-free office environment is one of the major factors that influences programming productivity.

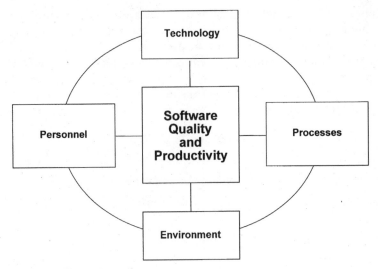

Figure 1.2   Key estimate factors.

The ability to include ergonomic factors in an estimate is an excellent example of the value of commercial software cost estimating tools. Not only do they contain the results of hundreds or thousands of completed projects, but they are also aware of influential factors that many human project managers may not fully understand.

The four key sets of attributes must be considered whether estimating manually or using an automated estimating tool. However, one of the key features of commercial software-estimating tools is the fact that they are repositories containing the results of hundreds or thousands of software projects, and so the effect of these four attribute areas can be examined, and their impacts can be analyzed.

There is a standard sequence for software cost estimation, which the author has used for more than 25 years. This sequence can be used with manual software cost estimates, and also mirrors the estimation stages in the software-estimation tools that the author has designed. There are nine steps in this sequence, although the sequence starts with 0 because the first stage is a preestimate analysis of the requirements of the application.

Step 0: Analyze the requirements

Software cost estimation at the project level cannot be performed unless the requirements of the project are well understood. Therefore, before estimating itself can begin, it is necessary to explore and understand the user requirements. At some point in the future it should be possible to create estimates automatically from the requirements specifications, but the current level of estimating technology demands human intervention.

A common estimating activity today is to analyze the software requirements and create function point totals based on those requirements. This provides the basic size data used for formal cost estimation. Function point analysis can be performed manually by certified function point counting personnel, or semiautomatically if the application is constructed using such tools as the Bachman Analyst or Texas Instruments Information Engineering Facility, which include function point sizing modules.

The time is rapidly approaching when function point totals can be assigned automatically from software requirements, and this method may appear in commercial software cost estimation tools within a few years.

Step 1: Start with sizing

Every form of estimation and every commercial software cost estimating tool needs the sizes of key deliverables in order to complete an estimate. Size data can be derived in several fashions, including the following:

1. Size prediction using an estimating tool's built-in sizing algorithms

2. Sizing by extrapolation from function point totals

3. Sizing by analogy with similar projects of known size

4. Guessing at the size using "project manager's intuition"

5. Guessing at the size using "programmer's intuition"

6. Sizing using statistical methods or Monte Carlo simulation

The basic size of the application being estimated is usually expressed in terms of function points, source code statements, or both. However, it is very important to size all deliverables and not deal only with code. For example, more than 50 kinds of paper documents are associated with large software projects, and they need to be sized also.

Source code sizing must be tailored to specific programming languages, and more than 500 languages are now in use. About one-third of software projects utilize more than a single programming language. More than a dozen kinds of testing occur, and each will require different volumes of test cases.

Sizing is a key estimating activity. If the sizes of major deliverables can be predicted within 5 to 10 percent, then the accuracy of the overall estimate can be quite good. If size predictions are wildly inaccurate, then the rest of the estimate will be inaccurate, too.

The technologies available for sizing have been improving rapidly. A little over 10 years ago, size data had to be supplied by users, using very primitive methods. Now modern software cost estimating tools have a number of sizing capabilities available, including support for very early size estimates even before the requirements are firm.

Step 2: Identify the activities to be included

Once the sizes of key deliverables are known, the next step is to select the set of activities that are going to be performed. In this context the term *activities* refers to the work that will be performed for the project being estimated, such as requirements, internal design, external design, design inspections, coding, code inspections, user document creation, change control, integration, quality assurance, unit testing, new function testing, regression testing, system testing, and project management. Accurate estimation is impossible without knowledge of the activities that are going to be utilized.

Activity patterns vary widely from project to project. Large systems utilize many more activities than do small projects. For projects of the same size, military and systems software utilize more activities than do information systems. Local patterns of activities are the ones to utilize, because they reflect your own enterprise's software development methodologies.

Modern software cost estimating tools have built-in logic for selecting the activity patterns associated with many kinds of software development projects. Users can also adjust the activity patterns to match local variations.

Step 3: Estimate software defect potentials and removal methods

The most expensive and time-consuming work of software development is the work of finding bugs and fixing them. It is not possible to create an accurate overall software cost estimate without also predicting defect potentials and knowing the effectiveness of the various kinds of reviews, inspections, and test stages that are planned.

All of the author's software cost estimating tools include full defect-estimation capabilities, and support all known kinds of defect-removal activity. This is necessary because the total effort, time, and cost devoted to a full series of reviews, inspections, and multistage tests will cost far more than source code itself.

Defect estimation includes predictive abilities for requirements defects, design defects, coding defects, user documentation defects, and a very troubling category called *bad fix defects*. The phrase *bad fix* refers to a new defect accidentally injected as a by-product of repairing a previous defect.

Some estimating tools that support commercial software can also predict duplicate defect reports, or bugs found by more than one customer. It is also possible to estimate *invalid defect reports,* or bug reports that turn out not to be the fault of the software, such as user errors or hardware problems.

The ability to predict software defects would not be very useful without another kind of estimation, which is predicting the *defect-removal efficiency* of various kinds of reviews, inspections, and test stages. Modern software cost estimating tools can predict how many bugs will be found by every form of defect removal, from desk checking through external Beta testing.

Step 4: Estimate staffing requirements

Every software deliverable has a characteristic *assignment scope,* or amount of work that can be done by a single employee. For example, an average assignment for an individual programmer will range from 5000 to 15,000 source code statements (from about 50 up to 2000 function points).

However, large systems also utilize many specialists, such as system architects, database administrators, quality assurance specialists, software engineers, technical writers, testers, and the like. Identifying each category of worker and the numbers of workers for the overall project is the next step in software cost estimation.

Staffing requirements depend upon the activities that will be performed and the deliverables that will be created, so staffing predictions are derived from knowledge of the overall size of the application and the activity sets that will be included.

For large systems, programmers themselves may comprise less than half of the workforce. Various kinds of specialists and project managers comprise the other half. Some of these specialists include quality assurance personnel, testing personnel, technical writers, systems analysts, database administrators, and configuration control specialists. If the project is big enough to need specialists, accurate estimation requires that their efforts be included. Both programming and other kinds of noncoding activities, such as production of manuals and quality assurance, must be included to complete the estimate successfully.

Step 5: Adjust assumptions based on capabilities and experience

Software personnel can range from top experts with years of experience to rank novices on their first assignment. Once the categories of technical workers have been identified, the next step is to make adjustments based on typical experience levels and skill factors.

Experts can take on more work, and perform it faster, than can novices. This means that experts will have larger assignment scopes and higher production rates than average or inexperienced personnel.

Other adjustments include work hours per day, vacations and holidays, unpaid and paid overtime, and assumptions about the geographic dispersal of the software team. Adjusting the estimate to match the capabilities of the team is one of the more critical estimating activities.

While estimating tools can make adjustments to match varying degrees of expertise, these tools have no way of knowing the specific capabilities of any given team. Many commercial estimating tools default to "average" capabilities, and allow users to adjust this assumption upward or downward to match specific team characteristics.

Step 6: Estimate effort and schedules

Effort and schedule estimates are closely coupled, and often are performed in an iterative manner.

Accurate effort estimation requires knowledge of the basic size of the application plus the numbers and experience levels of the software team members and the sizes of various deliverables they are expected to produce, such as specifications and user manuals.

Accurate schedule estimation requires knowledge of the activities that will be performed, the sizes of various deliverables; the overlap between activities with mutual dependencies, and the numbers and experience levels of the software team members.

Schedule and effort estimates are closely coupled, but the interaction between these two dimensions is complicated and sometimes is counterintuitive. For example, if a software project will take six months if it is developed by one programmer, adding a second programmer will not cut the schedule to three months. Indeed, a point can be reached where putting on additional personnel may slow down the project's schedule rather than accelerating it.

The complex sets of rules that link effort and schedules for software projects are the heart of the algorithms for software cost estimating tools. As an example of one of the more subtle rules that estimating tools contain, adding personnel to a software project within one department will usually shorten development schedules. But if enough personnel are added so that a second department is involved, schedules will stretch out. The reason for this is that software schedules, and also productivity rates, are inversely related to the number of project managers engaged. There are scores of rules associated with the interaction of schedules and effort, and some of these are both subtle and counterintuitive.

In fact, for very large software projects with multiple teams, the rate at which development productivity declines tends to correlate more closely to the number of managers that are engaged than to the actual number of programmers involved. This phenomenon leads to some subtle findings, such as the fact that projects with a small span of control (less than 6 developers per manager) may have lower productivity than similar projects with a large span of control (12 developers per manager).

This same phenomenon of productivity reduction correlated to the number of managers explains some otherwise curious observations, such as the fact that large software projects using matrix management principles often have lower productivity rates than similar projects using conventional hierarchical organization. The matrix style tends to inflate the number of managers and, hence, drive down productivity.

Indeed, the incidence of failure rates (canceled projects or severe cost and schedule overruns) is also higher under the matrix organization than under the hierarchical organization.

Step 7: Estimate development costs

Development costs are the next-to-last stage of estimation and are very complex. Development costs are obviously dependent upon the effort and schedule for software projects, so these factors are predicted first, and then costs are applied afterwards.

Costs for software projects that take exactly the same amount of effort in terms of hours or months can vary widely due to the following causes:

1. Average salaries of workers and managers on the project

2. The corporate burden rate or overhead rate applied to the project

3. Inflation rates, if the project will run for several years

4. Currency exchange rates, if the project is developed internationally

There may also be special cost topics that will have to be dealt with separately, outside of the basic estimate:

1. License fees for any acquired software needed

2. Capital costs for any new equipment

3. Moving and living costs for new staff members

4. Travel costs for international projects or projects developed in different locations

5. Contractor and subcontractor costs

6. Legal fees for copyrights, patents, or other matters

7. Marketing and advertising costs

8. Costs for developing videos or CD-ROM tutorial materials and training

On the whole, developing a full and complete cost estimate for a software project is much more complex than simply developing a resource estimate of the number of work hours that are likely to be needed. Many cost elements, such as burden rates or travel, are only indirectly related to effort and can impact the final cost of the project significantly.

The normal pattern of software estimation is to use hours, days, weeks, or months of effort as the primary estimating unit, and then apply costs at the end of the estimating cycle once the effort patterns have been determined.

Step 8: Estimate maintenance and enhancement costs

Software projects often continue to be used and modified for many years. Maintenance and enhancement cost estimation are special topics, and are more complex than new project cost estimation.

Estimating maintenance costs requires knowledge of the probable number of users of the application, combined with knowledge of the probable number of bugs or defects in the product at the time of release.

Estimating enhancement costs requires good historical data on the rate of change of similar projects once they enter production and start being used. For example, new software projects can add 10 percent or more in total volume of new features with each release for several releases in a row, but then slow down for a period of two to three years before another major release occurs.

Many commercial estimating tools can both estimate the initial construction costs of a project and estimate of maintenance and enhancement cost patterns for more than five years of usage by customers.

There is no actual limit on the number of years that can be estimated, but because long-range projections of user numbers and possible new features are highly questionable, the useful life of maintenance and enhancement estimates runs from three to five years. Estimating maintenance costs 10 years into the future can be done, but no estimate of that range can be regarded as reliable because far too many uncontrollable business variables can occur.

Cautions About Accidental Omissions from Estimates

Because software-estimating tools have such an extensive knowledge base, they are not likely to make the kinds of mistakes that inexperienced human managers make when they create estimates by hand or with general-purpose tools and accidentally omit activities from the estimate.

For example, when estimating large systems, coding may be only the fourth most expensive activity. Human managers often tend to leave out or underestimate the noncode work, but estimating tools can include these other activities.

- Historically, the effort devoted to finding and fixing bugs by means of reviews, walkthroughs, inspections, and testing take more time and cost more than any other software activities. Therefore, accurate cost estimates need to start with quality predictions, because defect-removal costs are often more expensive than anything else.

- In second place as major cost elements are the expenses and effort devoted to the production of paper documents, such as plans, specifications, user manuals, and the like. For military software projects, paperwork will cost twice as much as the code itself. For large civilian projects greater than 1000 function points or 100,000 source code statements, paper documents will be a major cost element and will approach or exceed the cost of the code.

- For some large distributed applications that involve multiple development locations or subcontractors, the costs of meetings and travel among the locations can cost more than the source code and may be in third place in the sequence of all software costs. A frequent omission from software cost estimates is the accidental exclusion of travel costs (airlines, hotels, etc.) for meetings among the development teams that are located in different cities or different countries. For very large kinds of systems, such as large operating systems, large telecommunication systems, or large defense systems, which may involve distributed development in half a dozen countries and a dozen cities, the costs of travel can exceed the cost of coding significantly, and this topic should not be left out by accident.

- For several kinds of massive software maintenance updates occurring near the end of the twentieth century, such as making year-2000 repairs and updating applications for the unified European currency, the latter stages of testing may involve an unusual form of testing between specific companies and their suppliers, their clients, the government agencies to whom they send or receive data, and perhaps even their direct competitors. It is easy to understate or omit this special kind of testing, because it is so unusual and has so little in the way of historical precedent. In the entire history of software, companies will pay more for year-2000 repairs than for any other software activity, while the Eurocurrency conversion work will be in second place. Each of these massive efforts is likely to cost more than 30 percent of a typical annual corporate software budget, so between the two, well over half of the software resources of many corporations will be preempted from all other tasks.

- Many software cost estimates—and many measurement systems, too—cover only the core activities of software development and ignore such topics as project management and support (i.e., program librarians, secretaries, administration, etc.). These ancillary activities are part of the project and can, in some cases, top 25 percent of total costs. This is far too much to leave out by accident.

- The software domain has fragmented into a number of specialized skills and occupations. It is very common to accidentally leave out the contributions of specialists if their skills are needed only during portions of a software development cycle. Some of the specialist groups that tend to be accidentally omitted from software cost estimates include quality assurance specialists, technical writing specialists, function point specialists, database administration specialists, performance tuning specialists, network specialists, and system administration specialists. The combined contributions of these and other specialists may total more than 20 percent of all software development costs and should not be omitted by accident.

- The most common omission from internal software cost estimates for information systems are the costs expended by users during requirements definition, prototyping, status reviews, phase reviews, documentation, inspections, acceptance testing, and other activities where the developers have a key role. Since user representatives are not usually considered to be part of the project team, their contributions to the project are seldom included in software cost estimates, and are seldom included in measurement studies, either. The actual amount of effort contributed by users to major software development projects can approach 20 percent of the total work in some cases, which is not a trivial amount and is far too significant to leave out by accident. Some commercial software cost estimating tools keep a separate chart of accounts for user activities and allow user efforts to be added to total project costs, if desired.

- For many projects, maintenance after delivery quickly costs more than the development of the application itself. It is unwise to stop the estimate at the point of delivery of the software without including several years of maintenance and enhancement estimates. Since maintenance (defect repairs) and enhancements (adding new features) have different funding sources, many estimating tools separate these two activities. Other forms of maintenance work, such as customer support or field service, may also be included in postrelease estimates.

A key factor that differentiates modern commercial software cost estimating tools from general-purpose tools, such as spreadsheets and project management tools, is the presence of full life-cycle historical data. This gives them the ability to estimate quality and to estimate both the sizes and costs of producing paper deliverables, as well as the costs of coding and testing.

When considering acquisition of a software cost estimating tool, be sure that the knowledge base includes the kind of software you are interested in. The real-life cost and schedule results of information systems, systems software, commercial software, military software, and embedded software are not identical, and you need to be sure the estimating tool contains data on the kinds of software you are concerned with. Some tools support all classes of software, but others are more narrow in focus.

Software Cost Estimating and Other Development Activities

Software cost estimating is not a "standalone" activity. The estimates are derived in large part from the requirements of the project, and will be strongly affected by the tools, process, and other attributes associated with the project. A cost estimate is a precursor for departmental budgets, and also serves as a baseline document for comparing accumulated costs against projected costs.

For any project larger than trivial, multiple cost estimates will be prepared during the course of development, including but not limited to the following:

- A rough prerequirements guesstimate
- An initial formal estimate derived from the project requirements
- One or more midlife estimates, which reflect requirements changes
- A final cost accumulation using project historical data

In addition, since the software industry is somewhat litigious, cost estimates may also be prepared as a by-product of several kinds of litigation, including the following:

- Litigation for breach of contract between software clients and outsource companies
- Litigation involving the taxable value of software in tax disputes

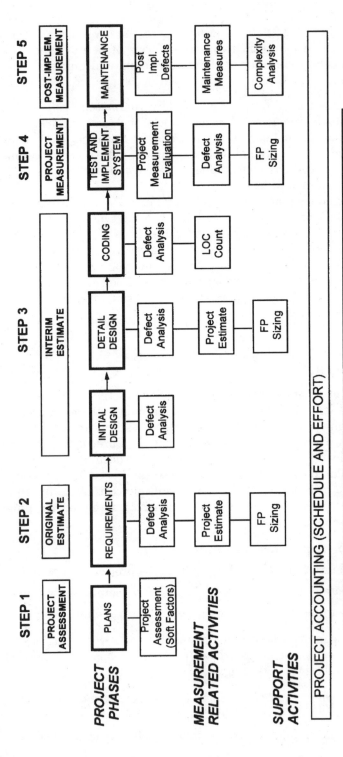

Figure 1.3 Software cost estimation and other activities.

18

In the course of developing a software project, historical data will steadily be accumulated. This means that after the first rough guesstimate and the initial requirements estimate, future estimates will need to interleave historical data with predicted data. Therefore, software-estimating tools need the ability to capture historical data and to selectively display both historical data and predicted values.

Figure 1.3 illustrates how software cost estimation fits into the context of other key software development activities.

As can be seen from Fig. 1.3, estimating is closely aligned with other key development phases. When done well, software cost estimates are among the most valuable documents in the entire software world, because they make a software project real and tangible in terms of the resources, schedules, and costs that will be required.

However, cost estimates that are poorly constructed and grossly inaccurate are key factors in almost every major software disaster. The best advice for those charged with constructing software cost estimate is the following:

1. Be accurate.

2. Be conservative.

3. Base the estimate on solid historical data.

4. Include quality, since software quality affects schedules and costs.

5. Include paper documents, since they can cost more than source code.

6. Include project management.

7. Include the effects of creeping requirements.

8. Do not exaggerate the effect of tools, languages, or methods.

9. Get below phases to activity-level cost estimates.

10. Be prepared to defend the assumptions of your estimate.

Even with the best estimating tools, accurate software cost estimating is complicated and can be difficult. But without access to good historical data, accurate software cost estimating is almost impossible. Measurement and estimation are twin technologies and both are urgently needed by software project managers.

Measurement and estimation are also linked in the commercial software cost estimation marketplace, since many of the commercial estimating companies are also benchmark and measurement companies. As better historical data becomes available, the features of the commercial software cost estimating tools are growing stronger.

Literature on Software Cost Estimating

The literature on the techniques of software cost estimating is somewhat sparse for such a mainstream activity. Because most of the commercial software cost estimating tool vendors regard their estimating methods and algorithms as trade secrets, the only book that actually explains the mechanics and algorithms of a software cost estimation model is Dr. Barry Boehm's classic *Software Engineering Economics* (Boehm 1981).

This book has been very influential in the commercial software cost estimating domain, and its published algorithms have been used in perhaps a score of commercial estimating tools and at least the same number of internal, proprietary estimating tools. Dr. Boehm's *constructive cost model* (COCOMO) has recently been updated and the new COCOMO II estimating model adds new features and capabilities, although Dr. Boehm's book has not yet been reissued.

Among the other developers of software cost estimating tools who have published books or articles, the work of Larry Putnam in *Measures for Excellence* (Putnam 1992) shows the strong relationship between measurement and estimation. Larry Putnam's *software-life-cycle model* (SLIM) is revised frequently, and new versions come out on an approximately annual basis as a result of continuous data-collection activities. Larry Putnam is one of the more prolific authors among the estimating tool developers.

Dr. Howard Rubin, the developer of the ESTIMACS software cost estimation tool, has published scores of journal articles and also publishes an annual benchmark survey of software productivity and quality rates, such as *Software Benchmark Studies for 1997*, which reflects the current year (Rubin 1997). Rubin's work is another clear example of the close linkage between measurement and estimation, since the historical data Rubin collects is one of the key information sources of the software industry. Dr. Rubin is also a prolific writer on software estimation and measurement topics.

Among the more recent books by software-estimating tool developers that can be found is *Best Practices in Software Cost and Schedule Estimation* by William Roetzheim and Reyna Beasley (Roetzhiem and Beasley 1998). Roetzheim is the developer of the Cost Xpert estimation tool.

Charles Symons, the developer of the Mark II function point method used widely in the United Kingdom, has not developed a commercial software cost estimating tool, but his book *Software Sizing and Estimating* contains many rules of thumb for procedures for manual estimation (Symons 1991). Several commercial software cost estimation tools do support the Mark II function point, especially in the United Kingdom and Europe. Symons's work concentrates on the estimation of information systems and is not as extensive when dealing with military software, embedded systems, or other more technical kinds of software applications.

Among the developers of commercial software cost estimating tools, the author of this book has published the largest number of related books, with 10 prior books and several hundred articles dealing with aspects of software estimation, software measurement, and software risk analysis. The companion book to the current volume, *Applied Software Measurement* (Jones 1996) illustrates the very close linkage between collecting historical data and the ability to derive estimating algorithms. A more recent book that deals with one of the hardest and most complex kinds of estimation is *The Year 2000 Software Problem—Quantifying the Costs and Assessing the Consequences* (Jones 1997). This is a particularly tricky estimation problem because it involves making simultaneous estimates for hundreds of applications, and year-2000 cost estimates also require the inclusion of such nonsoftware tasks as database repairs, hardware upgrades, chip replacement, financial reporting, and litigation, as well as the costs of pure software repairs.

The literature on estimating by academia and by users of estimating tools is fairly extensive but is not quite as focused on the principles of estimation as are the books by estimating developers themselves. Among the category of books by users or teachers of estimation can be found the excellent works of Dr. Norm Brown, dealing with topics of interest to the military and defense software community (Brown 1995); Dr. Daniel Ferens and Gerald Ourada (Ourada and Ferens 1992), who also are in the military and defense software domain; Tom DeMarco (DeMarco 1982), who covers many of the topics that influence software projects; Bob Grady of Hewlett Packard (Grady 1992); and at least a dozen others.

Also significant are a number of books on the risks and failures associated with poor estimating practices, such as the risk management works of Robert Charette (Charette 1989, 1990) and William Perry's *Handbook of Diagnosing and Solving Computer Problems* (Perry 1989).

A number of general-purpose books include chapters or sections on software cost estimating. Examples of this genre include John Marciniak's well-known *Encyclopedia of Software Engineering* (Marciniak 1994), Stephen Kan's *Metrics and Models in Software Engineering* (Kan 1995), and Ed Yourdon's *Death March* (Yourdon 1997). Also, Thomas Gulledge and his colleagues have created an interesting book on estimating, with chapters on software cost estimating and also on hardware and engineering estimating (Gulledge et al. 1992).

The military services and the Department of Defense have created an estimating genre all by themselves, since both software and software estimation are key topics in the defense domain. Many articles and technical reports have originated from the military sector, including some rare side-by-side comparisons of estimating tool capabilities, such as the work of Sherry Stukes and colleagues in *Air Force Cost Analysis Agency Estimating Model Analysis* (Stukes et al. 1996). An older but even more extensive study of some 20 estimation tools was prepared by Dean Barrow and colleagues for the Air Force Software Technology Support Center in Utah (Barrow et al. 1993).

An estimating genre that could be expanded is discussions of the available commercial estimating tools and how they operate with other project management tools. Both Lois Zells (Zells 1990) and Nicholas Zvegintzov (Zvegintzov 1994) have written useful books that discuss software estimating and project management tools, but this genre is very transient because new tools appear almost monthly. Therefore, books more than a year or two old tend to fall out of date.

The well-known catalog editor Alan Howard puts together an annual catalog of metrics and project management and estimation tools (Howard 1997), but even this catalog is only about 70 percent complete because new tools are being created so rapidly and so many mergers and acquisitions are sweeping through the software tool vendors.

Somewhat surprisingly, software estimating has even appeared in fiction. The well-known software consultant Tom DeMarco has written a tutorial novel for software project managers called *Deadline* (DeMarco 1997), which deals with estimation in the context of an interesting novel about how major software projects are developed.

Overall, the literature on estimating is somewhat fragmented but is increasing rapidly in volume and usefulness.

References

Barrow, Dean, Susan Nilson, and Dawn Timberlake: *Software Estimation Technology Report*, Air Force Software Technology Support Center, Hill Air Force Base, Utah, 1993.

Boehm, Barry: *Software Engineering Economics*, Prentice Hall, Englewood Cliffs, N.J., 1981.

Brown, Norm (ed.): *The Program Manager's Guide to Software Acquisition Best Practices*, Version 1.0, U.S. Department of Defense, Washington, D.C., July 1995.

Charette, Robert N.: *Software Engineering Risk Analysis and Management*, McGraw-Hill, New York, ISBN 0-07-010719-X, 1989.

———: *Application Strategies for Risk Analysis*, McGraw-Hill, New York, ISBN 0-07-010888-9. 1990.

DeMarco, Tom: *Controlling Software Projects*, Yourdon Press, New York. ISBN 0-917072-32-4, 1982.

———: *Deadline*, Dorset House Press, New York, 1997.

Department of the Air Force: *Guidelines for Successful Acquisition and Management of*

Software Intensive Systems; vols. 1 and 2, Software Technology Support Center, Hill Air Force Base, Utah, 1994.

Dreger, Brian: *Function Point Analysis,* Prentice Hall, Englewood Cliffs, N.J., ISBN 0-13-332321-8, 1989.

Garmus, David, and David Herron: *Measuring the Software Process: A Practical Guide to Functional Measurement,* Prentice Hall, Englewood Cliffs, N.J., 1995.

Grady, Robert B.: *Practical Software Metrics for Project Management and Process Improvement,* Prentice Hall, Englewood Cliffs, N.J., ISBN 0-13-720384-5, 1992.

―――― and Deborah L. Caswell: *Software Metrics: Establishing a Company-Wide Program,* Prentice Hall, Englewood Cliffs, N.J., ISBN 0-13-821844-7, 1987.

Gulledge, Thomas R., William P. Hutzler, and Joan S. Lovelace (eds.): *Cost Estimating and Analysis—Balancing Technology with Declining Budgets,* Springer-Verlag, New York, ISBN 0-387-97838-0, 1992.

Howard, Alan (ed.): *Software Metrics and Project Management Tools,* Applied Computer Research (ACR), Phoenix, Ariz., 1997.

IFPUG Counting Practices Manual, Release 4, International Function Point Users Group, Westerville, Ohio, April 1995.

Jones, Capers: *Critical Problems in Software Measurement,* Information Systems Management Group, ISBN 1-56909-000-9, 1993a.

――――: *Software Productivity and Quality Today—The Worldwide Perspective,* Information Systems Management Group, ISBN-156909-001-7, 1993b.

――――: *Assessment and Control of Software Risks,* Prentice Hall, Englewood Cliffs, N.J., ISBN 0-13-741406-4, 1994.

――――: *New Directions in Software Management,* Information Systems Management Group, ISBN 1-56909-009-2.

――――: *Patterns of Software System Failure and Success,* International Thomson Computer Press, Boston, ISBN 1-850-32804-8, 1995.

――――: *Applied Software Measurement,* 2d ed., McGraw-Hill, New York, ISBN 0-07-032826-9, 1996.

――――: *The Economics of Object-Oriented Software,* Software Productivity Research, Burlington, Mass., April 1997a.

――――: *Software Quality—Analysis and Guidelines for Success,* International Thomson Computer Press, Boston, ISBN 1-85032-876-6, 1997b.

――――: *The Year 2000 Software Problem—Quantifying the Costs and Assessing the Consequences,* Addison-Wesley, Reading, Mass., ISBN 0-201-30964-5, 1998.

Kan, Stephen H.: *Metrics and Models in Software Quality Engineering,* Addison-Wesley, Reading, Mass., ISBN 0-201-63339-6, 1995.

Kemerer, C. F.: "Reliability of Function Point Measurement—A Field Experiment," *Communications of the ACM,* **36:** 85–97 (1993).

Keys, Jessica: *Software Engineering Productivity Handbook,* McGraw-Hill, New York, ISBN 0-07-911366-4, 1993.

Marciniak, John J. (ed.): *Encyclopedia of Software Engineering,* vols. 1 and 2, John Wiley & Sons, New York, ISBN 0-471-54002, 1994.

Mertes, Karen R.: *Calibration of the CHECKPOINT Model to the Space and Missile Systems Center (SMC) Software Database (SWDB),* Thesis AFIT/GCA/LAS/96S-11, Air Force Institute of Technology (AFIT), Wright-Patterson AFB, Ohio, September 1996.

Ourada, Gerald, and Daniel V. Ferens: "Software Cost Estimating Models: A Calibration, Validation, and Comparison," in *Cost Estimating and Analysis: Balancing Technology and Declining Budgets,* Springer-Verlag, New York, 1992, pp. 83–101.

Perry, William E.: *Handbook of Diagnosing and Solving Computer Problems,* TAB Books, Blue Ridge Summit, Pa., ISBN 0-8306-9233-9, 1989.

Putnam, Lawrence H.: *Measures for Excellence—Reliable Software on Time, Within Budget:* Yourdon Press/Prentice Hall, Englewood Cliffs, N.J., ISBN 0-13-567694-0, 1992.

――――, and Ware Myers: *Industrial Strength Software—Effective Management Using Measurement,* IEEE Press, Los Alamitos, Calif., ISBN 0-8186-7532-2, 1997.

Reifer, Donald (ed.): *Software Management,* 4th ed., IEEE Press, Los Alamitos, Calif., ISBN 0-8186-3342-6, 1993.

Rethinking the Software Process, CD-ROM, Miller Freeman, Lawrence, Kans., 1996. (This CD-ROM is a book collection jointly produced by the book publisher, Prentice Hall, and the journal publisher, Miller Freeman. It contains the full text and illustrations of five Prentice Hall books: Capers Jones, *Assessment and Control of Software Risks*; Tom DeMarco, *Controlling Software Projects*; Brian Dreger, *Function Point Analysis*; Larry Putnam and Ware Myers, *Measures for Excellence*; and Mark Lorenz and Jeff Kidd, *Object-Oriented Software Metrics.*)

Rubin, Howard: *Software Benchmark Studies for 1997,* Howard Rubin Associates, Pound Ridge, N.Y., 1997.

Roetzheim, William H., and Reyna A. Beasley: *Best Practices in Software Cost and Schedule Estimation,* Prentice Hall PTR, Upper Saddle River, N.J., 1998.

Stukes, Sherry, Jason Deshoretz, Henry Apgar, and Ilona Macias: *Air Force Cost Analysis Agency Software Estimating Model Analysis—Final Report,* TR-9545/008-2, Contract F04701-95-D-0003, Task 008, Management Consulting & Research, Inc., Thousand Oaks, Calif., September 1996.

Symons, Charles R.: *Software Sizing and Estimating—Mk II FPA (Function Point Analysis),* John Wiley & Sons, Chichester, U.K., ISBN 0-471-92985-9, 1991.

Yourdon, Ed: *Death March—The Complete Software Developer's Guide to Surviving "Mission Impossible" Projects,* Prentice Hall PTR, Upper Saddle River, N.J., ISBN 0-13-748310-4, 1997.

Zells, Lois: *Managing Software Projects—Selecting and Using PC-Based Project Management Systems,* QED Information Sciences, Wellesley, Mass., ISBN 0-89435-275-X, 1990.

Zvegintzov, Nicholas: *Software Management Technology Reference Guide,* Dorset House Press, New York, ISBN 1-884521-01-0, 1994.

2

The Origins of Software Cost Estimation

Software development and maintenance are both difficult domains for cost-estimation purposes. Software is highly labor-intensive, so individual human variances exert a major impact. Also, unlike with many physical constructs, such as buildings or automobiles, the requirements and design for software projects tend to change significantly during the development cycle. Indeed, the average rate for new requirements after the requirements phase runs from 1 percent to more than 5 percent per month during the subsequent design and coding phases, and these changes may even continue into the testing phase.

There are also many different kinds of software, many different processes or methods for building software, and many hundreds of programming languages in which the code itself might be written. For example, the schedule and cost results of projects that are exactly the same size can vary widely for various kinds of software, such as the following:

1. End-user development projects

2. Internal information systems projects

3. External outsourced projects

4. Systems software projects

5. Embedded software projects

6. Commercial software projects

7. Military software projects

Within these seven discrete forms of software, schedules for exactly the same size of application can vary by more than three to one, and costs can vary by more than six to one.

Further, software projects do not scale up very well. The tools and methods needed to successfully build a large system of, say, 10,000 function points or 1 million source code statements are quite different from those needed for small applications of 10 function points or 1000 source code statements.

The overall result of the combination of these factors is that software cost estimating is a complicated activity that requires the ability to deal with a host of overlapping variables, including but not limited to the following:

- Requirements volatility

- Class and type of software being estimated

- Size of the final application

- Team capabilities

- Multiple occupation groups employed

- Standard and overtime pay required

- Processes and methods used

- Tools and equipment available

- Programming languages used

- Reusable artifacts available

From the start of the software era in the 1940s until roughly 1970, software cost estimating was performed manually, using simple rules of thumb or local estimating algorithms developed through trial and error methods. (Indeed, even today simple rules of thumb and manual methods are numerically the most frequently used methods of developing software cost estimates, in spite of the many problems of these crude approaches.)

By the late 1960s, computer usage had become widespread and therefore software applications were growing in both size and numbers. Software cost estimating first began to be discussed as an important technology in the late 1960s. For example, Joel Aron of IBM gave a presentation on software cost estimating at a NATO conference in 1969 (Aron 1970). Both of the estimating pioneers, Dr. Barry Boehm and Larry Putnam, first began to explore software cost estimation in the late 1960s.

By the late 1960s and early 1970s, a number of researchers independently began to explore the possibilities of building automated software cost estimating tools. It is no coincidence that the software cost estimating pioneers all worked for large corporations that were experiencing difficulties in building large software systems. For example, such large companies and organizations as the Army, the Air Force, IBM, RCA, TRW, and Hughes Aircraft were among the first to fund formal research studies for improved methods of software cost estimating.

Some of these pioneering researchers succeeded well enough to bring out internal estimating tools that later evolved into commercial software cost estimating tools, and thus created the modern software cost estimating industry. As this book is being written there are at least 50 commercial software cost estimating tools sold in the United States, and perhaps 25 sold elsewhere. However, the cost-estimating industry is young enough so that many of the software cost estimating pioneers are still active in the commercial estimating business.

Although they did not know one another at the time they began working on software cost estimation, a number of software cost estimation pioneers became interested in the problems of estimation in the late 1960s and began to produce estimation prototypes in the early 1970s. In alphabetical order, some of the pioneering estimating researchers included Allan Albrecht at IBM on the East Coast, Dr. Barry Boehm at TRW, Frank Freiman at RCA, Dr. Randall Jensen at Hughes, Capers Jones at IBM on the West Coast, and Colonel Larry Putnam in the U.S. Army. All of these estimating pioneers began their research into software cost estimation at roughly the same time. All of these estimation researchers were facing the same problem in their respective organizations: Software applications were growing in size and importance, and no one knew how to predict the costs of these troublesome projects.

In 1973, the author and his colleague Dr. Charles Turk at IBM San Jose built IBM's first automated estimation tool for systems software, although this tool was an IBM internal tool and was not put on the commercial market. This early software cost estimation tool was called *IPQ*, for *Interactive Productivity and Quality* estimator. Since that name proved awkward, an expanded version of the tool created in 1974 was renamed *DPS*, for *Development Planning System*.

Although the IBM DPS estimating tool was not released outside of IBM, a number of papers and reports on software cost estimation based on it were presented at external conferences and in a 1977 IBM Technical Report (Jones 1977), so some of the supporting data became widely known.

Although he did not develop a software-estimating tool himself, Dr. Fred Brooks of IBM captured the need for better software-estimating methods in his classic book *The Mythical Man-Month* (Brooks 1974). This book described the development problems of IBM's OS/360 operating system, which was the first software application built by IBM that topped 1 million source code statements in its first release, and was also the first IBM software product that missed its delivery date by a long enough period for the delay to be published in the major software journals and newspapers, to the considerable embarrassment of IBM executives.

Also around 1974, Dr. Randall Jensen and his colleagues at Hughes Aircraft were at work on the software cost estimating methodology that later grew into the commercial SEER software cost estimating tool. Some of this research was published by Jensen and Tonies in 1979 (Jensen and Tonies 1979).

Around 1975, Allan Albrecht and his colleagues at IBM White Plains were developing the original version of the function point metric, which has become a major feature of modern software estimation.

The function point metric is a synthetic metric based on five external attributes of software applications: (1) inputs, (2) outputs, (3) inquires, (4) logical files, and (5) interfaces.

The function point metric stays constant regardless of the programming language used to implement the software. This property of invariance across multiple programming languages greatly eased sizing and estimating the noncoding portions of software projects, such as requirements, design, specifications, creation of user manuals, and the like. As a result, most of the modern software cost estimating tools now support function point metrics as well as lines-of-code metrics.

In tracing the origins of software cost estimating, the commercial software-estimation business dates back only to the early 1970s. In 1977, the PRICE-S software-estimation model designed by Frank Freiman was marketed as the first commercial software-estimation tool in the United States. (The PRICE-H hardware-estimation tool had come out earlier, in 1973.)

The PRICE-S tool was originally developed and marketed by RCA. However, the tool has changed hands many times and is now marketed by Lockheed-Martin. It is a sign that cost estimating is important when a tool survives far longer than the company that first created it. In this case, RCA was acquired by General Electric, followed by Martin-Marietta, which became Lockheed-Martin after a merger.

In October 1979, Allan Albrecht, then at IBM, gave a paper on function point metrics at a joint IBM/SHARE/GUIDE conference in Monterey, California (Albrecht 1979). At the same time, IBM put the structure of the function point metric into the public domain. Since function point metrics are now supported by more than 30 software-estimation tools in the United States and by 15 overseas, the publication of function point metrics was a very significant step in software cost estimating.

In 1979, the second commercial estimation tool reached the U.S. market. This was the software life-cycle management (SLIM) tool developed by Larry Putnam of Quantitative Software Management (QSM). Putnam developed his original concepts for the SLIM model while serving in the U.S. Army, where he was often engaged in the estimation of military software projects. In 1978, Putnam published a report on a generalized macroestimating method in *IEEE Transactions on Software Engineering* (Putnam 1978).

In 1981, Dr. Barry Boehm, who worked at TRW at the time, published his monumental book on *Software Engineering Economics* (Boehm 1981) which contained the essential algorithms of the *constructive cost model* (COCOMO). Since the COCOMO algorithms were first described in print, at least a dozen commercial software-estimating tools have been derived from the COCOMO estimation method. Today, COCOMO remains the only software-estimating model whose algorithms are not treated as trade secrets. (As this book is being written, Dr. Boehm has developed a new COCOMO II software cost estimating model, which supports function point metrics and adds additional features, such as sizing logic, that were not part of the original COCOMO model.)

Also in 1981, the first worldwide publication of Allan Albrecht's paper on function points occurred when the paper was included in the present author's book *Programming Productivity—Issues for the Eighties* (Jones 1981). This same book included an article by the author describing a controlled study of the problems of using *lines-of-code* (LOC) metrics for evaluating productivity across multiple languages.

In 1982, Tom DeMarco, a well-known software management consultant, published his classic book *Controlling Software Projects* (DeMarco 1982), which contained an independent form of functional metric that, by coincidence, duplicated some of the features of Albrecht's function point. (This situation brings to mind the publication of two independent theories of evolution by Darwin and Wallace, with Darwin getting the most recognition because he published first.)

The DeMarco function point, sometimes called the *bang* metric, is supported by several software cost estimating tools. Several features of the original DeMarco function point have resurfaced in a recent metric termed *Boeing 3D function points* and in several other function point variants, as well.

In 1983, Charles Symons, a British software-estimating researcher working at the management consulting group of Nolan, Norton & Company (later acquired by KPMG Peat Marwick), published a description of an alternative function point metric that he termed *Mark II function points,* which became widely used in the United Kingdom (Symons 1991).

The Mark II method differed from the Albrecht function point in a number of respects, and it has become a popular metric for estimation and measurement in the United Kingdom, Canada, and Hong Kong. Further, the Mark II variant was the first of at least 36 other function point variations.

The Mark II function point metric includes entities and relationships as parameters, and also has an expanded set of adjustment factors for dealing with complexity, with the result that Mark II function point counts tend to be larger than Albrecht function point counts for many applications with complex data structures.

In 1983, Dr. Howard Rubin's ESTIMACS model reached the commercial market. Dr. Rubin is a professor at Hunter College, and is also a well-known software management consultant.

Dr. Rubin's original work on the ESTIMACS cost-estimating model was derivative of some of IBM's internal estimating methodology for information systems projects. ESTIMACS supported an early form of function point metric prior to IBM's major revision of function points in 1984, which is the basis of today's standard function point.

(The *MACS* portion of the name *ESTIMACS* refers to the MACS corporation, which was the original vendor of the ESTIMACS tool. This corporation was acquired by Computer Associates, but the name of the estimating tool was not changed.)

Starting in the 1970s, Albrecht and his colleagues at IBM measured the sizes of many projects using both LOC metrics and function point metrics. The results showed useful but not perfect correlations between the two metrics.

The dual measurement of both lines of code and function points led to *backfiring,* or direct conversion from LOC metrics to function point metrics and vice versa. The term *backfiring* denotes the direct mathematical conversion of logical source code statements into an equivalent volume of function points.

Backfiring is used primarily for estimating maintenance and enhancement projects for aging legacy applications, where the specifications may be missing and the original development personnel have changed jobs.

Backfiring was also adopted by both international benchmark consulting groups and many commercial software-estimating tool vendors.

In 1984, enough data had been collected that it was possible to start publishing conversion ratios between logical source code statements and function point metrics. The early reports covered only 20 of the more common programming languages. However, the use of backfiring became so common that the table of conversion rates between source code statements and function points now includes almost 500 programming languages (Jones 1996).

In 1985, the author's SPQR/20™ (for *software productivity, quality, and reliability*) estimation tool reached the commercial market. The SPQR/20 estimation tool was the first commercial software estimator built explicitly to support function point metrics and to include bidirectional backfiring support. That is, logical statements could be converted into equivalent function point totals, or vice versa. SPQR/20 was also the first software estimation tool to use function points for the sizing logic for specifications, user documents, and source code.

The SPQR/20 tool also integrated quality, risk, and reliability estimating with effort, cost, and schedule estimating, and it produced maintenance and enhancement estimates for five years after the initial deployment of a software project. This was a pioneering attempt to integrate all of the following key software predictable factors into a single tool:

- Sizing of all deliverables

- Staffing by activity

- Schedules by activity

- Effort by activity

- Costs by activity

- Quality and defect severity levels

- Defect removal efficiency

- Reliability

- Risks

- Maintenance

- Enhancements

By 1986, usage of function point metrics had grown so rapidly that the nonprofit International Function Point Users Group (IFPUG) was founded by a number of users of this metric. The IFPUG organization was started in Toronto, Canada, a city which has pioneered a number of interesting software technologies. (IFPUG moved its headquarters to Westerville, Ohio, in 1988 and became a nonprofit corporation in the United States.)

As function point usage grew, the IFPUG organization recognized that counting was complex enough that standards would be required. Also, it was desirable to develop a certification examination, to ensure that counting would be consistent from project to project. In 1986, Allan Albrecht, the inventor of function point metrics, developed the first IFPUG-certified course for function point counting.

Although Allan Albrecht, who is an electrical engineer, envisioned function points as a metric for all kinds of software, the historical fact that function points were first used for information systems slowed down the acceptance of functional metrics within the real-time and embedded-software domains.

In 1986, the author developed an alternative form of function point called *feature points* for use with real-time, embedded, and systems software. The feature point metric added a sixth parameter, *algorithms*, to the five standard function point parameters. Complex algorithmic processing is an important aspect of real-time and systems software, so the addition of this factor augmented the usage of functional metrics for real-time applications, such as weapons systems, telephone switching systems, operating systems, and the like. The development of the feature point metric was done with the cooperation of Allan Albrecht, the inventor of the original function point metrics.

Because the main reason for developing feature points was to overcome a psychological resistance to using function points, it was important that function point metrics and feature point metrics create similar or identical results for most kinds of software projects. Indeed, for more than 80 percent of software projects the function point and feature point totals were identical. Only in situations where the number of algorithms was extremely high would feature points generate larger totals than standard function points.

Between the early 1970s and 1987, the nucleus of the current software cost estimating industry was created. Most of the original estimating pioneers all developed their own estimating methods, which have become the basis of the current software-estimating business, as shown in Table 2.1.

TABLE 2.1   Commercial Software Estimation from 1974 Through 1986

Estimation pioneer	Methods or tools	Year of availability
Dr. Randall Jensen	SEER	1974
Frank Freiman	PRICE-S	1977
Allan Albrecht	IBM function points	1978
Larry Putnam	SLIM	1979
Dr. Barry Boehm	COCOMO	1981
Tom DeMarco	DeMarco function points	1982
Charles Symons	Mark II function points	1983
Dr. Howard Rubin	ESTIMACS	1983
Allan Albrecht and Capers Jones	Backfiring (LOC to function points)	1984
Capers Jones	SPQR/20	1985
Allan Albrecht and Capers Jones	SPR feature points	1986

These pioneering commercial software-estimating tools, plus the invention and publication of function point metrics, mark the emergence of the modern software cost estimation industry.

(In the course of preparing this book, all of the estimating pioneers who developed actual estimating tools were invited to contribute papers on why they became interested in software cost estimating. For biographical information contributed by Dr. Barry Boehm and Larry Putnam, refer to App. A.)

From 1986 to 1997, new commercial software-estimation tools were released so rapidly that it is now difficult to keep track of the growth of the estimating industry.

However, many of the more recent estimating tools are derived at least in part from the work of the software-estimating pioneers. For example, at least 20 commercial estimating tools (12 in the United States and 8 overseas) use portions of the COCOMO algorithms published by Dr. Barry Boehm.

About the same number of commercial estimating tools use the backfiring method published by Allan Albrecht and Capers Jones for converting lines-of-code data based on logical statement counts into equivalent function point data.

Because accurate software cost estimation depends upon data derived from accurate measurement of software projects, it is no coincidence that some of the software cost estimating pioneers are also well known as measurement experts. Indeed, a majority of the published books that contain quantitative measurement data for software projects have been written by the software cost estimating pioneers.

The total number of software project results published in the collected works of the software-estimating pioneers totals more than 20,000 and constitutes the bulk of all quantitative data yet published on software projects.

A search of software-estimating and measurement topics on the Internet reveals that the quantitative software measurement databases developed by such estimating researchers as Allan Albrecht, Dr. Barry Boehm, Tom DeMarco, Capers Jones, Larry Putnam, and Dr. Howard Rubin are cited in more than 50,000 research studies, and each of these authors individually are cited from about 10,000 to more than 20,000 times each.

The linkage between software measurement and software estimation is so strong that outside of the data collected and published by software cost estimating specialists, there are very few other industry collections of quantitative data on software productivity, costs, and quality.

Some of the function point groups, such as the IFPUG benchmark committee and the Australian function point users group, have published limited volumes of benchmark data.

There are some interesting military software data collections and also some government software data collected by the National Aeronautics and Space Administration (NASA). However, military software development and, to an extent, governmental software development use standards and approaches that are not totally commensurate with civilian methods or results. Also, comparatively little of the governmental software data has found its way into commercial books dealing with software productivity or quality.

Several Air Force databases contain significant quantities of project-level data and are sometimes used for calibrating software cost estimating tools: The Electronic Systems Center (ESC) and Space and Missile Systems Center (SMC) databases are good examples, as is the data collected by the Rome Air Development Center (RADC).

The only significant civilian databases of software effort, productivity, and quality information are the proprietary databases of software benchmarking and consulting organizations, such as the Real Decisions subsidiary of Gartner Group, the Computer Sciences Corporation (CSC) Index subsidiary, the Compass Group in Europe, Quantitative Software Management, and Software Productivity Research.

In recent years the nonprofit function point organizations in various countries have begun to publish collections of benchmark data, with the function groups in Australia (Australian Software Metrics Association [ASMA]), the Netherlands Function Point Users Group (NEFPUG), and the International Function Point Users Group (IFPUG) in the United States having the largest numbers of projects to date.

Function points have become so common that even the consulting groups that do not market estimating tools use function point metrics as the basis for their comparative benchmark studies, and they often compare their results against some of the published studies produced by the software-estimating companies.

Indeed, several of the estimating pioneers have also pioneered measurement and benchmarking services. Dr. Howard Rubin, Larry Putnam, and Capers Jones all have benchmarking and measurement divisions, as well as cost-estimating divisions, in their respective companies.

Although some of the proprietary consulting databases contain interesting and valuable information about software project costs, schedules, and quality, they are usually available only to the direct clients of the consulting companies. Many of the benchmark consulting organizations sell their data directly to their clients rather than making it available by means of general publication in books or articles.

The bulk of the published data on software productivity, costs, schedules, and quality still derives from the books and articles published by software-estimating tool developers, who continue to measure and collect data at a combined rate of several hundred software projects every month.

References

Albrecht, A. J.: "Measuring Application Development Productivity," *Proceedings of the Joint IBM/SHARE/GUIDE Application Development Symposium,* October 1979, reprinted in Capers Jones, *Programming Productivity—Issues for the Eighties,* IEEE Computer Society Press, New York, 1981, pp. 34–43.

Aron, J. D.: "Estimating Resources for Large Programming Systems," *Software Engineering Techniques,* NATO Conference Report, Rome, October 1969, April 1970, pp. 68–84.

Boehm, Barry: *Software Engineering Economics,* Prentice Hall, Englewood Cliffs, N.J., 1981.

Brooks, Fred: *The Mythical Man-Month,* Addison-Wesley, Reading, Mass., 1974, rev. 1995.

DeMarco, Tom: *Controlling Software Projects,* Yourdon Press, New York, ISBN 0-917072-32-4, 1982.

Jensen, R. W., and C. C. Tonies: *Software Engineering,* Prentice Hall, Englewood Cliffs, N.J., 1979.

Jones, Capers: *Program Quality and Programmer Productivity,* IBM Technical Report TR 02.764, IBM, San Jose, Calif., January 1977.

———: "Measuring Programming Quality and Productivity," *IBM Systems Journal,* **17**(1): 39–63 (1978).

———: *Programming Productivity—Issues for the Eighties,* IEEE Press, ISBN 0-8186-0681-9, 1981, rev. 1986.

———: *Programming Productivity,* 2d ed., McGraw-Hill, ISBN 0-070032811-0, 1986.

———: *Critical Problems in Software Measurement,* Information Systems Management Group, ISBN 1-56909-000-9. 1993a.

———: *Software Productivity and Quality Today—The Worldwide Perspective,* Information Systems Management Group, ISBN-156909-001-7, 1993b.

———: *Assessment and Control of Software Risks,* Prentice Hall, ISBN 0-13-741406-4, 1994.

———: *New Directions in Software Management,* Information Systems Management Group, ISBN 1-56909-009-2.

———: *Patterns of Software System Failure and Success,* International Thomson Computer Press, Boston, ISBN 1-850-32804-8, 1995.

———: *Applied Software Measurement,* 2d ed., McGraw-Hill, ISBN 0-07-032826-9, 1996.

Putnam, Lawrence H.: "A General Empirical Solution to the Macro Software Sizing and Estimation Problem," *IEEE Transactions on Software Engineering,* **SE-**4(4):345–361 (1978).

———: *Measures for Excellence—Reliable Software On Time, Within Budget,* Yourdon Press/Prentice Hall, Englewood Cliffs, N.J., ISBN 0-13-567694-0, 1992.

Rubin, Howard: *Software Benchmark Studies For 1997,* Howard Rubin Associates, Pound Ridge, N.Y., 1997.

Symons, Charles R.: *Software Sizing and Estimating—Mk II FPA (Function Point Analysis),* John Wiley & Sons, Chichester, U.K, ISBN 0-471-92985-9, 1991.

3

Features of Commercial Software Cost Estimating Tools

The explosive growth of the software industry has triggered the development of at least 50 commercial software estimation tools. As of 1998, the overall family of commercial software estimation tools tends to have these basic features:

- An on-board knowledge base of more than 1000 software projects
- Sizing logic for specifications, source code, and test cases
- Support for software process assessment questions
- Phase-level or activity-level effort, cost, and schedule estimation
- Support for both function point metrics and the older lines-of-code (LOC) metrics
- Support for *backfiring,* or conversion between LOC and function points
- Quality and reliability estimation, as well as cost and schedule estimation
- Interfaces to project management tools
- Support for dozens of standard development methods
- Customization support for unique development methods

These are the overall capabilities that basically any commercial software-estimating tool can be expected to have. However, in order to differentiate themselves from their competitors, a number of special features can be found in various software cost estimating tools.

As software estimation tools continue to evolve, these new features and capabilities will continue to be added. As of 1998, the total set of major features included in commercial software-estimating tools numbers close to 100, although not every feature is found in every commercial estimating tool. For detailed information on the specific features, it is best to contact the vendors themselves. Appendix B lists major software cost estimating tool vendors.

A very useful catalog of software cost estimating tools is produced annually by Alan Howard of Applied Computer Research (Howard 1997). The estimating-tool catalog is one volume of a multifaceted set of related catalogs that attempt to include all commercial software tools marketed in the United States.

There is no known comparative discussion of all known estimating tools, but the U.S. Air Force (Stukes et al. 1996) has published an interesting comparison of the features of seven software-estimating tools that are capable of estimating military software projects: CHECKPOINT, PRICE-S, REVIC, SASET, SEER, SLIM, and SOFT-COST in alphabetical order.

Accurate estimates for military software projects require factoring in the effects of Department of Defense standards, such as DoD 2167, DoD 498, and a number of others, so many civilian estimating tools are not calibrated for the special needs of military cost estimating.

Following is an alphabetical list of the major features now present in the family of commercial software cost estimating tools.

activity-based costing Cost estimates can be set to various degrees of granularity by user command, including total project costs and resources, phase-level costs and resources, and activity-level costs and resources. Activity- and task-level estimates are far more useful for contracts and business purposes than coarser project-level or phase-level estimates.

advice mode Software cost estimating tools are often expert systems that contain substantial information about best practices and the harmful effects of bad practices. Several software cost estimating tools can have *advice* modes, in which they will suggest methods that have been effective for similar projects, or offer warnings about methods, tools, languages, and so forth that may be inappropriate for the project being estimated. Users can, of course, disregard the advice, but much of the advice is actually pretty sound.

approximation modes Software projects must often be estimated even before requirements are fully known. Some estimating tools include powerful approximation modes for use when project attributes are still uncertain. One approximation method is a *browsing* mode that allows users to search the tool's knowledge base for similar projects. Another approximation mode is based on statistical reconstruction of missing attributes using the tool's knowledge base.

assessment support The outcomes of software projects are strongly determined by the processes used for development. Some estimating tools include process assessment questions, such as those used by the Software

Engineering Institute (SEI) or by Software Productivity Research (SPR). Some cost-estimating tools also sort assessment responses into ranked sets, so that factors that are better or worse than U.S. norms are highlighted. For example, CHECKPOINT and KnowledgePlan feature optional "strength" and "weakness" reports, which sort out responses into categories of better or worse than average performance, compared against similar projects contained in the tool's internal knowledge base.

automatic metric conversion   Estimating tools often support multiple metrics and can convert data back and forth between LOC metrics, IFPUG standard function points, Mark II function points, feature points, and sometimes other metrics also. Users can select any metric of their choice, and the estimating tool will automatically convert data into the chosen metric. This means that users who prefer LOC metrics can have the data normalized to LOC, and anyone interested in function points can have the same data converted to that metric automatically. Both function points and LOC metrics can be displayed simultaneously.

backfiring support   The term *backfiring* was first used circa 1985 to describe the ability to convert counts of source code statements into equivalent function point counts. (Bidirectional conversion from function points to LOC and from LOC to function points are common features in estimating tools.) The ability to do backfiring can be found in at least 30 commercial software-estimating tools. The ability to perform backfiring is based on empirical relationships derived from thousands of software projects and hundreds of programming languages. For example, COBOL averages about 106.7 statements per function point in the procedure and data divisions. This kind of relationship is now known for hundreds of programming languages, including Ada83, Ada95, Algol, Basic, Bliss, C, C++, CHILL, COBOL, Forth, Smalltalk, and hundreds more.

benchmark mode   Users often wish to compare their projects against the built-in knowledge base that comes with estimating tools, or against portfolios of their own projects. Therefore, estimating tools may allow comparisons against their own knowledge, or against other projects selected by the users. Powerful selection criteria are needed to ensure that the comparisons are valid. For example, military software projects might be compared against other military projects but not against civilian projects. Users can also construct their own databases of software projects, using the estimation tool as a corporate repository.

burden rates   In addition to basic salaries, enterprises accumulate the costs of doing business (taxes, rents, medical benefits, etc.) into a separate cost component termed the *burden rate*. This rate is added to basic compensation and is used for charge-out and billing purposes. Many software cost estimation tools allow independent adjustments to both the compensation and burden rate values, and display both separately. Burden rates are sometimes called the *overhead*.

calibration mode   Many software-estimating tools include a calibration mode that allows them to be custom-tailored to the specifics of a given way of building software. Several forms of calibration are found, but the most common method is to allow users to construct custom *templates* that include the activities and tasks they usually perform, sometimes accompanied by local default values for productivity rates. Other forms of calibration allow renaming of activities, and some estimating tools also allow activities to be added to or removed from the set of activities deployed on any given project.

client/server estimation   Estimating client/server applications is more difficult than estimating monolithic applications because the client portion and the server portion may use different methods, tools, and even programming languages. Modern estimating tools can estimate and measure client/server applications and integrate both the client and server results.

comparative mode   Some estimating tools feature a side-by-side comparative mode so that two separate estimates can be viewed at once, and the differences between the two are also displayed. This simplifies "what if" modeling by allowing things like an Ada version of a project and a C++ version of the same project to be displayed side by side with the variances highlighted.

complexity adjustments   One of the factors that influences both costs and schedules is that of *complexity,* or the difficulty of the problems facing the development team. Several forms of complexity are supported by software cost estimating tools, and responses to these complexity factors will partly determine schedules, effort, costs, and defect levels. Among the forms of complexity used as estimating adjustments are problem complexity, data complexity, code complexity, cyclomatic complexity, and essential complexity.

compensation and overhead   Software compensation levels vary widely from job to job, company to company, city to city, and country to country. Overhead costs, or the burden rate that companies apply to cover such factors as taxes, rent, medical coverage, and personnel functions, also vary widely. Modern cost-estimating tools provide default values for "average" compensation and overhead rates but allow both values to be adjusted by users to match local conditions.

confidence levels   Software estimates vary in accuracy with the amount of firm information that is known and used in establishing the estimate. A number of software cost estimating tools allow users to specify the certainty of input factors, and then calculate a confidence level for the resulting estimate.

conversion projects   As the twentieth century winds down, many software applications run on multiple platforms, such as Windows 95, Windows NT, OS/2, UNIX, MVS, and so forth. Several modern software-estimating tools can predict the costs of converting an application from one platform to another, such as moving a UNIX application to Windows NT, or vice versa.

cost to complete estimates   Some of the more powerful software cost estimating tools also have a measurement mode for collecting historical data. This means that for projects that are in middevelopment it is possible to perform *cost to complete* estimates for the unfinished work, and also show total anticipated costs by summing the actual accrued costs with the predicted costs. The related topic of *time to complete* estimates are also supported.

creeping requirements adjustments   One of the many problems associated with software cost estimation is the fact that software requirements tend to "creep" at a monthly rate of perhaps 1 to 2 percent after the initial requirements phase. Thus, for a 2-year project, perhaps 25 percent of the final functionality is added after the initial requirements and, hence, will be outside the scope of the first cost estimate. Some software cost estimation models have algorithms for predicting the probable rate of requirements creep, and then predicting the effort, costs, quality, and other factors that will be expended on these late features.

currency conversion   Since software development is a global activity, modern software-estimating tools include built-in currency conversion routines for supporting international software projects. Many estimating vendors are adding support for the new Eurocurrency, which starts to be utilized in 1999.

customer support   Software products require extensive customer support after deployment, in the form of personnel to handle incoming telephone calls and Internet queries, answer faxes and e-mail, and, in general, respond to customer's queries and bug reports. Several software-estimating tools aimed at the commercial software markets now estimate customer support requirements for phones, e-mail, and so forth.

domain adjustments   Since software development within various industries is often quite different, estimating tools can be set to match the normal methods and practices of military software, systems software, MIS projects, commercial software projects, scientific projects, and so forth. More than 200 class/type combinations are now supported.

early warnings   Software cost estimating tools are extremely useful for providing early warnings of potential cost and schedule overruns. Some software cost estimating tools can also issue warnings of other kinds of problems, including even sociological problems, such as excessive schedule pressure or potential staff burnout. The value of the early warnings from software cost estimating tools and software quality estimating tools can also head off potential litigation for breach of contract. Indeed, the power of the early warning information give quality- and cost-estimation tools excellent returns on investment.

Eurocurrency support   Starting in calendar year 1999, the European Union will be moving toward a single currency, called the *euro*. Many software cost estimating tools will support this currency, although as of 1998 the euro is a very troubling currency to deal with because of changing standards and requirements coupled with some ambiguity in the character codes for the euro. For example, Microsoft does not support the unicode, so software engineers need multiple encoding techniques to handle displaying the euro symbol.

full sizing logic   Modern estimating tools include source code sizing logic for all known languages (perhaps 500 at last count) and combinations of languages. Sizing logic also supports sizing for more than 50 kinds of specifications and paper documents, and supports test case sizing for about 20 different kinds of test operations. Estimating tools also include special "early sizing" capabilities for use during or before completion of a project's requirements phase.

function point support   Almost all commercial software-estimating tools support standard IFPUG function points. Some also support function point variations, such as Boeing 3D function points, British Mark II function points, SPR function points, and SPR feature points. Most commercial estimating tools also include bidirectional size conversion between IFPUG function points and other metrics, such as feature points or LOC metrics.

graphics and visualization   One of the cosmetic but interesting advantages of modern software cost estimating tools is their built-in graphical capabilities. Although columns of data with results shown to two or more decimal places are desirable for accuracy, it is much easier to visualize the significance of an estimate from graphs and diagrams. Many software cost estimating tools include very sophisticated graphical abilities and support bar charts, Gantt charts, pie charts, actual-versus-planned line charts, and a number of other graphical capabilities.

inflation rate adjustments   For long-range projects that may run up to five years or more during development, inflation must be factored into software cost estimates. Modern software cost estimating tools permit inflation rates to be set by users, and some also provide default values.

import and export of data   Although software cost estimating tools are a very important weapon in a software project manager's arsenal, cost-estimating tools are not the only tool used for modern projects. Therefore, most commercial software cost estimating tools can import and export data to other kinds of project management tools, such as planning tools like Andersen's METHOD/1; Microsoft Project; function point counting tools, such as Function Point Workbench; and methodology management tools, such as the LBMS Process Engineer or SHL Transform. Indeed, some software cost estimating tools have synergistic relationships with other kinds of project management tools, which greatly expand the capabilities available to software project managers.

Internet applications   Now that the Internet and the World Wide Web are being used for so many applications, modern software-estimating tools must be able to support applications aimed at the Internet. This also implies support for such languages as JAVA and HTML.

ISO standards support   Now that the ISO 9000–9004 standards are common, and ISO 9001 standards are used for many software projects, modern software cost estimating tools can adjust their assumptions for projects that are built using ISO 9001. (For example, there will be a marked increase in paperwork volume under ISO 9001.)

maintenance and enhancement estimates   Software maintenance and enhancements are now major activities, so many software-estimating tools can support these activities. Many estimating tools can estimate postrelease service and maintenance for a three- to five-year period. Some can estimate probable enhancements and maintenance (defect repairs) for up to 20 years, because the military services are interested in long-range maintenance costs, even though the reliability of long-range estimates is low. Maintenance estimation also deals with estimates for customer-support costs, field maintenance, invalid and duplicate defect reports, and many other factors of interest after deployment of software.

measurement mode   Since estimation and measurement are mirror images, many estimating tools also serve as powerful measurement tools. This capability allows the tools to mix historical data and estimated results, and deal with such topics as cost to complete and time to complete estimates for projects in the middle of their development cycles.

methodology adjustments   There are dozens of standard software-development methodologies and thousands of unique methods used by specific companies, and each has a characteristic profile of activities that are performed. Many modern software cost estimating tools can adjust their assumptions to match many common software-development methodologies, such as information engineering (IE), MERISE, rapid application development (RAD), and a number of others. In addition, some software cost estimation tools can support customized or unique methods by allowing users to add or remove tasks, rename activities, adjust rates, or modify standard assumptions in various ways.

metrics support   Software cost estimation tools and software-measurement tools are the primary working tools for software metrics. All of the major software metrics are supported by at least some of the commercial software estimation tools. Among the metrics with wide support in the estimation business are: (1) source code metrics in the form of logical statements, (2) source code metrics in the form of physical lines of code, (3) IFPUG function points at versions 1 through 4 levels, (4) Mark II function points, (5) SPR feature points for systems and embedded software, (6) SPR function points, (7) cyclomatic complexity metrics, and (8) essential complexity metrics. Some estimating tools also allow other metrics to be added, and several estimating tools feature metrics conversion logic, such as backfiring support for converting data between source code and function point metrics, or even for displaying both metrics simultaneously.

mixed programming languages   About one-third of U.S. software projects utilize two or more programming languages simultaneously, such as COBOL and SQL or C++ mixed with assembly language. A few large applications may have as many as a dozen programming languages within them. Some commercial software estimation tools include support for mixed-language estimates, and can show the proportion of both source code volumes and functionality (measured with function points) that each language comprises.

nationalization costs   Many software projects are marketed globally, so some modern software cost estimation tools can now handle the costs of converting the screens, user manuals, comments, and other materials into various languages, such as French, Japanese, Korean, German, and so forth.

object-oriented (OO) estimation   Modern software estimating tools can estimate applications in any known programming language, including C++, Objective C, Smalltalk, and other OO programming languages. Estimating tools can also deal with OO analysis and design, although the initial results of using OO analysis and design are not always favorable due to the steep learning curve. Users who have already developed OO applications can construct very accurate templates from their own historical data, and can then estimate using their own customized activities and factors.

occupation group estimation   The software industry now has more than 50 recognized occupations within it, such as database administrators, quality-assurance specialists, software engineers, systems analysts, technical writers, testing specialists, and the like. For large software projects, noncoding specialists may comprise more than one-third of the total staff. Modern software-estimating tools can predict both the kinds of specialists needed and the impact they may have compared to generalists.

package acquisition estimation Since package acquisition and modification are common, some estimating tools have a special set of features for estimating and measuring projects that are derived from commercial off-the-shelf (COTS) software. Some also support estimates for modifying and updating packages once they are acquired.

parent/child logic Many large software systems are comprised of a number of more or less independent components that may be under development simultaneously. For example, large operating systems and large switching systems may have from a dozen to more than 50 discrete components, each of which can be a significant project in its own right. Further, each of these components may be built using its own variety of tools, may be built in different cities, and may be on different schedules. Sometimes different components even use different programming languages.

To deal with this complex situation, some software cost estimating tools use *parent/child* logic. The overall system is defined as the *parent,* and the individual components are defined as *children.* Each of the child components will have its own unique estimate, but the overall system estimate will be constructed from the combined results of all of the component estimates, plus the special activities of system-level integration, system testing, and other functions that affect the parent outside the work needed to construct the children. This approach is also useful for projects with multiple subcontractors, or even for client/server projects, where the client portion and the server portion may be on separate schedules and use different tools and methods but eventually need to be integrated and tested simultaneously.

portfolio analysis Some estimating tools include built-in statistical processors that can average and perform various statistical functions on hundreds or thousands of software projects. Once clients enter a substantial volume of historical project data into the tool, the on-board statistical processor in the tool itself will generate averages, ranges, standard deviations, and so forth.

programming language support There are now hundreds of programming languages in use, ranging from assembly language at the low end through application generators, object-oriented languages, visual languages, and JAVA and its peers at the higher end. Modern software cost estimating tools support most or even all programming languages. Because new languages and dialects occur so often, some software-estimating tools include a language table that users can modify. In addition, many companies have built their own private programming languages, which are unknown outside of the enterprise. Some software cost estimating tools allow users to add languages at will, and adjust language levels to match local situations.

quality estimation Any effective modern software estimation tool must include quality estimation, since the costs and schedules for finding defects are major elements of software projects. The more powerful quality-estimation tools or features can estimate defect potentials, defect severity levels, defect origins, and the defect-removal efficiencies of any combination of review, inspection, and test.

Rayleigh curves   Lord Rayleigh was a pioneering nineteenth-century British physicist who explored the implications of an interesting family of curves that seem to be associated with many natural phenomena, such as the spread of epidemics and the population distributions of animal species. Larry Putnam introduced the concept of Rayleigh curves in his software life-cycle management (SLIM) estimating tool, and many other software cost estimating tools use a similar approach. Under the Rayleigh curve model, the *effort* and *schedule* dimensions of a project are not interchangeable. Attempting to compress schedules by adding people results in lower and lower productivity rates as the staffing level rises which, in turn, raises costs. In extreme conditions, the communication channels become so clogged that schedules are even extended rather than compressed.

reengineering and reverse engineering support   As the industry matures, more and more legacy systems become candidates for reengineering, reverse engineering, or other geriatric treatment. Modern estimating tools can estimate the most common forms of geriatric modification of aging legacy systems.

reliability estimation   Some software estimation tools include built-in software reliability models, which can predict reliability at the time of delivery, the stabilization period required to eliminate deployed errors, and the reliability interval after stabilization.

reusability support   Software reuse is a major technology. Modern estimating tools may include algorithms for estimating the probable quantity of reused material in any project, but users can override the predicted values and substitute their own assumptions for reuse. Software reuse includes much more than just source code, so reusable design, reusable source code, reusable user documents, and reusable test cases must all be supported. Some estimation tools can handle reuse for dozens of artifacts, including requirements, specifications, user manuals, plans, source code, test materials, and so forth.

risk analysis support   Software estimation tools with built-in assessment questions are an excellent choice for assisting in formal risk analysis. Several estimating tools can predict various risk probabilities when used in estimating mode, and can measure risk factors when in measurement mode. Some of the risks these tools handle include the risk of project failure, the risk of using inadequate tools, the risk of schedule overruns, the risk of cost overruns, the risk of poor quality, and even the risk of possible litigation.

SAP estimation   *Systems, Applications, Products* (SAP) is an integrated software package that is expanding rapidly in usage both in Europe and in the United States. The parent company SAP AG is a German company. Because SAP is so widely deployed, some commercial software-estimating tools now support various kinds of estimation in an SAP context, such as tailoring the SAP tables or programming using the special ABAP 4 programming language.

schedule estimation   The estimation of software schedules is a critical and important task. Because project planning tools predate software cost estimating tools by perhaps 10 years, many software cost estimating tools simply export data to project planning tools for scheduling purposes. However, some software-estimating tools, such as KnowledgePlan®, include powerful on-board scheduling capabilities. Such tools will predict overlaps between the starting point of activities and their logical predecessors and will perform critical path analysis. Many estimating tools also have close interfaces with project planning tools (i.e., project management tools), such as Microsoft Project or Project Manager's Workbench, and support bidirectional data interchange.

SEI CMM levels   Software-development practices and performance levels vary widely under the five levels of the Software Engineering Institute (SEI) capability maturity model (CMM). Therefore, modern software cost estimating tools will adjust their quality and productivity assumptions based on the CMM level of the organization unit producing the software being estimated.

sizing methods   Modern software cost estimating tools support a number of sizing methods for predicting the size or volume of various deliverables. Sizing support for requirements, specifications, source code in any known programming language, test case, user documents, and many kinds of supplemental documents, such as test plans, are now standard features. Several kinds of sizing logic are found in software-estimating tools, including sizing by analogy, sizing from function points, and sizing from partial or incomplete data. Sizing by analogy is the newest form of sizing logic and is based on providing users with a search or browse capability, which allows them to select projects with known sizes from the tool's on-board knowledge base and use them as the starting point for the current estimate.

special cost factors   No commercial software cost estimating tool supports every factor that can impact the costs of a software project. However, many estimating tools provide empty "buckets" that allow users to add special costs to the project and have these costs become part of the total costs. Some examples of these special costs outside the scope of normal cost estimating logic include travel costs for multisite or international projects; moving and living fees for new staff hired during the project; agency fees for personnel-recruitment companies; professional fees for attorneys, for such topics as trademark searching and patents; and professional fees for marketing and advertising agencies.

template construction   Some software-estimating tools allow users to convert historical data into customized estimating templates derived from their own projects and their own methodologies. Template construction is very useful for organizations that build many similar applications. Template construction can be based on a single project or on several similar projects averaged together. Some common uses for templates are establishing performance criteria for the five levels of the SEI capability maturity model and dealing with the software-quality approaches associated with the ISO 9001 standard. Templates can also be matched with various methods and techniques, such as templates for object-oriented development, for information engineering (IE), for clean-room development, and the like.

tool catalogs   Some estimating tools include built-in catalogs of hundreds or more software tools. When used in measurement mode, these catalogs allow the collection of data on the tools utilized, which can then be used to assess the impact of those tools on quality, productivity, schedules, and other dimensions.

value analysis   For many software projects, the costs of development and maintenance must be less than the anticipated value of the resulting application in order for the project to be funded. Several leading software cost estimating tools include value-analysis features, which allow users to input value factors, such as enhanced user performance, enhanced user satisfaction, faster business operations, or even direct revenues and indirect revenues, if the software being estimated is aimed at the market.

wizard support A modern full-featured estimating tool is a large and imposing tool that has at least as many features and options as a spreadsheet or project management tool. To facilitate getting up to speed, some software cost estimating tools feature *wizards,* which are guided instructions with default values for carrying out common forms of estimation. Some of the kinds of wizards that might be found in a modern estimating tool include sizing wizards, template construction wizards, and wizards associated with specific methodologies, such as ISO standards, military standards, client/server estimation, and the like.

work unit conversion Estimating tools allow users to select any standard work unit for expressing output data (i.e., work hours, days, weeks, months, or years). Users can also adjust the default assumptions on the number of productive hours per work period. This feature allows estimating tools to support national and local practices for work weeks, vacation lengths, holidays, and the like.

year-2000 software estimation The year-2000 software-repair problem is a special form of maintenance estimating, and a number of software-estimating tools can handle it on a project-by-project basis. Some estimating tools can even aggregate the costs to produce an overall estimate for the hundreds, or even thousands, of projects that may need modification. However, the year-2000 problem is very complex, and some of the year-2000 costs are outside the scope of any known software estimating tools—litigation expenses, hardware upgrade costs, database repairs, and repairs to physical devices with embedded year-2000 problems (fax machines, bank vaults, time locks, etc.).

zero-defect estimation For mission-critical software, it may be necessary to approach or achieve zero-defect levels in the delivered software packages. This is not an easy goal to accomplish, and it normally requires at least a dozen discrete forms of defect removal, including formal inspections and many kinds of testing. Some estimating tools can suggest quality-control strategies for achieving various desired quality levels, including zero-defect quality levels.

As can be seen from this listing of software estimating tool capabilities, there are a great many useful features available in commercial software estimation tools that are very difficult to imitate using manual approaches or general-purpose project management tools.

Developing the algorithms for estimating software projects well requires analysis of very large volumes of historical data. The more powerful commercial software estimating tools are derived from the analysis of at least 1000 projects, and some of them are derived from more than 5000 software projects.

The vendors of commercial software estimating tools tend to be very active in measurement, assessment, and benchmarking studies because a continuous stream of new data is needed in order to keep estimating tools current with changes in the industry, such as the explosive growth of Internet applications; the migration to client/server applications; the impact of ISO 9001 certification; and new languages, such as JAVA, Forte, and Realizer.

The literature on side-by-side comparisons of estimating-tool features is rather scarce. Most books by estimation-tool vendors or developers feature only their own tools and methods. Reports by academia are usually so limited and dated as to lack value in the commercial world.

Surprisingly, the military services have done the most rigorous comparisons of estimating-tool capabilities. These reports are aimed at tools that can estimate military projects, but with that caveat they do a good job of comparing features and functions. The reports of Dean Barrow and colleagues (Barrow et al. 1993) and Sherry Stukes and colleagues (Stukes et al. 1996) are both excellent examples of this genre.

Alan Howard's attempt to catalog metric, estimation, and project management tools (Howard 1997) is also useful, with the caveat that new tools come out so often that such catalogs need to be updated often.

Both Lois Zells (Zells 1990) and Nicholas Zvegintzov (Zvegintzov 1994) attempted to place estimation tools in context with other project management tools and did a good job at the time, but both books are in need of updating, because about 30 new tools have appeared since their publication.

References

Barrow, Dean, Susan Nilson, and Dawn Timberlake: *Software Estimation Technology Report,* Air Force Software Technology Support Center, Hill Air Force Base, Utah, 1993.

Howard, Alan (ed.): *Directory of Software Metrics and Project Management Tools,* Applied Computer Research, Phoenix, Ariz., 1997.

Stukes, Sherry, Jason Deshoretz, Henry Apgar, and Ilona Macias: *Air Force Cost Analysis Agency Software Estimating Model Analysis—Final Report,* TR-9545/008-2, Contract F04701-95-D-003, Task 008, Management Consulting & Research, Inc., Thousand Oaks, Calif., September 1996.

Zells, Lois: *Managing Software Projects—Selecting and Using PC-Based Project Management Systems,* QED Information Sciences, Wellesley, Mass., ISBN 0-89435-275-X, 1990.

Zvegintzov, Nicholas: *Software Management Technology Reference Guide,* Dorset House Press, New York, ISBN 1-884521-01-0, 1994.

4

Six Forms of
Software Cost Estimation

Software cost estimates can be created in a number of different fashions. In order of increasing rigor and sophistication, the following six general kinds of software cost estimates constitute the major estimating methods used by corporations and government groups that produce software.

Manual Software-Estimating Methods

1. Manual project-level estimates using rules of thumb
2. Manual phase-level estimates using ratios and percentages
3. Manual activity-level estimates using work-breakdown structures

Automated Software-Estimating Methods

1. Automated project-level estimates (macroestimation)
2. Automated phase-level estimates (macroestimation)
3. Automated activity-level or task-level estimates (microestimation)

The most accurate forms of software cost estimation are the last ones in each set: cost estimating at either the activity or the task level. Only the very granular forms of software cost estimation are usually rigorous enough to support contracts and serious business activities. Let us consider the pros and cons of each of these six estimating methods.

Overview of Manual
Software-Estimating Methods

Manual estimates for software projects using simple rules of thumb constitute the oldest form of software cost estimation, and this method is still the most widely used, even though it is far from the most accurate.

An example of an estimating rule of thumb would be "Raising the function point total of an application to the 0.4 power will predict the schedule of the project in calendar months from requirements until delivery."

Examples of rules of thumb using the obsolete lines-of-code metric might be "COBOL applications average 500 noncommentary code statements per staff month" or "COBOL applications cost an average of $10 per line of code to develop."

About the only virtue of this simplistic kind of estimation is that it is easy to do. However, simplistic estimates using rules of thumb should not serve as the basis of contracts or formal budgets for software projects.

Manual phase-level estimates using ratios and percentages are another common and long-lived form of software estimation. Usually the number of phases will run from five to eight, and will include such general kinds of software work as: (1) requirements gathering, (2) analysis and design, (3) coding, (4) testing, and (5) installation and training.

Manual phase-level estimates usually start with an overall project-level estimate and then assign ratios and percentages to the various phases. For example, suppose you were building an application of 100 function points, or roughly 10,000 COBOL source code statements in size. Using the rules of thumb from the previous example, you might assume that if this project will average 500 source code statements per month, then the total effort will take 20 months.

Applying typical percentages for the five phases previously shown, you might next assume that requirements would comprise 10 percent of the effort, analysis and design 20 percent, coding 30 percent, testing 35 percent, and installation and training 5 percent.

Converting these percentages into actual effort, you would arrive at an estimate for the project that showed the following:

Requirements	2 staff months
Analysis and design	4 staff months
Coding	6 staff months
Testing	7 staff months
Installation	1 staff month

The problems with simple phase-level estimates using ratios and percentages are threefold:

1. The real-life percentages vary widely for every activity.

2. Many kinds of software work span multiple phases or run the entire length of the project.

3. Activities that are not phases may accidentally be omitted from the estimate.

As an example of the first problem, for small projects of less than 1000 lines of code or 10 function points, coding can total about 60 percent of the total effort. However, for large systems in excess of 1 million lines of code or 10,000 function points, coding is often less than 15 percent of the total effort, and testing can top 50 percent.

As an example of the second problem, the phase-level estimating methodology is also weak for activities that span multiple phases or run continuously. For example, preparation of user manuals often starts during the coding phase and is completed during the testing phase. Project management starts early, at the beginning of the requirements phase, and runs throughout the entire development cycle.

As an example of the third problem, neither *quality assurance* nor *technical writing* nor *integration* are usually identified as phases, but the total amount of effort devoted to these three kinds of work can sometimes top 25 percent of the total effort for software projects. There is a common tendency to underestimate activities that are not phases, and this explains why most manual estimates tend toward excessive optimism for both costs and schedules.

The most that can be said about manual phase-level estimates is that they are slightly more useful than overall project estimates and are just about as easy to prepare. However, they are far from sufficient for contracts, budgets, or serious business purposes.

The third form of manual estimation, which is to estimate each activity or task using a formal work-breakdown structure, is far and away the most accurate of the manual methods.

This rigorous estimating approach originated in the 1960s for large military software projects and has proven to be a powerful and effective method that supports other forms of project management, such as critical path analysis. (Indeed, the best commercial estimating tools operate by automating software estimates to the level of activities and tasks derived from a work-breakdown structure.)

The downside of manual estimating via a detailed work-breakdown structure of perhaps 50 activities, or 250 or so tasks, is that it is very time-consuming to create the estimate initially, and it is even more difficult to make modifications when the requirements change or the scope of the project needs to be adjusted.

Overview of Automated
Software-Estimating Methods

The first two forms of automated estimating methods are very similar to the equivalent manual forms of estimation, only faster and easier to use. The forms of automated estimation that start with general equations for the staffing, effort, and schedule requirements of a complete software project are termed *macroestimation*.

These macroestimation tools usually support two levels of granularity: (1) estimates to the level of complete projects, and (2) estimates to the level of phases, using built-in assumptions for the ratios and percentages assigned to each phase.

Although these macroestimation tools replicate the features of manual estimates, many of them provide some valuable extra features that go beyond the capabilities of manual methods.

Recall that automated software-estimation tools are built on a knowledge base of hundreds, or even thousands, of software projects. This knowledge base allows the automated estimation tools to make adjustments to the basic estimating equations in response to the major factors that affect software project outcomes, such as the following:

- Adjustments for levels of staff experience

- Adjustments for software development processes

- Adjustments for specific programming languages used

- Adjustments for the size of the software application

- Adjustments for work habits and overtime

The downside of macroestimation tools is that they do not usually produce estimates that are granular enough to support all of the important software-development activities. For example, many specialized activities tend to be omitted from macroestimation tools, such as the production of user manuals, the effort by quality-assurance personnel, the effort by database administrators, and sometimes even the effort of project managers.

The automated estimating tools that are built upon a detailed work-breakdown structure are termed *microestimating* tools. The method of operation of microestimation is the reverse of that of macroestimation.

The macroestimation tools begin with general equations for complete projects, and then use ratios and percentages to assign resources and time to specific phases.

The microestimation tools work in the opposite direction. They first create a detailed work-breakdown structure for the project being estimated, and then estimate each activity separately. When all of the activity-level or task-level estimates are complete, the estimating tool then sums the partial results to reach an overall estimate for staffing, effort, schedule, and cost requirements. The advantages of activity-based microestimation are the following:

1. The granularity of the data makes the estimates suitable for contracts and budgets.

2. Errors, if any, tend to be local within an activity, rather than global.

3. New or unusual activities can be added as the need arises.

4. Activities not performed for specific projects can be backed out.

5. The impact of specialists, such as technical writers, can be seen.

6. Validation of the estimate is straightforward, because nothing is hidden.

A critical aspect of software estimation is the chart of accounts used, or the set of activities for which resource and cost data are estimated. The topic of selecting the activities to be included in software project estimates is a difficult issue and cannot be taken lightly. There are four main contenders:

1. Project-level measurements

2. Phase-level measurements

3. Activity-level measurements

4. Task-level measurements

Before illustrating these four concepts, it is well to begin by defining what each one means in a software context, with some common examples.

A *project* is defined as the implementation of software that satisfies a cohesive set of business and technical requirements. Under this definition, a project can be either a standalone program, such as an accounting application or a compiler, or a component of a large software system, such as the supervisor component of an operating system. The manager responsible for building the application, or one of the components of larger applications, is termed the *project manager.*

Software projects can be of any size, but those where software cost estimating and project management tools are utilized are most commonly those of perhaps 1000 function points, or 100,000 source code statements, and larger. Looking at the project situation from another view, in a cost-estimating and project management context, formal project estimates and formal project plans are usually required for projects that will require more than one full-time staff member and will run for more than about three calendar months.

A *phase* is a chronological time period during which much of the effort of the project team is devoted to completing a major milestone or constructing a key deliverable item. There is no exact number of phases, and their time intervals vary. However, the phase concept for software projects implies a chronological sequence starting with requirements and ending with installation or deployment.

An example of a typical phase structure for a software project might include the following:

1. The requirements phase

2. The analysis phase

3. The design and specification phase

4. The coding phase

5. The integration and testing phase

6. The installation phase

7. The maintenance phase

Of course, some kinds of work, such as project management, quality assurance, and the production of user documents, span multiple phases. Within a phase, multiple kinds of activities might be performed. For example, the testing phase might have as few as one kind of testing or as many as a dozen discrete forms of testing.

The phase structure is only a rough approximation that shows general information. Phases are not sufficient or precise enough for cost estimates that will be used in contracts or will have serious business implications.

An *activity* is defined as the sum of the effort needed to complete a key milestone or a key deliverable item. For example, one key activity is gathering user requirements. Other activities for software projects would be completion of external design, completion of design reviews on the external design, completion of internal or logical design, completion of design reviews on the logical design, completion of database design, completion of a test plan, completion of a user's guide, and almost any number of others.

There are no limits on the activities utilized for software projects, but from about 15 to 50 key deliverables constitute a normal range for software cost estimating purposes. Activities differ from phases in that they do not assume a chronological sequence; also, multiple activities are found within any given phase. For example, during a typical software project's testing phase it would be common to find the following six discrete testing activities:

1. New function testing

2. Regression testing

3. Component testing

4. Integration testing

5. Stress testing

6. System testing

A *task* is defined as the set of steps or the kinds of work necessary to complete a given activity. Using the activity of unit testing as an example, four tasks normally included in that activity might comprise the following:

1. Test case construction

2. Test case running or execution

3. Defect repairs for any problems found

4. Repair validation and retesting

There is no fixed ratio of the number of tasks that constitute activities, but from 4 to perhaps 12 tasks for each activity are very common patterns.

Of these four levels of granularity, only activity and task estimates will allow estimates with a precision of better than 10 percent in repeated trials. Further, neither project-level nor phase-level estimates will be useful in modeling process improvement strategies, or in carrying out "what if" alternative analysis to discover the impact of various tools, methods, and approaches. This kind of modeling of alternative scenarios is a key feature of automated software-estimating approaches, and a very valuable tool for software project managers.

Estimating only at the level of full projects or approximate phases correlates strongly with cost and schedule overruns, and even with litigation for breach of contract, since the data cannot be used for serious business purposes with safety.

This is not to say that phase-level or even project-level estimates have no value. These concise estimating modes are very often used for early sizing and estimating long before enough solid information is available to tune or adjust a full activity-level estimate.

Also, for in-house software where there are no legal liabilities or risks of being sued, phase-level estimates may well be sufficient for smaller projects involving only one or two people for no more than a few months of effort.

However, for projects that may involve large teams of people, have expenses of more than $1 million, or have any kind of legal liabilities associated with missed schedules, cost overruns, or poor quality, then a much more rigorous kind of estimating and planning will be necessary.

A fundamental problem with the coarse estimating approaches at the project and phase levels is that there is no way of being sure what activities are present and what activities (such as user manual preparation) might have been accidentally left out.

Also, data estimated to the levels of activities and tasks can easily be rolled up to provide phase-level and project-level views. The reverse is not true: You cannot explode project-level data or phase-level data down to the lower levels with acceptable accuracy and precision. If you start an estimate with data that is too coarse, you will not be able to do very much with it.

Table 4.1 gives an illustration that can clarify the differences. Assume you are thinking of estimating a project such as the construction of a small switching system. Shown are the activities that might be included at the levels of the project, phases, and activities for the chart of accounts used to build the final cost estimate.

Even more granular than activity-based cost estimates would be the next level, or task-based cost estimates. Each activity in Table 4.1 can be expanded down a level (or even more). For example, activity 16 in Table 4.1 is identified as *unit testing*. Expanding the activity of unit testing down to the task level might show six major tasks:

Activity	Tasks
Unit testing	1. Test case creation
	2. Test case validation
	3. Test case execution
	4. Defect analysis
	5. Defect repairs
	6. Repair validation

Assuming that each of the 25 activities in Table 4.1 could be expanded to a similar degree, then the total number of tasks would be 150. This level of granularity would lead to maximum precision for a software project estimate, but it is far too complex for manual estimating approaches, at least for ease and convenience of use.

Although some large software systems consisting of multiple components may actually reach the level of more than 3000 tasks, this is a misleading situation. In reality, most large software systems are

TABLE 4.1   Project-, Phase-, and Activity-Level Estimating Charts of Accounts

Project level	Phase level	Activity level
Project	1. Requirements	1. Requirements
	2. Analysis	2. Prototyping
	3. Design	3. Architecture
	4. Coding	4. Planning
	5. Testing	5. Initial design
	6. Installation	6. Detail design
		7. Design review
		8. Coding
		9. Reused code acquisition
		10. Package acquisition
		11. Code inspection
		12. Independent verification and validation
		13. Configuration control
		14. Integration
		15. User documentation
		16. Unit testing
		17. Function testing
		18. Integration testing
		19. System testing
		20. Field testing
		21. Acceptance testing
		22. Independent testing
		23. Quality assurance
		24. Installation
		25. Management

really comprised of somewhere between half a dozen and 50 discrete components that are built more or less in parallel and are constructed using very similar sets of activities. The absolute number of tasks, once duplications are removed, seldom exceeds 100, even for enormous systems that may top 10 million source code statements or 100,000 function points.

Only in situations where hybrid projects are being constructed so that hardware, software, microcode, and purchased parts are being simultaneously planned and estimated will the number of activities and tasks top 1000, and these hybrid projects are outside the scope of software cost estimating tools. Indeed, really massive and complex hybrid projects will stress any kind of management tool.

For day-to-day software estimation, somewhere between 10 and 30 activities and perhaps 30 to 150 tasks will accommodate almost any software application in the modern world and will allow estimates with sufficient precision for use in contracts and business documents.

If you estimate software cost data only to the project level, you will have no idea of the inner structure of the work that goes on. Therefore, the data will not give you the ability to analyze activity-based cost factors, and it will be almost useless for purposes of process improvement.

Estimating to the phase level is marginally better, but tends to be deceptive. The phase structure gives a false impression that everything is included, when in fact a number of major activities, such as production of user manuals, integration, and project management, span multiple phases and must not be left out by accident. Because they do span multiple phases, these "invisible" activities tend to confuse the estimate and make validation difficult.

Estimating to the activity level is the first level suitable for contracts, budgets, outsourcing agreements, and other serious business purposes. Indeed, the use of simplistic project or phase-level estimates for software contracts is very hazardous and may well lead to some kind of litigation for breach of contract.

Estimating at the activity level does not imply that every project performs every activity. For example, small MIS projects and client/server applications normally perform only 10 or so of the 25 activities that are shown previously. Systems software such as operating systems and large switching systems will typically perform about 20 of the 25 activities. Only large military and defense systems will routinely perform all 25.

However, it is better to start with a full chart of accounts and eliminate activities that will not be used. That way you will be sure that significant cost drivers, such as user documentation, are not left out accidentally because they are not part of just one phase.

Table 4.2 illustrates some of the activity patterns associated with six general kinds of software projects:

1. End-user applications

2. Management information systems (MIS)

3. Contract or outsourced projects

4. Systems software projects

5. Commercial software projects

6. Military software projects

TABLE 4.2 Typical Activity Patterns for Six Software Domains

Activities performed	End user	MIS	Outsource	Commercial	Systems	Military
01 Requirements		X	X	X	X	X
02 Prototyping	X	X	X	X	X	X
03 Architecture		X	X	X	X	X
04 Project plans		X	X	X	X	X
05 Initial design		X	X	X	X	X
06 Detail design		X	X	X	X	X
07 Design reviews		X	X	X	X	X
08 Coding	X	X	X	X	X	X
09 Reuse acquisition	X		X	X	X	X
10 Package purchase		X	X		X	X
11 Code inspections				X	X	X
12 Independent verification and validation						X
13 Configuration management		X	X	X	X	X
14 Formal integration		X	X	X	X	X
15 Documentation	X	X	X	X	X	X
16 Unit testing	X	X	X	X	X	X
17 Function testing		X	X	X	X	X
18 Integration testing		X	X	X	X	X
19 System testing		X	X	X	X	X
20 Field testing				X	X	X
21 Acceptability testing		X	X		X	X
22 Independent testing						X
23 Quality assurance			X	X	X	X
24 Installation and training		X	X		X	X
25 Project management		X	X	X	X	X
Activities	5	16	20	21	22	25

As can be seen from Table 4.2, activity-based costing makes visible some important differences in software-development practices. This level of granularity is highly advantageous in software contracts and is also very useful for preparing detailed schedules that are not likely to be exceeded for such trivial reasons as accidentally omitting an activity.

Now that the topic of activity-based estimating has been discussed, it is of interest to illustrate some of the typical outputs that are available from commercial software-estimating tools. Table 4.3 illustrates a hypothetical 1000–function point systems software project written in the C programming language.

TABLE 4.3   Example of Activity-Based Software Cost Estimating

Project type: Systems software of 1000 function points (125,000 C statements)
Project start: January 6, 1997
First delivery: July 15, 1998

Activity	Start date	End date	Schedule, months	Effort, months	Staffing	Cost, $
Planning	1/6/97	6/29/98	17.71	13.54	0.76	67,700
Management	1/6/97	8/15/98	17.40	19.45	1.12	97,250
Requirements	2/14/97	4/4/97	1.61	6.86	4.26	34,300
Prototyping	2/27/97	3/30/97	1.02	2.39	2.34	11,950
Configuration management	3/15/97	7/20/98	16.50	8.50	0.52	42,500
Functional design	3/6/97	5/12/97	2.20	15.72	7.15	78,600
Design reviews 1	3/24/97	5/12/97	1.61	3.92	2.43	19,600
Detail design	4/29/97	8/7/97	2.27	16.07	7.08	80,350
Design reviews 2	6/9/97	7/7/97	0.92	4.20	4.57	21,000
Quality assurance	4/3/97	7/28/98	15.80	5.50	0.35	27,500
Coding	5/15/97	4/15/98	9.01	64.44	7.15	322,200
Reuse acquisition	7/1/97	7/13/97	0.39	0.29	0.74	1,450
Code inspections	11/1/97	3/25/98	3.37	11.60	3.44	58,000
Unit test	11/13/97	4/8/98	4.89	5.19	1.06	25,950
Function test	1/30/98	5/5/98	5.01	16.08	3.21	80,400
System test	2/13/98	4/25/98	4.07	20.57	5.05	102,850
Field test	4/20/98	6/1/98	1.45	4.28	2.95	21,400
User documents	11/15/97	5/25/97	6.20	26.70	4.31	133,500
Document reviews	2/1/98	5/5/98	5.65	5.27	0.93	26,350
Installation	4/15/98	7/20/98	3.10	13.43	4.33	67,150
Average staff level					14.47	
Overlapped schedule			18.24			
Waterfall schedule			120.18			
Paid effort and costs				264.00		1,320,000
Unpaid overtime				41.64		
Total effort				305.64		
Cost per function point						1,320.00
Cost per SLOC						10.56

The granularity of the estimate is set at the activity level, and the project is assumed to have started on January 6, 1997. In this example, the average burdened salary level for all project personnel is set at $5000 per month.

Although most of the outputs from this illustrative example are straightforward, several aspects might benefit from a discussion. First, note that 20 out of the 25 activities are shown, which is not uncommon for systems software in this size range.

Second, note that the overlapped schedule and the waterfall schedule are quite different. The waterfall schedule of roughly 120 calendar months is simply the arithmetic sum of the schedules of the various activities used. This schedule would probably never occur in real life, because software projects always start activities before the previous activities are completed. As a simple example, design usually starts when the requirements are only about 75 percent complete. Coding usually starts when the design is less than 50 percent complete, and so on.

The overlapped schedule of just over 18 months reflects a much more common scenario, and assumes that nothing is really finished when the next activity begins.

The third aspect of this example that merits discussion is the fact that unpaid overtime amounts to almost 42 staff months, which is about 14 percent of the total effort devoted to the project. This much unpaid overtime is a sign of three important factors:

1. The software personnel are exempt, and don't receive overtime payments.

2. Schedule pressure is probably intense for so much unpaid overtime to accrue.

3. There are major differences between *real* and *apparent* productivity rates.

If the unpaid overtime is left out (which is a common practice), then the apparent productivity rate for this project is 3.78 function points per staff month, or 473 source code statements per staff month.

If the unpaid overtime is included, then the real productivity rate for this project is 3.27 function points per staff month, or 409 source code statements per staff month. It can easily be seen that the omission or inclusion of unpaid overtime can exert a major influence on overall productivity rates.

Although coding is the most expensive single activity for this project, and costs almost $322,200 out of the total cost of just over $1,320,000, that is still only a little over 24 percent of the total cost for the project.

By contrast, the nine activities associated with defect removal (quality assurance, reviews, inspections, and testing) total to about $383,000 or roughly 29 percent of the overall development cost.

The activities associated with producing paper documents (plans, requirements, design, and user manuals) total to more than $394,000 or about 30 percent of the development cost.

Without the granularity of going down at least to the level of activity-based costs, the heavy proportion of noncoding costs might very well be underestimated, and it would be difficult to ascertain if these costs were even present in the estimate. With activity-based costs, at least errors tend to be visible and, hence, can be corrected.

The overlap in project schedules is difficult to see from just a list of start and stop dates. This is why calendar intervals are usually shown visually in the form of Gantt charts, critical path networks, or PERT charts.

Figure 4.1 illustrates a Gantt chart that would accompany an activity-based cost estimate such as the one shown in Table 4.3. The provision of graphs and charts is a standard feature of a number of software cost estimating tools, because graphical outputs make the visualization of key information easier to comprehend.

Many estimating tools allow users to switch back and forth between numerical and graphical output, to print out either or both kinds, and in some cases, to actually make adjustments to the estimate by manipulating the graphs themselves.

Analyzing the Gantt chart, it is easy to see why the waterfall schedule and the overlapped schedule differ by a ratio of almost 8 to 1. The sum of the schedules for the individual software activities is never equal to the elapsed time, because most activities are performed in parallel and overlap both their predecessor and their successor activities.

Incidentally, the kinds of Gantt chart information shown in both Table 4.3 and Fig. 4.1 are standard output from such software-estimating tools as CHECKPOINT, KnowledgePlan, SLIM, and a number of others.

However, if schedule information were needed down to the level of tasks, or even below that to the level of individual employees, then the data would usually be exported from a cost-estimating tool and imported into a project-planning tool, such as Microsoft Project.

The kinds of information shown in Table 4.3 and Fig. 4.1 are only a few of the kinds of data that modern software cost estimating tools can provide. Many of the other capabilities will be illustrated later in this book, as will some of the many other kinds of reports and analyses.

For example, software cost estimating output reports also include quality and reliability estimates, maintenance and enhancement estimates, analyses of risks, and sometimes even evaluations of the

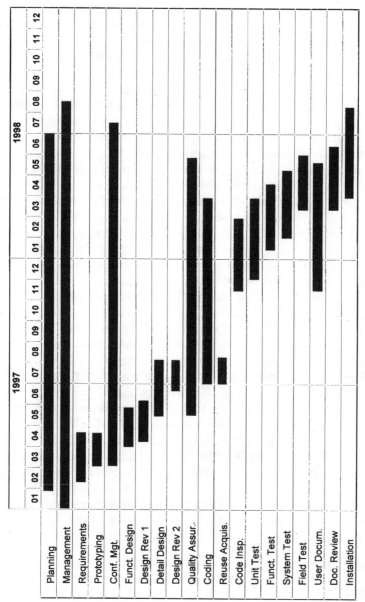

Figure 4.1　Sample Gantt chart output from a software cost estimating tool.

strengths and weaknesses of the methods and tools being applied to the software project being estimated.

Strength and weakness analysis is also a useful capability for other purposes, such as moving up the Software Engineering Institute (SEI) capability maturity model. Since modern software cost estimation tools, many of which include measurement capabilities, can include as many as a hundred or more influential factors, their ability to focus on topics where the project is either better or worse than industry norms is a great asset for process-improvement work.

In spite of the advantages derived from using software cost estimation tools, surveys by the author at software project management and metrics conferences indicate that the most accurate forms of software cost estimation are not the most widely used.

The frequency of use among a sample of approximately 500 project managers interviewed during 1996 and 1997 is as shown in Table 4.4.

The fact that manual estimating methods, which are known to be inaccurate, are the most widely utilized approach is one of the more troubling problems of the software project management domain. From interviews with software project managers, the main reasons for the continued use of manual methods are interesting.

As of 1998, there are 50 or so commercial software cost estimating tools on the market in the United States, and perhaps 25 overseas. However, most of them are sold by independent corporations with rather small advertising and marketing budgets. There has not yet been a major marketing push to make software cost estimating tools visible to a majority of software project managers.

A second reason concerns the pricing of commercial software cost estimating tools. Because of the value of the attached knowledge base, software cost estimating tools have traditionally been priced much higher than other project management tools. The first tier of top-selling commercial software-estimation tools, such as CHECK-POINT, ESTIMACS, PRICE-S, SEER, and SLIM, have been priced in the $5000- to $20,000-per-seat range from the 1970s through the mid-1990s.

The high prices of the first tier of commercial estimating tools reflect the value of the associated data derived from hundreds or

TABLE 4.4   Frequency of Usage of Software Cost Estimating Methods

Estimating methodology	Project management usage
Manual software estimating	63%
Automated software estimating	37%
Total	100%

thousands of software projects that comes with the cost-estimating tools, plus the value of the proprietary estimating algorithms. However, as the twentieth century winds down the prices for software cost estimating tools are beginning to decline, and some of the newer commercial estimating tools, such as ProQMS and KnowledgePlan, are now dropping below $2500 per seat even with extensive attached knowledge bases.

The reduction in prices for the newer estimating tools is due to increased competition in the estimating domain, plus a desire on the part of the vendors to reach the large market of clients in small companies who cannot afford the high costs of the earlier software cost estimation tools.

Below the first tier of commercial software estimation tools runs a second tier of lower-cost tools, often based at least in part on the published algorithms of Dr. Barry Boehm's constructive cost model (COCOMO; Boehm 1981). Tools in this category range from shareware to perhaps a few hundred dollars.

The second-tier tools often lack a number of the features of those in the first tier, such as quality estimation and activity-base costing, but they still provide useful capabilities and are often the entry point for organizations interested in improving their estimating abilities.

Some of the tools derived in part from the COCOMO algorithms include REVIC (for *revised COCOMO*), which is a military software estimation tool; Before You Leap (BYL), which is aimed at civilian software; and GECOMO (marketed by GE Marconi), which is also a general-purpose software-estimation tool.

Over and above standalone software cost estimation tools, many vendors of more general-purpose tools, such as computer-aided software engineering (CASE) and methodology management tools, have included at least rudimentary software cost estimation capabilities. For example, the Texas Instruments Information Engineering Facility (IEF) contains a function point–based estimation feature that estimates projects developed using the IEF itself. The LBMS Process Engineer methodology management tool also contains a basic estimating tool for information systems, although it does not perform activity- or task-level estimates or include quality and reliability estimates.

In general, the estimating tools that are embedded in other kinds of tools, such as CASE and methodology management tools, are not as complete as the more specialized standalone estimating tools, such as COCOMO II, SLIM, CHECKPOINT, and KnowledgePlan. However, in all its various forms, software cost estimation is a critical activity which needs to be carried out with professional competence.

The literature on estimating methods is divided fairly sharply into books that feature manual estimating approaches, and books that discuss estimating tools. Some books, such as Dr. Barry Boehm's *Software Engineering Economics* (Boehm 1981), bridge this gap, of course.

Tom DeMarco's excellent work *Controlling Software Projects* (DeMarco 1982) is in the set of books that discuss manual estimation. His later book with Tim Lister, *Peopleware* (DeMarco and Lister 1987), adds some insights into the human component of estimation and software engineering.

Dean Barrow and colleagues of the Air Force prepared an interesting study in 1993 that evaluated the features of about 20 software cost estimating tools (Barrow et al. 1993), which is probably as many estimating tools as has ever been examined in a single report.

Fred Brooks, in his classic *The Mythical Man-Month* (Brooks 1974) discusses the need for greater estimation accuracy in the context of IBM's development of OS/360.

The function point metric is now a mainstream tool for software cost estimation. The books of Brian Dreger (Dreger 1989) and Garmus and Herron (Garmus and Herron 1995) discuss estimation using function points, which is also the topic of Charles Symons, the well-known developer of the Mark II function point method (Symons 1991).

Watts Humphrey writes in the manual-estimating genre and discusses manual estimation models in both of his interesting books on software processes (Humphrey 1990, 1995). Humphrey is concerned with estimating programming and does not deal extensively with ancillary topics, such as user manuals and project management.

In his own prior books (Jones 1993, 1994, 1995, 1996, 1997) the author tries to deal with both manual estimation and automated estimation, with the caveat that automated estimation methods are preferred for large systems above 1000 function points in size. For small projects or those without any contractual obligations, manual methods are adequate.

References

Barrow, Dean, Susan Nilson, and Dawn Timberlake: *Software Estimation Technology Report,* Air Force Software Technology Support Center, Hill Air Force Base, Utah, 1993.

Boehm, Barry: *Software Engineering Economics,* Prentice Hall, Englewood Cliffs, N.J., 1981.

Brooks, Fred: *The Mythical Man-Month,* Addison-Wesley, Reading, Mass., 1974, rev. 1995.

Brown, Norm (ed.): *The Program Manager's Guide to Software Acquisition Best Practices,* Version 1.0, U.S. Department of Defense, Washington, D.C., July 1995.

DeMarco, Tom: *Controlling Software Projects,* Yourdon Press, New York, ISBN 0-917072-32-4, 1982.

——— and Tim Lister: *Peopleware,* Dorset House, New York, ISBN 0-932633-05-6, 1987.

————: *Why Does Software Cost So Much?,* Dorset House, New York, ISBN 0-932633-34-X, 1995.

Department of the Air Force, *Guidelines for Successful Acquisition and Management of Software Intensive Systems,* vols. 1 and 2, Software Technology Support Center, Hill Air Force Base, Utah, 1994.

Dreger, Brian: *Function Point Analysis,* Prentice Hall, Englewood Cliffs, N.J., 1989.

Garmus, David, and David Herron: *Measuring the Software Process: A Practical Guide to Functional Measurement,* Prentice Hall, Englewood Cliffs, N.J., 1995.

Humphrey, Watts: *Managing the Software Process,* Addison-Wesley, Reading, Mass., 1990.

————: *A Discipline of Software Engineering,* Addison-Wesley, Reading, Mass., 1995.

Jones, Capers: 1993, 1994. Author: Please add.

————: *Patterns of Software System Failure and Success,* International Thomson Computer Press, Boston, ISBN 1-850-32804-8, 1995.

————: *Applied Software Measurement,* 2d ed., McGraw-Hill, New York, ISBN 0-07-032826-9, 1996.

————: *Software Quality—Analysis and Guidelines for Success,* International Thomson Computer Press, Boston, ISBN 1-85032-867-6, 1997a.

————: *The Year 2000 Software Problem—Quantifying the Costs and Assessing the Consequences,* Addison-Wesley/Longman, Reading, Mass., ISBN 0-201-30964-5, 1997b.

Kan, Stephen H.: *Metrics and Models in Software Quality Engineering,* Addison-Wesley, Reading, Mass., ISBN 0-201-63339-6, 1995.

Symons, Charles R: *Software Sizing and Estimating—Mk II FPA (Function Point Analysis),* John Wiley & Sons, Chichester, U.K., ISBN 0-471-92985-9, 1991.

5

Software Cost Estimating and Other Software Project Management Tools

Modern software cost estimating tools are based on a number of technologies and a long stream of research dating back to the mid-1940s. Some of the underlying technologies that are now part of contemporary software cost estimation tools include the following:

- Operations research
- Multiple regression analysis
- Analysis of variance (ANOVA)
- Critical path analysis
- Program evaluation and review technique (PERT)
- Cost accounting
- Cost of quality analysis
- Root cause analysis
- Software measurement and metrics
- Function point analysis

These same underlying technologies are also part of project management tools outside the specialized domain of software. For example, there are project management and estimating tools available for civil engineering projects, mechanical engineering projects, electrical engineering projects, and the construction of various buildings, bridges, and the like.

As this book is being written, there are many kinds of both general and specialized tools available to software project managers. However, these tools tend to be produced by independent companies and are not integrated into a cohesive, total suite of software project management capabilities.

In order to give a context to software project management tools, an illustration of the various kinds of information that software project managers are concerned with and the business purposes to which this information might be put will supply a context to the overall universe of software project management tools.

As can easily be seen from Fig. 5.1, software project management is a complex, multifaceted activity. Indeed, software project management is one of the more difficult forms of project management because the primary artifact, software itself, is essentially an invisible and intangible substance that does not lend itself to visual examination.

While it is true that software can be visually inspected by trained personnel, the fact remains that software is a very abstract topic that is difficult to encompass either visually or mentally. This means that such project management functions as judging the stage of completeness of a product or the quality of software must rely on indirect methods.

An interesting approach is to examine the set of software project management tools utilized in order to see how software cost estimating tools fit into context with other kinds of software project management tools. There are 18 general kinds of tools available for software

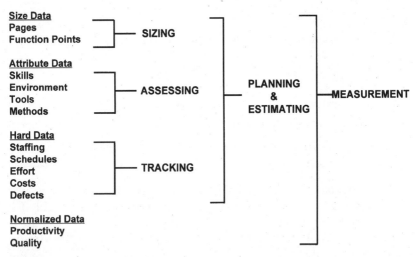

Figure 5.1   Software project management information categories.

project managers as this book is being written, and several more categories of experimental management tools may soon be deployed.

A recent usage of the function point metric is that of evaluating the capacities of various kinds of software tools. Table 5.1 shows an overall total of the 18 different kinds of software project management tools, ranked in descending order of tool capacities.

Table 5.1 also shows the patterns of project management tools noted in lagging, average, and leading software organizations as a by-product of performing software-assessment and benchmark studies. (Table 5.1 is derived from studies of large enterprises with more than 1000 software personnel.)

Although some of these independent capabilities may be found in the same tool, it is currently more common to have separate tools for most project management functions. It is also common to have gaps, or to lack tools for a number of management functions.

These separate tools may or may not share data and information, although there are some common kinds of linkages, such as the bidi-

TABLE 5.1 Software Project Management Tool Categories and Sizes Noted in Lagging, Average, and Leading Enterprises

Tool capacities are expressed in terms of function point size.

Tool category	Lagging	Average	Leading
Cost estimating	0	500	2,500
Project planning	1,000	1,500	2,500
Statistical analysis	0	750	2,500
Methodology management	0	1,250	2,500
Year-2000 analysis	0	0	2,000
Quality estimating	0	0	2,000
Risk analysis	0	0	1,500
Portfolio analysis	0	0	1,500
Assessment support	0	350	1,500
Project measurement	0	0	1,250
Complexity analysis	0	350	1,250
Value analysis	0	0	1,250
Budget support	0	500	1,000
Variance reporting	0	250	750
Project tracking	300	500	750
Defect tracking	0	125	750
Function point analysis	0	350	750
Source code counting	0	100	500
Total	1,300	6,525	26,750

rectional movement of data between cost-estimating and project-planning tools.

It would be interesting to create a complete listing of all known software project management tools. However, the total number of specific tools in the 18 categories discussed in this book would exceed 600. Even if each tool received only half a page of commentary, the total volume of information would be almost as large as this book. Further, it is certain that several new tools would appear while such a tool inventory was being created, and perhaps a few older tools would be withdrawn.

The closest approach to a full listing of project management tools is the Applied Computer Research (ACR) annual catalog of metrics and project management tools edited by Alan Howard (Howard 1997). This annual catalog is part of a larger set of linked catalogs that cover the following subjects:

Metrics and project management tools

Requirements analysis, design, and CASE tools

Application development systems

Testing and debugging tools

Database management and developer support tools

Data warehousing and user-support tools

Development support tools for programmers and designers

Programming languages and compilers

These catalogs have about 10 short tool discussions per page, and the total number of pages in the entire set totals to about 600 pages, which implies that there are at least 6000 commercial tools aimed at various aspects of software development, maintenance, and management.

Note that over and above the set of tools needed to manage software projects, project managers also have a need for tools to deal with personnel management. There are a number of commercial and proprietary tools available for handling appraisals, for salary planning, and for other human resource activities. However, those tools are not concerned with projects and, hence, are not discussed in this book.

There are also corporate functions that project managers participate in, such as annual budget cycles, office space planning, capital equipment leasing or purchasing, travel requests and approval, and general administrative work. Here, too, a number of proprietary and commercial tools support these activities, but since such corporate matters do not deal with specific projects, they are not discussed either.

The focus of this book is on the tools and methods for dealing with specific software projects.

Available Software Management Tools

Following are brief discussions of the 18 kinds of software project management tool categories that are now deployed and available. Although some specific tools are mentioned, there are far too many tools for a complete list. Therefore, the tools cited are merely representative of the kinds of tools in each category.

Software cost estimating tools

Software cost estimating tools are key weapons in the project management arsenal. Indeed, some large corporations own several different tools and run them on key projects to see if they reach a convergent result. Software cost estimating tools are specialized predictive tools aimed specifically at software projects.

Software cost estimating tools are derived from and accompanied by a knowledge base of software projects that may number in the thousands. The top-line software cost estimating tools can top 3000 function points, and they include many powerful features, such as full sizing capabilities, activity-based schedule and cost estimating capabilities, quality and reliability estimating capabilities, and many more.

Most modern software cost estimating tools support both function point and lines-of-code estimates and include automatic conversion in either direction.

Several software estimating tools include a side-by-side capability, which can show the same project as it might appear using two different development scenarios so that the value of effective QA methods can easily be seen.

Software cost estimating tools can provide schedule estimates too, but usually only to the phase or activity levels. To drop down to the scheduling of individual employees, it is usually necessary to export data to project-planning tools. Indeed, bidirectional data transfer between cost-estimating tools and project-planning tools is possible.

Examples of standalone commercial software cost estimating tools include the Adaptive Estimating Model (AEM), Before You Leap (BYL), Bridge Modeler, CHECKPOINT, COCOMO, COCOMO II, CoCoPro, COSTMODELER, COSTMODL, COSTAR, COSTEXPERT, ESTIMACS, GECOMO, KnowledgePlan, MicroMan, PRICE-S, ProQMS, REVIC, SASET, SOFTCALC, SOFTCOST, SEER, SLIM, SPQR/20, and perhaps 50 others in the United States alone.

There are other forms of software cost estimating tools embedded within a number of CASE and methodology management tools. For example, the Texas Instruments Information Engineering Facility (IEF) includes an embedded function point analysis and estimating tool for IEF projects. The LBMS methodology management tool, Process Engineer, also includes a form of software function point and estimating capability. Also, the Andersen METHOD/1 approach includes integral cost estimation.

Project-planning (project management) tools

Project-planning tools are standard general-purpose scheduling tools for performing critical path analyses, producing Gantt and PERT charts, and, in general, laying out the sequence of activities associated with a project of any type, including software projects. These tools can also accumulate costs and handle staffing patterns, but unlike software cost estimating tools, they lack an attached knowledge base of software project data.

The commercial project-planning tool market started more than 10 years before the commercial software cost estimating market, which explains in part the much larger numbers of users of planning tools. Also, many project-planning tool vendors are major powers in the software marketing world, such as Computer Associates and Microsoft.

These planning tools are often called "project management" tools, but for software projects they perform such a limited function that the term *project management* is actually something of a misnomer. For example, none of the commercial project management tools can deal with software quality, with different programming languages, or with the implications of various software styles, such as Rapid Application Development (RAD), object-oriented (OO) development, or the spiral method of development.

However, some of the leading-edge project-planning tools can top 2500 function points in size and have a number of other useful functions besides schedule planning, such as project tracking, cost accumulation, milestone tracking, and the like.

Examples of project-planning tools include Artemis, FastPROJECT, Computer Associates PLANMACS, Microsoft Project, MultiTrak, Primavera, Project Manager's Workbench (PMW), Time Line, and at least 80 others in the United States alone. These tools differ from the specialized software-estimating tools in that they are general-purpose tools which do not have an attached software project knowledge base containing data on thousands of software projects.

A major use for project management tools is to create plans down to the level of specific workers. For ease of use in producing very granular plans, modern project-planning tools are now standard management tools in most high-technology industries, including software.

Project-planning tools and software cost estimating tools are often closely coupled, and some support bidirectional data transfer. For example, the ABT Project Manager's Workbench (PMW) planning tool and the ABT Bridge Modeler estimating tool can share data in both directions. This kind of bidirectional data transfer can also occur for SPR's KnowledgePlan software cost estimating tool and Microsoft Project.

Statistical analysis tools

All measurement programs for either productivity or quality require at least rudimentary statistical analysis. There are at least a dozen excellent statistical tools on the market, and some are even available in the form of freeware or shareware from the Internet or bulletin boards, in addition to the larger and more sophisticated commercial statistical tools such as SAS® or StatPak. In addition, the statistical functions supported by such spreadsheets as Excel, Lotus, Quattro, and the like are also widely used for software analytical work.

Statistical tools are quite common in large and sophisticated companies that capture data from dozens, or even hundreds, of software projects and perform internal or external benchmark studies. The most common use for statistical tools is for producing averages for productivity and quality by organization unit and by time period. The larger and more complete statistical tools can exceed 2500 function points in size.

Methodology management (process management) tools

Methodology or process management tools are a fairly new category of software project management tool. Some of these methodology management tools may include planning and estimating support, and also aspects of risk management and even quality estimation.

The methodology management tools are usually keyed to one or more of the standard software development methodologies, such as information engineering, rapid application development (RAD), Merise, or conventional structured analysis and design. Within this context, they provide guidance for what deliverables are needed, for scheduling, for planning, and for other management topics.

The concept of the methodology management approach is to aggregate a number of managerial functions under one umbrella. Here, too, these tools may be coupled to software project planning and software-estimating tools, or planning and estimating capabilities may be integrated into the methodology management tool itself.

Some examples of methodology or process management tools include the LBMS Process Engineer, PLATINUM's Process Continuum, the TRANSFORM tools of the SHL Systems House, the ForeSight tool by Knowledgeware, the PRIDE tool from M. Bryce & Associates, and many more.

The term *methodology management* includes tools that span a range from somewhat rudimentary tools of less than 1000 function points to very comprehensive tools that can approach or exceed 3000 function points in size. The category of methodology management tools is growing rapidly in terms of both the number of available tools and also the capabilities of the tools themselves.

Year-2000 analysis tools

The onrushing year-2000 problem concerns the historical practice of storing calendar dates in two-digit formats, so that the year 1997 might be stored as 97 in computer software applications. At the end of the century, when 1999 switches to 2000, many applications will fail or produce incorrect results because their internal logic cannot deal with the fact that the year 99 will be followed by the year 00.

A host of new tools for analyzing the incidence of year-2000 hits has become commercially available within the past 18 months of this writing, and new tools are being announced almost daily. The general mode of these tools is to scan source code or data bases for instances of year-2000 hits. Sometimes these tools include automated or semi-automated repair logic. However, whether these tools can find 100 percent of the year-2000 hits is still unknown.

Also, there are dozens of year-2000 search engines aimed at common languages, such as COBOL, but for many languages, there are none at all. As this book is being written there are more than 500 programming languages in use, and the entire universe of year-2000 search engines seems to cover only about 50 of these languages. For software written in such languages as CHILL, CMS2, CORAL, JOVIAL, PLM, RATFOR, or hundreds of other specialized programming languages, there may be no automated year-2000 search tools available.

The year-2000 problem is going to occupy increasing amounts of software technical and project management time and effort, so year-2000 analysis tools are rapidly being added to the project management tool suites of almost every major corporation and government agency in the world.

There are hundreds of year-2000 tools and tool vendors, and almost every major software company now has year-2000 search engines, repair engines, or other specialized tools available. Companies marketing tools in the year-2000 domain include Ascent Logic, IBM,

Peritus, ViaSoft, Sterling, PLATINUM, SUN, Data Dimensions, and hundreds more.

However, estimating the costs of the year-2000 problem is a special situation, and here the tools are more limited. The full spectrum of year-2000 costs is one of the most difficult estimating challenges of all history, since the costs will include software repairs, database repairs, hardware upgrades, litigation expenses, and many other unusual elements. Further, year-2000 repairs are being made on hundreds or thousands of applications simultaneously, so not only the costs of individual application repairs but the overall aggregation of costs at the enterprise level need to be estimated and then measured.

Quality-estimating tools

Quality-estimating tools are sometimes custom or standalone tools, but more often occur as features of the previous category of software cost estimating tools. Indeed, several of the major cost-estimation tools, such as CHECKPOINT, KnowledgePlan, SPQR/20, and SLIM, include quality estimation as a standard feature.

Because the ability to predict quality is based on the ability to measure quality, most of the larger and more sophisticated corporations have developed internal quality-estimation, and reliability-estimation models, which are not marketed commercially. Tools of this kind are often found in such leading-edge organizations as AT&T, Bellcore, Hewlett-Packard, IBM, Microsoft, Motorola, Raytheon, and the like.

The main features of software quality estimating tools are the ability to predict *defect potentials* and *defect-removal efficiency* levels. The phrase *defect potentials* means the numbers of errors, bugs, or defects that are likely to be found in requirements, design, coding, user manuals, and *bad fixes,* or secondary bugs that are by-products of fixing prior defects. A few quality-estimation tools are also starting to deal with errors in test cases and with data errors.

The phrase *defect-removal efficiency* refers to the percentage of latent defects that are likely to be removed prior to the release of software to clients or customers. Each form of testing, for example, tends to remove about 30 percent of the bugs that are present, so to achieve very high quality levels it is necessary to plan for at least half a dozen different kinds of defect-removal operations in serial order.

These quality-estimation tools are particularly important for software quality because they include "what if" modeling capabilities that can demonstrate the impact of various software quality assurance (SQA) approaches, such as formal design inspections, formal code inspections, ISO certification, SEI CMM levels, testing specialists, and so forth. Since quality estimating and risk analysis overlap, this tool category and the following one may sometimes be found together.

Somewhat surprisingly, the companies that specialize in quality control, such as Mercury and Rational, which recently acquired Pure Atria and Software Quality Automation (SQA), offer little or nothing in the quality-estimation market. The bulk of the quality-estimation tools are sold by software cost estimating companies, such as Quantitative Software Management (QSM) or Software Productivity Research (SPR). These quality-estimation tools are multifaceted and can deal with defects in requirements, design, and documentation, as well as coding defects.

Quality-estimation tools can also estimate the very important topic of *bad fixes,* or the number of defect repairs that accidentally contain new defects. Defect-severity levels are also projected, and for commercial software with many clients, some of these tools can even estimate duplicates (multiple reports of the same defect) and invalids (defect reports caused by hardware problems or user errors).

There are also more specialized tools that deal only with coding defects, such as UX-Metric and VX-Metric by SET Laboratories, which combine code complexity and defect-estimation capabilities. Quality-estimation tools run from a low of less than 100 function points to more than 2000 function points in size.

Risk analysis tools

Risk analysis is one of the newer categories of software project management tools, and some new examples only appeared in 1997. The earliest software risk analysis tool appeared in 1985, so this form of tool is still in rapid evolution.

Risk analysis tools are either special custom-built tools, usually found within large corporations, or they are special features associated with software project estimating tools or methodology management tools.

Regardless of whether they work in standalone mode or as part of another tool, the risk analysis tools can usually predict many kinds of software technical risks (i.e., inadequate defect removal and requirements volatility). A few can also predict sociological risks (i.e., excessive schedule pressure and staff burnout). Some risk analysis tools can predict the probability that a software project will run late, exceed its budget, or even have a high probability of litigation.

The problem with standalone risk management tools is that many project managers tend to discount or disbelieve their warnings. The risk management features embedded in software cost and quality estimation tools are often more credible, because they include the ability to back up their warnings with tangible information. For example, if a project manager decides "we don't have time to do formal inspections," an obvious resulting risk will be degraded quality.

When this situation is modeled using a cost-estimating tool, a qualitative warning about quality degradation will be augmented by quantitative data, such as a side-by-side comparison that shows defect-removal efficiency dropping from 95 to 85 percent and delivered defects rising from 0.2 per function point to 0.7 per function point.

Risk analysis functions have been part of commercial software cost estimating tools since SPQR/20 in 1985 and are a common feature of such modern cost-estimating tools as Adaptive Estimating Model (AEM), CHECKPOINT, KnowledgePlan, SLIM, and others. Project management tools and process management tools have also offered risk analysis support, such as in the LBMS Process Engineer. In addition, more recent standalone risk management tools are starting to appear, such as RiskTrak from Risk Services and Technology, which appeared in 1997.

Portfolio analysis tools

The total volume of software owned by an enterprise is termed the *portfolio* of applications, and this is a very important kind of information. The total set of applications owned by a large corporation can be numbered in the thousands, and can total to more than a million function points and many millions of source code statements. No project manager owns more than a small fraction of the portfolio, but the overall portfolio itself is very important for many business reasons.

Two business reasons are becoming more important every day: (1) the Internal Revenue Service is interested in the taxable value of software assets represented by the overall portfolios and (2) the onrushing year-2000 problem will affect most of the software owned by an enterprise and, hence, demands portfolio-level cost analysis.

There is a shortage of commercial tools capable of dealing with entire portfolios of software, although some custom-built tools can be found within large corporations. A few commercial software cost estimating and measurement tools, such as CHECKPOINT, KnowledgePlan, and SLIM, have portfolio analysis capabilities, which allow the sizes and resources of all measured or estimated projects to be added together.

Since software portfolios of existing applications are in maintenance mode, the companies that specialize in maintenance or year-2000 repairs also offer portfolio analysis capabilities, such as those of the ViaSoft RECAP portfolio analysis tool, although this tool is aimed primarily at COBOL.

Assessment support tools

Assessment support tools are another fairly new class of automated tools that are keyed to one or more of the standard forms of evaluating software methods and approaches, such as the Bootstrap approach, the SPICE approach, the ISO 9001 approach, the Software Engineering Institute Capability Maturity Model (SEI CMM), or the Software Productivity Research (SPR) assessment method.

When used near the beginning of major projects (i.e., >5000 function points), assessment tools can highlight both strengths and weaknesses. Obviously, the weaknesses will need repair prior to moving into full development. Assessment tools can either be standalone tools or add-ons connected to software estimating tools or software methodology management tools.

The more sophisticated assessment tools can also serve to gather data that can modify cost, schedule, and quality estimates. In fact, several software cost estimating tools, such as CHECKPOINT, KnowledgePlan, SLIM, and COCOMO II, have assessment-gathering input capabilities, as do other forms of project management tools, such as the LBMS Process Engineer.

There are a number of kinds of software process assessments, which include the Software Engineering Institute's capability evaluation, the Software Productivity Research assessment and benchmark analyses, and the European TickIt and SPICE assessment methods; and then there are a number of more specialized forms of assessment, such as those associated with achieving certification for various International Organization of Standards topics, such as ISO 9001 or 9002. Not every assessment tool supports every form of assessment. You should contact the tool vendors or read reviews if you plan to use a specific form of assessment and want automated support.

Project measurement tools

Software project measurement is a complex activity that requires the collection of several different kinds of information in order for the resulting data to be truly useful. The first kind of data that is needed is accurate *size information* for the key deliverables, plus the function point total of the application being measured. The second kind of data that is needed is accurate *staffing, effort, and cost data* for all of the activities that are part of the software project. The third kind of data needed is that of *defects* or *bugs,* since the cost of defect repairs constitutes a major software cost driver.

However, even very accurate quantitative data does not explain why projects vary, so the fourth kind of data that is needed is information about the specific *methods, tools,* and *processes* used to develop the application, as well as information about such subjective factors as schedule pressures, rate of requirements creep, and many others.

The overall volume of information to fully measure a software project is roughly equivalent to the volume of information recorded about a patient who is undergoing a medical examination. From 20 to 50 pages of quantitative and qualitative information may be collected.

Project measurement tools are available as standalone tools or as separate features within related project management tools, such as cost-estimation tools. Indeed, since measurement and estimation are mirror images of each other, estimation tools that feature a measurement mode are often the best choice for effective measurement programs.

Measurement capabilities are often features of other kinds of project management tools, such as project-planning tools like Microsoft Project, cost-estimating tools like CHECKPOINT, or process management tools like the LBMS Process Engineer, or the Andersen METHOD/1 tool suite, and MultiTrak by Work Management Solutions.

There are also specialized measurement tools, such as Computer Associates FPExpert, which collects data in function point form, as does the similar Function Point Workbench (FPW) tool by InterMetrics. Computer Associates also markets the CA-METRICS tool, which collects a variety of data points, including productivity, quality, costs, and the like. There are also many other tools that collect multiple kinds of measurement data, such as QSM's Productivity Analysis Database System (PADS).

A rudimentary project measurement tool that collects only project-level resource data can be less than 10 function points in size. However, a more powerful measurement tool that collects activity-level information, and also includes various attribute information such as which tools or methods were utilized, can top 1000 function points in size.

Complexity analysis tools

There are no fewer than 24 discrete kinds of complexity that affect software projects, but software complexity analysis tools on the commercial market tend to concentrate only on a few kinds of complexity, such as *cyclomatic complexity* and *essential complexity* of source code. This is unfortunate, because many of the other kinds of complexity also affect software in important ways. The commercial software complexity analysis tools, such as McCabe's Analysis of Complexity Tool (ACT) or Battlemap, usually deal with complexity only in the sense of the control flow of the source code. Other forms of complexity, such as the difficulty of the underlying problem structure or the complexity of the design, are outside the scope of complexity analysis engines.

Surprisingly, there are also commercial tools used for measuring the complexity of text passages and calculating readability indexes, such as the FOG index, that might be very useful when applied to software specifications and user manuals, but the software community never seems to use such tools.

Some of the kinds of complexity that lack commercial tools for software purposes include algorithmic complexity, combinatorial complexity, computational complexity, fan complexity, flow complexity, graph complexity, Halstead complexity, mnemonic complexity, organizational complexity, perceptional complexity, semantic complexity, syntactic complexity, and topologic complexity.

On the whole, the topic of complexity is not well supported by software tools except for those dealing with the flow or graph complexity of source code, where there are perhaps 25 such tools available. Some of the tools that can measure source code complexity include the Complexity Measures Tool (CMP) of EVB Software Engineering, PC Metric (and several others) by SET Laboratories, QualGen for Ada by Software Systems Design, and the curiously named Tools of a Competent Craftsman by Gesink & Associates.

Value analysis tools

Value analysis for software is a primitive and unconvincing technology that lacks sophisticated commercial tools. This situation is because the fundamental issues for calculating the "value" of software have not yet been fully worked out and are not well understood.

If software is to be marketed, then the direct and indirect revenues can be predicted and compared to the development, maintenance, marketing, and support costs. This form of value analysis is well understood by commercial software vendors. However, companies such as Computer Associates, IBM, Cognos, Microsoft, Oracle, and other commercial vendors utilize their own proprietary tools and methods for estimating value.

For in-house software, outsource contracts, military software, and a host of other kinds of software, the value concepts are more ambiguous and difficult to enumerate. There are a number of tools, such as spreadsheets and statistical packages, which can calculate accounting rates of return, internal rates of return, and other forms of return on investment. But these are general-purpose tools and are not specifically aimed at software projects.

Some software cost estimating tools, such as CHECKPOINT, include value features. The topics usually included for software value analysis are the following:

1. The impact of the software on market share

2. The impact of the software on operating costs

3. The impact of the software on worker performance

4. The impact of the software on competitors

However, software value analysis is not a mature technology, and the fundamental methods of dealing with this topic are imperfect.

Budget support tools

Budget support tools are among the oldest forms of project management automation, and custom-developed mainframe budgeting tools have been in existence for more than 30 years.

The funding for departmental budgets and the funding for software projects have similar but not identical needs, so project management tools and departmental budgeting tools do not overlap exactly. For example, a single department might have multiple projects ongoing at any one time, so obviously a budgeting tool must be able to deal with continuous monthly expenditures.

Departmental budget costs also need to include such things as capital equipment, office supplies, furniture, hiring expenses, moving expenses, and a number of other elements that tend to be hidden in the overhead structure of project costs.

Most large corporations utilize custom mainframe budget tools which they have developed themselves. Some commercial software packages, such as the SAP tool suite, also include budgeting features. Other software-oriented tools with budgeting features include MultiTrak and SLIM. But most departmental budgets must be linked into corporate accounting systems, and these are general-purpose tools rather than being aimed specifically at software projects.

Variance-reporting tools

Associated with the budget process is the reporting of monthly variances, or the differences between anticipated expenditures and actual expenditures. Variance-reporting tools can be either standalone tools or embedded features within the overall budgeting support automation.

Variance reporting is usually an accounting function, so most variance tools are either proprietary custom features to accounting systems or are offered by accounting software vendors rather than by project management or estimating tool vendors.

There are some linked estimation and reporting tools, such as Digital Equipment's VAX Software Project Manager and Applied Business Technology's (ABT's) Total Project Management Suite.

Project milestone tracking tools

Milestone-tracking tools are one of the oldest forms of project management capability; they have existed in standalone mode since the late 1950s and have been a part of other project management tools ever since. The major forms of tracking include tracking of resources and tracking of milestones, or accomplishments.

Resource-tracking tools accumulate data on the human effort and costs expended on software projects. Ideally, these tools will support a very granular chart of accounts so that costs can be apportioned to specific activities. However, often the charts of accounts are too coarse to be really useful.

Even worse, SPR assessment and benchmark studies indicate that many software resource tracking tools "leak" substantial amounts of information and seldom accumulate total costs accurately. The problem of leakage is not because of the tools themselves, but because of the way the tools are administered and used in day-to-day project work. For example, sometimes the tracking tools are not even initialized or turned on until the requirements are done, so early requirements costs are missing.

Other sources of leakage include failure to record unpaid overtime, failure to record project management effort, and failure to record the work of specialists, such as quality assurance staffers and technical writers. A very common form of leakage is failure to record the work of clients or users when they are performing technical tasks, such as participating in design reviews or assisting with prototypes.

The average volume of leakage varies from industry to industry, but averages about 35 percent for management information systems software projects. This means that cost data must be validated and corrected before it can be used to develop accurate software-estimating algorithms.

Milestone-tracking tools record both planned and actual events that are deemed critical for software projects. Examples of typical milestones would include completion of high-level design, completion of design inspections, completion of low-level or detailed design, completion of coding, completion of code inspections, completion of first drafts of user manuals, and so forth.

Milestone-tracking tools are seldom found as standalone tools, although custom milestone-tracking tools from the 1970s are sometimes still used. More often, they are noted as add-ons to either project-planning tools, project-estimating tools, or methodology management tools. These tools have a significant role in software projects because they can highlight key events.

Indeed, within leading companies the various milestones are the major drivers of software development processes, and the rest of the development cycle is built around such key milestones as completion of design, completion of coding, completion of code inspections, completion of user manuals, and completion of various test stages.

Milestone-tracking capabilities are sometimes features of other kinds of project management tools, such as project-planning tools like Microsoft Project, cost-estimating tools like CHECKPOINT, or process management tools like the LBMS Process Engineer or the Andersen METHOD/1 tool suite, Ernst & Young's NAVIGATOR, and MultiTrak by Work Management Solutions. There are also standalone tracking tools, such as TRAK by MarCon & Associates.

Computer Associates also markets the CA-METRICS tool, which collects a variety of data points tracking productivity, quality, costs, and the like. There are also many other tools that collect multiple kinds of measurement data and perform milestone tracking, such as QSM's Productivity Analysis Database System (PADS) or PROJECT/2 by Project Software & Development.

Incidentally, the term *milestone* refers to some significant software event, such as finishing requirements, finishing internal and external design, finishing coding, or finishing testing.

These fairly coarse milestones are so far apart that the project can run out of control in between them. Some of the emerging work in the domain of military software involves establishing a host of smaller events, called *inch pebbles*. This curious term is intended to denote smaller and more closely spaced events.

As this book is being written, there are no specialized commercial inch-pebble tools available, but a number of general-purpose tools, such as spreadsheets and project-planning tools, can support customized sets of inch pebbles defined by project managers.

Defect-tracking and -measurement tools

Because finding and fixing software bugs or defects comprise the most expensive and time-consuming activities for large software projects, defect-estimation tools and defect-tracking tools are important weapons in the software project management arsenal.

It is important to realize that software defects are found in more than just the source code. There are six major sources of error that need to be predicted, tracked, and analyzed via root cause analysis:

1. Requirements defects
2. Design/specification defects
3. Coding defects
4. User documentation defects
5. Test case defects

6. Bad fixes, or secondary defects based on incorrect repairs to a prior defect

It is interesting that as this book is being written, the topic of data quality is expanding rapidly as a major industrial concern. However, there are currently no commercial tools that can measure data quality or track data-quality defects. It might be possible to force-fit data-quality defect counts into conventional defect-tracking tools, but these tools are not set up for data quality.

Many source code defect tracking tools are commercially available from such companies as Mercury Interactive, Software Research, and the Pure Atria and Software Quality Automation (SQA) subsidiaries of Rational, Inc. There are more generic defect-tracking tools that can handle additional kinds of errors besides coding errors, such as the PCMS tool by SQL Software and the defect-measurement capabilities of CHECKPOINT by Software Productivity Research.

Function point analysis tools

Function point analysis tools are now very common and serve a useful purpose for many project management purposes. These tools come in at least three different varieties, based upon how the function point totals are arrived at.

The most common form of function point tool automates the rather complex calculations involved in function point counting, and also allows function points to be apportioned or assigned to different business units or different segments of the overall software requirements. This form of function point analysis tool can be either a standalone tool, such as Function Point Workbench (FPW), or a part of some other project management or cost-estimating tool, such as the function point support found within CHECKPOINT, KnowledgePlan, or ProQMS.

A second form of function point analysis tool is an adjunct to software CASE or design tools, and derives function point totals semiautomatically from analyzing requirements or design, assuming that the design is performed via the design engine to which the function point tool is appended. This form of function point analysis tool is usually found as a feature within the CASE umbrella, such as the function point capabilities within the Texas Instruments Information Engineering Facility (IEF) or the Bachman Analyst tool.

A third form of function point analysis tool starts with source code parsing, and generates a rough approximation of equivalent function point totals for software by means of backfiring or direct conversion from logical source code statements. This form of tool can be either a standalone tool or a part of some other kind of tool that analyzes source code, such as a complexity analysis tool, a reverse-engineering tool, or a year-2000 analysis tool. An example of this form of tool, which starts with source code counts and delivers function point approximations, would be ViaSoft's RECAP tool.

Some of the standalone function point tools include Computer Associate's FPExpert; Function Point Workbench (FPW), marketed in the United States by Software Productivity Research; Function Point System II by the Development Support Center; and SIZE Plus by GEC Marconi.

Function points can also be derived by backfiring, or direct conversion from logical source code statements. As this book is being written, dozens of commercial software cost estimating tools support backfiring, including COCOMO II, CHECKPOINT, GECOMO, KnowledgePlan, ProQMS, SLIM, and SPQR/20 as representative examples.

Source code counting tools

Tools that count or parse source code have long been used for rough measurements of both productivity and quality. Source code counting tools that measure logical statements are somewhat rarer than tools that measure physical lines, but also are more useful for other purposes, such as backfiring from LOC data to function point data.

Many compilers and assemblers include code counting as a standard feature, although the rules by which the code is counted can vary from language to language and tool to tool.

Code-counting tools can either be standalone tools or features within other kinds of tools, such as compilers, code restructuring tools, or complexity analysis tools. For example, the complexity analysis tools, such as McCabe's Battlemap and Analysis of Complexity Tool (ACT), provide source code counts. The ViaSoft RECAP tool not only produces source code counts of COBOL, but also generates an estimate of equivalent function points.

The source code restructuring tools also provide counts of physical lines, logical statements, or both. Examples of this category include Superstructure, Structured Retrofit, and Recoder.

There are also other kinds of tools that produce source code counts as a by-product of other kinds of analysis. For example, Software Research has a tool called STW/Advisor, which is a static source code analysis tool that creates source code counts and also calculates Halstead software science metrics, cyclomatic complexity metrics, and some other useful information.

Although many code counting tools are available, there is little or no consistency in what they count. Any combination of physical lines and logical statements can be found within the code-counting domain.

This means that size comparisons from application to application using source code counts are rather difficult.

Emerging Software Management Tools

Over and above the 18 kinds of software management tools that have been discussed, there are several promising new kinds of management tools in the prototype or experimental stage. Because these tools are still experimental, it is too early to judge their impact and effectiveness, but they are attracting substantial interest.

Software war game tools

Dr. Tarik Abdel Hamid of the Naval Post Graduate School in Monterey, California has been pioneering a simulation model of software development processes. This model has been used at conferences and seminars by the well-known management consultants Ed Yourdon, Tom DeMarco, and Dr. Howard Rubin.

Dr. Hamid's tool is a flow-based mathematical model of software development that is sensitive to such factors as schedule pressure, quality approaches, staff experience, and a number of other variables. The tool uses and illustrates a complex net of software development activities, all of which are interrelated. The underlying logic of the tool somewhat resembles a popular family of games, such as SimCity.

This mode of using a game approach for software project management functions is starting to become popular, and other tools are being developed by such organizations as the SHL systems house. Indeed, there is even a Monopoly-style board game based on patterns of software project management, with the goal of the game to complete a project on time and within budget.

In playing management war games, teams of managers make various decisions about what quality methods to use or how many staff members to devote to tasks such as requirements gathering. These results then adjust the downstream activities, and managers can see the consequences of key decisions without having to wait for them to occur in real life.

Enterprise software planning tools

A number of software topics, such as ISO 9001 certification, total quality management (TQM), ascending the SEI capability maturity model, signing an outsourcing agreement, or applying for a Baldrige Award, affect the software practices of entire corporations rather than individual projects. This statement is also true of many other situations, such as the mass changes needed in response to the year-2000 problem.

The author and his colleagues have developed an experimental software-estimating tool that operates at the corporate level rather than at the project level. This tool can deal with such complex issues as the total investment that might be needed to move a company with 25,000 software professionals from Level 1 to Level 3 on the SEI capability scale (about $2.5 billion, as it turns out).

This tool is aimed at satisfying some of the planning and estimating needs of senior executive management rather than individual project managers, and it includes an extensive set of value analysis and return-on-investment (ROI) calculations. However, this is an experimental prototype and not a commercial product.

Enterprise-level year-2000 cost-estimating tools

There are specialized broad-band estimating tools that are starting to be used in the year-2000 domain. Year-2000 repairs involve the entire corporate portfolio, and also involve triage, database repairs, test library repairs, hardware upgrades, physical device repairs (such as fax machines and telephone PBX systems), and litigation preparation.

Further, year-2000 software repairs can vary widely, based on whether date field expansion, bridging, windowing, encapsulation, or compression is the strategy used. And many companies are using all of these, plus replacements and withdrawals, as part of their overall year-2000 containment strategies.

Suffice it to say that year-2000 estimation is a very complex, multifaceted problem which far exceeds the capacities of single-purpose project-level software cost estimating tools, although these tools can handle year-2000 repairs for key software applications.

As this book is being written, many year-2000 vendors, such as Andersen, IBM, SPR, and others, have developed year-2000 repair-estimation tools, but they are not being marketed commercially. Instead, the tools are used in the context of consulting and outsourcing agreements to inform clients of the probable magnitude of year-2000 costs.

Enterprise-level Eurocurrency-estimation tools

The simultaneous arrival of the year-2000 problem and the poorly timed choice of the European Union to introduce a unified currency starting in 1999 has triggered a need for software-estimation tools whose features expand the state of the art. Almost all of the current software cost estimation tools aim at individual, specific projects.

Both the euro-conversion work and the year-2000 repairs need tools that can estimate the costs of simultaneously updating hundreds, or even thousands, of software projects.

Of these two major software maintenance tasks, the Eurocurrency work has more estimation support than the year-2000 problem. The Eurocurrency work is primarily a form of software enhancement, while the year-2000 problem also involves hardware upgrades and database repairs, and has substantial risks of litigation expenses.

A number of software cost estimation tools can estimate the euro-conversion work for specific applications. Some of these can also accumulate the overall costs for making updates to many applications at the same time.

However, there is currently a gap in estimating-tool capabilities for creating estimates for work that affects scores of applications simultaneously.

Summary and Conclusions

As this book is being written, software project management tools are more powerful individually than collectively. There are dozens of kinds of project management tools that have individual functions that are quite valuable, but there is not yet a suite of project management tools that supports all necessary management functions in a consistent way, or that can share data across all of the diverse needs of the project manager's roles.

The model of office suites that integrate word processing, spreadsheets, graphics, a database, and the like has not yet arrived in the project management domain. The main reason for this is that the individual project management and estimating tools are currently built by companies that are small and lack the resources to put together entire suites. However, as mergers and acquisitions sweep through the project management tool domain, this problem will no doubt prove to be transient. By the early part of the twenty-first century, project managers may have the same set of integrated capabilities that is already available to those who use office suites or to software engineers. The era of standalone tools is nearing its end, and the era of integrated suites is on the rise.

In summary, the family of software project management tools can exert a major impact on the success rates of large software development and maintenance efforts. Indeed, software project managers supported by powerful cost-estimating, quality-estimating, and project-planning tools have much better track records for on-time, within-budget performance than similar projects using manual estimating and planning approaches.

The literature on how estimation tools relate to other kinds of project management tools is fairly sparse. Much of the literature on this topic comes from military and defense research, since the military software community tends to build very large systems and, hence, needs very complete suites of management tools. Examples of the military estimation genre would be the work of Dean Barrow and colleagues (Barrow et al. 1993), Dr. Norm Brown and colleagues (Brown 1995), and Sherry Stukes and colleagues (Stukes et al. 1996).

Also attempting to put estimation tools in context with other kinds of project management tools is the set of catalogs edited by Alan Howard (Howard 1997). These catalogs include project management, estimation, and metrics tools and are revised annually.

Some of the general-purpose books on project management include discussions of both estimation and other kinds of tools, such as the work of Richard Thayer (Thayer 1988) and Donald Reifer (Reifer 1993). Both Lois Zells (Zells 1990) and Nicholas Zvegintzov (Zvegintzov 1994) also attempted a survey of all forms of project management tools.

References

Barrow, Dean, Susan Nilson, and Dawn Timberlake: *Software Estimation Technology Report,* Air Force Software Technology Support Center, Hill Air Force Base, Utah, 1993.

Brown, Norm (ed.): *The Program Manager's Guide to Software Acquisition Best Practices,* Version 1.0, U.S. Department of Defense, Washington, D.C., July 1995.

Department of the Air Force: *Guidelines for Successful Acquisition and Management of Software Intensive Systems,* vols. 1 and 2, Software Technology Support Center, Hill Air Force Base, Utah, 1994.

Howard, Alan (ed.): *Software Metrics and Project Management Tools,* Applied Computer Research, Phoenix, Ariz., 1997.

Kan, Stephen H.: *Metrics and Models in Software Quality Engineering,* Addison-Wesley, Reading, Mass., ISBN 0-201-63339-6, 1995.

Oman, Paul, and Shari Lawrence Pfleeger (eds.): *Applying Software Metrics,* IEEE Press, Los Alamitos, Calif., ISBN 0-8186-7645-0, 1996.

Reifer, Donald (ed.): *Software Management,* 4th ed., IEEE Press, Los Alamitos, Calif., ISBN 0-8186-3342-6, 1993.

Rethinking the Software Process, CD-ROM, Miller Freeman, Lawrence, Kansas, 1996. (This CD-ROM is a book collection jointly produced by the book publisher, Prentice Hall, and the journal publisher, Miller Freeman. It contains the full text and illustrations of five Prentice Hall books: Capers Jones, *Assessment and Control of Software Risks*; Tom DeMarco, *Controlling Software Projects*; Brian Dreger, *Function Point Analysis*; Larry Putnam and Ware Myers, *Measures for Excellence*; and Mark Lorenz and Jeff Kidd, *Object-Oriented Software Metrics.*)

Stukes, Sherry, Jason Deshoretz, Henry Apgar, and Ilona Macias: *Air Force Cost Analysis Agency Software Estimating Model Analysis,* TR-9545/008-2, Contract F04701-95-D-0003, Task 008, Management Consulting & Research, Inc., Thousand Oaks, Calif., September 1996.

Symons, Charles R.: *Software Sizing and Estimating—Mk II FPA (Function Point Analysis),* John Wiley & Sons, Chichester, U.K., ISBN 0-471-92985-9, 1991.

Thayer, Richard H. (ed.): *Software Engineering and Project Management,* IEEE Press, Los Alamitos, Calif., ISBN 0-8186-075107, 1988.

Umbaugh, Robert E. (ed.): *Handbook of IS Management,* 4th ed., Auerbach Publications, Boston, ISBN 0-7913-2159-2, 1995.

Zells, Lois: *Managing Software Projects—Selecting and Using PC-Based Project Management Systems,* QED Information Sciences, Wellesley, Mass., ISBN 0-89435-275-X, 1990.

Zvegintzov, Nicholas: *Software Management Technology Reference Guide,* Dorset House Press, New York, ISBN 1-884521-01-0, 1994.

6

Patterns of Project Management Tool Usage By Industry and Project Size

There are interesting patterns in software project management tool usage that vary by industry, by company, and even by the size of a company. In this book six major industry segments are discussed. Although any kind of tool can be found within any company, it is interesting to note the kinds of tools that are used by a majority or a significant minority of enterprises within a group.

The data on tool usage is derived from Software Productivity Research (SPR) assessment and benchmarking studies, which include analyses of tool usage patterns. However, since most SPR assessments and benchmarking studies are performed for large organizations in the Fortune 500 class, our results are biased toward large enterprises with more than 1000 software personnel on board. The total number of enterprises whose information is condensed in this book is roughly 600; about 500 of them are United States organizations and 100 are from abroad.

Management Information System (MIS) Projects

Management information system software projects are those enterprises that build for their own internal use, such as accounting systems, sales support systems, customer information systems, and the like. Any kind of company or government agency can build its own software, and the kinds of enterprises found within this family include banks; insurance companies; financial services companies; manufacturing companies; entertainment organizations, such as Walt Disney; and even major-league sports organizations, such as professional football and baseball teams. The most common software project management tools found within the MIS community include the following:

- Project-planning tools are found in more than 70 percent of MIS organizations.

- Project cost estimating tools are found in about 45 percent of MIS organizations.

- Year-2000 analysis tools are found in about 40 percent of MIS organizations.

- Project measurement tools are found in about 35 percent of MIS organizations.

- Project-tracking tools are found in about 35 percent of MIS organizations.

- Function point analysis tools are found in about 30 percent of MIS organizations.

- Methodology management tools are found in about 30 percent of MIS organizations.

The MIS community tends to be very concerned about productivity and schedules, but unfortunately somewhat less concerned about quality and reliability. The MIS community leads all others in usage of function point metrics. However, in terms of other kinds of tools, such as those dealing with quality and risks, the MIS community is often underequipped.

Function point metrics have established a key role in both measurement and estimation within the MIS domain, so tools that support function points have wider penetration among MIS providers than among any other group.

The MIS domain is also heavily impacted by both the onrushing year-2000 problem and the ill-timed Eurocurrency conversion. Therefore, tools that can deal with mass updates are being developed and pressed into service to deal with these two enormous sets of software updates.

However, it is somewhat alarming that the incidence of year-2000 analysis tools in the MIS community was still below the 50 percent mark at the end of 1997, although it will grow rapidly in 1998 and beyond.

Outsourced or Contracted Projects

Outsourced and contracted software projects can be either MIS projects, systems software projects, or military projects. However, these projects have an urgent business need for accurate estimation since many of the contracts are fixed-price contracts.

Also, litigation between clients and software contractors are not uncommon, and are often triggered by schedule delays, cost overruns, or allegations of inadequate quality. Some of the major outsource contractors include Andersen, Computer Sciences Corporation (CSC), Electronic Data Systems (EDS), Keane, and IBM's ISSC division. The most common software management tools found within the outsource community include the following:

- Project-planning tools are found in more than 90 percent of outsource organizations.

- Project-tracking tools are found in about 60 percent of outsource organizations.

- Budget/variance-reporting tools are found in about 60 percent of outsource organizations.

- Project cost estimating tools are found in about 55 percent of outsource organizations.

- Year-2000 analysis tools are found in about 50 percent of outsource organizations.

- Defect-tracking tools are found in about 45 percent of outsource organizations.

- Project measurement tools are found in about 40 percent of outsource organizations.

- Function point analysis tools are found in about 40 percent of outsource organizations.

- Methodology management tools are found in about 35 percent of outsource organizations.

- Defect-estimating tools are found in about 25 percent of outsource organizations.

As outsourcing agreements increase in numbers and importance, the incidence of litigation between clients and outsource vendors is also increasing, although the percentage of agreements that go to litigation is still only about 1 percent.

The outsource community is aware that schedule overruns, cost overruns, and poor quality are serious concerns, and hence are moving to minimize the risks of these problems.

Also, an increasing number of outsourcing contracts are now based on cost per function point for development and maintenance, so the usage of function point analysis tools is rising within the outsource community.

Because international outsourcing to such countries as India and the Ukraine is increasing, many international outsource organizations are beginning to use function points for marketing and advertising purposes, as well as for contractual purposes. The rationale for this is because of the significant differential between offshore costs per function point and U.S. or Western European costs per function point.

End-User Software Applications

End-user software applications are small software projects built for private use by knowledge workers who are also computer literate, such as engineers, accountants, attorneys, and others who use computers for performing part of their daily jobs. Since most end-user applications are small (end-user applications average less than 10 function points or 1000 source code statements in size) there are usually no project management tools found in this category at all, except perhaps informal usage of project-planning tools or spreadsheets if the end users happen to own them for other purposes.

Commercial Software Projects

Commercial software projects are those built for lease or sale to other enterprises by software vendors. The commercial world also includes companies that build and market project management and cost-estimating tools. Examples of major commercial software houses include Computer Associates (CA), IBM, Oracle, SAP AG, and, of course, Microsoft. The management tool suites observed within the commercial software domain include the following:

- Project-planning tools are found in more than 90 percent of commercial organizations.

- Project-tracking tools are found in about 80 percent of commercial organizations.

- Defect-tracking tools are found in about 75 percent of commercial organizations.

- Complexity analysis tools are found in about 40 percent of commercial organizations.

- Source code counting tools are found in about 35 percent of commercial organizations.

- Project cost estimating tools are found in about 30 percent of commercial organizations.

- Project measurement tools are found in about 25 percent of commercial organizations.

- Defect-estimating tools are found in about 25 percent of commercial organizations.

- Function point analysis tools are found in about 20 percent of commercial organizations.

The commercial software world is heavily driven by schedules and time-to-market considerations, which often overshadow both cost factors and quality factors. However, customer support and maintenance are also important considerations. Also, the commercial software world tends to have a "not invented here" syndrome and, hence, often avoids tools built by other commercial software vendors.

Systems Software Projects

Systems software projects are those that control physical devices, such as telephone switching systems, operating systems, fuel-injection systems, flight-control systems, medical instruments, and the like. The larger systems software projects run on standalone computers or special computers, such as those built by telephone companies for switching systems.

The smaller systems software projects are often termed *embedded software* because the computer and its software is physically part of the device it controls. Examples of embedded software would include automotive fuel-injection controls, cruise missile navigation packages, and the software controlling such home appliances as microwave ovens.

Systems software companies include primarily groups that build large and complicated physical devices, such as Boeing, Ford, General Electric, General Motors, Lucent, and the like. For a variety of reasons, the systems software community is often the best equipped with project management tools. The set of project management tools noted within systems software organizations includes the following:

- Project-planning tools are found in more than 90 percent of systems organizations.

- Project-tracking tools are found in more than 85 percent of systems organizations.

- Defect-tracking tools are found in more than 80 percent of systems organizations.

- Complexity analysis tools are found in about 70 percent of systems organizations.

- Source code counting tools are found in about 65 percent of systems organizations.

- Statistical analysis tools are found in about 60 percent of systems organizations.

- Project cost estimating tools are found in about 55 percent of systems organizations.

- Year-2000 analysis tools are found in about 55 percent of systems organizations.

- Project measurement tools are found in about 50 percent of systems organizations.

- Risk analysis tools are found in about 45 percent of systems organizations.

- Assessment support tools are found in about 35 percent of systems organizations

- Methodology management tools are found in about 30 percent of systems organizations.

- Function point analysis tools are found in about 25 percent of systems organizations.

Since the main products of the systems software world are large and complex physical devices which need high-reliability software in order to operate, the systems software community is much more sophisticated in software quality control than most of the other industries (except the military industry). The pattern of management tool usage reflects a very strong interest in quality control, and, of course, a strong interest in schedule and cost control as well.

The large systems software companies, such as AT&T, IBM, Hewlett-Packard, and Motorola often have formal cost-estimating departments staffed by software cost estimating specialists. These departments provide estimation services to many engineering and software project managers, who may or may not be well trained in this rather complex discipline.

These cost-estimating groups in large systems software companies often have very complete tool suites, including quite a few software cost estimating tools. It is not uncommon for critical projects to have estimates produced using multiple cost-estimating tools, such as CHECKPOINT, COCOMO, KnowledgePlan, SEER, SLIM, and SOFT-COST. When these tools converge, the certainty of the estimating process is enhanced. When these tools differ markedly, it is sometimes useful to explore why, and use that analysis to refine a final estimate.

These cost-estimating departments in large systems software companies are more or less unique in being able to produce integrated cost estimates that span hardware, software, and microcode components.

Many of the most important products of high-technology corporations are hybrid products where hardware, microcode, and software are all being developed concurrently. Estimation of hybrid products is a very complicated and challenging kind of cost estimating, which can be done best by trained specialists supported by extensive predictive tool suites.

An eventual goal of software estimation is to be able to produce linked estimates that consolidate the work of software, microcode, database development, hardware development, and human activities, such as customer support.

Military Software Projects

Military software projects are defined as software projects that are constrained to follow various military standards, such as DoD 2167A or DoD 498. Military standards imply fairly rigorous development approaches and the production of enormous volumes of required paperwork in the forms of very detailed plans, specifications, and other documents. Examples of companies that build military software include Computer Sciences Corporation (CSC), Grumman, IBM, Litton, Raytheon, and TRW. The set of management tools found in the military software community is similar to the tools found in the systems software community, although the distributions vary:

- Project-planning tools are found in more than 90 percent of military organizations.

- Project-tracking tools are found in more than 75 percent of military organizations.

- Defect-tracking tools are found in about 70 percent of military organizations.

- Complexity analysis tools are found in about 65 percent of military organizations.

- Source code counting tools are found in about 65 percent of military organizations.

- Assessment support tools are found in about 55 percent of military organizations.

- Project cost estimating tools are found in about 55 percent of military organizations.

- Risk analysis tools are found in about 45 percent of military organizations.

- Year-2000 analysis tools are found in about 35 percent of military organizations.

- Statistical analysis tools are found in about 30 percent of military organizations.

- Project measurement tools are found in about 25 percent of military organizations.

- Function point analysis tools are found in about 20 percent of military organizations.

The military software community is heavily impacted by Department of Defense (DoD) standards. As a result, this community tends to be somewhat conservative and has lagged the civilian sector in some aspects of software project management, such as the adoption of function point metrics. On the other hand, the military community has pioneered software process assessments and has a long tradition of seeking excellence in quality control.

As with civilian systems software, the larger defense contractors and military establishments are likely to have specialized cost-estimating departments staffed by cost-estimating specialists and well equipped with software-estimating tools.

Military projects are often very expensive hybrid structures where hardware, software, and microcode must be developed concurrently. Consider the complexity of estimating a new kind of weapons system, a new kind of fighter aircraft, or a new kind of radar system. Successful estimating in this kind of complex environment implies both trained personnel and powerful planning and estimating tools.

The military community has a need for hybrid estimation that can deal with software, hardware, and microcode at the same time. As this book is being written, most of these complex hybrid estimates are produced in pieces using individual estimating tools for each component, and then the results are aggregated via a spreadsheet or similar general-purpose tool.

Overall Project Management Tool Usage Patterns

Overall patterns are difficult to enumerate because of the large variations from industry to industry and company to company. However, the following data is interesting even if it has a high margin of error. These results are found among medium to large software organizations that employ from 200 to more than 20,000 software personnel:

- Project-planning tools are found in more than 80 percent of software organizations.

- Project-tracking tools are found in about 60 percent of software organizations.

- Defect-tracking tools are found in about 55 percent of software organizations.

- Source code counting tools are found in about 45 percent of software organizations.

- Project cost estimating tools are found in about 40 percent of software organizations.

- Year-2000 analysis tools are found in about 40 percent of software organizations.

- Methodology management tools are found in about 25 percent of software organizations.

- Function point analysis tools are found in about 20 percent of software organizations.

The probable reasons that project-planning tools are used more widely than any other kind of management tool are the following:

- Commercial project-planning tools entered the market in the 1960s, more than 10 years before most other kinds of management tools.

- Many commercial project-planning tools are low-cost, and can be acquired for less than $500 per copy.

- Some of the project-planning tool vendors, such as Computer Associates and Microsoft, have very significant marketing budgets and extensive sales facilities.

It will be interesting to revisit these rankings of project management tool deployments at various intervals, such as every year, and note how changes occur. For example, as this book is being written, defect-tracking tools, cost-estimating tools, and methodology management tools appear to be on a very fast growth path, and so do function point analysis tools.

Software-Estimating and Project Management Tool Usage by Application Size

Another interesting way of examining the usage patterns of software-estimating and project management tools is to evaluate usage based on the sizes of software projects, and also on the sizes of software organization. Table 6.1 shows results from SPR assessments. The per-

TABLE 6.1   Software Project Management Tools and Enterprise Size Ranges from Small, Medium, Large, and Very Large Enterprises

(Percentages of managers using each tool)

Tool category	Total software personnel employed, %				
	Small, <10	Medium, 10–100	Large, 100–1000	Very large, >1000	Average
Project planning	20	45	65	95	56
Budget support	10	25	75	90	50
Variance reporting	10	25	75	90	50
Source code counting	35	40	50	60	46
Project tracking	10	30	45	65	38
Complexity analysis	15	25	35	50	31
Defect tracking	10	20	35	45	28
Year-2000 analysis	1	10	25	60	24
Cost estimating	1	5	15	55	19
Function point analysis	5	10	15	35	16
Project measurement	1	5	15	40	15
Statistical analysis	1	5	15	35	14
Methodology management	0	5	15	35	14
Quality estimating	1	10	15	25	13
Risk analysis	0	1	15	20	9
Value analysis	0	0	10	25	9
Assessment support	0	1	5	20	7
Portfolio analysis	0	1	5	15	5
Average	7	15	29	48	25

centages reflect the number of managers who use various categories of tools more or less regularly.

In general, large projects and large companies have a more extensive suite of project management capabilities than do small projects and small companies. Note that Table 6.1 shows the same sets of software management tools as Table 5.1, only sorted in order of frequency of usage among enterprises of various size.

Small companies, as a class, are often marginally funded and cannot afford the costs or licensing fees for an extensive suite of software project management tools. Fortunately for them, small companies are usually limited to below 1000 function points as the maximum size of software applications they can build.

As a general rule, the larger the organization the more extensive is the suite of software management tools. For that matter, large organizations typically have the most extensive suites of every kind of tool, including software CASE tools, quality-assurance tools, testing tools, and all other categories.

Not only do larger organizations have larger management tool suites, but they are much more likely to adopt the power end of the tool spectrum than the low-cost end of the tool spectrum.

Table 6.2 shows the approximate number of U.S. software project managers in the same four sizes of organizations just illustrated. The table also shows typical annual investments in project management tools, and then aggregates the overall investment to show approximate annual U.S. spending for software management tools of just over $1 billion.

Table 6.2 has a high margin of error, since management tool budgets vary widely from company to company and industry to industry. However, for illustrative purposes Table 6.2 shows some interesting trends.

A quick glance at this table explains why so many management tool vendors target the large Fortune 500–class corporations as their primary markets. The 500 largest organizations contain about one-third of the software managers in the United States, but spend more than half of the national annual investment in software management tools.

The obvious reason for this skew is that really large systems can be built only by really large organizations. It might be theoretically possible to develop large systems using hosts of small contract organiza-

TABLE 6.2   U.S. Software Project Managers and Management Tool Investments

| Enterprise size in software personnel | Total software personnel employed | | | | |
	Small, <10	Medium, 10–100	Large, 100–1000	Very large, >1000	Total
Information systems	15,000	3,500	750	200	19,450
Outsource software	2,500	500	100	50	3,150
Systems software	1,000	700	250	125	2,075
Commercial software	1,500	600	125	10	2,235
Military software	1,500	750	150	65	2,465
Other software types	2,500	500	200	50	3,250
Total U.S. enterprises	24,000	6,550	1,575	500	32,625
U.S. software managers	36,000	49,125	102,375	107,500	295,000
Annual tool investment per manager	$750	$1,750	$4,000	$5,500	$3,775
Total annual tool investment	$27,000,000	$85,968,750	$409,500,000	$591,250,000	$1,113,718,750
Percentage of Total	2.42%	7.72%	36.77%	53.09%	100%

TABLE 6.3   Approximate 1997 Purchases of Software
Management Tools, $ Million

Geographic region	Management tool purchases
North America	$1000
Western Europe	1250
South America	750
Pacific Rim	750
Eastern Europe	250
Total	4000

tions, but in fact most large systems development work remains concentrated in very large organizations employing tens of thousands of software technical staff personnel and thousands of software project managers.

This phenomenon of large systems being built within large corporations explains why the biggest software-producing companies usually have the most complete suites of software project management tools: Alcatel, Andersen, AT&T, Bellcore, Boeing, Computer Associates, EDS, GTE, Hewlett-Packard, IBM, Microsoft, Motorola, Nippon Telegraph, and Siemens-Nixdorf are samples of the kinds of corporations where the most extensive suites of management tools are likely to be found.

It is this same category of very large corporations that invented many of the project management tools and also built the first working versions, even though smaller companies may be the current leaders in the commercial software management tool domain.

Although this table illustrates the management tool market only in the United States (with a large margin of error, of course) the worldwide market for software management tools may approximate $4 billion per year as the century closes, as shown in Table 6.3.

In terms of market growth, all of these regions are capable of sustaining double-digit annual increases over the next 5 to 10 years. Software is now a global commodity, and software management is the factor that needs the greatest amount of improvement in order to move software from an art form to a solid business venture.

Software Management Tools and Software Project Size

Another way of looking at software management tool use is to consider the kinds of tools typically associated with software projects of six discrete size ranges, each an order of magnitude apart, starting with 1 function point and ending with 100,000 function points.

Software is highly labor intensive, and as a result, *large* software projects are among the most expensive undertakings of the twentieth century. For example, large software systems cost far more to build and take much longer to construct than the office buildings occupied by the companies that have commissioned the software.

Really large software systems in the 100,000–function point size range can cost more than building a domed football stadium, a 50-story skyscraper, or a 70,000-ton cruise ship.

Not only are large systems expensive, but they also have one of the highest failure rates of any manufactured object in human history. The term *failure* refers to projects that are canceled without completion due to cost or schedule overruns, or that run later than planned by more than 25 percent.

Let us consider what the phrase *large systems* means in the context of six different size plateaus separated by an order of magnitude for each plateau: 1 function point, 10 function points, 100 function points, 1000 function points, 10,000 function points, and 100,000 function points.

1 function point (125 C statements)

There are few software applications of this size except small enhancements to larger applications or minor personal applications. The schedules for such small programs are usually only from a day to perhaps a week.

Assuming that software staff compensation averages about $30 an hour, or just under $5000 per month, projects in this size range sometimes cost only a few hundred dollars.

In general, no management tools of any kind are associated with projects of this size category, although source code counting tools and complexity analysis tools may sometimes be used out of curiosity.

Function point metrics are seldom used for these small projects, because normal function point counting stops at about 15 function points—the weighting factors have minimum values and can't drop down below 5 function points at all. It is possible to use the backfiring method of converting logical source code statements into function points for smaller projects, however.

Project management tools and software cost estimating tools have trouble dealing with the work of a single individual. Factors such as a bout of flu, a major snowstorm, or a family emergency can throw off the estimate for one-person projects, and there are no ways of dealing with these personal situations without knowing the individual and the local conditions.

Usually, projects of this tiny size are exempt from formal cost estimates, formal plans, or most of the other rigors of larger application development. In fact, a 1–function point project is usually dealt with as part-time work, and the same programmer or technical staff member might have half a dozen or more such small projects under way in any average working month. Usually, milestone-tracking and cost-tracking software packages are not granular enough to even collect historical data for projects of this size, nor do the personnel doing such small projects try to record any historical data.

10 function points (1250 C statements)

This is the typical size of end-user applications, and also is a very frequent size plateau for enhancements to existing software. Development schedules are usually less than a month. The development costs for applications in this size range are often less than $5000.

In general, there are no common patterns of software management tools used for this size range, although sometimes formal budgets are assigned. Management tools associated with this size range include the following:

- Project planning
- Budget support
- Variance reporting
- Source code counting
- Defect tracking
- Complexity analysis

For this size range, manual estimation and automated estimation are roughly equivalent in accuracy, and there are usually no major failures or excessive risks observed.

100 function points (12,500 C statements)

This is the practical upper limit of end-user applications. There were few complete standalone applications of this size by 1997, but 10 years before there were a number of DOS applications in this size range, such as early Basic interpreters. However, there are many features of larger applications that approximate this size. Development schedules are usually from perhaps three to less than nine months. Development costs within this size range can top $100,000, which can be a significant investment for a small company, and is at least a noticeable investment within larger organizations. Individual programmers can handle applications of this size, although technical writers and other specialists may be involved, too.

This size plateau marks the lower boundary of projects where software cost estimation tools start coming into play. The management tools noted for applications within this size range include the following:

- Project planning
- Cost estimating
- Function point analysis
- Methodology management
- Budget support
- Variance reporting
- Source code counting
- Defect tracking
- Complexity analysis
- Year-2000 analysis

This size range also marks the boundary between sizes where casual development methods and informal processes can be utilized without excessive risk of delays, overruns, or outright failures. Above this size range, software starts to be a serious business undertaking.

1000 function points (125,000 C statements)

This size range exceeds the capabilities of end-user development. This is a fairly common entry-level size range for many commercial and internal Windows software applications. It is also a common size range for in-house client/server applications.

Schedules for software projects of this size are usually longer than 12 months. Costs for software in this size range can sometimes top $1 million, although most are only about half this cost or less. In this size range, the volume of specifications and user documentation becomes a significant contributor to software costs.

Quality control is a major requirement at this size range, also. Applications of this size range require development teams of 6 up to perhaps 12 staff members, since individual programmers cannot usually handle the volume of code and other deliverables. Also, at this size user manuals and paper documents become major items, so paperwork costs begin to balloon.

Specialists, such as quality-assurance personnel, technical writers, and database administrators, are often on the development team. With team development, issues of system segmentation and interfaces among components become troublesome. At this size range, management tools begin to play an increasingly important role. The tools noted for this size range include the following:

- Project planning
- Cost estimating
- Risk analysis
- Value analysis
- Function point analysis
- Defect estimating
- Complexity analysis
- Methodology management
- Budget support
- Variance reporting
- Source code counting
- Defect tracking
- Project tracking
- Year-2000 analysis

The 1000–function point plateau is the approximate upper limit for software projects that can be constructed by small corporations. Above this size plateau, software projects become a major undertaking that are usually found only within large corporations and large government agencies.

Also, the 1000–function point plateau marks a fairly sharp dividing line between the sizes where software projects can be built casually by a handful of developers and the larger sizes where large development teams, formal processes, and significant rigor are necessary for success.

Below 1000 function points, a few very bright developers can build software without any particular rigor except their own abilities and sometimes will succeed. Above this size, even the brightest will fail more often than not unless they adopt formal process controls.

10,000 function points (1.25 million C statements)

Applications of this size are usually termed *systems,* because they are far too large for individual programs. This size range is often troubled by cost and schedule overruns and by outright cancellations. Development teams of 100 or so members are common, so communication and interface problems are endemic.

Software schedules in this size plateau run from 3 to more than 5 years, although the initial planning for applications of this size range tends to naively assume schedules of 18 months or less. Since costs can top $10 million for civilian projects in this size range and $25 million for military projects, every kind of project management tool is often deployed.

The volume of paperwork in terms of plans, specifications, and user manuals is so large that production of documents is often more expensive than production of the source code. Because defect levels rise with application size, formal quality control, including pretest inspections, is necessary for successful completion. Configuration control and change management are also mandatory for this size plateau.

Basically, all known kinds of software management tools can and should be used for this size category:

- Cost estimating*
- Project planning*
- Methodology management*
- Quality estimating*
- Risk analysis*
- Project tracking*
- Project measurement*
- Defect tracking*
- Budget support
- Variance reporting
- Source code counting
- Complexity analysis
- Year-2000 analysis
- Value analysis
- Assessment support
- Function point analysis
- Statistical analysis

The management tools marked with an asterisk are those which the author regards as being mandatory for projects in the 10,000–function point or 1.25 million–source code statement size range. Without using this set of tools, the risk of failure or disaster is ominously high.

100,000 function points (12.5 million C statements)

Applications that approach 100,000 function points in size are among the most troubling constructs of the twentieth century. This is roughly the size range of Microsoft's Windows 95 product and IBM's MVS operating system. This is also the size range of major military systems.

Software-development schedules for systems of this size are usually from 5 to more than 8 years, although the initial development plans tend to assume 36 months or less. Development teams number in the hundreds of members, often in multiple locations that may even be in different countries. The costs of systems in this enormous size range can top $1 billion, which are major expenditures even for very large enterprises and for the Department of Defense. Communication problems are rampant. Paperwork and defect-removal operations absorb the bulk of development costs. Formal configuration control and change management are mandatory and expensive for this size plateau.

All known kinds of software management tools and technical tools can and many should be used for this size category. Indeed, even with all available tools failures tend to outnumber successes at this extreme upper limit of the software size spectrum. The following listing notes the management tools deployed within this size category:

- Cost estimating*
- Project planning*
- Methodology management*
- Quality estimating*
- Risk analysis*
- Project tracking*
- Project measurement*
- Defect tracking*
- Budget support
- Variance reporting
- Source code counting
- Complexity analysis
- Year-2000 analysis
- Value analysis
- Assessment support
- Function point analysis
- Statistical analysis

Here, too, the asterisks indicate tool categories that are mandatory if the project is to have any chance at all of being finished, to say nothing of finishing on time, finishing within budget, and actually working when finished.

Major systems in the 100,000–function point size domain are among the most troublesome artifacts of the twentieth century, and will probably remain troubling artifacts in the twenty-first century, too. Systems of this enormous size can only be constructed by the largest and most sophisticated software organizations in the world: Probably fewer than 100 organizations in the world can build systems of this size at all, and fewer than 20 can do it well.

The literature that correlates estimation tools with project sizes and project outcomes is fairly sparse. A classic in the field is Dr. Fred Brooks's *Mythical Man-Month* (Brooks 1974), which describes some of the problems IBM had building OS/360, where estimation was a key trouble zone. This book was revised and reissued in 1995.

Another useful source is the work of Loic Briand and Daniel Roy, *Meeting Deadlines in Hard Real-Time Systems* (Briand and Roy 1997).

The *best practices* genre is also a useful source of guidance. The best practice works of Dr. Norm Brown (Brown 1995) and Dr. William Roetzheim and Reyna Beasley (Roetzheim and Beasley 1998) are both useful sources.

The *risk* genre is a useful source of information, as well. There are dozens of risk books, but the works of Robert Charette are very well known in this field (Charette 1989, 1990). Ed Yourdon's new book on "death march" projects is an example of extreme risks (Yourdon 1997) and, as usual with Ed's work, is very interesting reading.

All of Tom DeMarco's books provide useful insights and guidance, and any of them can be recommended, such as *Controlling Software Projects* (DeMarco 1982), *Peopleware* (DeMarco and Lister 1990), and even the fictional *Deadline* (DeMarco 1997).

References

Briand, Loic, and Daniel Roy: *Meeting Deadlines in Hard Real-Time Systems,* IEEE Computer Society Press, Los Alamitos, Calif., ISBN 0-8186-406-7, 1997.
Brooks, Fred: *The Mythical Man-Month,* Addison-Wesley, Reading, Mass., 1974, rev. 1995.
Brown, Norm (ed.): *The Program Manager's Guide to Software Acquisition Best Practices,* Version 1.0, U.S. Department of Defense, Washington, D.C., July 1995.
Charette, Robert N.: *Software Engineering Risk Analysis and Management,* McGraw-Hill, New York, ISBN 0-07-010719-X, 1989.
———: *Application Strategies for Risk Analysis,* McGraw-Hill, New York, ISBN 0-07-010888-9, 1990.
DeMarco, Tom: *Controlling Software Projects,* Yourdon Press, New York, ISBN 0-917072-32-4, 1982.
———: *Why Does Software Cost So Much?,* Dorset House Press, New York, ISBN 0-932633-34-X, 1995.
———: *Deadline,* Dorset House Press, New York, 1997.
——— and Tim Lister: *Peopleware,* Dorset House Press, New York, ISBN 0-932633-05-6, 1987.
Department of the Air Force, *Guidelines for Successful Acquisition and Management of Software Intensive Systems,* vols. 1 and 2, Software Technology Support Center, Hill Air Force Base, Utah, 1994.

Roetzheim, William H., and Reyna A. Beasley: *Best Practices in Software Cost and Schedule Estimation,* Prentice Hall PTR, Upper Saddle River, N.J., 1998.

Yourdon, Ed: *Death March—The Complete Software Developer's Guide to Surviving "Mission Impossible" Projects,* Prentice Hall PTR, Upper Saddle River, N.J., ISBN 0-13-748310-4, 1997.

Zells, Lois: *Managing Software Projects—Selecting and Using PC-Based Project Management Systems,* QED Information Sciences, Wellesley, Mass., ISBN 0-89435-275-X, 1990.

Zvegintzov, Nicholas: *Software Management Technology Reference Guide,* Dorset House Press, New York, ISBN 1-884521-01-0, 1994.

7

Software Cost Estimating Tools and Project Success and Failure Rates

Several years ago, the author and his colleagues at Software Productivity Research (SPR) were commissioned to do a study of the patterns of failure and success associated with software projects. The full results were published in *Patterns of Software System Failure and Success* (Jones 1995).

The attributes of *success* included delivering the system on time or early, staying within budgets, providing high quality levels, and providing high levels of user satisfaction.

The attributes of *failure* included cancellation of the project in mid-development, or severe schedule or cost overruns, or both. Poor quality and low user satisfaction were also aspects of failure.

The study explored six kinds of large software projects: (1) systems software, (2) military software, (3) information systems software, (4) outsourced software, (5) commercial software, and (6) end-user software.

The study also explored six size ranges an order of magnitude apart, starting with very small projects of 1 function point in size and culminating with massive systems of 100,000 function points in size.

Using six size ranges from 1 to 100,000 function points (FP), Table 7.1 shows the approximate frequency of various kinds of outcomes, ranging from finishing early to total cancellation. This table is taken from *Patterns of Software Systems Failure and Success* (Jones 1995).

The study concentrated on the failures and successes of large systems in the 5000–function point (500,000–source code statement) and

TABLE 7.1   Software Project Outcomes by Size of Project

	Probability of selected outcomes, %				
	Early	On time	Delayed	Canceled	Total
1 FP	14.68	83.16	1.92	0.25	100
10 FP	11.08	81.25	5.67	2.00	100
100 FP	6.06	74.77	11.83	7.33	100
1,000 FP	1.24	60.76	17.67	20.33	100
10,000 FP	0.14	28.03	23.83	48.00	100
100,000 FP	0.00	13.67	21.33	65.00	100
Average	5.53	56.94	13.71	23.82	100

higher range, since failures are more common than successes for large systems, and large-system failures can be enormously expensive.

The root causes of software success and failure include technical factors, social and cultural factors, and management factors. The study found that there is an almost infinite number of ways to fail in building software applications, and only a few ways to succeed.

As can easily be seen from Table 7.1, small software projects are successful in the majority of instances, but the risks and hazards of cancellation or major delays rise quite rapidly as the overall application size goes up. Indeed, the development of large applications in excess of 10,000 function points is one of the most hazardous and risky business undertakings of the modern world.

Of the ways to succeed, the capabilities of the project management team had a very strong impact. Conversely, on the failures or projects that were canceled or ran very late, poor project management practices were universally noted.

The attributes most strongly associated with successful software projects include the use of automated software cost estimating tools and automated software project management tools, effective quality control, and effective tracking of software-development milestones.

For larger software projects in excess of 1000 function points, or roughly 100,000 source code statements, success rates correlate strongly with four kinds of estimation or prediction rigor and three kinds of measurement rigor:

Predictive Estimation Methods Correlating with Successful Software Projects

1. Formal sizing of major deliverables (specifications, source code, test cases, and user manuals)

2. Formal cost estimating down to the level of activities and tasks

3. Formal quality estimating for all defect categories (requirements, design, code, documentation, and bad-fix defects)

4. Formal schedule planning down to the level of individual workers

Measurement Methods Correlating with Successful Software Projects

1. Accurate resource and cost tracking during development

2. Accurate milestone tracking during development

3. Accurate defect tracking during development

The major difference between successful and unsuccessful software projects can be encapsulated by two key words: *no surprises*. With successful projects, development evolves painlessly from careful estimating, planning, and quality control. There are no unexpected delays due to sloppy planning, and no protracted nightmarish testing delays when the software is discovered not to work.

To summarize the kinds of tools most often associated with successful software projects, they include the following capabilities:

- Automated sizing of major deliverables
- Automated cost estimating
- Automated defect estimating
- Automated project planning
- Automated defect tracking
- Automated project resource tracking
- Automated project milestone tracking

Tools alone don't make a successful project, of course. In addition to sophisticated project management tools and development tools, successful software projects also make use of other rigorous approaches, including but not limited to the following:

- Careful requirements analysis
- Formal design and code inspections
- Testing by trained specialists
- Effective quality-assurance groups

As we have observed on hundreds of projects, effective estimating and planning methods, coupled with careful measurements and quality control, are high on the list of methods that can optimize software projects.

Probabilities of Software Project
Success or Failure

The author and his colleagues at Software Productivity Research often deal with topics where multiple factors simultaneously impact the outcome of a project. A useful way of showing the range of possible outcomes is to illustrate what happens when every factor is either the best that it can be or the worst, and to ignore intermediate situations.

The author has found that the upper limit of convenience and effectiveness for this approach is to deal with 4 factors. The various combinations of four factors result in 16 possible outcomes, and it is usually possible to assign failure or success probabilities to each of the 16 combinations. It is even possible to assign specific quality and productivity levels to the combinations, although that is not done in this book.

The reason that 4 factors is the convenient upper limit is that each additional factor would double the number of possible combinations, so that 5 factors would generate 32 possibilities, 6 factors would generate 64 combinations, and so on.

Table 7.2 illustrates the probability results of 16 combinations of 4 major management factors that affect software cancellations and schedules:

1. Use of automated versus manual estimating tools

2. Use of automated versus manual planning methods

3. Use of automated versus manual progress-tracking methods

4. Use of optimal versus minimal quality-control approaches

The phrase *automated estimating* implies usage of one or more of the commercial software-estimating tools, such as ABT Bridge Modeler, BYL, CHECKPOINT, COCOMO, GECOMO, ESTIMACS, KnowledgePlan, PRICE-S, ProQMS, SEER, SLIM, SOFTCOST, SPQR/20, or others within this class.

The phrase *automated planning* implies usage of one or more of the commercial software planning or project management tools, such as ABT Project Manager's Workbench (PMW), CA SUPERPROJECT, Microsoft Project, PINNACLE, Primavera, TIMELINE, or one of many others within this class.

The phrase *formal tracking* implies a monthly summation of accomplishments, milestones, and potential problems encountered by every manager on a project. The lower-level progress reports are summarized upward to provide an overall status report of the health of the project. Formal tracking also implies usage of automated tools that can produce variance reports showing the difference between budget-

TABLE 7.2   Probability of Canceled, Delayed, On-Time, or Early Software Project Completion Associated with Estimation and Project Management Factors

(Best-practice project management factors appear in boldface type)

	Probability of Selected Outcomes, %			
	Canceled	Delayed	On time	Early
Manual estimates Manual plans Informal tracking Minimal quality control	40	45	15	0
Manual estimates **Automated plans** Informal tracking Minimal quality control	37	42	20	1
Manual estimates Manual plans **Formal tracking** Minimal quality control	35	39	24	2
Automated estimates Manual plans Informal tracking Minimal quality control	33	36	28	3
Manual estimates Manual plans Informal tracking **Optimal quality control**	30	32	34	4
Manual estimates **Automated plans** **Formal tracking** Minimal quality control	27	28	40	5
Automated estimates **Automated plans** Informal tracking Minimal quality control	23	26	45	6
Automated estimates Manual plans **Formal tracking** Minimal quality control	20	23	50	7

TABLE 7.2   **Probability of Canceled, Delayed, On-Time, or Early Software Project Completion Associated with Estimation and Project Management Factors** (*Continued*)

(Best-practice project management factors appear in boldface type)

	Probability of Selected Outcomes, %			
	Canceled	Delayed	On time	Early
Manual estimates **Automated plans** Informal tracking **Optimal quality control**	18	20	54	8
Manual estimates Manual plans **Formal tracking** **Optimal quality control**	16	17	58	9
Automated estimates Manual plans Informal tracking **Optimal quality control**	13	15	62	10
Automated estimates **Automated plans** **Formal tracking** Minimal quality control	10	12	67	11
Manual estimates **Automated plans** **Formal tracking** **Optimal quality control**	8	10	69	13
Automated estimates Manual plans **Formal tracking** **Optimal quality control**	5	8	72	15
Automated estimates **Automated plans** Manual tracking **Optimal quality control**	3	6	74	17
Automated estimates **Automated plans** **Formal tracking** **Optimal quality control**	1	2	78	19

ed and actual expenditures, as well as variances in schedule and milestone achievement.

The phrase *optimal quality control* is defined to mean utilizing formal design and code inspections, formal and automated defect tracking, and formal testing by trained specialists as well as unit testing by the developers themselves.

The phrase *minimal quality control* is defined to mean a failure to utilize pretest inspections, a lack of effective defect tracking, and testing by ordinary generalists.

Although quality control is technical in nature, it is primarily driven by management decisions. In several significant disasters the technical staff recommended using such approaches as formal inspections and testing, but were overruled by management for the stated reason that "There is no time in the schedule."

Since the probability of a successful or unsuccessful outcome varies with the size range of the project being developed, the probabilities shown here are assumed to be for a system of nominally 5000 function points in size. This is roughly equivalent to about 525,000 source code statements in a procedural language such as COBOL or FORTRAN.

For smaller projects, successful outcomes would be more prevalent. For larger projects, unsuccessful outcomes would be more prevalent. There are commercial software estimating tools, such as CHECKPOINT, KnowledgePlan, SLIM, and SPQR/20, that can predict the specific failure probabilities of software projects of any arbitrary size and combination of technologies. It is recommended that tools such as these be utilized for dealing with the actual risk probabilities. The information in Table 7.2 simply indicates approximate outcomes and should not be used for serious planning purposes.

The margin of error in the information In Table 7.2 is high, but the overall combinations of factors are derived from empirical observations, and they illustrate that too much carelessness can lead to disaster.

Obviously this picture is incomplete and omits all midrange situations between the best and the worst. There are also many other factors that can affect software projects besides the four shown here.

However, the overall situation is quite clear and is supported by many empirical observations. Carelessness, poor estimating, poor planning, poor tracking, and minimal quality control are strongly associated with canceled projects, overruns, and various disasters.

Conversely, usage of automated estimating and planning tools, careful monthly tracking, and excellence in terms of software quality are strongly associated with software projects that are successful in terms of schedule adherence, cost control, customer satisfaction, and other beneficial attributes.

The seeds of major software disasters are usually sown in the first three months of commencing the software project. Hasty scheduling, irrational commitments, unprofessional estimating techniques, and carelessness of the project management function are the factors that tend to introduce terminal problems. Once a project blindly lurches forward toward an impossible delivery date, the rest of the disaster will occur almost inevitably.

The literature on software successes and failures is out of balance, in that books on failures outnumber books on successes by a huge margin. This is not necessarily bad, but it does imply that software is a very troublesome discipline.

The major references for this chapter are those that deal with risks of various kinds, such as the work of Fred Brooks (Brooks 1974), Bob Charette (Charette 1989, 1990), DeMarco (DeMarco 1997), and Ed Yourdon's new book on "death march" projects (Yourdon 1997). The author's own books on software risks are included, too (Jones 1994, 1995). The work of Bill Perry is also a valuable resource (Perry 1989).

References

Brooks, Fred: *The Mythical Man-Month,* Addison-Wesley, Reading, Mass., 1974, rev. 1995.

Charette, Robert N.: *Software Engineering Risk Analysis and Management,* McGraw-Hill, New York, ISBN 0-07-010719-X, 1989.

——: *Application Strategies for Risk Analysis,* McGraw-Hill, New York, ISBN 0-07-010888-9, 1990.

DeMarco, Tom: *Deadline,* Dorset House Press, New York, 1997.

Jones, Capers: *Assessment and Control of Software Risks,* Prentice Hall, ISBN 0-13-741406-4, 1994.

——: *Patterns of Software Systems Failure and Success,* International Thomson Computer Press, Boston, ISBN 1-850-32804-8, 1995.

Perry, William E.: *Handbook of Diagnosing and Solving Computer Problems,* TAB Books, Blue Ridge Summit, Pa., ISBN 0-8306-9233-9, 1989.

Yourdon, Ed: *Death March—The Complete Software Developer's Guide to Surviving "Mission Impossible" Projects,* Prentice Hall PTR, Upper Saddle River, N.J., ISBN 0-13-748310-4, 1997.

8

Investment Costs and Return on Investment (ROI) for Software Project Management Tools

One of the accidental by-products of the current state of software management tools is that the expenses required to fully equip software project managers with the best available tools are rather high. This is due in part to the fact that project management tools are not integrated into complete suites, but instead are marketed by a number of independent corporations as independent tools.

A second reason for the high cost of fully equipping software project managers is that the *cost per seat* for the upper tier of software management tools is rather expensive compared to programming tools or software-engineering tools. For cost-estimating tools, the high unit costs reflect the value of the attached knowledge bases and the historical data embedded within the tools.

Table 8.1 shows current U.S. ranges for the 18 kinds of software management tools discussed in this book. The lowest-cost range is for tools where shareware or even freeware versions are available for personal computers. The median range is for retail tools that are available on normal personal computer platforms. The high-cost range is for custom tools built to client specifications or for the most expensive kinds of tools within each category.

In Table 8.1, the top tier of software cost estimating tools stands out as having the highest cost per seat of almost any kind of tool in the world. This is due primarily to the value of the accompanying knowledge base, rather than to the size or difficulty of building the

TABLE 8.1   Approximate Cost per Seat for Software Management Tools

Tool category	Low-cost	Median-cost	High-cost
Cost estimating	$250	$2,500	$15,000
Quality estimating	150	500	5,000
Methodology management	0	1,250	3,500
Complexity analysis	75	500	3,000
Statistical analysis	0	750	2,500
Assessment support	0	750	2,000
Project planning	100	500	1,500
Risk analysis	0	500	1,500
Value analysis	0	500	1,500
Portfolio analysis	0	750	1,500
Year-2000 analysis	350	750	1,500
Project measurement	75	500	1,250
Budget support	0	500	1,000
Variance reporting	0	500	1,000
Project tracking	100	300	1,000
Defect tracking	200	500	1,000
Function point analysis	50	500	750
Source code counting	0	250	500
Total	$1,350	$12,300	$45,000
Average	$75	$683	$2,500

estimating tools themselves. Essentially, the costs are really for the data derived from more than 1000 projects and available only by means of the cost-estimating tools.

It can be hypothesized that, in common with all other kinds of software, business and economic pressures will bring these costs down, and will certainly bring down the high-cost range.

It can be predicted that an integrated suite marketed by a single vendor would probably be able to supply all of the tool capabilities shown in Table 8.1 for less than $5000 per seat. However, that level of integration is still some distance in the future as this book is being written.

The gaps with zero values in Table 8.1 reflect one of two different conditions: (1) tools are available as freeware or for no charge (as with source code counting tools), or (2) no low-cost tools are available at all for this category (as with portfolio analysis tools).

Some of the more expensive tools, such as cost-estimating tools, actually exceed the spending authority of most of the intended users.

The total costs for all of the project management tools in aggregate usually exceeds the spending authority of first-line managers, although most large companies buy multiple copies of common kinds of tools.

The rather high costs for a complete suite of software management tools goes far toward explaining why such tools are found more often in large and profitable corporations than they are in small companies or in government agencies.

Software cost estimating is valuable in direct proportion to the value of the software projects that are being estimated. Assume that a typical software cost estimating tool is in the $2500 range for a single copy or seat. If such a tool is acquired for software projects which themselves cost less than $10,000, then the value of the tool is negligible.

However, if the software project costs rise above $100,000, then the cost-estimating tool begins to generate positive value by reducing the chances of budget overruns, schedule overruns, or possible failure of the project.

Since $100,000 software projects estimated using manual methods typically overrun their budgets by perhaps $5000, purchasing a cost-estimating tool would probably generate a modest positive value by minimizing the chances of schedule and cost overruns.

If the project costs for software development rise above $1 million, then formal cost estimating is one of the most valuable investments that can be made for the project. For this range, manual estimating methods often result in 10 percent or $100,000 cost overruns, or even higher.

If the project costs for software development are going above $10 million, or above $100 million, then attempting to build the project without use of the formal cost-estimating tools can result in major disasters.

The topic of the return on investment (ROI) in various software tools is a difficult and complex issue with a significant margin of error. The author's 1994 book *Assessment and Control of Software Risks* (Jones 1994) utilized our large knowledge base of software projects to attempt a four-year ROI analysis of about 65 software technology and tool categories, including almost a dozen software management tools and methods.

The ROI calculations were based on analyzing sets of projects that used certain tools and methods, and comparing their costs, schedules, quality, and other factors against the results of similar projects that did not use the selected methods or tool classes.

For example, to evaluate the impact of formal design and code inspections, three samples of 50 projects each were contrasted:

1. Sample *A* used formal design and code inspections with experienced personnel.

2. Sample *B* used formal inspections for the very first time.

3. Sample *C* did not use formal inspections at all.

From analysis of the costs, schedules, defect counts, and maintenance costs, the approximate ROI for formal inspections could be worked out.

This same kind of analysis can be applied to software management tools, although the results are more problematic. For dealing with software management tools, four kinds of benefits were considered:

1. Does the tool reduce the risk of outright cancellation of software projects?

2. Does the tool reduce the risk of litigation between clients and contractors?

3. Does the tool reduce the risk of poor quality before and after deployment?

4. Does the tool reduce the risk of cost and schedule overruns?

Readers should be aware that the primary reason for software project cancellation is severe cost and schedule overruns, which approximate about 100 percent cost overruns and delays of about one calendar year at project termination.

However, root-cause analysis of canceled projects usually reveals that the delays were due to such poor quality control that when testing began, the project could not be made to work satisfactorily.

Table 8.2 illustrates the approximate impact of various software management tools on these four factors, using the subjective assertions of *excellent* through *fair* when the tool has any impact on the topic at all.

Note that gaps and blank columns in Table 8.2 indicate either that the tool has no impact on that topic, or that there is no available data from which to judge the impact.

Table 8.3, which shows return on investment, uses the same format as the tables in *Assessment and Control of Software Risks* and attempts to illustrate a four-year return on investment for every dollar invested initially.

Needless to say, the table has a very large margin of error and should not be used for any serious business purpose. Table 8.3 is based on partial and preliminary data, and the results can vary widely from case to case.

The overall rationale for the values shown in the table is based on

TABLE 8.2   Risk-Abatement Value of Selected Software Management Tools

Tool category	Risk of cancellation	Risk of litigation	Risk of poor quality	Risk of overruns	Overall
Quality estimating	Very good	Excellent	Excellent	Excellent	Very good
Cost estimating	Excellent	Excellent	Very good	Excellent	Very good
Methodology management	Good	Fair	Very good	Good	Good
Project measurement	Good	Very good	Very good	Good	Good
Project planning	Excellent	Good	Fair	Good	Good
Defect tracking	Fair	Good	Very good	Fair	Good
Year-2000 analysis		Excellent	Good	Good	Good
Assessment support	Good	Good	Good	Fair	Good
Project tracking	Very good	Fair	Fair	Good	Good
Value analysis	Very good				Good
Function point analysis			Good	Good	Good
Portfolio analysis					
Statistical analysis					
Risk analysis	Very good	Very good	Fair	Fair	Good
Complexity analysis			Good		Good
Variance reporting	Good	Good		Good	Good
Budget support	Good	Good		Good	Good
Source code counting			Fair		Fair

observations of canceled projects, lawsuits brought by disgruntled clients, and the potential impact of the tools for improving quality, schedules, and costs.

(As this book is being written, the author and his company have been involved as expert witnesses in several breach of contract lawsuits for software projects with combined values of about $300 million. Preventing the legal costs and damages for breach of contract suits explains why the ROI for project management tools is higher than might otherwise be expected.)

This means that if management tools are used primarily for small in-house projects with little or no chance of lawsuits or damages occurring, the return on investment will be substantially lower.

The ROI for most software management tools is favorable, but not so dramatic as a situation where a $10,000 software cost estimating tool can prevent a $10-million breach-of-contract lawsuit. In this extreme situation, the ROI would be roughly 1000 to 1.

It is obvious that quality is receiving preferential weighting, since poor quality is a primary causative factor of canceled projects, litiga-

TABLE 8.3   Approximate Four-Year Return on Investment in Software Management Tools

Tool category	Year 1	Year 2	Year 3	Year 4	Total
Quality estimating	$3.00	$4.50	$12.00	$18.00	$37.50
Cost estimating	2.50	5.00	12.00	17.50	37.00
Methodology management	2.00	3.50	10.00	16.00	31.50
Project measurement	1.50	3.50	8.50	13.00	26.50
Project planning	1.50	4.00	8.00	12.50	26.00
Defect tracking	2.00	3.00	7.00	13.00	25.00
Year-2000 analysis	15.00	5.00	2.00	0.00	22.00
Assessment support	1.50	3.00	6.00	10.00	20.50
Project tracking	1.75	3.50	6.00	9.00	20.25
Value analysis	1.50	3.00	5.00	8.00	17.50
Function point analysis	1.75	3.00	4.50	8.00	17.25
Portfolio analysis	1.75	2.50	5.00	7.50	16.75
Statistical analysis	1.75	2.75	4.50	6.00	15.00
Risk analysis	1.50	2.50	3.50	5.50	13.00
Complexity analysis	1.30	2.00	3.00	4.50	10.80
Variance reporting	1.00	1.50	2.50	3.50	8.50
Budget support	1.00	1.50	2.00	3.00	7.50
Source code counting	1.00	1.00	1.00	1.00	4.00
Total	$43.30	$54.75	$102.50	$156.00	$356.55
Average	$2.41	$3.04	$5.69	$8.67	$19.81

tion, schedule overruns, and cost overruns. However, if a software management tool does not benefit quality, then whatever else it does can be jeopardized if the software in question fails or does not operate correctly.

The literature on software ROI is very sparse for such a major topic. The topic of best practices is better covered, but exactly what constitutes a *best practice* is somewhat ambiguous without firm ROI data.

The citations used for this chapter include the work of Loic Briand and Daniel Roy on real-time deadlines (Briand and Roy 1997); Dr. Norm Brown on the Navy's set of best practices (Brown 1995); the author's own books on risk (Jones 1994, 1995); Mark Paulk's clear discussion of the Software Engineering Institute's capability maturity model (Paulk 1995); and the work of Larry Putnam (Putnam 1992) and Ed Yourdon (Yourdon 1997).

References

Briand, Loic, and Daniel Roy: *Meeting Deadlines in Hard Real-Time Systems,* IEEE Computer Society Press, Los Alamitos, Calif., ISBN 0-8186-406-7, 1997.

Brown, Norm (ed.): *The Program Manager's Guide to Software Acquisition Best Practices,* Version 1.0, U.S. Department of Defense, Washington, D.C., July 1995.

Jones, Capers: *Assessment and Control of Software Risks,* Prentice Hall, ISBN 0-13-741406-4, 1994.

———: *Patterns of Software System Failure and Success,* International Thomson Computer Press, Boston, ISBN 1-850-32804-8, 1995.

Paulk, Mark, et al.: *The Capability Maturity Model: Guidelines for Improving the Software Process,* Addison-Wesley, Reading, Mass., ISBN 0-201-54664-7, 1995.

Putnam, Lawrence H.: *Measures for Excellence—Reliable Software on Time, Within Budget,* Yourdon Press/Prentice Hall, Englewood Cliffs, N.J., ISBN 0-13-567694-0, 1992.

Yourdon, Ed: *Death March—The Complete Software Developer's Guide to Surviving "Mission Impossible" Projects,* Prentice Hall PTR, Upper Saddle River, N.J., ISBN 0-13-748310-4, 1997.

9

Sources of Error in Software Cost Estimation

A natural question that accompanies the growth of the software estimating market is that of how accurate the software cost estimating tools are. That question is surprisingly difficult to answer, since accuracy can be judged only in the context of precisely measured software projects. Most companies, universities, and government agencies do not have historical data that is precise enough to be used to judge the relative accuracy of software cost estimation tools.

Indeed, as determined by performing assessment and benchmark studies, the historical cost data for an average software project is only about 50 percent complete. Most cost-tracking systems omit early requirements, unpaid overtime, the work of specialists, the technical work performed by users, project management, travel costs, and many other factors that will be discussed later in this chapter.

A very common phenomenon occurs when companies or researchers first evaluate a software cost estimating tool. Comparisons are made between the estimating tool and locally available historical data. These estimates almost always show large discrepancies of 50 to 100 percent or more between what the estimating tool predicts and the historical results.

The variances are always in the same direction: The estimating tool predicts higher costs and longer schedules than what the local historical data indicates. The natural tendency is to assume that the estimating tool is inaccurate. However, it often happens that the error resides in the historical data itself. Most of what passes for historical data in the software industry is incomplete and omits from 30 percent to more than 70 percent of the real work performed on software projects.

Before the topic of software-estimation accuracy can be properly discussed, it is necessary to understand the gaps and errors that are endemic in software measurement data. Only when the errors of historical data have been corrected is it possible to judge the relative accuracy of estimation methods.

Following are the three major sources of error observed in software historical data. These three problems are almost universal, and unless they are corrected it is very difficult to utilize historical data for calibrating estimation tools. Observations on these problems have been made as a result of software process assessments, and are derived from studies within about 600 companies and government organizations. The three major problems are:

1. Failure to include all activities that were performed

2. Failure to include all classes of workers who participate

3. Failure to include unpaid overtime

Normally, software project historical data is accumulated in some kind of a general project cost tracking system. These cost-tracking systems are seldom designed for, or optimized for, collecting data on software projects. Their most common problem is that they lack an effective chart of accounts that matches a full software life cycle.

The most common omissions from cost-tracking systems include the following:

1. Work performed before the cost-tracking system was initialized, such as requirements determination

2. Work performed by nonprogramming personnel, such as technical writers, database administrators, or quality-assurance staffers

3. Work performed by project management, especially second-level or higher managers

4. Technical work performed by users, when they participate in testing or create their own user documentation

Note that it is intrinsically difficult to quantify activities that are omitted from formal cost-tracking systems. However, from interviewing several hundred project personnel and asking them to reconstruct how they spent their time, the following tentative values can be assigned to these missing elements:

- From 5 to 10 percent of a software project's effort will be expended before the cost-tracking system is turned on.

- From 15 to 30 percent of the work on a project will be performed by workers who are not included in typical cost-tracking systems.

- Management effort will amount to between 10 and 20 percent of the overall project and may not be tracked in some companies.

- User participation in the technical work of software projects amounts to between 5 and 20 percent of the total effort and is almost never tracked.

- Unpaid overtime by exempt professional staff and management amounts to between 5 and 15 percent of software project effort, with the largest amount of overtime being utilized on the most important and largest projects.

Other problems with historical data collection also occur. Here are a few observations that have been noted during software process assessments:

- When a project begins to run low on funding, there is a tendency to charge time to other projects.

- Some personnel refuse to use the cost-tracking system at all.

- Some complex systems projects utilize other kinds of personnel besides software engineers, such as electrical engineers or mechanical engineers. These engineers may be engaged in software design work and sometimes even in coding, but they do not regard themselves as software personnel and don't record their time when doing software work.

- Many enterprises have no cost-tracking systems at all and, hence, have no historical data of any kind.

Since problems with historical data are so endemic, it is a fair question to ask how software-estimating tool vendors accumulated enough information to build the tools in the first place. (Note that the author is also a developer of commercial software cost estimating tools.)

From informal conversations with competitive estimating-tool vendors (i.e., Dr. Barry Boehm of COCOMO, Larry Putnam of SLIM, and Dr. Howard Rubin of ESTIMACS), it appears that all have encountered problems of inaccurate historical data and have compensated for this problem in one or more of three ways:

1. By excluding projects where the data is incomplete

2. By correcting the missing data based on interviews with project team members

3. By building activity-based cost-estimating tools

As a general rule, historical data that is not granular should be avoided. Data collected only to the level of complete projects, for example, without any breakdown by activities or tasks, is seldom accurate enough to be useful for estimating purposes.

Also, data that is granular only to the level of phases (i.e., requirements, design, coding, testing, and installation) is also of questionable value. Many activities span multiple phases. To name but a few, configuration control, integration, and the preparation of user manuals normally span at least two phases. Therefore, phase-level data cannot be safely used for estimating multiphase work.

Some industries are better than others in recording software effort, schedule, cost, and quality information. Among the clients served by Software Productivity Research, the patterns of errors typically noted are presented in Table 9.1.

The problem of incomplete historical data is common enough that the patterns of gaps can be illustrated. Table 9.2 is derived from the companion volume to this book, *Applied Software Measurement* (Jones 1996a).

Only about 5 activities out of a possible 25 are routinely accurate enough that the data is usable for cost-estimation purposes. The effect of the missing or incomplete data is to drive up apparent productivity rates and make projects seem cheaper than they really are.

The chart of accounts shown in Table 9.2 illustrates the approximate level of granularity that is needed to accumulate historical data with enough precision to judge the accuracy of software-estimation tools.

Historical data that is only aggregated to the level of complete projects is not useful for serious study, since there is no way of knowing what activities were or were not performed and did or did not affect the total costs and resources.

There are at least two levels below the activity level that are necessary for really fine-tuning estimating tools: tasks and subtasks. For

TABLE 9.1   Patterns of Missing Software Cost Data by Industry

Software subindustry	Percentage of missing data	Most common omissions
Military software	10	Unpaid overtime
Contracted or outsourced software	10	Unpaid overtime
Systems software	12	Unpaid overtime and documentation
Commercial software	15	Unpaid overtime, noncode tasks, and requirements
Information systems	35	Unpaid overtime, user activities, noncode tasks, specialists, and project managers
End-user software	75	Everything but coding

TABLE 9.2   Common Gaps in Historical Software Cost and Resource Data

Activities performed	Completeness of historical data
01 Requirements	Missing or incomplete
02 Prototyping	Missing or incomplete
03 Architecture	Incomplete
04 Project planning	Incomplete
05 Initial analysis and design	Incomplete
06 Detail design	Incomplete
07 Design reviews	Missing or incomplete
08 Coding	Complete
09 Reusable code acquisition	Missing or incomplete
10 Purchased package acquisition	Missing or incomplete
11 Code inspections	Missing or incomplete
12 Independent verification and validation	Complete
13 Configuration management	Missing or incomplete
14 Integration	Missing or incomplete
15 User documentation	Missing or incomplete
16 Unit testing	Incomplete
17 Function testing	Incomplete
18 Integration testing	Incomplete
19 System testing	Incomplete
20 Field testing	Incomplete
21 Acceptance testing	Missing or incomplete
22 Independent testing	Complete
23 Quality assurance	Missing or incomplete
24 Installation and training	Missing or incomplete
25 Project management	Missing or incomplete
26 Total project resources, costs	Incomplete

example, if *unit testing* is considered to be a standard activity, then the following three tasks are the key subcomponents of normal unit testing:

1. Preparing test cases

2. Running test cases

3. Repairing bugs or defects

Because every activity will have from 3 to 5 tasks connected with it, and some tasks can have from 3 to 5 subtasks, the most granular level of precision can exceed 1000 data elements.

Judging the Accuracy of Software Cost Estimates

Because the author's company designs and builds software cost estimating tools, he is frequently asked three general questions about the accuracy of estimates:

1. How accurate are our company's tools in terms of how their results compare to historical data?

2. How accurate are our company's tools in terms of how their estimates compare to estimates from competitive estimating tools?

3. How accurate are our company's tools in terms of how their estimates compare to manual cost estimates?

The first question has already been discussed, with the surprising result that cost estimates both from our tools and from competitive estimating tools are often more accurate than historical data, due to "leakage" from cost-tracking systems.

A significant study was performed by Air Force Captain Karen R. Mertes as a master's thesis at the Air Force Institute of Technology, using validated Air Force data (Mertes 1996). This study showed that when the historical data is accurate, estimates usually come within 10 percent, and sometimes come closer than 5 percent.

The second question about competitive tools is difficult for the author to answer, since it involves comparing our products against our competitors'. That question obviously involves a conflict of interest, and it is better addressed by university studies or independent research.

Because the United States military services produce so much software and use so many estimating tools, much of the comparative research about software cost estimation is performed in a military context.

The Air Force Software Technology Support Center (STSC) at Hill Air Force Base in Utah produced an interesting comparison of no less than 31 software cost estimation tools that contrasts features and discusses partial accuracy from limited trials (Barrow et al. 1993).

The estimating tools included were ASSET-R, CA-ESTIMACS, CA-FPXpert, CB COCOMO, CEIS, CHECKPOINT, COCOMO1, COCO-MOID, CoCoPro, COSTAR, COSTEXPERT, COSTMODL, GECOMO Plus, GHL COCOMO, ESTI-MATE, PRICE-S, PROJECT BRIDGE, REVIC, SASET, SECOMO, SEER-SEM, SEER-SSM, SIZE PLANNER, SIZE Plus, SIZEEXPERT, SLIM, SOFTCOSST-R, SPQR/20, SWAN, and SYSTEM-4.

Another Air Force comparison using a smaller number of tools but a greater amount of validated data was performed jointly between Maxwell Air Force Base and the Air Force Institute of Technology

(Ourada and Ferens 1995). This study included eight estimating tools (REVIC, COCOMO, PRICE-S, SEER, SASET, SYSTM-4, CHECK-POINT, and COSTMODL).

Another interesting military estimating comparison, by the well-known software cost estimating expert, Professor Daniel Ferens of the Air Force Institute of Technology (AFIT), was published in one of the special cost-estimating issues of *American Programmer* magazine (Ferens 1996).

An older and fairly rare study of civilian software cost estimating models was performed by MIT and included six software cost models from the 1985 era (Kemerer 1987).

The third question has been answered independently by a number of software estimating tool vendors, and the results are identical:

- Manual estimates are usually highly optimistic for costs and schedules.

- Automated estimates are usually accurate or conservative for costs and schedules.

In 1994 the author collected a sample of 50 manual software cost estimates from our company's clients for projects where both the initial formal cost estimate and the final accumulated costs were known. Figure 9.1 shows that only 4 of these 50 manual estimates came with-

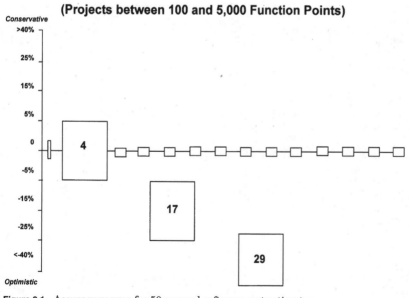

Figure 9.1   Accuracy ranges for 50 manual software cost estimates.

in plus or minus 5 percent of the historical costs, and the majority of manual estimates were optimistic to a significant degree.

Because the manual estimates were produced by colleagues and clients, interviews and discussions were able to pinpoint the reasons for the optimism. Here are some examples cited by project managers whose estimates proved to be optimistic:

"I could not get approval for an accurate estimate, so I had to change it."

"The project doubled in size after the requirements."

"Debugging and testing took longer than we thought."

"The new CASE tools we were using didn't work right and slowed us down."

"We didn't have any estimating tools available at the time the estimate was needed."

"I lost some of my developers and had to find replacements."

By contrast, Fig. 9.2 illustrates the accuracy ranges of 50 automated software cost estimates.

It is interesting that a much higher percentage of projects came within plus or minus 5 percent than with manual methods. Even more interesting is the fact that the direction of error is reversed.

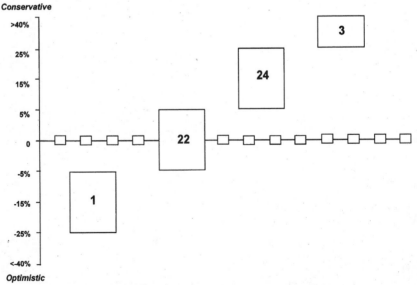

(Projects between 100 and 5,000 Function Points)

Figure 9.2   Accuracy ranges for 50 automated software cost estimates.

Automated estimating tools are usually conservative when they are not accurate, while manual methods are usually optimistic. Indeed, only 1 of the 50 automated estimates was on the optimistic side.

Accuracy within plus or minus 5 percent is the desired goal of estimating, but if errors do occur the fail-safe mode is to be conservative rather than optimistic. For bidding purposes, deliberate optimism is sometimes used, but in the long run accuracy and conservatism are the best choices.

Classes of Software Estimation Errors

Once the problem of incomplete or missing historical data has been overcome, it is possible to evaluate the accuracy of estimation tools and methods themselves. There are 12 common problems that tend to occur with software estimates:

1. Metrics errors

2. Scaling errors

3. Executive and client errors

4. Sizing errors

5. Activity-selection errors

6. Assignment-scope errors

7. Production-rate errors

8. Creeping user requirements

9. Critical path errors

10. Staffing build-up errors

11. Technology adjustment errors

12. Special or unique situations

Let us consider the implications of these sources of error individually.

Metrics errors

The most common error in software estimating is derived from the very common usage of *lines-of-code* (LOC) metrics. Although LOC metrics were proven to be unreliable for software estimation as long ago as 1978, the technique is still among the most widely utilized.

There are problems with LOC metrics associated with variations in the way code is counted, but these are not the source of the main problem. The main problem with LOC metrics is the fact that more than half of all software effort is not directly related to source code.

TABLE 9.3   Implementation of the Same Program in Three Languages

	Macro assembly	Ada 83	C++
Source code required, LOC	10,000	3,500	2,500
Effort per activity, staff months			
Requirements	1.0	1.0	1.0
Design	3.0	2.0	0.5
Coding	5.0	1.5	1.0
Testing	4.0	1.5	1.0
Documentation	2.0	2.0	2.0
Management	2.0	1.0	0.5
Total project, months	18.0	10.0	7.5
Total project, LOC/staff month	555	350	333
Coding and testing, % total project	28%	15%	13%

This means that LOC metrics tend to paradoxically move in the wrong direction when used with high-level languages.

To illustrate the problem with LOC metrics as an estimation method, Table 9.3 shows three examples of the same program. The first example is written in macro assembly language, the second is written in Ada 83, and the third example is written in C++. However, all three examples perform exactly the same functions.

As may be seen from the examples, apparent productivity expressed in LOC metrics declines as the power of the language increases. This phenomenon causes problems for estimation when LOC metrics are used by the unwary.

For example, suppose a manager has some historical data based on assembly language, with a rate of 600 LOC per month. It is natural to assume that more powerful languages such as Ada or C++ will improve productivity, as indeed they often do. (Note that pure coding for the prior examples had rates of 2000 LOC per month for assembly, 2300 for Ada, and 2500 for C++.)

It often happens that unwary or inexperienced software managers get trapped into making false estimating assumptions along these lines: "We've been getting 600 LOC per month for our assembly-language projects, and Ada is a much more powerful language. I'll use 700 LOC per month as the rate for estimating our new Ada project."

This common estimating problem can be seen to be comprised of two separate components:

1. Historical data that is not granular enough to show activities is dangerous for estimating work.

2. The LOC metric itself is flawed and dangerous for cross-language measurement or estimation purposes.

This problem is very common when estimates are performed manually. But it can also occur with some of the older LOC-based estimation tools that do not vary their assumptions from language to language. Most modern software-estimating tools allow the specific language or sets of languages used to be identified, and then adjust the estimation algorithms to match the specifics of the language set.

There are alternate metrics that do not exhibit the paradoxical rate reversal associated with lines of code. The function point metric, for example, is free from the distortions and errors that occur with LOC metrics.

As an example, since all three versions of the program in Table 9.3 are identical in functionality, their function point total would stay constant regardless of language. Assume that the program illustrated contains 50 function points. When productivity is expressed in terms of function points per staff month, the results correlate exactly with the increased power of the higher level languages:

Assembly-language version =	2.80 function points per staff month
Ada version	=	5.00 function points per staff month
C++ version	=	6.60 function points per staff month

The ability of function points to measure and estimate economic productivity across multiple languages is one of the reasons why the usage of this metric has been expanding at more than 50 percent per year. By about 1992, the nonprofit International Function Point Users Group (IFPUG) had become the largest software measurement association in the United States. When the membership of the 21 current international affiliates is considered, the function point metric is now the most widely used software metric in the world.

Scaling errors

Another common source of estimating error is the naive assumption that data collected from small programs can safely be used to estimate large systems. Large systems (more than 1 million source code statements or 10,000 function points) differ from small programs (less than 10,000 source code statements or 100 function points) in two major ways:

1. Large systems require more activities than small programs.

2. The costs of large systems do not follow the same profile as small programs.

TABLE 9.4   Variations in Software Effort Associated with Application Size

Size, function points	Size, KLOC	Coding, %	Paperwork, %	Defect removal, %	Management and support, %
1	0.1	70	5	15	10
10	1	65	7	17	11
100	10	54	15	20	11
1,000	100	30	26	30	14
10,000	1,000	18	31	35	16

Using the chart of accounts from Table 9.1 as a reference point, small programs seldom perform more than about 10 of the 25 activities that are listed. Large civilian systems, on the other hand, routinely perform at least 20 of the 25 activities, and large military projects perform all 25.

Not only do large systems perform more activities, but the effort required for various kinds of work changes notably as software projects grow in size. Table 9.4, derived from *Applied Software Measurement* (Jones 1996), highlights the distribution of effort for programs and systems of various sizes.

As may be seen from Table 9.4, it is not at all safe to use data taken from applications of one size range as the basis for estimating applications of a significantly different size.

The most common form of scaling error is the assumption that data from small projects of 100 function points or less (roughly 10,000 source code statements) can be used for large systems of 1000 function points or more (roughly 100,000 source code statements). The reason is that project managers see many more small projects than large systems. A project manager may be responsible for several small projects in the course of a typical business year, but be responsible for the estimation of a large system only a few times in an entire career. Therefore, project managers know quite a bit about small-project estimating, but very little about large-system estimating.

Executive and client errors

One of the most severe sources of software-estimation error centers around corporate politics, or the fact that senior executives and client executives have the authority to arbitrarily reject valid estimates. Most software cost estimates must go through several layers of management approval and client approval before being finalized.

What often happens is that the original estimate created by a software project manager is either accurate or conservative. However, this initial estimate is outside the envelope of an acceptable schedule or acceptable costs in the minds of the executives who must approve the estimate. Therefore, the project manager is directed to recast the estimate in order to lower costs or shorten schedules or both.

What has happened is that the real estimate is no longer the creation of the software project manager responsible for the project. The real estimate has become the subjective opinion of a client or senior executive. Usually, such mandated estimates are made in the total absence of any kind of serious, professional estimating methodology, and without any estimating tools at all.

When performing autopsies on canceled software projects or on projects that exceeded their schedules and budgets by more than 50%, more than half of these disasters are seen to have had initial conservative estimates that were arbitrarily rejected by senior executives or by client executives. Unfortunately, the project managers were still assigned the blame for the disaster or overrun even though they had tried to estimate accurately.

Sizing errors

Yet another common software-estimating error is that of mistakes in predicting the sizes of various deliverables. Sizing errors are very common for all external deliverables, including the quantity of source code, the number of screens, and the number of pages in both course materials and user documentation.

Sizing errors are also endemic when dealing with internal deliverables, such as pages of specifications, pages of planning documents, test cases, and the like.

Predicting source code size, predicting documentation quantities and sizes, and test-case prediction are standard functions of modern software-estimating tools, although they are missing from those developed prior to about 1985. (Historical note: SPQR/20, which was released in 1985, appears to be the first commercial software-estimating tool that included sizing logic for source code, documentation volumes, and test cases. This tool pioneered the usage of function points as the uniform basis for sizing all software deliverables.)

More recent software-estimating tools can predict the size of more than 50 paper documents, the number of test cases for 18 kinds of testing, and source code size for almost 500 programming languages.

Activity-selection errors

Activity-selection errors are those of omitting necessary work from an estimate, such as accidentally omitting the costs of user documentation. Activity selection from a repertoire of more than 20 activities (or even several hundred tasks), with the estimating tool automatically adjusting its selection to match military, civilian, and project class or type characteristics, is now a standard function of modern software-estimating tools.

Users can override activity-selection logic or produce custom activity lists. Several modern software cost estimating tools support the creation of *templates* that utilize historical projects or custom templates created by the user as the basis for activity and task selection.

Activity-selection errors are very common when performing manual estimates. For example, a project manager within a major computer company once received funding for a project with an approved estimate that accidentally omitted the costs of producing the user manuals.

Activity-selection errors also have another unfortunate manifestation: Software tool vendors and programming language vendors tend to make advertising claims based on comparisons of unlike activities.

For example, an ad for a fourth-generation language cited productivity results of more than 100 function points per staff month, and the ad claimed that these results were "10 times greater than COBOL."

However, when the vendor was queried about the activities that went into the claim, it was discovered that requirements, design, user documentation, and project management were not included. In fact, the only activities that were included for the language being advertised were coding and unit testing. However, the COBOL projects used for the comparison did include requirements, design, documentation, and other normal project activities.

Failure to define the tasks and activities when either measuring or estimating software is an embarrassingly common problem within the software industry. Table 9.5 shows the patterns of tasks that are typical for several kinds of software projects. Table 9.5 is also derived from the author's companion book, *Applied Software Measurement* (Jones 1996).

As can easily be seen, it would be dangerous to construct a formal software cost estimate without full and complete knowledge of the activities that are going to be part of the development cycle for the project in question.

The large variations in activity sets from class to class illustrate why gross estimates at the project or phase level are seldom as accurate as those at the activity level. It is too hard to validate gross estimates because the inner structure of the work to be performed is invisible.

Although project-level and phase-level estimates were the norm from the 1960s through the early 1990s, activity-level cost estimates are rapidly becoming the norm as the end of the century approaches. Activity-level estimates are also needed for the dreaded year-2000 problem, since the costs of this problem are complex and multifaceted.

TABLE 9.5   Software Development Activities Associated with Six Subindustries
(Percentage of staff months by activity)

Activities performed	End user	MIS	Outsource	Commercial	System	Military
01 Requirements		7.50	9.00	4.00	4.00	7.00
02 Prototyping	10.00	2.00	2.50	1.00	2.00	2.00
03 Architecture		0.50	1.00	2.00	1.50	1.00
04 Project plans		1.00	1.50	1.00	2.00	1.00
05 Initial design		8.00	7.00	6.00	7.00	6.00
06 Detail design		7.00	8.00	5.00	6.00	7.00
07 Design reviews			0.50	1.50	2.50	1.00
08 Coding	35.00	20.00	16.00	23.00	20.00	16.00
09 Reuse acquisition	5.00		2.00	2.00	2.00	2.00
10 Package purchase		1.00	1.00		1.00	1.00
11 Code inspections				1.50	1.50	1.00
12 Independent verification and validation						1.00
13 Configuration management		3.00	3.00	1.00	1.00	1.50
14 Formal integration		2.00	2.00	1.50	2.00	1.50
15 User documentation	10.00	7.00	9.00	12.00	10.00	10.00
16 Unit testing	40.00	4.00	3.50	2.50	5.00	3.00
17 Function testing		6.00	5.00	6.00	5.00	5.00
18 Integration testing		5.00	5.00	4.00	5.00	5.00
19 System testing		7.00	5.00	7.00	5.00	6.00
20 Field testing				6.00	1.50	3.00
21 Acceptance testing		5.00	3.00		1.00	3.00
22 Independent testing						1.00
23 Quality assurance			1.00	2.00	2.00	1.00
24 Installation and training		2.00	3.00		1.00	1.00
25 Project management		12.00	12.00	11.00	12.00	13.00
Total	100	100	100	100	100	100
Activities	5	16	20	21	22	25

Assignment-scope errors

Assignment-scope errors are those of miscalculating the quantity of work that can be handled by the staff, so that they become overloaded. The phrase *assignment scope* denotes the amount of work assigned to one staff member.

Assignment-scope prediction in terms of both natural metrics (pages of specifications, source code, and number of test cases) and synthetic metrics (function points and feature points) is now a standard function of modern software cost estimating tools. Templates defined by users or created from historical project data can also be used.

Assignment scopes have now been worked out from empirical observations for the following occupation groups:

- Software development engineers and/or programmers
- Software maintenance engineers and/or programmers
- Systems analysts
- Technical writers
- Quality-assurance specialists
- Configuration control specialists
- Integration specialists
- Testing specialists
- Customer-support specialists
- Project managers

However, there are almost 100 software occupations that can be found in large software-producing companies, such as IBM, AT&T, Microsoft, and the like. There are quite a few specialized occupation groups where the quantity of work that can be assigned to one person is still uncertain. Examples of occupations where assignment scopes fluctuate from project to project and company to company include the following:

- Administrative specialists
- Database administration specialists
- Network specialists
- Multimedia specialists
- Human factors specialists
- System performance specialists
- Process specialists

As of 1998, there are some unresolved problems surrounding specialists and assignment scopes. For example, how many different kinds of specialists are needed to support a general software population of 1000?

Research in this topic is made difficult by the fact that many companies do not even have records or job titles for some of the specialist occupations. For example, companies that use "member of the technical staff" as a blanket job title covering a host of occupations are essentially unable to do research into an important topic.

The topic of specialization and assignment scope is becoming more and more important in the context of four recent trends:

1. Downsizing, or major layoffs of personnel in large companies

2. Business process reengineering

3. The shortage of software personnel brought on by the year-2000 problem

4. The increasing frequency of outsourcing arrangements, which transfer employees to the outsource company

In all four situations, knowledge of the kinds and quantities of specialists employed by an enterprise is a significant factor.

Production-rate errors

The phrase *production rate* denotes the amount of work that one person can complete in a standard time period, such as an hour, a work day, a work week, or a work month.

Production-rate errors are those of excessive optimism, such as assuming coding rates in excess of 3000 statements per month. Production-rate estimation using both natural metrics, such as source code, and synthetic metrics, such as function points, is now a standard function of modern software cost estimating tools. Templates defined by users or created from historical data can also be used.

Production rates expressed in terms of natural metrics have long been a part of the software-estimation process. For example, estimating programming effort by lines of code per month, and estimating technical writing time by pages written per month, estimating testing by test runs per hour all date back to the 1950s. The problem with natural metrics is that they do not allow aggregation or summarization of unlike tasks.

More recently, the synthetic function point metric has been used to provide a uniform base for exploring the comparative performance of all activities and tasks. Table 9.6 shows current average production rates in function points for the 25-activity chart of accounts already discussed in Table 9.5.

TABLE 9.6   Productivity Ranges for Software Development Activities

Activities performed	Function points per month			Work hours per function point		
	Minimum	Mode	Maximum	Maximum	Mode	Minimum
01 Requirements	50.00	175.00	350.00	2.64	0.75	0.38
02 Prototyping	25.00	150.00	250.00	5.28	0.88	0.53
03 Architecture	100.00	300.00	500.00	1.32	0.44	0.26
04 Project plans	200.00	500.00	1500.00	0.66	0.26	0.09
05 Initial design	50.00	175.00	400.00	2.64	0.75	0.33
06 Detail design	25.00	150.00	300.00	5.28	0.88	0.44
07 Design reviews	75.00	225.00	400.00	1.76	0.59	0.33
08 Coding	15.00	50.00	200.00	8.80	2.64	0.66
09 Reuse acquisition	400.00	600.00	2000.00	0.33	0.22	0.07
10 Package purchase	350.00	400.00	1500.00	0.38	0.33	0.09
11 Code inspections	75.00	150.00	300.00	1.76	0.88	0.44
12 Independent verification and validation	75.00	125.00	200.00	1.76	1.06	0.66
13 Configuration management	1000.00	1750.00	3000.00	0.13	0.08	0.04
14 Formal integration	150.00	250.00	500.00	0.88	0.53	0.26
15 User documentation	20.00	70.00	100.00	6.60	1.89	1.32
16 Unit testing	70.00	150.00	400.00	1.89	0.88	0.33
17 Function testing	25.00	150.00	300.00	5.28	0.88	0.44
18 Integration testing	75.00	175.00	400.00	1.76	0.75	0.33
19 System testing	100.00	200.00	500.00	1.32	0.66	0.26
20 Field testing	75.00	225.00	500.00	1.76	0.59	0.26
21 Acceptance testing	75.00	350.00	600.00	1.76	0.38	0.22
22 Independent testing	100.00	200.00	300.00	1.32	0.66	0.44
23 Quality assurance	30.00	150.00	300.00	4.40	0.88	0.44
24 Installation and training	150.00	350.00	600.00	0.88	0.38	0.22
25 Project management	15.00	100.00	200.00	8.80	1.32	0.66
Cumulative results	1.90	6.75	13.88	69.38	19.55	9.51
Arithmetic mean	133	284.8	624	2.78	0.78	0.38

As can be seen, there are wide variances for every activity. However, it is very useful to be able to explore the relative productivity of every activity and task using a common metric. This kind of research is opening up many new avenues for improved estimation accuracy.

TABLE 9.7   Representative Software Work Hours per Day in Six Subindustries

Software class	Work hours per 8-h day	Unpaid overtime per day	Total work hours per day
End user	3.5	0.0	3.5
MIS	5.5	1.0	6.5
Outsource	7.0	1.5	8.5
Commercial	7.0	2.0	9.0
System	6.0	1.0	7.0
Military	6.5	1.0	7.5
Average	5.9	1.1	7.0

Another aspect of necessary production-rate adjustments are those required to deal with variances in the number of work hours per day and the probable amount of unpaid overtime applied.

Both work hours and unpaid overtime vary extremely from project to project, company to company, industry to industry, and country to country. Table 9.7 shows the approximate values for the United States for six subindustries.

As can be seen, the typical work-hour pattern for commercial software houses, such as Microsoft or Oracle, is quite a bit longer than for internal software producers. Variances such as this are even more extreme internationally, when it is necessary to include the very significant differences in vacation periods and holidays for projects that span the Atlantic or Pacific and involve European or Asian development teams as well as American development teams.

This kind of data on work patterns is so highly variable from company to company and country to country that it is unsafe to use "industry norms" for estimating actual projects. Instead, each estimate should use local values for work hours and effective work hours.

Creeping user requirements

Omission of creeping requirements refers to the very common phenomenon of failing to adjust an estimate for the growth rate in unplanned requirements after the conclusion of the formal requirements phase.

The phenomenon of creeping requirements is so common that predicting the amount of requirements creep, and adjusting the estimate accordingly, have become standard functions of modern cost-estimating tools.

One of the useful by-products of function points is their ability to perform direct measurement of creeping user requirements. Every change that a user might need after the initial requirements are agreed to will almost certainly affect one or more of the five basic function point parameters:

1. Inputs
2. Outputs
3. Inquiries
4. Logical files
5. Interfaces

From long-range observations of several hundred projects, it can be stated that creeping requirements average about 2 percent per month from the day of the initial agreement on requirements until the commencement of testing. Thus, for a project that has a schedule of 2 years or 24 months from requirements until testing, it can be expected that the functional content will grow by roughly 50 percent.

The utility of function points for monitoring and measuring project growth explains why so many consulting and outsourcing companies are adopting function points as the basis of their contracts. For example, the current average cost of building one function point in the United States is just over $1000.

Suppose a contract is agreed to for producing an application of 1000 function points in size for a cost of $1000 per function point, or $1 million in all. Now suppose that six months into the contract, the client identifies a need for an additional 100 function points. Under the basic terms of the contract, the new functionality might be added to the contract for a price of $100,000.

Some vendors are even adopting a sliding scale, with the cost per function point going up for changes added later in the development cycle. The methodology of using function points as the basis for software contracts is clarifying a number of important issues and making the contracts easier to administer.

However, vendors should be alerted to a new problem that is showing up in breach of contract lawsuits by unhappy clients. Usually the first year of an outsourcing arrangement is complex, with many personnel changing positions and needing time to adjust to the new arrangement. The outsource company's managers and technical staff also need time to understand the applications in depth. As a result, the first year of an outsource contract usually has a temporary reduction in productivity of perhaps 5 percent compared to the year preceding the outsourcing agreement.

However, it is not uncommon for outsource contracts to commit the vendor to annual improvements in development or maintenance productivity, or both. If the client has performed a function point baseline analysis prior to starting the outsource contract, then it will be easy to measure the performance of the outsourcer during the first year. If the outsource vendor promised to achieve, for example, a 5 percent increase in productivity in the first year but the actual results were a 5 percent reduction, then litigation for breach of contract is a common response by the client.

Outsource vendors should be aware that while using function points as the basis of contracts makes the contracts easy to administer and has many advantages, the function point metric is accurate enough that empty promises and false claims will quickly become visible.

Critical path errors

Software development is a complex net of hundreds of interlinked activities. A very common estimating problem is failure to identify the critical path though this network of activities, so that delays in some key component or deliverable ripples downstream and lengthens the final delivery schedule.

The most common variety of critical path error is associated with debugging and testing. It is obvious that final integration and delivery of a software project cannot occur if the software is not working. From a sample of 64 IBM software projects and 20 ITT software projects that ran late by at least six months, insufficient time was allowed in the schedule for debugging and testing on every project. The root cause of the problem was an unwise attempt by senior executives to compress schedules by skimping on quality control and testing. This approach usually backfires, and stretches out the schedule rather than shortening it.

These same projects exhibited an interesting pathology. Until testing began, there was no overt sign or evidence that the projects were in trouble; indeed, they seemed to be ahead of schedule. However, when the cost and time profiles of the late projects were examined and compared to similar projects that were delivered close to their nominal schedules, the true situation emerged.

The late projects had skimped on front-end reviews, inspections, and quality control. This gave a false appearance of speeding through the development cycle. When the problems were finally encountered as testing began, there were so many of them and they were so severe that schedule recovery was impossible. Figure 9.3 illustrates the very different curves that differentiate pathological projects from healthy projects.

Note how deceptive the early phases are for projects on the pathological curve. All of the short-cuts during requirements and design

How Quality Affects Software Estimation

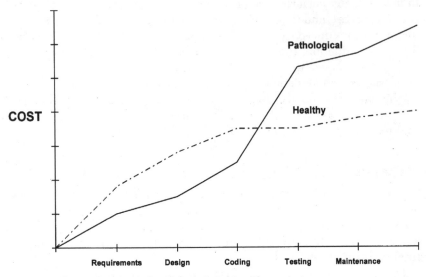

Figure 9.3 Cost comparison of pathological and healthy projects.

and the failure to utilize inspections come back to haunt testing and maintenance.

Staffing build-up errors

This problem is only intermittent, but can be severe when it occurs. For many military and defense contractors, and some civilian contractors, the total complement of personnel needed to complete a contract is not actually employed or available. When a contract is won, there is an immediate need to start a hiring campaign or find subcontractors to do the work.

The problem of staffing build-up errors can occur when there is a shortage of available personnel or the subcontracting process takes longer than anticipated. If a contract assumes, for example, that 100 software engineers will be available on a certain date, and only 20 are present on that date, all of the subsequent activities and schedules are likely to be thrown out of kilter.

As this book is being written, the growth of software and the onrushing year-2000 problem have created a global shortage of software personnel. As a result, software salaries are climbing at double-digit inflation rates, and even so it is hard to hire sufficient experienced personnel.

Indeed, a number of retired software professionals are being lured back to the job market with hefty bonuses and high salaries if they will commit to working through the solution of the year-2000 problem.

Technology adjustment errors

The most subtle and complex of the sources of estimating errors are those dealing with adjusting the estimate to match the effects of various tools, languages, and methodologies.

As of 1998 there are more than 500 programming languages in use, and more than 5000 tools aimed at aspects of software development. There are also more than 150 specification and design methods, and more than 50 varieties of software methodology, such as information engineering, the object-oriented paradigm, various structured approaches, and the like.

To add to the difficulty of this topic, many of the tools and approaches are being marketed with productivity or quality claims that lack any kind of empirical evidence. There is also a continuous influx of new topics, which as of 1998 have little or no supporting data of any kind.

For example, Quality Function Deployment (QFD) is now starting to be used for software, but most such usages are so new that the results are not yet known. Multimedia applications, virtual reality applications, and applications intended for massively parallel computing platforms are also too new to have accumulated much historical data.

There are also some important topics that have a very steep learning curve. For example, the object-oriented paradigm has such a steep learning curve that the first projects developed using various kinds of object-oriented analysis usually take longer and are more expensive than projects of the same size and nature developed using the older structured methods, such as the Yourdon or Warnier-Orr design approaches.

This means that both estimating-tool vendors and their clients can encounter situations that are outside the boundary of current versions of estimating tools. Although this is a regrettable situation, software is not unique in having to deal with new phenomena. Not many years ago, most patients with Lyme disease were misdiagnosed because that illness had not yet been identified or typed.

The best of the estimating tools and methods attempt to stay current with advances in technologies by implementing annual upgrades to the factors that are included. For example, 10 years ago, or even 5 years ago, there were no estimating tools that allowed client/server applications to be identified as a discrete type of project for estimating purposes. However, now that client/server applications are exploding in popularity, most estimating-tool vendors are preparing updates that support this technology.

As this book is being written, JAVA applications are just starting to be measured with enough precision to develop useful software cost estimating algorithms. There will always be an *event horizon* for software-estimating tools, or a gap between the newest software technologies and the algorithms used by the estimating tools.

Special or unique situations

The phrase *special or unique situations* refers to uncommon factors that can affect a specific project, but which do not occur with enough regularity to fit into standard estimating algorithms or common templates. A few examples of special situations which can affect project costs will clarify the point:

- Closure of an office or evacuation of staff due to weather conditions
- Closure of an office or evacuation of staff due to fire or natural disaster
- Voluntary termination of more than 50 percent of project team members
- Major layoffs or downsizing of project personnel
- Illness or incapacity of key team members
- Physical relocation of a project team from one city to another
- Injunctions or legal actions which freeze project specifications or source code
- Sale or merger of companies which affect specific projects
- Travel costs for trips among geographically dispersed projects
- Moving, living, and real-estate costs for hiring new employees
- Reassignment of key personnel to year-2000 repair work

These are only examples of special situations which, when they do occur, must be factored in to a final software cost estimate.

Range of Impact of Estimating Errors

Estimating-tool vendors are often asked questions about how accurate their tools are. It is even more significant to note how far out of balance an estimate can be if one or more of the 12 error conditions are present when the estimate is prepared. Following are the ranges of impact associated with each of the 12 problems.

When an estimate includes *metrics errors,* such as using LOC rates from one language for estimating productivity on a project using another language, the observed range of deviation can exceed 100 percent. That is, an error can be off by more than 100 percent if the languages vary widely, such as using data from assembly language to estimate projects written in an object-oriented language such as C++.

When an estimate includes *scaling errors,* such as using data from a small project to estimate a large system, the observed range of deviation can approach an order of magnitude, or 1000 percent. It might be thought that such errors would never occur in real life, but unfortunately they do. A major government software project in excess of 15,000 function points, or 15 million lines of code, was estimated using data drawn from projects of less than 500 function points, or 50,000 lines of code. This is one of the reasons why the project is running more than four years behind schedule: The schedule was absurd in the way it was developed.

When an estimate includes *executive errors,* where schedules or costs are constrained by executive or client decree, the results are always in the same direction: The projects take longer and cost more. The typical range of political errors is about 50 percent for schedules and 100 percent for costs. That is, the real project takes almost twice as long and costs almost as much as the forced estimate.

This phenomenon is associated with another troublesome situation: canceled projects. It often happens that the initial estimates of projects that are canceled without being completed had been subjected to political manipulation.

When an estimate includes *sizing errors,* the range of deviation is more or less proportional to the difference between the true size and the anticipated size. Experienced project managers have been observed to average about plus or minus 15 percent in estimating the size of deliverables, if the requirements are stable. Inexperienced managers can fluctuate widely, and have errors that approach 100 percent or more. Sizing errors are more common for manual estimates than for automated ones, but some of the older estimating tools, such as COCOMO clones, still require that users input size themselves. Modern estimating tools with full sizing logic derived from function points can usually (but not always) come within 15 percent of estimating key deliverables, such as the volume of source code and the size of user documentation.

When an estimate includes *task-selection errors,* the range of uncertainty can exceed an order of magnitude, or 1000 percent. The worst case would be to estimate only coding, and exclude all other activities. Task-selection errors are much more common for manual estimates than for automated ones. Most modern estimating tools have a full repertory of activities and tasks available and will suggest the appropriate set for any given project. The more sophisticated estimating tools will vary their task lists to match civilian or military norms and large systems or small projects.

When an estimate includes *assignment-scope errors*, the range of uncertainty can approach 100 percent. Normally, assignment-scope errors result in too few people for the work at hand. Here, too, the problem is more common for manual estimates than for automated ones. This problem is particularly severe for maintenance estimates and for estimates of customer support. In real life, some people are able to handle much larger assignment scopes than others. Experienced personnel, for example, can often handle tasks that are two or three times larger than those that novices can deal with.

When an estimate includes *production-rate errors*, the range of uncertainty usually matches the difference between the true rate and the anticipated rate. Suppose a technical writer is estimated to be able to write 75 pages per month, and can only average 50 pages per month. It is difficult to generalize the impact of production-rate errors, since production rates are highly specific to the activities being performed and to the skill and experience of the personnel doing the work.

When an estimate includes *creeping user requirements errors*, the range of uncertainty more or less matches the volume of unplanned functionality. As stated previously, function points are now being used to make direct measurements of unplanned functions, and the average is about 1 percent per month from the end of requirements to the commencement of testing. Thus, for a 2-year project, perhaps 25 percent requirements creep might occur. Some modern estimating tools can predict probable volume of creeping requirements.

When an estimate includes *critical path errors*, both the schedules and the costs will appear to be running better than planned until testing begins, whereupon the entire project comes to a shuddering halt for an indefinite period. This problem normally results in schedule slippages of about 25 percent and cost overruns in excess of 35 percent, although unpaid overtime is so enormous during the testing of projects with critical path errors that the cost overruns might be hidden.

When an estimate includes *staffing build-up errors*, the range of uncertainty matches the difference between the planned and available personnel. If you expect to have 10 people start a project and you only have 5 available, then the error is obviously 100 percent. This error condition does not lend itself to generalization and must be dealt with in the context of specific projects.

When an estimate includes *technology adjustment errors*, the observed range of uncertainty appears to be as much as 150 percent.

This problem is particularly severe when technologies are initially deployed. There is always a short-term reduction in productivity as personnel climb the learning curve. Unfortunately, there is a tendency by tool vendors and by project managers to assume that there will be immediate productivity gains. On the whole, estimating tools do a better job of dealing with this factor than do manual estimates, but this problem requires very thoughtful consideration.

When an estimate includes *special or unique situation errors,* there is usually no way of dealing with the problem ahead of time. Here is an example of a special and unique situation which could not be anticipated: The cooling pipe for an air conditioning system of an office building in Cambridge, Massachusetts burst and dropped over 500 gallons of cooling fluid onto the DEC VAX computer owned by a software company, shutting down development on a critical project for almost a week.

Another example of a special and unique situation occurred during one of the California earthquakes, when the roof of a programming laboratory in Palo Alto collapsed, causing software development to be temporarily suspended until the staff could be relocated to other quarters.

As another example of a special case, in litigation involving a payment dispute between a contract programmer and a small software company, the judge ordered the source code of the product to be frozen until the issue was decided. The case ran on for more than a year, and the company was unable to even fix bugs in the product, eventually resulting in bankruptcy.

Another special case involved a midwestern manufacturing company where a popular CIO was fired after a merger with another company, whose CIO took over the position. More than 50 percent of the software personnel in the original company resigned in protest, shutting down at least a dozen major software projects.

Software estimation is still a young technology, with only about 25 years of history as of 1998. Although the technology of software estimation is imperfect, it is rapidly improving. Of particular value in improving the ability to estimate projects has been the advent of better measurement, and also of functional metrics.

Better measurement is starting to provide a nucleus of firm schedule, resource, cost, and quality data that can be used as a jumping-off place for estimation. Functional metrics are free of the paradoxical quirks of the older LOC metrics, which produced erroneous results for high-level languages. Further, functional metrics are allowing research to occur on topics that were previously obscure, such as the impact of specialization. The overall prognosis for improved estimation is very favorable.

The literature on sources of error in software cost estimation is very sparse. In order to perform studies of estimation errors two critical pieces of data are needed: (1) the estimate itself, and (2) accurate historical data when the project is finished. Unfortunately, item number 2, accurate historical data, is not readily available.

The citations used for this chapter include the Air Force comparison of estimating tools by Dean Barrow and colleagues (Barrow et al. 1993), Professor Daniel Ferens's study of estimating in a DoD environment (Ferens 1996), and Air Force Captain Karen Mertes's calibration of the CHECKPOINT estimating tool against Air Force historical data (Mertes 1996).

Chris Kemerer's interesting but dated study on software cost estimating tools (Kemerer 1987) is also included, on the grounds that this may be the very first comparative study of estimating tools ever published.

Some of the author's books are included also (Jones 1995, 1996) because they discuss aspects of both estimation and measurement.

References

Barrow, Dean, Susan Nilson, and Dawn Timberlake: *Software Estimation Technology Report,* Software Technology Support Center, OO-ALC/TISE, Hill Air Force Base, Utah, March 1993.

Ferens, Daniel V.: "Software Cost Estimating in the DoD Environment," *American Programmer,* **9**(7):28–34 (1996).

Jones, Capers: *Patterns of Software System Failure and Success,* International Thomson Computer Press, Boston, ISBN 1-850-32804-8, 1995.

———: *Applied Software Measurement,* 2d ed., McGraw-Hill, New York, ISBN 0-07-032826-9, 1996a.

———: *Table of Programming Languages and Levels* (8 Versions from 1985 through July 1996), Software Productivity Research, Burlington, Mass., 1996b.

———: *Software Quality—Analysis and Guidelines for Success,* International Thomson Computer Press, Boston, ISBN 1-85032-876-6, 1997.

Kan, Stephen H.: *Metrics and Models in Software Quality Engineering,* Addison-Wesley, Reading, Mass., ISBN 0-201-63339-6, 1995.

Kemerer, Chris F.: "An Empirical Validation of Software Cost Estimation Models," *Communications of the ACM,* **30**:416–429 (1987).

Mertes, Karen R.: *Calibration of the CHECKPOINT Model to the Space and Missile Systems Center (SMC) Software Database (SWDB),* Thesis AFIT/GCA/LAS/96S-11, Air Force Institute of Technology (AFIT), Wright-Patterson AFB, Ohio, September 1996.

Ourada, Gerald L., and Daniel V. Ferens: "Software Cost Estimating Models: A Calibration, Validation, and Comparison," in *Cost Estimating and Analysis: Balancing Technology and Declining Budgets,* Springer-Verlag, New York, 1992, pp. 83–101.

Chapter

10

Software Project Management in the Twenty-First Century

Although software project management and software cost estimating tool capabilities are good as this book is being written, there is obviously room for improvement. Some of the new capabilities that are needed can be projected based on current trends, but other new capabilities may require invention and solid research.

Integration of Project Management Tool Suites

As the twentieth century winds down, there are more than 50 vendors marketing software cost estimating tools, more than 80 vendors marketing project-planning or project management tools, and at least 50 other vendors of other tools with project management implications, such as function point analysis, risk analysis, value analysis, assessment support, and the like.

In every industry where useful products are marketed by a large number of small independent manufacturers, consolidation tends to occur. For software project management and cost-estimating tools, consolidation is already starting to occur as cost-estimating tool vendors, project management tool vendors, methodology management vendors, and other kinds of tool vendors form strategic alliances or move toward mergers and acquisitions.

Within a few years, the large number of independent tools and independent tool vendors will probably give way to integrated management tool suites sharing common interfaces and common data repositories. The overall capabilities of these integrated tool suites will no doubt include the following:

- Cost estimating
- Schedule planning
- Quality estimation
- Reliability estimation
- Methodology management
- Assessment support
- Benchmarking support
- Resource tracking
- Defect tracking
- Variance reporting

The pattern of software project management tools may well follow the pattern of general office suites. Integrated suites consisting of word processors, spreadsheets, database applications, graphics packages, and the like now dominate the market for office work and independent products are becoming something of a rarity.

However, until a large corporation such as Microsoft or Computer Associates decides to concentrate on management tool integration and begins a wave of acquisitions, the small independent management tool vendors are still growing.

Internet-Enabled Estimation and Benchmarking Services

Software estimating and project management will be impacted by the explosive growth of the Internet as a business tool. One obvious opportunity will be to provide software cost estimation and planning services via the Internet and the World Wide Web, so that companies can use estimation tools remotely and indeed interact with expert estimating consultants.

An equally obvious companion service to software cost estimation and project planning would be the construction of a benchmarking service via the Internet, so that companies could compare their own projects against the historical results of thousands of projects. It is even possible to envision search and browsing capabilities, which might use various selection criteria to extract and aggregate results from perhaps 50 to 100 similar projects and create dynamic, on-the-fly benchmarking studies in real time.

More remote, but technically possible, would be the development of Web or Internet benchmarking groups where 10 or so companies in the same industry might submit data concurrently and have it compared against each other's. This approach would necessitate stringent security and confidentiality safeguards.

Data Metrics, Data Estimation, and Data Quality

The most visible and important gap in software project management capabilities concerns data and information. As this book is being written, many companies own multiple databases and are moving toward the concepts of integrated repositories or data warehouses. In addition, *online analytical processing* (OLAP) is an important emerging technology for dealing with aggregation of trends and information derived from multiple databases and long series of chronological changes to data.

Although the technologies for building databases are improving rapidly, there are no visible technologies for measuring the volumes of data that companies own, for estimating the costs of building databases, or for measuring the number of errors in databases and hence exploring data quality. These major gaps can be attributed to one critical missing factor: *data metrics*.

In addition, there are also gaps in the information contained in data dictionaries and even in the information headers within databases themselves. Quite a lot of valuable information, such as the identities of the applications that create or modify the data, the dates of changes, and prior values before changes could and should be recorded is often missing. Remedying this would greatly facilitate OLAP processing and, indeed, would create a new kind of application that is difficult today: analysis of the rates of change of data over long time periods.

It may well be that the onrushing year-2000 problem will trigger a serious exploration of data storage methods, and also of the kind of supporting information that goes into data dictionaries and data header records.

Since many companies often own larger volumes of data than of software, the year-2000 problem will generate tremendous data-quality problems as well as tremendous software-repair problems, although the data-quality aspects of the year-2000 issue are not as well understood due to the lack of a normalizing metric for data size and data quality.

Data has been a difficult topic for research. A major source of difficulty has been the lack of useful data-related metrics. Unfortunately, as this is being written there are no satisfactory normalizing metrics for expressing the volume of data a company uses, the quality levels of the data, and the costs of creating data, migrating data from platform to platform, correcting errors, or destroying obsolete data.

Also, unlike software errors, which are found only in computerized applications, data errors are not restricted to data stored magnetically or optically in computerized databases, repositories, and warehouses. Data errors can also occur in data stored on paper, on microfiche, on video or audio tape, on CD-ROM, or on any other known medium. Indeed, data errors are far older than the computer era and have been occurring since the invention of writing and symbolic representations for mathematics.

There are many data errors to be found in ordinary office file cabinets containing paper documents. Data quality is also of concern during transmission of data via optical or copper cable, microwave, or radio or television, because errors and noise can be introduced during the transmission process.

Even the word *data* itself is ambiguous and hard to pin down exactly. What the word *data* means in the context of data quality is symbolic representations of facts (i.e., $\pi = 3.14159265358$, etc.), encoded representations of objects (i.e., valves, bolts, chairs, etc.), or encoded representations of almost any kind of idea the human mind can envision.

Associated with the definition of data is the concept that data can be structured in the form of models that deal with various aspects of the world: physical objects, business rules, mathematics, images, and so forth.

Although the function point metric was created to measure the size of software applications, it is interesting to evaluate whether function points might be extended to deal with the size and quality of databases, or whether an equivalent *data point* metric might be developed for similar purposes.

Recall that the function point metric is comprised of the weighted totals of five external aspects of software applications:

Inputs	Forms, screens, sensor-based values, and so forth entering the application
Outputs	Reports, screens, electronic signals, and so forth leaving the application
Inquires	Question/answer pairs which the application responds to
Logical files	Record sets maintained within or by the application
Interfaces	Record sets passed to or received by external applications

These five elements are then adjusted for complexity to provide the final total of function points for the application. There are 14 adjustment factors for the U.S. function point defined by the International Function Point Users Group (IFPUG) and 19 adjustment factors for the British Mark II function point.

While all five of the function point elements overlap data to a certain degree, they do not seem to capture some of the topics of concern when exploring data size. Perhaps a set of factors similar to the following may move toward the development of a data point metric:

Logical files	The number of record sets maintained within or by the application
Entities	The number of kinds of objects within the database
Relationships	The number of kinds of intersections among the entities
Attributes	The number of qualifications for the entities within the database
Inquires	Question/answer pairs which the database responds to
Interfaces	Record sets passed to or received by the database

While the preceding is only a preliminary suggestion, there is an urgent need to develop a data point metric, without which research into data quality and database economics is severely handicapped.

Right now, there is so little empirical, quantified information on data quality that this topic is included primarily to serve as a warning flag that an important project management domain is emerging, and substantial research is urgently needed.

Estimation and Planning of Mixed Hardware, Software, and Microcode Projects

Many of the most important products of the twentieth and twenty-first centuries (i.e., aircraft, switching systems, weapons systems, etc.) are hybrid constructions that include hardware components, software components, database components, and microcode components. For example, the year-2000 repair cycle will include updates to software, databases, test libraries, and chip replacement and, hence, exceeds the capabilities of all single-purpose estimation tools.

Although there are commercial sizing, planning, and estimating tools that can handle each of these discrete kinds of components separately (except for the database component), it is still very difficult to perform integrated cost estimates across multiple domains.

In addition, each of these product components also includes a need for extensive human effort for customer support, field service, and other manual or semiautomated activities.

Because the technologies of hardware, software, database construction, and microcode development are quite different, a first stage for integration of cost estimates would be to agree on common interfaces that would allow aggregation of activity schedules and cost elements.

However, for early sizing and estimating, additional research is needed on the development of a family of related metrics that might include the following:

- Function points for the software component

- Data points for the database component

- Hardware points for the mechanical and electronic components

- Service points for the manual activities, such as support and repairs

The goal of a set of mutually compatible size metrics would be to facilitate sizing and cost-estimating of hybrid products with multiple kinds of components. It would be highly advantageous to be able to assert that a given project might contain 1000 function points, 2000 data points, 1500 hardware points, and will require 3500 service points per year after deployment.

Whether or not a family of unified cost metrics is developed, it would still be advantageous to have budget and estimating tools that can aggregate costs across software, hardware, database, and service activities.

Enterprise Estimation

Essentially all of the management tools on the commercial market today are aimed at specific software projects. This is true of software cost estimating tools, project-planning tools, defect-tracking tools, and the other forms of management tools.

There is a growing need to be able to deal with long-range estimating and measurement at the enterprise or corporate level. For example, many large companies own hundreds of software applications whose total volumes can exceed 2 million function points, or 250 million source code statements. There is a need for tools that can predict such factors as annual maintenance costs, annual enhancement costs, annual replacement frequency, latent defect levels, and other business topics for entire portfolios.

Two of the most massive software updates in history operate at the enterprise level:

- The year-2000 software problem

- The Eurocurrency conversion problem

Although many software cost estimating tools could handle these problems for individual applications, both of these massive sets of changes will affect hundreds, even thousands, of applications more or less concurrently. The need is for estimating methods that can create enterprisewide cost estimates.

Also, some large enterprises, such as Andersen, AT&T, Electronic Data Systems, IBM, Siemens-Nixdorf, and the like, employ more than 25,000 software personnel in aggregate. These same organizations may each employ as many as 50 to 75 discrete occupations within their overall software universe, such as database administrators, quality-assurance specialists, testing specialists, SAP specialists, ISO specialists, measurement specialists, cost-estimating specialists, and a host of others.

Here, too, there is a need for both predictive and measurement tools that can deal with software occupations at the enterprise level.

Several prototype enterprise-estimation tools have been constructed, but none have yet reached the commercial market. One of the more interesting prototypes was constructed by the author and his colleagues at the former ITT Programming Technology Center in Stratford, Connecticut.

This enterprise-estimation tool could predict the overall growth rate of software personnel and the ITT software portfolio for 10 years or more into the future. It could also deal with various initiatives and changes over time, such as the introduction of formal inspections, the migration to CASE, or the adoption of more powerful programming languages.

The onrushing year-2000 crisis emphasizes the need for enterprisewide estimation. The repairs to the year-2000 problem will affect more than 50 percent of the applications in corporate portfolios more or less simultaneously, and the estimates for hundreds, or even thousands, of applications need to be aggregated at the corporate level.

Another massive enterprise project is that of the European currency conversion work, which is now ongoing all over the world. Like the year-2000 effort, the Eurocurrency work tends to affect scores or hundreds of applications simultaneously. Indeed, the year-2000 repairs are the largest software-maintenance projects in history, and the Eurocurrency updates are the second largest.

Only politicians could manage to schedule the Eurocurrency work so that it competes directly with the year-2000 work for resources. If, as is likely, Europe enters a period of recession caused by the failure to achieve either year-2000 compliance or full Eurocurrency conversion success, it would be unfair to blame the software community. The blame must fall directly on the heads of state of the European Union, who have created one of the worst public policy decisions in all of human history.

Other massive enterprisewide topics that can influence software are Business Process Reengineering (BPR), downsizing, outsourcing, mergers and acquisitions, and even the adoption of such enterprisewide tools as SAP R/3.

Process-Improvement Estimation

One of the gaps in current software-estimation capabilities is that of estimating the impact of changing technologies over time. For example, when a company moves from Level 1 on the Software Engineering Institute (SEI) capability maturity model to Level 3, what will that mean in terms of productivity and quality improvements? Also, how long will it take to move from Level 1 to Level 3, and what investments will be needed in terms of tools, training, or other tangible factors?

Several commercial estimating tools can perform side-by-side estimates using two different sets of assumptions about tools, methods, and process rigor. Indeed, a few estimating tools, such as CHECKPOINT, COCOMO II, KnowledgePlan, and SLIM, even have templates for the five levels of the SEI CMM and can do side-by-side comparisons of the same project at different maturity levels.

However, these tools essentially provide snapshots of two different ways of building software. What is lacking in the industry is tools that can predict such factors as the following:

- The learning curve when moving to new tools or methods
- The number of days of staff training needed to acquire new skills
- The short-term reduction in productivity rates during the learning curve
- The annual or one-time investments needed to equip personnel with better tools
- The return on investment in improved methods and tools

Here, too, prototypes have been constructed, but none of these tools have yet reached the commercial market. As an example of such a prototype, the author has constructed a process-improvement estimator that can predict the calendar time and investments needed to move from Level 1 on the SEI CMM scale to any higher level.

The tool is sensitive to the size of the organization and will predict training days and even generate sample curricula associated with each level. In addition, probable investments in methods and tools are estimated, as are enhanced quality and productivity levels. The investments are compared with the anticipated gains, and the return on investment is also calculated, together with the interval required for the investment to receive positive returns.

Preliminary results from this tool indicate that an investment of more than $10,000 per staff member over a 3-year period may be needed to jump from SEI Level 1 up to Level 3, but the return on investment in some situations may top $10 for every dollar invested.

Other forms of improvement would also benefit from a process estimator, and would need to be included in commercial versions of such tools. Some of the other topics amenable to process-improvement estimation would include achievement of ISO 9001 certification, moving toward Baldrige Award criteria, and adoption of total quality management (TQM).

Outsource Estimation

Software outsourcing agreements are complex instruments that may include development, maintenance, and support of hundreds of applications, totaling more than 1 million function points in some cases.

As outsourcing agreements grow in numbers, it is obvious that a small but significant number of these agreements will be unsatisfactory to one side or the other. Indeed, about 1 percent of outsourcing agreements end up in court for breach of contract or some other assertion of poor performance.

It is obvious that individual project-estimating tools are not aimed at supporting the complexity of outsourcing contracts. What is needed is a higher-level form of estimation that can deal with trends over at least 10 years for such topics as the following:

- Portfolio growth, maintenance, and retirement
- Latent defects and the impact of quality control
- Staffing by occupation group
- Head-count of staffing by time period
- Effort by time period
- Costs by occupation group and time period
- Special factors, such as mass year-2000 upgrades
- Inflation rates

This form of estimation is actually technically possible today, but has not been turned into a commercial venture because the market size has been insufficient. That situation is now changing, and outsource-estimation tools may now be economically feasible.

Given the distressing tendency for perhaps 1 percent of outsourcing agreements to end up in court, and for almost 10 percent to cause dissatisfaction one side or the other, an outsource-estimating tool would appear to be a useful product.

Although only about 1 percent of outsourcing agreements actually go to litigation, almost 10 percent end up being renegotiated because of errors or omissions in the original agreement. Some of the more common reasons for renegotiation include the following:

- Omissions of major work, such as year-2000 repairs

- Unilateral expansion of the scope of work by the client

- Assertions of inadequate quality by the client to the vendor

Although outsource vendors usually outperform their clients, they are still capable of making mistakes. This is especially true when there are highly competitive bids involving multiple candidate outsource vendors, so margins are shaved to perhaps hazardous levels.

Management War Game Tools

In many ways, the software game industry is one of the most technically advanced sectors of the entire software domain. The game industry has pioneered a number of role-playing simulations in which players deal with many real-life problems, such as urban planning, and even with developing empires and becoming gods in their own universe.

The technology underlying these role-playing games is a natural vehicle for project management simulations, and a number of companies recognize that fact. It cannot be very long before several software project management role-playing games appear on the commercial market.

Although management games will probably start as low-cost independent products, their intrinsic usefulness and their ability to allow managers to take risks without having to face serious consequences in real life will make them very useful additions to methodology management tools, software cost estimating tools, and project-planning tools, and certainly will make them welcome as an alternative form of risk management tool.

Estimation on Handheld Computers

Several software-estimating and project management tools can work on DOS-based handheld computers, such as the Hewlett-Packard 100LX and 200LX. For example, the author's SPQR/20 tool works well on Hewlett-Packard computers, and even the DOS version of full-function estimation tools, such as CHECKPOINT, can work with larger flash disks installed, although performance is somewhat slow.

Some COCOMO implementations can also work on DOS-based hand-held computers.

The advent of Windows CE and the popularity of other small platforms, such as the Psion, Sharp Zaurus, and similar products, is likely to attract software-estimating and project management companies as these platforms grow in popularity and sales volumes.

Microsoft has produced special trimmed-down versions of several popular tools, such as Microsoft Word and Excel. It is very likely that trim versions of popular estimating tools, such as SLIM, KnowledgePlan, and CHECKPOINT, may also find their way onto these emerging platforms.

Summary and Conclusions

Software cost estimating is still a young technology, and the first commercial software cost estimating tool turns 25 in 1998, having initially gone on the market in 1973.

As software systems grow in numbers and frequency of release, software cost estimating is becoming a rapidly expanding industry. Only 10 years ago, the entire software cost estimating market had less than half a dozen vendors. Now, as this book is being written, there are at least 50 vendors in the United States and about half that number overseas.

From the fact that new software-estimating products are being announced at approximately monthly intervals, it can be seen that this technology is experiencing significant growth.

Software cost estimating tools are steadily improving in capability, accuracy, and ease of use. The better automated software cost estimating tools easily defeat manual estimates in accuracy for applications larger than about 500 function points. For large systems above 5000 function points, it is not even a fair contest: Manual estimates are almost never accurate enough to be used safely.

Although cost-estimating is a powerful and useful technology, estimating tools are not the only kinds of tools needed for successful management of large software systems. Software cost estimating, project-planning, methodology management, defect-estimating, defect-tracking, complexity analysis, and many others are needed to fully equip software project managers for the challenges of planning and controlling large software systems.

Suggested Readings

Abran, A., and P. N. Robillard: "Function Point Analysis: An Empirical Study of Its Measurement Processes," *IEEE Transactions on Software Engineering,* **22**(12):895–909 (1996).

Abreu, Fernando Brito e: "An e-mail information on MOOD," *Metrics News*, Otto-von-Guericke-Univeersitaat, Magdeburg, **7**(2):11 (1997).

Albrecht, Allan: *AD/M Productivity Measurement and Estimate Validation*, IBM Corporation, Purchase, N.Y., May 1984.

Barrow, Dean, Susan Nilson, and Dawn Timberlake: *Software Estimation Technology Report*, Air Force Software Technology Support Center, Hill Air Force Base, Utah, 1993.

Boehm, Barry: *Software Engineering Economics*, Prentice Hall, Englewood Cliffs, N.J., 1981.

Bogan, Christopher E., and Michael J. English: *Benchmarking for Best Practices*, McGraw-Hill, New York, ISBN 0-07-006375-3, 1994.

Briand, Loic, and Daniel Roy: *Meeting Deadlines in Hard Real-Time Systems*, IEEE Computer Society Press, Los Alamitos, Calif., ISBN 0-8186-406-7, 1997.

Brooks, Fred: *The Mythical Man-Month*, Addison-Wesley, Reading, Mass., 1974, rev. 1995.

Brown, Norm (ed.): *The Program Manager's Guide to Software Acquisition Best Practices*, Version 1.0, U.S. Department of Defense, Washington, D.C., July 1995.

Charette, Robert N.: *Software Engineering Risk Analysis and Management*, McGraw-Hill, New York, ISBN 0-07-010719-X, 1989.

——: *Application Strategies for Risk Analysis*, McGraw-Hill, New York, ISBN 0-07-010888-9, 1990.

Chidamber, S. R., and C. F. Kemerer: "A Metrics Suite for Object Oriented Design," *IEEE Transactions on Software Engineering*, **20**:476–493 (1994).

——, D. P. Darcy, and C. F. Kemerer: "Managerial Use of Object Oriented Software Metrics," Working Paper no. 750, Joseph M. Katz Graduate School of Business, University of Pittsburgh, Pittsburgh, Pa., November 1996.

Conte, S. D., H. E. Dunsmore, and V. Y. Shen: *Software Engineering Models and Metrics*, Benjamin Cummings, Menlo Park, Calif., ISBN 0-8053-2162-4, 1986.

DeMarco, Tom: *Controlling Software Projects*, Yourdon Press, New York, ISBN 0-917072-32-4, 1982.

——: *Why Does Software Cost So Much?*, Dorset House, New York, ISBN 0-932633-34-X, 1995.

Department of the Air Force, *Guidelines for Successful Acquisition and Management of Software Intensive Systems*, vols. 1 and 2, Software Technology Support Center, Hill Air Force Base, Utah, 1994.

Dreger, Brian: *Function Point Analysis*, Prentice Hall, Englewood Cliffs, N.J., ISBN 0-13-332321-8, 1989.

Fenton, Norman, and Shari Lawrence Pfleeger: *Software Metrics—A Rigorous and Practical Approach*, 2nd ed., IEEE Press, Los Alamitos, Calif., ISBN 0-534-95600-0, 1997.

Fetcke, Thomas, Alain Abran, and Tho-Hau Nguyen: *Mapping the OO-Jacobsen Approach into Function Point Analysis*, University du Quebec a Montreal, Software Engineering Management Research Laboratory.

Galea, R. B.: The Boeing Company: 3D Function Point Extensions, V2.0, Release 1.0, Boeing Information Support Services, Seattle, Wash., June 1995.

Garmus, David, and David Herron: *Measuring the Software Process: A Practical Guide to Functional Measurement*, Prentice Hall, Englewood Cliffs, N.J., 1995.

Grady, Robert B.: *Practical Software Metrics for Project Management and Process Improvement*, Prentice Hall, Englewood Cliffs, N.J., ISBN 0-13-720384-5, 1992.

——, and Deborah L. Caswell: *Software Metrics: Establishing a Company-Wide Program*, Prentice Hall, Englewood Cliffs, N.J., ISBN 0-13-821844-7, 1987.

Gulledge, Thomas R., William P. Hutzler, and Joan S. Lovelace (eds.): *Cost Estimating and Analysis—Balancing Technology with Declining Budgets*, Springer-Verlag, New York, ISBN 0-387-97838-0, 1992.

Halstead, Maurice H.: *Elements of Software Science*, North Holland, 1977.

Harmon, Paul, and David King: *Expert Systems*, John Wiley & Sons, New York, ISBN 0-471-81554-3, 1985.

Howard, Alan (ed.): *Software Metrics and Project Management Tools*, Applied Computer Research, Phoenix, Ariz., 1997.

IFPUG Counting Practices Manual, Release 3, International Function Point Users Group, Westerville, Ohio, April 1990.

———, Release 4, International Function Point Users Group, Westerville, Ohio, April 1995.

Jacobsen, Ivar, Martin Griss, and Patrick Jonsson: *Software Reuse—Architecture, Process, and Organization for Business Success,* Addison-Wesley/Longman, Reading, Mass., ISBN 0-201-92476-5, 1997.

Jones, Capers: *SPQR/20 Users Guide,* Software Productivity Research, Cambridge, Mass., 1986.

———: *Critical Problems in Software Measurement,* Information Systems Management Group, ISBN 1-56909-000-9, 1993a.

———: *Software Productivity and Quality Today—The Worldwide Perspective,* Information Systems Management Group, ISBN 1-56909-001-7, 1993b.

———: *Assessment and Control of Software Risks,* Prentice Hall, Englewood Cliffs, N.J., ISBN 0-13-741406-4, 1994.

———: *New Directions in Software Management,* Information Systems Management Group, ISBN 1-56909-009-2.

———: *Patterns of Software System Failure and Success,* International Thomson Computer Press, Boston, ISBN 1-850-32804-8, 1995.

———: *Applied Software Measurement,* 2nd ed., McGraw-Hill, New York, ISBN 0-07-032826-9, 1996a.

———: *Table of Programming Languages and Levels* (8 Versions from 1985 through July 1996), Software Productivity Research, Burlington, Mass., 1996b.

———: *The Economics of Object-Oriented Software,* Software Productivity Research, Burlington, Mass., April 1997a.

———: *Software Quality—Analysis and Guidelines for Success,* International Thomson Computer Press, Boston, ISBN 1-85032-876-6, 1997b.

———: *The Year 2000 Software Problem—Quantifying the Costs and Assessing the Consequences,* Addison-Wesley, Reading, Mass., ISBN 0-201-30964-5, 1998.

Kan, Stephen H.: *Metrics and Models in Software Quality Engineering,* Addison-Wesley, Reading, Mass., ISBN 0-201-63339-6, 1995.

Kemerer, C. F.: "Reliability of Function Point Measurement—A Field Experiment," *Communications of the ACM,* **36:**85–97 (1993).

Keys, Jessica: *Software Engineering Productivity Handbook,* McGraw-Hill, New York, ISBN 0-07-911366-4, 1993.

Love, Tom: *Object Lessons,* SIGS Books, New York, ISBN 0-9627477 3-4, 1993.

Marciniak, John J. (ed.): *Encyclopedia of Software Engineering,* vols. 1 and 2, John Wiley & Sons, New York, ISBN 0-471-54002, 1994.

McCabe, Thomas J.: "A Complexity Measure," *IEEE Transactions on Software Engineering,* 308–320 (December 1976).

Mertes, Karen R.: *Calibration of the CHECKPOINT Model to the Space and Missile Systems Center (SMC) Software Database (SWDB),* Thesis AFIT/GCA/LAS/96S-11, Air Force Institute of Technology (AFIT), Wright-Patterson AFB, Ohio, September 1996.

Mills, Harlan: *Software Productivity,* Dorset House Press, New York, ISBN 0-932633-10-2, 1988.

Muller, Monika, and Alain Abram (eds.): *Metrics in Software Evolution,* R. Oldenbourg Vertag GmbH, Munich, ISBN 3-486-23589-3, 1995.

Oman, Paul, and Shari Lawrence Pfleeger (eds.): *Applying Software Metrics,* IEEE Press, Los Alamitos, Calif., ISBN 0-8186-7645-0, 1996.

Paulk, Mark, et al.: *The Capability Maturity Model: Guidelines for Improving the Software Process,* Addison-Wesley, Reading, Mass., ISBN 0-201-54664-7, 1995.

Perlis, Alan J., Frederick G. Sayward, and Mary Shaw (eds.): *Software Metrics,* MIT Press, Cambridge, Mass., ISBN 0-262-16083-8, 1981.

Perry, William E.: *Data Processing Budgets—How to Develop and Use Budgets Effectively,* Prentice Hall, Englewood Cliffs, N.J., ISBN 0-13-196874-2, 1985.

——— *Handbook of Diagnosing and Solving Computer Problems,* TAB Books, Blue Ridge Summit, Pa., ISBN 0-8306-9233-9, 1989.

Putnam, Lawrence H.: *Measures for Excellence—Reliable Software on Time, Within*

Budget, Yourdon Press/Prentice Hall, Englewood Cliffs, N.J., ISBN 0-13-567694-0, 1992.

———, and Ware Myers: *Industrial Strength Software—Effective Management Using Measurement,* IEEE Press, Los Alamitos, Calif., ISBN 0-8186-7532-2, 1997.

Reifer, Donald (ed.): *Software Management,* 4th ed., IEEE Press, Los Alamitos, Calif., ISBN 0 8186-3342-6, 1993.

Rethinking the Software Process, CD-ROM, Miller Freeman, Lawrence, Kan., 1996. (This CD-ROM is a book collection jointly produced by the book publisher, Prentice Hall, and the journal publisher, Miller Freeman. It contains the full text and illustrations of five Prentice Hall books: Capers Jones, *Assessment and Control of Software Risks;* Tom DeMarco, *Controlling Software Projects;* Brian Dreger, *Function Point Analysis;* Larry Putnam and Ware Myers, *Measures for Excellence;* and Mark Lorenz and Jeff Kidd, *Object-Oriented Software Metrics.*)

Roetzheim, William H., and Reyna A. Beasley: *Best Practices in Software Cost and Schedule Estimation,* Prentice Hall PTR, Upper Saddle River, N.J., 1998.

Rubin, Howard: *Software Benchmark Studies For 1997,* Howard Rubin Associates, Pound Ridge, N.Y., 1997.

Shepperd, M.: "A Critique of Cyclomatic Complexity as a Software Metric," *Software Engineering Journal,* **3**:30–36 (1988).

Software Productivity Consortium, *The Software Measurement Guidebook,* International Thomson Computer Press, Boston, ISBN 1-850-32195-7, 1995.

St-Pierre, Denis, Marcela Maya, Alain Abran, and Jean-Marc Desharnais: *Full Function Points: Function Point Extensions for Real-Time Software, Concepts and Definitions,* TR 1997-03, University of Quebec, Software Engineering Laboratory in Applied Metrics (SELAM), March 1997.

Stukes, Sherry, Jason Deshoretz, Henry Apgar, and Ilona Macias: *Air Force Cost Analysis Agency Software Estimating Model Analysis,* TR-9545/008-2, Contract F04701-95-D-0003, Task 008, Management Consulting & Research, Inc., Thousand Oaks, Calif., September 1996.

Symons, Charles R.: *Software Sizing and Estimating—Mk II FPA (Function Point Analysis),* John Wiley & Sons, Chichester, U.K., ISBN 0-471-92985-9, 1991.

———: "ISMI—International Software Metrics Initiative—Project Proposal," private communication, June 15, 1997.

———: "Software Sizing and Estimating: Can Function Point Methods Meet Industry Needs?" (unpublished draft submitted to the IEEE for possible publication), Guild of Independent Function Point Analysts, London, U.K., August 1997.

Thayer, Richard H. (ed.): *Software Engineering and Project Management,* IEEE Press, Los Alamitos, Calif., ISBN 0-8186-075107, 1988.

Umbaugh, Robert E. (ed.): *Handbook of IS Management,* 4th ed., Auerbach Publications, Boston, ISBN 0-7913-2159-2, 1995.

Whitmire, S. A.: "3-D Function Points: Scientific and Real-Time Extensions to Function Points," *Proceedings of the 1992 Pacific Northwest Software Quality Conference,* June 1, 1992.

Yourdon, Ed: *Death March—The Complete Software Developer's Guide to Surviving "Mission Impossible" Projects,* Prentice Hall PTR, Upper Saddle River, N.J., ISBN 0-13-748310-4, 1997.

Zells, Lois: *Managing Software Projects—Selecting and Using PC-Based Project Management Systems,* QED Information Sciences, Wellesley, Mass., ISBN 0-89435-275-X, 1990.

Zvegintzov, Nicholas: *Software Management Technology Reference Guide,* Dorset House Press, New York, ISBN 1-884521-01-0, 1994.

Preliminary Estimation Methods

Software cost estimates must be produced long before there is sufficient knowledge about a software project to be truly accurate. Two forms of preliminary estimation are discussed in this section:

1. *Manual estimates using rules of thumb*
2. *Preliminary estimates using the approximation modes of commercial estimating tools*

Accurate software estimating is too difficult for simple rules of thumb. Yet in spite of the availability of more than 50 commercial software-estimating tools, simple rules of thumb remain the most common approach. The function point metric has now been used on many thousands of software projects. A family of simple rules of thumb based on function points can now be applied to estimating software sizes, schedules, effort, costs, and quality.

These simple rules of thumb are not a substitute for formal cost estimates produced using such tools as SPQR/20, CHECKPOINT, KnowledgePlan, or SLIM, but they are capable of providing rough early estimates or "sanity checks" for estimates produced using more formal methods. The more accurate forms of manual software cost estimating involve activity-based costing. These methods are more complex than simple rules of thumb, but are also more powerful.

Many commercial software-estimating tools recognize the fact that estimates must be created before there is adequate information about a project and the factors which will affect its outcome. Therefore, commercial estimating tools offer a variety of approximation modes for creating early estimates from partial knowledge. These early estimates are not particularly accurate, but they are usually better than wild guesses.

The most powerful of the preliminary estimating methods use templates derived from similar projects. With template estimation, at least the same kinds of projects are used as the starting point.

Manual Software Estimating Methods

The phrase *manual software cost estimation* refers to estimating methods that are simple enough that they can be performed mentally or, at least, using nothing more sophisticated than a pocket calculator.

Manual estimating methods are the most widely used approaches to software cost estimating as this book is being written. Manual estimating methods are useful for the following purposes:

- Early estimates before requirements are known

- Small projects needing only one or two programmers

- Low-value projects with no critical business impacts

However, there are a number of situations where manual estimates are not very useful and indeed may be hazardous:

- Contract purposes for software development or maintenance

- Projects larger than 100 function points or 10,000 source code statements

- Projects with significant business impact

Manual methods are quick and easy, but not very accurate. Accurate estimating methods are complex and require integration of many kinds of information. When accuracy is needed, avoid manual estimating methods.

As pointed out in Chap. 9, a comparative study of 50 estimates produced manually and 50 estimates produced by commercial estimating tools noted two significant results:

1. Manual estimates were wrong by more than 35 percent more than 75 percent of the time. The maximum errors exceeded 50 percent for both costs and schedules. The errors with manual estimates were always on the side of excessive optimism, or underestimating true costs and actual schedules.

2. Automated estimates came within 5 percent of actual costs about 45 percent of the time. The maximum errors were about 30 percent. When errors occurred, they were usually on the side of conservatism, or estimating higher costs and longer schedules than actually occurred.

Of course, automated estimating tools can achieve optimistic results, too, if users do things such as exaggerate staff experience, understate application complexity, minimize paperwork and quality control, and ignore learning curves. These are common failures with manual estimates, and they can be carried over into the automated estimation domain, too.

In spite of the plentiful availability of commercial software-estimating tools, the author receives dozens of e-mail and phone messages containing requests for simple rules of thumb that can be used manually or with pocket calculators.

This chapter provides a number of rules of thumb that are interesting and sometimes useful. Readers are cautioned that rules of thumb are not suitable for formal estimates, major projects, or software with important schedule, cost, or business implications.

Rules of Thumb Based on Lines-of-Code (LOC) Metrics

For many years manual estimating methods were based on the *lines-of-code* (LOC) metric, and a number of workable rules of thumb were developed for common procedural programming languages, such as Assembly, COBOL, FORTRAN, PASCAL, PL/I, and the like.

These LOC rules of thumb usually start with basic assumptions about coding productivity rates for various sizes of software projects, and then use ratios or percentages for other kinds of work, such as testing, design, quality assurance, project management, and the like.

Tables 11.1 and 11.2 illustrate samples of the LOC-based rules of thumb for procedural languages in two forms: Table 11.1 uses *months* as the unit for work, while Table 11.2 uses *hours* as the unit for work. Both hourly and monthly work metrics are common in the software literature, with the hourly form being common for small programs and the monthly form being common for large systems.

Both tables show seven size ranges for software, with each one being an order of magnitude larger than its predecessor.

TABLE 11.1 Rules of Thumb Based on LOC Metrics for Procedural Languages
(Assumes 1 work month = 132 work hours)

Size of Program, LOC	Coding, LOC per month	Coding effort, months	Testing effort, %	Noncode effort, %	Total effort, months	Net LOC per month
1	2500	0.0004	10.00	10.00	0.0005	2083
10	2250	0.0044	20.00	20.00	0.0062	1607
100	2000	0.0500	40.00	40.00	0.0900	1111
1,000	1750	0.5714	50.00	60.00	1.2000	833
10,000	1500	6.6667	75.00	80.00	17.0000	588
100,000	1200	83.3333	100.00	100.00	250.0000	400
1,000,000	1000	1000.0000	125.00	150.00	3750.0000	267

TABLE 11.2 Rules of Thumb Based on LOC Metrics for Procedural Languages
(Assumes 1 work month = 132 work hours)

Size of Program, LOC	Coding, LOC per hour	Coding effort, hours	Testing effort, %	Noncode effort, %	Total effort, hours	Net LOC per hour
1	18.94	0.05	10.00	10.00	0.06	15.78
10	17.05	0.59	20.00	20.00	0.82	12.18
100	15.15	6.60	40.00	40.00	11.88	8.42
1,000	13.26	75.43	50.00	80.00	173.49	5.76
10,000	11.36	880.00	75.00	100.00	2,420.00	4.13
100,000	9.09	11,000.00	100.00	150.00	38,500.00	2.60
1,000,000	7.58	132,000.00	125.00	150.00	495,000.00	2.02

The column labeled "Testing effort, %" denotes the relative amounts of time for testing versus coding. As can be seen, the larger the project, the greater the amount of testing required.

The column labeled "Noncode effort, %" denotes the host of activities other than pure programming that are associated with software projects and need to be included in the estimate:

- Requirements definition
- External design
- Internal design
- Change management
- User documentation
- Project management

As software applications grow in size, a larger and larger proportion of total effort must be devoted to paperwork and other noncoding activities.

As can be seen, the *monthly* form of normalizing effort is fine for large systems but is not very convenient for the smaller end of the spectrum. Conversely, the *hourly* form is inconvenient at the large end.

Also, the assumption that a work month comprises 132 hours is a tricky one, since the observed number of hours actually worked in a month can run from less than 120 to more than 170. Because the actual number of hours varies from project to project, it is best to replace the generic rate of *132* with an actual or specific rate derived from local conditions and work patterns.

While LOC-based estimating rules of thumb served for many years, they are rapidly dropping from use because software technologies have changed so much that it is difficult, and even dangerous, to apply them under some conditions.

Usage of the LOC metric obviously assumes the existence of some kind of procedural programming language where programmers develop code using some combination of alphanumeric information, which is the way such languages as COBOL, C, FORTRAN, and hundreds of others operate.

However, the development of Visual Basic and its many competitors, such as Realizer, has changed the way many modern programs are developed. Although these visual languages do have a procedural source code portion, quite a bit of the more complex kinds of "programming" are done using button controls, pull-down menus, visual worksheets, and reusable components. In other words, programming is being done without anything that can be identified as a *line of code* for measurement or estimation purposes.

Also, the object-oriented programming languages and methods, such as Objective C, Smalltalk, Eiffel, and the like, with their class libraries, inheritance, and polymorphism, have also entered a domain where attempting to do estimates using conventional lines of code is not a very effective approach.

As the twentieth century ends, the volume of programming done using languages where the LOC metric no longer works well for estimating purposes is rising rapidly. By the end of the century, perhaps 30 percent of the new software applications will be developed using either object-oriented languages or visual languages, or both.

Over and above the fact that the LOC metric is difficult to apply for many modern programming languages, there are deep and serious economic problems with attempting to use LOC metrics for measurement and estimation purposes.

Most of the important kinds of software, such as operating systems,

TABLE 11.3   Rank Order of Large System Software Cost Elements

1. Defect removal (inspections, testing, and finding and fixing bugs)
2. Producing paper documents (plans, specifications, and user manuals)
3. Meetings and communication (clients, team members, and managers)
4. Programming or coding
5. Project management
6. Change management

billing systems, aircraft navigation systems, word processors, spreadsheets, and the like, are quite large compared to the sizes of applications built 20 years ago.

Twenty years ago, a programming application of 100,000 LOC was viewed as rather large. Even IBM's main operating system, OS/360, was only about 1 million LOC in size during its first year of release, although the modern incarnation, MVS, now tops 10 million LOC.

Today, a size of 100,000 LOC is more or less an entry-level size for a modern Windows 95 application. Many software packages can top 250,000 LOC, while things like major operating systems are in the 10-million-LOC domain and up.

For large systems in the 1 million–source code statement size range, programming itself is only the fourth most expensive activity. The three higher-cost activities can not really be measured or estimated effectively using the LOC metric. Also, the fifth and sixth major cost elements, project management and change management, cannot easily be estimated or measured using the LOC metric, either. (See Table 11.3.)

If these noncoding activities are not measured separately, the overall project can be measured using LOC, but such measures have a disturbing property: They will penalize high-level languages and make low-level languages seem to have higher productivity rates than high-level languages.

As can easily be seen, the usefulness of a metric such as lines of code, which can only measure and estimate one out of the six major software cost elements, is a significant barrier to economic understanding.

Rules of Thumb Based on Ratios and Percentages

Software projects obviously include a lot more kinds of work than just coding. A fairly large family of manual estimating methods has developed based on the use of ratios and percentages.

These rules assume a *cascade* form of estimation. First, the overall project is estimated in its entirety. Second, ratios and percentages are applied to apportion the overall effort into the desired sets of phases or activities.

The basic problem with ratio-based estimation is the false assumption that there are constant ratios between coding and other key activities, such as testing, project management, integration, and the like. In fact, the ratios vary significantly, based on four sets of independent variables:

1 The class of the application

2. The size of the application

3. The programming language or languages utilized

4. The presence or absence of reusable materials

The complexity of the interactions of these four sets of variables is why commercial software cost estimating tools contain hundreds of rules and adjustment factors.

There are too many combinations of factors to illustrate all of them, but it is instructive to view how the percentages applied to key software activities vary in response to the class of the application and to the size of the application.

Table 11.4 uses only seven major activities in order to highlight the percentage of coding effort against the background of noncoding activities.

Table 11.4 shows some of the changes in ratios among five different classes of applications. Note that for end-user applications there is very little work except coding and testing, because when users are building their own software they obviously know what their own requirements are, and they don't need personal user's guides.

TABLE 11.4   Percentages of Development Effort by Software Class

(Assumes application of 1000 function points or 100,000 source code statements)

Activity	End-user projects	MIS projects	Systems projects	Commercial projects	Military projects
Requirements definition	0	7	8	4	10
Design	10	12	15	10	15
Coding	60	25	18	25	18
Testing	30	30	30	36	22
Change management	0	6	10	5	12
Documentation	0	8	7	10	10
Project management	0	12	12	10	13
Total	100	100	100	100	100

TABLE 11.5   Percentages of Development Effort by Software Size
(Assumes procedural languages, such as COBOL or C)

Activity	10-FP projects	100-FP projects	1,000-FP projects	10,000-FP projects	100,000 FP projects
Requirements definition	5	5	7	8	9
Design	5	6	10	12	13
Coding	50	40	30	20	15
Testing	27	29	30	33	34
Change management	1	4	6	7	8
Documentation	4	6	7	8	9
Project management	8	10	10	12	12
Total	100	100	100	100	100

By contrast, for military software projects, the activities associated with requirements, design, and documentation total roughly twice the effort devoted to coding itself: 35 percent versus 18 percent.

When we consider ratios based on various size ranges of applications, we also see huge differences that prevent any single ratio or percentage from being a safe general estimating method.

Table 11.5 shows five size plateaus an order of magnitude apart, starting with small applications of 10 function points (roughly 1000 source code statements) and running up to enormous systems of 100,000 function points (roughly 10 million source code statements).

At the small end of the spectrum, coding is the dominant activity in terms of effort, but at the large end of the spectrum, coding itself is only 15 percent of the total effort. The main cost drivers at the large end of the spectrum are the activities associated with finding and fixing bugs and the activities associated with producing various kinds of paper documents, such as requirements, plans, specifications, and user manuals.

At the intersection between rules of thumb based on ratios and those based on lines of code is an important topic that is not well covered in the software literature: the amount of reusable source code taken from similar applications or from other sources.

Table 11.6 gives reuse percentages noted among SPR's clients for a variety of programming languages. It is interesting that in spite of the emphasis which the object-oriented community places on software reuse, the language that typically has the largest volume of reusable code for common applications is Visual Basic.

When reusable material is present in substantial volumes during a software development project, it will obviously affect the schedule, effort, and cost results from an estimating standpoint.

TABLE 11.6   Approximate Amount of
Reusable Code by Language

Language	Average reuse, %
Visual Basic	60.00
Eiffel	55.00
Smalltalk	50.00
Objective C	45.00
Ada 95	35.00
C++	27.50
SQL	25.00
Ada 83	25.00
COBOL	17.50
FORTRAN	15.00
Macro assembly	15.00
C	12.50
Pascal	12.50
Jovial	10.00
CMS2	10.00
PL/I	7.50
Basic assembly	5.00
Average	25.15

Software reusability is an important topic with many poorly understood aspects. For example, software reuse is only valuable if the reused material approaches zero-defect quality levels. Reusing poor-quality source code is dangerous and expensive.

The ratios for software reuse shown in Table 11.6 are only approximate and can vary widely. For example, there can be Visual Basic applications with less than 10 percent reused code, while some basic assembly applications can top 40 percent in terms of code reuse.

In general, the languages that endorse and facilitate reuse, such as the object-oriented family of languages and the Visual Basic family, have far more sources of reusable code than do such languages as COBOL, where reuse is merely accidental.

The overall conclusion is that the use of simplistic ratios and percentages for software cost estimating is a very hazardous practice unless the estimator has experience-based ratios derived from projects of the same size, same class, same programming language, and that utilize the same volume of reusable materials.

There is no single set of ratios or percentages that can be universally applied to software projects. This lack of universal constants is true in every other human activity. Knowing the average cost of buying an automobile in the United States is obviously irrelevant to buying your own personal automobile. You start with the kind of automobile and set of features that you want, check the averages for that combination, and then try to negotiate with dealers for a better cost.

It is astonishing that project managers would use simple ratios and percentages for software projects that cost millions of dollars, and yet use much more sophisticated costing techniques for buying automobiles, home appliances, houses, clothes, food, or any other personal purchases.

Rules of Thumb Based on Function Point Metrics

Since function point metrics were first published in the late 1970s, their use has swept through the software world, and function points are now among the most widely used of any metric in all countries that develop significant volumes of software, such as the United States, Japan, Germany, Australia, and Canada.

Function point metrics solve some of the more difficult problems for software cost estimation and cost measurement, and it is interesting to explore the origin and evolution of functional metrics.

In the middle 1970s, the IBM corporation was the world's largest and most successful producer of mainframe software. However, IBM's success and innovation led to some new and unexpected problems.

By the middle 1970s, IBM's software community was topping 25,000 members, and the costs of building and maintaining software were becoming a significant portion of the costs and budgets for new products.

Programming languages were exploding in number, and within IBM applications were being developed in assembly language, APL, COBOL, FORTRAN, RPG, PL/I, PL/S (a derivative of PL/I), and perhaps a dozen others. Indeed, many software projects at IBM and elsewhere used several languages concurrently, such as COBOL, RPG, and SQL, as part of the same system.

Also, the sizes of IBM's average software applications were growing from the 10,000 lines of code typical for the old IBM 1401 computers to well over 100,000 lines of code for the IBM 360 and IBM 370 computers.

The combination of larger applications and dozens of programming languages meant that manual estimates based on the lines of code metric were causing cost and schedule overruns of notable proportions. The problems of IBM in this era are captured very well in Dr. Fred Brooks's classic book *The Mythical Man-Month* (Brooks 1974), which was revised and reissued to commemorate the twentieth anniversary of its first publication.

Allan J. Albrecht and his colleagues at IBM White Plains were tasked with attempting to develop an improved methodology for sizing, estimating, and measuring software projects. The method they developed is now known as *function point analysis,* and the basic metric they developed is termed a *function point.*

Although the actual rules for counting function points are rather complex, the essential concepts behind the function point metric are simple: Base the size of applications on external characteristics that do not change because of the programming language or languages used.

In essence, a *function point* consists of the weighted totals of five external aspects of software applications:

1. The types of *inputs* to the application

2. The types of *outputs* that leave the application

3. The types of *inquiries* that users can make

4. The types of *logical files* that the application maintains

5. The types of *interfaces* to other applications

In October 1979, Allan Albrecht presented the function point metric at a conference in Monterey, California sponsored jointly by IBM and two IBM user groups, SHARE and GUIDE. Concurrently, IBM placed the basic function point metric into the public domain.

What Albrecht and his colleagues at IBM were attempting to do was to create a software metric that had the following 10 important attributes.

Design Goals of Function Point Metrics

1. The metric can be used to measure software productivity.

2. The metric can be used to measure software quality.

3. The metric can be used to measure software in any known programming language.

4. The metric can be used to measure software in any combination of languages.

5. The metric can be used to measure all classes of software (real-time, MIS, systems, etc.)

6. The metric can be used to measure any software task or activity and not just coding.

7. The metric can be used in discussions with clients.

8. The metric can be used for software contracts.

9. The metric can be used for large-scale statistical analysis.

10. The metric can be used for value analysis.

On the whole, the function point metric meets all 10 goals fairly well. This is not to say that function points have no problems of their own, but they meet the 10 criteria far better than the older lines-of-code metric. Indeed, given the advent of visual languages and object-oriented software, the lines-of-code metric does not currently meet any of the 10 criteria at all.

As the usage of function points expanded, a nonprofit organization, the International Function Point Users Group (IFPUG), was formed. IFPUG has now become one of the largest measurement associations in the world, and there are affiliated organizations in at least 20 other countries.

IFPUG took over responsibility from IBM for modernizing and updating the basic counting rules for function points, which have gone through four major sets of revisions. The current set of IFPUG counting rules is Version 4, and this set of rules can handle modern software, such as applications with graphical user interfaces (GUIs) as well as conventional software, object-oriented applications, real-time applications, and essentially all other kinds of software applications.

This chapter contains a set of simple rules of thumb that cover various aspects of software development and maintenance. The rules assume the Version 4.0 function point counting rules published by IFPUG. Adjustments would be needed for the British Mark II function point rules or the older Version 3.4 IFPUG rules. Also, these rules would need adjustments for some of the many function point variations, such as the Boeing 3D function point or the DeMarco *bang* function point.

However, rules of thumb are far too limited to cover every aspect of software development. So this section also discusses the usage of simple table-driven *templates* that allow somewhat finer levels of estimation. Here, too, the table-driven method is not as accurate as a commercial estimating tool, but can be performed quickly and can provide a rough check on more formal and rigorous estimating approaches.

Strong cautions must be given yet again:

1. Simple rules of thumb are *not* accurate.

2. Simple rules of thumb should *not* be used for contracts, bids, or serious business purposes.

3. No manual software-estimating methodology can give rapid response when assumptions change and requirements creep.

The following rules of thumb are known to have a high margin of error. They are being published in response to many requests to the author for simple methods that can be used manually or with pocket calculators. Also, an understanding of the limitations of manual estimating methods can give a greater appreciation for the need for more formal automated methods.

The best that can be said is that the rules of thumb are easy to use, and can provide a "sanity check" for estimates produced by other and hopefully more rigorous methods.

Function Point Sizing Rules of Thumb

Predicting the sizes of various deliverables is the usual starting point for software cost estimating. The function point metric has transformed sizing from a very difficult task into one that is now both easy to perform and comparatively accurate, although the accuracy of early sizing methods applied prior to the availability of information that can lead to function point analysis is not great.

Sizing function point totals prior to completion of requirements

It often happens that software cost estimates are required long before there is enough solid information to actually create an accurate estimate. Since the function point metric is the basis for so many subsequent estimating stages, it is very difficult to produce a reasonable software cost estimate prior to the completion of the requirements, which comprise the first software document with enough information to derive function point totals.

However, there are function point sizing methods that can be used to create a rough approximation of function point totals long before requirements are complete, although this method has a high margin of error.

Software Productivity Research (SPR) uses a multipart taxonomy for defining software projects in terms of scope, class, and type, in order to identify a project when entering information into the software cost estimating tools.

These project-identification checklists are organized using more or less the same principle as the Richter scale for earthquakes; that is, the larger numbers have more significance than the smaller numbers.

This property can be utilized to produce very early size approximations of function points before almost any other facts are known about the software projects in question. Admittedly, this crude form of sizing is far too inaccurate for serious cost-estimating purposes, but it has the virtue of being usable before any other known form of sizing is possible.

To use the scope, class, and type of taxonomy for guessing at the approximate size of the software, it is only necessary to sum the list values for the scope, class, and type and raise the total to the 2.35 power. This calculation sequence will yield a rough approximation of function points, assuming IFPUG Version 4 is the counting method. Table 11.7 summarizes the scope, class, and type lists in numeric order.

The kind of information needed to use this sizing approximation method is usually known on the very first day that requirements begin, so very early sizing is possible even if the size approximation is rather imprecise. To utilize this rough sizing method, it is only necessary to do three things:

1. Apply the numeric list values to the project to be sized in terms of the scope, class, and type factors.

TABLE 11.7   Examples of Scope, Class, and Type Values

	Scope		Class		Type
1	Subroutine	1	Individual software	1	Nonprocedural
2	Module	2	Shareware	2	Web applet
3	Reusable module	3	Academic software	3	Batch
4	Disposable prototype	4	Single location—internal	4	Interactive
5	Evolutionary prototype	5	Multilocation—internal	5	Interactive GUI
6	Standalone program	6	Contract project—civilian	6	Batch database
7	Component of system	7	Time sharing	7	Interactive database
8	Release of system	8	Military services	8	Client/server
9	New system	9	Internet	9	Mathematical
10	Compound system	10	Leased software	10	Systems
		11	Bundled software	11	Communications
		12	Marketed commercially	12	Process control
		13	Outsource contract	13	Trusted system
		14	Government contract	14	Embedded
		15	Military contract	15	Image processing
				16	Multimedia
				17	Robotics
				18	Artificial intelligence
				19	Neural net
				20	Hybrid: mixed

2. Sum the numeric values from the three lists.

3. Raise the total to the 2.35 power.

For example, assume you are building an application with the following three attributes:

Scope = 6 (standalone program)

Class = 4 (internal—single site)

Type = 8 (client/server)

Sum = 18

Raising 18 to the 2.35 power yields a value of 891, which can be utilized as a very rough approximation of function points, assuming the IFPUG Version 4 rules. Incidentally, client/server applications are often in the 1000–function point range, so this is not a bad starting point.

Let us try this method again on a different form of application. Suppose you were building a small personal application with the following properties:

Scope = 4 (disposable prototype)

Class = 1 (individual program)

Type = 1 (nonprocedural)

Sum = 6

Raising 6 to the 2.35 power gives a value of 67, which can serve as a rough approximation of the application's function point total. Here, too, since most personal applications are less than 100 function points in size, this is not a bad way of beginning even if the true size will vary.

Applying this same method to a more significant military software project, the results might be the following:

Scope = 9 (new system)

Class = 15 (military contract)

Type = 13 (trusted system)

Sum = 37

Raising 37 to the 2.35 power gives a value of 4844 function points, which again can serve as a rough approximation of the application's function point total until enough information is available to perform a proper function point analysis. Here, too, military software projects at the system level are often in the 5000–function point range in size (or larger), so this approximation method is enough to see that the application will not be a trivial one.

This very crude function point size approximation method is not recommended for any purpose other than estimating size prior to full requirements definition, when almost nothing is known about a software project and some form of sizing is needed to complete an early estimate.

It should be noted that the SPR scope, class, and type lists are changed from time to time to add new kinds of software or to adjust the rank placements as empirical evidence suggests that changes are needed. These changes mean that users of the methods should feel free to experiment with other power settings besides 2.35, or even to develop their own list sequences.

It is technically possible to develop a rule-based method for early sizing that would utilize the scope, class, and type information in a more sophisticated way than simply summing the scores and raising the results to a power.

The fundamental operating principle of this early sizing method is that useful information about software projects can be derived from a taxonomy that can rank a software application in a fashion that allows rough size information to be derived merely from the ranking itself.

Even the first column, or scope portion, of this taxonomy can be used for rough sizing purposes. Table 11.8 shows the "average" sizes of various kinds of projects, assuming a rough expansion factor of 100 logical source code statements for every function point.

In Table 11.8, most of the terms are self-explanatory. However, item 10, *compound system,* is a large system which is actually comprised of several systems linked together. An example of a compound system

TABLE 11.8   Size Approximations Using Only the Scope Factor

	Application scope	Size, function points	Size, source lines of code
1	Subroutine	1	100
2	Module	3	300
3	Reusable module	5	500
4	Disposable prototype	7	700
5	Evolutionary prototype	10	1,000
6	Standalone program	25	2,500
7	Component of system	100	10,000
8	Release of system	1,200	120,000
9	New system	5,000	500,000
10	Compound system	15,000	1,500,000

would be the SAP R3 integrated business suite, although that is much larger than 15,000 function points (closer to 250,000 function points)—it is comprised of a number of linked *systems,* which taken together constitute the entire SAP product.

A smaller example of a compound system would be Microsoft Office, which comprises the separate applications of word processing, spreadsheet, database, graphics, and personal scheduler, all integrated and working together. In fact, Microsoft Office is in the 20,000–function point size range, with each of the individual applications running about 3000 function points, plus the OLE capabilities to share information making up the total.

Because triangulating a software project in terms of its scope, class, and type is possible as early as the first day that requirements definition begins, this method can be utilized very early in a development cycle, long before any other kind of information is available.

However, this early sizing method is experimental and is still being developed. Users are urged to experiment with their own ranking systems and taxonomies, and also with varying the power used to achieve the function point approximations.

Although this sizing method is experimental, the early results indicate that the method is potentially quite useful. However, the software industry needs a standard taxonomy for software scope, class, and type. If such a standard taxonomy can be developed, then early sizing of applications would be facilitated.

Indeed, a standard taxonomy would allow historical data to be assigned to each of the major combinations, and this would greatly facilitate benchmarking studies.

Sizing by analogy

Another form of rapid sizing is simply browsing a list of the sizes of applications that have been measured and selecting one or more similar projects to serve as an approximate size basis for the new project that is about to be estimated, as shown by Table 11.9.

Sizing by analogy is a feature of automated cost-estimating models, but as more and more projects are measured, it will be increasingly common to see published tables of applications sizes using both function points and source code statements. Table 11.9 gives an example of such a table.

Sizing source code volumes

Now that thousands of software projects have been measured using both function points and lines of code (LOC), empirical ratios have been developed for converting LOC data into function points, and vice

TABLE 11.9 **Approximate Sizes of Selected Software Applications**
(Sizes based on IFPUG Version 4 and SPR logical statement rules)

Application	Type	Purpose	Primary language	Size, KLOC	Size, FP	LOC per FP
Graphics Design	Commercial	CAD	Objective C	54	2,700	20.00
IEF	Commercial	CASE	C	2,500	20,000	125.00
Visual Basic	Commercial	Compiler	C	375	3,000	125.00
IMS	Commercial	Database	Assembly	750	3,500	214.29
CICS	Commercial	Database	Assembly	420	2,000	210.00
Lotus Notes	Commercial	Groupware	Mixed	350	3,500	100.00
MS Office Professional	Commercial	Office tools	C	2,000	16,000	125.00
SmartSuite	Commercial	Office tools	Mixed	2,000	16,000	125.00
MS Office Standard	Commercial	Office tools	C	1,250	10,000	125.00
Word 7.0	Commercial	Office tools	C	315	2,500	126.00
Excel 6.0	Commercial	Office tools	C	375	2,500	150.00
MS Project	Commercial	Project management	C	375	3,000	125.00
KnowledgePlan	Commercial	Project management	C++	134	2,500	56.67
CHECKPOINT	Commercial	Project management	Mixed	225	2,100	107.14
Function Point Control	Commercial	Project management	C	56	450	125.00
SPQR/20	Commercial	Project management	Quick Basic	25	350	71.43
WMCCS	Military	Defense	Jovial	18,000	175,000	102.86
Aircraft Radar	Military	Defense	Ada 83	213	3,000	71.00
Gun Control	Military	Defense	CMS2	250	2,336	107.00
Airline Reservation	MIS	Business	Mixed	2,750	25,000	110.00
Insurance Claims	MIS	Business	COBOL	1,605	15,000	107.00
Telephone billing	MIS	Business	C	1,375	11,000	125.00
Tax Preparation (Personal)	MIS	Business	Mixed	180	2,000	90.00
General Ledger	MIS	Business	COBOL	161	1,500	107.00
Order Entry	MIS	Business	COBOL/SQL	106	1,250	85.00
Human Resource	MIS	Business	COBOL	128	1,200	107.00
Sales Support	MIS	Business	COBOL/SQL	83	975	85.00
Budget Preparation	MIS	Business	COBOL/SQL	64	750	85.00

TABLE 11.9　Approximate Sizes of Selected Software Applications (Continued)
(Sizes based on IFPUG Version 4 and SPR logical statement rules)

Application	Type	Purpose	Primary language	Size, KLOC	Size, FP	LOC per FP
Windows 95	Systems	Operating system	C	11,000	85,000	129.41
MVS	Systems	Operating system	Assembly	12,000	55,000	218.18
UNIX V5	Systems	Operating system	C	6,250	50,000	125.00
DOS 5	Systems	Operating system	C	1,000	4,000	250.00
5ESS	Systems	Telecommunication	C	1,500	12,000	125.00
System/12	Systems	Telecommunication	CHILL	800	7,700	103.90
Total				68,669	542,811	126.51
Average				2,020	15,965	126.51

versa. The following rules of thumb are based on *logical statements* rather than *physical lines*.

(The physical LOC metric has such wide and random variations from language to language and programmer to programmer that it is not suited for sizing, for estimating, or for any other serious purpose.)

For similar information on almost 500 programming languages, refer to the McGraw-Hill companion book, *Applied Software Measurement* (Jones 1996).

Rule 1: Sizing Source Code Volumes

One function point = 320 statements for basic assembly language
One function point = 213 statements for macro assembly language
One function point = 128 statements for the C programming language
One function point = 107 statements for the COBOL language
One function point = 107 statements for the FORTRAN language
One function point = 80 statements for the PL/I language
One function point = 71 statements for the ADA 83 language
One function point = 53 statements for the C++ language
One function point = 15 statements for the Smalltalk language

The overall range of noncommentary logical source code statements to function points ranges from more than 300 statements per function point for basic assembly language to less than 15 statements per function point for object-oriented languages and many program generators.

However, since many procedural languages, such as C, Cobol, Fortran, and Pascal, are close to the 100-to-1 mark, that value can serve as a rough conversion factor for the general family of procedural source code languages.

For object-oriented programming languages with full class libraries, such as Actor, Eiffel, Objective-C, C++, and Smalltalk, the range is from perhaps 14 to about 50 statements per function point, and a value such as 20 statements per function point can serve as a rough approximation.

These code-sizing rules of thumb have a high margin of error, and need specific adjustments based on individual *dialects* of programming languages. Also, individual programming styles can vary significantly. Indeed, in a controlled study within IBM where eight programmers implemented the same specification using the same language, a 5-to-1 variation in the number of source code statements was noted, based on individual interpretations of the specification.

Note that these rules for sizing source code can also be reversed. It often happens when dealing with aging legacy applications, and sometimes for small enhancement and maintenance projects, that source code volumes are known earlier in the development cycle than is possible to calculate function points.

Direct conversion from source code volumes to an equivalent count of function points is termed *backfiring*. Although the accuracy of backfiring is not great, because individual programming styles can cause wide variations in source code counts, it is easy and popular.

Indeed, for some aging legacy applications where the specifications are missing and the source code is the only remaining artifact, backfiring provides the only effective method for arriving at function point values.

There is another situation where backfiring is very popular, too: small enhancements and maintenance projects. The normal method of calculating function points has trouble with small projects below about 15 function points in size because the weighting factors have lower limits; this creates a floor at about 15 function points, below which the normal method ceases to work effectively.

However, the backfiring method of conversion between logical statements has no lower limit and can even be used for sizes as small as a fraction of a function point. For example, making a 1–source code statement change to a COBOL application has a size of about 0.001

function points. There is no way to calculate such a tiny fraction of a function point using normal methods.

Because maintenance and enhancement projects are very common, and because aging legacy applications are also common, the backfiring method for approximating function points is actually the most widely used method in the world for deriving function point totals.

Backfiring is a common feature of software cost estimating tools, and is found in at least 30 commercial software cost estimating tools in the United States, as well as in those developed in Europe and elsewhere.

Note that for backfiring to work well, the starting point should be *logical statements* rather than physical lines of source code. However, it is possible to cascade from physical lines to logical statements, although the accuracy is reduced somewhat.

Sizing paper deliverables

Software is a very paper intensive industry. More than 50 kinds of planning, requirements, specification, and user-related document types can be created for large software projects. For many large systems, and especially for large military projects, producing paper documents costs far more than producing the source code.

Paperwork volumes correlate fairly closely to the size of the application, using either function points or source code metrics. Small projects create comparatively few paper documents, and they themselves are not very large.

However, large systems in the 10,000–function point or 1 million–source code statement range often produce large numbers of documents, and some of these are very large indeed. For example, some sets of specifications have topped 60,000 pages.

For a few really large systems in the 100,000–function point range, the specifications can actually exceed the lifetime reading speed of a single person, and could not be finished even by reading 8 hours a day for an entire career!

The following rule of thumb encompasses the sum of the pages that will be created in requirements, internal and external specifications, development and quality plans, test plans, user manuals, and other business-related software documents.

However, if you are following ISO 9000–9004 standards, you should use 1.17 as the power rather than 1.15. If you are following older military standards, such as DoD 2167, you should use 1.18 as the power rather than 1.15, because military projects produce more paperwork than any other kind of software application.

Rule 2: Sizing Software Plans, Specifications, and Manuals

Function points raised to the 1.15 power predict approximate page counts for paper documents associated with software projects.

A simple corollary rule can be used to predict the approximate volume of text that the pages will contain: Pages multiplied by 400 words per page predict the approximate number of English words created for the normal page size used in the United States (i.e., 8.5- by 11-in paper stock) with single-spaced type, using a 12-point type such as Times Roman. The actual capacity is greater than 400 words, but the inclusion of graphics and tables must be factored in.

Obviously, adjustments must be made for European A4 paper, where the capacity is closer to 500 words, once again assuming that graphic elements and tables will also be present, and that a 12-point type is selected.

Paperwork is such a major element of software costs and schedules that it cannot safely be ignored. Indeed, one of the major problems with the LOC metric is that it tends to conceal both the volumes of paper deliverables and the high costs of software paperwork.

Sizing creeping user requirements

One of the most severe problems of the software world is that of dealing with the emergence of new and changing requirements after the completion of the initial requirements phase.

The function point metric is extremely useful in measuring the rate at which requirements creep. In fact, the usage of *cost per function point* is now starting to occur in software contracts and outsourcing agreements. For contract purposes, cost per function point is used with a sliding scale that becomes more expensive for features added later in the development cycle.

Rule 3: Sizing Creeping User Requirements

Creeping user requirements will grow at an average rate of 2 percent per month from the design through coding phases.

Assume that you and your clients agree during the requirements definition to develop an application of exactly 1000 function points. This rule of thumb implies that every month thereafter during the subsequent design and coding phases, the original requirements will grow by a rate of 20 function points.

Since the overall schedule for a generic 1000–function point project would be about 16 calendar months, and the design and coding phases would be about half that, or 8 calendar months, this rule implies that about 16 percent new features would be added due to creeping requirements. The final total for the application would be 1160 function points rather than the initial value of 1000 function points.

In real life, the observed range of creeping requirements ranges from close to 0 to more than 5 percent per month. The better requirements methods, such as joint application design (JAD), prototypes, and requirements inspections, can reduce the rate of creep to well below 1 percent per month.

However, quick and dirty requirements methods, such as those often found with rapid application development (RAD) or client/server projects, can cause the rate of creep to top 5 percent per month and throw the project into such turmoil that a successful completion becomes unlikely.

Because internal information systems have no visible penalties associated with creeping requirements, they tend to grow almost uncontrollably. For contract software and outsourcing arrangements, there may be financial penalties for adding requirements late in the development cycle.

For software development contracts, perhaps the most effective way of dealing with changing user requirements is to include a sliding scale of costs in the contract itself. For example, suppose a hypothetical contract is based on an initial agreement of $500 per function point to develop an application of 1000 function points in size, so that the total value of the agreement is $500,000.

The contract might contain the following kind of escalating cost scale for new requirements added downstream:

Initial 1000 function points	$500 per function point
Features added more than 3 months after contract signing	$600 per function point
Features added more than 6 months after contract signing	$700 per function point
Features added more than 9 months after contract signing	$900 per function point
Features added more than 12 months after contract signing	$1200 per function point

Features deleted or delayed at user request $150 per function point

Similar clauses can be utilized with maintenance and enhancement outsource agreements, on an annual or specific basis such as the following:

Normal maintenance and defect repairs	$125 per function point per year
Mainframe to client/server conversion	$200 per function point per system
Eurocurrency conversion	$115 per function point per system
Special year-2000 search and repair	$65 per function point per system

The advantage of the use of function point metrics for development and maintenance contracts is that they are determined from the user requirements and cannot be unilaterally added or deleted by the contractor.

One of the many problems with the older LOC metric is that there is no objective way of determining the minimum volume of code needed to implement any given feature. This means that contracts based on cost per LOC could expand without any effective way for the client to determine whether the expansions were technically necessary.

Function points, on the other hand, cannot be unilaterally determined by the vendor and must be derived from explicit user requirements. Also, function points can easily be understood by clients, while the LOC metric is difficult to understand in terms of why so much code is needed for any given contract.

Sizing test-case volumes

The function point metric is extremely useful for test-case sizing, since the structure of function point analysis closely parallels the items that need to be validated by testing.

Commercial software-estimating tools can predict the number of test cases for more than 15 discrete forms of testing, and can deal with the specifics of unit testing, new function testing, system testing, and all of the other varieties. This simple rule of thumb encompasses the sum of all test cases in all forms of testing, which is why rules of thumb should be used with caution.

Rule 4: Sizing Test-Case Volumes

Function points raised to the 1.2 power predicts the approximate number of test cases created.

A simple corollary rule can predict the number of times each test case will be run or executed during development: Assume that each test case would be executed approximately four times during software development.

Of course, there are at least 18 separate forms of testing used for software projects. In addition, companies are split between those where developers perform testing, where professional test personnel perform testing, and even where independent test organizations perform testing. The true complexity of testing requires much more work than a simple rule of thumb for acceptable precision in estimating results.

Sizing software defect potentials

The *defect potential* of an application is the sum of bugs or errors that will occur in five major deliverables:

1. Requirements errors

2. Design errors

3. Coding errors

4. User documentation errors

5. Bad fixes, or secondary errors introduced in the act of fixing a prior error

One of the many problems with LOC metrics is the fact that more than half of all software defects are found in requirements and design, and hence the LOC metric is not capable of either predicting or measuring their volume with acceptable accuracy.

Because the cost and effort for finding and fixing bugs is usually the largest identifiable software cost element, ignoring defects can throw off estimates, schedules, and costs by massive amounts.

Rule 5: Sizing Software Defect Potentials

Function points raised to the 1.25 power predict the approximate defect potential for new software projects.

A similar corollary rule can predict the defect potentials for enhancements. In this case, the rule applies to the size of the enhancement rather than to the base that is being updated: Function points raised to the 1.27 power predict the approximate defect potential for enhancement software projects, using the enhancement (and not the base system) as the basis for applying the rule. The higher power used in the enhancement rule is because of the latent defects lurking in the base product that will be encountered during the enhancement process.

The function point metric has been very useful in clarifying the overall distribution of software defects. Indeed, almost the only literature on the volume of noncode defects uses function point metrics for expressing the results. The approximate U.S. average for software defects during development for new projects is shown in Table 11.10.

As can easily be seen from Table 11.10, there are more software defects found outside the code than within it. Data expressed using the older LOC metric almost never deals with noncoding defects, such as those in requirements, specifications, and user manuals.

There are two other important categories of defects where empirical evidence has not yet accumulated enough data to derive useful rules of thumb: (1) errors in databases, and (2) errors in test cases themselves.

Research on database errors is handicapped by the fact that there is no *data point* metric for normalizing database sizes or defect rates.

This same problem is true for test cases. However, assessments and interviews with commercial software companies indicate that errors in test cases are sometimes more plentiful than errors or bugs in the software itself!

A very preliminary rule of thumb for test-case errors would be about 1.8 defects per function point. This rule is derived by simply dividing the function point total of the application by the number of errors fixed in test cases.

Hopefully, more reliable data will become available for test-case errors in the future, and data quality will be able to be measured if a data point size metric can be created.

TABLE 11.10   U.S. Averages for Software Defect Levels During Development

Defect origin	Defects per function point
Requirements	1.00
Design	1.25
Code	1.75
User documents	0.60
Bad fixes	0.40
Total	5.00

Sizing software defect-removal efficiency

The defect potential is the life-cycle total of errors that must be eliminated. The defect potential will be reduced by somewhere between 85 percent (approximate industry norms) and 99 percent (best-in-class results) prior to actual delivery of the software to clients. Thus, the number of delivered defects is only a small fraction of the overall defect potential.

An interesting set of rules of thumb can size the numbers of defects that might be found and can approximate the defect-removal efficiency of various reviews, inspections, and tests.

Rule 6: Sizing Testing Defect-Removal Efficiency

Each software test step will find and remove 30 percent of the bugs that are present.

Testing has a surprisingly low efficiency in actually finding bugs. Most forms of testing will find less than one bug or defect out of every three that are present. The implication of this fact means that a series of between 6 and 12 consecutive defect-removal operations must be utilized to achieve very high quality levels.

This is why major software producers normally use a multistage series of design reviews, code inspections, and various levels of testing from unit test through system test.

This rule may require an example to clarify how it works. Suppose you are developing a new application of 100 function points in size. Applying Rule 4 and raising 100 function points to the 1.25 power yields a possible bug total of 316 bugs or defects.

Applying Rule 5, your first testing step (unit testing) will find about 30 percent of the bugs, or 95 bugs out of 316, leaving a residue of 221 bugs. Your second test stage (new function testing) will find 30 percent of the 221 bugs left after unit testing, or 66 more bugs. Thus, you will have 155 bugs left after two testing stages.

You can continue with this same sequence of consecutive 30 percent reductions until you reach the end of your normal series of testing stages. Incidentally, if you depend only upon testing for achieving high levels of quality, plan on performing at least a 6-stage series, and more likely a 10-stage series, of test operations.

The rather low defect-removal efficiency level of most common forms of testing explains why the U.S. average for defect-removal efficiency is only about 85 percent unless formal design and code inspections are utilized.

In fact, the defect-removal efficiency of formal design and code inspections is so much higher than testing that it is useful to show a separate rule for these activities.

Rule 7: Sizing Formal Inspection Defect-Removal Efficiency

Each formal design inspection will find and remove 65 percent of the bugs present.
Each formal code inspection will find and remove 60 percent of the bugs present.

It is easy to see from Rule 7 why most of the software organizations that produce really high quality software with more than 95 percent cumulative defect-removal efficiency utilize formal pretest inspections at the design and code levels.

Incidentally, although formal inspections are not inexpensive, they have such a strong effect on defect removal that the increase in testing speed and reduction in testing and maintenance costs that they trigger give them one of the best returns on investment of any known software technology.

To complete the set of quality-related rules of thumb, the following rule deals with the rate at which bugs can be repaired after software applications are released.

Rule 8: Postrelease Defect-Repair Rates

Maintenance programmers can repair 8 bugs per staff month.

Rule 8, or maintenance repair rates, has been around the software industry for more than 30 years and still seems to work. However, some of the state-of-the-art maintenance organizations that utilize complexity analyzers and code restructuring tools and have sophisticated maintenance work benches available can double the rate and may even top 16 bugs per month.

Rules of Thumb for Schedules, Resources, and Costs

After the sizes of various deliverable items and potential defects have been quantified, the next stage in an estimate is to predict schedules, resources, costs, and other useful results.

Some of the rules of thumb for dealing with schedules, resources, and costs are compound, and require joining several individual rules together. However, these combinations are simple enough to be done with a pocket calculator, spreadsheet, or even in your head if you are good with mental calculations.

Assignment scope and production-rate logic

Software rules of thumb and both manual and automated estimating methods utilize algorithms and relationships based on two key concepts:

1. The *assignment scope* (A scope) is the amount of work for which one person will be responsible on a software project.

2. The *production rate* (P rate) is the amount of work that one person can perform in a standard time period, such as a work hour, work week, work month, or work year.

Both assignment scopes and production rates can be expressed using any convenient metric, such as function points, source code statements, or "natural" deliverables, such as words or pages.

For example, assume that you are responsible for estimating an application of 50,000 source code statements in size using the C programming language. If an average assignment for programmers in your organization is 10,000 source code statements, then this project will require 5 programmers.

If an average programmer in your organization can code at a rate of 2000 C statements each month, then the project will require 25 months of effort.

By combining the results of the assignment-scope and production-rate rules, you can derive useful estimates with a pocket calculator.

Let us look at the kinds of information which can be derived using A-scope and P-rate logic. We will also include an average monthly salary rate in order to derive a complete cost estimate.

Monthly pay	$6,000
Project size	50,000 C statements
A scope	10,000 C statements
P rate	2,000 C statements per month
Staff	5 programmers (50,000 divided by the A scope of 10,000)
Effort	25 months (50,000 divided by the P rate of 2,000)
Schedule	5 months (25 months of effort divided by 5 programmers)
Cost	$150,000 (25 months of effort at $6000 per month)

This logic is not foolproof, but is often useful for creating quick and rough estimates. However, to use assignment scopes and production rates well, you need to know the averages and ranges of these factors within your own organization. This is one of the reasons why software measurements and software cost estimating are so closely aligned. Measurements supply the raw materials needed to construct accurate cost estimates.

Indeed, companies that measure software projects well can create local rules of thumb based on their own data that will be much more useful than generic rules of thumb based on overall industry experience.

Estimating software schedules

Schedule estimation is usually the highest priority topic for clients, project managers, and software executives. Rule 9 calculates the approximate interval from the start of requirements until the first delivery to a client.

Rule 9: Estimating Software Schedules

Function points raised to the 0.4 power predict the approximate development schedule in calendar months.

Note that Rule 9 is a generic rule that would need adjustment between civilian and military projects. Because military software usually takes more time, raising function point totals to about the 0.45 power gives a better result.

Among our clients, the range of observed schedules in calendar months varies from a low of about 0.32 to a high of more than 0.45. In general, smaller, simpler projects would match the lower power levels, while larger, more complex projects would match the higher power levels. Also, standards that add complexity and extra paperwork to software development, such DoD 2167 or ISO 9001, tend to push the schedule power level above the 0.4 average value.

Table 11.11 illustrates the kinds of projects whose schedules are typically found at various power levels, assuming a project of 1000 function points in size.

The use of function points for schedule estimation is one of the more useful by-products of function points that has been developed in recent years. As with all rules of thumb, the results are only approximate and should not be used for serious business purposes such as

TABLE 11.11   Software Schedules in Calendar Months
from Start of Requirements to Delivery

(Assumes 1000 function points from requirements to
delivery)

Power	Schedule in calendar months	Projects within range
0.32	9.12	
0.33	9.77	
0.34	10.47	
0.35	11.22	
0.36	12.02	O-O software
0.37	12.88	Client/server software
0.38	13.80	Outsourced software
0.39	14.79	MIS software
0.40	15.85	Commercial software
0.41	16.98	Systems software
0.42	18.20	
0.43	19.50	Military software
0.44	20.89	
0.45	22.39	

contracts. However, as a sanity check these rules of thumb are fairly useful. Readers are urged to explore historical data within their own organizations and to develop schedule power tables based on their own local results, rather than on industry averages.

Estimating software staffing levels

The next rule of thumb is concerned with how many personnel will be needed to build the application. Rule 10 is based on the concept of *assignment scope* or the amount of work for which one person will normally be responsible.

Rule 10 includes software developers, quality assurance, testers, technical writers, database administrators, and project managers.

Rule 10: Estimating Software Development Staffing Levels

Function points divided by 150 predict the approximate number of personnel required for the application.

The rule of 1 technical staff member per 150 function points obviously varies widely based on the skill and experience of the team and the size and complexity of the application. This rule simply provides an approximate starting point for more detailed staffing analysis.

A corollary rule can estimate the number of personnel required to maintain the project during the maintenance period.

Rule 11: Estimating Software Maintenance Staffing Levels

Function points divided by 750 predict the approximate number of maintenance personnel required to keep the application updated.

The implication of Rule 11 is that 1 person can perform minor updates and keep about 750 function points of software operational. (Another interesting maintenance rule of thumb is: Raising the function point total to the 0.25 power will yield the approximate number of years that the application will stay in use.)

Among our clients, the best-in-class organizations are achieving ratios of up to 3500 function points per staff member during maintenance. These larger values usually indicate a well-formed geriatric program, including the use of complexity analysis tools, code restructuring tools, reengineering and reverse engineering tools, and full configuration control and defect tracking of aging legacy applications.

Estimating software development effort

The last development rule of thumb in this chapter is a hybrid rule that is based on the combination of Rules 9 and 10.

Rule 12: Estimating Software Development Effort

Multiply software development schedules by number of personnel to predict the approximate number of staff months of effort.

Since this is a hybrid rule, an example can clarify how it operates. Assume you are concerned with a project of 1000 function points in size.

- Using Rule 7, or raising 1000 function points to the 0.4 power, indicates a schedule of about 16 calendar months.

- Using Rule 8, or dividing 1000 function points by 150, indicates a staff of about 6.6 full-time personnel.

- Multiplying 16 calendar months by 6.6 personnel indicates a total of about 106 staff months to build this particular project.

(Incidentally, another common but rough rule of thumb defines a *staff month* as consisting of 22 working days with 6 productive hours each day, or 132 work hours per month.)

Hybrid rules are more complex than single rules, but at least this hybrid rule includes the two critical factors of staffing and schedules.

Rules of Thumb Using Activity-Based Cost Analysis

There are manual software cost estimating methodologies that are more accurate than simple rules of thumb, but they require work sheets and more extensive calculations in order to be used. Of these more complex manual methods, the approaches that lead to activity-based cost estimates are often the most useful and also the most accurate in the hands of experienced project managers.

It has been known for many years that military software projects have much lower productivity rates than civilian software projects. It has also been known for many years that large systems usually have much lower productivity rates than small projects. A basic question which our measurement methods should be able to answer is, "Why do these productivity differences occur?"

It is the ability to explore some of the fundamental reasons why productivity rates vary that gives activity-based measurements a strong advantage that can lead to significant process improvements.

Data measured only to the project level is inadequate for any kind of in-depth economic analysis or process comparison. This is also true for data based on rudimentary phase structures, such as "requirements, design, coding, integration and testing."

However, when activity-based cost analysis is used, it becomes fairly easy to answer questions such as the one posed at the beginning of this section. For example, military software projects have lower productivity rates than civilian software projects because military software projects perform many more activities than do civilian projects of the same size.

SPR has analyzed many software development methodologies from around the world, and has constructed a generic checklist of 25 activities that occur with high frequency. This list of activities is used for baseline cost collection, for schedule measurement, and as the basis for exploring the effectiveness of various kinds of tools and practices.

One of the interesting by-products of exploring software projects down to the activity level is the set of *patterns* that are often associated with various sizes and kinds of software projects.

To illustrate some of the variations at the activity level, Table 11.12 gives examples of activity pattern differences noted during SPR assessment and baseline studies for various classes of software based on the checklist of 25 activities that SPR utilizes for data collection.

Table 11.12 illustrates the patterns noted for six general kinds of software: (1) end-user software, (2) management information systems

TABLE 11.12   Typical Activity Patterns for Six Software Domains

Activities performed	End user	MIS	Outsource	Commercial	Systems	Military
01 Requirements		X	X	X	X	X
02 Prototyping	X	X	X	X	X	X
03 Architecture		X	X	X	X	X
04 Project plans		X	X	X	X	X
05 Initial design		X	X	X	X	X
06 Detail design		X	X	X	X	X
07 Design reviews		X	X	X	X	X
08 Coding	X	X	X	X	X	X
09 Reuse acquisition	X		X	X	X	X
10 Package purchase		X	X		X	X
11 Code inspections				X	X	X
12 Independent verification and validation						X
13 Configuration management		X	X	X	X	X
14 Formal integration		X	X	X	X	X
15 Documentation	X	X	X	X	X	X
16 Unit testing	X	X	X	X	X	X
17 Function testing		X	X	X	X	X
18 Integration testing		X	X	X	X	X
19 System testing		X	X	X	X	X
20 Field testing				X	X	X
21 Acceptance testing		X	X		X	X
22 Independent testing						X
23 Quality assurance			X	X	X	X
24 Installation and training		X	X		X	X
25 Project management		X	X	X	X	X
Activities	5	18	21	20	23	25

(MIS), (3) outsource projects, (4) commercial software vendors, (5) systems software, and (6) military software.

It is very interesting to realize that much of the observed difference in productivity rates among various industries and kinds of software is due to the fact that they do not all build software using the same sets or patterns of activities. It takes much more work to build U.S. military software than any other kind of software in the world. This is because Department of Defense standards mandate activities such as *independent verification and validation* and *independent testing* that civilian software projects almost never use.

Over and above the average values shown, there can be other significant variations. For example, small client/server projects may only perform 8 of the 16 activities listed under the MIS domain, which simultaneously explains why client/server productivity can be high and client/server quality low, since many of the quality-related activities are conspicuously absent in the client/server domain.

From activity-based analysis such as this, it becomes easy to understand a number of otherwise ambiguous topics. For example, it can easily be seen why U.S. military software projects are more expensive than any other kind of software, since they perform more activities.

Variation in activity patterns is not the only factor that causes productivity differences, of course. The experience and skill of the team, the available tools, programming languages, methods, processes, and a host of other factors are also important. However, the impact of these other factors cannot be properly understood unless the cost and effort data for the project is accurate and is also granular down to the level of the activities performed.

If your software cost tracking system "leaks" large but unknown amounts of effort, and if you collect data only to the level of complete projects, you will not have enough information to perform the kind of multiple regression analysis necessary to evaluate the impact of the other factors that influence software productivity and cost results.

To illustrate the approximate amount of effort and costs required for specific activities, Table 11.13 shows the average amount of work hours per function point for each of the 25 activities in the standard SPR chart of accounts for software projects, although there are, of course, large variations for each activity.

The information shown in Table 11.13 illustrates the basic concept of activity-based costing. It is not a substitute for one of the commercial software cost estimating tools that support activity-based costs in a much more sophisticated way, such as allowing each activity to have its own unique cost structure and varying the nominal hours expended based on experience, methods, tools, and so forth.

In this table, the "Staff FP assignment" column represents the average number of function points assigned to one staff member.

TABLE 11.13   **Example of Activity-Based Chart of Accounts**
(Assumes new development projects)

Assumptions	
Work hours per month	132
Unpaid overtime per month	0
Average monthly salary	$5,000
Burden rate	100%
Burdened monthly rate	$10,000
Burdened hourly rate	$76

	Activities	Staff FP assignment	Monthly FP production	Work hours per FP	Burdened cost per FP	Staffing per 1000 FP
01	Requirements	250.00	175.00	0.75	$57.14	4.00
02	Prototyping	350.00	150.00	0.88	66.67	2.86
03	Architecture	2000.00	300.00	0.44	33.33	0.50
04	Project plans	1000.00	500.00	0.26	20.00	1.00
05	Initial design	250.00	175.00	0.75	57.14	4.00
06	Detail design	250.00	150.00	0.88	66.67	4.00
07	Design reviews	200.00	225.00	0.59	44.44	5.00
08	Coding	150.00	50.00	2.64	200.00	6.67
09	Reuse acquisition	250.00	600.00	0.22	16.67	4.00
10	Package purchase	5000.00	400.00	0.33	25.00	0.20
11	Code inspections	150.00	150.00	0.88	66.67	6.67
12	Independent verification and validation	2000.00	125.00	1.06	80.00	0.50
13	Configuration management	1000.00	1750.00	0.08	5.71	1.00
14	Integration	2000.00	250.00	0.53	40.00	0.50
15	User documentation	750.00	70.00	1.89	142.86	1.33
16	Unit testing	150.00	150.00	0.88	66.67	6.67
17	Function testing	350.00	150.00	0.88	66.67	2.86
18	Integration testing	700.00	175.00	0.75	57.14	1.43
19	System testing	2500.00	200.00	0.66	50.00	0.40
20	Field (beta) testing	1500.00	225.00	0.59	44.44	0.67
21	Acceptance testing	750.00	350.00	0.38	28.57	1.33
22	Independent testing	2500.00	200.00	0.66	50.00	0.40
23	Quality assurance	2000.00	150.00	0.88	66.67	0.50
24	Installation and training	5000.00	350.00	0.38	28.57	0.20
25	Project management	750.00	100.00	1.32	100.00	1.33
	Cumulative results	203.39	6.75	19.55	1481.03	4.92

The "Monthly FP production" column represents the typical amount of a particular activity that one person can accomplish in one month.

The "Work hours per FP" column represents the number of hours for each function point, assuming in this case that 132 hours are worked each month. Obviously, this column will change if the number of available monthly hours changes.

To use the data in Table 11.13, you need to know at least the approximate function point size of the application in question. Then, select the set of activities that you believe will be performed for the application. After that, you can add up the work hours per function point for each activity.

You can do the same kind of selection and aggregation with costs, of course, but you should replace the default compensation level of $5000 per staff month and the default burden or overhead rate of 100 percent with the appropriate values from your own company or organization.

Note that Table 11.13 uses a generic chart of accounts that includes both civilian and military activities. For example, activity 12 is *independent verification and validation,* which is required by many military contracts but is seldom or never used for civilian projects.

Once activity-based costing is started, it can be extended to include many other activities in a similar fashion. For example, the set of activities shown here is common for development projects. If you are concerned with the maintenance of aging legacy applications, with porting software from one platform to another, or with bringing out a new release of a commercial software package, then you will need to deal with other activities outside of those shown in the table.

Table 11.14 illustrates a similar chart of accounts as might be used for an enhancement project in the civilian software domain. While some of the activities are identical between new projects and enhancements, enhancements often have some unique activities, such as analyzing the base system, restructuring the base system (if necessary), regression testing, and several others. These *enhancement-only* activities are shown in boldface type in the table to set them off from common activities.

Neither table should be regarded as anything more than an example to illustrate the concept of activity-based cost estimating. What are actually needed are similar tables that match your organization's charts of accounts and substitute your organization's data for generic industry data.

However, both tables do illustrate the levels of granularity that are needed to really come to grips with the economic picture of software development. Data collected only to the level of projects or a few phases

TABLE 11.14   Example of Activity-Based Chart of Accounts

(Assumes enhancement projects)

Assumptions	
Work hours per month	132
Unpaid overtime per month	0
Average monthly salary	$5,000
Burden rate	100%
Burdened monthly rate	$10,000
Burdened hourly rate	$76

Activities	Staff FP assignment	Monthly FP production	Work hours per FP	Burdened cost per FP	Staffing per 1000 FP
01 Requirements	250.00	175.00	0.75	$57.14	4.00
02 **Base analysis**	1000.00	300.00	0.44	33.33	1.00
03 **Restructuring base**	3000.00	1000.00	0.13	10.00	0.33
04 Project plans	1000.00	500.00	0.26	20.00	1.00
05 Initial design	300.00	200.00	0.66	50.00	3.33
06 Detail design	300.00	175.00	0.75	57.14	3.33
07 Design reviews	200.00	225.00	0.59	44.44	5.00
08 Coding	150.00	50.00	2.64	200.00	6.67
09 Reuse acquisition	250.00	600.00	0.22	16.67	4.00
10 New inspections	150.00	150.00	0.88	66.67	6.67
11 **Base inspections**	500.00	150.00	0.88	66.67	2.00
12 Configuration management	1000.00	1750.00	0.08	5.71	1.00
13 Integration	2000.00	250.00	0.53	40.00	0.50
14 User documentation	750.00	70.00	1.89	142.86	1.33
15 Unit testing	150.00	150.00	0.88	66.67	6.67
16 New function testing	350.00	150.00	0.88	66.67	2.86
17 **Regression testing**	1000.00	150.00	0.88	66.67	1.00
18 Integration testing	700.00	175.00	0.75	57.14	1.43
19 System testing	2500.00	200.00	0.66	50.00	0.40
20 **Repackaging**	2500.00	300.00	0.44	33.33	0.40
21 Field (beta) testing	3000.00	225.00	0.59	44.44	0.33
22 Acceptance testing	2500.00	200.00	0.66	50.00	0.40
23 Quality assurance	2000.00	150.00	0.88	66.67	0.50
24 Installation and training	5000.00	350.00	0.38	28.57	0.20
25 Project management	750.00	100.00	1.32	100.00	1.33
Cumulative results	218.18	6.94	19.02	1496.48	4.58

is too coarse to really understand software economics with enough precision to plan significant process improvements.

Tables 11.13 and 11.14 are generic in nature and do not assume any particular methodology or formal process.

However, there are also specific activity patterns associated with object-oriented (OO) development, with information engineering (IE), with rapid application development (RAD), and with a host of methodologies and software processes. The fundamental concept of activity-based costing can still be used, even though the activities and their patterns will vary, as will the specific values for the activities in question.

Rules of Thumb for Year-2000 Repair Estimation

Accurate cost estimating for year-2000 repairs is extremely complicated, because it involves software repairs, database repairs, test library repairs, tool purchases, hardware upgrades, contracts, and a host of other factors.

The following rough rules of thumb are derived from our clients and from other year-2000 resource reports, and are merely starting points that year-2000 managers can use until they begin to substitute their own data. For a more complete picture of year-2000 costs on a global basis, refer to the author's book *The Year 2000 Software Problem* (Jones 1997).

- Assume that 50 percent of the applications in your portfolio are dormant and do not need repairs, and that 50 percent are active applications which do need repairs.

- Assume that the source code is missing or uncompilable for about 15 percent of the aging legacy applications in your active portfolio, so either replacement or object-code repairs will be necessary.

- Assume that dead code, comments, and blank lines in your applications, for which you should not have to pay repair costs, total 30 percent of the total volume of physical lines in every application undergoing year-2000 repairs.

- Assume that the amount of code in your active applications that needs repair is about 5 percent of the total code measured in physical lines.

- Assume that your initial year-2000 software repairs, based on the number of lines of code needing repair (5 percent of the total), will proceed at a rate of 1500 lines of code per month, or 15 function points per month.

- Assume that you would need at least 1 full-time year-2000 repair specialist for every 5000 function points (roughly 500,000 source code statements) in your active portfolio if you had 36 months in which to accomplish year-2000 repairs. As the elapsed time passes, your staffing needs are rising accordingly. If you start year-2000 repairs in 1998, you will need one full-time specialist for about every 3000 function points (roughly 300,000 source code statements) in your active portfolio.

- In the absence of data point metrics, assume that your database repairs and your source code repairs will take roughly the same amount of effort; that is, one month of database repair work for every month of software repair work.

- Assume that true date field expansion for databases is so complex that alternatives, such as data duplexing or bridging, are the most common strategies for year-2000 database repairs.

- Assume that testing and regression testing your year-2000 repairs will each take about 60 percent as much effort as the repairs themselves, and will take more than half of the calendar time.

- Assume that approximately 10 percent of your initial defect repairs will be bad fixes, and hence those repairs will have to be done over.

- Assume that 10 percent of your year-2000 test cases are incorrect and will need to be repaired themselves.

- Assume that your year-2000 repairs will be about 95 percent efficient, but that 5 percent of the total possible number of year-2000 hits will be missed before the end of the century, and will not be discovered until after the year-2000 itself.

- Assume that year-2000 repairs will degrade application performance and throughput by 10 to 20 percent unless performance monitoring, careful tuning, and extensive testing are used to regain performance.

- If your enterprise average for software compensation levels is about $60,000 per year, expect your year-2000 repair costs to run from $0.25 to $1.00 per physical line of code. This is equivalent to $25 to $100 per function point.

- If you outsource your year-2000 repairs to a contractor, expect your year-2000 repair costs to run from $1.00 to $2.50 per physical line of code. This is equivalent to $100 to $250 per function point.

- Assume that year-2000 software repairs will require about four months of effort on the part of every software professional in your enterprise. Expressed another way, assume that year-2000 repairs will cost about 30 percent of your annual software budget.

- Assume that the damages, litigation, and recovery costs from unrepaired year 2000 problems in software and databases will cost about $3 to more than $20 per physical line of code. This is equivalent to between $30 and $2000 per function point.

- Do *not* assume that any cost data about year-2000 repair costs will be accurate for your enterprise unless the data uses the same compensation rates, burden rates, and work-pattern assumptions that your enterprise uses. This is an obvious fact and does not require a specific source of information.

Once again, these rules of thumb are not safe for serious year-2000 estimating purposes, but are included for the benefit of year-2000 project managers and enterprise executives who are seeking some kind of general guidance about potential resources for dealing with the year-2000 issues.

Rules of Thumb for Eurocurrency Conversion

The European Union has scheduled the implementation of a unified currency for Western Europe, the *euro,* to begin on January 1, 1999 and then expand until 2002. Of course, this puts the euro-conversion work in conflict with the much more serious year-2000 repair work. It is hard to imagine a more serious public policy mistake than scheduling the second-largest software project in history so that it conflicts with the largest software project in history.

This is such a serious error that it lowers the probability that the European Union will be able to finish either its year-2000 repairs or their Eurocurrency work on schedule. In fact, the timing of the Eurocurrency work is bad enough to lead to a recession in Western Europe. However, politicians seem to know and care little about technical problems, so Europe is going to have to live with their errors.

The following rules of thumb are only approximate and are not a replacement for a full-featured cost-estimating tool.

- Assume that the amount of code in your active applications that needs Eurocurrency modification repair is about 7 percent of the total code of financial applications, measured in physical lines.

- Assume that your initial euro-conversion work, based on the number of lines of code needing repair (7 percent of the total), will proceed at a rate of 1200 lines of code per month, or 12 function points per month.

- Assume that you would need at least 1 full-time euro-conversion specialist for every 2500 function points (roughly 250,000 source code statements) in your active portfolio if you had 24 months in which to accomplish euro-conversion repairs. As the elapsed time passes, your staffing needs are rising accordingly. If you start euro conversion in 1998, you will need 1 full-time specialist for about every 1500 function points (roughly 150,000 source code statements) in your active portfolio.

- In the absence of data point metrics, assume that your database updates and your source code updates will take roughly the same amount of effort; that is, one month of database repair work for every month of software repair work.

- Assume that testing and regression testing your euro-conversion work will each take about 45 percent as much effort as the repairs themselves, and will take just under half of the calendar time.

- Assume that approximately 10 percent of your euro updates will be bad fixes, and hence those repairs will have to be done over.

- Assume that 10 percent of your euro-conversion test cases are incorrect and will need to be repaired themselves.

- Assume that your Eurocurrency conversion work will be about 90 percent efficient, but that 10 percent of the total possible number of euro hits will be missed and will not be discovered until the software fails or produces erroneous results.

- If your enterprise average for software compensation levels is about $60,000 per year, expect your euro-conversion costs to run from $0.50 to $1.25 per physical line of code. This is equivalent to $50 to $125 per function point.

- If you outsource your euro updates to a contractor, expect your costs to run from $1.15 to $2.75 per physical line of code. This is equivalent to $115 to $275 per function point.

- Assume that Eurocurrency conversion repairs will require about four months of effort on the part of every software professional in your enterprise. Expressed another way, assume that euro-conversion repairs will cost about 30 percent of your annual software budget.

- Do *not* assume that any cost data about Eurocurrency costs will be accurate for your enterprise unless the data uses the same compensation rates, burden rates, and work-pattern assumptions that your enterprise uses. This is an obvious fact and does not require a specific source of information.

Summary and Conclusions

Simple rules of thumb are never very accurate, but continue to be very popular. The main sizing and estimating rules of thumb and the corollary rules presented here are all derived from the use of the function point metric. Although function point metrics are more versatile than the older lines-of-code metric, the fact remains that simple rules of thumb are not a substitute for formal estimating methods.

These rules of thumb and their corollaries have a high margin of error and are presented primarily to show examples of the kinds of new project management information that function point metrics have been able to create. At least another dozen or so rules of thumb also exist for other predicting phenomena, such as annual software enhancements, optimal enhancement sizes, software growth rates during maintenance, and many other interesting topics.

Software estimating using rules of thumb is not accurate enough for serious business purposes. Even so, rules of thumb continue to be the most widely used estimating mode for software projects. Hopefully, the limits and errors of these simplistic rules will provide a motive for readers to explore more accurate and powerful estimation methods, such as commercial estimating tools.

Manual estimating methods using work sheets that drop down to the level of activities, or even tasks, are more accurate than simple rules of thumb, but they require a lot more work to use. They also require a lot more work when assumptions change.

Replacing work sheets with automated spreadsheets eliminates some of the drudgery, but neither worksheets nor spreadsheets can deal with some of the dynamic estimating situations, such as creeping user requirements or improvements in tools and processes during project development. This is why automated estimating tools usually outperform manual estimating methods.

Software measurement and estimation are becoming mainstream issues as software becomes a major cost element in corporations and government organizations. In order to use collected data for process improvements or industry benchmark comparisons, it is important to address and solve three problems:

1. Leakage from cost-tracking systems must be minimized or eliminated.

2. Accurate normalization metrics, such as function points, are needed for benchmarks to be economically valid.

3. Cost and effort data needs to be collected down to the level of specific activities to understand the reasons for software cost and productivity-rate variances.

Activity-based software costing is not yet a common phenomenon in the software industry, but the need for this kind of precision is already becoming critical.

The literature on manual estimating methods is the largest of almost any project management topic, with a number of books offering algorithms, rules of thumb, or empirical results taken from historical data.

Among the early authors who published useful information on manual estimation methods prior to 1985 can be found Alan Albrecht, the inventor of function point metrics (Albrecht 1981); Dr. Barry Boehm, author of the *Software Engineering Economics* (Boehm 1981); and Tom DeMarco, author of the classic *Controlling Software Projects* (DeMarco 1982).

Among the authors who use IFPUG-defined U.S. function points for estimation can be found Dr. Brian Dreger (Dreger 1989), the coauthors David Garmus and David Herron (Garmus and Herron 1995), and the present author (Jones, 1995, 1996a, 1997a). Also in the function point genre are the IFPUG counting manuals, which provide the basis for many U.S. estimation methods. Among the authors using function point metrics for estimating object-oriented projects can be found Dr. Tom Love (Love 1993).

In the United Kingdom, Charles Symons's work on estimation using Mark II function points is widely cited (Symons 1991), although U.S. and U.K. function points differ by about 20 percent in some cases.

An interesting author whose work includes estimation and data using both lines-of-code and function point metrics is Stephen Kan (Kan 1995); his book is an interesting bridge between the function point and lines-of-code camps. William Roetzheim also uses both function points and LOC metrics for estimation algorithms (Roetzheim and Beasley 1998), and Dr. Howard Rubin deals with estimation using both LOC metrics and function point metrics, as well (Rubin and Robbins 1997).

The authors whose estimation models are based primarily on lines-of-code metrics include the well-known Watts Humphrey of SEI fame (Humphrey 1995); Bob Grady of Hewlett-Packard (Grady 1992); and Larry Putnam (Putnam 1992), the chairman of QSM.

Among the authors who deal with the special problems of year-2000 estimation can be found various consulting groups, such as the Gartner Group (Hall and Schick 1996), Leon Kappelman (Kappelman 1997), Dick Lefkon (Lefkon 1997), and the present author (Jones 1997b). However, the year-2000 literature is exploding, and more than 25 books on year-2000 issues will be in print before the end of 1998.

References

Albrecht, A. J.: "Measuring Application Development Productivity," *Proceedings of the Joint IBM/SHARE/GUIDE Application Development Symposium,* October 1979, reprinted in Capers Jones, *Programming Productivity—Issues for the Eighties,* IEEE Computer Society Press, New York, 1981, pp. 34–43.

Boehm, Barry: *Software Engineering Economics,* Prentice Hall, Englewood Cliffs, N.J., 1981.

Brooks, Fred: *The Mythical Man-Month,* Addison-Wesley, Reading, Mass., 1974, rev. 1995.

DeMarco, Tom: *Controlling Software Projects,* Yourdon Press, New York, ISBN 0-917072-32-4, 1982.

Dreger, Brian: *Function Point Analysis,* Prentice Hall, Englewood Cliffs, N.J., 1989.

Garmus, David, and David Herron: *Measuring the Software Process: A Practical Guide to Functional Measurement,* Prentice Hall, Englewood Cliffs, N.J., 1995.

Grady, Robert B.: *Practical Software Metrics for Project Management and Process Improvement,* Prentice Hall, Englewood Cliffs, N.J., ISBN 0-13-720384-5, 1992.

———, and Deborah L. Caswell: *Software Metrics: Establishing a Company-Wide Program,* Prentice Hall, Englewood Cliffs, N.J., ISBN 0-13-821844-7, 1987.

Hall, B., and K. Schick: *The Year 2000 Crisis—Estimating the Cost,* Application Development and Management Group (ADM) Research Note, Gartner Group, Stamford, Conn., Key Issue Analysis KA 21-1262, 1996 (periodically revised).

Humphrey, Watts: *A Discipline of Software Engineering,* Addison-Wesley, Reading Mass., 1995.

IFPUG Counting Practices Manual, Release 3, International Function Point Users Group, Westerville, Ohio, April 1990.

———, Release 4, International Function Point Users Group, Westerville, Ohio, April 1995.

Jones, Capers: *Critical Problems in Software Measurement,* Information Systems Management Group, ISBN 1-569011-000-9, 1993a.

———: *Software Productivity and Quality Today—The Worldwide Perspective,* Information Systems Management Group, ISBN 1-569011-001-7, 1993b.

———: *Assessment and Control of Software Risks,* Prentice Hall, Englewood Cliffs, N.J., ISBN 0-13-741406-4, 1994.

———: *New Directions in Software Management,* Information Systems Management Group, ISBN 1-569011-0011-2.

———: *Patterns of Software System Failure and Success,* International Thomson Computer Press, Boston, ISBN 1-850-32804-8, 1995.

———: *Applied Software Measurement,* 2d ed., McGraw-Hill, New York, ISBN 0-07-032826-9, 1996a.

———: *Table of Programming Languages and Levels* (8 Versions from 1985 through July 1996), Software Productivity Research, Burlington, Mass., 1996b.

———: *Software Quality—Analysis and Guidelines for Success,* International Thomson Computer Press, Boston, 1997a.

———: *The Year 2000 Software Problem—Quantifying the Costs and Assessing the Consequences,* Addison-Wesley/Longman, Reading, Mass., ISBN 0-201-30964-5, 1997b.

Kan, Stephen H.: *Metrics and Models in Software Quality Engineering,* Addison-Wesley, Reading, Mass., ISBN 0-201-633311-6, 1995.

Kappelman, Leon: *Year-2000 Problem,* International Thomson Computer Press, Boston, ISBN 1-85302-913-3, 1997. (Includes a CD-ROM of year-2000 vendors.)

Lefkon, Dick: *Year 2000: Best Practices for the Y2K Millennium,* Association of Information Processing Professionals (AITP)/SIG Mainframe, New York, 1997.

Love, Tom: *Object Lessons,* SIGS Books, New York, ISBN 0-9627477 3-4, 1993.

Rethinking the Software Process, CD-ROM, Miller Freeman, Lawrence, Kans., 1996. (This CD-ROM is a book collection jointly produced by the book publisher, Prentice Hall, and the journal publisher, Miller Freeman. It contains the full text and illustrations of five Prentice Hall books: Capers Jones, *Assessment and Control of Software Risks*; Tom DeMarco, *Controlling Software Projects*; Brian Dreger, *Function Point Analysis*; Larry Putnam and Ware Myers, *Measures for Excellence*; and Mark Lorenz and Jeff Kidd, *Object-Oriented Software Metrics.*)

Putnam, Lawrence H.: *Measures for Excellence—Reliable Software on Time, Within Budget,* Yourdon Press/Prentice Hall, Englewood Cliffs, N.J., ISBN 0-13-567694-0, 1992.

Robbins, Brian, and Howard Rubin: *The Year 2000 Planning Guide,* Rubin Systems, Pound Ridge, N.Y., 1997.

Roetzheim, William H., and Reyna A. Beasley: *Best Practices in Software Cost and Schedule Estimation,* Prentice Hall PTR, Upper Saddle River, N.J., 1998.

Rubin, Howard: *Software Benchmark Studies for 1997,* Howard Rubin Associates, Pound Ridge, N.Y., 1997.

Symons, Charles R.: *Software Sizing and Estimating—Mk II FPA (Function Point Analysis),* John Wiley & Sons, Chichester, U.K., ISBN 0-471-92985-9, 1991.

Chapter

12

Automated Estimates from Minimal Data

Among software project managers, having full information about a software project to create an initial cost is a rarity. Estimates are demanded by both clients and senior management before the requirements are known, before the team is assembled, and before the tools and methods are selected. The majority of early cost estimates have to be produced in a hurry with less than complete information about the factors that will influence the outcome of the project.

This chapter discusses some of the estimating features that commercial estimating-tool vendors have developed to allow useful estimates from imperfect and partial information. These early estimates have the advantage of being easy and very quick to create. Often, from the time an estimating tool is turned on until the estimate is finished is a matter of less than five minutes. Of course, no one can expect high precision from estimates that are based only on a few known factors.

Whether software cost estimation is performed manually or via automated means, it is still a complex technical activity that requires dealing with a large number of rules and with many kinds of adjustment factors. However, with estimating tools many of the factors are assigned default values or can be inherited from similar projects.

The commercial software-estimating tools are usually calibrated so that *average* performance is the assumed value for all settings and adjustments. This means that when you are creating an initial cost estimate and don't yet know all of the information needed for high precision, you can simply accept the average settings for such topics as assignment scopes, available work hours, or team experience levels and create preliminary estimates using these default settings until more accurate information is known later.

To give a framework for discussing the sequence of activities that must be completed when constructing an initial software cost estimate for a project, three stages can highlight the basic sequence of software-estimating activities:

Stage 1: Recording administrative and project information

Stage 2: Preliminary sizing of key deliverables

Stage 3: Producing a preliminary cost estimate

As a general sequence describing the way early software estimation works, these three stages apply both to software cost estimation tools and to manual software cost estimation methods.

As we move through the stages of preparing software cost estimates, note that the same factors that influence the outcome of the estimate are also key factors for software measurement purposes. This explains why so many of the software cost estimating vendors are also measurement experts and have benchmarking services: You cannot build an effective software cost estimating tool without substantial historical data from which to derive the algorithms.

For any kind of software cost estimate, some kind of input information has to be provided by the users, sizing of various deliverables must occur, adjustments to basic estimates for experience and complexity and other factors must be made, and all of the pieces of the estimate must be totaled at the end to produce the final estimate.

We'll begin our tour of automated estimating by examining the minimum kinds of information needed to do preliminary, early estimates. Then we will move to the more extensive kinds of information needed to calibrate and adjust the estimate for optimal precision.

Let us now consider the three software cost estimating stages in sequence, starting with the minimum amount of information that has to be provided in order to allow at least a rough estimate using commercial software-estimating tools.

Stage 1: Recording Administrative and Project Information

Since software cost estimates will have a life expectancy that can run from weeks up to several years, the first kind of information that needs to be recorded is administrative information, such as the name of the project for which the estimate is being prepared, and some information about the participants in the estimating process so that they can be contacted if needed.

Most items of administrative information are straightforward and readily available and are known even before the requirements begin. A few optional topics are exceptions, however, such as recording a *standard industry classification* or identifying the starting date of the project in question.

Following are samples of some of the questions used by the author and other vendors of commercial software cost estimating tools to collect basic administrative information when performing software cost estimates.

This administrative information is optional in terms of getting some kind of estimate out of a commercial software-estimating tool. However, to keep one project's estimate from being confused with another, at least the names of the project, the project manager, and the person preparing the estimate should be recorded. Also, this kind of administrative information will allow an estimate to be picked up after a period of weeks or months without confusion as to which project it deals with.

Software Estimating Administrative Information

Security level   _____

Project name   _____

Estimate number   _____

Estimating tool   _____

Project description   _____

Standard industry classification (SIC)   _____

Organization   _____

Location   _____

Project manager   _____

Estimate completed by   _____

Current date (mm/dd/yyyy)   _____

Project start (mm/dd/yyyy)   _____

Desired delivery (mm/dd/yyyy)   _____

The *security level* is optional for many estimates, but is an important item for military and classified software projects. Security may also have relevance for software estimates in competitive situations, such as bids, or for software estimates being prepared in the course of litigation, such as tax cases or breach of contract cases.

The *project name* is included for convenience in telling one estimate from another, since any large company may have dozens of ongoing software projects in any given month.

The *estimate number* is useful in distinguishing early estimates from later estimates. For example, an estimate numbered *1* for a particular project is not likely to be as firm as an estimate numbered *6* for the same project.

For estimates that are being prepared for litigation, it is important to record the name of the *estimating tool.* Also, some large enterprises have as many as half a dozen different software cost estimating tools available, so it is useful to record which tool is used for which estimate. Of course, most of the commercial software cost estimating tools identify themselves on their printed outputs and also on screen, but some in-house estimation tools may not do this.

The *project description* is optional and, of course, does not affect the outcome of a project at all. Its purpose is to facilitate separating one project from another if a company does a lot of similar kinds of work. For example, as the Eurocurrency conversion work expands throughout the world, project descriptions might be used for such purposes as "Euro conversion for project A," "Euro conversion for project B," and so on.

The *standard industry classification (SIC) code* is optional, but can be very useful. The SIC coding method was developed by the U.S. Department of Commerce to assist in performing statistical studies of trends within industries. Many large-scale economic studies utilize SIC codes, including software benchmarking studies.

There are two-digit and four-digit versions of the SIC code, with the four-digit form giving greater granularity. The full set of SIC codes and their definitions are available from the Government Printing Office in Washington, D.C., or even as advertisements from such companies as Dun and Bradstreet.

The purpose of recording the optional SIC codes is to allow benchmark comparisons of your projects with similar projects within the same industry. Although use of the SIC code is purely optional, if you want to compare your projects against a knowledge base of projects from within your own industry, then use of the SIC code is recommended.

Some of the two-digit SIC codes for industries that tend to have large populations of software personnel and, hence, large inventories of software applications for benchmarking purposes are shown in Table 12.1.

TABLE 12.1   Two-Digit Standard Industry Classification (SIC) Codes for Industries that Use Software Extensively

13	Oil and gas extraction
20	Food and kindred products
21	Tobacco products
27	Printing, publishing, and allied industries
28	Chemicals and allied products
29	Petroleum refining and related industries
33	Primary metal industries
35	Industrial and commercial machinery
36	Electronic and electrical equipment and components
37	Transportation equipment
40	Railroad transportation
42	Motor freight transportation
45	United States Postal Service
44	Water transportation
45	Transportation by air
47	Transportation services
48	Communications
49	Electric, gas, and sanitary services
50	Wholesale trade—durable goods
51	Wholesale trade—nondurable goods
53	General merchandise stores
60	Depository institutions
61	Nondepository credit unions
62	Security and commodity brokers and dealers
63	Insurance carriers
64	Insurance agents and broker services
67	Holding and other investment offices
70	Hotels and lodging
73	Business services
80	Health services
87	Engineering, accounting, and research services
91	Executive, legislative, and general government
92	Justice, public order, and courts
93	Public finance, taxation, and monetary policy
94	Human resource programs
95	Environmental programs
96	Economic programs
97	National security

Examples of some of the four-digit SIC codes for industries that contain significant software personnel populations and large inventories of applications are shown in Table 12.2.

Although the four-digit form of SIC encoding is more precise, usually the two-digit form is easier to use and provides an adequate basis for benchmark comparisons.

The *current date* in most commercial software cost estimating tools is automatically taken from the internal date field of the computer

TABLE 12.2   Four-Digit Standard Industry Classification (SIC) Codes for Industries that Use Software Extensively

3571	Electronic computers
3572	Computer storage devices
3575	Computer terminals
3613	Switchgear and switching apparatus
3661	Telephone and telegraph apparatus
3711	Motor vehicles and car bodies
3721	Aircraft
3724	Aircraft engines and engine parts
3761	Guided missiles and space equipment
4512	Air transportation, scheduled
4812	Radiotelephone communication
4813	Telephone communication
4911	Electric services
5045	Computers, peripherals, and software
5311	Department stores
6011	Federal Reserve banks
6021	National commercial banks
6022	State commercial banks
6211	Security brokers and dealers
6311	Life insurance
6321	Accident and health insurance
7371	Custom computer programming services
7372	Prepackaged software
7373	Computer integrated system design
7374	Data processing and preparation
7375	Information retrieval services
7376	Computer facilities management
8062	General medical and surgical hospitals
8742	Management consulting services

itself, although users can, of course, change this if they wish. Sometimes 15 or 20 "what if" estimates may be run for the same project on the same day, so it can even be useful to record the time of day for a specific estimate. Some commercial software cost estimating tools will utilize the current date for the start date of the project unless the user inputs a specific start date.

A very important piece of information for software cost estimating is the *project start date* of the project being estimated. However, the start date of a project is also one of the most tricky and elusive pieces of information in the entire domain of software cost estimating.

The reason that determining the start date of a project is ambiguous is because quite a lot of informal exploratory work can take place before it is decided that a software application should be built or is required.

Ideally, the start date reflects the date on which effort on the formal requirements gathering commenced. However, in real-life estimating, the best that can usually be achieved is a more or less arbitrary starting point selected by the project manager, a client, or technical staff members who pick a date that approximates the kickoff point for the project being estimated.

If the start date is omitted as a specific input, the usual default by commercial software cost estimating tools is to use the current day's date as the starting date.

The *desired delivery date* for the software project is optional but can also be very useful. If the delivery date predicted by the estimating tool is much longer than the desired delivery date, then obviously the project has to be speeded up, cut down in size, or both.

Some commercial software cost estimating tools include an *advice* mode. If the predicted date for the completion of the project is significantly later than the desired delivery date, the estimating tool will offer suggestions about approaches that might bring the two closer together or make them identical.

A software taxonomy: Defining the nature, scope, class, and type of project

After recording basic (and largely optional) administrative information about the project being estimated, the next kind of input information to consider is the fundamental issue of taxonomy, that is, "What kind of a software project is this one?"

Software projects come in a wide variety of classes and types—systems software, embedded software, civilian projects, military projects, and a host of other designations.

Each of these variations in terms of the class and type of the application can affect the outcome of the project in real life, and hence must be considered when performing a software cost estimate.

At least some kind of information about the nature of a software project must be supplied, in order to achieve estimates of even marginal precision. It is also important to record this information for measurement purposes.

In the domain of defining a taxonomy for pinning down the exact form of a software project, there are many variations from estimating tool to estimating tool. In the estimating tools which the author has designed and built, four terms are used to differentiate software projects into families or categories with enough precision to use the results for software-estimation purposes:

1. Project nature

2. Project scope

3. Project class

4. Project type

The term *project nature* refers to whether the application being estimated is a new project, an enhancement to existing software, a maintenance project, or a conversion project.

This question is important when using automated estimating tools, because different factors will affect each choice. For example, estimating an enhancement project requires dealing with the size and complexity of an existing software application.

The term *project scope* refers to whether the estimate is to be performed for something small, such as a module, or something large, such as a system. This question is also important when using automated estimating tools, because here, too, different factors will be evaluated for large systems that may not be present when estimating small projects.

The term *project class* refers to the business arrangement under which the project is to be built; that is, whether it will be built for internal purposes or for delivery to clients, or whether it will be built to civilian or military norms.

The term *project type* refers to the nature of the software itself; that is, whether the software will be an information system, systems software, or embedded software that might reside on board an airplane, or something else.

Although in real life there may be unlimited possibilities for these four terms, when using an automated estimating tool it is necessary to limit the choices to those that the rules of the estimating tool are capable of evaluating.

The most convenient way of keeping the choices within the bounds

PROJECT NATURE: _____

1. New program development
2. Enhancement (new functions added to existing software)
3. Maintenance (defect repair to existing software)
4. Conversion or adaptation (migration to new platform)
5. Reengineering (reimplementing a legacy application)
6. Package modification (revising purchased software)

recognized by a software-estimating tool is to use multiple-choice questions. The following questions on project nature are fairly typical of the range covered by software-estimation tools.

The *nature* question occurs early in the sequence of gathering information, because it is used to guide the choice of further questions later on. For example, if the project being estimated is identified as an *enhancement,* then obviously information will be needed about the existing software that is being updated.

The second topic of importance is the *scope* of the project, or whether the estimate is being prepared for something small, like a module, or something large, like a major software system.

The *scope* topic is not a substitute for detailed size information, but serves to narrow the set of downstream factors that need to be evaluated. For example, if a project is identified as a *system,* then activities such as architecture, user documentation, and system testing are likely to be performed.

PROJECT SCOPE: _____

1. Subroutine
2. Module
3. Reusable module
4. Disposable prototype
5. Evolutionary prototype
6. Standalone program
7. Component of a system
8. Release of a system
9. New system (initial release)
10. Compound system (linked integrated systems)

On the other hand, if the project is identified as a *module,* then many system-level activities, such as architecture, system testing, and creation of a user's guide, are not likely to occur.

The next topic of concern is a very important one for software cost estimating purposes: the *class,* or business rationale, for the project being estimated. The software class is one of the factors that has real-life implications as well as implications in software cost estimating.

As a general rule, the further down the class list a project is placed, the more expensive it becomes and the greater the proportion of costs associated with the production of paper documents becomes.

Also, the set of projects identified as *external* differ in many important ways from the set of projects identified as *internal.* The external projects are designed to be delivered to customers or clients, and, hence, often have more extensive testing and more complete sets of user documentation.

Also, the set of external projects are much more likely to end up in some kind of litigation or arbitration should major quality flaws or other deficiencies slip out into production. The class of an application is very important for both measurement and estimation purposes.

Consider the implications of the class parameter on real-life software cost elements. For the first class on the list, *personal programs,* there may be no written requirements, no specifications, no user doc-

PROJECT CLASS: _____

1. Personal program, for private use
2. Personal program, to be used by others
3. Academic program, developed in an academic environment
4. Internal program, for use at a single location
5. Internal program, for use at a multiple location
6. Internal program, developed by external contractor
7. Internal program, with functions used via time sharing
8. Internal program, using military specifications
9. External program, to be put in public domain or on the Internet
10. External program, leased to users
11. External program, bundled with hardware
12. External program, unbundled and marketed commercially
13. External program, developed under commercial contract
14. External program, developed under government contract
15. External program, developed under military contract

umentation, and no project paperwork of any kind, and the entire costs of the project may be devoted to coding and debugging.

For the last class on the list, *military contract software,* the production of paper documents will absorb more than 50 percent of the total cost of building the application, while coding costs will usually be less than 20 percent.

There are other important assumptions that can be derived from the class parameter. For example, the class of *internal software projects* usually has smaller and less sophisticated user manuals than the class of *external software projects.*

Another significant piece of information that needs to be recorded is the *type* of software, or whether the software is real-time, embedded, or perhaps even a hybrid project consisting of multiple categories of software under the same system umbrella.

The type parameter is a very troubling one and also is quite volatile. Many new kinds or types of software projects tend to appear, and it is tough work for estimating vendors to stay current with all possible types. For example, as this book is being written, a fairly new type, the World Wide Web application, is exploding through the software world. Ten years ago this type did not even exist, and now it is becoming a major category.

The type parameter is significant in evaluating the kind of quality-control approaches that are likely to be associated with the software projects. Before a new type parameter can be added to a software cost estimating tool, enough projects of that type must be measured so that estimating algorithms can be developed and refined.

As can be seen, the general rankings of the nature, scope, class, and type parameters more or less follow the pattern of the Richter scale for evaluating earthquake power. In other words, the larger numbers have more serious consequences than the smaller numbers.

Also, the combination of nature, scope, class, and type parameters provides a useful *signature* for browsing a cost-estimation knowledge base and selecting similar projects that can be used as a starting point for sizing by analogy or even as a jumping-off place for performing a rough early version of the current estimate.

To leave software for a moment and consider other human activities where approximation and preliminary estimates occur, think of the stages of purchasing an automobile or building a home. For example, consider the differences in Case X and Case Y for purchasing an automobile.

If your criteria for purchasing an automobile approximates Case X, then you can probably acquire one for less than $15,000. However, if your criteria are similar to Case Y, you will no doubt have to spend more than $30,000 and possibly more than $50,000.

PROJECT TYPE: _____

1. Nonprocedural (generated, query, spreadsheet)
2. World Wide Web application
3. Batch applications program
4. Interactive applications program
5. Interactive GUI applications program
6. Batch database applications program
7. Interactive database applications program
8. Client/server applications program
9. Scientific or mathematical program
10. Systems or support program
11. Communications or telecommunications program
12. Process-control program
13. Trusted system
14. Embedded or real-time program
15. Graphics, animation, or image-processing program
16. Multimedia program
17. Robotics, or mechanical automation program
18. Artificial intelligence program
19. Neural net program
20. Hybrid project (multiple types)

For hybrid projects:

Primary type:_____   Secondary type:_____

	Case X	Case Y
Nature	Used automobile	New automobile
Class	U.S. manufacture	German manufacture
Type	4 cylinders; economy	8 cylinders; luxury
Scope	2-door coupe	4-door station wagon

Simply placing your choices into a taxonomy of possibilities is enough to understand the probable cost ranges for the kinds of automobiles you are interested in. There is a great deal of useful information contained in a well-formed taxonomy, and for software cost estimating the ability to slot a proposed project into the right combination of nature, class, type, and scope is sufficient to estimate the probable costs and schedules within tolerable boundaries.

However, when you actually set out to purchase an automobile you need more than just general information. You need to examine the specific automobile that you have selected, and probably have a mechanic examine it also.

In addition, you have to negotiate with a specific dealer, and you have to reach final agreement on any options that you select, such as leather seats, upgraded stereo equipment, special suspension, and the like.

Software cost estimating is similar in concept. Simply knowing the nature, scope, class, and type can give you a useful range of costs and schedules for a project. But in order to deal with the exact schedule and costs for a specific software application with a unique set of features and a unique development team, more information is necessary.

From a real-life standpoint, consider the huge differences in costs and schedules that are likely to be found between the following two combinations of software estimating input parameters, even if nothing else is known about the projects except these four topics:

	Case A	Case B
Project name	Travel expenses	Gun Control System
Project nature	1 (new program)	1 (new program)
Project scope	4 (disposable prototype)	9 (new system)
Project class	1 (personal program)	15 (military contract)
Project type	1 (nonprocedural)	14 (embedded software)

Although there is not yet enough information to produce a formal cost estimate, it is obvious that Case B is going to cost a lot more than Case A. Without even knowing any more details than the combinations of nature, scope, class, and type, we can already draw some useful inferences.

For example, it is probable that Case A will be less than 50 function points or 5000 source code statements in size, since more than 95 percent of programs identified as *personal* and *prototypes* are below this size.

Case B, on the other hand, will probably be larger than 5000 function points or 500,000 source code statements in size, since more than 50 percent of military applications identified as *systems* are above this size range.

Further, it is also obvious that Case A is going to be developed in a way that will differ in many important ways from that of Case B. For example, Case B will no doubt follow various military development standards, such as DoD 2167A or DoD 498, while Case A may follow no standards of any kind.

Not only that, but we can begin to extract similar projects from our cost-estimation database in order to evaluate them as potential templates for use in estimating the current project.

We can also begin to see why manual software cost estimating is a complex activity that is easy to get wrong, and rather difficult to get right. The permutations of the 6 nature questions, 8 scope questions, 15 class questions, and 20 type questions lead to 14,400 possible combinations. Each of these 14,400 possibilities will have a characteristic set of activities, methods, languages, and tools that can further impact the results of a cost estimate.

And we have not yet even started to consider other important topics, such as the size of the application, its complexity, the rate at which requirements are likely to change, and the experience levels of the development team!

There is now another important piece of information to consider: the *project goals* of the project as given to the project manager by the clients or by higher management.

This factor is very important in real life, and hence is important to know when performing software cost estimates, also. Six varieties of goals are found for software projects, but unfortunately Goal 2, or *shortest schedule,* is perhaps the most common even though it is one of the most dangerous of all.

When using automated software estimating these six goals exert a considerable impact on estimating assumptions, as follows:

- For Goal 1, or *standard estimate,* normal staffing complements and no excessive schedule pressure are assumed.

- For Goal 2, or *shortest schedule with extra staff,* there is an implied assumption that staffing complements will be expanded by perhaps a ratio of 2 to 1. More subtle, there is also an assumption that management does not know or understand much about software quality, so such activities as formal inspections will probably be absent or truncated. This goal would often be found on "good enough"–style projects, and sometimes on rapid application development projects.

PROJECT GOALS: _____

1. Find the standard estimate of schedule, staff, and quality.
2. Find the shortest development schedule with extra staff.
3. Find the lowest effort with reduced staff.
4. Find the highest quality with normal staff.
5. Find the highest quality with shortest schedule.
6. Find the highest quality with least effort.

- For Goal 3, or *lowest effort,* there is an assumption that this is a background project with no great rush to have it completed. Therefore, the smallest staffing complement noted on similar projects will be assumed.

- Goal 4, or *highest quality,* combines the assumption of normal staffing complements with the assumption that quality is significant, and hence assumes that such approaches as specifications and inspections will be followed more or less rigorously.

- Goal 5, or *highest quality with shortest schedule,* is not a bad choice, and is often used for outsource projects, systems software, and commercial software. This goal assumes additional staffing, but does not assume that quality-control approaches will be bypassed or abbreviated.

- Goal 6, or *highest quality and least effort,* seldom occurs because schedule pressure is so endemic in the software industry. When it does occur, the assumptions are for a reduced staffing complement coupled with significant attention to quality control. This goal is sometimes used after a major round of downsizing, when many personnel have been laid off more or less concurrently.

Work patterns, staff salaries, and overhead rates

Most commercial software cost estimating tools provide default values for such topics as compensation, burden rates, and work patterns. However, the range of possible values for each of these factors is very broad, so it is normal to make adjustments for local conditions.

This kind of information is very important for software cost estimating purposes. In real life as well as in setting up an estimating tool, it is important to know if the personnel will be available full time or will have other commitments.

It is also important to know typical work patterns, in terms of the length of the normal working week, normal working day, and vacations; number of holidays; and so forth.

Most software cost estimating tools provide some kind of default values for these assumptions, but defaults and average values should really be replaced by actual local information if it is available.

In companies that use commercial software-estimating tools, basic information about work patterns and compensation rates can be inherited from project to project or can be set up as corporate default values for use by all estimates within a given company, or at least within a given location, where such attributes are likely to be more or less constant from project to project.

The need for accurate data on these topics is vital for estimates of critical projects where unpaid or paid overtime is likely to be needed. There can be a tremendous difference in both schedules and costs between a project that is averaging 10 hours of unpaid technical staff overtime every week and a project of the same size and kind with no overtime, or even with part-time personnel who divide the work day with other projects.

This kind of information is also very important for estimates that are international, since work patterns vary widely between North America, Europe, the Pacific Rim, and South America.

For example, overtime is very common in the United States and Japan, but is much less common in Germany and Canada. Indeed, in Germany some computer facilities close down on weekends and even shut down the power to their computer systems, so that weekend work is almost impossible.

Examples of typical software cost estimating information dealing with personnel costs, work patterns, and overtime follow.

The *availability* factor deals with whether project personnel will be fully assigned to the current project or will be splitting their time among multiple projects.

Exempt is the term used by the U.S. Bureau of Labor Statistics for salaried personnel who do not receive overtime payments. Most U.S.

Staff availability: _____
(Default = 100%)

Exempt technical staff: _____
(Default = 100%)

Average work week: _____
(Default = 5 days)

Work hours per day: _____
(Default = 8.0)

Effective work hours per day: _____
(Default = 6.0)

Overtime hours per week: _____
(Default = 0 hours)

Work days per year: _____
(Default = 220)

Overtime premium pay: _____
(Default = 50%)

Average salary (monthly):   _____
(Default = $5,000)

software technical personnel fall into this category, and also tend to work rather long weeks. Personnel who are paid on an hourly basis and do receive overtime pay are termed *nonexempt*.

The *work week* parameter is very significant for international cost estimates. For example, the normal U.S. work week consists of 5 days of 8 hours duration, or 40 hours in all. The normal Japanese work week, on the other hand, consists of 5.5 days of 8 hours duration, or 44 hours in all. The normal Canadian work week consists of 5 days but only 7 hours duration, or 35 hours in all, although the Canadian work week can vary between summer and winter.

The *work hours per day* parameter deals with the nominal amount of time during which employees are expected to be present and available for work assignments. However, in real life most of us don't actually work that amount of time on a daily basis.

The *effective work hours per day* parameter deals with the amount of effective time available, once lunch periods, coffee breaks, and other nonwork activities are backed out.

The *overtime hours* parameter is a key factor for dealing with project schedules and also project costs. In spite of the importance of this parameter, it is often ignored or set to zero value, when in fact extensive overtime occurs on many software projects.

The *work days per year* parameter is very significant for international estimates, since the number of public holidays and vacation days varies widely from country to country. Although the nominal work year in the United States is about 220 days, the nominal work year in much of Western Europe is only about 200 days due to much longer vacation periods.

The *overtime premium pay* parameter is the adjustment to base pay rates for normal, scheduled overtime by nonexempt employees. Overtime can become very complicated, and sometimes will have different rates on holidays from normal weekday rates, and Sundays may also have different rates from Saturdays.

The *average salary* parameter is really an oversimplification used primarily for early software cost estimates before the staff complement is fully known. This parameter is simply the average monthly compensation rate for all project personnel, including both managers and technical staff members.

The phrase *burden rate* refers to the costs for taxes, medical benefits, building rents, utilities and a host of other indirect items that are needed to keep a company running. These costs are usually applied on top of staff compensation, and the total is then used for contracts and cost-estimating purposes. The range of burden rates is very wide, and can run from less than 15 percent for companies operating out of small home offices to more than 300 percent for large defense contractors.

The *burdened compensation* parameter refers to the sum of salary expenses plus administrative expenses that must be factored into the cost estimate.

The *currency* parameter is important for international cost estimates, because, for example, the values of Australian, Canadian, and American dollars are not the same. The currency parameter is now being updated in many commercial software cost estimating tools in order to support the new unified European currency, which will be phased in over several years, beginning on January 1, 1999.

The work pattern and compensation information is an example of the kind of data that is often inherited from other projects, using the ability to construct templates offered by many software estimating tools.

Stage 2: Preliminary Sizing of Key Deliverables

We're now almost at the point where we can provide a rough or preliminary estimate for the project, but before we can do this we need to determine at least the approximate size of the project.

Size determination has long been one of the most difficult and troublesome aspects of software cost estimating, although technical advances over the last 20 years have made sizing easier and more accurate than in the early days of the industry.

Modern software cost estimating tools support a variety of sizing methods, including but not limited to the following:

1. Size supplied by users as explicit inputs

2. Size approximations based on scope, class, and type

3. Size approximations based on function points

4. Size approximations based on statistical reconstruction

5. Sizing by analogy with previously measured projects

6. Size approximations based on business situations

7. Size approximations based on Monte Carlo simulations

8. Size approximations based on physical lines of source code

9. Size approximations based on logical source code statements

Software project sizing provided by users

The oldest method used by software cost estimating tools for dealing with size was to ask that size information be provided by the users as an explicit input, in the form of the estimated volume of source code.

This method was common in the software-estimating tools that came out in the 1970s, such as PRICE-S, SLIM, and COCOMO, and it is still supported in more recent software cost estimating tools, such as SPQR/20, CHECKPOINT, and Knowledgeplan, although advanced sizing logic is now available, too.

Many of the older software cost estimating tools had a required input parameter for sizes that dealt with source code volumes, usually in the form of noncommentary code statements or the common variant, source code statements in groups of 1000 identified by the letter K. (Thus, an application of 10,000 source code statements in size could be entered directly as 10,000 statements, or could be entered using the abbreviated form of 10K.)

Although many modern estimating tools now include sizing logic and can help the user to determine project sizes, all of them still allow users to input an explicit size value if they wish to do so. Most commercial estimating tools permit the size to be expressed in terms of function points, source code volumes, or both. Indeed, many modern software cost estimating tools can convert size between function points and source code statements in either direction.

Of course, for size information using source code to be used for estimating purposes, it is also necessary to know the programming languages involved. Therefore, a corollary piece of information would be to identify the languages for the project, usually by means of some kind of checklist of the languages supported by the estimating tool.

Today these checklists run up to more than 500 languages, but the earlier software cost estimating tools usually supported between 10 and 30 programming languages.

The language tables are usually listed both alphabetically and in order of the *level* of the programming languages. Although the concept of a language *level* is somewhat ambiguous, a method developed by the author and his colleagues within IBM circa 1965 has become widely used in software cost estimating tools.

The original IBM concept of language levels was based on the number of statements in basic assembly language that might be required to encode the same function as a single statement in some other language.

Thus, under the IBM level concept, COBOL and FORTRAN were both *level 3* languages, because it took roughly three statements in assembly language to perform the same function as one statement in either COBOL or FORTRAN.

After the function point metric was put into the public domain by IBM in 1978, software-sizing methods began to include both function points and lines-of-code (LOC) metrics. That is, the language level concept began to include the number of source code statements required to encode one function point as well as the number of assembly statements required to replicate a statement in the target language.

By 1985, software-estimating tools began to appear that could accept size information entered using either lines of code or function points, and the tool itself would convert data in both directions. This was made possible by a technique called *backfiring,* which was developed via empirical observations of the number of source code statements required to encode one function point in various languages.

The backfiring method is almost as old as the function point metric itself, and indeed some of the early studies that included both source code counts and function point counts were published by Allan Albrecht, the inventor of function point metrics.

In spite of the long history of the backfiring approach and its wide usage, this method has been underreported in the software metrics literature and has essentially been ignored by metrics organizations, such as the International Function Point Users Group (IFPUG) and the metrics research group at the Software Engineering Institute (SEI).

The development of the backfiring methodology meant that size information could initially be stated either in terms of source code counts or function point counts, based on the preference of the estimating-tool users. Typical generic size questions might resemble the following:

With question sets such as the preceding, the user could supply partial information and the estimating tool would complete the missing elements. For example, a user who supplied only source code statement counts would also be able to see size expressed in terms of function points, and vice versa. However, a user would have to supply either source code size or function point size, because the backfire size

---

Software Application Size Assumptions

Programming language(s): _____

Application size in noncommentary source code statements: _____

Application size in physical lines of code: _____

Source code statements per function point: _____

Source code counting method: _____

Application size in function points: _____

Function point counting method: _____

conversion equations needed a starting point of one form or the other.

Because many estimating tools contain built-in sizing features, it is not absolutely necessary to provide size as an explicit input. However, all software cost estimating tools permit the user to input size, since user-supplied sizes may be known with high precision (even if this seldom occurs in real life).

If the application being estimated uses only a single programming language, then entering explicit size data is straightforward, if not always easy. However, about one-third of the applications in the United States and elsewhere use multiple programming languages. Indeed, sometimes as many as a dozen discrete languages can be found within the same application, although two-language pairs are far more common.

Mixed language applications are very common among all classes of software—systems, military, information systems, and commercial. Some of the more common programming language combinations include the following:

- Ada and CMS2
- Ada and Jovial
- Ada and assembly
- Basic and assembly
- Basic and C
- C and assembly
- C and C++
- + and assembly
- COBOL and database languages
- COBOL and PL/I
- COBOL and Query languages
- COBOL and RPG
- COBOL and SQL
- COBOL, SQL, and database languages
- Generators mixed with procedural languages

The presence of combinations of programming languages makes sizing using the LOC metric more complicated, but software-estimating tools now support mixed language sizing and also size conversions between source code volumes and equivalent function point totals in situations where as many as a dozen languages might be in use within the same application.

Although the methods for dealing with multiple programming languages vary from tool to tool, the following example of a mixed-language worksheet would not be uncommon. This sample worksheet shows an application of 500 function points that uses four different languages: COBOL, SQL, RPG II, and FOCUS.

Users of estimating tools cannot be expected to know the levels of programming languages nor the number of statements required to encode one function point. Therefore, the software cost estimating tools usually provide some kind of pull-down menu with this kind of information.

The information on the ratios of source code statements to function points are sometimes expressed in terms of maximum, average, and minimum values, or sometimes in terms of only a single default value. In either case, users can adjust the ratio in response to local conditions or in situations where they feel the default value may be incorrect.

Users can input any of the factors that they know, and the estimating tool will solve for the unknown factors. For example, users could supply size in KLOC, and the estimating tool would produce function points, or vice versa.

The four languages shown here are merely an example of how mixed-language applications are dealt with in terms of sizing. Essentially any combination involving any number of programming languages can be dealt with by modern software cost estimating tools. Note that both source code and function point metrics are now supported by the great majority of software-estimating tools, so sizing can be based on either metric or on both concurrently.

It is possible to do the same kind of conversion between source code

---

Multiple Language Size Aggregation

Number of languages: 4

Function point method: IFPUG Version 3.4

Language	KLOC	Language levels	Source statements per function point	Function points
COBOL	15.00	3.00	106.67	141
SQL	1.00	25.00	12.80	78
RPG II	10.00	5.00	64.00	156
FOCUS	5.00	8.00	40.00	125
Total	31.00	5.16	62.00	500

and function points for mixed languages using a pocket calculator if the language levels are known, but one of the advantages of automated software cost estimating tools is that they can do this set of calculations in a fraction of a second, while it takes human beings a great deal longer even if they know all of the language levels.

With automated software estimating tools, factors such as the ratio of source code statements to function points are normally provided by the tools themselves, using pull-down lists or tables similar to Tables 12.3 and 12.4.

Table 12.3 illustrates a small sample of 15 programming languages listed in alphabetical order, with both the level and the approximate number of source code statements per function point illustrated.

Tables 12.3 and 12.4 use IFPUG Version 3.4 as the basis of the expansion factors. Adjustments to such a table for IFPUG Version 4.0 or for other variants, such as the British Mark II function point method, are also possible, but they require somewhat different ratios of source code to function points. This rather complex issue will be dealt with further on in the book.

The information in Tables 12.3 and 12.4 merely represents typical languages and values that can be found in dozens of commercial software-estimating tools. Many other kinds of information may also be

TABLE 12.3 Software Language Levels in Ascending order of Alphabetic Sequence

Language	Level	Source code statements per function point
Ada 83	4.50	71.12
Ada 95	6.00	53.33
Algol	3.00	106.67
Assembly (basic)	1.00	320.00
Assembly (macro)	1.50	213.33
C	2.50	128.00
C++	5.00	64.00
COBOL	3.00	106.67
FORTRAN	3.00	106.67
Jovial	3.00	106.67
Objective C	12.00	26.67
PowerBuilder	20.00	16.00
Smalltalk	15.00	21.33
SQL	25.00	12.80
Visual Basic	10.00	32.00
Average	7.63	92.35

TABLE 12.4   Software Language Levels in Ascending Order of Level or Statements per Function Point

Language	Level	Source code statements per function point
Assembly (basic)	1.00	320.00
Assembly (macro)	1.50	213.33
C	2.50	128.00
Algol	3.00	106.67
COBOL	3.00	106.67
FORTRAN	3.00	106.67
Jovial	3.00	106.67
Ada 83	4.50	71.12
.C++	5.00	64.00
Ada 95	6.00	53.33
Visual Basic	10.00	32.00
Objective C	12.00	26.67
Smalltalk	15.00	21.33
PowerBuilder	20.00	16.00
SQL	25.00	12.80
Average	7.63	92.35

shown, such as the range of possible values for each language, the number of projects in the sample for each language, complexity assumptions, and so forth.

The same set of 15 languages is shown in another format, listed in descending order by language level, in Table 12.4.

Both alphabetic and numeric sequences are supported by modern software-estimating tools, and the tables of languages and dialects can now top 500 listings.

In addition, users of software cost estimating tools also have the ability to modify the language tables by adding languages of their choice, or by changing the default values for the levels of programming languages that are contained in the table.

A surprisingly large number of companies have developed unique, proprietary languages which only they use. For example, the ITT corporation developed a variant of PL/I for electronic switching systems, called *ESPL/I,* which was only used within ITT. Many other companies have also created unique languages which they alone utilize.

Over and above the 500 or so programming languages that are available in commercial form, such as C, COBOL, and Smalltalk, the author and his colleagues have encountered at least another 200 proprietary languages in the course of their assessment and benchmarking studies.

Proprietary languages are hard to deal with in the context of software cost estimation, because their levels or the numbers of source code statements per function point are seldom known, and the proprietary languages are not included as standard choices in the estimating tools. However, about 99 percent of these proprietary languages are actually minor variants to *public* languages, such as PL/I, so it is practical to assume that the levels of the public and private languages are in the same general range.

(Proprietary languages will also be troublesome in another context—year-2000 date repairs, because there will be no automated tools available.)

Software cost estimation developers and software-estimating tools must be flexible and open-ended when dealing with programming languages, because new languages tend to be announced at roughly monthly intervals, and there are many proprietary languages as well.

Indeed, many of the more common programming languages used today did not even exist 10 years ago, although some languages, such as COBOL and FORTRAN, have been in continuous use for more than 30 years.

As the end of the century approaches, a host of newer languages have joined the traditional languages, so that applications in such recent languages as ABAP/4, C++, Eiffel, Forte, Java, Realizer, and Visual Basic comprise a significant percentage of modern applications.

A quick analysis of the most common programming languages at 10-year intervals between 1967 and 1997 illustrates the rapid evolution of programming languages, as shown in Table 12.5.

Although the backfiring method for converting size between source code statements and function points is useful, it is not highly accurate unless the ratios of source code statements to function points are adjusted for specific instances. However, the convenience is so great that it has become the most common way of deriving function point totals for the following kinds of software situations:

TABLE 12.5   Most Common Programming Languages from 1967 to 1997

Year	Languages
1967	Assembly
1977	COBOL and FORTRAN
1987	COBOL, C, and Ada
1997	Visual Basic and Java

- Aging legacy applications
- Small enhancements
- Maintenance or defect repairs

In addition, the backfiring method is very useful for normalizing data using common metrics, function points, and lines of code.

It should be noted that the range of possibilities for assigning levels to any language varies widely. Taking COBOL as an example, although the average value is about 106.7 source code statements in the procedure and data divisions to encode one function point, the range runs from 57 statements per function point up to perhaps 165 statements per function point when all counts follow the SPR method of using logical statements.

Because language levels are derived from empirical observations and programming styles can vary from person to person, most software cost estimating tools allow users to override or adjust the levels to match the characteristics of local styles and conventions. Estimating tools also allow users to add other languages that may not be known to the estimating tool, such as customized dialects or proprietary languages used only within a specific company.

Although size data supplied by users is quite common, modern estimating tools now offer a variety of size approximation methods.

Automated sizing approximation methods

While size data supplied by users is fairly common, it often happens that project managers, who are the most common users of estimating tools, don't have enough information to determine the size of the application.

In this situation, the user could guess at the size, but guesses are seldom satisfactory. Modern commercial software cost estimating tools provide a wide variety of sizing approximation methods that can be used for early estimates before requirements are firm. Not every software-estimating tool supports every method, but some form of size approximation is a common feature.

The sizing problem is usually dealt with in a series of sequential operations. The first step in the sequence is to determine the size of the overall application in terms of a major metric, such as function points, source code statements, or both.

Once this overall size is determined, the sizes of a variety of other artifacts and deliverables can be projected, including but not limited to the following:

- The sizes of specifications

- The sizes of user manuals
- The number of test cases to be created
- The probable numbers of defects or bugs

The sizing of these secondary items will be discussed later in the book. However, before the secondary topics can be considered it is necessary to deal with the primary size topics of function point totals and source code volumes.

Sizing based on scope, class, and type.   Recall that the SPR scope, class, and type checklists are organized using more or less the same principle as the Richter scale for earthquakes; that is, the larger numbers have more significance than the smaller numbers.

This property can be utilized to produce very early size approximations in function points before almost any other facts are known about the software project in question.

Admittedly, this crude form of sizing is far too inaccurate for serious cost-estimating purposes, but it has the virtue of being usable before any other known form of sizing is possible.

To use the scope, class, and type taxonomy for guessing at the approximate size of the software, it is only necessary to sum the list values for the scope, class, and type and raise the total to the 2.35 power. This calculation sequence will yield a rough approximation of function points, assuming that IFPUG Version 4 is the counting method.

Table 12.6 summarizes the scope, class, and type lists in numerical order.

To utilize this rough sizing method, it is only necessary to sum the numeric values from the three lists and raise the total to the 2.35 power. For example, assume you are building an application with the following three attributes:

Scope $\doteq$ 5 (single program)

Class = 4 (single location)

Type = 8 (client/server)

Sum = 17

Raising 17 to the 2.35 power yields a value of 779, which can be utilized as a very rough approximation of function points, assuming the IFPUG Version 4 rules.

Later in this chapter a pair of estimating examples will be presented: Case A and Case B. *Case A* is a small personal application developed as a prototype. Applying the preceding approximation method to

TABLE 12.6   Examples of Scope, Class, and Type Values

Scope		Class		Type	
1	Disposable prototype	1	Individual software	1	Nonprocedural
2	Evolutionary prototype	2	Shareware	2	Web applet
3	Module	3	Academic software	3	Batch
4	Reusable module	4	Single location	4	Interactive
5	Single program	5	Multilocation	5	Interactive GUI
6	System component	6	Contract	6	Batch database
7	Major system	7	Time sharing	7	Interactive database
8	System release	8	Military services	8	Client/server
		9	Internet	9	Mathematical
		10	Leased software	10	Systems
		11	Bundled software	11	Communications
		12	Marketed	12	Process control
		13	Outsourced	13	Trusted system
		14	Government contract	14	Embedded
		15	Military contract	15	Image processing
				16	Multimedia
				17	Robotics
				18	Artificial Intelligence
				19	Neural net
				20	Hybrid: mixed

Case A, the personal software project, the following size can be derived:

Scope = 1 (prototype)

Class = 1 (personal program)

Type = 1 (nonprocedural)

Sum = 3

Raising 3 to the 2.35 power gives a value of 13, which can serve as a rough approximation of the application's function point total.

Case B is a military application: a shipboard gun control system. Applying this same method to Case B, the military software project discussed later in this chapter, the results are as follows:

Scope = 7 (system)

Class = 15 (military contract)

Type = 14 (embedded)

Sum = 36

Size = 4542 function points (sum raised to the 2.35 power)

This very early size approximation method is not recommended for any purpose other than estimating when almost nothing is known about a software project, and some form of sizing is needed to complete a rough estimate.

It is technically possible to develop a rule-based method for early sizing that would utilize the scope, class, and type information in a more sophisticated way than simply summing the scores and raising the results to a power.

However, extracting useful information using rule-based logic goes beyond simple calculations that can be performed on a pocket calculator, although some of the other approximations are rule-based methods that use scope, class, and type information.

Sizing based on function point ranges.   There are several forms of size approximation based on the usage of function point metrics in a more subjective way than a formal function point analysis.

These approximation methods do not require that users have enough information at hand to actually perform accurate counts of the real function point totals of the applications in question.

An early form of function point sizing that utilized approximate ranges instead of exact counts was developed in 1985 as a feature of the SPQR/20 software-estimating tool.

This approximation methodology only asked that the user select an approximate range for each of the function point methods, and then the tool itself would narrow down the choices based on nature, class, and type logic, as follows.

To use this form of approximation, the user would simply select one of

Probable Values for Function Point Input Parameters				
	None	<10	11–25	26–50	>50
Inputs	1	2	3	4	5
Outputs	1	2	3	4	5
Logical Files	1	2	3	4	5
Inquiries	1	2	3	4	5
Interfaces	1	2	3	4	5

the five integer values from 1 through 5, and the estimating tool would examine the choices and select a value for the factors in question.

Since this method has been in use for more than 10 years, it has been utilized hundreds or even thousands of times. When comparing the early approximation results against final sizes, after function points have actually been counted, the approximated values tend to be on the low side.

Analysis reveals that the difference between the initial approximation and the final size often vary because of creeping requirements, or features added later in the development cycle after the first or early estimate is performed. Interestingly, the approximate size estimate and the first actual count of function points tend to be rather close, but after that point creeping requirements need to be dealt with.

The realization that creeping user requirements need to be included in software size estimating methodology is an important topic, and has led to some useful methods for approximating the rate at which requirements creep is likely to occur, which will be discussed later.

While this rough approximation method from the mid 1980s has the virtue of simplicity and ease of use, it is obvious that the range of uncertainty is rather broad. However, this approximation method is intended only for use before the requirements of a project are far enough along to enable any kind of more formal function point analysis.

Sizing based on function point reconstruction.   A second form of early approximation based on function point logic was developed for SPR's CHECKPOINT estimating tool in 1989, although it can also be performed manually if historical data is readily available.

This form of approximate sizing from function point metrics is based on the existence of a knowledge base of projects within the estimating tool itself. This second form of approximation assumes that users might know some of the function point information, but not all of it. By examining similar projects within the knowledge base, it becomes possible to reconstruct the missing function point elements using the statistics of similar projects.

This second approximation method is based on pattern-matching concepts. For software applications of significant size ranges, such as those larger than 1000 function points, there is a natural sequence during the requirements phase in which the elements of function point counting are uncovered.

The output types are usually the first item known or defined during the requirements phase, while the inquiry types are often the last. Table 12.7 shows the usual sequence.

Suppose you were concerned with creating a preliminary estimate for a software project that has the set of known attributes following,

TABLE 12.7   Normal Sequence of Function Point Discovery

Function point element	Normal sequence of enumeration	Normal chronology from start of project
Outputs	Usually known first	Within the first month
Inputs	Usually known second	Within two months
Interfaces	Usually known third	Within three months
Logical files	Usually known fourth	Within four months
Inquiries	Usually known last	Within five months

Case A

Project name	New Account Entry
SIC code	60 (depository Institutions)
Start date	January 6, 1997
Burdened cost	$7500
Project goals	1 (normal effort)
Project nature	1 (new program)
Project scope	5 (standalone program)
Project class	5 (internal, multiple locations)
Project type	8 (client/server)
Language	PowerBuilder
FP method	IFPUG Version 4
Project size	?
External inputs	?
External outputs	30
External inquiries	?
Internal logical files	?
External interface files	?

---

shown for Case A, but not yet enough information to attempt a formal function point analysis.

However, at this point in the requirements cycle a need for 30 kinds of outputs has been identified.

Surprisingly, although only the number of outputs has been enumerated, this partial information is enough to produce a preliminary size estimate by analysis of projects that share the same kinds of overall attributes, such as nature, scope, class, and type, and that also have about 30 external outputs.

In fact, so long as any one of the attributes is known, then the missing attributes can be created by statistical analysis of similar applica-

Statistical Reconstruction of Missing Function Point Elements

Function types	Number		Weight		Raw total
External inputs	35	×	4	=	140*
External outputs	30	×	5	=	150
External inquiries	45	×	4	=	180*
Internal logical files	10	×	10	=	100*
External interfaces	5	×	7	=	35*
Raw total					605*
Complexity adjustment					105%
Adjusted function points					636*

*Omitted values synthesized from similar projects.

tions. Should the user know two or more of the missing attributes, the accuracy of the preliminary size estimate can improve to acceptable levels.

By aggregating other projects in the knowledge base that have the same signatures in terms of nature, scope, class, and type and averaging their function point elements, it is possible to create a *synthetic* size estimate that might resemble the above, although this particular example is hypothetical and merely represents what might occur.

This method of approximation works reasonably well for projects that plan to use function point metrics but are simply too early in defining requirements to be able to derive accurate counts.

But there are many projects where neither the project managers nor the technical staff are familiar with function points, and they may not have a clue as to any of the function point parameters at all. Obviously, this form of approximation is not effective for such projects.

However, the next form of approximation, *sizing by analogy,* can be utilized regardless of whether function points or source code metrics (or neither) constitute the starting point.

This method can also be performed manually, but it requires access to a significant amount of historical data for similar projects that can be scanned.

Sizing by analogy.   One of the conveniences of automated estimating tools is that their built-in knowledge bases can ease some of the more difficult aspects of software-cost estimation.

Size approximation by analogy is based on browsing a catalog of similar projects and seeking examples similar to the one being estimated as the starting point for size analysis. Sizing by analogy is an excellent example of how estimation tools can ease a tricky problem.

Sizing by analogy is the last of the approximation methods that will be discussed, and it is the most useful and potentially the most accurate of any of the approximate sizing methods.

Any software cost estimation and/or measurement tool that keeps a directory of projects already estimated or measured can assist in performing at least a rudimentary form of sizing by analogy.

However, in order to make the sizing task easy, the tool should also offer a summary list of projects with helpful identifying information, such as the type of project and the business purpose. The list in Table 12.8 is derived from the SPR historical data files and illustrates the kind of information needed to make sizing by analogy convenient.

This list covers only a small set of generic projects, simply to illustrate some of the kinds of information that are useful when browsing through sets of software projects. Of course, software-estimating tools can also provide subsets of projects to cut down on the amount of work needed to find useful analogies.

It would obviously be tedious to browse through huge lists of 1000 or more projects, so using search logic to subset the overall listing into more manageable segments is a more convenient approach.

For example, a user might restrict the search logic to include only those projects with selected characteristics, such as the following set:

1. MIS project types
2. Business purposes
3. COBOL programming language

On the other hand, another user might wish to restrict the search logic to a totally different set of criteria, such as the following:

1. Military project types
2. Defense purposes
3. Ada 83 programming language

Although the current discussion deals only with using similar projects as the basis for sizing new projects, the same fundamental concept of starting with projects stored in an estimating tool's knowledge base can also be used to construct estimation templates that include not only size data but also attribute and adjustment factors. Building templates from historical project data will be discussed more fully in the next section, which discusses detailed estimating methods.

Sizing by analogy need not be limited to a single project. It might be of interest to evaluate half a dozen or more similar projects and use the average size of this sample as the starting point for estimating a new project.

Several commercial software-estimation tools have built-in statistical features that can easily handle aggregation and averaging of sizes and other quantifiable data, and that can also produce standard deviations and other statistical information of possible value.

Table 12.8 illustrates a small generic sample of the kinds of information that are useful for sizing by analogy. Table 12.8 is sorted in alphabetic sequence by the "Purpose" column. The data in the table is simply for illustrative purposes to indicate the kinds of information that make sizing by analogy an interesting and useful method.

By contrast, Table 12.9 shows the same sets of projects sorted by the "Size, FP" column. It should be noted that the sizes indicated are rounded to integer values in order to fit the table onto a printed page.

The kinds of information shown in Tables 12.8 and 12.9 can, of course, be sorted by any column of interest, although sorting by class, purpose, language, and size is the most common approach for exploring this kind of information.

In order for the tables to fit on a printed page, some of the other kinds of information often displayed have been left out. For example, the level of the programming language is usually displayed, and the ranges of application sizes may also be shown if more than one kind of sample application is included for the same kind of product. Other kinds of useful information, such as SIC codes, are also not shown, in order to fit the needs of a printed page.

The data in these tables shows only a few samples of sizing by analogy, abbreviated for publication purposes. Larger collections, with hundreds or thousands of software projects, coupled with search logic tools to facilitate collecting the data into useful subsets is what makes sizing by analogy the most useful of the approximation methods.

Sizing the impact of creeping requirements.   One of the classic problems of software size estimation is that of *creeping requirements,* or new features added in middevelopment after the first software cost estimate has been created.

The software requirements gathering process can affect the rate at which requirements creep if methods of proven effectiveness are known. The most effective techniques for minimizing the disruptive effect of uncontrolled creeping requirements include the following:

1. Joint application design (JAD)

2. Prototyping of key features and outputs

TABLE 12.8 Approximate Sizes of Selected Software Applications

(Sizes based on IFPUG 4 and SPR logical statement rules)

Application	Type	Purpose	Primary language	Size, KLOC	Size, FP	LOC per FP
Airline Reservations	MIS	Business	Mixed	2,750	25,000	110.00
Insurance Claims	MIS	Business	COBOL	1,605	15,000	107.00
Telephone Billing	MIS	Business	C	1,375	11,000	125.00
Tax Preparation (Personal)	MIS	Business	Mixed	180	2,000	90.00
General Ledger	MIS	Business	COBOL	161	1,500	107.00
Order Entry	MIS	Business	COBOL/SQL	106	1,250	85.00
Human Resource	MIS	Business	COBOL	128	1,200	107.00
Sales Support	MIS	Business	COBOL/SQL	83	975	85.00
Budget Preparation	MIS	Business	COBOL/SQL	64	750	85.00
Graphics Design	Commercial	CAD	Objective C	54	2,700	20.00
IEF	Commercial	CASE	C	2,500	20,000	125.00
Visual Basic	Commercial	Compiler	C	375	3,000	125.00
IMS	Commercial	Database	Assembly	750	3,500	214.29
CICS	Commercial	Database	Assembly	420	2,000	210.00
WMCCS	Military	Defense	Jovial	18,000	175,000	102.86
Aircraft Radar	Military	Defense	Ada 83	213	3,000	71.00
Gun Control	Military	Defense	CMS2	225	2,336	107.00
Lotus Notes	Commercial	Groupware	Mixed	350	3,500	100.00
MS Office Professional	Commercial	Office tools	C	2,000	16,000	125.00
SmartSuite	Commercial	Office tools	Mixed	2,000	16,000	125.00
MS Office Standard	Commercial	Office tools	C	1,250	10,000	125.00
Word 7.0	Commercial	Office tools	C	315	2,500	126.00
Excel 6.0	Commercial	Office tools	C	375	2,500	150.00
Windows 95	Systems	Operating system	C	11,000	85,000	129.41
MVS	Systems	Operating system	Assembly	12,000	55,000	218.18
UNIX V5	Systems	Operating system	C	6,250	50,000	125.00
DOS 5	Systems	Operating system	C	1,000	4,000	250.00
MS Project	Commercial	Project management	C	375	3,000	125.00

TABLE 12.8 (*Continued*)

(Sizes based on IFPUG 4 and SPR logical statement rules)

Application	Type	Purpose	Primary language	Size, KLOC	Size, FP	LOC per FP
KnowledgePlan	Commercial	Project management	C++	134	2,500	56.67
CHECKPOINT	Commercial	Project management	Mixed	225	2,100	107.14
Function Point Control	Commercial	Project management	C	56	450	125.00
SPQR/20	Commercial	Project management	Quick Basic	25	350	71.43
5ESS	Systems	Telecommunication	C	1,500	12,000	125.00
System/12	Systems	Telecommunication	CHILL	800	7,700	103.90
Total				68,669	542,811	126.51
Average				2,020	15,965	126.51

3. Quality function deployment (QFD)

4. Formal requirements inspections

5. Contractual penalties for late requirements

6. Automated configuration control tools

7. Software-estimating tools with creep-prediction features

8. Use of function point metrics during development

Fortunately, the advent of function point metrics allows the rate of creeping requirements to be measured directly. Recall that the function point sizes of software projects are normally enumerated four times during software development:

1. A rough function point approximation before requirements are complete

2. A formal function point sizing at the end of the requirements phase

3. A midcourse function point sizing at the end of the design phase

4. A final function point sizing at the end when the software is delivered

These four points of reference, coupled with other kinds of information, such as project schedules, allow the rate of requirements creep to be anticipated with reasonable, but not perfect, precision.

TABLE 12.9 **Approximate Sizes of Selected Software Applications**

(Sizes based on IFPUG 4 and SPR logical statement rules)

Application	Type	Purpose	Primary language	Size, KLOC	Size, FP	LOC per FP
WMCCS	Military	Defense	Jovial	18,000	175,000	102.86
Windows 95	Systems	Operating system	C	11,000	85,000	129.41
MVS	Systems	Operating system	Assembly	12,000	55,000	218.18
UNIX V5	Systems	Operating system	C	6,250	50,000	125.00
Airline Reservation	MIS	Business	Mixed	2,750	25,000	110.00
IEF	Commercial	CASE	C	2,500	20,000	125.00
MS Office Professional	Commercial	Office tools	C	2,000	16,000	125.00
SmartSuite	Commercial	Office tools	Mixed	2,000	16,000	125.00
Insurance Claims	MIS	Business	COBOL	1,605	15,000	107.00
ESS	Systems	Telecommunication	C	1,500	12,000	125.00
Telephone Billing	MIS	Business	C	1,375	11,000	125.00
MS Office Standard	Commercial	Office tools	C	1,250	10,000	125.00
System/12	Systems	Telecommunications	CHILL	800	7,700	103.90
DOS 5	Systems	Operating system	C	1,000	4,000	250.00
IMS	Commercial	Database	Assembly	750	3,500	214.29
Lotus Notes	Commercial	Groupware	Mixed	350	3,500	100.00
Visual Basic	Commercial	Compiler	C	375	3,000	125.00
Aircraft Radar	Military	Defense	Ada 83	213	3,000	71.00
MS Project	Commercial	Project management	C	375	3,000	125.00
Graphics Design	Commercial	CAD	Objective C	54	2,700	20.00
Word 7.0	Commercial	Office tools	C	315	2,500	126.00
Excel 6.0	Commercial	Office tools	C	375	2,500	150.00
KnowledgePlan	Commercial	Project management	C++	134	2,500	56.67
Gun Control	Military	Defense	CMS2	250	2,336	107.00
CHECKPOINT	Commercial	Project management	Mixed	225	2,100	107.14
Tax Preparation (Personal)	MIS	Business	Mixed	180	2,000	90.00
CICS	Commercial	Database	Assembly	420	2,000	210.00
General Ledger	MIS	Business	COBOL	161	1,500	107.00
Order Entry	MIS	Business	COBOL/SQL	106	1,250	85.00

TABLE 12.9 (*Continued*)
(Sizes based on IFPUG 4 and SPR logical statement rules)

Application	Type	Purpose	Primary language	Size, KLOC	Size, FP	LOC per FP
Human Resource	MIS	Business	COBOL	128	1,200	107.00
Sales Support	MIS	Business	COBOL/SQL	83	975	85.00
Budget Preparation	MIS	Business	COBOL/SQL	64	750	85.00
Function Point Control	Commercial	Project management	C	56	450	125.00
SPQR/20	Commercial	Project management	Quick Basic	25	350	71.43
Total				68,669	542,812	126.51
Average				2,020	15,965	126.51

TABLE 12.10 Approximate Rate of Creeping Software Requirements

Delivered size, FP	Schedule, months	Planned size, FP	Creep size, FP	Percentage of requirements creep
1	1.00	1.00	0.00	0.00
10	2.51	9.50	0.50	5.00
100	6.31	92.00	8.00	8.00
1000	15.85	850.00	150.00	15.00
10000	39.81	6500.00	3500.00	35.00
100000	100.00	55000.00	45000.00	45.00

Table 12.10 shows the approximate rate at which software requirements creep for 6 size ranges an order of magnitude apart, from 1 function point through 1000 function points.

Table 12.10 illustrates typical scenarios where no concentrated effort has been applied to reducing the impact of creeping user requirements. In situations where effective requirements approaches are used, such as JAD sessions and requirements inspections, the rate of creeping requirements can be much lower than the data shown.

Of course, the opposite case may be true as well: The rate of creeping requirements growth may sometimes be *worse* than Table 12.10 indicates. This situation can be devastating for fixed-price contracts, and greatly troubling for any kind of schedule and cost-containment method.

In the absence of any other information, it can be assumed that software requirements will creep or grow at an average monthly rate of about 1 to 2 percent from the end of the requirements phase through the design and coding phases. This situation may be tolerable for applications with development schedules of less than 12 months, but for major systems with 3- to 5-year development cycles, the steady accumulation of unplanned requirements can be a major contributing factor to cost and schedule overruns.

Incidentally, changes in software project requirements can be negative as well as positive. It often happens that towards the end of the design or coding phases, when it becomes apparent that planned schedules will be missed, it may be necessary to defer some features to a follow-on release.

The combination of growth in unplanned requirements coupled with abrupt decisions to defer features to later releases are difficult problems even for sophisticated software cost estimating tools. Of course, these situations are difficult for any other kind of project management tool and for manual estimating methods, too.

Table 12.11 illustrates a typical pattern of both growth and deferral in function point totals for an application of a nominal 1000 function points at delivery with an 18-month development cycle.

Note that the growth pattern for function points illustrated by Table 12.11 represents the function point total as defined in the appli-

Table 12.11   Growth and Deferral Pattern of Function Point Volumes for an Application of 1000 Function Points

Month	Phase	FP per month	Cumulative FP	Percent per month
January	Requirements	250	250	25.0
February		350	600	35.0
March		350	950	35.0
April	Design	75	1025	7.50
May		38	1063	3.80
June		24	1087	2.40
July		45	1132	4.50
August	Coding	25	1157	2.50
September		18	1175	1.80
October		10	1185	1.0
November		10	1195	1.0
December	Testing	5	1200	0.50
January		−200	1000	−20.0
February		0	1000	0.0
March		0	1000	0.0
April		0	1000	0.0
May		0	1000	0.0
June	Deployment	0	1000	0.0
Total		1000	1000	100

cation's requirements and specifications. The function point metric is not an appropriate tool for monitoring the rate at which software applications are constructed, because software is not built one function point at a time.

Consider the analogy with *cost per square foot* or *cost per square meter* for dealing with the costs of building a new home. Costs per square unit are very useful for determining the approximate costs for building a house, but obviously homes are not constructed one square foot or square meter at a time.

An examination of Table 12.11 reveals some common but interesting trends. Note that at its peak in the month of December, the project is actually up to 1200 function points in total size.

At that point, it is suddenly realized that the project will miss its schedule severely, so it is decided to defer features which total 200 function points to a later release.

This combination of functional expansion and contraction is very common for applications in the 1000–function point size range and larger. In fact, our assessment and benchmarking studies indicate that less than 25 percent of projects larger than 1000 function points actually contain all of the intended features in the initial release.

Since creeping software requirements are an endemic problem for the software industry, modern software cost estimating tools can offer at least some assistance by predicting the probable volume of unplanned requirements and their consequences on schedules and costs.

During early estimating sessions, these creeping requirements predictions can either be ignored or can be added to the final estimate, based on the preference of the user of the estimating tool.

Once the programming languages and size of the application have been entered into a cost-estimating tool, there is enough information to produce a rough but useful software cost estimate.

However, to create a software estimate at this point, the size information must be provided by the user of the estimating tool. If size must be approximated or derived, then additional kinds of information will be needed, as will be shown later.

At this point, the estimating tool has knowledge of only 10 kinds of information: nature, scope, class, type, goals, programming language, burdened salary rate, size of the application in terms of either function points or source code (or both), and the start date of the project.

Therefore, early cost estimates will not include adjustments based on team experience, complexity, tools, methods, or any of several hundred factors that are known to influence the outcomes of software projects.

In spite of the need to further refine the estimate with adjustment factors, the fact that it is now possible to create a rough estimate using only 10 parameters is a useful feature of modern software cost estimating tools.

It should be noted as an important fact that the same parameters that are useful for early software cost estimating should also be recorded when projects are measured and historical data is collected.

In the context of using the estimate for comparison purposes, it is also useful to record the SIC code. This will facilitate comparing the estimate against similar projects from the same industry. The SIC code does not affect the outcome of an estimate, but does make it easier to do comparisons with like projects.

Stage 3: Producing a Preliminary Cost Estimate

Once the administrative data for a software project, the cost and burden-rate data, work-habit data, and user-supplied size data have been provided, there is enough information available to create a rough preliminary cost estimate.

This preliminary estimate based on minimal information cannot be very accurate, because none of the major adjustment factors have been dealt with. However, the fact that preliminary estimates at this point can be done at all is encouraging.

The early estimating situation brings to mind Samuel Johnson's observation made while looking at a dog that had been trained to walk on its hind legs: "It isn't done well, but it is surprising that it can be done at all."

Once the 10 basic inputs have been entered into a software cost estimating tool, it is very easy to create a preliminary estimate.

Usually it is only necessary to switch the tool from *input* mode to *estimate* mode. Some software cost estimating tools even support concurrent inputs and estimates, so that the effect of each new or changed input shows up at once in an immediate, real-time revision of the estimated results.

Consider the same two Cases A and B that were discussed earlier. The following example illustrates the minimum amount of 10 kinds of information needed to produce early software cost estimates for these two projects.

	Case A	Case B
Project Name	Travel Expenses	Gun Control System
SIC code	73 (Services)	97 (national security)
Start date	January 6, 1997	January 6, 1997
Burdened cost	$6000	$12,000
Project goals	1 (normal effort)	4 (highest quality)
Project nature	1 (new program)	1 (new program)
Project scope	1 (disposable prototype)	7 (major system)

	Case A	Case B
Project class	1 (personal program)	15 (military contract)
Project type	1 (nonprocedural)	14 (embedded software)
Language	Visual Basic	Ada 95
FP method	IFPUG Version 4	IFPUG Version 4
Project size	15 FP 480 LOC	250 KLOC (4688 FP)
Count method	SPR logical statements	SEI physical lines

Five of the 10 factors are always known even very early in the requirements phase, and only the start date, burdened salary rate, choice of programming languages, and the size of the application are problematic. The SIC code is not always readily known, but some software-estimating tools provide a pull-down list of these codes.

While all of the factors are of use, the factors that actually affect the numeric results of an estimate are the following:

1. Project goals
2. Project nature
3. Project scope
4. Project class
5. Project type
6. Project size

At this point, the user can actually create a rough preliminary estimate for both Case A and Case B. There is not much point in dropping down to a task-level estimate at this point, because none of the adjustment factors that can influence project outcomes, such as complexity, experience, tools, methods, processes, and the like, have yet been dealt with.

The usual mode of cost-estimating tools when presented with incomplete adjustment information is to assume that the project will be *average* in terms of the missing elements. That is, there will be no adjustments of any kind based on complexity, experience, or the other key adjustment parameters.

At this point, if the estimating tool is switched from *input* to *estimate* mode, a preliminary software cost estimate can be created from the minimum information that has been provided.

Table 12.12 illustrates Case A, which is a simple travel expense application produced as a prototype.

Although this project is a comparatively small one, the cost estimate still provides some useful information. For example, the esti-

TABLE 12.12   **Preliminary Estimate for Case A (Personal Software)**

	Project information		
Category	Input	Category	Input
Project name	Travel Expenses	Start date	January 6, 1997
Project class	Personal	Project scope	Disposable prototype
Project type	Nonprocedural	Project goals	Normal
Language	Visual Basic	SIC code	73 (services)
Monthly Rate	$6,000		
Source code size	480 (SPR logical statements)		
Function point size	15 (IFPUG 4)		

Activity	Start date	Completion date	Schedule, days	Staff	Effort, days	Cost
Coding	1/6/97	1/8/97	3	1	3	$818.18
Testing	1/7/97	1/9/97	2	1	2	545.45
Total/average	1/6/97	1/9/97	5	1	5	1363.64

Rate summary	
FP per month	66.00
LOC per month	2114.00
Cost per FP	$90.91
Cost per LOC	$2.84

mated cost of the project is $1363.64. This is not terribly expensive for custom software, but since it is possible to buy travel accounting software packages for less than $100, it may be that building a custom one might be construed as a waste of time. This simple example illustrates one of the useful properties of software cost estimating tools: They facilitate business decisions, such as make-or-buy analyses.

In fairness, it is highly unlikely that anyone would bother to run a small personal application through a commercial software cost estimating tool. However, commercial software cost estimating tools can handle projects as small as a 1-line maintenance change (equivalent to perhaps 1 one-hundredth of a function point) to as large as a 30 million–source code statement defense system (equivalent to perhaps 300,000 function points).

Now let us examine the estimate for Case B, which is a much larger and more serious undertaking. Recall that Case B is a military software project produced under military specifications and standards.

For larger projects such as this, the normal work metric would be *months* rather than *days*, although users can select whatever work metric they wish to see (i.e., hours, days, months, or years), and the estimating tool will handle the conversion automatically.

As can be seen when examining Table 12.13, this project will not be

TABLE 12.13   Preliminary Estimate for Case B (Military Software)

Project information			
Category	Input	Category	Input
Project name	Gun Control System	Start date	January 6, 1997
Project class	Military	Project scope	System
Project type	Embedded	Project goals	Highest quality
Language	Ada 95	SIC code	97 (national security)
Monthly rate	$12,000		
Source code size	250,000 (SEI physical lines)		
Function point size	4,688 (IFPUG 4)		

Activity	Start date	Completion date	Schedule, months	Staff	Effort, months	Cost
Requirements	1/6/97	6/20/97	6.13	19.00	116.50	$1,398,000
Prototype	2/6/97	7/27/97	6.35	10.00	63.50	762,000
Design	5/15/97	12/20/97	9.43	20.00	188.50	2,262,000
Critical design review	12/10/97	1/20/98	1.20	26.00	31.25	375,000
Coding	9/15/97	7/15/98	10.02	23.50	235.40	2,824,800
Code inspections	5/3/98	7/20/98	2.70	26.00	70.25	843,000
Testing	6/10/98	1/20/99	8.67	31.00	268.75	3,225,000
Independent verification and validation	10/2/98	2/12/99	4.71	7.00	33.00	396,000
Independent testing	11/1/98	1/27/99	2.96	8.00	23.70	284,400
Quality assurance	3/15/98	4/20/99	13.05	4.00	52.20	626,400
User documents	3/1/98	4/10/99	13.45	7.75	104.25	1,251,000
Management	/6/97	4/26/99	28.00	5.00	140.00	1,680,000
Total/average	1/6/97	4/26/99	28.00	15.60	1327.30	15,927,600

Rate summary	
FP per month	$3.53
LOC per month	188.35
Cost per FP	3397.53
Cost per LOC	63.71

a trivial one in terms of effort, schedules, and costs, even though all of the information is not yet at hand to refine the estimate.

The *latent* information derived merely from knowing the scope, nature, class, and type plus preliminary size data is quite enough to draw useful conclusions and generate a rough estimate.

Although only a few basic facts about both applications have been provided, the knowledge base and rules within the cost-estimating tool know that military projects utilize several activities that are rare or nonexistent in the civilian world, as follow:

1. Critical design reviews

2. Independent verification and validation

3. Independent testing

These three activities are applied to the estimate simply because the project is identified as a military project. If the estimate was to be produced for the same kind of application, but it was identified as a civilian project, then these three activities would not be automatically included.

Note that in Case A, size was originally provided by the user in the form of function points and was then converted into the equivalent size in terms of SPR logical source statements, using a backfiring utility function found within most commercial software estimating tools.

In Case B, size was originally provided in the form of SEI-style physical lines of code, or KLOC (units of 1000 LOC), and was then converted into the equivalent size in terms of function points, also using the backfiring size-conversion feature.

However, backfiring from physical lines is very problematic because individual programming styles vary so widely. For accuracy when backfiring, logical statement counts rather than physical line counts should be used whenever possible.

This form of bidirectional backfiring conversion between function point metrics and logical statement counts of software is a standard feature of perhaps 30 commercial software cost estimating tools and is rapidly becoming a universal project management approach.

Neither the estimate for Case A nor for Case B is very accurate at this point, but both are probably useful for considering the general effort, cost, and schedule situations for the projects in question.

Note also that both estimates were produced using minimal information and, hence, minimal time on the part of the project manager or person producing the estimate. Preliminary estimates of this kind can be created in less than a minute if the 10 basic facts for the projects being estimated are known and automated estimating tools are available.

Summary and Conclusions

Sizing approximations and preliminary cost estimates are not particularly accurate, but they are accurate enough for gross business decisions, such as whether to proceed with a project into the requirements phase, where more details will become available.

If preliminary estimates are used only as gates to determine whether projects should proceed or be terminated, they serve a useful purpose.

However, preliminary estimates using minimal information should definitely *not* serve as the basis for contracts, outsourcing agreements, or budgets for major projects.

In order to achieve a level of estimating accuracy suitable for important business decisions, many more factors need to be considered and included in the estimate. Actual software projects are built by real people, using tools and development processes that can affect the outcome of the project in significant ways. Here, too, general information can get the estimate started, but in order to achieve a satisfactory precision, a number of adjustments and refinements need to be made.

None of the approximation methods discussed thus far in this book are perfect or can offer great precision. But all are useful and have a place in software-cost estimation. However, early estimates using approximate information are only the beginning stage of software-cost estimation. Let us now explore how to refine the estimate by dealing with some of the more detailed sizing and adjustment factors.

The literature on early estimation and approximation is sparse, but is growing fairly rapidly under the influence of the usage of function point metrics. The authors who provide useful rules of thumb for early estimation can be divided into such sets as: (1) those who use lines-of-code metrics; (2) those who use function point metrics; (3) those who use both lines-of-code and function point metrics; and (4) those who use something else, which is a very mixed category including object-oriented metrics, Halstead software-science metrics, and a variety of other metrics, such as simply using number of personnel or number of work hours.

Among the LOC authors may be found Dr. Barry Boehm (Boehm 1981), Larry Putnam, and Ware Myers (Putnam 1992; Putnam and Myers 1997), Watts Humphrey (Humphrey 1995), and Bob Grady and Deborah Caswell (Grady 1992; Grady and Caswell 1987).

Among the authors who discuss estimation using function point metrics can be found Allan Albrecht (Albrecht 1984), Brian Dreger (Dreger 1989), David Garmus and his colleague David Herron (Garmus and Herron 1995), and many publications of the International Function Point Users Group (IFPUG 1990, 1995).

Also in the function point genre are a number of the present author's books (Jones 1993, 1994, 1995, 1996a, 1996b, 1997b), which apply function points to estimating schedules, effort, costs, quality, and even risks.

Also writing in the function point genre are the authors using function point variants, such as Charles Symons of the United Kingdom (Symons 1991) and Scott Whitmire, who uses a variation termed *3D function points* (Whitmire 1992).

Among the authors who discuss estimation using multiple metrics or both LOC and function points can be found Stephen Kan (Kan 1995), Dr. Howard Rubin (Rubin 1997), and William Roetzheim (Roetzheim and Beasley 1998). Also in this category can be found Tom DeMarco (DeMarco 1982, 1995) who uses function points, lines of code, and DeMarco *bang* metrics as the need applies.

Among the authors who use something else can be found those using various flavors of object-oriented metrics, Halstead software-science metrics, or local metrics used only within a single company. There is not enough empirical data within this genre to include many citations.

References

Albrecht, Allan: *AD/M Productivity Measurement and Estimate Validation,* IBM Corporation, Purchase, N.Y., May 1984.

Boehm, Barry: *Software Engineering Economics,* Prentice Hall, Englewood Cliffs, N.J., 1981.

DeMarco, Tom: *Controlling Software Projects,* Yourdon Press, New York, ISBN 0-917072-32-4, 1982.

———: *Why Does Software Cost So Much?,* Dorset House, New York, ISBN 0-932633-34-X, 1995.

Department of the Air Force, *Guidelines for Successful Acquisition and Management of Software Intensive Systems,* vols. 1 and 2, Software Technology Support Center, Hill Air Force Base, Utah, 1994.

Dreger, Brian: *Function Point Analysis,* Prentice Hall, Englewood Cliffs, N.J., ISBN 0-13-332321-8, 1989.

Galea, R. B.: The Boeing Company: 3D Function Point Extensions, V2.0, Release 1.0, Boeing Information Support Services, Seattle, Wash., June 1995.

Garmus, David, and David Herron: *Measuring the Software Process: A Practical Guide to Functional Measurement,* Prentice Hall, Englewood Cliffs, N.J., 1995.

Grady, Robert B.: *Practical Software Metrics for Project Management and Process Improvement,* Prentice Hall, Englewood Cliffs, N.J., ISBN 0-13-720384-5, 1992.

———, and Deborah L. Caswell: *Software Metrics: Establishing a Company-Wide Program,* Prentice Hall, Englewood Cliffs, N.J., ISBN 0-13-821844-7, 1987.

Humphrey, Watts S.: *Managing the Software Process,* Addison Wesley/Longman, Reading, Mass., 1989.

———: *A Discipline of Software Engineering,* Addison-Wesley, Reading, Mass., 1995.

IFPUG Counting Practices Manual, Release 3, International Function Point Users Group, Westerville, Ohio, April 1990.

———: Release 4, International Function Point Users Group, Westerville, Ohio, April 1995.

Jones, Capers: *SPQR/20 Users Guide,* Software Productivity Research, Cambridge, Mass., 1986.

————: *Critical Problems in Software Measurement,* Information Systems Management Group, ISBN 1-56909-000-9, 1993.

————: *Assessment and Control of Software Risks,* Prentice Hall, ISBN 0-13-741406-4, 1994.

————: *New Directions in Software Management,* Information Systems Management Group, ISBN 1-56909-009-2.

————: *Patterns of Software System Failure and Success,* International Thomson Computer Press, Boston, ISBN 1-850-32804-8, 1995.

————: *Applied Software Measurement,* 2d ed., McGraw-Hill, New York, ISBN 0-07-032826-9, 1996a.

————: *Table of Programming Languages and Levels* (8 Versions from 1985 through July 1996), Software Productivity Research, Burlington, Mass., 1996b.

————: *The Economics of Object-Oriented Software,* Software Productivity Research, Burlington, Mass., April 1997a.

————: *Software Quality—Analysis and Guidelines for Success,* International Thomson Computer Press, Boston, ISBN 1-85032-876-6, 1997b.

————: *The Year 2000 Software Problem—Quantifying the Costs and Assessing the Consequences,* Addison-Wesley, Reading, Mass., ISBN 0-201-30964-5, 1998.

Kan, Stephen H.: *Metrics and Models in Software Quality Engineering,* Addison-Wesley, Reading, Mass., ISBN 0-201-63339-6, 1995.

Kemerer, C. F.: "Reliability of Function Point Measurement—A Field Experiment," *Communications of the ACM,* **36:**85–97 (1993).

Putnam, Lawrence H.: *Measures for Excellence—Reliable Software on Time, Within Budget,* Yourdon Press/Prentice Hall, Englewood Cliffs, N.J., ISBN 0-13-567694-0, 1992.

————, and Ware Myers: *Industrial Strength Software—Effective Management Using Measurement,* IEEE Press, Los Alamitos, Calif., ISBN 0-8186-7532-2, 1997.

Rethinking the Software Process, CD-ROM, Miller Freeman, Lawrence, Kans., 1996. (This CD-ROM is a book collection jointly produced by the book publisher, Prentice Hall, and the journal publisher, Miller Freeman. It contains the full text and illustrations of five Prentice Hall books: Capers Jones, *Assessment and Control of Software Risks;* Tom DeMarco, *Controlling Software Projects;* Brian Dreger, *Function Point Analysis;* Larry Putnam and Ware Myers, *Measures for Excellence;* and Mark Lorenz and Jeff Kidd, *Object-Oriented Software Metrics.*)

Roetzheim, William H., and Reyna A. Beasley: *Best Practices in Software Cost and Schedule Estimation,* Prentice Hall PTR, Upper Saddle River, N.J., 1998.

Rubin, Howard: *Software Benchmark Studies for 1997,* Howard Rubin Associates, Pound Ridge, N.Y., 1997.

Symons, Charles R.: *Software Sizing and Estimating—Mk II FPA (Function Point Analysis),* John Wiley & Sons, Chichester, U.K., ISBN 0 471-92985-9, 1991.

Symons, Charles R.: "ISMI—International Software Metrics Initiative—Project Proposal" (private communication), June 15, 1997.

————: "Software Sizing and Estimating: Can Function Point Methods Meet Industry Needs?" (unpublished draft submitted to the IEEE for possible publication), Guild of Independent Function Point Analysts, London, U.K., August 1997.

Whitmire, S. A.: "3-D Function Points: Scientific and Real-Time Extensions to Function Points," *Proceedings of the 1992 Pacific Northwest Software Quality Conference,* June 1, 1992.

3

Sizing Software Deliverables

Software projects consist of far more than just source code. A modern software project is surrounded by a host of artifacts and deliverable items that need to be both sized and estimated. Software projects can include text-based documents, graphical and multimedia materials, source code, and test cases and test scripts. In addition, although these are not planned artifacts, software projects are also accompanied by large numbers of bugs or defects. Here, too, both sizing and estimating technologies are needed.

This section discusses the kinds of sizing methods that are found in software cost estimating tools for dealing with all classes of deliverable items and all major kinds of software artifacts. However, in spite of the improvements introduced by functional metrics, sizing remains an immature and incomplete area of cost estimating.

Sizing Software Deliverables

Up until this point our discussion of software cost estimating has dealt primarily with surface issues that are not highly complex. We are now beginning to deal with some of the software cost estimating issues that are very complex indeed.

It will soon be evident why software cost estimating tools either must be limited to a small range of software projects or else must utilize hundreds of rules and a knowledge base of thousands of projects in order to work well.

It is easier to build software-estimating tools that aim at specific domains, such as those aimed only at military projects (such as the REVIC estimating tool) or at management information systems projects (such as the original ESTIMACS estimating tool), than to build estimating tools that can work equally well with information systems, military software, systems and embedded software, commercial software, Web applets, object-oriented applications, and the myriad of classes and types that comprises the overall software universe.

The first estimating tool the author built at IBM concentrated primarily on IBM's systems software. However, his estimating interests expanded widely while working for the ITT corporation, which was a conglomerate owning more than 100 companies that built software. Some of the larger companies owned by ITT at the peak of its diversity included the following:

- Avis rental cars
- Bell Telephone Manufacturing (BTM)
- Bobbs Merrill Publishing

- Burpee Seeds
- Continental Baking
- Courier
- Defense Communications
- Hartford Insurance
- Howard Sams Publishing
- ITT Financial Services
- Morton Frozen Foods
- QUME
- Scotts Fertilizer
- Sheraton Hotels
- Standard Telephone Lorenz
- Standard Telephone and Cables

Within the various locations that built software in the ITT system it was possible to find every conceivable kind of software, including the following:

1. Management information systems
2. Systems software
3. Telecommunication software
4. Military software projects
5. Internal tool development for ITT's use
6. Contract software for external clients
7. Contract software from external vendors for ITT
8. Commercial software packages
9. Decision-support software
10. Manufacturing automation software
11. Computer-aided design and manufacturing software
12. End-user developed software

Not only did the ITT corporation build every known kind of software, but it used almost every possible tool, programming language, and process variation. For example, ITT software operated on more than 20 hardware platforms, including several custom-built computers, such as ITT's own switching computers.

ITT software was coded in more than 100 programming languages (including several proprietary ones developed by ITT itself), ran under a dozen or more operating systems, and used more than 50 kinds of design approaches, and used more than 25 development process variations.

This kind of estimating situation is very complex, but in the long run it is the kind of situation which all software project management tools should be able to deal with: Software project management should be able to work for any size, nature, class, and type of software application that exists in the world. If a project management tool does have limits to its applicability, then those limits should be clearly identified by the tool vendor.

In this section we will begin to delve into some of the harder problems of software cost estimating that the vendors in the software cost estimating business attempt to solve, and then we will place the solutions into our commercial software cost estimating tools.

General Sizing Logic for Key Deliverables

One of the first and most important aspects of software cost estimating is that of *sizing*, or predicting the volumes of various kinds of software deliverable items. Sizing is a very complex problem for software cost estimating, but advances in sizing technology over the past 20 years have been impressive.

Software cost estimating tools usually approach sizing in a sequential or *cascade* fashion. First, the overall size of the application is determined, using source code volumes or function point totals, and then the sizes for other kinds of artifacts and deliverable items are predicted based on the primary size in terms of LOC, function points, or both.

Assume that a software application's basic size is 100 function points or 10,250 logical statements in the C programming language. Once either of these basic sizes has been determined, then a host of other sizes can be derived. For example, the functional specifications might be sized by applying a ratio, such as 1 page per function point or 8.5 pages per KLOC.

Sizing software deliverable items is a major feature of modern software cost estimating tools. It is also a feature where automated software cost estimating tools can often outperform either manual sizing approaches or even any other kind of project management tool. The success of software cost estimating tools as sizing engines is primarily due to their attached knowledge bases of historical project data.

Although software sizing is a key feature of software cost estimating tools, the number and kinds of items that need to be sized are highly variable from project to project. Therefore, users should review the size predictions carefully and make any overrides or adjustments that seem to be needed to match local conditions. Three forms of sizing adjustments are usually supported by software cost estimating tools:

1. Users can add or remove items from the list of artifacts being sized.

2. Users can change the size predictions for specific artifacts to match local values.

3. Users can convert sizes from one metric to another using built-in conversion logic.

Although some of the major commercial software cost estimating tools include powerful sizing algorithms for many deliverables, the vendors of the commercial software-estimating tools (including the author's own company) regard these algorithms as being proprietary, even trade secrets. Therefore, discussions of sizing in this book will of necessity be general ones.

Before discussing how sizing is performed, it is useful to consider some examples of the kinds of software artifacts for which sizing may be required. The main software artifacts can be divided into a number of categories for discussion purposes, as shown in Table 13.1.

Although this list is fairly extensive, it covers only the more obvious software artifacts that need to be dealt with. Let us now consider the sizing implications of these various software artifacts at a somewhat more detailed level.

Sizing Based on Function Point Analysis of Software Applications

The first sizing task of most commercial software cost estimating tools in the 1990s begins with function point analysis. Software sizing from the basis of function point sizing dates back to October 1979, when Allan Albrecht of IBM gave a public lecture on the function point metric at a conference in Monterey, California (Albrecht 1981). Concurrently, IBM placed the basic function point metric in the public domain.

Function point sizing support in the context of software cost estimation tools was present in the ESTIMACS tool circa 1983, but that tool used a specialized variant of IBM's function point, and its function point size predictions did not exactly match IBM's method after IBM's 1984 revision of function point counting.

In 1982, the well-known management consultant Tom DeMarco published an independent form of function point metric in his book

TABLE 13.1   Software Artifacts for Which Size Information Is Useful

1. Function point sizes for new development
2. Function point sizes for reused material and packages
3. Function point sizes for changes and deletions
4. Function point sizes for creeping requirements
5. Function point sizes for reusable components
6. Function point sizes for object-oriented class libraries
7. Source code to be developed for applications
8. Source code to be developed for prototypes
9. Source code to be extracted from a library of reusable components
10. Source code to be updated for enhancement projects
11. Source code to be changed or removed during maintenance
12. Source code to be updated from software packages
13. Text-based paper documents, such as requirements and specifications
14. Text-based paper documents, such as test plans and status reports
15. Percentages of text-based paper documents that are reused
16. Graphics-based paper documents, such as data flow diagrams or control flows
17. Percentages of graphics elements that are reused
18. On-line HELP text
19. Graphics and illustrations
20. Multimedia materials (music and animation)
21. Defects or bugs in all deliverables
22. New test cases
23. Existing test cases from regression test libraries
24. Database contents
25. Percentage of database contents that are reused

Controlling Software Projects (DeMarco 1982). Interestingly, DeMarco and Albrecht both performed their primary research during the mid-1970s, although the publication of their results was separated by three years.

At the time of publication, DeMarco was unfamiliar with the work of Allan Albrecht, and vice versa. The DeMarco and Albrecht function points are similar in concept but not identical in form. However, a subset of the DeMarco function point is a near match to the original Albrecht function point.

The simultaneous creation of function point metrics by two independent researchers appears to be a case of independent invention—similar, perhaps, to the joint discovery of the principles of evolution by Charles Darwin and Alfred Wallace.

The DeMarco function point appeared in several software cost estimating tools but was rapidly replaced by the Albrecht function point, which was easier to automate and had the aura of IBM behind it. However, the DeMarco function point has recently reappeared as the basis for a number of function point variations, such as Boeing 3D function points (Galea 1995) and full function points (St-Pierre et al. 1997).

In 1983, British management consultant Charles Symons gave a public lecture in London about a modified form of Albrecht/IBM function point, which he termed *Mark II* function points. This variation to the basic function point metric has become widely used in the United Kingdom, and was the first of more than 35 published function point variations (Symons 1991).

A number of software cost estimating tools now support both U.S. function points as defined by the International Function Point Users Group (IFPUG) and British Mark II function points. However, these two metrics often differ in apparent size for the same application by as much as 20 percent, so knowledge of the specific form of function point metric is quite important.

In 1984, IBM made a major revision to the rules for counting function points (Albrecht 1984). The revised rules added a more rigorous way of evaluating complexity, and the 1984 IBM revision became the basic method of counting function points when the nonprofit IFPUG was formed and began to assume responsibility for function point counting rules.

In 1985, the author's SPQR/20 tool (Jones 1986) was the first U.S. commercial software cost estimating tool which created function point totals that correlated to the IBM function point metric following the major revision to function point counting which Allan Albrecht and his colleagues at IBM carried out in 1984.

Although this tool gave function point totals that matched the IBM method to within about 1.5 percent, it utilized a simplified set of only three adjustment factors rather than the 14 used by IBM. This was to facilitate automation of the function point metric and speed up the estimation process.

In 1986, the responsibility for defining function point metrics in the United States and Canada left IBM and was taken over by the IFPUG.

Also in 1986, the Software Productivity Research (SPR) feature point variation on function point metrics was developed to assist in moving functional metrics to the real-time and systems software domains. Feature points added a new parameter, *algorithms* to the set of basic function point metric elements (Jones 1991).

Today most U.S. commercial software cost estimating tools include explicit support for IFPUG function point metrics, and some also support other variations, such as Mark II function points or SPR feature points.

However, the success and expansion of function points and the IFPUG organization has created a very tricky and complicated international situation which affects software sizing and cost estimating in major ways.

IFPUG is not a true standards-issuing organization, such as the Institute of Electrical and Electronic Engineers (IEEE) or the International Organization of Standards (ISO). This means that the function point counting rules defined by IFPUG are not true standards in the sense of ISO standards, IEEE standards, or Department of Defense (DoD) standards. As a result, a host of alternative function point counting methods have been created over the past 10 years.

Function point variations

Over and above the *standard* function point metric defined by IFPUG, there are perhaps 35 other variants that do not necessarily give the same results as the IFPUG method. Further, many of the minor function point variants have no published conversion rules to standard IFPUG function points or much data of any kind in print.

This means that the same application can appear to have very different sizes, based on whether the function point totals follow the IFPUG counting rules, the British Mark II counting rules, the SPR feature point counting rules, the Boeing 3D counting rules, or any of the other function point clones. Thus, application sizing and cost estimating based on function point metrics must also identify the rules and definitions of the specific form of function point being utilized.

Also, IFPUG itself introduced a major change in function point counting rules in 1994, when Version 4 of the rules was published. The Version 4 changes eliminated counts of some forms of error messages (over substantial protest, it should be noted) and, hence, reduced the counts from the prior Version 3.4 by perhaps 20 percent for projects with significant numbers of error messages.

The function point sizes in this book are based on IFPUG counts, with Version 4 being the most commonly used variant. However, from time to time points require that the older Version 3.4 form be used. The text will indicate which form is utilized for specific cases.

Over and above the need to be very clear as to which specific function point is being used, there are also some other issues associated with function point sizing that need to be considered.

The rules for counting function points using most of the common function point variants are rather complex. This means that attempts to count function points by untrained individuals generally lead to major errors. This is unfortunate, but is also true of almost any other significant metric.

Both the IFPUG and the equivalent organization in the United Kingdom, the United Kingdom Function Point (Mark II) Users Group, offer training and certification examinations. Other metrics organizations, such as the Australian Software Metrics Association (ASMA) and the Netherlands Function Point Users Group (NEFPUG), may also offer certification services. However, most of the minor function point variants have no certification examinations and have very little published data.

When reviewing data expressed in function points, it is important to know whether the published function point totals used for software cost estimates are derived from counts by certified function point counters, from attempts to create totals by untrained counters, or from four other common ways of deriving function point totals:

1. Backfiring from source code counts, either manually or using tools such as those marketed by ViaSoft

2. Automatic generation of function points from requirements and design, using tools such as those of Bachman or Texas Instruments

3. Deriving function points by analogy, such as assuming that Project B will be the same size as Project A, a prior project which has a function point size of known value

4. Counting function points using one of the many variations in functional counting methods (i.e., SPR feature points, Boeing 3D function points, Nokia function points, Netherlands function points, etc.)

(Of course it is also important to know whether data expressed in lines of code is based on counts of physical lines or logical statements, just as it is important to know whether distance data expressed in *miles* refers to statute miles or nautical miles, or whether volumetric data expressed in terms of *gallons* refers to U.S. gallons or Imperial gallons.)

In terms of accuracy, the preferred method for calculating function points is to utilize the services of certified function point counting personnel, and to derive the counts from the software specifications augmented by the formal written requirements, plus interviews with user representatives.

Also, the training courses themselves should be certified by the function point associations. Unfortunately, these methods, which yield the highest accuracy, also mean delays in arriving at function point totals, and some not insignificant expenses.

Since manual function point counts by a single counter usually proceed at rates of less than 1000 function points a day, the costs and time for enumerating the function point totals for a major system can be in excess of $25,000 in fees and a month in time.

Unfortunately, for analysis of historical projects and legacy systems, normal function point counting may be impossible or, certainly, extremely difficult. Often the original specifications are missing or were never updated. The original development team members have been reassigned, been downsized, or have changed companies and, therefore, are no longer available.

As a result of the lack of written information for legacy projects, the method called *backfiring,* or direct conversion from source code statements to equivalent function point totals, has become the most widely used method for determining the function point totals of legacy applications. Since legacy applications far outnumber new software projects, this means that backfiring is actually the most widely used method for deriving function point totals.

Backfiring is highly automated, and a number of vendors provide tools that can convert source code statements into equivalent function point values. Backfiring is very easy to perform, so that the function point totals for applications as large as 1 million source code statements can be derived in only a few minutes of computer time.

The downside of backfiring is that it is based on highly variable relationships between source code volumes and function point totals. Although backfiring may achieve statistically useful results when averaged over hundreds of projects, it may not be accurate by even plus or minus 50 percent for any specific project. This is due to the fact that individual programming styles can create very different volumes of source code for the same feature. Controlled experiments by IBM in which 8 programmers coded the same specification found variations of about 5 to 1 in the volume of source code written by the participants.

In spite of the uncertainty of backfiring, it is supported by more tools and is a feature of more commercial software-estimating tools than any other current sizing method. The need for speed and low sizing costs explains why many of the approximation methods, such as backfiring, sizing by analogy, and automated function point derivations, are so popular: They are fast and cheap, even if they are not as accurate. It also explains why so many software-tool vendors are actively exploring automated rule-based function point sizing engines that can derive function point totals from requirements and specifications, with little or no human involvement.

Since function point metrics have splintered in recent years, the family of possible function point variants used for estimation and measurement include at least 36 choices (see Table 13.2).

TABLE 13.2   Function Point Counting Variations, Circa 1998

1. The 1975 internal IBM function point method
2. The 1979 published Albrecht IBM function point method
3. The 1982 DeMarco bang function point method
4. The 1983 Rubin/ESTIMACS function point method
5. The 1983 British Mark II function point method (Symons)
6. The 1984 revised IBM function point method
7. The 1985 SPR function point method using three adjustment factors
8. The 1985 SPR backfire function point method
9. The 1986 SPR feature point method for real-time software
10. The 1994 SPR approximation function point method
11. The 1997 SPR analogy-based function point method
12. The 1997 SPR taxonomy-based function point method
13. The 1986 IFPUG Version 1 method
14. The 1988 IFPUG Version 2 method
15. The 1990 IFPUG Version 3 method
16. The 1995 IFPUG Version 4 method
17. The 1989 Texas Instruments IEF function point method
18. The 1992 Reifer coupling of function points and Halstead metrics
19. The 1992 ViaSoft backfire function point method
20. The 1993 Gartner Group backfire function point method
21. The 1994 Boeing 3D function point method
22. The 1994 unadjusted function point method
23. The 1994 Bachman Analyst function point method
24. The 1995 Compass Group backfire function point method
25. The 1995 Air Force engineering function point method
26. The 1995 Oracle function point method
27. The 1995 NEFPUG method
28. The 1995 ASMA method
29. The 1995 Finnish method
30. The 1996 CRIM micro–function point method
31. The 1996 object point method
32. The 1997 data point method for database sizing
33. The 1997 Nokia function point approach for telecommunications software
34. The 1997 full function point approach for real-time software
35. The 1997 ISO working group approach for functional sizing
36. The 1997 Symons-ISMI proposed function point approach

Note that this listing is not stated to be 100 percent complete. The 36 variants shown in Table 13.2 are merely the ones that have surfaced in the software measurement literature or been discussed at metrics conferences. No doubt, at least another 20 or so variants may exist that have not yet published any information or been presented at metrics conferences.

Reasons cited for creating function point variations

The reasons why there are at least 36 variations in counting function points deserve some research and discussion. First, it was proven long ago in the 1970s that the lines-of-code metric cannot measure software productivity in an economic sense and is harmful for activity-based cost analysis. Therefore, there is a strong incentive to adopt some form of functional metric because the older methods have been proven to be unreliable.

However, the mushrooming growth of function point variations can be traced to other causes. From meetings and discussions with the developers of many function point variants, the following reasons have been noted as to why variations have been created.

First, a significant number of variations were created due to a misinterpretation of the nature of function point metrics. Because the original IBM function points were first applied to information systems, a belief has grown up that standard function points don't work for real-time and embedded software. This belief is caused by the fact that productivity rates for real-time and embedded software are usually well below the rates for information systems of the same size in function points.

The main factors identified as differentiating embedded and real-time software from information systems applications include the following:

1. Embedded software is high in algorithmic complexity.

2. Embedded software is often limited in logical files.

3. Embedded software's inputs and outputs may be electronic signals.

4. Embedded software's interfaces may be electronic signals.

5. The user view for embedded software may not reflect human users.

These differences are great enough that the real-time and systems community has been motivated to create a number of function point variations that give more weight to algorithms, give less weight to logical files, and expand the concept of inputs and outputs to deal with electronic signals and sensor-based data rather than human-oriented inputs and outputs, such as forms and screens.

Some of the possible changes to function points in behalf of real-time, systems, and embedded software may have enough merit to be considered as possible modifications to the counting rules of standard function points. The problem is that having dozens of function point variations that produce different counts is harmful to the overall concept of function points.

About half a dozen variants for counting function points were created to serve the real-time software and embedded software communities. Rather than explore the reasons why real-time and embedded software projects typically have lower productivity rates than information systems (it is due to more extensive specifications and more extensive quality control in the real-time domain), some researchers have developed function point variations that simply assign larger totals to real-time and embedded applications by including additional parameters or assigning higher adjustment factors for the kinds of complexity noted on systems software projects.

Another phenomenon noted when exploring function point variations is the fact that many function point variants are aligned to national borders. The IFPUG is headquartered in the United States, and most of the current officers and committee chairs are U.S. citizens.

There is a widespread feeling in Europe and elsewhere that in spite of the association having *international* in its name, IFPUG is dominated by the United States and may not properly reflect the interests of Europe, South America, the Pacific Rim, or Australia.

Incidentally, the arrival of the unified European currency in 1999 is leading to the suggestion by some European function point analysts that perhaps a unified European function point might be appropriate, following roughly the same adoption schedule as the euro.

A third common reason for developing function point variants has to do with the perception that the IFPUG counting practices committee tends to reject suggested expansions and refinements to function point metrics other than those originated by the committee itself. At least a dozen function point researchers have expressed frustration at the IFPUG's response to suggested modifications to the counting rules.

This last perception may be close enough to the mark that IFPUG might do well to evaluate an alternative method for dealing with suggested expansions and refinements of function point metrics. Rather than limiting the evaluation of proposed metric expansions to the counting practices committee, it might be well to deal with proposed function point changes in the same way that Congress deals with proposed legislation. The proposed modifications to the counting rules for functional metrics could be put to a vote of the entire IFPUG membership.

Indeed, if function points and the IFPUG organization are to remain viable into the next century, it is urgent to focus energies on perfecting one primary form of functional metric rather than dissipating energies into the creation of scores of minor function point variants, many of which have no published data and have only a handful of users.

Unfortunately, so long as all function point counting proposals can only be dealt with by one small committee, the validity of function point metrics will be questioned. Since the members of the IFPUG counting practices committee do not speak for the majority of function point users, it would seem reasonable to follow the pattern of the official standards bodies, such as IEEE and ISO, and allow voting on proposed changes rather than simply having the IFPUG counting practices committee issue changes in an arbitrary manner.

There is an urgent need to move IFPUG toward the operational characteristics of other nonprofit standards organizations, such as the IEEE and ISO standards bodies. In other words, expansions to function point metrics must become subject to the power of the democratic ballots of knowledgeable members rather than being the exclusive preserve of a small group of committee members, many of whom are vendors with a vested interest in their own proposals. Unless IFPUG begins to operate as a true nonprofit organization, there is some reason to suggest that IFPUG should give up its nonprofit status.

Regardless of the reasons, the existence of so many variations in counting function points is damaging to the overall software metrics community and is not really advancing the state of the art of software measurement.

As the situation currently stands, the overall range of apparent function point counts for the same application can vary by perhaps two to one, based on which specific varieties of function point metrics are utilized. This situation obviously requires that the specific form of function point be recorded in order for the size information to have any value.

Although the large range of metric choices all using the name *function points* is a troublesome situation, it is not unique to software. Other measurements outside the software arena also have multiple choices for metrics that use the same name. For example, it is necessary to know whether statute miles or nautical miles are being used; whether American dollars, Australian dollars, or Canadian dollars are being used; and whether American gallons or Imperial gallons are being used. It is also necessary to know whether temperatures are being measured in Celsius or Fahrenheit degrees. There are also three ways of calculating the octane rating of fuel, and several competing methods for calculating fuel efficiency or miles per gallon. There are even multiple ways of calculating birthdays.

However, the explosion of the function point metric into 36 or so competitive claimants must be viewed as an excessive number of choices. Hopefully the situation will not reach the point seen among programming languages, where 500 or more languages are competing for market share.

Volume of Function Point Data Available

The next table is an attempt to quantify the approximate number of software projects that have been measured using various forms of function point metrics. No single function point counting method is in the majority, but due to the global preponderance of aging legacy applications, various forms of backfiring appear to be the major sources of global function point data.

The information in Table 13.3 is derived from discussions with various benchmarking companies, from the software metrics literature,

TABLE 13.3   Approximate Distribution of Function Point Methods, Circa 1997

Function point counting method	New projects	Maintenance projects	Total projects	Percent of total
SPR backfire	1,000	17,000	18,000	13.98
Gartner backfire	1,000	17,000	18,000	13.98
IFPUG 3	15,000	2,500	17,500	13.59
Uncertified counters	1,000	5,000	15,000	11.65
IFPUG 4	12,500	1,500	14,000	10.87
ViaSoft backfire	1,000	10,000	11,000	8.54
Mark II	7,500	1,000	8,500	6.60
Compass backfire	500	5,000	5,500	4.27
IBM 1984	3,500	1,000	4,500	3.50
IEF	2,500	500	3,000	2.33
DeMarco bang	2,000	500	2,500	1.94
Other	1,500	500	2,000	1.55
SPR function point	1,000	750	1,750	1.36
Bachman	1,500	200	1,700	1.32
IBM 1979	1,000	500	1,500	1.17
Unadjusted	1,000	500	1,500	1.17
SPR feature point	750	300	1,050	0.82
Australian	500	200	700	0.54
3D Function point	500	150	650	0.50
Netherlands	250	150	400	0.31
Total	64,500	64,250	128,750	100

and from informal discussions with function point users and developers during the course of software assessment and benchmarking studies. The table has a high margin of error and is simply a rough attempt to evaluate the size of the universe of function point data when all major variations are included.

Note that some of the minor variations are not included in Table 13.3 because usage of the minor variations is very sparse, published results are nonexistent, and, hence, it is not easy to gather information on the number of projects measured.

Because aging legacy applications comprise the bulk of all software projects in the world, the various forms of backfiring, or direct conversion between source code statements and function points, is the most widely utilized method for enumerating function points. All of the major software benchmarking companies (i.e., Compass Group, Gartner Group, SPR, etc.) utilize backfiring for their client studies and, hence, have substantial data derived from backfiring.

Curiously, none of the major function point groups, such as IFPUG or the United Kingdom Function Point Users Group, have attempted any formal studies of backfiring, or even made any visible contribution to this popular technology. The great majority of reports and data on backfiring come from the commercial benchmark consulting companies, such as Gartner Group, Rubin Systems, Meta Group, Compass Group, and Software Productivity Research.

As stated, the margin of error with Table 13.3 is very high, and the information is derived from informal surveys at various function point events in the United States, Europe, and the Pacific Rim. However, there seems to be no other source of this kind of information on the distribution of software projects among the various forms of function point analysis.

It is also curious that none of the function point user associations, such as IFPUG or the United Kingdom Function Point Users Group, have attempted to quantify the world number of projects measured using function points. IFPUG has attempted some minor benchmarking work, but only in the context of projects measured using the IFPUG Version 4 counting rules.

Unfortunately, the major function point associations, such as IFPUG in the United States, and the British Mark II users group, NEFPUG, ASMA, and others, tend to view each other as political rivals and, hence, ignore one another's data or sometimes even actively disparage one another.

Another aspect of using function point metrics for benchmarking studies is to consider the approximate distribution of projects that have been measured into various types of applications.

As can be seen from Table 13.4 the great majority of applications

TABLE 13.4   Approximate Distribution of Software Project Types, Circa 1997

Software project type	New projects	Maintenance projects	Total projects	Percent of total
Information systems	45,150	44,975	90,125	70
Systems software	6,450	6,425	12,875	10
Embedded software	3,225	3,213	6,438	5
End-user applications	645	643	1,288	1
Commercial packages	1,290	1,285	2,575	2
Other	7,740	7,710	15,450	12
Total	64,500	64,250	128,750	100

measured using functional metrics are information systems. However, from about 1995 through the present the application of function point metrics to real-time, embedded, and systems software has increased significantly.

Although information systems comprise the largest volume of projects that have been measured using function points, both systems software and embedded applications are present in significant numbers. Indeed, membership in function point users groups is growing faster for systems and embedded software practitioners than for any other kind of software professional.

One striking anomaly can be seen in Table 13.4, and that is the fact that commercial software vendors, such as Microsoft, SAP, and Computer Associates, are severely underrepresented. Not only do commercial vendors lag in membership in function point associations, but they also lag in utilization of function point metrics.

Consider yet another issue associated with function point metrics. The minimum weighting factors assigned to standard IFPUG function points have a lower limit or cutoff point. These limits mean that the smallest practical project where such common function point metrics as IFPUG and Mark II can be used is in the vicinity of 10 to 15 function points. Below that size, the weighting factors tend to negate the use of the function point metric.

Because of the large number of small maintenance and enhancement projects, there is a need for some kind of *micro–function point* that can be used in the zone that runs from a fraction of a single function point up to the current minimum level where normal function points apply.

Since it is the weighting factors that cause the problem with small projects, one obvious approach would be to use unadjusted function point counts for small projects without applying any weights at all. However, this experimental solution would necessitate changes in the logic of software-estimating tools to accommodate this variation.

The huge numbers of possible methods for counting function points are very troublesome for software cost estimating tool vendors and for all those who build metrics tools and software project management tools. None of us can support all 36 variations in function point counting, so most of us support only a subset of the major methods.

It is easy to find support for backfiring, for IFPUG function points, for Mark II function points, and for SPR feature points in many software cost estimating tools. Indeed, some software cost estimating tools support all four of these common methods and can convert data back and forth among them.

However, none of the current generation of software cost estimating tools support the more obscure or localized variations, nor are any likely to do so in the future. Unless the function point community can learn to cooperate instead of creating new function point variations for little or no technical reason, the function point method will lose its overall business value as a better standard than lines of code for software economic studies.

Backfiring—Direct Conversion from Lines of Code to Function Points

The many variations in methods of counting function points have a significant impact on the mathematics of *backfiring*, or direct conversion from source code statements into equivalent function point values.

Recall that the backfiring method originated in the 1970s when the pioneering IBM function point counting method was first being published. Indeed, some of the pioneering studies of backfiring were performed by Allan Albrecht, the inventor of function points, and were carried out even before function points were announced to the general public in the autumn of 1979.

When IBM made its major revision to function point counting in 1984, that method was adopted by the IFPUG at its formation in 1986 and stayed more or less constant until Version 4 of the IFPUG rules was published in 1994.

Thus, the original values for the ratios of source code statements per function point were more or less constant for perhaps 10 years.

The IFPUG Version 4 rules eliminated counts for error messages; hence, the function point totals for many applications are about 20 percent lower using Version 4 rules than they would have been under the previous Version 3 rules.

On the other hand, the British Mark II method, with 19 adjustment factors rather than the 14 used by IFPUG, tends to create function point totals that are about 15 to 20 percent higher than the IFPUG Version 3 counts.

TABLE 13.5   Backfiring Ranges Associated with Function Point Methods

(Source code statements per function point)

Language	Level	IFPUG 4 (80%)	IFPUG 3 (100%)	Mark II (115%)
Assembly (basic)	1.00	400.00	320.00	278.26
Assembly (macro)	1.50	266.67	213.33	185.51
C	2.50	160.00	128.00	111.30
Algol	3.00	133.33	106.67	92.75
COBOL	3.00	133.33	106.67	92.75
FORTRAN	3.00	133.33	106.67	99.13
Jovial	3.00	133.33	106.67	92.75
Ada 83	4.50	88.89	71.11	61.84
C++	5.00	80.00	64.00	55.65
Ada 95	6.00	66.67	53.33	46.38
Visual Basic	10.00	40.00	32.00	27.83
Objective C	12.00	33.33	26.67	23.19
Smalltalk	15.00	26.67	21.33	18.55
PowerBuilder	20.00	20.00	16.00	13.91
SQL	25.00	16.00	12.80	11.13
Average	7.63	115.44	92.35	80.73

Table 13.5 illustrates how the volume of source code needed to implement one function point can vary, based upon whether IFPUG 3, IFPUG 4, or Mark II function points are used as the basis for the conversion.

The column of data called "Level" needs a word of explanation. The original concept of language levels is much older than any form of function point metric, having originated in the 1960s at IBM.

The original meaning was the number of statements in basic assembly language needed to encode one statement in the target language. Thus, COBOL was termed a *level-3 language* because it took about three assembly statements to perform an action that could be performed by one COBOL statement. That original definition is still a good approximation and is still used for converting source code sizes between one language and another.

When function point metrics appeared, the concept of language levels was extended slightly so that it also included the number of source code statements required to implement one function point. For example, COBOL requires about 107 logical statements in the procedure and data divisions to encode one function point using the 1984 IBM function point method or the IFPUG methods through Version 3.4.

It is obvious from a study of standard economics that some form of functional metric is highly advantageous for economic and quality studies that span multiple programming languages. However, it is not obvious that many of the more recent variants to the original function point concept really have much merit.

Before function points were invented, the only method that could yield accurate productivity and quality metrics where multiple languages were involved was to convert the sizes of all languages into the *equivalent* size in a single language, usually basic assembly language. This method of converting the sizes of various languages into equivalent size in assembly language thus provided a constant basis for doing productivity and quality comparisons.

In a sense, the situation is very similar to trying to do economic studies involving multiple currencies. Obviously, it is impossible to do direct comparisons of costs between dollars, yen, pounds, pesos, and other international currencies. All of the information has to be converted into a single currency before any kind of economic comparison can be performed. (Indeed, the emergence of the new unified European currency in 1999 is leading to more emphasis on accurate currency conversion than in perhaps any prior era in human history.)

Thus, while the ratio of source code statements to function points can vary between the IFPUG and Mark II function point methods, or between IFPUG 3 and IFPUG 4, the COBOL language itself remains a level-3 language under the original definition of the level concept, because it still takes about three assembly-language statements to encode the features that can be coded in one COBOL statement.

Although Table 13.5 illustrates how several of the variations in function points affect backfiring, it should be noted that there are also variations in how source code is counted. Indeed, the many variations in the way source code is counted have an even wider range of uncertainty than the variations in the way function points are counted. The two major variations in source code counting methods are the following:

1. The Software Productivity Research (SPR) method, based on *logical statements*

2. The Software Engineering Institute (SEI) method, based on *physical lines*

There can be as much as a 500-percent difference in the apparent size of a software application, based on whether the SPR method or the SEI method is utilized. Unfortunately, this 500 percent variation can run in either direction, depending upon which language is utilized.

When the variations in how function point methods are counted are

TABLE 13.6   COBOL Backfiring Ranges and Counting Method Combinations
(Source code statements per function point)

Method		IFPUG 4 (80%)	IFPUG 3 (100%)	Mark II (115%)
SPR Logical Statements	(100%)	133.33	106.67	92.75
SEI Physical Lines	(300%)	400.00	320.00	278.26

joined to the variations in how source code might be counted, the results are very broad indeed.

Table 13.6 illustrates the ranges of source code statements needed to encode one function point for a typical COBOL application when both the function point method and the code counting method vary simultaneously. It shows three of the common function point variants, coupled with two of the common source code variants—the SPR method of counting logical statements and the SEI method of counting physical lines.

As can easily be seen from the large range of possible results, it is very important to record the exact counting methodology utilized when dealing with function points, source code, or any other software metric. Unless the exact counting rules are identified, the resulting information is little better than worthless for exploring productivity, quality, costs, or any other business purpose.

In fact, without recording the counting rules used, the information is actually harmful because it may lead to serious errors in cost estimates that attempt to use the data without knowledge of the counting rules on which the data is based.

As an example of possibilities, a software project where the productivity rate is 10 function points per staff month using IFPUG Version 3.4 counting rules might have a productivity rate of only 8 function points per staff month using IFPUG Version 4 counting rules.

However, if the same project is evaluated using the Mark II counting rules, productivity might be 12 function points per staff month, and if other variants, such as the Boeing 3D function point, are used, the productivity might top 15 function points per staff month.

All of these variations are for the same project, the same people, and exactly the same number of work months.

In spite of the possible ambiguity associated with backfiring, there is no question but that this method has established a dominant place in determining the function point sizes of aging legacy applications. Indeed, there are not even any other major contenders for this particular task. In summary, the main strengths of backfiring function points are as follows:

1. Backfiring is extremely quick and easy to perform.

2. Backfiring automation is commercially available.

3. Backfiring is supported by many software cost estimating tools.

4. Backfiring is used in many software benchmarking studies.

The main weaknesses of backfiring function point metrics are as follows:

1. Backfiring is of lower accuracy than normal function point counting.

2. Backfiring is ambiguous if the starting point is physical lines of code (LOC).

3. Backfiring may be ambiguous for mixed-language applications.

4. Backfiring results may vary based on individual programming styles.

5. Backfiring is not endorsed by any of the major function point associations.

Although backfiring has both strengths and weaknesses, the strengths include speed and low cost, and these are such substantial advantages that no other method is likely to overcome them in the near future.

It is possible to increase the accuracy of backfiring by analysis of the causes of coding variations. Indeed, this kind of analysis would also increase the accuracy of estimation based on lines of code. It is surprising, therefore, that only a handful of research studies on coding variations have ever been produced and that the topic does not appear to be a subject of investigation by any of the estimating vendors whose tools are based primarily on source code sizes.

The International Organization of Standards (ISO) Functional Size Standard

As this book is being written, the International Organization of Standards (ISO) is attempting to define an overall standard for sizing software using function points as the start. However, the ISO size metric is not yet available, and even when it becomes available, it is not clear that it will be universally adopted.

Hopefully, the ISO working group can create a useful standard for functional size metrics. However, given the prevalence of backfiring and the ambiguity of source code counting rules, those aspects of the software metrics problem need to be addressed also.

Other topics that the ISO working group might well address include the following problem areas that are currently tricky for both estimation and measurement purposes:

- The need for a *data point* metric for sizing database volumes
- The need for a *service point* metric for sizing manual activities
- The need for a *micro–function point* for small maintenance projects
- The need for published conversion rules between various metrics
- The need to deal with the backfiring technology or conversion from code counts
- The need to define the sizes of all major software deliverables
- The need to deal with reusability of various software artifacts
- The need to address such adjustments as for complexity

The latter point—size adjustments in response to complexity—is actually a major topic in its own right and one which deserves much more research than has yet been given to such a critical factor. Let us consider the implications of all of the known forms of complexity and how they relate to software sizing.

Software Complexity Analysis

The topic of complexity is very important for software cost estimation because it affects a number of independent and dependent variables, such as the following:

- High complexity levels can increase bug or defect rates
- High complexity levels can lower defect-removal efficiency rates
- High complexity levels can decrease development productivity rates
- High complexity levels can raise maintenance staffing needs
- High complexity levels can lengthen development schedules
- High complexity levels increase the number of test cases needed

Unfortunately, the concept of *complexity* is an ambiguous topic that has no exact definition agreed upon by all software researchers. When we speak of complexity in a software context, we can be discussing the difficulty of the problem that the software application will attempt to implement, the structure of the code, or the relationships among the data items that will be used by the application. In other words, the term *complexity* can be used in a general way to discuss problem complexity, code complexity, and data complexity.

The scientific and engineering literature encompasses no fewer than 30 different flavors of complexity, some or all of which may be found to be relevant for software applications. Unfortunately, most of the forms of scientific complexity are not even utilized in a software context.

In a very large book on software complexity, Dr. Horst Zuse (Zuse 1990) discusses about 50 variants of structural complexity for programming alone. It is perhaps because of the European origin—functional metrics are not as dominant there as in the United States—but in spite of the book's large size and fairly complete treatment, Zuse seems to omit all references to function point metrics and to the forms of complexity associated with functional metrics.

When software sizing and estimating tools utilize complexity as an adjustment factor, the methods tend to be highly subjective. Some of the varieties of complexity encountered in the scientific literature that show up in a software context include the following:

Algorithmic complexity concerns the length and structure of the algorithms for computable problems. Software applications with long and convoluted algorithms are difficult to design, to inspect, to code, to prove, to debug, and to test. Although algorithmic complexity affects quality, development productivity, and maintenance productivity, it is utilized as an explicit factor by only a few software cost estimating tools.

Code complexity concerns the subjective views of development and maintenance personnel about whether the code they are responsible for is complex or not. Interviewing software personnel and collecting their subjective opinions is an important step in calibrating more formal complexity metrics, such as cyclomatic and essential complexity. A number of software-estimating tools have methods for entering and adjusting code complexity based on ranking tables that run from *high* to *low* complexity in the subjective view of the developers.

Combinatorial complexity concerns the numbers of subsets and sets that can be constructed out of N components. This concept sometimes shows up in the way that modules and components of software applications might be structured. From a psychological vantage point, combinatorial complexity is a key reason why some problems seem harder to solve than others. However, this form of complexity is not utilized as an explicit estimating parameter.

Computational complexity concerns the amount of machine time and the number of iterations required to execute an algorithm. Some problems are so high in computational complexity that they are considered to be noncomputable. Other problems are solvable but require enormous quantities of machine time, such as cryptanalysis or meteorological analysis of weather patterns. Computational complexity is sometimes used for evaluating the performance implications of software applications, but not the difficulty of building or maintaining them.

Cyclomatic complexity is derived from graph theory and was made popular for software by Dr. Tom McCabe (McCabe 1976). Cyclomatic complexity is a measure of the control flow of a graph of the structure of a piece of software. The general formula for calculating cyclomatic complexity of a control flow graph is edges − nodes + unconnected parts × 2. Software with no branches has a cyclomatic complexity level of 1. As branches increase in number, cyclomatic complexity levels also rise. Above a cyclomatic complexity level of 20 path flow testing becomes difficult and, for higher levels, probably impossible.

Cyclomatic complexity is often used as a warning indicator for potential quality problems. Cyclomatic complexity is the most common form of complexity analysis for software projects and the only one with an extensive literature. At least 20 tools can measure cyclomatic complexity, and these tools range from freeware to commercial products. Such tools support many programming languages and operate on a variety of platforms.

Data complexity deals with the number of attributes associated with entities. For example, some of the attributes that might be associated with a human being in a typical medical office database of patient records could include date of birth, sex, marital status, children, brothers and sisters, height, weight, missing limbs, and many others. Data complexity is a key factor in dealing with data quality. Unfortunately, there is no metric for evaluating data complexity, so only subjective ranges are used for estimating purposes.

Diagnostic complexity is derived from medical practice, where it deals with the combinations of symptoms (temperature, blood pressure, lesions, etc.) needed to identify an illness unambiguously. For example, for many years it was not easy to tell whether a patient had tuberculosis or histoplasmosis because the superficial symptoms were essentially the same. For software, diagnostic complexity comes into play when customers report defects and the vendor tries to isolate the relevant symptoms and figure out what is really wrong. However, diagnostic complexity is not used as an estimating parameter for software projects.

Entropic complexity is the state of disorder of the component parts of a system. Entropy is an important concept because all known systems have an increase in entropy over time. That is, disorder gradually increases. This phenomenon has been observed to occur with software projects because many small changes over time gradually erode the original structure. Long-range studies of software projects in maintenance mode attempt to measure the rate at which entropy increases and determine whether it can be reversed by such approaches as code restructuring. Surrogate metrics for evaluating entropic complexity are the rates at which cyclomatic and essential complexity change over time, such as on an annual basis. However, there are no direct measures for software entropy.

Essential complexity is also derived from graph theory and was made popular by Dr. Tom McCabe (McCabe 1976). The essential complexity of a piece of software is derived from cyclomatic complexity after the graph of the application has been simplified by removing redundant paths. Essential complexity is often used as a warning indicator for potential quality problems. As with cyclomatic complexity, a module with no branches at all has an essential complexity level of 1. As unique branching sequences increase in number, both cyclomatic and essential complexity levels will rise. Essential complexity and cyclomatic complexity are supported by a variety of software tools.

Fan complexity refers to the number of times a software module is called (termed *fan in*) or the number of modules that it calls (termed *fan out*). Modules with a large fan-in number are obviously critical in terms of software quality, since they are called by many other modules. However, modules with a large fan-out number are also important, and they are hard to debug because they depend upon so many extraneous modules. Fan complexity is relevant to exploration of reuse potentials. Fan complexity is not used as an explicit estimating parameter, although in real life this form of complexity appears to exert a significant impact on software quality.

Flow complexity is a major topic in the studies of fluid dynamics and meteorology. It deals with the turbulence of fluids moving through channels and across obstacles. A new subdomain of mathematical physics called *chaos theory* has elevated the importance of flow complexity for dealing with physical problems. Many of the concepts, including chaos theory itself, appear relevant to software and are starting to be explored. However, the application of flow complexity to software is still highly experimental.

Function point complexity refers to the set of adjustment factors needed to calculate the final adjusted function point total of a software project. Standard U.S. function points as defined by the IFPUG have 14 complexity adjustment factors. The British Mark II function point uses 19 complexity adjustment factors. The SPR function point and feature point metrics use 3 complexity adjustment factors. Function point complexity is usually calculated by reference to tables of known values, many of which are automated and are present in software-estimating tools or function point analysis tools.

Graph complexity is derived from graph theory and deals with the numbers of edges and nodes on graphs created for various purposes. The concept is significant for software because it is part of the analysis of cyclomatic and essential complexity, and also is part of the operation of several source code restructuring tools. Although derivative metrics, such as cyclomatic and essential complexity, are used in software estimating, graph theory itself is not utilized.

Halstead complexity is derived from the *software-science* research carried out by the late Dr. Maurice Halstead (Halstead 1977) and his colleagues and students at Purdue University. The Halstead software science treatment of complexity is based on four discrete units: (1) number of unique operators (i.e., verbs), (2) number of unique operands (i.e., nouns), (3) instances of operator occurrences, and (4) instances of operand occurrences.

The Halstead work overlaps linguistic research, in that it seeks to enumerate such concepts as the vocabulary of a software project. Although the Halstead software-science metrics are supported in some software cost estimating tools, there is very little recent literature on this topic.

Information complexity is concerned with the numbers of entities and the relationships between them that might be found in a database, data repository, or data warehouse. Informational complexity is also associated with research on data quality. Unfortunately, all forms of research into database sizes and database quality are handicapped by the lack of metrics for dealing with data size, or for quantifying the forms of complexity which are likely to be troublesome in a database context.

Logical complexity is important for both software and circuit design. It is based upon the combinations of AND, OR, NOR, and NAND logic conditions that are concatenated together. This form of complexity is significant for expressing algorithms and for proofs of correctness. However, logical complexity is utilized as an explicit estimating parameter in only a few software cost estimating tools.

Mnemonic complexity is derived from cognitive psychology and deals with the ease or difficulty of memorization. It is well known that the human mind has both temporary and permanent memory.

Some kinds of information (i.e., names and telephone numbers) are held in temporary memory and require conscious effort to be moved into permanent memory. Other kinds of information (i.e., smells and faces) go directly to permanent memory.

Mnemonic complexity is important for software debugging and during design and code inspections. Many procedural programming languages have symbolic conventions that are very difficult to either scan or debug because they oversaturate human temporary memory. Things such as nested loops that use multiple levels of parentheses—that is, (((...)))—tend to swamp human temporary memory capacity.

Mnemonic complexity appears to be a factor in learning and using programming languages, and is also associated with defect rates in various languages. However, little information is available on this potentially important topic in a software context, and it is not used as an explicit software estimating parameter.

Organizational complexity deals with the way human beings in corporations arrange themselves into hierarchical groups or matrix organizations. This topic might be assumed to have only an indirect bearing on software, except for the fact that many large software projects are decomposed into components that fit the current organizational structure rather than the technical needs of the project. For example, many large software projects are decomposed into segments that can be handled by eight-person departments, whether or not that approach meets the needs of the system's architecture.

Although organizational complexity is seldom utilized as an explicit estimating parameter, it is known that large software projects that are well organized will outperform similar projects with poor organizational structures.

Perceptional complexity is derived from cognitive psychology and deals with the arrangements of edges and surfaces that appear to be simple or complex to human observers. For example, regular patterns appear to be simple while random arrangements appear to be complex. This topic is important for studies of visualization, software design methods, and evaluation of screen readability. Unfortunately, the important topic of the perceptional complexity of various software design graphics has only a few citations in the literature, and none in the cost-estimating literature.

Problem complexity concerns the subjective views of people asked to solve various kinds of problems about their difficulty. Psychologists know that increasing the number of variables and the length of the chain of deductive reasoning usually brings about an increase in the subjective view that the problem is complex. Inductive reasoning also adds to the perception of complexity. In a software context, problem complexity is concerned with the algorithms that will become part of a program or system. Determining the subjective opinions of real people is a necessary step in calibrating more objective complexity measures.

Process complexity is mathematically related to flow complexity, but in day-to-day software work it is concerned with the flow of materials through a software development cycle. This aspect of complexity is often dealt with in a practical way by project management tools that can calculate critical paths and program evaluation and review technique (PERT) diagrams of software development processes.

Semantic complexity is derived from the study of linguistics and is concerned with ambiguities in the definitions of terms. Already cited in this book are the very ambiguous terms *quality, data,* and *complexity*. The topic of semantic complexity is relevant to software for a surprising reason: Many lawsuits between software developers and their clients can be traced back to the semantic complexity of the contract when both sides claim different interpretations of the same clauses. Semantic complexity is not used as a formal estimating parameter.

Syntactic complexity is also derived from linguistics and deals with the grammatical structure and lengths of prose sections, such as sentences and paragraphs. A variety of commercial software tools are available for measuring syntactic complexity, using such metrics as the FOG index. (Unfortunately, these tools are seldom applied to software specifications, although they would appear to be valuable for that purpose.)

Topologic complexity deals with rotation and folding patterns. This topic is often explored by mathematicians, but it also has relevance for software. For example, topological complexity is a factor in some of the commercial source code restructuring tools.

As can be seen from the variety of subjects included under the blanket term *complexity,* this is not an easy topic to deal with. From the standpoint of sizing software projects, 6 of the 24 flavors of complexity stand out as being particularly significant:

1. Cyclomatic complexity
2. Code complexity
3. Data complexity
4. Essential complexity

5. Function point complexity

6. Problem complexity

Each of these six tends to have an effect on the either the function point total for the application, the volume of source code required to implement a set of software requirements, or both. Although not every software-estimating tool uses all six of these forms of complexity, the estimating tools that include sizing logic utilize these complexity methods more often than any of the others.

If these six aspects of complexity are rated as high, based on either the subjective opinions of the technical staff who are building the software or on objective metrics, then application sizes are likely to be larger than if these topics are evaluated as being of low complexity.

These same topics also affect software quality, schedules, and costs. However, many other aspects of complexity affect the effort to build software. For estimating the costs and schedules associated with software projects, all 24 of the forms of complexity can be important, and the following 12 of them are known to affect project outcomes in significant ways:

1. Algorithmic complexity

2. Cyclomatic complexity

3. Code complexity

4. Data complexity

5. Entropic complexity

6. Essential complexity

7. Function point complexity

8. Mnemonic complexity

9. Organizational complexity

10. Problem complexity

11. Process complexity

12. Semantic complexity

It has been known for many years that complexity of various forms tends to have a strong correlation with elevated defect levels, reduced levels of defect-removal efficiency, elevated development and maintenance costs, lengthened schedules, and the probability of outright failure or cancellation of a software project.

The correlations between complexity and other factors are not perfect, but are strong enough so that best-in-class companies utilize automated tools for measuring the complexity of source code. As complexity rises, the probability of errors also tends to rise, although the data on the correlations between complexity and defect rates has some exceptions.

Complexity analysis is an intermediate stage of another software technology, too. Most of the commercial code restructuring tools begin with a complexity analysis using cyclomatic complexity or essential complexity, and then automatically simplify the graph of the application and rearrange the code so that cyclomatic and essential complexity are reduced.

Although complexity analysis itself works on a wide variety of programming languages, the code restructuring tools were originally limited to COBOL. In recent years, C and FORTRAN have been added, but there are many hundreds of languages for which automatic restructuring is not possible.

Complexity analysis plays a part in backfiring, or direct conversion from lines-of-code (LOC) metrics to function point metrics. Because the volume of source code needed to encode one function point is partly determined by complexity, it is useful to have cyclomatic and essential complexity data available when doing backfiring. In principle, the complexity-analysis tools could generate the equivalent function point totals automatically, and some vendors are starting to do this.

Much of the literature on software complexity concentrates only on code, and sometimes concentrates only on the control flow or branching sequences. While code complexity is an important subject and well worthy of research, it is far from the only topic that needs to be explored.

Software Productivity Research uses multiple-choice questions to elicit information from software development personnel about their subjective views of several kinds of complexity. SPR normally interviews half a dozen technical personnel for each project and questions their perceptions of the factors that influenced the project, using several hundred multiple-choice questions.

It is relevant to show how perceived complexity increases with some tangible examples. Five plateaus for problem complexity, code complexity, and data complexity, illustrating examples of the factors at play in the ranges between simple and highly complex in the three domains are shown in Table 13.7.

Over the years thousands of software development personnel have been interviewed using this form of complexity questionnaire, and data has also been collected on schedules, costs, defect levels, and defect-removal efficiency levels.

As might be suspected, software projects where the answers are on the high side of the scale (4s and 5s) for problem, code, and data complexity tend to have much larger defect rates and much lower defect

TABLE 13.7   Examples of Software Complexity Analysis Questions

Problem complexity

1. Simple algorithms and simple calculations
   All problem elements are well understood.
   Logic is primarily well understood.
   Mathematics are primarily addition and subtraction.

2. Majority of simple algorithms and simple calculations
   Most problem elements are well understood.
   Logic is primarily deductive from simple rules.
   Mathematics are primarily addition and subtraction, with few complex operations.

3. Algorithms and calculations of average complexity
   Some problem elements are "fuzzy" and uncertain.
   Logic is primarily deductive, but may use compound rules with IF, AND, OR, or CASE conditions.
   Mathematics may include statistical operations, calculus, or higher math.

4. Some difficult and complex calculations
   Many problem elements are "fuzzy" and uncertain.
   Logic is primarily deductive, but may use compound rules with IF, AND, OR, or CASE conditions; some inductive logic or dynamic rules may be included; some recursion may be included.
   Mathematics may include advanced statistical operations, calculus, simultaneous equations, and nonlinear equations.

5. Many difficult and complex calculations
   Most problem elements are "fuzzy" and uncertain.
   Logic may be inductive as well as deductive. Deductive logic may use compound, multilevel rules involving IF, AND, OR, or CASE conditions; recursion is significant.
   Mathematics includes significant amounts of advanced statistical operations, calculus, simultaneous equations, nonlinear equations, and noncommutative equations.

Code complexity

1. Nonprocedural (generated, database, spreadsheet)
   Simple spreadsheet formulas or elementary queries are used.
   Small modules with straight-through control flow are used.
   Branching logic use is close to zero.

2. Built with program skeletons and reusable modules
   Program or system is of a well-understood standard type.
   Reusable modules or object-oriented methods are used.
   Minimal branching logic is used.

3. Well structured (small modules and simple paths)
   Standard IF/THEN/ELSE/CASE structures are used consistently.
   Branching logic follows structured methods.

TABLE 13.7   (*Continued*)

Code complexity

---

4. Fair structure, but some complex paths or modules
    Partial use of IF/THEN/ELSE/CASE structures.
    Some complicated branching logic is used.
    Memory or timing constraints may degrade structure.

5. Poor structure, with many complex modules or paths
    Random or no use of IF/THEN/ELSE/CASE structures.
    Branching logic is convoluted and confusing.
    Severe memory or timing constraints degrade structure.

Data complexity

---

1. Simple data, few variables, and little complexity
    Single file of basic alphanumeric information is used.
    Few calculated values are used.
    Minimal need for validation.

2. Several data elements, but simple data relationships
    Single file of primarily alphanumeric information is used.
    Some calculated values are used.
    Some interdependencies among records and data.
    Some need for validation.

3. Multiple files, switches, and data interactions
    Several files of primarily alphanumeric information are used.
    Some calculated or synthesized values are used.
    Substantial need for validation.
    Some data may be distributed among various hosts.

4. Complex data elements and complex data interactions
    Multiple file structures are used.
    Some data may be distributed among various hosts.
    Some data may not be alphanumeric (i.e., images or graphics).
    Many calculated or synthesized values are used.
    Substantial need for validation.
    Substantial interdependencies among data elements.

5. Very complex data elements and complex data interactions
    Multiple and sometimes incompatible file structures are used.
    Data is distributed among various and incompatible hosts.
    Data may not be alphanumeric (i.e., images or graphics).
    Many calculated or synthesized values are used.
    Substantial need for validation.
    Substantial interdependencies among data elements.

---

removal efficiency levels than projects on the lower end of the scale (1s and 2s).

However, some interesting exceptions to this rule have been observed. From time to time highly complex applications have achieved remarkably good quality results with few defects and high levels of defect-removal efficiency. Conversely, some simple projects have approached disastrous levels of defects and achieved only marginal levels of defect removal efficiency.

The general reason for this anomaly is because software project managers tend to assign the toughest projects to the most experienced and capable technical staff, while simple projects are often assigned to novices or those with low levels of experience.

The SPR complexity factors also play a key role in the logic of backfiring or direct conversion from logical source code statements into equivalent function points. For the purposes of backfiring, the sum of the problem, code, and data complexity scores are used to provide a complexity adjustment multiplier (see Table 13.8).

For example, a COBOL application of average complexity with a sum of 9 for the individual complexity scores will probably require approximately 107 source code statements in the procedure and data divisions to encode 1 function point.

TABLE 13.8   SPR Backfire Complexity Adjustments

Sum of problem, data, and code complexity scores	Code size adjustment multiplier
3	0.70
4	0.75
5	0.80
6	0.85
7	0.90
8	0.95
9	1.00
10	1.05
11	1.10
12	1.15
13	1.12
14	1.25
15	1.30

A low-complexity application with a sum of 3 for the complexity factors might require only about 75 source code statements in the procedure and data divisions to encode 1 function point.

A high-complexity application with a sum of 15 for the factors might require as many as 140 source code statements in the procedure and data divisions to encode 1 function point.

Complexity is a very important topic for software. Indeed, the complexity of some software applications appears to be as great as that of almost any kind of product constructed by the human species.

A great deal more research is needed on all forms of software complexity, and particularly on complexity associated with algorithms, visualization, software requirements, specifications, test cases, and data complexity.

Software Sizing with Reusable Components

As the twentieth century winds down, an increasingly large number of software projects are being constructed using reusable components of various kinds. The topic of reuse is very large and includes many more artifacts than source code alone. For example, it is possible to reuse any or all of the following software artifacts:

- Reusable architectures
- Reusable requirements
- Reusable designs
- Reusable class libraries
- Reusable source code modules
- Reusable source code components
- Reusable cost estimates
- Reusable project plans
- Reusable data
- Reusable user manuals
- Reusable graphics
- Reusable test plans
- Reusable test cases

Sizing methods for dealing with reusable artifacts are not yet perfected as this book is being written, but they are starting to evolve. The eventual solution will probably be to enumerate function point totals for all major reusable artifacts, so that when software projects are constructed from reusable components their overall size can be summed from the function point sizes of the individual components.

Thus, it might be possible in the future to estimate a project that consists of 7 reusable components each of 100 function points in size, plus a separate portion that must be developed uniquely which is 300 function points in size. Thus the overall project as delivered will be 1000 function points, but it will be constructed from 700 function points of reusable components and one unique component of 300 function points.

A basic difficulty of this approach is the fact that generic reusable components may have features which are not needed or used by a specific application. For example, suppose that for a reusable component of 100 function points only half of these, or 50 function points, are actually going to be utilized in the application being estimated.

The current solution to this problem is to assign a size label to the overall reusable component, and then use percentages to deal with the portions being used. For example, in the case just cited the gross size of the component is 100 function points, and if 50 percent of these features are to be utilized, then the net size in the current application would be 50 function points.

However, the introduction of percentages is intellectually unsatisfying and lacks precision. As this book is being written, there are no other available methods for dealing with partial utilization of reusable artifacts.

Since functional metrics reflect the user's view of the features needed or desired, it is obvious that if 1000 users are going to utilize portions of the same artifact, their personal needs will vary widely.

Consider a basic application, such as a modern Windows-based word processor, whose total size in terms of all features is perhaps 3000 function points. Modern word processors are so feature rich that it is doubtful if any single user utilizes more than a fraction of their available capacity. For example, in writing this book using Microsoft Word it is unlikely that the author utilized more than about 10 percent of the total feature set of this product, or perhaps 300 function points out of a possible 3000 function points.

However, on any given business day millions of people are using Microsoft Word simultaneously, so all of us together probably exercise every known feature of this product on a daily basis, even though no single user needs more than a small fraction of the total capabilities.

This simple example illustrates a key point when dealing with software reusability. It is important to keep separate records for what is *delivered* to clients, what is *developed* by the project team, and what is *reused* from component or class libraries.

In the past, the size of what got delivered and the size of what was developed were close to being the same, and reuse usually amounted to less than 15 percent by volume. As component reuse, patterns, frameworks, object-oriented class libraries, and other forms of reuse become common there will be a marked transformation in the ratios of reused material to custom development. It is not impossible to envision future software projects where close to 100 percent of the major artifacts are reused and custom development hovers below 1 percent.

Incidentally, the use of ratios and percentages to distinguish the proportion of reused material for any given artifact is now a feature of the sizing logic of several commercial software cost estimating tools. Users can now specify the percentage of reuse for such key artifacts as specifications, source code, user manuals, test cases, and so forth. The estimating tools will suggest default values based on empirical data, but users are free to modify the default assumptions for each artifact.

Overview of the Basic Principles of Function Point Metrics

Since not every reader is familiar with function points it may be of interest to illustrate the basics of function point analysis, in order to demonstrate why this is a useful but complex activity.

There are many complicated metrics that are used in daily life which we have learned to utilize and often take for granted, although few of us actually know how these metrics are counted or derived. For example, in the course of a normal day we may use the metrics of horsepower, octane ratings, and perhaps British thermal units (BTUs). We might discuss caloric content or cholesterol levels in various kinds of food. We may also discuss wind-chill factors. For day-to-day purposes, it is only sufficient that we know how to use these metrics and understand their significance. Very few people actually need to know how to calculate octane ratings or horsepower, so long as we feel fairly confident that published data is calculated honestly.

For that matter, those who invest in the stock market use the Dow Jones stock averages as a daily indicator, but few investors know how these averages are calculated. In a similar vein, the national rates of inflation and unemployment are difficult to calculate, but easy to understand.

In the same vein, very few people need to understand how to count function points, but every software project manager and technical staff member should understand how to use them and should know ranges of productivity and quality results.

For example, every project manager should understand the following generic ranges of software productivity levels:

- Projects of less than 5 function points per staff month (more than 26 work hours per function point) indicate performance that is below U.S. averages for all software projects.

- Projects between 5 and 10 function points per staff month (13 to 26 work hours per function point) approximate the normal range for U.S. software projects.

- Projects between 10 and 20 function points per staff month (7 to 13 work hours per function point) are higher than U.S. averages for software projects.

- Projects above 20 function points per staff month (7 work hours per function point) are significantly better than U.S. averages for software projects.

Of course, this kind of generic information needs to be calibrated for the specific class of software being considered, and also for the size of specific applications. Small projects of less than 100 function points in size often top 20 function points per staff month, but for larger projects above 1000 function points in size such results are extremely rare.

Function point metrics are difficult to calculate but easy to understand. The basic range of performance using function point metrics should be known by all software practitioners even if they only know such generalities as the following:

- A delivered defect rate of more than 1.50 bugs per function point is very bad.

- A delivered defect rate of less than 0.75 bugs per function point is normal.

- A delivered defect rate of less than 0.10 bugs per function point is very good.

The following overview is not intended as a function point counting manual leading to the development of actual counting skills. It is merely a summary of basic principles so that readers with no knowledge of what a function point is will be able to understand the basics of how they are calculated.

Let us turn to an overview of function point fundamentals. Recall from prior discussions that function points are based purely on the external attributes of a software project, and that the fundamental units of function point analysis consist of five primary elements:

1. Inputs
2. Outputs
3. Inquiries
4. Logical files
5. Interfaces

Function Point Types

- **External Inputs**

- **External Outputs** } **Transaction Function Types**

- **External Inquiries**

- **Internal Logical Files**

- **External Interface Files** } **Data Function Types**

Figure 13.1   Primary function point attributes.

Three of these five external attributes deal with the transactions that software performs, and two deal with the kinds of data utilized by the application. (See Fig. 13.1.)

These various external attributes are normally abbreviated when counting because using the whole name for each attribute quickly becomes cumbersome. Therefore, readers can expect to see the following abbreviations in the function point literature:

External inputs   EI

External outputs   EO

External inquiries   EQ

Internal logical files   ILF

External interface files EIF

The first aspect of using function points on a real project is to define the boundary of the application itself that needs to be sized. While this is simple enough in theory, it can be rather tricky in real life. (See Fig. 13.2.)

As an example of defining the boundary of an application, this manuscript is produced using Microsoft Word for Windows. This word processing application is part of a connected suite of applications that includes the Excel spreadsheet, the Access database, the PowerPoint graphics tool, and the Schedule Plus personal information manager.

Each of these separate applications would comprise a separate software project with its own boundaries and each could be enumerated using function points (in fact, each of these applications is about 3000 function points in size). However, each application can share information with the others, and the overall suite of applications is marketed as a set.

Identifying Application Boundaries

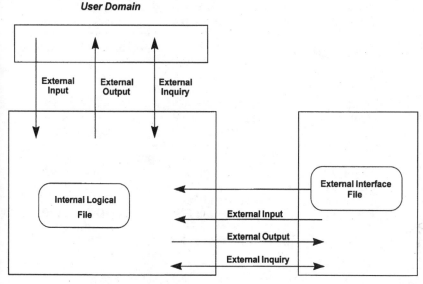

Figure 13.2   Application boundaries for function point analysis.

Once the boundary of the application has been determined, then the actual numbers of inputs, outputs, inquires, logical files, and interfaces are enumerated. It is at this point that the services of a certified function point counting expert are often utilized; or, alternatively, a function point counting tool may be invoked.

In any real-life software project, the work of development comprises not just writing new software; it also includes changes and modifications to existing software and, sometimes, deleting features that are being replaced.

All of these activities can be enumerated using function points, but doing so requires careful analysis of a number of variables, as shown in Fig. 13.3.

Since there are many kinds of inputs, outputs, inquiries, interfaces, and logical files used with software projects, consider some of the possible examples of each of these basic parameters, starting with some of the kinds of things that constitute *inputs* to software projects.

Figure 13.4 and the following illustrate some of the possibilities for each parameter, and also illustrate the kind of diagrams that are often used for function point analysis.

As can be expected, the accuracy of function point analysis depends to a certain degree upon the completeness and the form of the

Determine Type of Count

Type of Project	Project Function Points	Application Function Points
		Installed Function Pts. (IFP)
Development Project	Project FP = New (Added) FP + Conversion FP	Application FP = New (Added) FP
Enhancement Project	Project FP = Added FP + Changed FP + Deleted FP + Conversion FP	Application FP = Original FP - Deleted FP + Added FP + Δ Changed FP

Figure 13.3   Function point enumeration for new and modified projects.

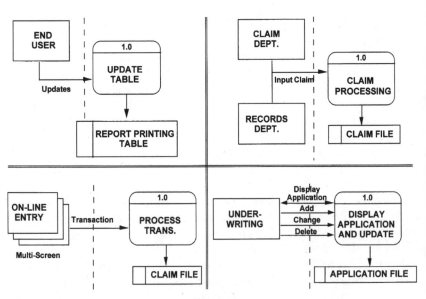

Figure 13.4   Examples of external input (EI) types.

requirements and the external specifications from which the function point totals are to be derived.

Although the military community has lagged somewhat in using function point analysis, the completeness of military specifications actually provides a very solid base for function point counting.

Specifications produced using any of the standard design methodologies provide a suitable basis for function point analysis; methods such as Warnier-Orr design, Merise, Yourdon structured design, or the Booch-Rumbaugh-Jacobsen Universal Modeling Language (UML) are all perfectly good starting places for function point analysis.

Although there are often questions from the OO community about the suitability of function point analysis for object-oriented projects, it is often easier to derive function points for OO projects than for many other kinds of software.

What is a troubling situation in terms of function point analysis is that some of the rapid application development (RAD) variants more or less dispense with written requirements and written specifications and plunge directly into some form of high-speed evolutionary prototype. Under such casual methods, there is little or no basis for accurate function point enumeration.

Also, this kind of casual development that truncates or eliminates written requirements and specifications is also difficult in the context of inspections and testing, and explains why such RAD variants have a distressing tendency to be unsatisfactory in terms of quality and maintainability.

Figure 13.5 shows some examples of typical output situations as might be used for function point analysis.

The outputs of a software application are quite important for sizing and cost estimating, because they are often the first topic that is explored in sufficient depth to actually begin the process of function point analysis. This phenomenon can be useful for some of the forms of function point approximation, where function point totals are estimated in the absence of complete information.

Inquiries (see Fig. 13.6) are the most tricky and subtle of the basic function point parameters because they consist of two linked portions, a query followed by a response. Indeed, it has been observed more than once that inquiries are basically nothing more than special cases of inputs and outputs.

Internal logical files (see Fig. 13.7) are key components of information systems, and the effort associated with building, serving, and utilizing logical files is a dominant portion of the development of information systems. This fact explains why logical files have the greatest weights assigned to them in function point analysis.

The last of the five function point parameters to be illustrated is

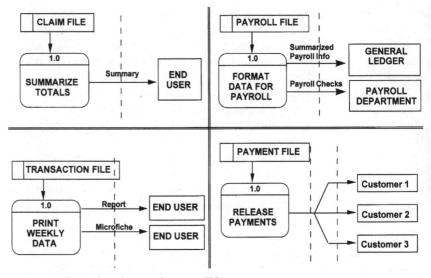

Figure 13.5 Examples of external output (EO) types.

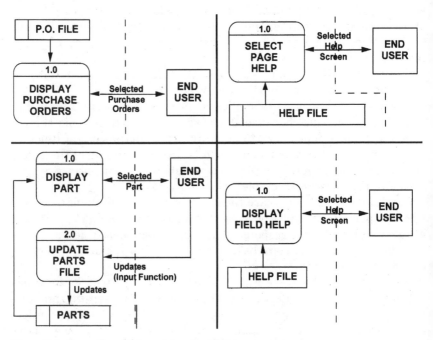

Figure 13.6 Examples of external inquiry (EQ) types.

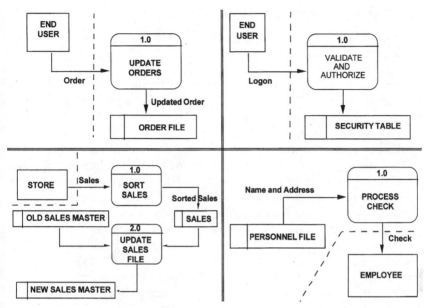

Figure 13.7 Examples of internal logical file (ILF) types.

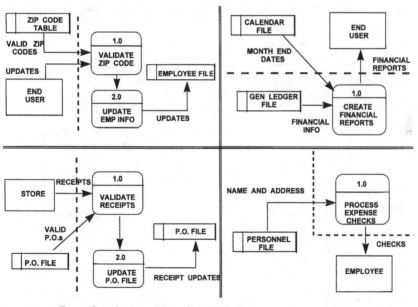

Figure 13.8 Examples of external interface (EIF) files.

the external interfaces to other applications (see Fig. 13.8). Interfaces are also rather difficult to implement, and, hence, the weighting factors for interfaces are higher than for any other of the five parameters, except for logical files.

Function Point Complexity Adjustments

It is an interesting sociological topic that the methods of evaluating *complexity* in a function point context and the 24 kinds of complexity discussed earlier in this chapter are only loosely connected.

The word *complexity* in function point analysis is somewhat restricted and deals primarily with methods for determining whether the five function point elements should be ranked as being of low, average, or high complexity.

Dealing with the function point methods of complexity adjustment is another aspect of function point counting that requires training. The complexity of counting the specific numbers of elements is because each element must be evaluated in terms of whether its complexity is *average,* or *low,* or *high.* Normally, a preliminary function point count is made using a worksheet as represented in Fig. 13.9.

The rules for determining whether an attribute should rank high or low in complexity are rather complicated and lengthy. On the other hand, the rules for determining our annual income tax are much more complex than the rules for determining function points, and many of us deal with the tax rules once a year.

The determinations for high, low, or average complexity for each of the five elements are made by evaluating the numbers of files and

Unadjusted Function Point Count

	USER FUNCTION LEVEL			
	Low (L)	Average (A)	High (H)	TOTAL
Input	___ x 3 = ___	___ x 4 = ___	___ x 6 = ___	_____
Output	___ x 4 = ___	___ x 5 = ___	___ x 7 = ___	_____
Inquiry	___ x 3 = ___	___ x 4 = ___	___ x 6 = ___	_____
Internal Logical File	___ x 7 = ___	___ x 10 = ___	___ x 15 = ___	_____
External Interface File	___ x 5 = ___	___ x 7 = ___	___ x 10 = ___	_____
Unadjusted Function Point Total				_____

Figure 13.9 Example of a function point counting worksheet.

Reference Table - External Inputs (EI)

File Types Referenced	Data Elements		
	1 - 4	5 - 15	16 +
< 2	Low - 3 FP	Low - 3 FP	Avg - 4 FP
2	Low - 3 FP	Avg - 4 FP	High - 6 FP
> 2	Avg - 4 FP	High - 6 FP	High - 6 FP

Figure 13.10 Example of a function point adjustment table for external inputs.

data elements that are referenced. For example, the worktable for dealing with the complexity of the internal input parameters resembles Fig. 13.10.

Without going to extremes, it should be obvious why the manual counting of the function point totals of an application usually proceeds at a rate of no more than 500 to perhaps 1000 function points per day. The rules are complex enough and the effort is time-consuming enough to make the work rather taxing.

Once the preliminary totals are accumulated, another set of adjustments then are made to deal with the 14 adjustment factors utilized by the IFPUG method, the 19 adjustment factors utilized by the British Mark II function point method, the 3 adjustment factors utilized by the SPR feature point metric, the 22 adjustment factors utilized by the DeMarco function point, or any of the adjustments used by the many other function point variants.

Other function point methods utilize variations in the number and significance of the final complexity adjustments. The overall range of the final complexity adjustments can change the function point total for an application by about plus or minus 35 percent, so the results are not insignificant.

The variations in complexity adjustments for function point totals have been a troublesome and contentious aspect of function point analysis. Indeed, the ambiguity and partial subjectivity of the adjustments have led several researchers to assert that the counts might be more accurate if the complexity adjustments were dispensed with and not even used at all.

**TABLE 13.9   Function Point
Complexity Adjustment Weights**

0	Not present or no influence at all
1	Minor influence
2	Moderate influence
3	Average influence
4	Significant influence
5	Strong, pervasive influence

Let us consider how these complexity adjustments operate, and the readers can see for themselves why the adjustment factors have been frequent subjects of debate and dispute. The purpose of the complexity adjustment factors is to modify the function point size of the application upward or downward based on the perceived impact of the adjustment parameters. Each adjustment parameter receives a score that can run from 0 in the case of *not present at all* through 5 for a *strong, pervasive influence*. The overall scoring method for the adjustment factors is shown in Table 13.9.

Let us examine the adjustment factors for three common variations of function point analysis. SPR adjustments, the IFPUG adjustments, and the British Mark II adjustments are shown in Table 13.10:

It is obvious from this table why it is important to know which function point method is being used to determine the size of the application, because the adjustment factors can lead to rather different final sizes. To apply the adjustments, the IFPUG and Mark II methods use a similar formula:

- Sum the total score for the adjustment factors.

- Convert the score to a decimal value by dividing by 100.

- Add a constant value of 0.65 to create an adjustment multiplier.

- Multiply the unadjusted function points by the adjustment multiplier.

- Use the final result as the adjusted function point total.

An example can perhaps clarify the adjustment situation. Suppose you have an unadjusted raw total of function points that is equal to exactly 100. Now you wish to apply the final complexity adjustments using the IFPUG method.

Suppose you assign every one of the 14 IFPUG factors a weight of 4. The sum for the adjustment factors would obviously be 56, since each of the 14 factors receives a weight of 4.

TABLE 13.10   Complexity Adjustments for SPR, IFPUG, and Mark II Function Points

SPR function points	IFPUG function points	Mark II function points
1 Problem complexity	Data communications	Data communications
2 Code complexity	Distributed functions	Distributed functions
3 Data complexity	Performance goals	Performance goals
4	Configuration usage	Configuration usage
5	Transaction rates	Transaction rates
6	Online data entry	Online data entry
7	End-user efficiency	End-user efficiency
8	Online update	Online update
9	Complex processing	Complex processing
10	Reusability	Reusability
11	Installation ease	Installation ease
12	Operational ease	Operational ease
13	Multiple-site usage	Multiple-site usage
14	Facilitate change	Facilitate change
15		Synchronization
16		Security, privacy
17		User training
18		Third-party usage
19		Documentation
Plus or minus 40%	Plus or minus 35%	Plus or minus 60%

Converting the total of 56 to a decimal value yields a result of 0.56. Adding the constant of 0.65 now gives you a multiplier of 1.21.

The last step is to multiply the original unadjusted total of 100 function points by the multiplier of 1.21 which brings the adjusted function point total to 121.

If you were to follow the same pattern using the British Mark II function point method, the results would be higher for the same application. Assuming that you scored each of the 19 Mark II factors with the same weight, or 4, your sum total would be 76.

Converting 76 to a decimal value yields 0.76, and adding the constant value of 0.65 brings the adjustment multiplier to 1.41.

Multiplying your unadjusted total of 100 raw function points by the adjustment multiplier would yield a final adjusted total of 141 Mark II function points for the same application.

The SPR method of complexity adjustment achieves results that are very close to the IFPUG method, but it goes about it in quite a different manner.

The IFPUG and Mark II function point methods were designed for manual counts by human function point experts. The SPR method, on the other hand, was never intended for manual counting but was designed to be used in a rule-based expert system.

Like the IFPUG and Mark II methods, the SPR complexity adjustments utilize a five-point weighting scale as follows:

SPR Function Point Complexity Adjustment Factors

Problem complexity　　　　　　　　　　　_____

1. All simple algorithms and simple calculations
2. Majority of simple algorithms and simple calculations
3. Algorithms and calculations of average complexity
4. Some difficult or complex algorithms or calculations
5. Many difficult algorithms and complex calculations

Code complexity　　　　　　　　　　　_____

1. Nonprocedural (generated, spreadsheet, query, etc.)
2. Well-structured code with simple control flows
3. Average structure, but some complex control flows
4. Fair structure, but some complex flows and branch logic
5. Poor structure, with very complex control flow and branch logic

Data complexity　　　　　　　　　　　_____

1. Simple data with few elements and relationships
2. Numerous variable and constant data items, but simple relationships
3. Average complexity with multiple files, fields, and data relationships
4. Complex file structures and complex data relationships
5. Very complex file structures and very complex data relationships

For normal forward function point calculations using the SPR complexity adjustments, the sum of the *problem complexity* and *data complexity* scores are utilized. For backfiring, or converting logical source code statements into equivalent function point counts, the *code complexity* parameter is also used. (see Table 13.11.)

Continuing the same example used for the IFPUG and Mark II adjustments, assuming that a user scored both the problem complex-

TABLE 13.11   SPR Function Point Complexity Adjustment Values

Sum of problem and data complexity	Adjustment Multiplier
1	0.5
2	0.6
3	0.7
4	0.8
5	0.9
6	1.0
7	1.1
8	1.2
9	1.3
10	1.4
11	1.5

ity and data complexity values as 4, then the sum of these two factors is 8.

Using the SPR adjustments in Table 13.11, the adjustment multiplier would be 1.2 and the final adjusted function point total would be 120. As can be seen, the SPR method and the IFPUG method often achieve similar results, and many times the results are identical.

Although this discussion does not illustrate it, the fact that the SPR method was designed for automated counting rather than manual counting allows decimal values to be used. For example, using the SPR approach, problem complexity scores of 2.45 or even 5.95 are valid and permitted values.

The use of decimal places allows fine tuning of responses. The SPR function point enumeration software, such as SPQR/20, CHECK-POINT, and KnowledgePlan, evaluates the user-supplied decimal place values and creates adjustment multipliers with three-decimal-place precision, such as 1.215.

This quick tour through the intricacies of function point analysis explains why the method is somewhat daunting and intimidating to first-time users. It also illustrates why manual function point analysis is rather time-consuming and can be expensive for large software projects.

It might be thought that the complexity of the function point counting rules would lead to huge variations in function point totals simply due to individual, personal interpretations of the counting rules. However, a study commissioned by IFPUG and performed by Dr. Chris Kemerer when he was at MIT's Sloan School found only about a

9 percent variance when the same application was counted by certified function point specialists.

Of course, attempts to count function points by untrained, uncertified personnel can lead to variations of several hundred percent, which is about the range of variation noted with counts of source code volumes, where there are multiple standards and no certification programs.

Unfortunately, the many variations in the basic function point rules are the real problem with function point analysis. The host of possible function point methods, such as IFPUG, Mark II, the Boeing 3D method, SPR function points, SPR feature points, Netherlands function points, backfired function points, and many others, are causing the entire function point community to be regarded as confused and unfocused.

Possibly the work of the ISO can lead to a unified form of function point analysis that will eliminate some or all of the many variations. However, this is a best-case scenario.

The worst-case scenario is that the ISO standard for function point sizing will merely become yet another variation in the huge family of current variations. As this book is being written, the ISO version is still under construction and it is premature to judge either its technical merits or its success in standardizing a rather confusing set of local variations.

In summary, the main strengths of function point metrics are the following:

1. Function points stay constant regardless of the programming languages used.

2. Function points are a good choice for full-life-cycle analysis.

3. Function points are a good choice for software reuse analysis.

4. Function points are a good choice for object-oriented economic studies.

5. Function points are supported by many software cost estimating tools.

6. Function points can be mathematically converted into logical code statements for many languages.

The main weaknesses of function point metrics are the following:

1. Accurate counting requires certified function point specialists.

2. Function point counting can be time-consuming and expensive.

3. Function point counting automation is of unknown accuracy.

4. Function point counts are erratic for projects below 15 function points in size.

5. Function point variations have no conversion rules to IFPUG function points.

6. Many function point variations have no backfiring conversion rules.

Although the technical strengths of function points are greater than their weaknesses, the politics and disputes among the function point splinter groups and the failure of the IFPUG organization to meet the needs of the entire function point community are likely to damage the prospects of functional metrics in the future.

On the other hand, the problems of using lines-of-code metrics for sizing and estimating are even greater than those of functional metrics. The most effective strategy would probably be to concentrate on developing one or more *standard* functional metrics with rigorous conversion logic between the standard and older alternatives.

Source Code Sizing

Source code sizing is the oldest sizing method for software and has been part of the feature sets of software cost estimating tools since the 1970s. In general, for such common programming languages as COBOL or C, automated software cost estimating tools can now do a very capable job of source code size prediction as early as the requirements phase, and often even before that, by using some of the approximation methods discussed earlier.

However, sizing for modern *visual* programming languages has added some complexity and some ambiguity to the source code sizing domain. For such languages as Visual Basic, Realizer, Forte, PowerBuilder, and many others, some of the "programming" does not utilize source code statements at all.

Sizing source code when the language utilizes button controls, pull-down menus, or icons in order to create functionality is a difficult task that taxes software cost estimating tools. But the usage of such controls for programming development is a fast-growing trend that will eventually dominate the software language world. It is also a trend that basically negates the use of source code metrics for some of the languages in question, although function points work perfectly well.

When the software industry began in the early 1950s, the first metric developed for quantifying the output of a software project was the metric termed *lines of code* (LOC). Almost at once some ambiguity occurred, because a *line of code* could be defined as either of the following:

- A physical line of code.
- A logical statement.

Physical lines of code are simply sets of coded instructions terminated by pressing the enter key of a computer keyboard. For some languages physical lines of code and logical statements are almost identical, but for other languages there can be major differences in apparent size based on whether physical lines or logical statements are used.

Table 13.12 illustrates some of the possible code counting ambiguity for a simple COBOL application, using both logical statements and physical lines.

As can be seen from this simple example, the concept of what actually comprises a line of code is surprisingly ambiguous. The size range can run from a low of 700 LOC if you select only logical statements in the procedure division to a high of 2500 LOC if you select a count of total physical lines. Almost any intervening size is possible, and most variations are in use for productivity studies, research papers, journal articles, books, and so forth.

Bear in mind that Table 13.12 is a simple example using only one programming language for a new application. The SPR catalog of programming languages (Jones 1996b) contains almost 500 programming languages, and more are being added on a daily basis. Furthermore, a significant number of software applications utilize two or more programming languages at the same time. For example, such combinations as COBOL and SQL or Ada and Jovial are very common. SPR has observed one system that actually contains 12 different programming languages.

There are other complicating factors, too, such as the use of macro instructions and the inclusion of copybooks, inheritance, class

TABLE 13.12   Sample COBOL Application Showing Sizes of Code Divisions Using Logical Statements and Physical Lines of Code

Division	Logical statements	Physical lines
Identification division	25	25
Environment division	75	75
Data division	300	350
Procedure division	700	950
Dead code	100	300
Comments	200	700
Blank lines	100	100
Total lines of code	1500	2500

libraries, and other forms of reusable code. There is also ambiguity when dealing with enhancements and maintenance, such as whether to count the base code when enhancing existing applications.

Obviously, with so many variations in how lines of code might be counted, it would be useful to have a standard for defining what should be included and excluded. Here we encounter another problem. There is no true international standard for defining code counting rules. Instead, there are a number of published local standards which, unfortunately, are in conflict with one another.

Citing just two of the more widely used local standards, the Software Productivity Research (SPR) code counting rules published in 1991 are based on logical statements (Jones 1991) while the Software Engineering Institute (SEI) code counting standards are based on physical lines of code. Both of these conflicting standards are widely used and widely cited, but they differ in many key assumptions.

As an experiment, the author carried out an informal survey of code counting practices in such software journals as *American Programmer, Byte, Application Development Trends, Communications of the ACM, IBM Systems Journal, IEEE Computer, IEEE Software, Software Development,* and *Software Magazine.*

About a third of the published articles using LOC data used physical lines, and another third used logical statements, while the remaining third did not define which method was used and, hence, were ambiguous in results by several hundred percent. While there may be justifications for selecting physical lines or logical statements for a particular research study, there is no justification at all for publishing data without stating which method was utilized!

To summarize, the main strengths of physical LOC are as follows:

1. The physical LOC metric is easy to count.

2. The physical LOC metric has been extensively automated for counting.

3. The physical LOC metric is used in a number of software estimating tools.

The main weaknesses of physical LOC are as follows:

1. The physical LOC metric may include substantial dead code.

2. The physical LOC metric may include blanks and comments.

3. The physical LOC metric is ambiguous for mixed-language projects.

4. The physical LOC metric is ambiguous for software reuse.

5. The physical LOC metric is a poor choice for full-life-cycle studies.

6. The physical LOC metric does not work for some visual languages.

7. The physical LOC metric is erratic for direct conversion to function points.

8. The physical LOC metric is erratic for direct conversion to logical statements.

The main strengths of logical statements are as follows:

1. Logical statements exclude dead code, blanks, and comments.

2. Logical statements can be mathematically converted into function point metrics.

3. Logical statements are used in a number of software-estimating tools.

The main weaknesses of logical statements are as follows:

1. Logical statements can be difficult to count.

2. Logical statements are not extensively automated.

3. Logical statements are a poor choice for full-life-cycle studies.

4. Logical statements are ambiguous for some visual languages.

5. Logical statements may be ambiguous for software reuse.

6. Logical statements may be erratic for direct conversion to the physical LOC metric.

Although not as exotic as the modern visual programming languages, a number of important business applications have been built with such spreadsheets such as Excel and Lotus. The mechanics of entering a spreadsheet formula are more or less equivalent to using a *statement* in a programming language. The spreadsheet macro languages actually are programming languages, even if not very elegant ones. However, using the built-in spreadsheet facilities for creating graphs from numeric tables is not really *programming* as it is traditionally defined.

Even more troublesome in the context of sizing are some of the add-on features associated with spreadsheets, such as templates, back-solving features, functions for statistical operations, for "what you see is what you get" printing, and a host of others.

For example, Case Study A earlier in this book illustrated a cost estimate for a small personal travel-expense program that was to be created in Visual Basic. Several commercial spreadsheets already have travel expense templates available, so that if the application were intended for a spreadsheet rather than for Visual Basic, little or no programming would even be needed.

Indeed, even in the context of Visual Basic, travel-expense controls are available from commercial vendors, which would cut down on the amount of procedural code that might have to be created.

Of course, reused software code in any fashion adds complexity to the task of software sizing also. Spontaneous reuse by programmers from their own private libraries of algorithms and routines has been part of programming since the industry began.

More extensive, formal reuse of software artifacts from certified libraries or commercial sources is not as common as private reuse, but is rapidly becoming a trend of significant dimensions.

As mentioned previously, there are more than 500 variations and dialects of commercial programming languages in existence, and perhaps another 200 or so proprietary "private" languages have been developed by corporations for their own use.

Also, many software applications utilize multiple languages concurrently. About one-third of U.S. software projects contain at least two programming languages, such as COBOL and SQL. Perhaps 10 percent of U.S. software applications contain three or more languages, and a few may contain as many as a dozen languages simultaneously.

The technology of source code size prediction for traditional procedural programming languages has been eased substantially by the advent of function point metrics. Because function points are normally calculated or derived during requirements definition, and because source code volumes can be predicted once function point totals are known, it is now possible to create reasonably accurate source code size estimates much earlier in the development cycle than ever before.

However, even with the help of function points source code sizing has some problems remaining, as shown in Table 13.13.

The same application can vary by as much as 500 percent in apparent size depending upon which code counting method is utilized. Consider the following example in the BASIC programming language:

```
BASEPAY = 0: BASEPAY = HOURS*PAYRATE: PRINT BASEPAY
```

This example is obviously one physical line of code. However, this example contains three separate logical statements. The first statement sets a field called *BASEPAY* to zero value. The second statement performs a calculation and puts the result in the field called *BASE-PAY.* The third statement prints out the results of the calculation.

It is clearly important to know whether physical lines or logical statements are implied when using the phrases *lines of code* (LOC),

TABLE 13.13   Software Sizing Problems, Circa 1998

1. Sizing source code volumes for proprietary programming languages
2. Sizing source code volumes for visually oriented programming languages
3. Sizing source code volumes for spreadsheet applications
4. Sizing source code volumes for microcode programming languages
5. Sizing very small updates below the levels at which function points are accurate
6. Sizing the volume of reusable code from certified component libraries
7. Sizing the volume of borrowed code taken from other applications
8. Sizing the volume of base, existing code when updating legacy applications
9. Sizing the volume of commercial software packages when they are being modified
10. Sizing changes and deletions to legacy applications, rather than new code
11. Sizing temporary scaffold code that is discarded after use
12. Sizing code volumes in disposable prototypes
13. Standardizing the forms of complexity that affect sizing logic
14. Validating or challenging the rules for backfiring lines of code to function points
15. Measuring the rate of unplanned growth to software artifacts during development

1000 lines of code (KLOC), and *1000 source lines of code* (KSLOC). (There is no difference numerically between KLOC and KSLOC.)

For a detailed look at the variations in the rules associated with counting source code volumes, refer to App. A, which shows the range of possible rules and also the specific subsets of rules that the author's company has adopted for use in its software cost estimating tools.

As a general rule, sizing source code volumes lends itself to rule-based parsing engines that can examine large volumes of source code quickly. While such engines are commercially available for such common languages as COBOL and C, the organizations that utilize proprietary or obscure languages often build their own counting tools.

Unfortunately, there is little or no consistency in the rules themselves, and almost every conceivable variation can be and has been utilized. The wide variations in methods for enumerating source code volumes cast severe doubts on the validity of large-scale statistical studies based on LOC metrics.

If one-third of the journal articles use physical lines of code, one-third use logical statements, and one-third don't state which method is used, then it is obvious that the overall data based on LOC metrics needs some serious scrubbing before any valid conclusions might be derived from it.

Once the primary size of a software project is determined using function points, source code statements, or both, then a host of other software artifacts can be sized in turn. Let us now consider some of the sizing ranges for such derivative software artifacts as paper documents, test cases, and bugs or defects.

Sizing Object-Oriented Software Projects

The object-oriented (OO) paradigm has been expanding rapidly in terms of numbers of projects developed. The OO paradigm presents some unique challenges to software cost estimating and sizing tool vendors, since OO development methods are not perfectly congruent with the way software is developed outside of the OO paradigm.

The OO community has been attempting to quantify the productivity and quality levels of OO projects, but because of the special needs of the OO paradigm the traditional LOC metric was not a suitable choice.

Although function point metrics can actually demonstrate the productivity advantages of the OO paradigm (Love 1993) and have been used for OO economic analysis (Jones 1997a) knowledge of functional metrics remains sparse among the OO community.

Curiously, the function point community is very knowledgeable about the OO paradigm, but the reverse is not true. For example, Software Engineering Management Research Lab at the University of Montreal has produced an interesting report (Fetchke et al. 1997) which maps the Jacobsen OO design method into equivalent function point analysis and generates function point sizes from Jacobsen's design approach.

A fairly extensive form of software research has started among OO metrics practitioners to develop a new and unique kind of sizing and estimating for OO projects, based on a specialized suite of metrics that are derived from the OO paradigm itself. For example, research at the University of Pittsburgh (Chidamber, Darcy, and Kemerer 1996) is attempting to build a complete OO metrics suite.

Similar research is ongoing in Europe, and a suite of OO metrics termed MOOD has been developed in Portugal (Abrieu 1997). There are also *object point* metrics, which attempt to build a special kind of function point keyed to the OO paradigm (Gupta 1996).

In the United States the work of Chidamber and Kemerer is perhaps the best known. Some of the OO metrics suggested by Chidamber, Darcy, and Kemerer include the following:

Weighted methods per class (WMC).   This metric is a count of the number of methods in a given class. The *weight* portion of this metric is still under examination and is being actively researched.

Depth of inheritance tree (DIT).   This is the maximum depth of a given class in the class hierarchy.

Number of children (NOC).   This is the number of immediate sub-classes of a given class.

Response for a class (RFC).   This is the number of methods that can execute in response to a message sent to an object within this class, using up to one level of nesting.

Lack of cohesion of methods (LCOM).   This metric is a count of the number of disjoint method pairs minus the number of similar method pairs. The disjoint methods have no common instance variables, while the similar methods have at least one common instance variable.

As this book is being written, the OO metrics are still highly experimental and, so far as can be determined, none are yet present in any of the major commercial software sizing and cost-estimating tools, such as (in alphabetical order) Bridge Modeler, CHECKPOINT, COCOMO, COCOMO II, ESTIMACS, KnowledgePlan, PRICE-S, REVIC, SEER, SLIM, SOFTCOST, and so forth.

In the past, both LOC and function point metrics have splintered into a number of competing and semiincompatible metric variants. There is some reason to believe that the OO metrics community will also splinter into competing variants, possibly following national boundaries. The main strengths of OO metrics are as follows:

1. The OO metrics are psychologically attractive within the OO community.

2. The OO metrics appear to be able to distinguish simple from complex OO projects.

The main weaknesses of OO metrics are as follows:

1. The OO metrics do not support studies outside of the OO paradigm.

2. The OO metrics do not deal with full-life-cycle issues.

3. The OO metrics have not yet been applied to testing.

4. The OO metrics have not yet been applied to maintenance.

5. The OO metrics have no conversion rules to LOC metrics.

6. The OO metrics have no conversion rules to function point metrics.

7. The OO metrics lack automation.

8. The OO metrics are difficult to enumerate.

9. The OO metrics are not supported by software-estimating tools.

Because of the rapid growth of the OO paradigm, the need for sizing and estimating metrics within the OO community is fairly urgent. Unfortunately, the OO metrics researchers are not as conversant with the standard metrics, such as function points, as might be desired.

Sizing Text-Based Paper Documents

Software is a very paper-intensive occupation and tends to put out massive quantities of paper materials. In fact, for large military software projects the creation and production of paper documents is actually the major cost element; it is more expensive than the source code itself and is even more expensive than testing and defect removal.

For civilian projects, paperwork is not quite as massive as for military projects, but it can still run up to many thousands of pages for large systems above 5000 function points in size.

Some of the major categories of paper documents produced for software projects include but are not limited to the following 10 categories:

1. Planning documents
2. Requirements
3. Specifications
4. User manuals
5. Training materials
6. Marketing materials
7. Defect reports
8. Financial documents
9. Memos and correspondence
10. Contracts and legal documents

Sizing paper deliverables is a major feature of software cost estimating tools and is a major topic for real-life software projects.

Sizing paper documents is especially important in a military software context, because military standards trigger the production of more paper than any other triggering factor in human history. The classic DoD 2167 standard has probably caused the creation of more pages of paper than any other technical standard in the world. Even the newer DoD 498 standard tends to generate significant volumes of paper materials.

Interestingly, the newer ISO 9000–9004 quality standards are giving DoD 2167 quite a good race for the record for most paperwork produced for a software project.

Curiously, many of these required military software documents are not really needed for technical reasons, but are there because the Department of Defense has a long-standing distrust of its many vendors. This distrust has manifested itself in the extensive oversight requirements and the massive planning, reporting, and specification sets mandated by such military standards as DoD 2167 or DoD 498.

The same sense of distrust is also found in the ISO 9000–9004 standard set and in ISO 9001 in particular. For an activity as common as performing software inspections and testing software applications, it should not be necessary to create huge custom test plans for every application. What the ISO standards and the DoD standards might have included, but did not, are the skeleton frameworks of review, inspection, and test plans with an assertion that special test-plan documentation would be needed only if the standard plans were *not* followed.

For commercial software projects, the internal specifications are not as bulky as for military or for systems software, but the external user manuals and the tutorial information are both large and sometimes even elegant, in terms of being produced by professional writers and professional graphics artists.

Among our civilian client organizations paperwork production ranks as the second most expensive kind of work on large systems, and is outranked only by the costs of defect removal, such as testing.

(Coding, by the way, is often as far down the list of software elements as fourth place. Coding expenses on large systems often lag behind paperwork costs, defect-removal costs, and meetings and communications costs.)

A minor but tricky issue for sizing software paperwork volumes is that of adjusting the size estimate to match the kind of paper stock being used.

For example, a normal page of U.S. office paper in the 8.5- by 11-in format holds about 500 English words, although the inclusion of graphics and illustrations lowers the effective capacity to around 400 words. However, the common European A4 page size holds about 600 English words, while legal paper holds about 675 English words.

By contrast, the smaller page size used by the U.S. civilian government agencies only holds about 425 words. Thus, in order to predict the number of pages in specifications and user manuals, it is obvious that the form factor must be known.

Of course, the full capacity of a printed page for holding text is seldom utilized, because space is often devoted to the inclusion of graphical materials, which will also be discussed as an interesting sizing problem.

Table 13.14 illustrates how function point metrics are now utilized for producing size estimates of various kinds of paper documents. The

TABLE 13.14   Number of Pages Created per Function Point for Software Projects

	Systems software	MIS software	Military software	Commercial software	Average
Project plans	0.30	0.20	0.45	0.25	0.30
Requirements	0.45	0.50	0.85	0.30	0.53
Functional specifications	0.80	0.55	1.75	0.60	0.93
Logic specifications	0.85	0.50	1.65	0.55	0.89
Test plans	0.25	0.10	0.55	0.25	0.29
User tutorials	0.30	0.15	0.50	0.85	0.45
User reference	0.45	0.20	0.85	0.90	0.60
Online HELP	0.15	0.30	0.25	0.65	0.34
Total	3.55	2.50	6.85	4.35	4.31

table assumes normal 8.5- by 11-in U.S. paper and IFPUG Version 4 function point rules.

Table 13.14 and the following illustrate the major benefit of function point metrics in the context of software sizing and cost estimating. Because the function point total for an application stays constant regardless of which programming language or languages are utilized, function points provide a very stable platform for sizing and estimating noncode artifacts, such as paper documents.

In fact, some of the LOC-based estimating tools don't deal with paper deliverables or noncoding work at all.

Table 13.14 shows selected size examples, drawn from systems, MIS, military, and commercial software domains. In this context, *systems software* is that which controls physical devices, such as computers or telecommunication systems.

MIS stands for *management information systems software* and refers to the normal business software used by companies for internal operations.

Military software constitutes all projects that are constrained to follow various military standards.

Commercial software refers to ordinary packaged software, such as word processors, spreadsheets, and the like.

This kind of sizing for software documentation is now a standard feature of several commercial software cost estimating tools. Indeed, as many as 50 discrete document types may be found on very large software projects. Table 13.15 is a summary list of the various kinds of paper documents associated with software projects.

Although few projects will produce all of the kinds of information listed in Table 13.15, many software projects will create at least 20 discrete kinds of paper and online documentation. Given the fact that

TABLE 13.15   Examples of Paper Documents Associated with Software Projects

Requirements and Specification Documents

1. Normal requirements specifications
2. Joint application design (JAD) requirements specifications
3. Quality function deployment (QFD) requirements specifications
4. Rapid application development (RAD) requirements specifications
5. Initial functional specifications
6. Final functional specifications
7. Internal logic specifications
8. Software reuse specifications
9. State-change specifications
10. Interface and dependency specifications
11. Security and confidentiality specifications
12. Database design specifications

Planning and control documents

1. Software project development schedule plans
2. Software project development tracking reports
3. Software project development cost estimates
4. Software project development cost-tracking reports
5. Software project milestone reports
6. Software project value analysis
7. Software project marketing plans
8. Software project customer support plans
9. Software project documentation plans
10. Software ISO 9000–9004 supporting documents
11. Software project inspection plans
12. Software project inspection tracking reports
13. Software project internal test plans
14. Software project test result reports
15. Software project external test plans
16. Software project external test results
17. Software prerelease defect-tracking reports
18. Software postrelease defect-tracking reports
19. Software project development contracts
20. Software litigation documentation

TABLE 13.15 (*Continued*)

User reference and training documents
1. Installation guides
2. User tutorial manuals
3. User reference manuals
4. Programmers guides
5. System programmers guides
6. Network administration guides
7. System maintenance guides
8. Console operators guides
9. Messages and return codes manuals
10. Quick reference cards
11. Online tutorials
12. Online HELP screens
13. Error messages
14. Icon and graphic screens
15. READ-ME files
16. Audio training tapes
17. Video training tapes
18. CD-ROM training materials

between 20 percent and more than 50 percent of software project budgets can go to the production of paper and online documents, it is obvious that paperwork sizing and cost estimating are important features of modern software cost estimating tools.

Several commercial software-estimating tools can even predict the number of English words in the document set, and also the numbers of diagrams that are likely to be present, and can change the page-count estimates based on type size or paper size.

Since the actual sizing algorithms for many kinds of paper documents are proprietary, Table 13.16 is merely derived by assuming a ratio of 500 words per page, taken from Table 13.15.

As can easily be seen from Tables 13.15 and 13.16, software is a very paper-intensive occupation, and accurate software cost estimating cannot ignore the production of paper documents and achieve acceptable accuracy. Far too great a percentage of overall software costs are tied up in the creation, reviewing, and updating of paper documents for this cost factor to be ignored.

TABLE 13.16   Number of English Words per Function Point for Software Projects

	Systems software	MIS software	Military software	Commercial software	Average
Project plans	120	80	180	100	120
Requirements	180	200	340	120	210
Functional specifications	320	220	700	240	370
Logic specifications	340	200	660	220	355
Test plans	100	40	220	100	115
User tutorials	120	60	200	340	180
User reference	180	80	340	360	240
Online HELP	60	120	100	260	135
Total	1420	1000	2740	1740	1725

To illustrate the overall magnitude of software paperwork, the author has worked on several large systems in the 10,000–function point category where the total volume of pages in the full set of design and specification documents exceeded 60,000 pages.

As a more extreme case, the sum of the paper documents for a proposed new operating system that IBM was considering would have totaled more than 1 million pages. The specifications would have been so large that reading them would exceed the lifetime reading speed of normal adults if they read steadily for eight hours every day for an entire career!

Should it have gone to completion, the full set of paper documents for the "Star Wars" strategic defense initiative, following normal military standards, would have exceeded 1 billion pages, and the sum of the English words would have exceeded 500 billion.

Although the document size information in this book is based on U.S. paper sizes and English words, software is an international discipline. Some software cost estimating tools can deal with the same problems as they might be encountered in France, Germany, Japan, or other countries that both use different languages and have different conventions for paper sizes.

In addition, some kinds of software, such as commercial packages, need to be *nationalized,* or translated into multiple languages. For example, the author's own CHECKPOINT cost-estimating tool is available in English, Japanese, and French versions.

Large commercial software vendors, such as Computer Associates, IBM, and Microsoft, may have software materials translated into more than a dozen languages.

Another tricky but important aspect of dealing with software paperwork costs is producing estimates for multinational projects, where the primary specifications are in a single language, such as English, but the development team may comprise personnel from France, Japan, Russia, the Ukraine, and many other countries as well. Although the developers may be able to deal with English-language specifications, there may be a need for supplemental materials created in other languages.

Some cost-estimating tools can also estimate the added costs for translating tutorial materials, HELP screens, and even source code comments from one natural language to another.

Translation costs can be a rather complicated topic for languages which do not use the same kinds of symbols for representing information. For example, translating materials from English into Japanese or Chinese written forms is a great deal more costly than merely translating English into French or Spanish. Indeed, automated translation tools are available that can facilitate bidirectional translations between English and many European languages.

Another critical aspect of sizing software paperwork volumes is the fact that the volumes are not constant, but grow during the development cycle (and afterwards) in response to creeping user requirements.

Thus, software paperwork sizing algorithms and predictive methods must be closely linked to other estimating capabilities that can deal with creeping user requirements, deferrals of features, and other matters that cause changes in the overall size of the application.

It is obvious why visualization is such an important technology for software, and why software cost estimating tools need to be very thorough in sizing and estimating paperwork for large software applications. Indeed, for almost all large systems in excess of 1000 function points in size, the total effort devoted to the construction of paper documents is actually greater than the effort devoted to coding. In the case of large military systems, the effort devoted to the creation of paper documents can be more than *twice* as costly as coding.

Sizing Graphics and Illustrations

Software specifications, software user manuals, software training materials, and sometimes online software tutorials often make extensive use of graphics and visual information. The kinds of graphical materials associated with software projects include but are not limited to the following categories:

1. Application design graphics
2. Planning and scheduling graphics
3. Charts derived from spreadsheets

4. Illustrations in user manuals

5. Graphical user interfaces (GUIs)

6. Photographs and clip art

Graphics sizing is a complicated undertaking because there are so many possibilities. For example, in just the software design category alone there are at least 50 major dialects of graphical software specification methods in existence, such as those listed in Table 13.17.

Not only are there many different dialects or flavors of graphics-based software specification methods, but many projects use combina-

TABLE 13.17   Forms of Graphical Software Design Representations

1. Conventional flowcharts

2. Control-flow diagrams

3. Data-structure diagrams

4. Gane & Sarson data-flow diagrams

5. DeMarco bubble diagrams

6. Entity-relationship diagrams

7. Chen entity-relationship diagrams

8. James Martin entity-relationship diagrams

9. James Martin information engineering diagrams

10. Texas Instruments information engineering diagrams

11. Nassi-Shneiderman diagrams

12. Chapin chart diagrams

13. Decision tables

14. Hierarchy plus input, output, process (HIPO) diagrams

15. Yourdon structured design diagrams

16. Yourdon object-oriented diagrams

17. Shlaer-Mellor object-oriented analysis diagrams

18. Booch object-oriented diagrams

19. Rumbaugh object-oriented diagrams

20. Jacobsen object-oriented diagrams

21. Universal modeling language (UML) diagrams

22. Petri nets

23. State-transition diagrams

24. Warnier-Orr diagrams

25. Structured analysis and design technique (SADT) diagrams

26. Merise diagrams

27. Quality function deployment (QFD) house diagrams

28. Root-cause analysis fishbone diagrams

tions of these diverse approaches rather than a single pure approach. For example, it is very common to see a mixture of flowcharts, one or more of the object-oriented specification methods, and some kind of entity-relationship charts all in the specifications for a single project.

Even more difficult from the standpoint of software sizing and cost estimating, a significant number of companies have developed unique and proprietary variants of common design methods which only they utilize. For example, the ITT corporation used the structured analysis and design technique (SADT) in both its pure form, and also in the form of a customized ITT variation created for switching software projects.

Table 13.18 illustrates the approximate volumes of graphic items per function point in various document types. A *graphic item* can be any of the following:

- A flowchart page
- An entity-relationship chart
- A data-flow diagram
- A control-flow diagram
- A Gantt chart
- A PERT chart
- A Kiviat Graph
- A graph from a spreadsheet, such as Excel or Lotus
- An illustration from a graphics package, such as PowerPoint
- A photograph

TABLE 13.18   Number of Graphics Items per Function Point for Software Projects

	Systems software	MIS software	Military software	Commercial software	Average
Plan graphics	0.30	0.20	0.45	0.25	0.30
Requirements graphics	0.15	0.20	0.35	0.15	0.21
Function graphics	0.30	0.25	0.60	0.25	0.35
Logic graphics	0.45	0.25	1.00	0.30	0.50
Test graphics	0.10	0.03	0.25	0.10	0.12
Tutorial graphics	0.25	0.10	0.30	0.60	0.31
Reference graphics	0.25	0.10	0.50	0.60	0.36
HELP graphics	0.10	0.20	0.20	0.40	0.23
Total	1.90	1.33	3.65	2.65	2.38
Graphics per page	0.54	0.53	0.53	0.61	0.55
Graphics per 1000 words	1.34	1.33	1.33	1.52	1.38

Needless to say, Table 13.18 has a significant margin of error and should be used only to gain an understanding of the significant volumes of graphical materials that are likely to be produced for software projects.

The ability of modern software cost estimating tools to deal with the size ranges of both text and graphics is one of the features that makes such tools useful.

Too often, manual estimates by software project managers tend to ignore or understate the noncoding portions of software projects, because the managers have comparatively little familiarity with the paper and graphics side of software.

Sizing Bugs or Defects

As software projects grow from less than 1000 function points to more than 10,000 function points in size, the costs, effort, and schedules associated with defect-removal operations tend to become the largest and costliest component of the entire project.

Also, when software projects miss their schedules (as in the case of the Denver airport) it is almost always due to a quality problem that keeps the software from running well enough to go into full production.

Of all of the factors that need to be estimated carefully, the number of bugs or errors is the most critical. Two major aspects of bug or defect prediction are now features of several software cost estimating tools:

1. Predicting the number of bugs by origin point and severity levels.

2. Predicting the efficiency of various inspections and tests in removing bugs.

Software defect prediction is another area where commercial software cost estimating tools can outperform even experienced human managers. The reason is that software cost estimating tools are operating from the basis of several thousand projects, while human managers may see fewer than 50 projects in their entire careers.

The function point metric has expanded the ability to create accurate quality estimates and defect predictions. Prior to the advent of function point metrics, much of the software quality literature and most of the defect-prediction algorithms dealt only with coding defects. Now that function points are widely used, the ability to measure and predict software defects has expanded to include five significant categories:

1. Requirements defects

2. Design and specification defects

3. Coding defects

4. User documentation defects

5. Bad fixes, or secondary defects

Two new kinds of software defect prediction capabilities are not yet found in commercial software cost estimating tools, but research is nearing the stage where predictive algorithms can be developed:

1. Test-case defects

2. Database defects

Both of these new categories of software defects have cost and schedule implications. Research performed at IBM indicates that software test cases sometimes contain more defects or errors than the software the test cases have been created to test!

The whole topic of *data quality* is becoming increasingly important. Research into data quality has suffered from the fact that there is no known metric for normalizing database volumes or data defects. In other words, there is no *data point* metric that is the logical equivalent to the *function point* metric.

The well-known aphorism that "you can't manage what you can't measure" has long been true for software quality. For about 50 years, less than 5 percent of U.S. companies had measurement programs for software quality. Similar proportions have been noted in the United Kingdom and in Europe. Therefore, attempts to improve software quality tended to resemble the classic probability example called the *drunkard's walk*. Quality improvements would lurch erratically in different directions and not actually get very far from the origin point.

When exploring why software quality measurements have seldom been performed, a basic issue has always been that the results were not very useful. A deeper analysis of this problem shows that an important root cause of unsuccessful quality measurement can be traced to the use of the flawed LOC metric.

Quality measurements based on lines of code have tended to ignore quality problems that originate in requirements and design and are of no use at all in measuring defects in related documents, such as user manuals. When the problems and errors of noncode software deliverables were accumulated, it was discovered that more than half of all software errors or defects were essentially invisible using LOC metrics.

Historically, software quality was measured in terms of defects per 1000 source code statements, or 1000 lines of code (KLOC).

Unfortunately, the KLOC metric contains a built-in paradox that causes it to give erroneous results when used with newer and more powerful programming languages, such as Ada, object-oriented languages, or program generators.

The main problem with the KLOC metric is that this metric conceals, rather than reveals, important quality data. For example, suppose a company has been measuring quality in terms of defects per KLOC. A project coded in FORTRAN might require 10,000 LOC, and might contain 200 bugs, for a total of 20 defects per KLOC.

Now, suppose the same project could be created using a more powerful language, such as C++, which would require only 2000 lines of code and contain only 40 bugs. Here, too, there are 20 defects per KLOC, but the total number of bugs is actually reduced by 80 percent.

In the preceding FORTRAN and C++ examples, both versions provide the same functions to end users, and so both contain the same number of function points. Assume both versions contain 100 function points.

When the newer defects per function point metric is used, the FORTRAN version contains 2.00 defects per function point, but the C++ version contains only 0.40 defects per function point. With the function point metric, the substantial quality gains associated with more powerful high-level languages can now be made clearly visible.

Another problem with LOC metrics is the difficulty of measuring or exploring defects in noncode deliverables, such as requirements and specifications. Here, too, function point metrics have illuminated data that was previously invisible.

Based on a study published in the author's book *Applied Software Measurement* (Jones 1996a), the average number of software errors in the United States is about five per function point. Note that software defects are not found only in code, but originate in all of the major software deliverables, in approximately the quantities shown in Table 13.19.

These numbers represent the total numbers of defects that are found and measured from early software requirements definitions throughout the remainder of the life cycle of the software. The defects

TABLE 13.19   U.S. Averages in Defects per Function Point

Defect origins	Defects per function point
Requirements	1.00
Design	1.25
Coding	1.75
Documentation	0.60
Bad fixes	0.40
Total	5.00

are discovered via requirement reviews, design reviews, code inspections, all forms of testing, and user problem reports.

U.S. averages using function points lend themselves to graphical representation. The graph in Fig. 13.11 shows defect-potentials and defect removal efficiency levels as the two axes. The graph also identifies three zones of some significance:

1. The central zone of average performance, where most companies can be found.

2. The zone of best-in-class performance, where top companies can be found.

3. The zone of professional malpractice, where companies that seem to know nothing at all about quality can be found.

It is very revealing to overlay a sample of an enterprise's software projects on this graph. Note that the *defects per FP* axis refers to the total defect potential, which includes errors in the requirements, specifications, source code, user manuals, and bad fix categories.

Complementing the function point metric are measurements of defect-removal efficiency, or the percentages of software defects removed prior to delivery of the software to clients.

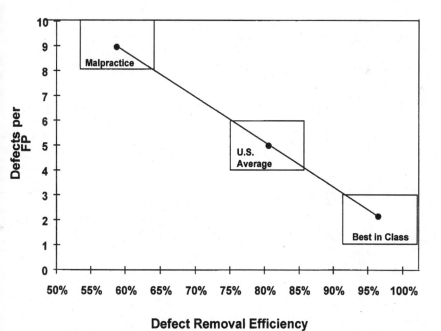

Figure 13.11   U.S. software quality performance ranges.

The U.S. average for defect-removal efficiency, unfortunately, is currently only about 85 percent, although top-ranked projects in such leading companies as AT&T, IBM, Motorola, Raytheon, and Hewlett-Packard achieve defect-removal efficiency levels well in excess of 99 percent on their best projects and average close to 95 percent.

All software defects are not equally easy to remove. Requirements errors, design problems, and bad fixes tend to be the most difficult. Thus, on the day when software is actually put into production, the average quantity of latent errors or defects still present tends to be about 0.75 per function point, distributed as shown in Table 13.20, which also shows approximate ranges of defect-removal efficiency by origin point of software defects.

Note that at the time of delivery, defects originating in requirements and design tend to far outnumber coding defects. Data such as this can be used to improve the upstream defect-prevention and defect-removal processes of software development.

The best results in terms of defect removal are always achieved on projects that utilize formal pretest inspections of design, code, and other major deliverables, such as user manuals, and even test cases.

It is obvious that no single defect-removal operation is adequate by itself. This explains why best-in-class quality results can be achieved only from synergistic combinations of defect prevention, reviews or inspections, and various kinds of test activities.

The best software projects within the organizations that constitute roughly the upper 10 percent of the groups that SPR has assessed have achieved remarkably good quality levels. Following are software quality targets derived from best-in-class software projects and organizations:

- Defect potentials of less than 2.5 defects per function point. (Sum of defects found in requirements, design, code, user documents, and bad fixes.)

TABLE 13.20   Defect Removal Efficiency by Origin of Defect
(Expressed in defects per function point)

Defect origins	Defect potentials	Removal efficiency	Delivered defects
Requirements	1.00	77%	0.23
Design	1.25	85%	0.19
Coding	1.75	95%	0.09
Documentation	0.60	80%	0.12
Bad fixes	0.40	70%	0.12
Total	5.00	85%	0.75

- Cumulative defect-removal efficiency averages higher than 95 percent. (All defects found during development, compared to first year's customer-reported defects.)

- Average less than 0.025 user-reported defects per function point per year. (Measured against valid, unique defects.)

- Achieve 90 percent *excellent* ratings from user-satisfaction surveys. (Measured on topics of product quality and service.)

- Allow zero error-prone modules in released software. (Modules receiving more than 0.8 defects per function point per year.)

- Improve software quality via defect prevention and defect removal at more than 40 percent per year. (Baseline is the current year's volume of customer-reported defects.)

If your organization is approaching or achieving these results, then you are part of a *world-class* software production organization.

There are thousands of ways to fail when building software applications, and only a very few ways to succeed. It is an interesting phenomenon that the best-in-class companies in terms of quality all use essentially similar approaches in achieving their excellent results. The 12 attributes of the best-in-class quality organizations are listed in Table 13.21.

The similarity of approaches among such companies as AT&T, Bellcore, Hewlett-Packard, IBM, Microsoft, Motorola, Raytheon, and so forth is quite striking when side-by-side benchmark comparisons are performed.

There are over 250 operational industries in the United States that

TABLE 13.21   Common Attributes Noted in Best-in-Class Software Organizations

1. Effective quality and removal efficiency measurements
2. Effective defect prevention (i.e., JAD, QFD, etc.)
3. Automated defect and quality estimation
4. Automated defect tracking
5. Complexity analysis tools
6. Test coverage analysis tools
7. Test automation tools
8. Test library control tools
9. Usage of formal design and code inspections
10. Formal testing by test specialists
11. Formal quality-assurance group
12. Executive and managerial understanding of quality

produce software. Software Productivity Research has collected data from only about 50 of these industries, so there are plainly major gaps in this research. Nonetheless, six U.S. industries stand out as being much better than average in terms of software quality control.

In general, these six best industries are those that have the following factors in common:

1. The software produced is an integral part of the equipment the industry markets.

2. The equipment will not operate successfully unless the software quality levels are high.

3. Either human life or major business functions or both depend upon the reliability of the marketed products and equipment.

Table 13.22 lists the six industries with much better than average quality levels.

Within these industries, it is the systems and embedded software that have the best overall quality levels. (Note that *systems software* is defined as programs or systems that control physical devices, such as a telephone switch, a computer, or a radar set. *Embedded software* is that which is resident within a physical device, such as on board a cruise missile.)

The Software Engineering Institute (SEI) maturity level concept is one of the most widely discussed topics in the software literature. During calendar year 1994, Software Productivity Research was commissioned by the U.S. Air Force to perform a study on the economic impact of various SEI capability maturity levels (CMM). Raw data was provided to SPR on levels 1, 2, and 3 by an Air Force software location.

In terms of quality, the data available indicated that for maturity levels 1, 2, and 3 average quality tends to rise with CMM maturity level scores. However, this study had a limited number of samples. By contrast, the U.S. Navy has reported a counterexample, and has stat-

---

TABLE 13.22   Industries with Better Than
Average Software Quality

---

1. Computer manufacturers

2. Defense and military software manufacturers

3. Medical instrument manufacturers

4. Telecommunication equipment manufacturers

5. Avionics and aircraft equipment manufacturers

6. Software manufacturers

TABLE 13.23 SEI CMM Software Quality Targets for Each Level

(Expressed in defects per function point)

SEI CMM Levels	Defect potentials	Removal efficiency	Delivered defects
SEI CMM 1	5.00	85%	0.75
SEI CMM 2	4.00	90%	0.40
SEI CMM 3	3.00	95%	0.15
SEI CMM 4	2.00	97%	0.06
SEI CMM 5	1.00	99%	0.01

ed that at least some software produced by a level-3 organization was observed to be deficient.

There is clearly some overlap among the various SEI levels. Some of the software projects created by organizations at SEI level 2 are just as good in terms of quality as those created by SEI level 3. Indeed, there are even good- to excellent-quality projects created by some SEI level 1 organizations. Table 13.23 shows some suggested quality targets for the five plateaus of the SEI capability maturity model.

Above level 3 these targets are somewhat hypothetical, but from observations of organizations at various CMM levels the results would seem to be within the range of current technologies through level 4.

For level 5, the hardest part of the target would be dropping the potential defect level down to 1 per function point. Achieving a 99 percent cumulative defect removal efficiency level is actually possible with current technologies for projects using formal inspections, testing specialists, and state-of-the-art testing tools.

As can be seen, the combination of function point metrics and defect-removal efficiency metrics are beginning to clarify quality topics that have long been ambiguous and intangible. Some of the examples shown here are now standard features of software cost estimating tools.

It cannot be overemphasized that quality estimates and cost estimates are closely coupled, because the costs and schedule time required for defect-removal operations make up the largest component of software expense elements.

Software quality measurement and estimation should not be limited only to source code. Every major software deliverable should be subject to careful quality analysis, including but not limited to software requirements, specifications, planning documents, and user manuals. However, the LOC metric is not effective in dealing with noncode software deliverables.

The combination of function point metrics coupled with direct measurement of defect-removal efficiency levels is making software quality results tangibly demonstrable. Now that software quality can be measured directly and predicted accurately, significant improvements are starting to occur.

Sizing Test Cases

The effort, costs, and schedule time devoted to testing software can, in some cases, exceed the effort, costs, and time devoted to coding the software. This situation means that test-case sizing and testing estimation are critical features of software cost estimating tools.

Fortunately, the function point metric has made a useful contribution to the ability to predict test-case volumes. Recall the fundamental structure of function points:

1. Inputs

2. Outputs

3. Logical files

4. Inquiries

5. Interfaces

These factors are the very aspects of software that need to be tested, and, hence, the function point metric is actually one of the best tools ever developed for predicting test case volumes, because derivation from function points is an excellent way of dealing with a problem that was previously quite difficult.

An emerging and very important topic in the context of test estimating is that of predicting the number of bugs or errors in test cases themselves. As many commercial software vendors have come to realize, the error density of software test cases may actually exceed the error density of the software being tested.

Because function points can be derived during both the requirements and early design stages, this approach offers a method of predicting test-case numbers fairly early. The method is still somewhat experimental, but the approach is leading to interesting results and its usage is expanding.

Table 13.24 shows preliminary data for 18 kinds of testing on the number of test cases that have been noted among SPR's clients, using test cases per function point as the normalizing metric.

This table has a high margin of error, but as with any other set of

TABLE 13.24   Range of Test Cases per Function Point for 18 Forms of Software-Testing Projects in the United States

Testing stage	Minimum	Average	Maximum
Clean-room testing	0.60	1.00	3.00
Regression testing	0.40	0.60	1.30
Unit testing	0.20	0.45	1.20
New function testing	0.25	0.40	0.90
Integration testing	0.20	0.40	0.75
Subroutine testing	0.20	0.30	0.40
Independent testing	0.00	0.30	0.55
System testing	0.15	0.25	0.60
Viral testing	0.00	0.20	0.40
Performance testing	0.00	0.20	0.40
Acceptance testing	0.00	0.20	0.60
Lab testing	0.00	0.20	0.50
Field (Beta) testing	0.00	0.20	1.00
Usability testing	0.00	0.20	0.40
Platform testing	0.00	0.15	0.30
Stress testing	0.00	0.15	0.30
Security testing	0.00	0.15	0.35
Year-2000 testing	0.00	0.15	0.30
Total	2.00	5.50	13.25

preliminary data points, it is better to publish the results in the hope of future refinements and corrections than to wait until the data is truly complete.

It should be noted that no project in our knowledge base has utilized all 18 forms of testing concurrently. The maximum number of test stages that the author has observed has been 16.

Much more common is a series of about half a dozen discrete forms of testing, which would include the following:

1. Subroutine testing

2. Unit testing

3. New function testing

4. Regression testing

5. System testing

6. Acceptance or field testing

TABLE 13.25   Number of Test Cases Created per Function Point

	Systems software	MIS software	Military software	Commercial software
Unit testing	0.30	0.20	0.50	0.30
New function testing	0.35	0.25	0.35	0.25
Regression testing	0.30	0.10	0.30	0.35
Integration testing	0.45	0.25	0.75	0.35
System testing	0.40	0.20	0.55	0.40
Total test cases	1.80	1.00	2.45	1.65

Another way of looking at test-case sizing is in terms of the patterns of testing by industry, rather than simply examining all 18 kinds of testing (see Table 13.25).

As can be seen, the numbers of test cases produced will vary widely, but quite a bit of this variance can be reduced by utilizing the typical patterns found in the class and type of software application.

To a very significant degree, modern software cost estimating tools operate as pattern-matching engines. Once the nature, scope, class, and type parameters are known to the software cost estimating tool, it can begin to extract and utilize similar projects from its built-in knowledge base or from the portfolio of projects stored by users.

Of course, there is always a finite probability that any given project will deviate from the normal patterns of its class and type. This is why software cost estimating tools allow users to override many predictions and make adjustments to the estimating assumptions.

Although functional metrics are not perfect, the advent of function points has expanded the number of software artifacts that can be sized, and has greatly simplified the tasks of sizing multiple deliverables.

The Event Horizon for Sizing Software Artifacts

We are now approaching the event horizon for software sizing technology. Beyond this horizon are a number of software artifacts where sizing is outside the scope of current software estimation capabilities.

Sizing database volumes

The technology for sizing database volumes is far less sophisticated than the technology for sizing other artifacts, such as documents, source code, test cases, and defects. The reason for this is because there are no current metrics for enumerating either the size of a database or for normalizing the number of errors that a database may contain.

Sizing multimedia artifacts

Modern software packages distributed and executed via CD-ROM are no longer severely limited by storage constraints and storage costs. As a result, software packages are no longer restricted to static displays of graphics and to the use of alphanumeric information for tutorial information.

These very modern multimedia artifacts are currently the edge of the event horizon for software cost estimating tools. Recall that before accurate cost-estimating algorithms can be developed, it is necessary to have a solid body of empirical data available from accurate project measurements.

Since many of the advanced multimedia applications are being produced by the entertainment segment of the software industry, such as game vendors, these companies have seldom commissioned any kind of measurement or benchmarking studies. Therefore, there is an acute shortage of empirical data available on the effort associated with the creation of multimedia applications.

Some of these exotic technologies will move into business software. The business software community does tend to commission benchmarking and measurement studies, so in the future enough empirical data may become available to create estimating algorithms for software projects that feature multimedia, animation, music and voice soundtracks, and three-dimensional graphics.

It is entirely possible to build business software applications that have features which were quite impossible 10 years ago, including but not limited to the following:

- Audio soundtracks with instruction by human voices
- Music soundtracks
- Full animation for dynamic processes
- Three-dimensional graphics
- Photographs or video clips
- Neural-net engines that change the software's behavior

As this book is being written, these multimedia artifacts are outside the scope of current software cost estimating tools and are also outside the scope of software-measurement technology.

There are a few other topics that are also outside the event horizon for commercial estimating tools, but are probably known by those with a need for this kind of information. Many military, defense, and intelligence software packages utilize very sophisticated protective methods, such as encryption and multiple redundancy of key components.

Some of these critical applications may even execute in from read-only memory (ROM) in order to minimize the risks of viral intrusion, so the software may have to be burned into special secure ROM devices. For obvious reasons of security, these methods are not widely discussed, and the specific approaches utilized are not covered by normal commercial software estimating tools and methods.

Suffice it to say that software applications with significant national security implications will include activities and forms of representation that are beyond the event horizon of standard estimating methods, and this is by reason of deliberate policy.

What Is Known as a Result of Sizing Software Projects

Because the main work of software estimating requires some kind of size information in order to proceed, sizing is a very important preliminary stage of constructing software cost estimates.

When using an automated estimating tool, users supply quite a bit of data by means of checklists or multiple-choice questions that enable the estimating tools to produce size predictions and later to produce full estimates.

Assuming that a user is working with one of the many commercial estimating tools, the list in Table 13.26 shows the kinds of information that are normally used to prime the estimating engine and allow the estimating tool to perform sizing and estimating tasks.

Note that much of the information is optional or the estimating tools include default values, which the users can either accept or override by substituting their own values.

If the estimating tool includes sizing logic, it can produce project size estimates that the users can either accept or adjust as appropriate. However, in order to generate an accurate cost estimate, the commercial software-estimating tools utilize the kinds of size information shown in Table 13.27, regardless of whether the information is generated by the tool itself, is supplied by the user, or both in some cases (the tool predicts a suggested value and the user may adjust or replace the value if desired).

Software projects have many different kinds of deliverable artifacts besides the code itself, and accurate software cost estimates must include these noncode deliverables in order to ensure that the estimate is complete and useful.

Similar kinds of information are required for estimating other types of projects besides software projects. For example, if you were

TABLE 13.26   Project Information Normally Provided by Users

Project name	Optional
Project manager's name	Optional
Project estimator's name	Optional
Standard industry classification (SIC)	Optional
Project start date	Optional; default is "today"
Desired delivery date	Optional
Salary levels	Optional or default value
Burden rates	Optional or default value
Burdened salary	Optional or default value
Inflation rate	Optional or default value
Special costs	Optional
Project goals	Optional or default value
Project nature	Required or default value
Project scope	Required or default value
Project class	Required or default value
Project type	Required or default value
Programming languages	Optional or default value
Complexity of problem	Optional or default value
Complexity of source code	Optional or default value
Complexity of data elements	Optional or default value

working with an architect on designing and building a custom home, you would have to provide the architect with some basic information on how many square feet you wanted the house to be. A luxury house with 6000 square feet of living space and a three-car garage will obviously be more expensive to construct than a starter home with 1500 square feet and a one-car carport.

Strengths and Weaknesses of Software Size Metrics

Unfortunately, the current conflict between warring metrics enthusiasts is slowing down progress in software sizing and estimating technology. In fact, the conflicts are so sharp that it often escapes notice that none of the currently available metrics can measure every important aspect of software.

- The LOC metrics have major problems for dealing with noncoding activities and for comparisons between unlike programming languages. Also, for certain languages, such as Visual Basic and its

TABLE 13.27 Predicted Size Information or User-Supplied Size Information

Size in function points/feature points (initial value)	Approximated or supplied by user
Algorithms	Approximated or supplied by user
Inputs	Approximated or supplied by user
Outputs	Approximated or supplied by user
Inquiries	Approximated or supplied by user
Logical files	Approximated or supplied by user
Interfaces	Approximated or supplied by user
Rate of function point creep	Predicted—adjusted by user
Size in function points/feature points (final value)	Predicted—adjusted by user
Size in physical lines of source code	Predicted—adjusted by user
Size in logical source code statements	Predicted—adjusted by user
Size in terms of input/output screens	Predicted—adjusted by user
Size in terms of database volumes	Predicted—adjusted by user
Number of probable defects or bugs	Predicted—adjusted by user
Number of probable test cases	Predicted—adjusted by user
Size of initial requirements	Predicted—adjusted by user
Rate of requirements creep	Predicted—adjusted by user
Size of final requirements	Predicted—adjusted by user
Size of external specifications	Predicted—adjusted by user
Size of internal specifications	Predicted—adjusted by user
Size of planning documents	Predicted—adjusted by user
Size of quality control documents	Predicted—adjusted by user
Size of user manuals	Predicted—adjusted by user
Size of training and tutorial information	Predicted—adjusted by user

competitors, coding is only one way of developing applications. The LOC metric has no relevance for software constructed using button control and pull-down menus.

- The function point metrics in all varieties have problems with counting precision for any specific variant, and even larger problems with converting data between variants. There are also severe problems across all function point variants for very small projects where certain constants in the counting rules tend to artificially inflate the results below about 15 function points.

- The object-oriented (OO) metrics are totally devoid of relevance for non-OO projects, and do not seem to deal with OO analysis or design or any of the noncode aspects of software development. There are no known conversion rules between the OO metrics and the other size metrics.

- The more obscure size metrics, such as the Halstead software-science metrics, are yet additional variants. The original studies for software science appear to have methodological flaws, and the volume of published data for software-science metrics is only marginally greater than zero.

- In addition to basic size metrics, there are also metrics that are used for size adjustments, such as complexity. Of the 24 known forms of complexity that influence software projects, only two (cyclomatic and essential complexity) have significant literature. Unfortunately, many of the more critical complexity metrics have no literature in a software context, although psychologists and linguists deal with them.

- There are also attempts to use "natural" metrics, such as number of pages of specifications or number of staff hours. Here, too, there are problems with accuracy and with data conversion from these metrics to any other known metric.

- There are no known metrics of any form that can deal with the topic of the size of databases, nor with the important topic of data quality. Fundamental metrics research is needed in the database arena.

- The literature on metrics conversion between the competing function point methods, the competing LOC methods, and the other methods (object-oriented metrics, software-science metrics, etc.) is only marginally better than a null set.

The following would be advantageous to the software industry overall:

1. A complete analysis of the strengths and weaknesses of all current metrics

2. A concerted effort to develop industrial-strength function metrics that can support all software activities

3. Development of a standard activity table for the major software activities, so that such terms as *requirements* or *design* have the same general meaning and include the same task sets

4. The elimination of the scores of minor function point variants with few users and little published data or, at the very least, publication of conversion rules between minor variants and major function point forms

5. A consistent set of source code counting rules that could be applied to all programming languages, including visual languages

6 Development of a *data point* metric derived from the structure of function point metrics, but aimed at quantifying the sizes of databases, repositories, data warehouses, and flat files

In order to make significant progress in software metrics and measurements, it will be necessary to arrange a truce, or at least a cease-fire, among the warring metrics camps and meet together to deal with software measurement and metrics as a key discipline that needs to be improved as rapidly as possible.

If multiple and conflicting metrics continue to be used, then metrics-conversion tools should be added to the software management tool kit to facilitate international comparisons when the data originates using multiple metrics.

The eventual goal of metrics research would be to facilitate the sizing and estimating of complex hybrid systems where software, microcode, hardware, data, and service components all contribute to the final constructed artifact.

In any case, it may be helpful that the International Organization of Standards is beginning to explore software size metrics. However, international politics and a host of vested interests will probably slow down ISO's progress.

What would probably be of more immediate use to the software industry would be to publish formal rules for conversion logic between the major competing metrics. Even better would be automated metrics conversion tools that could handle a broad range of current metrics problems, such as the following:

1. Rules for size conversion between IFPUG Versions 3.4 and 4 counting methods

2. Rules for size conversion between IFPUG and Mark II counting methods

3. Rules for size conversion between source code and function point metrics

4. Rules for code size conversion between SPR and SEI code counting methods

5. Rules for size conversion between object-oriented metrics and any other metric

6. Rules for size conversion between two unlike programming languages

As an experiment, the author has constructed a prototype metric conversion tool that can handle some of these conversion problems, such as conversion between the SPR logical statement counts and the SEI physical line counts for selected programming languages.

While the prototype demonstrates that automatic conversion is feasible, the total number of variations in the industry is so large that a full-scale metric-conversion tool that can handle all common variants would be a major application in its own right. For such a tool to stay current, it would be necessary to keep it updated on an almost monthly basis, as new languages and new metrics appear.

Summary and Conclusions

Software sizing is a critical but difficult part of software cost estimating. The invention of function point metrics has simplified the sizing of noncode artifacts, such as specifications and user documents, but sizing is still a complicated and tricky undertaking.

While function points in general have simplified and improved software sizing, the unexpected fragmentation of function point metrics into more than 35 variants has added an unnecessary amount of confusion to the task of sizing, without contributing much in terms of technical precision.

The most accurate and best method for software sizing is to keep very good historical data of the sizes of software project deliverables. This way it will be possible to use the known sizes of artifacts from completed projects as a jumping-off place for predicting the sizes of similar artifacts for projects being estimated.

References

Abran, A., and P. N. Robillard: "Function Point Analysis: An Empirical Study of Its Measurement Processes," *IEEE Transactions on Software Engineering,* **22**(12):895–909 (1996).

Abrieu, Fernando Brito e: "An email information on MOOD," *Metrics News,* Otto-von-Guericke-Univeersitaat, Magdeburg, **7**(2):11 (1997).

Albrecht, A. J.: "Measuring Application Development Productivity," *Proceedings of the Joint IBM/SHARE/GUIDE Application Development Symposium,* October 1979, reprinted in Capers Jones, *Programming Productivity—Issues for the Eighties,* IEEE Computer Society Press, New York, 1981, pp. 34–43.

———: *AD/M Productivity Measurement and Estimate Validation,* IBM Corporation, Purchase, N.Y., May 1984.

Boehm, Barry: *Software Engineering Economics,* Prentice Hall, Englewood Cliffs, N.J., 1981.

Bogan, Christopher E., and Michael J. English: *Benchmarking for Best Practices,* McGraw-Hill, New York, ISBN 0-07-006375-3, 1994.

Brown, Norm (ed.): *The Program Manager's Guide to Software Acquisition Best Practices,* Version 1.0, U.S. Department of Defense, Washington, D.C., July 1995.

Chidamber, S. R., D. P. Darcy, and C. F. Kemerer: "Managerial Use of Object Oriented Software Metrics," Working Paper no. 750, Joseph M. Katz Graduate School of Business, University of Pittsburgh, Pittsburgh, Pa., November 1996.

Chidamber, S. R., and C. F. Kemerer: "A Metrics Suite for Object Oriented Design," *IEEE Transactions on Software Engineering,* **20**:476–493 (1994).

DeMarco, Tom: *Controlling Software Projects,* Yourdon Press, New York, ISBN 0-917072-32-4, 1982.

———: *Why Does Software Cost So Much?,* Dorset House, New York, ISBN 0-932633-34-X, 1995.

Department of the Air Force: *Guidelines for Successful Acquisition and Management of Software Intensive Systems,* vols. 1 and 2, Software Technology Support Center, Hill Air Force Base, Utah, 1994.

Dreger, Brian: *Function Point Analysis,* Prentice Hall, Englewood Cliffs, N.J., ISBN 0-13-332321-8, 1989.

Fenton, Norman, and Shari Lawrence Pfleeger: *Software Metrics—A Rigorous and Practical Approach,* 2d ed., IEEE Press, Los Alamitos, Calif., ISBN 0-534-95600-0, 1997.

Fetchke, Thomas, Alain Abran, Tho-Hau Nguyen: *Mapping the OO-Jacobsen Approach into Function Point Analysis,* University du Quebec a Montreal, Software Engineering Management Research Laboratory, 1997.

Galea, R. B.: The Boeing Company: 3D Function Point Extensions, V2.0, Release 1.0, Boeing Information Support Services, Seattle, Wash., June 1995.

Garmus, David, and David Herron: *Measuring the Software Process: A Practical Guide to Functional Measurement,* Prentice Hall, Englewood Cliffs, N.J., 1995.

Grady, Robert B.: *Practical Software Metrics for Project Management and Process Improvement,* Prentice Hall, Englewood Cliffs, N.J., ISBN 0-13-720384-5, 1992.

————, and Deborah L. Caswell: *Software Metrics: Establishing a Company-Wide Program,* Prentice Hall, Englewood Cliffs, N.J., ISBN 0-13-821844-7, 1987.

Halstead, Maurice H.: *Elements of Software Science,* North Holland, 1977.

Howard, Alan (ed.): *Software Metrics and Project Management Tools,* Applied Computer Research (ACR), Phoenix, Ariz., 1997.

IFPUG Counting Practices Manual, Release 3, International Function Point Users Group, Westerville, Ohio, April 1990.

————, Release 4, International Function Point Users Group, Westerville, Ohio, April 1995.

Jones, Capers: *SPQR/20 Users Guide,* Software Productivity Research, Cambridge, Mass., 1986.

————: *Critical Problems in Software Measurement,* Information Systems Management Group, ISBN 1-56909-000-9, 1993a.

————: *Software Productivity and Quality Today—The Worldwide Perspective,* Information Systems Management Group, ISBN 1-56909-001-7, 1993b.

————: *Assessment and Control of Software Risks,* Prentice Hall, Englewood Cliffs, N.J., ISBN 0-13-741406-4, 1994.

————: *New Directions in Software Management,* Information Systems Management Group, ISBN 1-56909-009-2,

————: *Patterns of Software System Failure and Success,* International Thomson Computer Press, Boston, ISBN 1-850-32804-8, 1995.

————: *Applied Software Measurement,* 2d ed., McGraw-Hill, New York, ISBN 0-07-032826-9, 1996a.

————: *Table of Programming Languages and Levels* (8 Versions from 1985 through July 1996), Software Productivity Research, Burlington, Mass., 1996b.

————: *The Economics of Object-Oriented Software,* Software Productivity Research, Burlington, Mass., April 1997a.

————: *Software Quality—Analysis and Guidelines for Success,* International Thomson Computer Press, Boston, ISBN 1-85032-876-6, 1997b.

————: *The Year 2000 Software Problem—Quantifying the Costs and Assessing the Consequences,* Addison-Wesley, Reading, Mass., ISBN 0-201-30964-5, 1998.

Kan, Stephen H.: *Metrics and Models in Software Quality Engineering,* Addison-Wesley, Reading, Mass., ISBN 0-201-63339-6, 1995.

Kemerer, C. F.: "Reliability of Function Point Measurement—A Field Experiment," *Communications of the ACM,* **36:**85–97 (1993).

Love, Tom: *Object Lessons,* SIGS Books, New York, ISBN 0-9627477 3-4, 1993.

Marciniak, John J. (ed.): *Encyclopedia of Software Engineering,* vols. 1 and 2, John Wiley & Sons, New York, ISBN 0-471-54002, 1994.

McCabe, Thomas J.: "A Complexity Measure," *IEEE Transactions on Software Engineering,* pp. 308–320 (December 1976).

Muller, Monika, and Alain Abram (eds.): *Metrics in Software Evolution,* R. Oldenbourg Vertag GmbH, Munich, ISBN 3-486-23589-3, 1995.

Oman, Paul, and Shari Lawrence Pfleeger (eds.): *Applying Software Metrics,* IEEE Press, Los Alamitos, Calif., ISBN 0-8186-7645-0, 1996.

Putnam, Lawrence H.: *Measures for Excellence—Reliable Software on Time, Within Budget,* Yourdon Press/Prentice Hall, Englewood Cliffs, N.J., ISBN 0-13-567694-0, 1992.

———, and Ware Myers: *Industrial Strength Software—Effective Management Using Measurement,* IEEE Press, Los Alamitos, Calif., ISBN 0-8186-7532-2, 1997.

Rethinking the Software Process, CD-ROM, Miller Freeman, Lawrence, Kans., 1996. (This CD-ROM is a book collection jointly produced by the book publisher, Prentice Hall, and the journal publisher, Miller Freeman. It contains the full text and illustrations of five Prentice Hall books: Capers Jones, *Assessment and Control of Software Risks*; Tom DeMarco, *Controlling Software Projects*; Brian Dreger, *Function Point Analysis*; Larry Putnam and Ware Myers, *Measures for Excellence*; and Mark Lorenz and Jeff Kidd, *Object-Oriented Software Metrics.*)

Shepperd, M.: "A Critique of Cyclomatic Complexity as a Software Metric," *Software Engineering Journal,* **3:**30–36 (1988).

St-Pierre, Denis, Marcela Maya, Alain Abran, and Jean-Marc Desharnais: *Full Function Points: Function Point Extensions for Real-Time Software, Concepts and Definitions,* TR 1997-03, University of Quebec, Software Engineering Laboratory in Applied Metrics (SELAM), March 1997.

Stukes, Sherry, Jason Deshoretz, Henry Apgar, and Ilona Macias: *Air Force Cost Analysis Agency Software Estimating Model Analysis—Final Report,* TR-9545/008-2, Contract F04701-95-D-0003, Task 008, Management Consulting & Research, Inc., Thousand Oaks, Calif., September 1996.

Symons, Charles R.: *Software Sizing and Estimating—Mk II FPA (Function Point Analysis),* John Wiley & Sons, Chichester, U.K., ISBN 0 471-92985-9, 1991.

———: "ISMI—International Software Metrics Initiative—Project Proposal" (private communication), June 15, 1997.

———: "Software Sizing and Estimating: Can Function Point Methods Meet Industry Needs?" (unpublished draft submitted to the IEEE for possible publication), Guild of Independent Function Point Analysts, London, U.K., August 1997.

Whitmire, S. A.: "3-D Function Points: Scientific and Real-Time Extensions to Function Points," *Proceedings of the 1992 Pacific Northwest Software Quality Conference,* June 1, 1992.

Cost Estimating Adjustment Factors

Software cost estimating is a complex activity with a host of interlocking factors and hundreds of adjustment rules to evaluate. In general, commercial software cost estimation tools assume that a project is average in every major factor unless the users state otherwise. This means that users need deal only with topics where they know their project will be much better or much worse than normal.

However, there are some adjustments that are so important that industry averages should not be used, and, indeed, may even be hazardous. Some of these critical factors where local information should be used in place of industry averages include the following:

- *Compensation levels for project personnel*
- *Burden or overhead rates to be applied to the projects*
- *Work patterns in terms of paid and unpaid overtime*
- *Specific methodologies to be used*
- *Specific tools to be used*
- *Specific programming languages to be used*
- *The specific kinds of reviews and inspections to be used*
- *The specific kinds of testing to be used*

The normal method of operation of dealing with programming adjustments is to present the users of estimating tools with the current default values, which they can either accept or modify as the situation warrants.

14

Compensation and Work Pattern Adjustments

Estimating software development projects and the related topic of estimating software maintenance and enhancement projects are the real heart of commercial software-estimating tools. Hundreds of factors can influence the outcomes of software projects for better or for worse. Modern software-estimating tools are designed to deal with three classes of adjustment factors:

1. Average situations where tools or methods have no significant impact

2. Situations where the project is much better than average in key areas

3. Situations where the project is much worse than average in key areas

The factors that influence the outcomes of software projects number in the hundreds, but for convenience in evaluating them they can be placed into seven main topical areas:

1. Attributes of the project itself (novelty, complexity, and size)

2. Personnel and management experience levels (similar projects, tools, and languages)

3. Methodology and development processes utilized (requirements, design, etc.)

4. Tools utilized (management, development, quality, maintenance, etc.)

5. Office ergonomics and geographic separation of team members

6. Programming languages utilized

7. Reusable materials available

The default value for most software cost estimating tools is to assume that the project is average for all topics, unless the user states otherwise. But accurate estimation depends upon more than default values and average assumptions. Users of software cost estimation tools must deal truthfully with situations where the project is worse than normal, and should also identify situations where the project may be better than average.

One of the advantages of using computers and commercial software-estimating tools is that really accurate estimation for software projects is very complicated and involves hundreds of rules. Commercial software-estimation tools can handle many factors and adjustments quickly, and can also deal with the more granular activity-based and task-based cost estimates much more conveniently than would be possible using manual approaches.

However, even with automated software cost estimating tools managerial experience and judgment are helpful, as is input by the technical staff members who must actually do the work in real life.

Software cost estimates are important business tools, but important business decisions depend upon human judgment. It is interesting to examine a detailed work-breakdown structure of software estimating itself and evaluate whether automated or manual methods are most appropriate for each step (see Table 14.1).

As can easily be seen, for all of the steps that depend primarily on calculations and rule-based decisions, the automated approach is preferred. However, for the steps where judgment and business knowledge come into play, the human mind is preferred.

In addition, there are many activities where an automated cost-estimating tool can provide a default or starting value, but manual adjustments and overrides to match specific situations may be desirable.

For example, determining whether to build a software application or buy a commercial package remains a human choice. Also, while automated estimating tools may have adjustments for staff experience levels and expertise, human performance varies so widely that it is useful to allow project managers to override default assumptions and substitute their own values for teams of exceptional capabilities.

In addition, the amount of overtime applied to a software project can only be approximated by software cost estimating tools. The work ethics of the team and the amount of schedule pressure applied by clients or executives remain factors that must be interpreted by human minds.

TABLE 14.1   A 35-Step Breakdown for Constructing Software Cost Estimates

Step	Definition	Method preferred for maximum accuracy
Step 1	Understanding software requirements	Manual
Step 2	Evaluating creeping user requirements	Automated
Step 3	Exploring similar historical projects	Automated/manual
Step 4	Sizing software deliverables	Automated/manual
Step 5	Preliminary estimates and rules of thumb	Automated/manual
Step 6	Make or buy decisions based on estimate	Manual
Step 7	Identifying activities to be performed	Automated/manual
Step 8	Estimating the impact of reusable materials	Automated
Step 9	Estimating software defect potentials	Automated
Step 10	Estimating software defect removal efficiency	Automated
Step 11	Estimating staffing needs based on project size	Automated
Step 12	Staffing adjustments based on schedule pressure	Automated
Step 13	Staffing adjustments based on specialists	Automated
Step 14	Staffing adjustments based on team experience	Automated/manual
Step 15	Estimating software effort (hours/days/months)	Automated
Step 16	Effort adjustments based on unpaid overtime	Automated
Step 17	Effort adjustments based on class and type	Automated
Step 18	Effort adjustments based on team capability	Automated/manual
Step 19	Effort adjustments based on process	Automated
Step 20	Effort adjustments based on tools	Automated
Step 21	Effort adjustment based on languages	Automated
Step 22	Estimating software schedules	Automated
Step 23	Schedule adjustments based on scope creep	Automated/manual
Step 24	Schedule adjustments based on overtime	Automated/manual
Step 25	Schedule adjustments based on critical paths	Automated
Step 26	Applying basic salary cost structures	Automated
Step 27	Cost adjustments based on unpaid overtime	Automated
Step 28	Cost adjustments based on paid overtime	Automated
Step 29	Cost adjustments based on compensation levels	Automated
Step 30	Cost adjustment based on burden rate levels	Automated
Step 31	Cost adjustments based on inflation rates	Automated
Step 32	Cost adjustments based on special factors	Automated
Step 33	Estimating postrelease maintenance	Automated
Step 34	Estimating postrelease enhancements	Automated
Step 35	Validating software cost estimates	Automated/manual

TABLE 14.2   Software-Estimating Activities Depending upon Human Judgment

Step	Definition	Method preferred for maximum accuracy
Step 1	Understanding software requirements	Manual
Step 3	Exploring similar historical projects	Automated/manual
Step 4	Sizing software deliverables	Automated/manual
Step 5	Preliminary estimates and rules of thumb	Automated/manual
Step 6	Make or buy decisions based on estimate	Manual
Step 7	Identifying activities to be performed	Automated/manual
Step 14	Staffing adjustments based on team experience	Automated/manual
Step 18	Effort adjustments based on team capability	Automated/manual
Step 23	Schedule adjustments based on scope creep	Automated/manual
Step 24	Schedule adjustments based on overtime	Automated/manual
Step 35	Validating software cost estimates	Automated/manual

It is interesting to focus on the activities where human judgment is often used to override the default values provided by software estimating tools (see Table 14.2).

As can be seen, almost a third of the activities associated with software cost estimating benefit from the experience and judgment of human participants in the estimating process. Only for activities that are purely rule-based or mechanical, such as applying inflation rates, performing currency conversions, or dealing with critical path analysis, can software-estimating tools work in a wholly automated fashion.

Software cost estimates must also deal with a number of specific technologies which are known to affect the projects where these technologies come into play. A few examples of the technical factors that can affect the outcome of software projects both in real life and in the context of cost estimates are shown in Table 14.3.

With commercial software-estimating tools, the normal mode for dealing with specific technologies is that of either constructing or acquiring a *template* that includes the activities and default values associated with the technology in question.

A software cost estimating template for a technology is a kind of special estimating *object* that includes the set of development activities associated with the technology and default or starting values for assignment scopes, production rates, and other key factors.

Some of the standard software-estimating templates available with commercial software estimating tools include but are not limited to those shown in Table 14.4.

In addition to commercial estimating templates created by estimating-tool vendors, a number of commercial software-estimating tools

TABLE 14.3   Special Factors and Adjustments
for Software Cost Estimation

Application generators
CASE and I-CASE tools
Client/Server project estimation
Component-based software development
Deferral or deletion of planned project functions
Distributed international development
Department of Defense standards
Eurocurrency support
Frame-based development
Hybrid hardware/firmware/software projects
Hypertext links in text files
Information-engineering (IE) project estimation
International projects and translation expenses
Interactive tutorials on CD-ROM or DVD
ISO 9000–9004 standards
Music or special soundtracks
Pattern-based design methods
Processes or methodologies utilized
Prototyping before main project commences
Object-oriented (OO) analysis and design methods
Object-oriented (OO) programming languages
Object-oriented (OO) metrics
Migration to multiple platforms
Multiplatform projects
Multicompany projects
Multimedia software project estimation
Rapid application development (RAD) projects
Reusable design
Reusable source code
Reusable test cases
Reusable user information
SAP R3 deployment
SEI CMM level of the development organization
Training and tutorial material
Videotape tutorials
World Wide Web applets
Year-2000 software repairs
Year-2000 database repairs
Year-2000 contract adjustments

TABLE 14.4   Software-Estimating Templates for Specific Methods and Processes

---

Clean-room development

Client/server development

Eurocurrency updates

Information engineering (IE)

Object-oriented (OO) Development

Rapid application development (RAD)

SAP R3 installation and development

SEI CMM level 1

SEI CMM level 2

SEI CMM level 3

SEI CMM level 4

SEI CMM level 5

Year-2000 software repairs

---

include a template construction utility that allows users to create custom templates for technologies that are used locally.

It is also significant that even with very powerful automated software cost estimating tools, there are a number of cost topics which are usually excluded from general-purpose software cost estimates because they either occur infrequently or vary so widely that no overall rules have been developed for predicting their outcomes (see Table 14.5).

Although these activities are outside the scope of normal software cost estimates, some of the expenses can be very significant. Indeed, the costs of travel for projects involving multiple locations can actually achieve third place out of the top six major software cost elements:

1. Defect-removal costs

2. Paperwork costs

3. Travel and meeting costs

4. Coding costs

5. Project management costs

6. Change-control costs

A number of software cost estimating tools allow these special costs to be added to the overall project by providing empty "cost buckets" that can be filled with whatever special costs are known to be included for the project but are outside the scope of the normal estimate.

Some of these cost buckets are even identified and set up for various kinds of costs that often occur, but that are too variable and irreg-

TABLE 14.5   Normal Exclusions from Software Cost
Estimates

Advertising costs for commercial software

Assessments of projects during development

Benchmark studies of projects during development

Bonuses or awards to key employees

External management consultants

Legal expenses for trademark searches

Legal expenses for patent filings

Legal expenses for copyright filings

Legal expenses for any litigation affecting the project

Nationalization or translating material into other languages

Moving and living expenses for new hires

Postmortem analyses of projects after completion

Signing bonuses for new hires

Stock or equity awarded to employees

Travel expenses for meetings and conferences

Transfer costs for moving projects

Staff training expenses associated with the project

Personnel hiring expenses and agency fees

Capital equipment such as new computers

Software licenses and maintenance fees for tools

Marketing and advertising fees

Work performed by clients or customers

Focus group expenses

Customer survey expenses

Customer association funding

Online forum costs

---

ular for rule-based estimation. Some examples of these prepared cost
buckets include the following:

- Hiring expenses for the project
- Legal expenses for the project
- Travel expenses for the project
- Nationalization expenses for the project
- Assessment expenses for the project
- Management consulting fees for the project

Without multiplying examples, it can be seen that software cost estimating requires dealing with a very large number of factors. One of the advantages of automated cost estimating as opposed to manual cost estimating is that the obscure and infrequent factors are not likely to be forgotten or left out by accident.

Setting Up the Initial Conditions for a Cost Estimate

Once a user has turned on a cost-estimating tool and entered administrative information such as the name of the project, the next step is to establish the initial conditions for the project being estimated.

Although commercial estimating tools vary in how they deal with the initial conditions, many of them operate in a similar manner. By means of pull-down menus, buttons, or explicit statements, users need to narrow down the universe of all possible projects to the specific kind of project for which the estimate is to be made. The estimating tools narrow their focus with such basic kinds of topics as the following:

- Is the project a military project or a civilian project?
- Is the project for internal use or for delivery to external customers?
- Is the project a new project or an enhancement project?
- Is the project a small program or a large system?
- Is the project embedded software, an information system, or something else?
- Will the staff receive payment for overtime work or not?
- Will the project involve work in more than one city or country?
- Are subcontracts or multiple companies involved in the project?
- Are there schedule or cost limits for completing this project?
- Should the estimate to be set at project, phase, activity, or task level?

These are the kinds of factors with such an obvious impact on the outcome of the project that it is apparent why the information is needed. To ease the work of users, however, some commercial estimating tools have default or assumed settings so that the only information that users have to supply is regarding things that are different from the default values.

For example, the estimating tools that the author's company builds includes the following set of assumptions as the initial default values, although every factor in the list can be changed by users if needed:

Project nature	New project
Project scope	Standalone program
Project class	Internal software
Project type	Information system
Staff availability	100%
Staff compensation	$5000 per month
Burden rate	50%
Burdened compensation	$7500
Overtime premium	50%
Annual inflation rate	5%
Exempt personnel (no overtime pay)	100%
Nonexempt personnel (overtime pay)	0%
Overtime premium	100%
Hiring costs	0
Moving and living costs	0
Development locations	1
Maintenance locations	1
Work days per week	5.00
Work hours per day	8.00
Effective hours per day	6.00
Unpaid overtime hours per day	1.00
Holidays per year	10.00
Vacation days per year	15.00
Sick days per year	3.00
Education/training days per year	10.00
Meetings/travel days per year	5.00
Work days per calendar year	218

The purpose of providing default values is to simplify estimating mechanics by having at least reasonable information available for topics which not every project manager will know or have immediate access to.

Although these are reasonable default values for software projects produced in the United States, they are by no means absolute values that can safely be applied to projects in every country. Even in the United States, the ranges of possible values are extremely broad and users will need to replace such default assumptions with their own organization's real values.

There are several major problems in the cost domain that have existed for more than 50 years, but which escaped notice so long as software used inaccurate metrics like lines of code that tended to mask a host of other important problems. These same problems occur for other industries besides software, incidentally. They tend to be more troublesome for software than for most other industries because software is so labor intensive.

The topic of software costs has a very large range of variability within any given country, and an even larger range for international software studies. There are seven interconnected sets of cost factors that need to be evaluated to determine software costs, and every one is an independent variable, as shown in Table 14.6.

A fundamental problem with software cost measures is the fact that salaries and compensation vary widely from job to job, worker to worker, company to company, region to region, industry to industry, and country to country.

In calendar years 1997 and 1998, an added problem has been the fact that the global shortage of software personnel is pushing software salary rates upwards at double-digit inflation rates, and even with excellent compensation packages software personnel are hard to find. Indeed, as of 1997 and 1998, some software engineers with critical skills may receive signing bonuses in excess of $10,000. This is such a new topic that it is not a standard assumption in commercial software cost estimating tools.

For example, among SPR's clients in the United States the basic salary for software project managers ranges from a low of about $42,000 per year to a high of more than $100,000 per year. When international clients are included, the range for the same position runs from less than $10,000 per year to more than $120,000 a year.

As this is being written, annual data is available only through calendar year 1996. Table 14.8 shows 1996 averages and ranges for project management compensation for 20 U.S. industries taken from among SPR's client organizations.

However, as this book is being finished (early 1998) the software

---

TABLE 14.6   Compensation Variations That Impact
Software Cost Estimates

1. Variations due to industry compensation averages

2. Variations due to sizes of companies

3. Variations due to geographic regions or locations

4. Variations due to merit appraisals or longevity

5. Variations due to burden rate or overhead differences

6. Variations due to work patterns and unpaid overtime

7. Variations due to bonuses or special one-time payments

industry is in the throes of a huge personnel shortage. The combination of the onrushing year-2000 problem coupled with the European currency conversion problem has created a shortage of software personnel estimated to be about 35 percent in the industrialized nations.

For software-intensive industries, such as banks, insurance companies, and telecommunications companies, personnel shortages are reaching critical levels and are lowering the chances of completing such key tasks as year-2000 repairs and Eurocurrency conversion work in the time remaining.

This means that compensation levels for experienced software personnel are moving up at double-digit inflation rates. Using 1996 as the base year, software salaries can be expected to rise by these approximate amounts over the next five years (see Table 14.7).

Of course, if the probable failure to repair the year-2000 problem in time causes a global recession, then even software personnel will be affected and the rapid increase in software salaries can plummet starting in 2000.

Table 14.8 shows average compensation in the left column, and then ranges based on company size and geographic region. As can be expected, large corporations pay more than small companies.

For example, large urban areas, such as the San Francisco Bay area or the urban areas in New York and New Jersey, have much higher pay scales than do more rural areas or smaller communities in other locations, such as Arkansas, Nebraska, or West Virginia.

Also, some industries, such as banking and financial services and telecommunications manufacturing, tend to have compensation levels that are far above U.S. averages, while other industries, such as government service and education, tend to have compensation levels that are significantly lower than U.S. averages.

TABLE 14.7   Expected Inflation in Software Salaries for Five Years

Year	Inflation rate, %	Major reason
1996	Base year	Startup of year-2000 and Eurocurrency work
1997	11	Year-2000 and Eurocurrency staffing grows
1998	13	Major year for Eurocurrency conversion
1999	16	Peak year for year-2000 repairs
2000	17	Peak year for year-2000 damage recovery
2001	15	Both year-2000 and Eurocurrency work
2002	12	Both year-2000 and Eurocurrency work
2003	10	Possible return to normal staffing
2004	7	Probable return to normal staffing
2005	5	Normal staffing

TABLE 14.8   1996 Annual Compensation Levels for Software Project Managers in 20 Industries in the United States

Industry	Average annual salary	Range by company size, ±	Range by geographic region, ±	Maximum annual salary	Minimum annual salary
Banking	$72,706	$18,000	$6,000	$96,706	$48,706
Electronics	71,750	15,000	6,000	92,750	50,750
Telecommunications	71,500	15,000	6,000	92,500	50,500
Software	71,250	15,000	6,000	92,250	50,250
Consumer products	69,929	14,000	5,500	89,429	50,429
Chemicals	68,929	13,000	5,500	87,429	50,429
Defense	65,828	13,000	5,500	84,328	47,328
Food and beverages	63,667	12,000	5,000	80,667	46,667
Media	62,125	12,000	5,000	79,125	45,125
Industrial equipment	62,009	12,000	5,000	79,009	45,009
Distribution	60,900	11,000	5,000	76,900	44,900
Insurance	59,117	10,000	5,000	74,117	44,117
Public utilities	57,214	7,500	4,500	69,214	45,214
Retail	57,105	7,000	4,500	68,605	45,605
Health care	55,459	7,500	4,500	67,459	43,459
Nonprofits	53,883	7,500	4,500	65,883	41,883
Transportation	53,448	7,000	4,500	64,948	41,948
Textiles	52,583	7,000	4,500	64,083	41,083
Government	51,990	6,000	4,000	61,990	41,990
Education	50,176	6,000	4,000	60,176	40,176
Average	$61,578	$11,026	$5,079	$78,284	$46,073

The huge variances in basic compensation mean that it is unsafe and inaccurate to use "U.S. averages" for cost comparisons of software. In fact, although "average cost per function point" is the single question that is most often posed to software cost estimating companies, that specific factor is one of the most volatile and unreliable of all metrics.

At the very least, cost comparisons should be within the context of the same or related industries, and comparisons should be made against organizations that are of similar size and are located in similar geographic areas.

Other software-related positions besides project management have similar ranges, and there are now more than 50 software-related occupations in the United States. This means that in order to do software cost studies it is necessary to deal with major differences in

TABLE 14.9   1996 Variations in Compensation for Selected Software Occupation Groups in the United States

Occupation	Average annual salary	Range by company size, ±	Range by geographic location, ±	Range by industry, ±	Maximum annual salary	Minimum annual salary
Software architect	$77,000	$13,000	$4,500	$7,500	$102,000	$52,000
Senior systems programmer	75,000	12,000	4,500	6,000	97,500	52,500
Senior systems analyst	67,000	11,000	4,000	6,000	88,000	46,000
Systems programmer	60,000	11,000	4,000	5,500	80,500	39,500
Systems analyst	55,000	10,500	3,750	5,000	74,250	35,750
Process Analyst	53,000	10,500	3,750	5,000	72,250	33,750
Database analyst	52,000	12,000	3,750	6,000	73,750	30,250
Metrics specialist	50,000	12,000	3,750	5,000	70,750	29,250
Programmer/ analyst	50,000	11,000	3,500	5,000	69,500	30,500
Applications programmer	50,000	10,000	3,500	5,000	68,500	31,500
Maintenance programmer	50,000	10,000	3,500	5,000	68,500	31,500
Quality assurance	49,000	7,500	3,500	5,000	65,000	33,000
Testing specialist	49,000	7,500	3,500	5,000	65,000	33,000
Technical writer	40,000	5,000	3,500	3,000	51,500	28,500
Customer support	37,000	2,000	3,500	2,000	44,500	29,500
Average	$54,267	$9,667	$3,767	$5,067	$72,767	$35,767

costs based on industry, on company size, on geographic location, on the kinds of specialists that are present on any given project, and on years of tenure or merit appraisal results.

Table 14.9 illustrates the 1996 ranges of basic compensation (exclusive of bonuses or merit appraisal adjustments) for 15 software occupations in the United States. As can be seen, the range of possible compensation levels runs from less than $30,000 to more than $100,000.

Over and above the basic compensation levels shown in Table 14.9, a number of specialized occupations are now offering even higher compensation levels than those illustrated. For example, programmers who are familiar with SAP R/3 integrated systems and the ABAP programming language can expect compensation levels about 10 percent higher than average, and may even receive signing bonuses similar to those offered to professional athletes.

Special premiums are also being paid to those with other rare or needed skills, such as webmasters and year-2000 repair specialists. As this book is being written, the global shortage of software professionals is artificially raising compensation rates faster than at almost any time in the history of the software occupation.

Even if only basic compensation is considered, it can easily be seen that software projects developed by large companies in such large cities as New York, Chicago, and San Jose will have higher cost structures than the same applications developed by small companies in smaller cities.

Although the topic is not illustrated and the results are often proprietary, there are also major variations in compensation based on merit appraisals and/or longevity within grade. This factor can add about plus or minus $7500 to the ranges of compensation for technical positions, and even more for executive and managerial positions.

Also not illustrated are the bonus programs and stock equity programs that many companies offer to software technical employees and to managers. For example, the stock equity program at Microsoft has become famous for creating more millionaires than any similar program in U.S. industry.

Although technical software personnel seldom have access to all of them, there are also a number of other perks that may affect the compensation package and burden rate, such as the following:

- Automobiles leased by the corporation
- Health or athletic club memberships
- Membership fees for premium airline clubs and facilities
- Education and tuition refund programs

One of the more complex issues of software cost estimating is dealing with all of the elements that actually go into the cost structures of modern corporations and their payment and benefit plans.

Variations in Burden Rates or Overhead Costs

An even more significant problem associated with software cost studies is the lack of generally accepted accounting practices for determining the burden rate or overhead costs that are added to basic salaries to create a metric called the *fully burdened salary rate,* which corporations use for determining topics business such as the charge-out rates for cost centers. The fully burdened rate is also used for other business purposes, such as contracts, outsourcing agreements, and return on investment (ROI) calculations.

The components of the burden rate are highly variable from company to company. Some of the costs included in burden rates can be social security contributions, unemployment benefit contributions, various kinds of taxes, rent for office space, utilities, security, postage, depreciation, portions of mortgage payments on buildings, various fringe benefits (medical plans, dental plans, disability, moving and living, vacations, etc.), and sometimes the costs of indirect staff (human resources, purchasing, mail room, etc.)

One of the major gaps in the software literature as this is being written, and for that matter in accounting literature as well, is the almost total lack of international comparisons of the typical burden rate methodologies used in various countries. So far as can be determined, there are no published studies that explore burden rate differences between countries, such as the United States, Canada, India, the European Union countries, Japan, China, and so forth.

Among SPR's clients, the range of burden rates runs from a low of perhaps 15 percent of basic salary levels to a high of approximately 300 percent. In terms of dollars, that range means that the fully burdened charge rate for the position of senior systems programmer in the United States can run from a low of about $15,000 per year to a high of $350,000 per year.

Unfortunately, the software literature is almost silent on the topic of burden or overhead rates. Indeed, many articles on software costs not only fail to detail the factors included in burden rates, but often fail to even state whether the burden rate itself was used in deriving the costs that the articles discuss.

Of all of the cost-estimating adjustment factors, there is the greatest scarcity of industry average data for burden rates. This is because many companies regard the structure of their burden or overhead rates as being proprietary information.

Table 14.10 illustrates some of the typical components of software burden rates, and also shows how these components might vary between a large corporation with a massive infrastructure and a small startup corporation that has very few overhead cost elements.

When the combined ranges of basic salaries and burden rates are applied to software projects in the United States, they yield almost a 6 to 1 variance in personnel costs for projects where the actual number of work months or work hours are identical.

When the salary and burden rate ranges are applied to international projects, they yield about a 15 to 1 variance between such countries as India or the Ukraine at the low end of the spectrum and Germany or Switzerland or Japan at the high end of the spectrum.

Hold in mind that this 15 to 1 range of cost variance is for projects where the actual number of hours worked is identical. When produc-

TABLE 14.10   Generic Components of Typical Burden or Overhead Costs in Large and Small Companies

Component	Large company		Small company	
	Cost	Percentage	Cost	Percentage
Average annual salary	$50,000	100.0	$50,000	100
Personnel burden				
Payroll taxes	5,000	10	$5,000	10
Bonus	5,000	10	0	0
Benefits	5,000	10	2,500	5
Profit sharing	5,000	10	0	0
Subtotal	$20,000	40	$7,500	15
Office burden				
Office rent	$10,000	20	$5,000	10
Property taxes	2,500	5	1,000	2
Office supplies	2,000	4	1,000	2
Janitorial service	1,000	2	1,000	2
Utilities	1,000	2	1,000	2
Subtotal	$16,500	33	$9,000	18
Corporate burden				
Information systems	$5,000	10	0	0
Finance	5,000	10	0	0
Human resources	4,000	8	0	0
Legal	3,000	6	0	0
Subtotal	$17,000	34	0	0
Total burden	$53,500	107	$16,500	33
Salary + burden	$103,500	207	$66,500	133
Monthly rate	8,625		5,542	

tivity differences are considered, too, there can be more than a 100 to 1 variance between the most productive projects in companies with the lowest salaries and burden rates and the least productive projects in companies with the highest salaries and burden rates.

On the whole, throughout the world, large corporations in major metropolitan areas have higher compensation and burden rates than smaller corporations in rural areas. Consider a plain ordinary management information system of 1000 function points written in COBOL. It might cost $1500 per function point for a major corporation to build this application in New York or San Francisco, but only

$600 per function point for a small company to build it in St. Petersburg, Florida or Lincoln, Nebraska, with exactly the same number of people and exactly the same number of work hours for the project. The large metropolitan version will be built by personnel whose salaries are 10 to 15 percent higher than the rural version, while the overhead factors of rent, taxes, utilities, and other components may be 100 percent greater in the large metropolitan areas.

Variations in Work Habits and Unpaid Overtime

From an estimating viewpoint, one of the most troublesome aspects of software cost estimating is predicting the work patterns of the development team. Software development and maintenance are very labor intensive. So long as software is built using human effort as the primary tool, all of the factors associated with work patterns and overtime will continue to be significant.

Assume that a typical month contains four work weeks, each comprised of five 8-hour working days. The combination of 4 weeks · 5 days · 8 hours = 160 available hours in a typical month. However, at least in the United States, the *effective* number of hours worked each month is often less than 160, due to such factors as coffee breaks, meetings, slack time between assignments, interruptions, and the like.

Thus, in situations where there is no intense schedule pressure, the effective number of work hours per month may only amount to about 80 percent of the available hours, or about 128 hours per calendar month.

On the other hand, software projects are often under intense schedule pressures and overtime is quite common. The majority of professional U.S. software personnel are termed *exempt,* which means that they do not receive overtime pay for work in the evening or on weekends. Indeed, many software cost tracking systems do not even record overtime hours.

Thus, for situations where schedule pressures are intense, not only might the software team work the available 160 hours per month, but they might also work late in the evenings and on weekends, too. Thus, on crunch projects the work might amount to 110 percent of the available hours, or about 176 hours per month.

Table 14.11 compares two versions of the same project, which can be assumed to be a 1000–function point information systems application written in COBOL.

The first version, shown in the left column, is a *normal* version, where only about 80 percent of the available hours each month are worked. The second version, shown in the right column, is the same project in *crunch mode,* where the work hours total 110 percent, with

TABLE 14.11   Differences Between Normal and Intense Work Patterns

Activity	Work habits			
	Project 1, normal	Project 2, intense	Difference	Percentage
Size, FP	1,000	1,000	0	0.00
Size, LOC	100,000	100,000	0	0.00
LOC per FP	100	100	0	0.00
A scope, FP	200	200	0	0.00
Nominal P rate, FP	10	10	0	0.00
Availability	80.00%	110.00%	30.00%	37.50
Hours per month	128.00	176.00	48.00	37.50
Salary per month	$5,000.00	$5,000.00	$0.00	0.00
Staff	5.00	5.00	0.00	0.00
Effort months	125.00	90.91	−34.09	−27.27
Schedule months	31.25	16.53	−14.72	−47.11
Cost	$625,000	$454,545	−$170,455	−27.27
Cost per FP	$625.00	$454.55	−$170.45	−27.27
Work hours per FP	16.00	16.00	0.00	0.00
Virtual P rate, FP	8.00	11.00	3.00	37.50
Cost per LOC	$6.25	$4.55	−$1.70	−27.27
LOC per month	800	1100	300	37.50

all of the extra hours being in the form of unpaid overtime by the software team.

Since exempt software personnel are normally paid on a monthly basis rather than an hourly basis, the differences in apparent results between normal and intense work patterns are both significant and tricky when performing software cost analysis.

As can be seen from Table 14.11, applying intense work pressure to a software project in the form of unpaid overtime can produce significant and visible reductions in software costs and software schedules. (However there may also be invisible and harmful results in terms of staff fatigue and burnout.)

Table 14.11 introduces five terms that are significant in software measurement and also cost estimating, but which need to be defined.

The first term is *assignment scope* (A scope), which is the quantity of function points normally assigned to one staff member. The assignment scope varies from activity to activity, but in general is approximately one staff member for every 150 function points for new development projects. During maintenance, one staff member is needed for about every 750 function points of deployed software. Both variables can vary significantly.

The second term is *production rate* (P rate), which is the monthly rate in function points at which the work will be performed. Here, too, there are major variations based on the expertise of the staff members, and the reusable materials and overtime applied to the project. (Other metrics are also used for production rates, such as lines of code for programmers, pages for technical writers, or bugs fixed per month for maintenance specialists.)

The third term is *nominal production rate,* which is the rate of monthly progress measured in function points without any unpaid overtime being applied.

The fourth term is *virtual production rate,* which is the apparent rate of monthly productivity in function points that will result when unpaid overtime is applied to the project or activity.

The fifth term is *work hours per function point,* which simply accumulates the total number of work hours expended and divides that amount by the function point total of the application. In the more sophisticated corporate measurement programs, normal paid hours, unpaid overtime hours, and paid overtime hours would be recorded separately.

Because software technical staff members are usually paid monthly but work hourly, the most visible impact of unpaid overtime is to decouple productivity measured in work hours per function point from productivity measured in function points per staff month. This is a complicated topic, and an illustration can clarify what happens.

Assume that a small 60–function point project would normally require 2 calendar months, or 320 work hours, to complete. Now assume that the programmer assigned works double shifts and finishes the project in 1 calendar month, although 320 work hours are still needed.

If the project had been a normal one stretched over 2 months, the productivity rate would have been 30 function points per staff month and 5.33 work hours per function point.

By applying unpaid overtime to the project and finishing in 1 month instead of 2, the virtual productivity rate appears to be 60 function points per staff month, but the actual number of hours required remains 5.33 work hours per function points—only a large portion of these work hours are in the form of unpaid overtime, and hence, have no effect on the costs of the project. The unpaid overtime hours tend to elevate productivity rates when measured at monthly intervals.

Variations in work patterns are extremely significant variations when dealing with international software projects. There are major national differences in terms of work hours per week, quantities of unpaid overtime, numbers of annual holidays, and annual vacation periods.

In fact, it is very dangerous to perform international studies without taking this phenomenon into account. Variations in work practices are a major differentiating factor for international software productivity and schedule results.

Table 14.12 makes a number of simplifying assumptions and does not deal with the specifics of sick time, lunch and coffee breaks, meetings, courses, and nonwork activities that might occur during business hours.

Table 14.12 is derived from basic assumptions about national holidays and average annual vacation times. Table 14.12 also ignores telecommuting, home offices, flex time, and a number of other factors that are important for detailed analyses.

Since there are significant local and industry differences within every country, the data in Table 14.12 should be used as just a starting point for more detailed exploration and analysis.

This table has a very large margin of error, because within any given country there are significant variances in work habits and compensation by industry, by geographic region, and by size of the organization.

Software is currently among the most labor-intensive commodities on the global market. Therefore, work practices and work effort applied to software exerts a major influence on productivity and schedule results. In every country, the top software personnel tend to work rather long hours, so Table 14.13 can only be used for very rough comparisons.

TABLE 14.12   Approximate Number of Work Hours per Year in 10 Countries

Country	Work days per year	Work hours per day	Overtime per day	Work hours per year	Percentage of U.S. results
Japan	260	9.00	2.5	2990	139
China	260	9.00	1.5	2730	127
India	245	8.50	2	2573	120
Italy	230	9.00	1	2300	107
United States	239	8.00	1	2151	100
Brazil	234	8.00	1	2106	98
United Kingdom	232	8.00	1	2088	97
France	230	8.00	1	2070	96
Germany	228	8.00	0	1824	85
Russia	230	7.50	0	1725	80
Average	238.8	8.30	1.1	2245	104

TABLE 14.13   International Cost Comparison for Software Projects of 1000
Function Points

Country	Work hours per FP	Effort, work hours	Cost per work hour	Project cost	Cost per FP	Percentage of U.S. results
Germany	20	20,000	$57.56	$1,151,200	$1,151.20	129
France	20	20,000	46.92	938,400	938.40	105
United States	20	20,000	44.74	894,800	894.80	100
United Kingdom	20	20,000	41.09	821,800	821.80	92
Brazil	20	20,000	37.60	752,000	752.00	84
Italy	20	20,000	37.30	746,000	746.00	83
Japan	20	20,000	36.70	734,000	734.00	82
Russia	20	20,000	10.08	201,600	201.60	23
India	20	20,000	4.46	89,200	89.20	10
China	20	20,000	3.70	74,000	74.00	8
Average	20	20,000	$57.56	$640,300	$640.30	72

The differences in national work patterns compounded with differences in burdened cost structures can lead to very significant international differences in software costs and schedules for the same size and kind of application.

Table 14.13 illustrates how wide the global cost variances can actually be. This table examines the cost ranges of building exactly the same 1000–function point software project in 10 countries throughout the world.

Table 14.13 artificially holds the effort constant at 20 work hours per function point, and then applies typical local compensation levels and burden rates for the 10 countries illustrated.

Although there are very large ranges within each country, it can be seen that there also are very large national differences, as well. Expressed in terms of cost per function point, the observed range for exactly the same size and kind of software projects around the world spans amounts that run from less than $75 per function point on the low end to more than $1500 per function point on the high end.

Although it is easily possible to calculate the arithmetic mean, harmonic mean, median, and mode of software costs, any such cost value would be dangerous to use for estimating purposes when the ranges are so broad.

This is why the author has always been reluctant to publish general software cost data, and instead uses costs only in the context of country, industry, regional, and project norms. In fact, cost data varies so much that work hours or person months are much more stable for software productivity studies.

Obviously, for international comparisons the daily fluctuations in currency exchange rates and the longer fluctuations in national rates of inflation also need to be considered.

When clients ask for data on average cost per function point so that they can use this data for estimating purposes, the only safe answer is that costs vary so much due to compensation and burden rate differences that it is better to base the comparison on the client's own industry and geographic locale. General industry cost data is much too variable for casual comparisons at national levels.

The literature on adjustment factors for software costs is somewhat sparse, and much of the available information is not as current as it should be. For an interesting discussion of how various estimation tools deal with adjustments, the Air Force comparative report of Dean Barrow and colleagues is useful (Barrow et al. 1993).

The pioneering work of Dr. Barry Boehm in *Software Engineering Economics* (Boehm 1981) is dated, but still valuable reading. Also, Tom DeMarco has a very solid way of dealing with adjustments, including social and ergonomic factors (DeMarco 1982, DeMarco 1995).

Because software-estimation tools are expert systems, the ways that other expert systems adjust themselves is relevant, and Paul Harmon's work on this is interesting (Harmon and King 1985).

Because the rigor of the development process is a key adjustment factor for estimation, all of the work of Watts Humphrey is relevant (Humphrey 1989). Also, many of the author's own books deal with estimating adjustments derived from SPR's benchmark studies (Jones 1994, 1995, 1996, 1997).

For an interesting treatment of adjustment factors in an object-oriented context, the work of Dr. Tom Love is very relevant (Love 1993). The OO domain is unique in several respects, but working long hours and plenty of unpaid overtime crosses all software domains.

Although there are business competitors with SPR in the estimation world, the work of Larry Putnam and his colleagues at QSM on estimation and adjustments are well worth reading (Putnam 1992; Putnam and Myers 1997). Larry Putnam is well known for his method of assigning aggregate weights to combinations of adjustment factors to create an overall productivity multiplier which can be used to estimate projects that are better or worse than industry norms.

Another researcher whose work on estimation and whose work on measurement provide deep insights into the significance of adjustment factors is the well-known speaker and management consultant Dr. Howard Rubin (Rubin 1997; Robbins and Rubin 1997). As this book is being finished, Dr. Rubin is chairman of a national task force on the software labor shortage and has collected very current data on work habits of software professionals (Rubin 1998).

William Roetzheim and Reyna Beasley also discuss adjustment factors for software cost estimation in their recent book on estimating best practices (Roetzheim and Beasley 1998).
Charles Symons, the well-known U.K. management consultant and developer of the Mark II function point metric, also discusses estimating adjustment factors (Symons 1991).
On the whole, a great deal more work is needed on software adjustment factors in terms of showing their impacts in both positive and negative directions. The current literature sometimes exaggerates the impact of positive factors, and is extremely limited in empirical findings on negative factors which can degrade productivity and stretch out schedules.

References

Barrow, Dean, Susan Nilson, and Dawn Timberlake: *Software Estimation Technology Report,* Air Force Software Technology Support Center, Hill Air Force Base, Utah, 1993.

Boehm, Barry: *Software Engineering Economics,* Prentice Hall, Englewood Cliffs, N.J., 1981.

DeMarco, Tom: *Controlling Software Projects,* Yourdon Press, New York, ISBN 0-917072-32-4, 1982.

———: *Why Does Software Cost So Much?,* Dorset House, New York, ISBN 0-932633-34-X, 1995.

Harmon, Paul, and David King: *Expert Systems,* John Wiley & Sons, New York, ISBN 0-471-81554-3, 1985.

Humphrey, Watts S.: *Managing the Software Process,* Addison-Wesley/Longman, Reading, Mass., 1989.

———: *A Discipline of Software Engineering,* Addison-Wesley, Reading, Mass., 1995.

Jones, Capers: *Critical Problems in Software Measurement,* Information Systems Management Group, ISBN 1-56909-000-9, 1993a.

———: *Software Productivity and Quality Today—The Worldwide Perspective,* Information Systems Management Group, ISBN 1-56909-001-7, 1993b.

———: *Assessment and Control of Software Risks,* Prentice Hall, Englewood Cliffs, N.J., ISBN 0-13-741406-4, 1994.

———: *New Directions in Software Management,* Information Systems Management Group, ISBN 1-56909-009-2.

———: *Patterns of Software System Failure and Success,* International Thomson Computer Press, Boston, ISBN 1-850-32804-8, 1995.

———: *Applied Software Measurement,* 2d ed., McGraw-Hill, New York, ISBN 0-07-032826-9, 1996.

———: *The Economics of Object-Oriented Software,* Software Productivity Research, Burlington, Mass., April 1997a.

———: *Software Quality—Analysis and Guidelines for Success,* International Thomson Computer Press, Boston, ISBN 1-85032-876-6, 1997b.

———: *The Year 2000 Software Problem—Quantifying the Costs and Assessing the Consequences,* Addison-Wesley, Reading, Mass., ISBN 0-201-30964-5, 1998.

Love, Tom: *Object Lessons,* SIGS Books, New York, ISBN 0-9627477 3-4, 1993.

Putnam, Lawrence H.: *Measures for Excellence—Reliable Software on Time, Within Budget,* Yourdon Press/Prentice Hall, Englewood Cliffs, N.J., ISBN 0-13-567694-0, 1992.

———, and Ware Myers: *Industrial Strength Software—Effective Management Using Measurement,* IEEE Press, Los Alamitos, Calif., ISBN 0-8186-7532-2, 1997.

Rethinking the Software Process, CD-ROM, Miller Freeman, Lawrence, Kans., 1996. (This CD-ROM is a book collection jointly produced by the book publisher, Prentice Hall, and the journal publisher, Miller Freeman. It contains the full text and illustrations of five Prentice Hall books: Capers Jones, *Assessment and Control of Software Risks*; Tom DeMarco, *Controlling Software Projects*; Brian Dreger, *Function Point Analysis*; Larry Putnam and Ware Myers, *Measures for Excellence*; and Mark Lorenz and Jeff Kidd, *Object-Oriented Software Metrics*.)

Robbins, Brian, and Howard Rubin: *The Year 2000 Planning Guide*, Rubin Systems, Pound Ridge, N.Y., 1997.

Roetzheim, William H., and Reyna A. Beasley: *Best Practices in Software Cost and Schedule Estimation*, Prentice Hall PTR, Upper Saddle River, N.J., 1998.

Rubin, Howard: *Worldwide Software Benchmark Report for 1997*, Rubin Systems, Pound Ridge, N.Y., 1997.

————: *Study of the Global Software Shortage*, Rubin Systems, Pound Ridge, N.Y., 1998. (Study produced for the ITAA.)

Symons, Charles R.: *Software Sizing and Estimating—Mk II FPA (Function Point Analysis)*, John Wiley & Sons, Chichester, U.K., ISBN 0 471-92985-9, 1991.

15

Activity Pattern
Adjustment Factors

It is obvious that serious studies of software processes and practices need data that gets down to the levels of activities and tasks. Data measured only to the project level is inadequate for any kind of in-depth economic analysis, and is worthless for process improvement analysis. This is also true for phase-level measurements based on rudimentary phase structures, such as *requirements, design, coding, integration,* and *testing.* However, as of 1998, there are no standard definitions for the sets of activities that should be included in activity-based software measurement studies.

It is very interesting to realize that much of the observed difference in productivity rates among various industries and kinds of software is due to the fact that not all software is built using the same sets of activities. For example, it takes much more work to build U.S. military software than any other kind of software in the world. This is because Department of Defense standards mandate activities, such as *independent verification and validation,* that civilian software projects almost never use.

Further, the intensive oversight requirements in military contracts cause various specifications and control documents on military software projects to be two to three times larger than equivalent documents on civilian projects. Among SPR's military clients, the effort associated with producing paper documents on software projects often exceeds 50 percent of the entire work of the project. In some military software projects, as many as 400 English words are written for every line of Ada code produced!

Some software methodologies include more than 50 activities and tasks, and there are countless variations when local customizations of methodologies are considered. For example, all of these methodologies have specialized activity sets associated with them: information engineering (IE), rapid application development (RAD), object-oriented (OO) analysis and design, and the European Merise and SPICE methodologies; and both the traditional waterfall and more recent spiral and iterative models have activity patterns that are partly unique and partly generic.

There are also specialized activities outside the scope of normal project development work that need to be considered. For example, some of the specialized activities are those associated with formal design and code inspections, with ISO 9000–9004 certification, with SEI assessments and the capability maturity model (CMM), with capturing *cost of quality* information, with total quality management (TQM), and with business process reengineering (BPR) studies.

SPR has analyzed many software development methodologies from around the world, and has constructed a generic checklist of 25 activities that occur with high frequency. This list of activities is used for our baseline and benchmark cost collections, for schedule measurement, and as the basis for exploring the effectiveness of various kinds of tools and practices.

One of the interesting by-products of exploring software projects down to the level of activities is the set of *patterns* that are often associated with various sizes and kinds of software projects.

To illustrate some of the variations at the activity level, Table 15.1 gives examples of activity pattern differences noted during SPR assessment and baseline studies for various classes of software, based on the checklist of 25 activities that SPR utilizes for data collection. These same patterns are discussed in previous sections, but they remain key differentiating factors which explain much of the cost variances among different software classes.

Table 15.1 illustrates the patterns noted for end-user software, management information systems (MIS), outsourced software, commercial software, systems software, and military software.

Note that over and above the average values shown, there can be significant variations. For example, small client/server projects may only perform 8 of the 16 activities listed under the MIS domain, which simultaneously explains why client/server productivity can be high and client/server quality can be low.

From activity-based analysis such as this, it becomes easy to understand a number of otherwise ambiguous topics. For example, it can easily be seen why U.S. military software projects are more expensive than any other kind of software. For a project of any given size, military standards trigger the performance of more activities

TABLE 15.1   Typical Activity Patterns for Six Software Domains

Activities performed	End-user	MIS	Outsource	Commercial	Systems	Military
01 Requirements		X	X	X	X	X
02 Prototyping	X	X	X	X	X	X
03 Architecture		X	X	X	X	X
04 Project plans		X	X	X	X	X
05 Initial design		X	X	X	X	X
06 Detail design		X	X	X	X	X
07 Design reviews		X	X	X	X	X
08 Coding	X	X	X	X	X	X
09 Reuse acquisition	X		X	X	X	X
10 Package purchase		X	X		X	X
11 Code inspections				X	X	X
12 Independent Verification and Validation						X
13 Configuration management		X	X	X	X	X
14 Formal integration		X	X	X	X	X
15 Documentation	X	X	X	X	X	X
16 Unit testing	X	X	X	X	X	X
17 Function testing		X	X	X	X	X
18 Integration testing		X	X	X	X	X
19 System testing		X	X	X	X	X
20 Field testing				X	X	X
21 Acceptance testing		X	X		X	X
22 Independent testing						X
23 Quality assurance			X	X	X	X
24 Installation and training		X	X		X	X
25 Project management		X	X	X	X	X
Activities	5	16	20	21	22	25

and tasks than any other software methodology or process of development.

It can also be seen why the quality levels of client/server projects often tend to be embarrassingly bad, and why client/server maintenance costs are alarmingly high. The processes used to build client/server applications are among the skimpiest and least rigorous of any kind of software yet analyzed.

Some questions frequently asked of software cost estimating

experts are "What percentage of effort goes to testing?" and "What percentage of effort goes to programming?" Unfortunately, these questions are dangerous ones either to ask or to answer.

There are no fixed percentages for any known activity that can safely be used for estimating software projects of all sizes and kinds. It is much better to consider the percentages associated with specific activities, and to do so in the context of a specific type of application and a specific size range.

To illustrate the reasons for the hazards of using simple ratios and percentages, Table 15.2 shows the approximate percentages of effort associated with six different kinds of software projects.

As can be seen from Table 15.2, it is folly to assume that any single activity will absorb a fixed percentage of development effort from project to project or industry to industry.

When variations in costs and variations in activity patterns are melded together, the overall results are very broad indeed. Table 15.3 illustrates the burdened and unburdened costs per function point for the same six industries shown in Tables 15.1 and 15.2.

Table 15.3 illustrates average U.S. data circa 1997, and the ranges would be even broader if global data were used. The projects in Table 15.3 run from 1 function point to 100,000 function points.

Table 15.3 is somewhat misleading because it uses simple arithmetic averages, rather than weighted averages. However, it is only included to illustrate the basic fact that variations in compensation levels by industry, and variations in burden rates or overhead structures, can exert a significant impact. Indeed, the impact is so significant that it is quite unsafe and hazardous to use *average cost per function point* for any business purpose unless the average in question is taken from information that meets the following restrictions:

- Similar companies
- Similar geographic region
- Similar staffing patterns
- Similar work habits
- Similar burden rate structures

Cost data is far too variable for more global averages to be valid for specific projects or estimating purposes.

Table 15.3 originally appeared in the companion book *Applied Software Measurement* (Jones 1996) and is repeated with the same message: Software costs are highly variable and unstable. Variations are so large from region to region, industry to industry, and company to company that only local cost data should be used for estimating purposes.

TABLE 15.2   Software Development Activities Associated with Six Subindustries
(Percentage of staff months by activity)

Activities performed	End-User	MIS	Outsource	Commercial	Systems	Military
01 Requirements		7.50	9.00	4.00	4.00	7.00
02 Prototyping	10.00	2.00	2.50	1.00	2.00	2.00
03 Architecture		0.50	1.00	2.00	1.50	1.00
04 Project plans		1.00	1.50	1.00	2.00	1.00
05 Initial design		8.00	7.00	6.00	7.00	6.00
06 Detail design		7.00	8.00	5.00	6.00	7.00
07 Design reviews			0.50	1.50	2.50	1.00
08 Coding	35.00	20.00	16.00	23.00	20.00	16.00
09 Reuse acquisition	5.00		2.00	2.00	2.00	2.00
10 Package purchase		1.00	1.00		1.00	1.00
11 Code inspections				1.50	1.50	1.00
12 Independent verification and validation						1.00
13 Configuration management		3.00	3.00	1.00	1.00	1.50
14 Formal integration		2.00	2.00	1.50	2.00	1.50
15 User documentation	10.00	7.00	9.00	12.00	10.00	10.00
16 Unit testing	40.00	4.00	3.50	2.50	5.00	3.00
17 Function testing		6.00	5.00	6.00	5.00	5.00
18 Integration testing		5.00	5.00	4.00	5.00	5.00
19 System testing		7.00	5.00	7.00	5.00	6.00
20 Field testing				6.00	1.50	3.00
21 Acceptance testing		5.00	3.00		1.00	3.00
22 Independent testing						1.00
23 Quality assurance			1.00	2.00	2.00	1.00
24 Installation and training		2.00	3.00		1.00	1.00
25 Project management		12.00	12.00	11.00	12.00	13.00
Total	100.00	100.00	100.00	100.00	100.00	100.00
Activities	5	16	20	21	22	25

TABLE 15.3   U.S. Cost per Function Point in 1996 with and without Burden Rates

	End-User	MIS	Outsource	Commercial	Systems	Military	Average
Compensation	$6,000	$4,750	$4,500	$5,000	$5,250	$4,500	$5,000
Burdened cost	9,600	7,600	13,500	8,000	8,400	14,625	10,288
Unburdened, $/FP	145	1,053	890	1,281	1,733	2,601	1,284
Burdened, $/FP	232	1,684	2,671	2,049	2,773	8,453	2,977

Of course, Table 15.3 does not show the full range of costs for software, since there are also major variations by size of the application, as well as variations due to the industry, the geographic region, the company size, and the variations in occupations utilized on the projects in question.

Software costs have a very wide range of possible results, although the reasons for the variations are at last starting to be well understood. For every item in Table 15.2, the range in the United States can run from less than 50 percent of the nominal average value to more than 150 percent of the nominal average value.

To illustrate the approximate amount of effort and costs for specific activities, Table 15.4 shows the approximate average amount of work hours per function point for each of the 25 activities in the standard SPR chart of accounts for software projects.

The information shown in Table 15.4 illustrates one basic form of activity-based software costing. It is not a substitute for one of the commercial software cost estimating tools that support activity-based costs in a much more sophisticated way, such as allowing each activity to have its own unique cost structure and to vary the nominal hours expended based on experience, methods, tools, and so forth.

Note that only large military projects will use all of the 25 activities shown in Table 15.4. Indeed, small civilian client/server projects or World Wide Web applets may utilize only a few of the 25 activities, which simultaneously explains their high productivity levels but often questionable quality levels.

Here, too, these default values are a good starting point, but the range around every value is at least 2 to 1 and not every activity will be used on every project. Software cost estimating is a very complex task, and involves thousands of rules and hundreds of adjustments if it is to be done with high precision.

Once activity-based costing is started, it can be extended to include many other activities in a similar fashion. For example, the set of activities shown here is common for development projects.

If you are concerned with maintenance of aging legacy applications, with porting software from one platform to another, or with bringing out a new release of a commercial software package, then you will need to deal with other activities outside of those shown in the tables.

There are also specific activity patterns associated with OO development, with IE, with RAD, and with a host of methodologies and software processes. The fundamental concept of activity-based costing can still be used, even though the activities and their patterns may vary.

The literature on adjustments to match specific activity patterns is very poorly covered in a software cost estimation context. Indeed,

TABLE 15.4   Example of Activity-Based Costs for Software Development

Average monthly salary	$5000
Burden rate	50%
Fully burdened monthly rate	$7500
Work hours per calendar month	132

	Activities	Staff assignment scope, FP	Monthly production rate, FP	Work hours per FP	Salary cost per FP	Burdened cost per FP
01	Requirements	333	175	0.75	$28.57	$42.86
02	Prototyping	500	150	0.88	33.33	50.00
03	Architecture	1000	300	0.44	16.67	25.00
04	Project plans	1000	500	0.26	10.00	15.00
05	Initial design	250	175	0.75	28.57	42.86
06	Detail design	250	150	0.88	33.33	50.00
07	Design reviews	200	225	0.59	22.22	33.33
08	Coding	175	50	2.64	100.00	150.00
09	Reuse acquisition	500	600	0.22	8.33	12.50
10	Package purchase	2000	400	0.33	12.50	18.75
11	Code inspections	150	150	0.88	33.33	50.00
12	Independent verification and validation	500	125	1.06	40.00	60.00
13	Configuration management	1000	1750	0.08	2.86	4.29
14	Integration	1000	250	0.53	20.00	30.00
15	User documentation	1000	70	1.89	71.43	107.14
16	Unit testing	200	150	0.88	33.33	50.00
17	Function testing	200	150	0.88	33.33	50.00
18	Integration testing	250	175	0.75	28.57	42.86
19	System testing	250	200	0.66	25.00	37.50
20	Field (beta) testing	1000	250	0.53	20.00	30.00
21	Acceptance testing	1000	350	0.38	14.29	21.43
22	Independent testing	750	200	0.66	25.00	37.50
23	Quality assurance	1000	150	0.88	33.33	50.00
24	Installation and training	2000	350	0.38	14.29	21.43
25	Project management	1000	100	1.32	50.00	75.00
	Cumulative results	130.18	6.77	19.49	$738.29	$1107.44

many books on software cost estimation do not even deal with activity-based costs but stop at the level of complete projects or rudimentary phase structures.

The worst result of this lack of empirical data on activity-based costs is the false belief that a small set of ratios and percentages can be used as estimating rules of thumb for any class, size, and type of software project. This is roughly the equivalent of assuming that any U.S. citizen could fit into a size 40-regular suit of clothes with a 34-inch waist. Both in software estimation and in buying clothes, it is important to have the results custom-fitted to match the reality of the client.

Among the authors who deal with the topic of activity-based costing, Dr. Barry Boehm's work in *Software Engineering Economics* (Boehm 1981) is dated but still useful. Also useful, although not exclusively about software benchmarking, is Christopher Bogan's work on best-practice analysis (Bogan and English 1994).

Tom DeMarco's work on software projects is always readable and interesting, and even though his book *Controlling Software Projects* was published more than 15 years ago, it still has valid insights (DeMarco 1982).

The Air Force has perhaps published more on software topics than any other service, and the Air Force guide to software acquisition is quite useful because military projects often make use of activity-based cost analysis (Department of the Air Force 1994). The Navy is not far behind in software publications, and Dr. Norm Brown's well-known project on best-practice analysis is also valuable (Brown 1995).

Many of the author's previous books utilize and illustrate activity-based cost approaches for various kinds and sizes of software projects (Jones 1993, 1994, 1995, 1996, 1997).

Much of the literature that discusses activity-based costing has been written by estimating-tool developers. Among these writings can be found the work of Larry Putnam (Putnam 1992, 1997), William Roetzheim (Roetzheim and Beasley 1998), and Howard Rubin (Rubin 1997, 1998).

The domestic function point literature in the United States seldom reaches the level of activity-based costs, but Charles Symons, from the United Kingdom, touches upon this in his book on estimating with Mark II function points (Symons 1991).

References

Boehm, Barry: *Software Engineering Economics,* Prentice Hall, Englewood Cliffs, N.J., 1981.

Bogan, Christopher E., and Michael J. English: *Benchmarking for Best Practices,* McGraw-Hill, New York, ISBN 0-07-006375-3, 1994.

Brown, Norm (ed.): *The Program Manager's Guide to Software Acquisition Best Practices,* Version 1.0, U.S. Department of Defense, Washington, D.C., July 1995.

DeMarco, Tom: *Controlling Software Projects,* Yourdon Press, New York, ISBN 0-917072-32-4, 1982.

Department of the Air Force: *Guidelines for Successful Acquisition and Management of Software Intensive Systems,* vols. 1 and 2, Software Technology Support Center, Hill Air Force Base, Utah, 1994.

Jones, Capers: *Critical Problems in Software Measurement,* Information Systems Management Group, ISBN 1-56909-000-9, 1993a.

———: *Software Productivity and Quality Today—The Worldwide Perspective,* Information Systems Management Group, ISBN 1-56909-001-7, 1993b.

———: *Assessment and Control of Software Risks,* Prentice Hall, Englewood Cliffs, N.J., ISBN 0-13-741406-4, 1994.

———: *New Directions in Software Management,* Information Systems Management Group, ISBN 1-56909-009-2.

———: *Patterns of Software System Failure and Success,* International Thomson Computer Press, Boston, ISBN 1-850-32804-8, 1995.

———: *Applied Software Measurement,* 2d ed., McGraw-Hill, New York, ISBN 0-07-032826-9, 1996.

———: *The Economics of Object-Oriented Software,* Software Productivity Research, Burlington, Mass., April 1997a.

———: *Software Quality—Analysis and Guidelines for Success,* International Thomson Computer Press, Boston, ISBN 1-85032-876-6, 1997b.

———: *The Year 2000 Software Problem—Quantifying the Costs and Assessing the Consequences,* Addison-Wesley, Reading, Mass., ISBN 0-201-30964-5, 1998.

Putnam, Lawrence H.: *Measures for Excellence—Reliable Software on Time, Within Budget,* Yourdon Press/Prentice Hall, Englewood Cliffs, N.J., ISBN 0-13-567694-0, 1992.

———, and Ware Myers: *Industrial Strength Software—Effective Management Using Measurement,* IEEE Press, Los Alamitos, Calif., ISBN 0-8186-7532-2, 1997.

Roetzheim, William H., and Reyna A. Beasley: *Best Practices in Software Cost and Schedule Estimation,* Prentice Hall PTR, Upper Saddle River, N.J., 1998.

Rubin, Howard: *Worldwide Software Benchmark Report for 1997,* Rubin Systems, Pound Ridge, N.Y., 1997.

———: *Study of the Global Software Shortage,* Rubin Systems, Pound Ridge, N.Y., 1998. (Study produced for the ITAA.)

Symons, Charles R.: *Software Sizing and Estimating—Mk II FPA (Function Point Analysis),* John Wiley & Sons, Chichester, U.K., ISBN 0 471-92985-9, 1991.

16

Software Technology Adjustment Factors

Once we have completed the administrative, sizing, and chart of accounts selection aspects of our estimate, we are ready to deal with one of the most important of all estimating tasks, which is that of dealing with software technology adjustment factors.

Here the commercial estimating tools really come into their own, because knowledge of how any particular tool, method, programming language, or skill set can affect the outcome of a software project is obviously a job for a rule-based expert system, where the rules themselves are derived from empirical data taken from hundreds, or even thousands, of software projects.

The methodology for dealing with adjustment factors varies widely from tool to tool. Since most commercial estimating-tool vendors regard their knowledge of adjustment factors as being a proprietary trade secret (including the author of this book), this discussion will of necessity deal with the ways of adjustment in general rather than with the specific adjustments of individual tools, which are often closely guarded trade secrets.

In one sense it is unfortunate that the software industry's most useful information is not more widely available. However it must be recalled that the estimating and software project management business is highly competitive. Software estimating tool vendors earn many millions of dollars every year primarily from their proprietary knowledge of how to deal with such complex topics as technology adjustment factors. If everyone knew how technology affects software projects, selling estimating tools would be difficult or impossible.

Software estimating tool vendors are usually for-profit corporations rather than nonprofit corporations. Although it would be very beneficial if the knowledge of adjustment factors were in the public domain, the value of this kind of information is so high that it is unlikely that the details of more than a few adjustment factors will be made publicly available.

Not only do the software estimating tool companies derive revenues from their proprietary knowledge bases, but so do some other kinds of information service providers. Companies such as Gartner Group, Meta Group, and Giga Group (all offshoots of a concept pioneered by Gideon Gartner) also sell proprietary data for many millions of dollars in annual revenues.

Although universities are often the source of new information on many topics, universities have not been very effective in dealing with either software measurement or with software estimation and adjustment factors.

The reason for this situation is a practical one. Estimation adjustment factors are derived from empirical data from hundreds, or even thousands, of software projects. Only the commercial measurement and estimation vendors have access to this kind of information; universities seldom have data on more than a few kinds of limited software projects. In fact, some of the estimating vendors actually derive significant portions of their annual revenues from performing assessment and benchmarking studies for their clients.

Adjustment Factors and Macroestimation Tools

In the commercial software-estimating domain, the way macroestimation tools and microestimation tools deal with adjustments is rather different. The macroestimation tools typically accumulate information from various kinds of adjustments, such as skill levels, tools, and methods, and create a single value which is used as a multiplier over the entire project.

For example if an average team using average tools and methods has a monthly productivity rate of 10 function points or 1000 lines of code, then a superstar team equipped with state-of-the-art tools and methods might experience a doubled productivity rate of 20 function points per staff month or 2000 lines of code per month.

Conversely, a novice team equipped with marginally adequate tools and methods might experience a monthly productivity rate of only 5 function points or 500 lines of code.

In this situation, team abilities and methodological sophistication have been converted into productivity multipliers, which span a range of 2 to 1. Inside the estimating tool itself may be found a table of values similar to the following.

Although these nine combinations are not taken from any specific

Example of Macroestimating Adjustment Assumptions

Factor combinations	Multiplier
Superior team with superior tools	2.00
Superior team with average tools	1.75
Average team with superior tools	1.50
Superior team with marginal tools	1.25
Average team with average tools	**1.00**
Average team with marginal tools	0.90
Novice team with superior tools	0.75
Novice team with average tools	0.65
Novice team with marginal tools	0.50

estimating tool, they show how various combinations of factors might be converted into productivity adjustments by means of a table-lookup function.

Assuming that an average team with average tools has a productivity rate of 10 function points per staff month, then a superior team with superior tools would have a productivity rate of 20 function points per staff month, while a novice team with marginal tools might have a productivity rate of only 5 function points per staff month.

As can be seen, the nine permutations of these two factors yield an average central value, and then four adjustments on either side of the average value for dealing with situations that are either better or worse than average. This illustration of how adjustments might be made is only an example and is not intended to provide actual estimating adjustment weights or multipliers, although in fact these combinations are not unreasonable in their range of impact.

Microestimation tools also deal with adjustment factors, but typically apply each factor independently rather than developing an aggregated adjustment that covers multiple factors concurrently.

Example of Microestimating Adjustment Assumptions

Evaluation	Team capability multiplier	Tool capability multiplier
Excellent	1.50	1.20
Good	1.25	1.10
Average	**1.00**	**1.00**
Below average	0.75	0.90
Poor	0.50	0.80

This microestimating method of applying each factor individually allows specific factors to be included or excluded as the situation warrants. This is a useful feature, because software productivity is a complex phenomenon with at least 100 known factors at play which can influence the outcomes of software projects.

Further, applying each factor individually opens up the range of possible outcomes. For example, it is now possible to consider what happens when an excellent team has poor tools, or what happens when a poor team is given excellent tools.

For example, assuming that an average team with average tools has a productivity rate of 10 function points per staff month, any of the following combinations can be explored:

Excellent team	$10*1.5 = 15$ function points per staff month
Excellent tools	$15*1.2 = 18$ function points per staff month
Excellent team	$10*1.5 = 15$ function points per staff month
Poor tools	$15*0.8 = 12$ function points per staff month
Poor team	$10*0.5 = 5$ function points per staff month
Excellent tools	$5*1.2 = 6$ function points per staff month
Poor team	$10*0.5 = 5$ function points per staff month
Poor tools	$5*0.8 = 4$ function points per staff month

This methodology of applying each factor in sequence can be continued indefinitely. But note that if a factor is average it is assumed to have a multiplying effect of 1 so that only factors where the project is better or worse than normal need to be dealt with.

Since there are more than 100 factors that can influence the outcome of software projects, it can be expected that the overall range of possible results is quite large, and indeed it is: The total range of possible outcomes over the entire universe of software projects spans more than four orders of magnitude.

The SPR knowledge base of roughly 8000 software projects spans a range that runs from a low of 0.13 function points per staff month to a high of about 140 function points per staff month. Figure 16.1 shows the approximate distribution of 1500 software development projects from the years 1991 through 1997 from the SPR knowledge base.

As can be seen from Fig. 16.1, the range of software productivity results is very broad. This brings up a key question: What causes productivity to be significantly better or worse than average results?

Some of the factors that influence software productivity results are outside the control of the software project team. Although these factors are important, there is little ability to change them. For example:

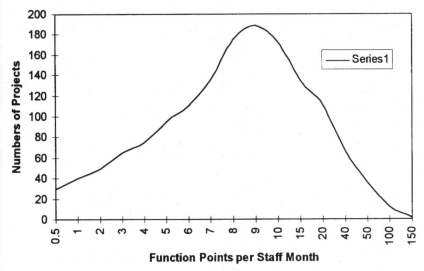

Figure 16.1 Distribution of productivity rates of 1500 software projects.

■ Large systems of more than 10,000 function points in size have lower productivity rates than small projects of less than 100 function points in size.

■ Military software projects that follow the older Department of Defense standards, such as DoD 2167, have lower productivity than similar civilian projects because of the huge volume of required paperwork.

There is little value in discussing factors that are outside the control of the software development team. What this section is concerned with are the factors over which there is a measure of control, such as the choice of tools, programming languages, and development processes.

Before discussing the positive and negative factors, it may be of interest to show a relatively typical average project, such as a COBOL application of 1000 function points in size, in order to give a context of why changes can occur in both positive and negative directions (See Table 16.1).

Because Table 16.1 is being used for illustrative purposes, it simplifies a number of topics and uses rounded data in order to arrive at a net productivity result of exactly 8 function points per staff month, which is a very representative average value for COBOL applications on mainframe computers.

Table 16.1 also uses an even value of 100 COBOL statements per function point even though the real-life results for COBOL applica-

TABLE 16.1 Example of an Average COBOL Application of 1000 Function Points

Assumptions	
Application class	Information system
Programming language(s)	COBOL
Size in function points	1,000
Source lines per function point	100
Size in source code statements	100,000
Average monthly salary	$5,000
Burden rate percent	50%
Fully burdened compensation	$7,500
Nominal work hours per month	160
Effective work hours per month	128

Activity	Assignment scope	Production rate	Hours per FP	Staff	Effort months	Schedule months	Burdened cost	Cost per FP	Cost per LOC	Percent of total
Requirements	333	95.00	1.35	3.00	10.53	3.51	$78,947	$78.95	$0.79	8.42
Prototyping	500	60.00	2.13	2.00	1.67	0.83	12,500	12.50	0.13	1.33
Design	250	75.00	1.71	4.00	13.33	3.33	100,000	100.00	1.00	10.66
Design inspections	200	150.00	0.85	5.00	6.67	1.33	50,000	50.00	0.50	5.33
Coding	200	25.00	5.12	5.00	40.00	8.00	300,000	300.00	3.00	31.99
Code inspections	165	150.00	0.85	6.06	6.67	1.10	50,000	50.00	0.50	5.33
Change control	1000	175.00	0.73	1.00	5.71	5.71	42,857	42.86	0.43	4.57
Testing	200	60.00	2.13	5.00	16.67	3.33	125,000	125.00	1.25	13.33
User documents	1000	140.00	0.91	1.00	7.14	7.14	53,571	53.57	0.54	5.71
Project management	1500	60.00	2.13	0.67	16.67	25.00	125,000	125.00	1.25	13.33
Net result	199	8.00	17.93	5.02	125.05	24.93	$937,876	$937.88	$9.38	100.00

tions average about 107 statements per function point. This approach serves to make the "Cost per FP" and "Cost per LOC" columns more comprehensible by having the two values differ by 100 to 1.

The main point to be gained from examining the table is that for typical software projects coding may be the largest single activity, but it constitutes only a relatively small percentage of total effort and expense. This means that the productivity improvement or degradation can affect some activities more than others, or may affect only one activity.

A strong lesson from the table is that productivity estimates or measurements which center on coding and do not include paper-based software work, such as specifications and user documents, are not complete enough for serious business purposes, such as contracts and budgets.

Factors That Influence Software Development Productivity

We turn now to the factors that can exert either a positive or negative influence on software development projects.

Table 16.2 shows a number of factors that can exert a positive impact on software productivity and raise results higher than average values.

The three most influential factors for elevating software productivity are the use of *high-quality reusable materials* and the *experience levels of both the managers and the technical staff,* respectively, in building similar kinds of applications.

Let us now consider some of the factors that can reduce or degrade software productivity and cause it to lag average values (see Table 16.3).

What is most interesting about Table 16.3 is that the same factor, *software reuse,* that can exert the largest positive impact on improving software productivity can also exert the largest negative impact on reducing productivity. How is it possible for software reuse to exert such a large influence in both directions?

The critical difference between the positive and negative influences of software reuse can be expressed in one word: *quality.* The positive value of software reuse occurs when the reusable artifacts approach or achieve zero-defect levels.

The negative value of software reuse, on the other hand, will occur if the reusable materials are filled with errors or bugs. Imagine the result of reusing a software module in 50 applications only to discover that it contains a number of high-severity errors which trigger massive recalls of every application!

Note that software reuse encompasses much more than just source code. An effective corporate reuse program will include at least the following five reusable artifacts:

TABLE 16.2   Impact of Key Adjustment Factors on Productivity
(Sorted in order of maximum positive impact)

New development factors	Plus range, %
Reuse of high-quality deliverables	350
High management experience	65
High staff experience	55
Effective methods or process	35
Effective management tools	30
Effective technical CASE tools	27
High-level programming languages	24
Quality estimating tools	19
Specialist occupations	18
Effective client participation	18
Formal cost and schedule estimates	17
Unpaid overtime	15
Use of formal inspections	15
Good office ergonomics	15
Quality measurement	14
Low project complexity	13
Quick response time	12
Moderate schedule pressure	11
Productivity measurements	10
Low requirements creep	9
Annual training of >10 days	8
No geographic separation	8
High team morale	7
Hierarchical organization	5
Total	800

1. Reusable requirements
2. Reusable designs
3. Reusable source code
4. Reusable test materials
5. Reusable user documentation

In order to gain the optimum positive value from software reuse, each major software deliverable should include at least 75 percent reused material, which is certified and approaches zero-defect levels.

TABLE 16.3   **Impact of Key Adjustment Factors on Productivity**
(Sorted in order of maximum negative impact)

New development factors	Minus range, %
Reuse of poor-quality deliverables	−300
Management inexperience	−90
Staff inexperience	−87
High requirements creep	−77
Inadequate technical CASE tools	−75
No use of inspections	−48
Inadequate management tools	−45
Ineffective methods or process	−41
No quality estimation	−40
High project complexity	−35
Excessive schedule pressure	−30
Slow response time	−30
Crowded office space	−27
Low-level programming languages	−25
Geographic separation	−24
Informal cost and schedule estimates	−22
Generalist occupations	−15
No client participation	−13
No annual training	−12
No quality measurements	−10
Matrix organization	−8
No productivity measurements	−7
Poor team morale	−6
No unpaid overtime	0
Total	−1067

Another interesting aspect of Table 16.3 is that the negative cumulative results are much larger than those of Table 16.2, which shows positive results. Essentially, this means that it is far easier to make mistakes and degrade productivity than it is to get things right and improve productivity.

In general, there is often a lack of symmetry between the positive influences and the negative influences. For example, a good development process will exert a moderate positive influence on software productivity, but a really bad development process can exert a very severe negative impact on productivity.

Consider a topic unrelated to software for a moment: the use of tobacco. Heavy use of tobacco products exerts a severe negative impact on human tissues and causes a number of medical problems. On the other hand, not using tobacco will not make a person healthy, but will simply minimize the risk of becoming unhealthy. Here, too, there is a lack of symmetry between positive and negative impact. Use of tobacco has a severe negative impact, but not using tobacco has no particular positive impact, as might regular exercise or a diet high in vegetables.

Factors That Influence Software Maintenance Productivity

The word *maintenance* is highly ambiguous in the software domain. The common meaning for the term *maintenance* includes both repair of defects and making enhancements in response to new requirements. Sometimes the term *maintenance* also includes customer support. A recent inclusion to the meaning of the term is the special effort required to repair instances of the year-2000 problem, or convert date formats from two-digit to four-digit formats. Although this general definition of maintenance is not perfect, it will serve to show the positive and negative factors that influence the modification of existing software applications.

Table 16.4 illustrates a number of factors which have been found to exert a beneficial positive impact on the work of updating aging applications.

Because software reuse is not a factor in either repairing defects or adding features to existing applications, the overall positive impacts in the maintenance domain are not as strong as those for new development projects.

The top three factors that exert a positive influence are those associated with the use of *full-time maintenance specialists,* with having extensive *experience in the application* being updated, and with the use of *tables for holding variables and constants* rather than embedding them in the source code itself.

Let us now consider some of the factors that exert a negative impact on the work of updating or modifying existing software applications (see Table 16.5). Note that the top-ranked factor which reduces maintenance productivity, the presence of *error-prone modules,* is very asymmetrical.

The top-ranked factor that degrades maintenance productivity is the presence of *error-prone modules* in the applications being updated. Indeed, as a class, error-prone modules are the most expensive artifacts in the software world and can cost as much as five times more than high-quality modules.

TABLE 16.4 Impact of Key Adjusment Factors on Productivity
(Sorted in order of maximum positive impact)

Maintenance factors	Plus range, %
Maintenance specialists	35
High staff experience	34
Table-driven variables and data	33
Low complexity of base code	32
Year-2000 search engines	30
Code restructuring tools	29
Reengineering tools	27
High-level programming languages	25
Reverse-engineering tools	23
Complexity-analysis tools	20
Defect-tracking tools	20
Year-2000 specialists	20
Automated change-control tools	18
Unpaid overtime	18
Quality measurements	16
Formal base code inspections	15
Regression-test libraries	15
Excellent response time	12
Annual training of >10 days	12
High management experience	12
HELP desk automation	12
No error-prone modules	10
Online defect reporting	10
Productivity measurements	8
Excellent ease of use	7
User satisfaction measurements	5
High team morale	5
Total	503

Error-prone modules were discovered in the 1960s when IBM began a methodical study of the factors that influence software maintenance. It was discovered that errors or bugs in IBM software products, such as the Information Management System (IMS) database and the Multiple Virtual Storage (MVS) operating system tended to clump in a very small number of modules which were extremely buggy indeed.

TABLE 16.5   Impact of Key Adjustment Factors on Productivity
(Sorted in order of maximum negative impact)

Maintenance factors	Minus range, %
Error-prone modules	−50
Embedded variables and data	−45
Staff inexperience	−40
High complexity of base code	−30
No year-2000 search engines	−28
Manual change-control methods	−27
Low-level programming languages	−25
No defect-tracking tools	−24
No year-2000 specialists	−22
Poor ease of use	−18
No quality measurements	−18
No maintenance specialists	−18
Poor response time	−16
Management inexperience	−15
No base code inspections	−15
No regression-test libraries	−15
No HELP desk automation	−15
No online defect reporting	−12
No annual training	−10
No code restructuring tools	−10
No reengineering tools	−10
No reverse-engineering tools	−10
No complexity-analysis tools	−10
No productivity measurements	−7
Poor team morale	−6
No user satisfaction measurements	−4
No unpaid overtime	0
Total	−500

In the case of MVS, about 38 percent of customer-reported errors were found in only 4 percent of the modules. In the case of IMS, an even more extreme skew was noted. There were 300 zero-defect modules out of a total of 425, and 57 percent of all customer-reported errors were found in only 31 modules, which coincidentally were in 1 department under 1 manager.

Although IBM first discovered the existence of error-prone modules, they are remarkably common and have been found by dozens of companies and government agencies, too. Wherever they are found, they are expensive and troublesome.

Fortunately, error-prone modules are a completely curable problem, and the usage of formal design and code inspections has the effect of completely immunizing software projects against these troublesome entities.

Patterns of Positive and Negative Factors

The author's company, Software Productivity Research (SPR) collects quantitative and qualitative data on about 50 to 70 software projects every month, and has been doing so for about 12 years. Software projects and software organizations tend to follow relatively normal bell-shaped curves. There are comparatively few projects and companies that are good in almost every aspect of software, and also few that are really bad in almost every aspect of software.

The most common pattern that SPR encounters is that of projects and companies where the technical work of building software in terms of design and coding are reasonably good, but project management factors and quality control factors are fairly weak. This combination of factors is a reasonable characterization of the information systems domain, which numerically is the most common form of software development.

A variant of information systems projects, those produced by outsource contractors, have a somewhat better chance of having good project management methods than do the other forms of information systems development. However, not all outsource projects use good project management tools and methods, either.

For a variety of reasons, the systems software domain has a greater likelihood of having fairly good quality control as well as fairly good development skills. Here, too, project management is often the weak link. Quality control is better in the systems software domain because the hardware devices that the software controls (switching systems, computers, aircraft, etc.) need stringent quality control in order to operate.

The military software domain, like the systems software domain, is often characterized by rather good development methods and fairly good quality control methods, but marginal or deficient project management methods.

The large commercial software vendors tend to have better than average software development methods and much better than average maintenance methods. Here, too, quality control and project management are the weaknesses noted most often in assessment and benchmarking studies.

Among the organizations whose productivity rates are in the top 10 percent of SPR's client's results, there is a very strong tendency for most of the following factors to be better than average:

- Project management tools and methods are excellent
- Quality control tools and methods are excellent
- Maintenance tools and methods are excellent
- Development tools and methods are excellent

Conversely, among the clients who bring up the rear in terms of productivity, there is a strong tendency for this pattern to be noted:

- Poor project management tools and methods
- Poor quality control tools and methods
- Poor maintenance tools and methods
- Adequate development tools and methods

On the whole, those in the software technical community of analysts and programmers seem to be better trained and equipped for their jobs than do those in the software project management community.

Most of the adjustment factors are treated as independent variables, and their impact is then calculated and used to adjust the overall productivity multiplier. Essentially, the macroestimating tools start with a null productivity multiplier of 1.00 and then apply the results of various plus or minus adjustment factors to reach a final productivity multiplier, which can range from a low or minimum value of about 0.1 to a high or maximum value of perhaps 10.

However, since any real-life set of adjustments will include both positive and negative changes, the most common range of adjustments is much narrower and usually runs from about 0.75 to 1.25 for most projects.

For example, using the familiar five stages of the SEI capability maturity model, a macroestimating tool might yield overall productivity adjustments for each level that resemble the following.

Macroestimating Productivity Adjustments for the Five Levels of the SEI CMM

SEI CMM level	Multiplier	Nominal rate, FP per month
SEI CMM level 1	1.00	5.00
SEI CMM level 2	1.10	5.50
SEI CMM level 3	1.25	6.25
SEI CMM level 4	1.50	7.50
SEI CMM level 5	2.00	10.00

It is interesting to compare SEI CMM assumptions against the five-point software excellence scale that SPR uses. With the SEI CMM, about 75 percent of all organizations assessed are at level 1, which actually has a very broad range of accomplishment.

With the SPR assessment scale, the results move in the opposite direction from the SEI CMM scale; in addition, the SPR scale includes an average midpoint, with deviations in both positive and negative directions.

The SEI and SPR results are similar at the high, or good, end of the scales, but not at the low, or bad, end of the scales. This is because the SEI level 1 category covers such a very broad range of accomplishment that it is difficult to use that level for any kind of economic, productivity, or quality analysis.

Macroestimating Productivity Adjustments for the Five Levels of the SPR Software Excellence Scale (SES)

SPR SES level	Multiplier	Nominal rate, FP per month
SPR level 1 (excellent)	2.00	10.00
SPR level 2 (above average)	1.50	7.50
SPR level 3 (average)	1.00	5.00
SPR level 4 (marginal)	0.75	3.75
SPR level 5 (poor)	0.50	2.50

The SPR software excellence scale is not really used for estimating, since the company builds and uses microestimating tools. However, the SPR scale and associated values are sometimes used for quick estimates with a pocket calculator or to illustrate the range of performance differences at various levels of software excellence.

Incidentally, the results shown here are really only applicable to fairly large applications in excess of 1000 function points in size. This is true of both the SPR and the SEI illustrative data.

Although the overall adjustments with macroestimating tools are reasonable and easy to understand, they tend to make some simplifying assumptions, such as a more or less equal rate of improvement across every activity.

In real life, some activities can improve much further than others. Indeed, some activities can even regress or get worse while others improve significantly. To deal with this phenomenon, it is necessary to move to the way adjustment factors are handled by the microestimating tools.

Adjustment Factors and Microestimating Tools

The activity-based microestimating tools deal with adjustments at a more granular level than do the macroestimating tools. For the microestimating tools, each activity is adjusted separately, although there are some factors that tend to affect every activity, such as *team experience.*

The microestimating adjustment factors can have an impact on any combination of these four dimensions of a software project:

1. The *assignment scope,* or the amount of work that is normally assigned to one person

2. The *production rate,* or amount of work that one person can perform in a standard time period such as an hour, a day, a week, a month, or a year

3. The *defect potential,* or probable number of errors or bugs that might be created

4. The *defect-removal efficiency,* or probable number of errors or bugs that will be detected and removed prior to external deployment of the software package

The microestimating tools usually have many more adjustment factors than the macroestimating tools. Sometimes more than 100 factors can be adjusted.

It would obviously be inconvenient to adjust 100 factors every time an estimate is made, so the normal mode of operation for microestimating tools is to provide a nominal or default value for every factor. That way, only factors that are significantly better or worse than average need to be entered: Sometimes, fewer than 10 out of 100 may require adjustment above or below nominal values.

It is also possible for users to establish custom templates with adjustments preset to match local conditions. For example, a telecommunications company with a stable personnel group which has been building switching software for a number of years might preset the factor for *application experience* to *all experts.* This way the number of adjustments that have to be made to estimate a specific project is reduced. Sometimes 50 percent or more of the variable adjustments might be preset to match local conditions, which greatly speeds up the amount of setup work needed to complete an estimate.

The estimating tools designed by the author use a five-point scale for adjustment factors, with the following meaning for each point of the five-point scale:

1 = Much better than average   (Excellent)

2 = Better than average   (Very good)

3 = Average or nominal value   (Average)

4 = Worse than average   (Marginal)

5 = Much worse than average   (Poor)

(The five-point scale is not the only kind used for adjustments. Some estimating tools use binary adjustment factors, such as yes or no answers to adjustment questions; some estimating tools use a three-point scale; and a very few use a seven-point scale.)

However, the five-point adjustment scale on the author's estimating tools do allow two-decimal-place precision to fine-tune the responses. Thus responses of 3.25 or 3.75 are perfectly acceptable inputs, and allow fine adjustments between integer scores. To illustrate how the author's estimating tools capture adjustment data, following are sample adjustment factors that deal with various aspects of management, staff, and client experience levels.

Examples of the Software Productivity Research Method for Capturing Adjustment Data

PROJECT MANAGEMENT EXPERIENCE   _____

    1 Experts (implemented many priority projects).

    2 Extensive experience (implemented some projects).

    3 Average experience (implemented some priority projects).

    4 Limited experience (previous project management experience).

    5 Novice experience (has never managed a project).

DEVELOPMENT PERSONNEL APPLICATION EXPERIENCE

    _____

    1 All are experts in the type of program being developed.

    2 Majority are experts, but some are new hires or novices.

    3 Even mixture of experts, new hires, and novices.

    4 Majority are new hires or novices, with few experts.

    5 All personnel are new to this kind of program.

DEVELOPMENT PERSONNEL TOOL AND METHOD EXPERIENCE   _____

    1 All are experts in the tools and methods for the project.

    2 Majority are experts in the tools and methods.

    3 Even mixture of experts, new hires, and novices.

    4 Majority are new hires or novices in tools and methods.

5 All personnel are new to the tools and methods.

DEVELOPMENT PERSONNEL ANALYSIS AND DESIGN EXPERIENCE _____

1 All are experts in analysis and design methods.
2 Majority are experts in analysis and design methods.
3 Even mixture of experts, new hires, and novices.
4 Majority are new hires or novices in analysis and design.
5 All personnel are inexperienced in analysis and design.

DEVELOPMENT PERSONNEL PROGRAMMING LANGUAGE EXPERIENCE _____

1 All are experts in the languages used for the project.
2 Majority are experts in the hardware used for the project.
3 Even mixture of experts, new hires, and novices.
4 Majority are new hires or novices in the languages.
5 All personnel are new to the languages used.

DEVELOPMENT PERSONNEL HARDWARE EXPERIENCE

_____

1 All are experts in the hardware used for the project.
2 Majority are experts in the hardware used for the project.
3 Even mixture of experts, new hires, and novices.
4 Majority are new hires or novices in the hardware.
5 All personnel are new to the hardware for the project.

PRETEST DEFECT-REMOVAL EXPERIENCE _____

1 All personnel are experienced in reviews/inspections.
2 Most personnel are experienced in reviews/inspections.
3 Even mixture of experienced and inexperienced personnel.
4 Most personnel are inexperienced in reviews/inspections.
5 All personnel are inexperienced in reviews/inspections.

TESTING DEFECT-REMOVAL EXPERIENCE _____

1 All personnel are experienced in software test methods.
2 Most personnel are experienced in software test methods.
3 Even mixture of experienced and inexperienced personnel.
4 Most personnel are inexperienced in test methods.
5 All personnel are inexperienced in software test methods.

USER PERSONNEL EXPERIENCE WITH SOFTWARE PROJECTS

_____

1 User experience with software is not a key factor.
2 All or a majority of users have software experience.
3 Even mixture of experts and inexperienced users.
4 Majority of users have no prior software experience.
5 All personnel have no prior software experience.

USER PERSONNEL EXPERIENCE WITH APPLICATION TYPE

_____

1 User expertise is not a major factor for the project.
2 All or a strong majority of users are experts.
3 Even mixture of experts, new hires, and novices.
4 Majority are new hires and novices, with few experts.
5 All personnel are new to this kind of program.

MAINTENANCE PERSONNEL STAFFING   _____
1 All are full-time professional maintenance personnel.
2 Majority are full-time professional maintenance personnel.
3 Some are full-time professional maintenance personnel.
4 Most maintenance is done by development personnel.
5 All maintenance is done by development personnel.

MAINTENANCE PERSONNEL EXPERIENCE   _____
1 All are experts in system being maintained.
2 Majority are experts, but some are new hires or novices.
3 Even mixture of experts, new hires, and novices.
4 Majority are new hires, with few experts.
5 All maintenance personnel are new to the system.

MAINTENANCE PERSONNEL EDUCATION   _____
1 Maintenance training is not required for the project.
2 Adequate training in projects and tools is available.
3 Some training is available in projects and tools.
4 Some training in projects to be maintained is available.
5 Little or no training in projects or tools is available.

As can be seen, these questions use a scoring pattern resembling the Richter scale for earthquakes. Low numbers are the safe direction, while larger numbers represent the dangerous or hazardous direction. In all of these questions, the approximate average value is set at 3.00. Lower scores of 1.00 through 2.50 indicate better than average performance, while scores of 3.50 through 5.00 represent worse than average performance.

However, if the project hovers around average or 3.00 for most responses, the user of an estimating tool does not have to take any overt action because average values are the default, or nominal, assumption.

As with the macroestimating adjustments, the direction of the adjustment can be either positive or negative. However, the microestimating adjustment factors do not provide universal adjustments but are used to adjust specific activities, such as requirements, specifications, coding, unit testing, or user documentation.

The range of impact of each adjustment factor varies, and indeed the impacts are often regarded as proprietary trade secrets. However, most factors will have a small adjustment of about 5 percent, while only a few factors can exert a really major impact and can top a range of plus or minus 10 to 15 percent from the midpoint or nominal default value.

A typical pattern of adjustments might span a range of plus or minus 10 percent, as shown in Table 16.6. Assume that the range in the table is associated with the following question about software development process rigor:

SYSTEM DEVELOPMENT PROCESS _____
    1 Automated and effective system development process
    2 Automated but cumbersome system development process
    3 Manual and effective system development process
    4 Manual and cumbersome system development process
    5 Informal development: no formal system development process

Assuming that these five questions reflect the topic, then the range of impact of how the questions are answered might exert the range of productivity adjustments shown in Table 16.6.

Obviously, there will be interpolation for scores with decimal values, such as 2.35 or 4.50, but these are exactly the kinds of calculations at which automated estimating tools excel.

Incidentally, the microestimating adjustment factors are applied independently and, hence, have a cumulative impact. For example, if every one of the experience adjustment factors is in the good to excellent range, then the cumulative impact of all of these factors can generate results that are more than 60 percent better than average values, and more than 120 percent better than marginal to poor adjustment values.

Of course, a random combination of good and bad factors can achieve an effective adjustment that is close to zero in its impact. However, random factors seldom occur in real-life software projects.

Software projects usually follow typical patterns where many adjustments are either average, better than average, or worse than

TABLE 16.6 Typical Ranges of Software Adjustment Factors

Score	Definition	Productivity impact, %
1	Excellent	+10
2	Good	+5
3	Average	0
4	Below average	−5
5	Poor	−10

average depending upon the company, its culture, and the importance of software to corporate operations.

Let us examine some typical microestimating adjustments and also nominal or default values for a sample of 10 common software development activities that occur on many different classes, types, and sizes of software applications.

1. Requirements

2. Prototyping

3. Specifications and design

4. Design inspections

5. Coding

6. Code inspections

7. Change management

8. Testing

9. User documentation

10. Project management

These 10 activities occur with high enough frequency that almost every commercial estimating tool can deal with them. Certainly, all of the microestimating tools can deal with them.

It should be noted that there are no constant or fixed ratios for the expense patterns of these 10 activities. Indeed, if there were constant ratios, then there would be no need for software cost estimating tools, and there would be no software cost estimating industry. Each of these 10 can range from less than 10 percent of development expenses to more than 50 percent, depending upon the nature, scope, class, and type of the software application in question.

For example, the generic topic of *testing* actually encompasses no less than 18 discrete kinds of software testing. The observed range of costs for the testing of software applications runs from a low of about 5 percent for small personal applications to more than 70 percent for large and complex systems with stringent safety or reliability requirements.

It is obvious that there are huge ranges for every activity, and this is why adjustments are necessary. However, these 10 are also major components of software development schedules and expenses, although there are certainly other important activities besides these 10, such as quality assurance, integration, independent verification and validation, and many others.

Before considering the details of how each of these activities might be estimated, let us consider what a complete estimate might look

TABLE 16.7 Examples of Estimating Values for 10 Software Activities

Assumptions

Application class	Systems software
Programming language(s)	C
Size in function points	1,500
Source lines per function point	125
Size in source code statements	187,500
Average monthly salary	$5,000
Burden rate percent	100%
Fully burdened compensation	$10,000
Work hours per month	160
Effective work hours per month	128

Activity	Assignment scope	Production rate	Hours per FP	Staff	Effort months	Schedule months	Burdened cost	Cost per FP	Cost per LOC	Percent of total
Requirements	500	75.00	1.71	3.00	20.00	6.67	$200,000	$133.33	$1.07	9.16
Prototyping	750	50.00	2.56	2.00	3.00	1.50	30,000	20.00	0.16	1.37
Design	300	60.00	2.13	5.00	25.00	5.00	250,000	166.67	1.33	11.45
Design inspections	250	150.00	0.85	6.00	10.00	1.67	100,000	66.67	0.53	4.58
Coding	250	25.00	5.12	6.00	60.00	10.00	600,000	400.00	3.20	27.48
Code inspections	200	100.00	1.28	7.50	15.00	2.00	150,000	100.00	0.80	6.87
Change control	1500	150.00	0.85	1.00	10.00	10.00	100,000	66.67	0.53	4.58
Testing	200	50.00	2.56	7.50	30.00	4.00	300,000	200.00	1.60	13.74
User documents	750	125.00	1.02	2.00	12.00	6.00	120,000	80.00	0.64	5.50
Project management	1500	45.00	2.84	1.00	33.33	33.33	333,333	222.22	1.78	15.27
Net result	245	6.87	20.94	6.13	218.33	35.65	2,183,333	1,455.56	11.64	100.00

like with all 10 activities displayed simultaneously. Table 16.7 illustrates a systems software project of 1500 function points constructed in the C programming language.

Table 16.7 differs from Table 16.1, which uses the same format. Table 16.7 assumes a systems software project in C rather than an MIS project in COBOL, and the size is 1500 function points rather than 1000 function points. More significant, Table 16.7 assumes a different company and, hence, uses a burden rate of 100 percent rather than 50 percent.

The columns in Table 16.7 reflect a number of basic kinds of information which the family of automated cost-estimating tools can usually provide.

Column 1, "Activity," is self-explanatory and simply lists the activities included in the software estimate.

Column 2, "Assignment scope," is the amount of work normally assigned to one technical staff member. Although the table expresses the assignment scope in terms of function point metrics, assignments in real life are often given in terms of natural metrics, such as pages of specifications, screens, volumes of source code, number of customers supported, and a host of other possibilities.

Column 3, "Production rate," is the amount of work that a staff member can be expected to complete in a standard time period. In this table the standard time period is the *month,* which the table itself defines as consisting of 128 hours of effective work time, once coffee breaks, meetings, and other nonwork tasks have been backed out. Here, too, it is possible to substitute natural metrics for function points, such as pages of specifications, screens, source code, and the like.

Column 4, "Hours per FP," provides the same information as column 3, but expresses the results in a different mathematical form. Rather than expressing the results in terms of *function points per staff month,* column 4 uses the reciprocal value of *work hours per function point* derived by dividing the number of effective work hours per month by the nominal rate. That is, a productivity rate of 100 function points and a rate of 128 work hours per month yields the result of 1.28 work hours per function point.

Column 5, "Staff," is a predicted value of the number of full-time personnel required for the project. Since some staff members will work only part-time, this information is normally expressed using decimal values. For example, 1 person working half-time would be expressed as a staffing level of 0.5.

Column 6, "Effort months," is also a predicted value, and shows the amount of effort for each activity. Although effort in the table is expressed in months, it could also have been expressed in terms of any other work period: hours, days, weeks, months, or years.

Column 7, "Schedule months," is also a predicted value, and shows the schedule in terms of calendar months. Since activities overlap and never really follow a "waterfall" model, the actual schedule for software projects is always shorter than the sum of the activity schedules. For example, if requirements takes 2 months and design takes 4 months, the arithmetic sum of these two activities would be 6 months. However, design usually starts when requirements are about 50 percent complete, so the effective schedule would be 5 months rather than 6, because design overlaps requirements by 50 percent, meaning that half of the requirements are still unfinished at the time design commences.

Column 8, "Burdened cost," shows the cost for the activity, which is calculated by multiplying the "Effort" column by the burdened compensation rate. If there were more space on the page, it might also be possible to show the costs without burden rates.

Column 9, "Cost per FP," shows the normalized data of cost per function point. Since this is a 1500–function point example, the costs of each activity are simply divided by 1500.

Column 10, "Cost per LOC," shows the normalized data of cost per line of code. Since this project is written in the C programming language and requires 187,500 source code statements, each data item in column 7 is divided by 187,500. This column will obviously vary widely from language to language. If the application had been written in Smalltalk rather than in C, then the amount of source code might have only been around 30,000 source code statements. If it had been written in assembly language, the volume of source code might have been 320,000 source code statements. This is one of the reasons why function points are preferred for normalizing data across different languages.

Column 11, "Percent of total," shows the percentage of the total effort devoted to each activity. Readers should be cautioned that percentages are not a safe method for estimating software effort or costs. Because of wide ranges and fluctuations in many factors, percentages vary far too widely to be used for software cost estimating. For example, the percentage of testing for this project is only 13.74 percent of the total effort. This is due to the use of formal design and code inspections. If inspections were absent, then testing could easily absorb 35 percent to more than 50 percent of the total effort.

Table 16.7 reveals quite a few interesting facts at the same time, and is a useful example of the kinds of outputs available from commercial software cost estimating tools. One of the advantages of using estimating tools is that they can produce all kinds of useful information very easily. For example, commercial software-estimating tools can easily show cost per function point, cost per line of code, and percentage of costs simultaneously.

Because Table 16.7 illustrates microestimation where each activity is subject to multiple adjustment factors, it is interesting to consider some of the factors that affect each row of the estimate, as follows:

Requirements adjustment factors

1. Overall size of the project
2. Experience of the clients in working with software teams
3. Experience of the clients in the knowledge that is to be automated
4. Experience of the development team with similar applications
5. Availability of commercial software that satisfies some requirements
6. Rate of creeping requirements after requirements phase
7. Use of prototyping
8. Use of joint application design (JAD)
9. Use of quality function deployment (QFD)

Prototyping adjustment factors

1. Experience of the prototype developers
2. Experience of the clients
3. Percentage of total features included in prototype
4. Programming languages utilized for the prototype
5. Reusable materials utilized within the prototype
6. Time allowed to construct the prototype

Design adjustment factors

1. Experience of the development team
2. Geographic separation of the team
3. Reusable materials utilized for the design
4. Use of formal or informal design methodologies
5. Use or failure to use design-automation tools
6. Use or failure to use design inspections

Design inspections

1. Size of specifications
2. Schedule pressure applied by management or clients
3. Geographic dispersal of the design team
4. Percentage of specifications to be inspected, up to 100 percent
5. Experience of the development team in inspections
6. Design representation methods utilized
7. Use or failure to use automated inspection tools

Coding

1. Experience of the development team with similar applications
2. Schedule pressure applied to developers by management or clients
3. Programming languages utilized
4. Experience of the team with the programming languages
5. Use or failure to use program structuring techniques
6. Programming environment and automated tools available
7. Volume of reusable source code utilized
8. Programming office space and ergonomics

Code inspections

1. Experience of the development team
2. Schedule pressure applied to developers by management or client
3. Programming languages utilized
4. Percentage of code inspected, up to 100 percent
5. Structure and complexity of the code being inspected
6. Use or failure to use code inspection automation

Change control

1. Presence or absence of a change-control board
2. Rate of requirements creep during development
3. Rate of design changes during development
4. Rate of coding development
5. Use or failure to use change-control automation
6. Continuous or discrete build strategy
7. Geographic dispersal of the development groups

Testing

1. Experience of the test personnel
2. Number and kind of test stages utilized
3. Number and severity levels of defects found during testing
4. Rate at which discovered defects are repaired
5. Schedule pressure applied by managers or clients
6. Number of existing regression tests
7. Structure and complexity of the code being tested
8. Use or failure to use test-automation tools
9. Use or failure to use test-coverage analysis
10. Use of failure to use defect tracking

User documentation

1. Experience of the technical writers
2. Communication between technical writers and developers
3. Schedule pressure applied by managers or clients
4. Nature of documentation to be produced (tutorial, reference, etc.)
5. Mixture of text and graphics utilized
6. Use or failure to use document-automation tools
7. Volume of reusable document items available

Project management

1. Experience of the project managers
2. Presence or absence of historical data from similar projects
3. Schedule and other pressures applied by higher management or clients
4. Use or failure to use software cost estimating tools
5. Use of failure to use software project planning tools

As can easily be seen, each software development activity is sensitive to a large number of adjustment factors. Further, there are complex interactions among the activities themselves. For example, source code that is well structured and has few defects is easier and quicker to inspect and to test than source code that is poorly structured and buggy.

Table 16.8 shows a general ranking of eight key adjustment factors in terms of their overall impacts. As might be expected using just common sense, small projects with capable teams and excellent tools will be much more productive than large systems with marginal teams and questionable tools.

Because activity-based costing is the heart of modern software cost estimation, let us now explore a selection of key activities in depth to

TABLE 16.8   General Ranking of Key Adjustment Factors

1. Size of project
2. Team experience
3. Reusable material
4. Schedule pressure
5. Creeping changes
6. Methodologies
7. Tools
8. Ergonomics

discover the nature of the problems which cost-estimation tool vendors are attempting to solve.

The most effective mode of software cost estimation is to estimate each activity individually, and then consolidate the overall estimate from the partial estimates of discrete activities.

This method ensures that no important activities will be accidentally omitted. Further, estimating each activity individually minimizes the chances that estimating errors will flow from activity to activity. In other words, estimating errors may occur, but they will tend to be localized to specific activities.

The literature on software technology adjustment factors is voluminous, but not scientifically rigorous. Mixed in with reports based on actual empirical data can be found pseudoreports by tool or methodology vendors that tend to make exaggerated claims with little or no evidence behind them. Any article or advertisement that features such phrases as "achieve 10 to 1 improvements in productivity" or "achieve 100 to 1 improvements in productivity" is probably spurious and nothing more than hype.

Among the works where the technology adjustment discussions are based on multiple regression analysis rather than wishful thinking can be found the very solid analysis of Dr. Barry Boehm (Boehm 1981), who is one of the pioneers of technology adjustment research in an estimating context.

Several other estimating-tool authors also discuss technology adjustments using empirical data and solid research, such as Larry Putnam (Putnam 1992), Dr. Howard Rubin (Rubin 1997), William Roetzheim (Roetzheim and Beasley 1998), and Charles Symons (Symons 1991).

Because the capabilities of the software personnel are key issues, the work of the cognitive psychologist Dr. Bill Curtis (Curtis et al. 1995) and his colleagues are recommended. Dr. Curtis was formerly at SEI and was one of the primary authors of the new people capability model, although he has been doing research on software skill issues for more than 20 years.

Since development processes and methodologies are also key technology adjustment factors, the solid work of some of the SEI research team members should be reviewed, such as the work of Watts Humphrey (Humphrey 1992) and Mark Paulk (Paulk et al. 1995). In this same vein, the work of Dr. Norm Brown of the Navy on best practices is also interesting in terms of the impact of technology on software (Brown 1995).

Tom DeMarco and his colleague Tim Lister have done extensive research into the factors that influence software projects, and their work is particularly strong in some of the sociological issues (DeMarco 1982, 1995; DeMarco and Lister 1987).

Many of the author's books discuss technology adjustment factors, since SPR's main business includes baseline and benchmarking studies for thousands of projects (Jones 1993, 1994, 1995, 1996, 1997). Jessica Keys has produced an interesting discussion of technology factors (Keys 1993) and Dr. Tom Love is one of the few authors in the object-oriented (OO) domain to actually quantify the impact of the OO paradigm (Love 1993).

The well-known author and consultant John Marciniak edited a very useful two-volume encyclopedia of software engineering which includes many useful sources of information about software technology adjustments (Marciniak 1994).

The work of Ed Yourdon is always interesting, and in his new book *Deathmarch* (Yourdon 1997) he discusses the impact of irrational schedule pressure on software projects.

References

Boehm, Barry: *Software Engineering Economics,* Prentice Hall, Englewood Cliffs, N.J., 1981.

Brown, Norm (ed.): *The Program Manager's Guide to Software Acquisition Best Practices,* Version 1.0, U.S. Department of Defense, Washington, D.C., July 1995.

Curtis, Bill, William E. Hefley, and Sally Miller: *People Capability Maturity Model,* Software Engineering Institute, Carnegie Mellon University, Pittsburgh, Pa., 1995.

DeMarco, Tom: *Controlling Software Projects,* Yourdon Press, New York, ISBN 0-917072-32-4, 1982.

————: *Why Does Software Cost So Much?,* Dorset House, New York, ISBN 0-932633-34-X, 1995.

————, and Tim Lister: *Peopleware,* Dorset House Press, New York, ISBN 0-932633-05-6, 1987.

Humphrey, Watts S.: *Managing the Software Process,* Addison-Wesley/Longman, Reading, Mass., 1989.

Jones, Capers: *SPQR/20 Users Guide,* Software Productivity Research, Cambridge, Mass., 1986.

————: *Critical Problems in Software Measurement,* Information Systems Management Group, ISBN 1-56909-000-9, 1993a.

————: *New Directions in Software Management,* Information Systems Management Group, ISBN 1-56909-009-2, 1993b.

————: *Assessment and Control of Software Risks,* Prentice Hall, Englewood Cliffs, N.J., ISBN 0-13-741406-4, 1994.

————: *Patterns of Software System Failure and Success,* International Thomson Computer Press, Boston, ISBN 1-850-32804-8, 1995.

————: *Applied Software Measurement,* 2d ed., McGraw-Hill, New York, ISBN 0-07-032826-9, 1996a.

————: *Table of Programming Languages and Levels* (8 Versions from 1985 through July 1996), Software Productivity Research, Burlington, Mass., 1996b.

————: *The Economics of Object-Oriented Software,* Software Productivity Research, Burlington, Mass., April 1997a.

————: *Software Quality—Analysis and Guidelines for Success,* International Thomson Computer Press, Boston, ISBN 1-85032-876-6, 1997b.

————: *The Year 2000 Software Problem—Quantifying the Costs and Assessing the Consequences,* Addison-Wesley, Reading, Mass., ISBN 0-201-30964-5, 1998.

Keys, Jessica: *Software Engineering Productivity Handbook,* McGraw-Hill, New York, ISBN 0-07-911366-4, 1993.

Love, Tom: *Object Lessons,* SIGS Books, New York, ISBN 0-9627477 3-4, 1993.

Marciniak, John J. (ed.): *Encyclopedia of Software Engineering,* vols. 1 and 2, John Wiley & Sons, New York, ISBN 0-471-54002, 1994.

Paulk Mark, et al.: *The Capability Maturity Model: Guidelines for Improving the Software Process,* Addison-Wesley, Reading, Mass., ISBN 0-201-54664-7, 1995.

Putnam, Lawrence H.: *Measures for Excellence—Reliable Software on Time, Within Budget,* Yourdon Press/Prentice Hall, Englewood Cliffs, N.J., ISBN 0-13-567694-0, 1992.

———, and Ware Myers: *Industrial Strength Software—Effective Management Using Measurement,* IEEE Press, Los Alamitos, Calif., ISBN 0-8186-7532-2, 1997.

Rethinking the Software Process, CD-ROM, Miller Freeman, Lawrence, Kans., 1996. (This CD-ROM is a book collection jointly produced by the book publisher, Prentice Hall, and the journal publisher, Miller Freeman. It contains the full text and illustrations of five Prentice Hall books: Capers Jones, *Assessment and Control of Software Risks*; Tom DeMarco, *Controlling Software Projects*; Brian Dreger, *Function Point Analysis*; Larry Putnam and Ware Myers, *Measures for Excellence*; and Mark Lorenz and Jeff Kidd, *Object-Oriented Software Metrics.)*

Roetzheim, William H., and Reyna A. Beasley: Best Practices in Software Cost and Schedule Estimation, Prentice Hall PTR, Upper Saddle River, N.J., 1998.

Rubin, Howard: *Software Benchmark Studies For 1997,* Howard Rubin Associates, Pound Ridge, N.Y., 1997.

Stukes, Sherry, Jason Deshoretz, Henry Apgar, and Ilona Macias: *Air Force Cost Analysis Agency Software Estimating Model Analysis—Final Report,* TR-9545/008-2, Contract F04701-95-D-0003, Task 008, Management Consulting & Research, Inc., Thousand Oaks, Calif., September 1996.

Symons, Charles R.: *Software Sizing and Estimating—Mk II FPA (Function Point Analysis),* John Wiley & Sons, Chichester, U.K., ISBN 0 471-92985-9, 1991.

Yourdon, Ed: *Death March—The Complete Software Developer's Guide to Surviving "Mission Impossible" Projects,* Prentice Hall PTR, Upper Saddle River, N.J., ISBN 0-13-748310-4, 1997.

5

Activity-Based Software Cost Estimating

Software cost estimating at the activity level, or microestimating, is far more accurate than macroestimating, but is also more difficult. The advantages of activity-based estimation are twofold: (1) key activities will not be accidentally left out, and (2) estimating errors, if they occur, tend to stay local within a specific activity rather than affecting the entire suite of activities.

This section explores the software cost estimating implications of 10 key software development activities:

1. Requirements

2. Prototyping

3. Design and specifications

4. Design inspections

5. Coding

6. Code inspections

7. Change management and configuration control

8. Testing

9. User documentation and project documentation

10. Project management

These 10 activities comprise a minimum set for activity-based software cost estimating, although not every one of these activities occurs on every project. Also, most of these 10 activities occur with very high frequency and, hence, can be encountered on many large software development projects.

However, the maximum set of activities for very large systems is more than 25 activities, which can be decomposed into many hundreds of subactivities and tasks. Discussing the implications of estimating 25 or more software activities would require a book more than twice as large as the current volume.

Estimating Software Requirements

Software requirements are the starting point for every new project, and are a key contributor to enhancement projects, as well. Software requirements are also very ambiguous, often filled with bad assumptions and severe errors, and are unusually difficult to pin down in a clear and comprehensive way.

From a software cost estimating standpoint, the most tricky part of estimating requirements is the fact that requirements are usually unstable and grow steadily during the software development cycle in the coding and even the testing phases.

The observed rate at which requirements change after their initial definition runs between 1 percent and more than 3 percent per month during the subsequent analysis, design, and coding phases. Equally as troublesome, software requirements are the source of about 20 percent of all software bugs or defects, and are the source of more than 30 percent of really severe and difficult defects. (For example, the year-2000 software problem was a standard requirement for military software projects, even though many programmers knew that two-digit date fields would eventually cause trouble.)

Because software projects depend heavily upon the accuracy and completeness of software requirements, it is urgent that requirements be done well. Both software sizing and software cost estimates are derived from the requirements themselves, so the precision with which requirements are defined affects the accuracy of the software size and cost estimates. Unfortunately, the available technologies for gathering and analyzing software requirements are troublesome and incomplete, although some progress is under way.

One of the more interesting early attempts to improve software requirements was described by Ken Orr in *Structured Requirements Definition* (Orr 1981). A more recent and very thoughtful analysis of software requirements fundamentals is the book by the well-known authors Don Gause and Gerry Weinberg, *Exploring Requirements—Quality Before Design* (Gause and Weinberg 1989).

A number of books on software requirements attempt to survey the entire literature on this topic. For example, Dr. Alan Davis and his colleagues at the University of Colorado have been doing substantial research into improving the state of the art of software requirements gathering and analysis. Dr. Davis's book *Software Requirements* (Davis 1993) fans out and covers almost 600 references and citations, including a very interesting annotated bibliography.

The IEEE Press often features books that consolidate state-of-the-art data from multiple sources. One of their books which consolidates a great deal of information on software requirements is Richard Thayer and Merlin Dorfman's *Software Requirements Engineering* (Thayer and Dorfman 1997).

Although many books on requirements contain thoughtful analyses of requirements methods and offer interesting suggestions for improving software requirements gathering and analysis, they tend to omit two key topics:

1. Quantification of requirements sizes, schedules, effort, and costs

2. Quantification of requirements errors and defect-removal efficiency

For books that contain quantitative data on requirements sizes, costs, and defects, some of the author's previous books might be cited, such as *Assessment and Control of Software Risks* (Jones 1994), *Patterns of Software Systems Failure and Success* (Jones 1996), and *Software Quality—Analysis and Guidelines for Success* (Jones 1997).

From a software cost estimating viewpoint, the nominal or default values for producing software requirements specifications are shown in Table 17.1.

If you were to utilize these nominal default values for a case study software project of 1500 function points, the results would approximate the following, assuming systems software as the class of the application.

For a 1500–function point systems software project, the nominal or average requirements would be about 375 pages in size and would be produced by a team of three technical personnel (working with about the same number of client personnel). The effort would amount to about 9 staff months. The schedule would be about 3 calendar months.

TABLE 17.1 Nominal Default Values for Requirements Estimates

Activity sequence	Initial activity of software projects
Performed by	Client representatives and development representatives
Predecessor activities	None
Overlap	None
Concurrent activities	Prototyping
Successor activities	Analysis, specification, and design
Initial requirements size	0.25 U.S. text pages per function point
Graphics volumes	0.01 illustrations per function point
Reuse	10% from prior or similar projects
Assignment scope	500 function points per technical staff member
Production rate	175 function points per staff month
Production rate	0.75 work hours per function point
Schedule months	Function points raised to the 0.15 power
Rate of creep or change	2.0% per month
Defect potential	1.0 requirements defects per function point
Defect removal	75% via requirements inspections
Delivered defects	0.25 requirements defects per function point
High-severity defects	30% of delivered requirements defects
Bad fix probability	10% of requirements fixes may yield new errors

More ominously, there would be about 1500 potential defects in the requirements themselves. About 30 percent of the requirements errors or bugs would be very serious, which would amount to about 450 high-severity requirements errors—more than any other source of serious error.

Since many companies are careless about attempting to remove errors or defects in software requirements, defect-removal efficiency levels against requirements are lower than for other sources of error and average only about 75 percent.

A nominal defect-removal efficiency of only 75 percent means that when the project is deployed there will still be about 375 requirements defects and about 112 high-severity defects still latent. Indeed, latent requirements defects comprise the most troublesome form of after-deployment defects in software systems, because they are highly resistant to defect-removal methods.

Among the more sophisticated software companies the significance of requirements and requirements errors is recognized. Several defect-prevention technologies that are deployed fairly widely are available:

- Joint application design (JAD) for gathering user requirements

- Quality function deployment (QFD) for focusing on quality issues
- Prototyping of key application features

Formal requirements inspections are useful and can top 75 percent defect-removal efficiency, but this powerful method is seldom deployed because too many companies have adopted the false concept that *quality* means *conformance to requirements*. The problem with this concept is that it ignores the volume and severity levels of errors in requirements themselves and, hence, leads to downstream problems with incorrect and ambiguous requirements.

The growth in unplanned creeping requirements would amount to about 20 percent during the analysis, design, and coding stages, which is equivalent to a monthly change rate of about 2 percent. The growth in unplanned new requirements affects the size of the requirements themselves, affects the size of the internal and external specifications, and also increases the source code size and ups the number of test cases that must be constructed. Also, the unplanned new requirements will have at least as many defects as the original requirements, and probably more.

Although the default or nominal values for requirements estimates provide a useful starting place, the range of variance around each of the default values can be more than 3 to 1. The adjustment factors account for much of the variance, but other factors, such as whether the requirements are being created for a military or a civilian project, also exert an impact.

Military software projects usually have much larger and more formal requirements than similar civilian projects of the same size, and also require much more extensive work in order to define the requirements than is normal for civilian projects.

In real-life situations, the effort for requirements definition fluctuates more than almost any other software activity, and can range from close to zero effort for small personal applications to more than 3.0 work hours per function point for large military software systems.

Table 17.2 illustrates some of the ranges in requirements productivity rates associated with various sizes and kinds of software projects.

In addition to the initial default assumptions, software requirements also have a number of attributes associated with them which should be recorded, including but not limited to the following.

Performed by. Clients, marketing staff, sales staff, engineering staff, systems analysts, programmers, quality-assurance staff, and software project managers are the normal participants in requirements, although not every category will be present on every project. It is useful to record who provided the basic set of application requirements.

TABLE 17.2   Ranges in Requirements Productivity Rates by
Class of Software

Software class	Requirements productivity, FP/staff month	Requirements productivity, hours/FP
End user	1000	0.128
Commercial	200	0.640
Small MIS	175	0.750
Large MIS	75	1.710
Outsource	90	1.422
Systems	75	1.710
Military	35	3.657

Formal methodologies. Numerous requirements methods exist, including those of information engineering (IE), rapid application development (RAD), object-oriented (OO) design, quality function deployment (QFD), joint application design (JAD), finite-state machines, and state transition diagrams. Since these methods affect both the error density and the productivity of requirements, it is useful to record which method is utilized, if any.

Requirements tools. Software requirements automation is only just becoming a major product arena, and a host of new tools, such as Rational's Requisite, are beginning to speed up the effort of requirements management. However, the next generation of requirements tools should include additional features, such as automatic derivation of function points and linkages to software sizing, cost estimating, and project management tools, which are often lacking. Indeed, some tools, such as the Bachman Analyst Workbench and the Texas Instruments Information Engineering Facility (IEF) do provide automatic derivation of function point metrics from requirements. The derivation of function point metrics from software requirements also facilitates software contracts, since function points are now the standard metric for measuring creeping requirements after the initial requirements-gathering phase.

Defect prevention. The most effective defect-prevention method for requirements defects is the construction of a working prototype. Disposable prototypes are much more effective than evolutionary prototypes. (Disposable prototypes typically contain about 10 percent of the functionality of the final product.) Time-box prototypes are also successful in preventing requirements defects. The methods of JAD and QFD are also effective in preventing requirements defects. If any of these are used, the fact should be recorded.

Defect removal. Requirements defects are highly resistant to removal (consider the year-2000 problem). However, formal requirements inspections have been successfully utilized and deserve more widespread usage. After requirements are complete, downstream activities, such as design inspections, code inspections, and testing, are not very effective in removing requirements defects. Indeed, once major defects (such as the year-2000 problem) are embedded in requirements, they tend be immune to most standard forms of defect removal and are especially resistant to being found via testing.

Requirements Defects   Software requirements errors comprise about 20 percent of the total errors found in software applications, but comprise more than 30 percent of the intractable, difficult errors.

The current U.S. averages for software defect origins, expressed in terms of defects per function point, are shown in Table 17.3.

Software requirements are the third highest source of all defects, but the second highest source of major defects that are likely to cause serious trouble after the application is deployed. It should not be forgotten that the year-2000 problem originated as a requirement rather than as a coding error, and it has become the most expensive software problem in human history.

Some examples of the kinds of errors that can be found in software requirements include but are not limited to the following:

Errors of omission.   The most common problem with requirements is that they are incomplete for any application larger than trivial. Given the number of permutations of features possible with large software projects, it is very likely that incompleteness will always occur, because a complete requirements specification might approach infinite size.

TABLE 17.3   Requirements Defects and Other Categories

Defect origins	Total Defects per FP	High-severity defects per FP
Requirements	1.00	0.30
Design	1.25	0.50
Code	1.75	0.25
Documentation	0.60	0.10
Bad fixes	0.40	0.15
Total	5.00	1.30

Errors of ambiguity.   Because requirements specifications are usually expressed using natural languages, such as English, Japanese, German, or Spanish, they are subject to all of the sources of ambiguity and misunderstanding of any other text document. For example, such phrases as "high-speed transaction processing" or "very high reliability" will be understood differently by almost everyone who reads them.

Errors of commission.   It is very common for software requirements to insist that the application do something that may be incorrect or hazardous. The famous year-2000 problem originated as a specific requirement to "economize storage by recording year dates using only the last two digits."

Conflicting requirements.   Some software requirements for applications where several or many users are contributing their specific needs may end up with conflicts. For example, the requirements for a state motor vehicle registration system contained conflicting requirements in two sections: (1) proof of insurance had to be input before a registration could be issued, and (2) a registration had to be input before a proof of insurance certificate could be granted. These two requirements were in direct conflict, and yet both were actually implemented!

The most important aspect of requirements errors is that if they escape detection, it is very difficult to find them downstream via testing. Usually, if an incorrect requirement eludes removal, subsequent testing will confirm the error rather than find it. For example, once the requirement to use two-digit date formats was accepted, then no test cases were ever created that could find this problem. Now that the century is ending, an entirely new suite of test cases is being built specifically in response to this classic requirements problem.

Creeping requirements.   The rate of *creeping requirements,* or changes after the initial set of requirements are defined, is a major software problem. The U.S. average is about 2 percent per month during the design and coding phases. The maximum amount of creep has sometimes topped 150 percent, so this is a major consideration. Prototyping plus such methods as JAD can reduce this rate down to a small fraction, such as 0.5 percent per month.

The fundamental root cause of changing requirements is that software applications are expanding the horizon of the ways companies operate. In a sense, the creation of software requirements is reminiscent of hiking in a fog that is gradually lifting. At first only the immediate surroundings within a few feet of the path are visible, but as the fog lifts more and more of the terrain can be seen.

Reuse of software requirements. In theory, software requirements should be one of the key artifacts of a formal software reuse program. Indeed, because so many software applications are so similar, the level of requirements reuse should top 75 percent for many software applications, although the actual volume of reuse hovers around only 10 percent or so.

Unfortunately, the technologies of requirements gathering, using primarily natural-language text and documents with random formats, makes effective reuse of software requirements rather difficult. As a result, the requirements for far too many applications are treated as being unique when in fact they may be only minor variations of existing software applications. One of the most important software technologies of the twenty-first century would be to improve the methodology of software requirements so that reusability becomes a standard attribute.

Function Points and Software Requirements

The function point metric has proven to be a useful tool for gathering requirements, and also for exploring the impact and costs of creeping requirements. Recall that the function point metric is a synthetic metric derived from the following five external attributes of software systems:

1. Inputs

2. Outputs

3. Inquiries

4. Logical files

5. Interfaces

The normal reason that requirements grow or creep is that one or more of the five attributes also associated with function points grows. The single most common growth factor is the need for additional outputs, but any of the five function point elements can and do expand as software projects proceed through development.

In the context of exploring creeping requirements, the initial use of function point metrics is simply to size the application at the point where the requirements are first considered to be firm. At the end of the development cycle, the final function point total for the application will also be counted.

For example, suppose the initial function point count is for a project of 100 function points, and at delivery the count has grown to 125. This provides a direct measurement of the volume of creep in the requirements.

TABLE 17.4   Monthly Growth Rate of Software Creeping Requirements

Software type	Monthly rate of requirements change, %
Contract or outsource software	1.0
Information systems software	1.5
Systems software	2.0
Military software	2.0
Commercial software	3.5

From analysis of the evolution of requirements during the development cycle of software applications, it is possible to show the approximate rates of monthly change. The changes in Table 17.4 are shown from the point at which the requirements are initially defined through the design and development phases of the software projects.

Table 17.4 is derived from the use of function point metrics, and the data is based on differences in function point totals between: (1) the initial estimated function point total at the completion of software requirements, and (2) the final measured function point total at the deployment of the software to customers.

If the first quantification of function points at requirements definition is 1000 function points and the final delivered number of function points is 1120, that represents a 12 percent net growth in creeping requirements. If the time span from completing the requirements through the design and code phases is a 12-month period, then it can be seen that the rate of growth in creeping requirements averages 1 percent per month.

In Table 17.4 the changes are expressed as a percentage change to the function point total of the original requirements specification. Note that there is a high margin of error, but even so it is useful to be able to measure the rate of change at all.

It is interesting that although the rate of change for contract software is actually less for many other kinds of applications, the changes are much more likely to lead to disputes or litigation. The data in these tables is taken from the author's book, *Patterns of Software Systems Failure and Success* (Jones 1996).

Since the requirements for more than 90 percent of all software projects change during development, creeping user requirements is numerically the most common problem of the software industry, which should not be a surprise to anyone.

A number of technologies have been developed that can either reduce the rate at which requirements change or, at least, make the changes less disruptive. Space does not permit a full discussion of each, but following are the technologies with positive value in terms of easing the stress of creeping user requirements.

Joint application design (JAD)

Joint application design (JAD) is a method for developing software requirements under which user representatives and development representatives work together with a facilitator to produce a joint requirements specification that both sides agree to.

The JAD approach originated in Canada in the 1970s and has now become very common for information systems development. Books, training, and consulting groups that offer JAD facilitation are also very common.

Compared to the older style of adversarial requirements development, JAD can reduce creeping requirements by almost half. The JAD approach is an excellent choice for large software contracts that are intended to automate information systems.

In order to work well, JAD sessions require active participation by client representatives, as well as by the development organization. This means that JAD technology may not be appropriate for some kinds of projects. For example, for projects such as Microsoft's Windows 95, where there are many millions of users, it is not possible to have a small subset of users act for the entire universe.

The JAD method works best for custom software, where there is a finite number of clients and the software is being built to satisfy their explicit requirements. It does not work well for software with hundreds or thousands of users, each of whom may have slightly different needs.

Prototypes

Since many changes don't start to occur until clients or users begin to see the screens and outputs of the application, it is obvious that building early prototypes can move some of these changes to the front of the development cycle instead of leaving them at the end.

Prototypes are often effective in reducing creeping requirements, and they can be combined with other approaches, such as JAD. Prototypes by themselves can reduce creeping requirements by somewhere between 10 and about 25 percent.

There are three common forms of software prototypes:

1. Disposable prototypes

2. Evolutionary prototypes

3. Time-box prototypes

Of these three, the disposable and time-box methods have the most favorable results. The problem with evolutionary prototypes that grow to become full projects is that during the prototyping stage, too many short cuts and too much carelessness is usually present. This means that evolutionary prototypes seldom grow to become stable, well-structured applications that are easy to maintain.

Use cases

The technique termed *use cases* originated as a method for dealing with the requirements of object-oriented applications, but has subsequently expanded and is moving toward becoming a formal approach for dealing with software requirements.

The use-case technique deals with the patterns of usage that typical clients are likely to have and, hence, concentrates on clusters of related requirements for specific usage sequences. The advantage of the use-case approach is that it keeps the requirements process at a practical level and minimizes the tendency to add "blue sky" features that are not likely to have many users.

Change-control boards

Change-control boards are not exactly a technology, but rather a group of managers, client representatives, and technical personnel who meet and decide which changes should be accepted or rejected.

Change-control boards are often encountered in the military software systems domain, although they are not common for information systems. Such boards are most often encountered for large systems in excess of 10,000 function points in size.

In general, change-control boards occur within large organizations and are utilized primarily for major systems. These boards are seldom encountered within small companies and are almost never utilized for small projects.

Change-control boards are at least twice as common among military software procedures as they are among civilian software producers. Within the civilian domain, change-control boards are more common for systems, commercial, and outsourced software projects than they are for internal management information systems.

The members of a change-control board usually represent multiple stakeholders and include client representatives, project representatives, and sometimes quality-assurance representatives. For hybrid projects that include hardware, microcode, and software components, the change-control board for software is linked to similar change-control boards for the hardware portions.

The change-control board concept has been very successful whenever it has been deployed, and tends to have long-range value across multiple releases of evolving systems. Change-control boards are now a standard best practices for the construction of large and complex applications, such as telephone switching systems, operating systems, defense systems, and the like.

Quality function deployment (QFD)

The technique called *quality function deployment* (QFD) originated in Japan as a technique for exploring the quality needs of engineered products, and then moved to software. QFD is now expanding globally, and many of SPR's high-technology clients who build hybrid products, such as switching systems and embedded software, have found QFD to be a valuable method for exploring and controlling software quality issues during requirements.

Procedurally, QFD operates in a fashion similar to JAD in that user representatives and design team representatives work together with a facilitator in focused group meetings. However, the QFD sessions center on the quality needs of the application rather than on general requirements.

The QFD method has developed some special graphical design methods for linking quality criteria to product requirements. One of these methods shows product feature sets linked to quality criteria. Visually, this method resembles the peaked roof of a house, so QFD drawings are sometimes termed *the house of quality*.

Sliding cost per function point scales

For software development contracts, perhaps the most effective way of dealing with changing user requirements is to include a sliding scale of costs in the contract itself. For example, suppose a hypothetical contract is based on an initial agreement of $500 per function point to develop an application of 1000 function points in size, so that the total value of the agreement is $500,000.

The contract might contain the following kind of escalating cost scale for new requirements added downstream:

Initial 1000 function points	$500 per function point
Features added more than 3 months after contract signing	$600 per function point
Features added more than 6 months after contract signing	$700 per function point
Features added more than 9 months after contract signing	$900 per function point

Features added more than 12 months after contract signing	$1200 per function point
Features deleted or delayed at user request	$150 per function point

Similar clauses can be utilized with maintenance and enhancement out-source agreements, on an annual or specific basis, such as the following:

Normal maintenance and defect repairs	$125 per function point per year
Mainframe to client/server conversion	$200 per function point per system
Special year-2000 search and repair	$65 per function point per system

(Note that the actual cost per function point for software produced in the United States runs from a low of less than $100 per function point for small end-user projects to a high of more than $5000 per function point for large military software projects. The data shown here is for illustrative purposes, and should not actually be used in contracts as it stands.)

The advantage of the use of function point metrics for development and maintenance contracts is that they are determined from the user requirements and cannot be unilaterally added by the contractor.

One of the many problems with the older lines-of-code (LOC) metric is that there is no objective way of determining the minimum volume of code needed to implement any given feature. This means that contracts based on cost per LOC could expand without any effective way for the client to determine whether the expansions were technically necessary.

Function points, on the other hand, cannot be unilaterally determined by the vendor and must be derived from explicit user requirements. Also, function points can easily be understood by clients while the LOC metric is difficult to understand in terms of why so much code is needed for any given contract.

Gathering and understanding software requirements has been a weak link in the software development process since the industry began more than 50 years ago, and shows signs of staying trouble-some for the foreseeable future. The basic problems with software requirements are the following four:

1. The clients who provide requirements vary widely in their under-standing of fundamental business processes and the rules for the activities needing automation.

2. The clients who provide requirements vary widely in their ability to explain the requirement clearly, even if they understand the requirements.

3. Requirements-gathering methodologies and requirements repre-sentation methods are not as well formed or sophisticated as soft-ware design approaches. For many projects, requirements are

casually collected and expressed primarily in natural-language text documents. Such requirements are highly ambiguous, contain many severe errors, and tend to creep at alarming rates.

4. Because clients are seldom software professionals, they may lack understanding of key topics such as development schedules and quality control, and, hence, may make impossible or even dangerous demands.

The topic of errors in requirements is often ignored under the common software aphorism that *quality* means *conformance to requirements*. In fact, requirements errors are plentiful and often are very severe.

It should never be forgotten that the very serious year-2000 problem originated as an explicit requirement. This is why all test libraries and test cases throughout the world failed to identify this problem for 15 years.

Only in about 1995 did the software world wake up to the fact that the end of the century would lead to catastrophic failure of software applications if calendar-year dates were recorded in two-digit format (i.e., 97 for the year 1997).

Conformance to the requirement that calendar years be recorded in two-digit rather than four-digit form is about to become the most expensive single problem in human history. This should be a lesson to us to examine requirements very carefully in terms of possible errors and long-range consequences.

The ability to measure the rate at which requirements creep is due to the advent of the function point metric. At the end of the requirements phase the function point total of the application can be quantified with high precision. Then, each change in requirements is evaluated in terms of how the function point total will be adjusted in response. When the application is delivered to users the final total is enumerated, and the difference between the initial and final totals is then noted.

Primary Topics for Software Requirements

By fortunate coincidence, the structure of the function point metric and the related feature point metric are a good match to the fundamental issues that should be included in software requirements. In chronological order, these seven fundamental topics should be explored as part of the requirements process:

1. The *outputs* that should be produced by the application

2. The *inputs* that will enter the software application

3. The *logical files* that must be maintained by the application

4. The *entities and relationships* that will be in the logical files of the application

5. The *inquiry types* that can be made to the application

6. The *interfaces* between the application and other systems

7. Key *algorithms* that must be present in the application

Five of these seven topics are the basic elements of the International Function Point Users Group (IFPUG) function point metric. The fourth topic, *entities and relationships,* is part of the British Mark II function point metric. The seventh topic, *algorithms,* is a standard factor of the feature point metric, which adds a count of algorithms to the five basic function point elements used by IFPUG.

The similarity between the topics that need to be examined when gathering requirements and those used by the functional metrics makes the derivation of function point totals during requirements a straightforward task.

Indeed, several companies, such as Bachman and Texas Instruments, have automated requirements tools which can also calculate function point totals directly from the requirements themselves.

There is such a strong synergy between requirements and function point analysis that it would be possible to construct a combined requirements-analysis tool with full function point sizing support as a natural adjunct, although the current generation of automated requirements tools is not quite at that point.

Secondary Topics for Software Requirements

In addition to the 7 fundamental requirements topics, there are also 12 other ancillary topics that should be resolved during the requirements-gathering phase:

1. The *size* of the application in function points and source code

2. The *schedule* of the application from requirements to delivery

3. The *cost* of the application by activity and also in terms of cost per function point

4. The *quality levels* in terms of defects, reliability, and ease of use criteria

5. The *hardware platform(s)* on which the application will operate

6. The *software platform(s),* such as operating systems and databases

7. The *security criteria* for the application and its companion databases

8. The *performance criteria,* if any, for the application

9. The *training requirements* or form of tutorial materials that may be needed

10. The *installation requirements* for putting the application onto the host platforms

11. The *reuse criteria* for the application in terms of both reused materials going into the application and also whether features of the application may be aimed at subsequent reuse by downstream applications

12. The *use cases* or major tasks users are expected to be able to perform via the application

These 12 supplemental topics are not the only items that can be included in requirements, but none of these 12 should be omitted by accident since they can all have a significant effect on software projects.

Positive and Negative Requirements Adjustment Factors

For estimating software requirements, schedules, effort, costs, and quality, both positive and negative factors must be considered.

Positive requirements factors

Among the positive factors that can benefit software requirements production by perhaps 10 percent for assignment scopes, production rates, and defect potentials may be found in the following:

- High client experience levels
- High staff experience levels
- Joint application design (JAD)
- Prototyping
- Quality function deployment (QFD)
- Use cases
- Requirements inspections
- Reusable requirements (patterns or frameworks)
- Requirements derived from similar projects
- Requirements derived from competitive projects
- Effective requirements representation methods

Negative requirements factors

Among the negative factors that can slow down or degrade the software requirements production by perhaps 5 percent, or that can raise defect potentials, may be found in the following:

- Inexperienced clients
- Inexperienced development team
- Novel applications with many new features
- Requirements creep of more than 3 percent per month
- Ineffective or casual requirements-gathering process
- Failure to prototype any part of the application
- Failure to review or inspect the requirements
- No reusable requirements

The way the author's estimating tools collect data about requirements approaches can be illustrated by the following sample questions using SPR's standard five-point weighting scale. These questions are not the only ones that affect software requirements, of course.

DEVELOPMENT PERSONNEL APPLICATION EXPERIENCE _____

    1 All are experts in the type of program being developed.
    2 Majority are experts, but some are new hires or novices.
    3 Even mixture of experts, new hires, and novices.
    4 Majority are new hires or novices, with few experts.
    5 All personnel are new to this kind of program.

DEVELOPMENT PERSONNEL REQUIREMENTS EXPERIENCE _____

    1 All are experts (have successfully gathered requirements from many projects).
    2 Majority are experts but some are new hires or novices.
    3 Even mixture of experts, new hires, and novices.
    4 Majority are new hires or novices, with few experts.
    5 All personnel are inexperienced in requirements analysis.

REQUIREMENTS ANALYSIS PROCESS _____

    1 Formal methods are used rigorously, such as JAD, QFD, Warnier-Orr, and the like.
    2 Formal methods are used in a semirigorous manner.
    3 Formal methods are mixed with informal methods.
    4 Requirements methods are primarily informal and unstructured.
    5 Requirements methods are informal and unstructured.

REQUIREMENTS PROTOTYPING PROCESS   _____

1 Application is too small to need prototyping or prototyping is not necessary.
2 Formal prototyping of key features, algorithms, and interfaces.
3 Informal prototyping of selected features, algorithms, and interfaces.
4 Partial prototyping of a few features or algorithms.
5 No prototyping at all for this project.

REQUIREMENTS INSPECTION EXPERIENCE   _____

1 All personnel are experienced in requirements reviews/inspections.
2 Most personnel are experienced in requirements reviews/inspections.
3 Even mixture of experienced and inexperienced personnel.
4 Most personnel are inexperienced in requirements reviews/inspections.
5 All personnel are inexperienced in requirements reviews/inspections.

USER PERSONNEL EXPERIENCE WITH SOFTWARE PROJECTS   _____

1 User experience with software is not a key factor.
2 All or a majority of users have software experience.
3 Even mixture of experts and inexperienced users.
4 Majority of users have no prior software experience.
5 All personnel have no prior software experience.

USER PERSONNEL EXPERIENCE WITH APPLICATION TYPE   _____

1 User expertise is not a major factor for the project.
2 All or a strong majority of users are experts.
3 Even mixture of experts, new hires, and novices.
4 Majority are new hires and novices, with few experts.
5 All personnel are new to this kind of program.

USER INVOLVEMENT DURING REQUIREMENTS   _____

1 User involvement is not a major factor for this project.
2 Users are heavily involved during requirements.
3 Users are somewhat involved during requirements.
4 Users are seldom involved during requirements.
5 Users are not involved during requirements.

As can be seen, projects whose responses to these questions are in the range of 1.00 through 2.00 are much more likely to succeed than similar projects where the responses are in the upper range of 4.00 and 5.00

Software requirements are a pivotal topic for software projects. If requirements are done well, the rest of the project has a good chance of being done well. If requirements are poorly formed, incomplete, or highly unstable, then it will be very difficult to have a successful project no matter what kinds of tools and methods or processes are utilized later on.

There are a number of interesting differences in how requirements are gathered and analyzed based on industry differences, and also on differences in the type of software being produced.

Requirements and End-User Software

There is very little to say about requirements when the application is being developed for the personal use of the developer.

Except for a few notes on possible alternatives, the requirements for end-user software exit primarily in the mind of the developer. This is not to say that the user can't change his or her mind during development. However, changes in end-user requirements usually have no serious implications.

Requirements and Management Information Systems (MIS) Projects

MIS projects usually derive software requirements directly from users or the users' authorized representatives.

For MIS projects the most effective methods for gathering requirements include JAD, prototypes, and requirements reviews. The combination of JAD sessions plus prototyping can reduce the rate of creeping requirements from 2 percent per month down to perhaps 0.5 percent per month.

The older method of gathering MIS requirements consisted of drafting a basic set of requirements more or less unilaterally by the client organization, and then presenting them to the software development organization. This method leads to a high rate of requirements creep, and also to adversarial feelings between the clients and the developers.

The requirements approach with the RAD methodology leads to a form of evolutionary prototyping without much in the way of written requirements. While the RAD approach is acceptable for small or simple applications, the results are not usually satisfactory for large applications above 1000 function points, nor for critical applications with stringent security, safety, performance, or reliability criteria.

MIS requirements can begin by exploring either the functions that the software is intended to perform or the data that is intended to be utilized. On the whole, beginning the requirements by exploring data and defining the outputs appears to give the best results.

Several well-known requirements approaches are in this general domain, including the Warnier-Orr method, the Jackson method, and several varieties of the information engineering (IE) method. Some of the object-oriented (OO) requirements approaches meet the general criteria, although as usual with OO methods there are also unique attributes due to the OO class and method concepts.

Even if user requirements can be satisfied by a package, it is still important to gather them, evaluate them, and review them in a careful manner. This means that even when commercial software is planned, such as SAP R/3, Oracle, IBM, or Computer Associates products, it is still desirable to match package capabilities against fundamental needs and requirements.

Requirements and Outsourced Projects

Outsourced projects in the MIS domain are similar in style and content to normal MIS projects with two important exceptions:

1. Outsource vendors often apply a cost per function point rate to the initial requirements in order to give the clients a good idea of the costs of the project. Some modern outsource contracts also include a sliding cost scale, so that the costs of implementing creeping requirements will be higher than the costs of the initial set of requirements.

2. Outsource vendors that serve many clients within the same industry often have substantial volumes of reusable materials and even entire packages available that might be utilized with minor or major customization. For certain industries, such as banking, insurance, telecommunications, and health care, almost every company uses software with the same generic feature sets, so reusable requirements are possible.

Requirements and Systems Software

In the author's books the phrase *systems software* is defined as software that controls a physical device, such as a computer, switching system, fuel injection system, or aircraft controls.

Because of the close and intricate relationship between the hardware and software, many requirements changes in the systems software domain are due to changes in the associated hardware. This close linkage between hardware and software requirements is one of the reasons why QFD technology has been effective in the systems software domain.

Requirements gathering in the systems software domain seldom comes directly from the users themselves. Instead the software requirements usually come in from hardware engineers and/or the marketing organization that is in direct contact with the users, although for custom software applications users may be direct participants in requirements sessions.

Requirements, and also specification methods, in the system software domain are closely linked to hardware requirements, and the approaches for the software and hardware domains overlap. Special representation methods, such as Petri nets or state-transition diagrams, are sometimes used in the context of systems software requirements, and even hardware representation methods, such as the Verilog design language, may be applied to software requirements.

Because quality is a key criterion for systems software, approaches that can deal with quality issues during the requirements phase are common practices for systems software.

Traditional quality-assurance methods for systems software include formal inspections, full configuration control, and sometimes JAD that may include both hardware and software requirements.

An interesting new approach called *quality function deployment* (QFD) is starting to move rapidly through the systems software domain. The QFD approach is similar to JAD in structure, although the primary emphasis of the QFD approach is on the quality and reliability of the application.

The usual starting point for the analysis of systems software requirements is determining the functions and features that are needed by the system.

Requirements and Commercial Software

Gathering requirements for commercial software has some unique aspects that are not found with the requirements for the other kinds of software projects.

For some kinds of commercial software products there may be hundreds, thousands, or even millions of possible users. There may also be many competitors whose software has features that might also have to be imitated.

These two factors imply that commercial software requirements seldom come directly from one or two actual clients. Instead, commercial software requirements may arrive from any or all of the following channels:

1. From the minds of creative development personnel who envision new products or useful new features

2. From customer surveys aimed at eliciting customer needs and requests for new features

3. From marketing and sales personnel, based on their perceptions of what users have requested

4. From sophisticated customer support personnel who recognize needed improvements due to incoming customer complaints

5. From user associations, focus groups, and online product forums on such services such as CompuServe or the World Wide Web, where inputs from thousands of customers may be received

6. From focus groups—selected sets of customers who volunteer to meet with design representatives and discuss the features which they like or dislike about possible new products

7. From analyzing the feature sets of competitive packages and imitating the more useful competitive features

Because the seven channels are more or less independent, the requirements for commercial software packages tend to be highly volatile. For example, if a competitor comes out with a striking new feature, a vendor may well have to implement a similar feature even if a product release is rather far along.

Requirements and Military Software Projects

Military software requirements are usually the most precise and exacting of any class of software. This phenomenon is due to the long-standing military requirement of *traceability,* or the need to identify exactly which requirement triggered the presence of any downstream design feature or source code module.

The military form of requirements tends toward large, even cumbersome, requirements specifications that are about three times larger than civilian norms. Although these military requirements documents are large and sometimes ambiguous, the specificity and completeness of military software requirements makes it easier to derive function point totals than for any other kind of software application.

On the whole, military software requirements have somewhat more positive attributes than negative for major systems that affect national defense or weapons. For smaller and less serious projects, the military requirements methods are something of an overkill.

Evaluating Combinations of Requirements Factors

The author and his colleagues at Software Productivity Research are often asked to deal with combinations of factors at the same time. SPR has developed a useful method of showing how a number of separate topics interact.

SPR's method is to show the 16 permutations that result from changing 4 different factors. This method is not perfect and makes some simplifying assumptions, but it is useful to show the ranges of possible outcomes.

Table 17.5 shows the 16 permutations that result from 4 key factors that affect software requirements:

1. The use of or failure to use prototypes

2. The use of or failure to use joint application design (JAD)

3. The use of or failure to use formal requirements inspections

4. The presence or absence of experienced staff familiar with the application type

In this table we assume fairly complex applications of at least 1,000 function points or 125,000 C statements in size. For smaller projects, requirements defects and rates of change would be less, of course. For really large systems in excess of 10,000 function points or 1,125,000 C statements, requirements errors would be larger and removal efficiency would be lower.

The table shows polar extreme conditions; that is, each factor is illustrated in binary form and can switch between best-case and worst-case extremes.

Note that the function point (FP) values used in the table assume the IFPUG Version 4 counting rules.

As can be inferred from the 16 permutations, software requirements outcomes cover a very broad range of possibilities. The combination of effective requirements-gathering technologies coupled with effective defect-removal technologies and a capable team lead to a very different outcome from casual requirements methods utilized by inexperienced staff.

The best-in-class technologies for dealing with requirements are highly proactive, and include the following components:

- Formal requirements gathering, such as JAD
- Augmentation of written requirements with prototypes
- Use of requirements-automation tools

TABLE 17.5   Sixteen Permutations of Software Requirements Technologies
(Data expressed in defects per function point; best-case options appear in boldface type)

	Defect potential per FP	Defect-removal efficiency, %	Residual defects per FP	Rate of creep, % monthly
No prototypes No use of JAD No inspections Inexperienced staff	2.00	60	0.80	4.0
No prototypes No use of JAD No inspections **Experienced staff**	2.00	65	0.70	3.5
Prototypes used No use of JAD No inspections Inexperienced staff	1.50	70	0.45	1.5
No prototypes No use of JAD **Inspections used** Inexperienced staff	2.00	80	0.40	3.0
No prototypes **JAD used** No inspections Inexperienced staff	1.50	75	0.38	1.0
Prototypes used No use of JAD No inspections **Experienced staff**	1.50	77	0.35	0.9
No prototypes No use of JAD **Inspections used** **Experienced staff**	2.00	84	0.32	1.0
No prototypes **JAD used** No inspections **Experienced staff**	1.50	80	0.30	0.9
Prototypes used **JAD used** No inspections Inexperienced staff	1.00	77	0.23	0.6

TABLE 17.5   Sixteen Permutations of Software Requirements Technologies
(*Continued*)

(Data expressed in defects per function point; best-case options appear in boldface type)

	Defect potential per FP	Defect-removal efficiency, %	Residual defects per FP	Rate of creep, % monthly
Prototypes used No use of JAD **Inspections used** Inexperienced staff	1.50	86	0.21	0.6
No prototypes **JAD used** **Inspections used** Inexperienced staff	1.50	86	0.21	0.5
No prototypes **JAD used** **Inspections used** **Experienced staff**	1.35	88	0.16	0.5
Prototypes used **JAD used** No inspections **Experienced staff**	1.00	87	0.13	0.3
Prototypes used No use of JAD **Inspections used** **Experienced staff**	1.50	94	0.09	0.3
Prototypes used **JAD used** **Inspections used** Inexperienced staff	1.00	94	0.06	0.2
Prototypes used **JAD used** **Inspections used** **Experienced staff**	0.70	97	0.02	0.1

- Attention to requirements quality control using such methods as quality function deployment and requirements inspections.

- Use of function point metrics based on requirements to determine overall application size, schedules, and costs

- Use of requirements change-control approaches, such as change-control boards, change-control tools, and the use of a sliding *cost per function point* scale

- Use of *reusable requirements* from similar or competitive projects

If the initial requirements for a software project are done well, the project has a fair chance to succeed regardless of size. If the requirements are done poorly and are filled with errors and uncontrolled changes, the project has a distressingly large chance of being canceled or running out of control.

References

Davis, Alan M.: *Software Requirements—Objects, Functions, and States,* 2d ed., Prentice Hall, Englewood Cliffs, N.J., ISBN 0-13-805763-x, 1993.

Gause, Donald C., and Gerald M. Weinberg: *Exploring Requirements—Quality Before Design,* Dorset House Press, New York, ISBN 0-932633-13-7, 1989.

Jones, Capers: *Assessment and Control of Software Risks,* Prentice Hall, Englewood Cliffs, N.J., ISBN 0-13-741406-4, 1994.

———: *Patterns of Software Systems Failure and Success,* International Thomson Computer Press, Boston, ISBN 1-850-32804-8, 1995.

———: *Software Quality—Analysis and Guidelines for Success,* International Thomson Computer Press, Boston, ISBN 1-85032-867-6, 1997.

Orr, Ken: *Structured Requirements Definition,* Ken Orr & Associates, Topeka, Kans., ISBN 0-99605884-0-X, 1981.

Thayer, Richard H., and Merlin Dorfman: *Software Requirements Engineering,* 2d ed., IEEE Computer Society Press, Los Alamitos, Calif., ISBN 0-8186-7738-4, 1997.

18

Estimating Software Prototypes

Prototyping and requirements gathering are often parallel activities. In some situations, the prototypes may even substitute for other forms of requirements gathering, although this is not a safe practice.

Among SPR's clients, prototyping is a very common practice. For projects between about 100 and 5000 function points in size, about 80 percent of them have had some form of prototype development prior to full development. Of the prototypes, about 65 percent were disposable, 10 percent were time-box, and 25 percent were evolutionary in nature.

To have an optimal effect, prototypes should serve as a method for augmenting written requirements and written specifications, not for replacing them. When prototypes are used in place of written specifications, the results are hazardous rather than beneficial. The reason for the hazard is because the prototype is not a sufficient source of information to enable formal design and code inspections, effective test case construction, or to facilitate later downstream maintenance.

High-speed prototypes can be useful adjuncts to both joint application design (JAD) sessions and quality function deployment (QFD) sessions, but prototypes are not a substitute for written requirements because prototypes have no long-range archival value. Also, for military and defense projects, prototypes have no traceability, so they do not support the military requirement of a backwards linkage between application features and specific requirements.

Prototypes are an interesting technology because they are most successful for midsized projects. For very small projects of less than 100 function points, they are usually not needed. For very large systems in excess of 10,000 function points, they may not be effective.

Prototypes are seldom used below a size of about 100 function points, although a few screens or user sequences might be constructed. Above 10,000 function points, prototypes are used but may be large projects in their own right. For example, prototyping 10 percent of a 10,000–function point application would yield a project of 1000 function points, which is an application of substantial size in its own right and might take a year to complete.

Although prototyping is very common, the topic of prototyping is underreported in the software engineering literature, and the discussion of prototyping in the software cost estimating literature is almost nil. The bulk of the literature on prototyping consists of how-to-do-it books, such as Bernard Boar's *Application Prototyping* (Boar 1984), John Reilly's *Rapid Prototyping* (Reilly 1997) or Scott Isensee and Jim Rudd's *The Art of Rapid Prototyping* (Isensee and Rudd 1997). In a previous book on software quality (Jones 1997) the author discusses the impact of prototypes on design defects, as well as defects in prototypes themselves.

In every engineering field a *prototype* is an early or partial version of a complex artifact assembled to test out design principles and, sometimes, operational characteristics. The same concept is true for software projects. A software prototype is an early and partial replica of a software application constructed to test out design principles and operational characteristics.

Prototyping is usually carried out with fairly high level languages of level 5 or higher because lower-level programming languages are too cumbersome for high-speed prototypes. (The level of a language is defined in Chap. 3 and refers to the number of source code statements required to encode 1 function point. Level 1 starts with basic assembly language where about 320 statements are needed for each function point. As language levels go up, fewer statements are needed, so that for level-10 languages only 32 statements are needed for each function point.)

Table 18.1 illustrates the ranges of possibilities for creating a prototype of 100 function points in size using language levels which range from 1 through 20. To simplify the situation, the coding rate is held constant at a fairly representative rate of 1600 lines of code per month for all 20 examples. The size of the prototype is also held constant at 100 function points. However, the volume of source code varies significantly, as does apparent productivity when considering the effort required or productivity rates expressed in terms of *function points per person month* (FP/PM).

As can be seen, the volume of source code needed to implement a constant size of 100 function points declines as the level of the language rises. This, in turn, translates into less effort to produce the

TABLE 18.1   Relationship Between Function Point and Lines-of-Code Productivity Rates for Software Prototypes by Language Level

Language level	Size, FP	Size, LOC	Monthly coding rate, LOC/PM	Effort to code prototype, months	Function point productivity, FP/PM
1	100	32,000	1,600	20.00	5
2	100	16,000	1,600	10.00	10
3	100	10,667	1,600	6.67	15
4	100	8,000	1,600	5.00	20
5	100	6,400	1,600	4.00	25
6	100	5,333	1,600	3.33	30
7	100	4,571	1,600	2.86	35
8	100	4,000	1,600	2.50	40
9	100	3,556	1,600	2.22	45
10	100	3,200	1,600	2.00	50
11	100	2,909	1,600	1.82	55
12	100	2,667	1,600	1.67	60
13	100	2,462	1,600	1.54	65
14	100	2,286	1,600	1.43	70
15	100	2,133	1,600	1.33	75
16	100	2,000	1,600	1.25	80
17	100	1,882	1,600	1.18	85
18	100	1,778	1,600	1.11	90
19	100	1,684	1,600	1.05	95
20	100	1,600	1,600	1.00	100

prototype and, hence, leads to higher productivity rates when the results are expressed in terms of function points per person month. In general, the economics of prototyping favors using languages of level 5 and higher regardless of the language used to create the actual application.

Incidentally, the ease of constructing prototypes is greatly facilitated when reusable artifacts are also available. Thus, prototyping derived from patterns, frameworks, class libraries, and the like can have even higher productivity rates than prototypes based on "pure coding" approaches.

Languages often used for prototyping include Visual Basic, Realizer, Eiffel, Smalltalk, JAVA, and a host of other languages whose nominal levels range between 5 and 20. In general, low-level languages, such as assembly, C, Fortran, and COBOL, are not used very often for prototyping purposes because these languages are bulky in terms of code volumes and hence low in productivity for quick and dirty work, such as prototyping.

The phrase *software prototyping* actually encompasses a number of discrete forms of prototype, including but not limited to the following:

- Disposable prototypes
- Time-box prototypes
- Evolutionary prototypes

Let us consider the pros and cons of these three forms of software project prototyping from the standpoint of how to estimate not only the prototypes themselves, but also their impact on downstream development.

Disposable Prototypes

As the name implies, disposable prototypes are created to demonstrate aspects of a software project, and when they have served that purpose they are no longer needed, so they are discarded.

Many of SPR's client companies do not limit the development of prototypes to the requirements phase of software development. If at any point in the development cycle an algorithm is difficult or there is some question as to how a screen element should appear, they continue to build disposable prototypes as the need arises.

Disposable prototypes are usually done rapidly, without formal specifications or much in the way of up-front planning. High-speed prototyping using such tools as Visual Basic and Realizer, or even special prototyping tools, such as the Bricklin Demo tool, is rather common.

The observed effects of disposable prototyping are a reduction in requirements defects and a very significant reduction in the rate of creeping requirements. Requirements creep for prototyped projects is usually well below the 1 to 2 percent per month range noted for conventional requirements gathering. Indeed, prototypes often reduce downstream requirements creep during design and coding to less than 0.5 percent per month.

Interestingly, disposable prototypes also yield a reduction in design defects and coding defects, although they yield no discernible impact on the user documentation or bad fix defect categories. Prototypes also seem to have little or no impact on bad test case defects or data errors, either.

Disposable prototypes interact in a synergistic fashion with two other requirements approaches: JAD and QFD. Indeed, disposable prototypes are often produced in real time during JAD or QFD sessions.

Disposable prototypes are usually only partial replicas of the software applications themselves, and usually contain only 10 to 25 percent of the features of the final product. Their main purpose is to test out interfaces, usability, and perhaps try out key algorithms or complex processing sequences.

Time-Box Prototypes

So far as can be determined, the concept of time-box prototypes originated circa 1986 at Du Pont. A specific time period, such as one month or six weeks, is dedicated to developing a prototype of the final project, in order to demonstrate that it is feasible and implementable.

Compared to disposable prototypes, which are often discrete and not unified, time-box prototypes are often partial replicas of full applications and are intended to show how the features and functions interact.

If the average size of disposable prototypes totals 10 to 15 percent of the eventual features, the average size of time-box prototypes is about 15 to 25 percent of the eventual features.

Because the time-box period may be less than a month and is almost never more than 3 months, it is obvious that time-box prototypes are most effective for projects that range from about 500 function points up to a maximum of about 5000 function points, with an optimal node point of about 1000 function points.

For really large systems that top 10,000 function points, the time-box would have to stretch out to more than 12 months to prototype 10 percent of the system, and the prototype would be 1000 function points in size, which is a significant application itself.

Time-box prototyping works best for new kinds of applications where the development team needs to practice in order to be sure that it can build the final product. While time-box prototypes are often constructed using such languages as Visual Basic, Realizer, or Objective C, they are sometimes built using conventional procedural languages, such as C.

The observed effects of time-box prototypes are twofold: (1) many requirements defects are prevented, and (2) the rate of requirements creep is significantly reduced and is often less than 0.5 percent per month after the prototype is finished.

Although harder to validate, time-box prototypes also seem to benefit design and coding defects slightly, although perhaps not as much as a staggered set of disposable prototypes.

Time-box prototypes are usually too extensive to be part of JAD or QFD sessions. Often the time-box method serves as a replacement for JAD, although QFD can still be included for high-technology projects.

The time-box concept sometimes overlaps the hazardous *evolutionary prototype* form if the time-box prototype is used as the actual base for growing a final product. This situation is dangerous for a number of reasons, as will be explained in the section on evolutionary prototypes.

A time-box prototype is usually a disposable prototype constructed during a specific time interval inserted into the overall project schedule. Typical time-box intervals might be 1 week for prototypes of less than 10 function points in size, 1 month for prototypes of less than 50 function points in size, or 3 months for prototypes of really massive systems where the prototype itself tops 100 function points.

Evolutionary Prototypes

As their name implies, evolutionary prototypes are intended to grow into finished products. Often the evolutionary prototypes are used as parts of various methodologies, such as RAD. Whether the evolutionary prototype is labeled RAD or not, there are some decided hazards associated with the approach that need to be dealt with very carefully.

By definition, *prototypes* are built without formal specifications or much in the way of quality control, such as design or code inspections. This carelessness means that the structure of the application may be far from optimal, the comment density may be below safe levels, and the number of latent defects in the application may be significant.

For low-end applications below 1000 function points in size, the carelessness of the evolutionary prototype can be partially offset by testing, although in fact this seldom occurs.

However, for really large systems in the 10,000–function point range and higher, attempting to grow a prototype into a final product is a very dangerous practice. Indeed, for contracted software, such systems show up in court often enough that evolutionary prototyping can be considered professional malpractice on larger applications.

The evolutionary prototype method leaves a lot of important issues more or less unresolved until late in the coding and testing phases. This means that testing itself is severely handicapped by the lack of any kind of formal specification document for the basis of constructing test cases.

Indeed, unless the development personnel are also the test personnel, it is difficult to do any serious testing at all, because the details of the evolutionary prototypes are not stable and may not even have been worked out at the normal time when test-case construction should be ramping up during the design and coding phases.

Also, the evolutionary prototype method usually does not have any finished materials that are capable of going through formal design and code inspections. This explains why inspections are almost never used in conjunction with evolutionary prototypes.

Obviously users and developers have whatever levels of prototypes are available at the moment, but a casual examination of a prototype is far less efficient in finding errors than are formal design and code inspections.

The hazards of evolutionary prototyping and of the related RAD approach for software applications larger than roughly 1000 function points are the following:

- Design rigor is often absent.
- Design inspections are seldom utilized.
- Written specifications are missing or perfunctory.
- Coding structure may be questionable.
- Code inspections are seldom utilized.
- Both cyclomatic and essential complexity levels may be high.
- Comments in code may be sparse.
- Test plan development is difficult and uncertain.
- Test cases may have major gaps in coverage.
- Quality and reliability levels are usually below average.
- Maintenance costs are usually well above average.
- Follow-on releases are expensive and troublesome.
- Customer support is difficult.
- User satisfaction levels are often below average.
- Litigation probability is alarmingly high.

These problems occur most severely at the larger end of the size spectrum. It is not fair to be totally dismissive of the evolutionary prototyping approach because it has been used more or less successfully on hundreds of applications by SPR's clients.

However, the literature on both RAD and evolutionary prototyping has manifested a common software flaw. There has been a tendency to assume that because the evolutionary prototype method works well on smaller applications of less than 1000 function points, it can be scaled up for larger applications of more than 10,000 function points. This is a dangerous fallacy, although it is a common failing in the software engineering literature.

Also, the evolutionary prototype method would be very dangerous to use for software that affects the operation of complex physical devices. This means that extreme caution is indicated when attempting evolutionary prototypes for weapons systems, aircraft flight control applications, medical instrument systems, or any other kind of application where failure can mean death, injury, or the probability of a major disaster.

Against the background of average results for MIS projects using disposable prototypes, evolutionary prototypes are a decided step backward in terms of quality results. Using COBOL information systems as an example, evolutionary prototypes tend to yield defect potentials about 15 percent higher than projects using JAD, while defect-removal efficiency levels are about 15 percent lower than average and may drop below 80 percent. This is a hazardous combination of results.

With evolutionary prototypes, the short-term advantages derived from working out the requirements early are quickly offset by sloppy design and poor coding structure, which elevates overall defect volumes and degrades defect-removal efficiency levels.

An evolutionary prototype is an attempt to build a full product by constructing a series of successively more complete partial versions, each of which includes features that are operational and usable by the intended clients.

The first stage of a series of evolutionary prototypes might include perhaps 25 percent of the features of the final product, and successive prototypes would then be constructed at the 50-, 75-, and 100-percent levels.

Default Values for Estimating Disposable Prototypes

The default values and initial assumptions shown here are for the *disposable prototype* form, which implies that the prototype is intended to clarify key algorithms or interfaces and, once it has served its purpose, will be replaced by a more rigorous version developed using normal quality controls.

Software-estimating tools can also deal with the more complex forms of prototyping associated with time-box prototypes, disposable prototypes, and the form of prototyping associated with RAD, which is another variant on the evolutionary prototyping form. The initial assumptions for creating disposable prototypes are shown in Table 18.2.

Prototyping is a highly variable activity, and in particular, the size range of software prototypes can vary by more than 50 to 1. The smallest prototypes observed are only a fraction of a function point and may be only 10 to 20 source code statements in size. These prototypes are typically created for proving key algorithms.

TABLE 18.2 Nominal Default Values for Disposable Prototypes

Activity sequence	Initial or second activity of software projects
Performed by	Development software engineers; client representatives
Predecessor activities	Early requirements or none
Overlap	50% with normal requirements
Concurrent activities	Requirements
Successor activities	Analysis, specification, and design
Initial prototype size	25 function points or 10% of final application size
Initial prototype size	750 source code statements
Reuse	35% from prior or similar projects
Assignment scope	500 function points or actual prototype
Production rate	75 function points per staff month
Production rate	1.76 work hours per function point
Production rate	2500 LOC per staff month (level-5 languages)
Language level	Level 5 or higher
Schedule months	Function points raised to the 0.1 power
Rate of creep or change	5% per month
Defect potential	1.5 defects per function point
Defect removal	90%
Delivered defects	0.15 defects per function point
High-severity defects	15% of delivered requirements defects
Bad fix probability	10% of prototype fixes may yield new errors

The largest prototypes, on the other hand, can almost be applications in their own right and can exceed 500 function points or 15,000 source code statements in size.

To illustrate the range of variability of prototypes, Table 18.3 illustrates three typical forms of prototyping: (1) disposable, (2) time-box, and (3) evolutionary.

Assume that the total size of the project for which the prototypes are being constructed will be 1000 function points. The prototypes are constructed using Visual Basic, which is one of the more common programming languages for prototyping.

One of the reasons why evolutionary prototypes are often hazardous is because prototypes of any kind are often built with casual development processes and no particular rigor during testing. Usually no formal inspections or other quality-control approaches will be used, so the removal of prototype errors will depend primarily on desk checking and unit testing by the developers themselves.

For disposable and time-box prototypes, the value of the prototypes for revealing possible requirements and design problems out-

TABLE 18.3   Three Forms of Prototypes
(Size expressed in both function points and source code statements)

Assumptions	
Programming language	Visual Basic
Project size in function points	1,000
Lines of code per function point	30
Source code size	30,000
Work hours per staff month	132
Burdened salary rate	$10,000

Factor	Disposable prototype	Time-Box prototype	Evolutionary prototype
Prototype percent	10.00%	15.00%	100.00%
Prototype FP	100	150	1000
Source code size	3000	4500	30000
Assignment, LOC	3000	2250	10000
Production, LOC	2500	2500	2000
Assignment, FP	150	112.5	500
Production, FP	125	125	100
Staff	1.00	2.00	3.00
Effort months	1.20	1.80	15.00
Schedule months	1.20	0.90	5.00
Cost	$12,000.00	$18,000.00	$150,000.00
Cost per FP	$120.00	$120.00	$150.00
Cost per LOC	$4.00	$4.00	$5.00
Defect potential per KLOC	50	50	75
Defect potential per FP	1.5	1.5	2.25
Defects	150	225	2250
Removal efficiency	90.00%	92.00%	93.00%
Delivered defects	15	18	158
per FP	0.15	0.12	0.16
per KLOC	5.00	4.00	5.25

weighs the number of errors or defects in the prototypes themselves.

But if the prototype is aimed at actually being grown into the final, finished product, the casual development approaches and lack of rigorous quality-control methods become a cause for concern.

As can be seen, the outcomes of software prototypes vary significantly based on which specific kind of prototype is being constructed.

Positive and Negative Factors That Influence Software Prototypes

The major positive adjustment factors for prototyping include the following:

- The prototyping language itself, if it is a high-level language
- Experience in the programming language used to construct the prototype
- Experience in the application or problem domain being prototyped
- Available reusable materials from similar projects or commercial sources

Some of the negative adjustment factors for prototyping include the following:

- Clients who are unsure of what features they want in the prototype
- Inadequate development tools
- The prototyping language itself, if it is a low-level language
- Inadequate computer power or response time
- Inexperience of various kinds
- No reusable artifacts available

To illustrate some of the adjustment factors that affect prototyping, consider the impact of the following topics.

DEVELOPMENT PERSONNEL APPLICATION EXPERIENCE

_____

1 All are experts in the type of program being developed.
2 Majority are experts, but some are new hires or novices.
3 Even mixture of experts, new hires, and novices.
4 Majority are new hires or novices, with few experts.
5 All personnel are new to this kind of program.

DEVELOPMENT PERSONNEL TOOL AND METHOD EXPERIENCE

_____

1 All are experts in the tools and methods for the project.
2 Majority are experts in the tools and methods.
3 Even mixture of experts, new hires, and novices.
4 Majority are new hires or novices in tools and methods.
5 All personnel are new to the tools and methods.

DEVELOPMENT PERSONNEL PROGRAMMING LANGUAGE EXPERIENCE _____

1 All are experts in the languages used for the project.

2 Majority are experts in the languages used for the project.

3 Even mixture of experts, new hires, and novices.

4 Majority are new hires or novices in the languages.

5 All personnel are new to the languages used.

DEVELOPMENT PERSONNEL HARDWARE EXPERIENCE _____

1 All are experts in the hardware used for the project.

2 Majority are experts in the hardware used for the project.

3 Even mixture of experts, new hires, and novices.

4 Majority are new hires or novices in the hardware.

5 All personnel are new to the hardware for the project.

USER PERSONNEL EXPERIENCE WITH APPLICATION TYPE _____

1 User expertise is not a major factor for the project.

2 All or a strong majority of users are experts.

3 Even mixture of experts, new hires, and novices.

4 Majority are new hires and novices, with few experts.

5 All personnel are new to this kind of program.

USER INVOLVEMENT DURING REQUIREMENTS _____

1 User involvement is not a major factor for this project.

2 Users are heavily involved during requirements.

3 Users are somewhat involved during requirements.

4 Users are seldom involved during requirements.

5 Users are not involved during requirements.

PROGRAM DEBUGGING TOOLS _____

1 Full screen editor and automated testing tool are used.

2 Full screen editor, traces, and cross-references are used.

3 Full screen editor traces, but little else, is used.

4 Full screen editor, but no trace or other flow aids, is used.

5 Line editor with little or no trace and flow aids is used.

DEVELOPMENT PLATFORM NOVELTY _____

1 All hardware is familiar and well understood by staff.

2 Most hardware is familiar and well understood by staff.

3 Mixture of familiar and new or unfamiliar hardware.

4 Most hardware is new or unfamiliar to staff.

5 Hardware is new or experimental or unfamiliar.

DEVELOPMENT HARDWARE STABILITY

1 Stable, single-vendor hardware with high compatibility is used.

2 Single-vendor hardware with moderate compatibility is used.

3 Mixed-vendor hardware with high mutual compatibility is used.

4 Mixed-vendor hardware with moderate compatibility is used.

5 Unstable, changing, or incompatible development hardware is used.

RESPONSE TIME OF DEVELOPMENT ENVIRONMENT

1 Response time is not a factor for this project.

2 Subsecond response time is the norm.

3 One- to five-second response time is the norm.

4 Five- to ten-second response time is the norm.

5 More than 10-second response time is the norm.

DEVELOPMENT COMPUTING SUPPORT

1 Computer support is ample, reliable, and effective.

2. Computer support is adequate, reliable, and effective.

3 Computer support is usually adequate and effective.

4 Computer support is sometimes inadequate or ineffective.

5 Computer support is seriously deficient for the project.

WORKSTATION ENVIRONMENT

1 Individual workstations networked with LAN and mainframe are used.

2 Individual workstations on LAN are used.

3 Individual workstations for all staff members are used.

4 Shared workstations (two employees per workstation) are used.

5 Batch development/more than two employees per workstation.

Here, too, a pattern of responses that are in the range of 1 or 2 indicates above-average performance levels, while a pattern of responses that sags into the 4 and 5 range indicates below-average responses.

References

Boar, Bernard: *Application Prototyping,* John Wiley & Sons, New York, ISBN 0-471-89317-X, 1984.

Isensee, Scott, and Jim R. Rudd: *The Art of Rapid Prototyping,* International Thomson Computer Press, Boston, ISBN 1-85032-215-5, 1997.

Jones, Capers: *Software Quality—Analysis and Guidelines for Success,* International Thomson Computer Press, Boston, ISBN 1-85032-867-6, 1997.

Reilly, John P.: *Rapid Prototyping,* International Thomson Computer Press, Boston, ISBN 1-85032-193-0, 1997.

Estimating Software Specifications and Design

Software specifications and design are a technical response to the user requirements, and serve to describe the way the user requirements will be handled in an automated fashion by the software application that is being constructed.

The term *specifications and design* covers a very broad range of actual forms of design, including but not limited to the following:

- Rough preliminary specifications
- Detailed final specifications
- External specifications of the features visible and usable by clients.
- Internal specifications of the control flow and structure of the application.
- Data specifications of the information created, used, or modified by the application.

Also, prior to the commencement of design itself, there may be a moderate to lengthy period of systems analysis, which is sometimes subsumed under the design phase, too.

Estimating software design and specification activities is complicated by the fact that there are a host of formal and semiformal methodologies, each of which will produce a somewhat different volume of design materials and also will trigger somewhat different work patterns.

The list in Table 19.1 of 40 different forms of specification representation methods illustrates some of the diversity of the software design situation.

TABLE 19.1   Forty Common Software Design Methods

1. Conventional flowcharts
2. Natural language text
3. Control-flow diagrams
4. Data-structure diagrams
5. Gane & Sarson data-flow diagrams
6. DeMarco bubble diagrams
7. DeMarco structured English
8. Entity-relationship diagrams (generic)
9. Chen entity-relationship diagrams
10. Action diagrams
11. Structured analysis and design technique (SADT)
12. James Martin entity-relationship diagrams
13. James Martin information engineering (IE) diagrams
14. Texas Instruments information engineering (IE) diagrams
15. Nassi-Shneiderman diagrams
16. Chapin chart diagrams
17. Decision tables
18. Jackson design diagrams
19. Hierarchy plus input, output, and process (HIPO) diagrams
20. Yourdon-Constantine structured design diagrams
21. Yourdon object-oriented diagrams
22. Shlaer-Mellor object-oriented analysis diagrams
23. Booch object-oriented diagrams
24. Rumbaugh object-oriented diagrams
25. Jacobsen object-oriented diagrams
26. Universal modeling language (UML) diagrams
27. Petri nets
28. Leighton diagrams
29. State-transition diagrams
30. Warnier-Orr diagrams
31. Structured analysis and design technique (SADT) diagrams
32. Merise diagrams
33. Three-dimensional control structure diagrams
34. Animated (dynamic) flow diagrams
35. Quality function deployment (QFD) house of quality diagrams
36. Root-cause analysis fishbone diagrams
37. Text-based specifications
38. Formal notation-based specifications
39. Pseudocode design
40. Z

This list of 40 methods of dealing with software specifications and design is not a complete list of all possible methods, which might well exceed 100 alternatives in all. It merely reflects the fact that the phrase *software design* can mean a very wide range of topics, and the huge number of possibilities represents a challenge to software cost estimating vendors.

The literature on software design methods is quite extensive and totals more than 250 books. However, the great bulk of the software design literature concentrates on how-to-do-it treatments of specific design representation methods. Books that deal with the interaction of software design issues with software cost estimating are far more limited. Also limited are books that attempt to relate various software design approaches to the development of function point analysis.

Some of the books that attempt to correlate software design issues with software cost estimating include Barry Boehm's *Software Engineering Economics* (Boehm 1981); Charles Symons's *Software Sizing and Estimating* (Symons 1991); Tom DeMarco's *Controlling Software Projects* (DeMarco 1982); Brian Dreger's *Function Point Analysis* (Dreger 1989); Larry Putnam and Ware Myers's *Industrial Strength Software* (Putnam and Myers 1997); and several of the author's previous books, including *Applied Software Measurement* (Jones 1996) and *Software Quality—Analysis and Guidelines for Success* (Jones 1997). Also, Howard Rubin often discusses the intersection of estimating with other disciplines, such as design, in his annual benchmark reports (Rubin 1997).

The usual estimating response to the very large number of software design and specification approaches is to utilize templates for the more common design methods. However, templates are not a perfect solution for several reasons:

- A significant number of software projects use multiple or hybrid design methods rather than one "pure" design method. For many projects, designers may start using one of the object-oriented design methods, such as the universal modeling language (UML), but find that it has such a steep learning curve that they augment it with something else, such as the Yourdon structured design approach.

- A significant number of software projects utilize private or custom specification methods for which no published general data is available. Although templates are possible for private design methods, they must be constructed by users of estimating tools rather than by vendors, who may not even be aware of their existence.

However, clients of software cost estimating tool vendors can construct software cost estimating templates no matter what combinations of specification methods they use. But if an enterprise uses its own proprietary or highly modified design approach, then commercial templates from software cost estimating tool vendors will obviously not be available.

As an example of a proprietary custom design method, the ITT corporation used the structured analysis and design technique (SADT) both in its pure form and in the form of a customized ITT variation created and used for switching software projects.

As an example of multiple design methods, it is very common to see a mixture of flowcharts, one or more of the object-oriented specification methods, and some kind of entity-relationship charts all in the specifications for a single project.

The nominal or default values for software specifications and design are not the same for every class and type of software project. The major variants are those of: (1) civilian versus military software projects, (2) systems software versus information systems projects, and (3) new applications versus enhancements to existing software.

The default values shown in Table 19.2 are for civilian systems software projects using conventional structured design methods, such as those defined by the late Wayne Stevens (Stevens 1981). The conven-

TABLE 19.2   Nominal Default Values for Systems Software Specifications and Design

Activity sequence	Third with prototypes; second without prototypes
Performed by	Systems analysts; development staff; architects
Predecessor activities	Requirements and prototypes
Overlap	75% with requirements and with prototypes
Concurrent activities	Reverse engineering for enhancement projects
Successor activities	Coding
Initial size	0.50 pages per function point
Graphics	0.25 illustrations per function point
Reuse	35% from prior or similar projects
Assignment scope	250 function points
Production rate	125 function points per staff month
Production rate	1.06 work hours per function point
Schedule months	Function points raised to the 0.25 power
Rate of creep or change	2% per month for 6 months; then 1% per month
Defect potential	1.25 defects per function point
Defect removal	90%
Delivered defects	0.125 defects per function point
High-severity defects	15% of delivered defects
Bad fix probability	5% of design fixes may yield new errors

tional structured design methods are the most widely deployed for systems software, and have default values in many commercial software cost estimating tools.

For military projects, the size would be two to three times larger than for civilian projects. If the older DoD 2167 standard is followed, then the designs are about three times larger than civilian norms. If the newer DoD 498 standard is followed, the design is roughly twice as large as civilian norms.

Using the default values for a systems software project of 1500 function points, the size of the design specifications would amount to perhaps 750 pages. The design team would consist of about 6 people, and the effort would amount to about 30 staff months. The schedule for the design would amount to roughly 5 calendar months.

Alarmingly, the design will contain about 1875 bugs or defects, and around 5 percent of these, or 94 of them, will be high-severity bugs that can have very serious consequences if they are not removed.

Assuming a 90 percent defect-removal efficiency, the number of residual design errors at the time of deployment will be about 190, and perhaps 10 of them will be quite serious. Design defects are often pervasive and require extensive changes, unlike coding defects, which are typically localized and concise.

Table 19.3 illustrates some of the nominal or default estimating

TABLE 19.3   Estimating Assumptions for Software Design Methods

Design method	Size, pages per FP	Graphics content, %	Defect potential per FP	Defect-removal efficiency, %	Residual defects deployed
Booch	1.50	50.00	1.35	80.00	0.27
Constantine	1.20	45.00	1.25	87.00	0.16
DoD 2167	2.75	25.00	1.10	90.00	0.11
Gane and Sarson	1.20	45.00	1.25	80.00	0.25
HIPO	1.15	60.00	1.30	75.00	0.33
Information Engineering	1.25	45.00	1.15	85.00	0.17
Merise	1.50	40.00	1.15	85.00	0.17
RAD	0.35	60.00	1.75	70.00	0.53
Rumbaugh	1.50	50.00	1.35	80.00	0.27
SADT	1.25	50.00	1.10	90.00	0.11
Shlaer-Mellor	1.50	50.00	1.35	80.00	0.27
UML	2.00	50.00	1.45	80.00	0.29
Warnier-Orr	1.20	60.00	1.00	90.00	0.10
Yourdon	1.20	35.00	1.25	87.00	0.16
Average	1.40	47.50	1.27	82.79	0.23

variations associated with a number of widely utilized software design methodologies. Table 19.3 is merely a rough approximation of samples of various design methodologies. Actual cost estimates would require further adjustment based on such factors as the experience of the design team, the use or absence of design automation, and the rate at which requirements change during the design phase. Table 19.3 is in alphabetical order by the name of the design method.

As can easily be seen, estimating software specifications and design requires knowledge of the specific kinds of design methods that are going to be utilized.

Positive Design Adjustment Factors

As the century winds down, software projects have been designed and developed continuously for almost 40 years. This means that quite a few applications in the late 1990s are actually third- or fourth-generation applications whose "grandparents," so to speak, were originally conceived for such computers as the IBM 650 or IBM 1401, more than 25 years ago.

As a result, comparatively few applications are truly new in the sense that they represent novel uses of computers which have never been seen before. Because so many new applications are basically replacements of prior applications, the topic of reusable design material is now quite common. Among SPR's clients in 1997, more than two-thirds of the software design projects consisted of either:

- Designing modern replacements for aging legacy software
- Designing new features and enhancements to existing applications
- Designing customized features for such packages as SAP R/3

Unfortunately, the original specifications are seldom useful as they stand, but the existence of the aging software itself provides at least a starting point. Also, the usage of such tools as reverse engineering and reengineering tools also facilitates capturing some of the original design assumptions, which may not even exist in paper form any more.

The general impact of reusable material from previous projects is to streamline and truncate the analytical portion of the design process, and also to reduce the overall bulk of written specifications that need to be created. Table 19.4 shows a rough approximation of software design from 1960 forward at 10-year intervals for a hypothetical 1000–function point billing application.

By the time an enterprise is on its fourth or fifth generation of billing software, the accumulated knowledge of what needs to be done is quite extensive, and this tends to shrink the size of the paper specifications.

TABLE 19.4   Evolution of Software Design Reuse at 10-Year Intervals

Year	Application generation	Size, FP	Size of new design, pages	Percent of reusable materials
1960	First	1000	600	0
1970	Second	1000	600	10
1980	Third	1000	500	25
1990	Fourth	1000	350	60
2000	Fifth	1000	200	75

Staff and client experience with similar applications is a major benefit for software design work, and can have an impact of 15 percent or more.

Software design methodologies also have an impact, although this impact can swing between positive and negative directions.

For information systems design methods that deal with data flow, such as the Warnier-Orr and Jackson design methods, have a positive impact, as do several of the variants of IE.

For systems, embedded, and real-time software, design methods that deal with control flow and state changes, such as finite-state design and Petri nets, have a beneficial impact.

As this book is being written, design patterns and frameworks are beginning to achieve publicity in the software press, while the topic of component-based development is now a standard topic. After many years of false starts, it appears that software reuse is finally beginning to move from a research topic to a day-to-day development approach.

Negative Design Adjustment Factors

For large systems, one of the major negative factors is the failure to utilize formal design methods. Surprisingly, exactly which formal design method is comparatively unimportant, but a total lack of rigor exerts a significant downward trend in design completion coupled with an upward trend in serious design defects.

Perhaps the most significant factor of all is failure to utilize formal design inspections, or at least some form of design review. Design defects are both plentiful and serious, and are highly resistant to later discovery via testing.

Other negative influences on the software design process include the following:

- Using natural language as the primary medium of expressing design.

- Using graphical design approaches without automated tools.
- Failure to place specifications under formal configuration control.
- Failure to utilize formal design inspections.
- Substituting prototypes for specifications.
- Inappropriate use of RAD.
- The very steep learning curve for OO design methods.

As a prime example, consider the implications of the year-2000 problem. Once this problem moved from requirements (where it originated) into design, it was no longer possible to find it via testing because test cases are derived from design specifications. Hence, major errors in the design tend to be *tested into* a project rather than being *tested out*.

Some of the factors that influence software specifications and design, either for good or for ill, include the following:

PROJECT ORGANIZATION STRUCTURE _____

1 Individual project.
2 Small team project (less than four staff members).
3 Conventional departments, with hierarchical organization.
4 Conventional departments, with matrix organization.
5 Ambiguous or uncertain organization.

DEVELOPMENT PERSONNEL APPLICATION EXPERIENCE _____

1 All are experts in the type of program being developed.
2 Majority are experts, but some are new hires or novices.
3 Even mixture of experts, new hires, and novices.
4 Majority are new hires or novices, with few experts.
5 All personnel are new to this kind of program.

DEVELOPMENT PERSONNEL ANALYSIS AND DESIGN EXPERIENCE _____

1 All are experts in analysis and design methods.
2 Majority are experts in analysis and design methods.
3 Even mixture of experts, new hires, and novices.
4 Majority are new hires or novices in analysis and design.
5 All personnel are inexperienced in analysis and design.

DEVELOPMENT PERSONNEL HARDWARE EXPERIENCE _____

1 All are experts in the hardware used for the project.
2 Majority are experts in the hardware used for the project.
3 Even mixture of experts, new hires, and novices.

4 Majority are new hires or novices in the hardware.
5 All personnel are new to the hardware for the project.

DESIGN REVIEW DEFECT-REMOVAL EXPERIENCE   _____

1 All personnel are experienced in reviews/inspections.
2 Most personnel are experienced in reviews/inspections.
3 Even mixture of experienced and inexperienced personnel.
4 Most personnel are inexperienced in reviews/inspections.
5 All personnel are inexperienced in reviews/inspections.

USER PERSONNEL EXPERIENCE WITH APPLICATION TYPE

   _____

1 User expertise is not a major factor for the project.
2 All or a strong majority of users are experts.
3 Even mixture of experts, new hires, and novices.
4 Majority are new hires and novices, with few experts.
5 All personnel are new to this kind of program.

USER INVOLVEMENT DURING DESIGN REVIEWS   _____

1 User involvement is not a major factor for the project.
2 Users are heavily involved during design reviews.
3 Users are somewhat involved during design reviews.
4 Users are seldom involved during design reviews.
5 Users are not involved during design reviews.

DESIGN AUTOMATION ENVIRONMENT   _____

1 Design-to-code automation with reusable code library is applied.
2 Formal design methods and automated text/graphics support are applied.
3 Semiformal design with some text/graphics support is applied.
4 Semiformal design with text automation only is applied.
5 Informal design with no automation is applied.

CASE INTEGRATION   _____

1 Integration across all phases of life cycle is achieved.
2 Integration across multiple phases is achieved.
3 Integration between phases is achieved.
4 Integration within a phase is achieved.
5 No integration is achieved.

PROJECT DOCUMENTATION LIBRARY   _____

1 Full project library with automated support is used.
2 Partial project library with automated support is used.
3 Minimal automated library for documentation is used.
4 Manual documentation control is used.
5 No formal library control for documentation is used.

DEVELOPMENT PLATFORM NOVELTY _____

1 All hardware is familiar and well understood by staff.
2 Most hardware is familiar and well understood by staff.
3 Mixture of familiar and new or unfamiliar hardware.
4 Most hardware is new or unfamiliar to staff.
5 Hardware is new or experimental or unfamiliar.

DEVELOPMENT HARDWARE STABILITY _____

1 Stable, single-vendor hardware with high compatibility is used.
2 Single-vendor hardware with moderate compatibility is used.
3 Mixed-vendor hardware with high mutual compatibility is used.
4 Mixed-vendor hardware with moderate compatibility is used.
5 Unstable, changing, or incompatible development hardware is used.

WORKSTATION ENVIRONMENT _____

1 Individual workstations networked with LAN and mainframe are used.
2 Individual workstations on LAN are used.
3 Individual workstations for all staff members are used.
4 Shared workstations (two employees per workstation) are used.
5 Batch development/more than two employees per workstation.

Here, too, projects with a majority of answers in the 1.0 to 2.5 range will end up with significantly better results than projects with a majority of answers in the 3.5 to 5.0 range.

Software specifications and design are critical aspects of software development projects, and, hence, critical to software cost estimation methods, too. However, the variations and ranges associated with software specifications and design make this a particularly difficult estimating domain.

Also, the fact that neither the size nor the effort associated with most forms of specification and design can be measured using the traditional lines-of-code metric has led to a shortage of solid empirical data. Only studies using natural metrics (such as pages of text) have function point metrics have been published.

References

Boehm, Barry: *Software Engineering Economics,* Prentice Hall, Englewood Cliffs, N.J., 1981.

DeMarco, Tom: *Controlling Software Projects,* Yourdon Press, New York, ISBN 0-917072-32-4, 1982.

Dreger, Brian: *Function Point Analysis,* Prentice Hall, Englewood Cliffs, N.J., ISBN 0-13-332321-8, 1989.

Jones, Capers: *Assessment and Control of Software Risks,* Prentice Hall, Englewood Cliffs, N.J., ISBN 0-13-741406-4, 1994.

————: *Patterns of Software System Failure and Success,* International Thomson Computer Press, Boston, ISBN 1-850-32804-8, 1995.

————: *Applied Software Measurement,* 2d ed., McGraw-Hill, New York, ISBN 0-07-032826-9, 1996.

————: *Software Quality—Analysis and Guidelines for Success,* International Thompson Computer Press, Boston, ISBN 1-85032-867-6, 1997.

Putnam, Lawrence H.: *Measures for Excellence—Reliable Software on Time, Within Budget,* Yourdon Press/Prentice Hall, Englewood Cliffs, N.J., ISBN 0-13-567694-0, 1992.

————, and Ware Myers: *Industrial Strength Software—Effective Management Using Measurement,* IEEE Computer Society Press, Washington, D.C., ISBN 0-8186-7532-2, 1997.

Rubin, Howard: *Software Benchmark Studies for 1997,* Howard Rubin Associates, Pound Ridge, N.Y., 1997.

Stevens, Wayne: *Using Structured Design,* John Wiley & Sons, Chichester, U.K., ISBN 0 471-08198-1, 1981.

Symons, Charles R.: *Software Sizing and Estimating—Mk II FPA (Function Point Analysis),* John Wiley & Sons, Chichester, U.K., ISBN 0 471-92985-9, 1991.

20

Estimating Design Inspections

The defect-removal method of formal inspections was developed at IBM Kingston in the 1970s by Michael Fagan and his colleagues (Fagan 1976). The inspection process has more than 25 years of continuous data available and has proven to be one of the most effective and efficient defect-removal operations ever developed. As a general rule, formal inspections are about twice as effective in finding bugs as any known form of testing. Most forms of testing are less than 30 percent efficient in finding bugs, but formal inspections are more than 60 percent efficient.

The phrase *defect-removal efficiency* refers to the percentage of latent errors actually detected. For example, if a formal inspection is 60 percent efficient, that implies that it found 6 out of 10 errors that were actually present. Obviously, it is necessary to measure defects over a lengthy period to calibrate defect-removal efficiency rates.

There is an extensive literature on both design and code inspections, but much of the literature is devoted to how-to-do-it books, such as the excellent handbook of inspections by Gerald Weinberg and Daniel Friedman (Friedman and Weinberg 1990) and the more recent treatment by Tom Gilb and D. Graham in *Software Inspections* (Gilb and Graham 1993), although this book does deal with the defect-removal results of formal inspections.

There are few books that attempt to quantify the economics of inspections, such as Robert Dunn and Richard Ullman's *Quality Assurance for Computer Software* (Dunn and Ullman 1982) and the author's own more recent *Patterns of Software Systems Failure and Success* (Jones 1995) and *Software Quality—Analysis and Guidelines for Success* (Jones 1997). Also, Larry Putnam has discussed inspections in an estimating context (Putnam and Myers 1997), and Howard Rubin usually includes interesting data on inspections in his annual benchmark handbooks (Rubin 1997).

Not every software cost estimating tool can deal with the impact of inspections. For example, some of the older cost-estimating tools, such as COCOMO, did not deal with quality or inspection technologies.

Because quality plays such a major role in software schedules and costs, and because formal inspections are a leading quality method, modern software cost estimating tools deal explicitly with inspections and can predict the following data points:

1. The number of defects in the application

2. The defect-removal efficiency of formal inspections

3. The bad fix injection of defect repairs, which leads to new errors

4. The number of latent defects still present at delivery of the software

5. The severity levels of latent defects

6. The postrelease discovery rate of defects by users of the software

7. The postrelease maintenance costs to repair latent defects

The term *inspection* refers to a formal procedure in which a trained group of practitioners examine a software artifact, such as a specification, page by page in a planned fashion. Each inspection session is limited to a two-hour duration, and no more than two such sessions can be held in any business day. Prior to the inspection, each participant will have received the material to be inspected no less than a week prior to the start of the first inspection process.

The participants in the inspection process normally include the following set, although there is some flexibility and doubling up, such as having one person perform two roles:

- The *producer* of the material being inspected
- A *moderator,* charged with keeping the inspection on track
- A *recorder,* charged with keeping track of problems identified
- A *reader,* charged with paraphrasing each section
- One or more *reviewers,* charged with performing the inspection
- One or more *observers,* normally novices there to learn how inspections operate

In really large organizations that use inspections, such as IBM or AT&T, there are other specialized personnel associated with the inspection process, too:

- A *coordinator*, charged with scheduling inspections and reserving rooms

- One or more *trainers*, charged with instructing novices in the inspection protocols

The minimum number of participants needed to actually perform a formal inspection is three: the producer, the moderator, and the recorder. In this minimum complement, the moderator and recorder are, of course, also serving as reviewers.

For an average inspection held within a major corporation on specifications associated with large systems, the normal complement is five personnel: the producer, the moderator, the recorder, and two reviewers.

The maximum number of participants in formal inspections is limited to no more than eight. This is a practical limitation caused by the fact that large meetings tend to be discursive and inefficient, coupled with the fact that rooms big enough to hold more than eight people are not readily available in many corporations.

The most difficult role to fill when performing inspections is that of the moderator, because the moderator must deal with rather delicate human relationship issues. It is sometimes stressful to have other individuals performing a close scrutiny of one's work, and from time to time producers challenge the validity of whether or not a particular finding is really an error or defect or not. The moderator has to keep such disagreements from growing into full-scale disputes.

The reviewers also must be selected carefully, since they have to understand the work being inspected. For large projects, the reviewers are normally selected from the project team for the practical reason that other team members have the best prospect of being able to contribute meaningful observations.

From an estimating standpoint, there is a substantial body of empirical data available on both inspection effort and inspection effectiveness. However, in spite of the available data, inspections are somewhat tricky and complex to estimate. The reason for the difficulty is because inspections are intermittent activities that occur in a series of discrete two-hour packets that may occur at almost random intervals due to the need to juggle the schedules of the participants. The nominal default values for design inspections are the parameters shown in Table 20.1.

Estimating inspections often use natural metrics, such as pages. Typical rules of thumb using pages of specifications might be the following:

Preparation	10 to 15 pages per hour
Inspection sessions	5 to 10 pages per hour

TABLE 20.1   Nominal Default Values for Design Inspections

Activity sequence	Fourth
Performed by	Developers; quality assurance; testing staff; observers
Predecessor activities	Requirements, prototypes, design, and specification
Overlap	75% with specification and design
Concurrent activities	Both design and code
Successor activities	Coding
Initial size	1.50 pages per function point
Graphics	0.25 illustrations per function point
Reuse	15% from prior or similar projects
Assignment scope	200 function points
Assignment scope	200 specification pages
Production rate	225 function points per staff month
Production rate	0.59 work hours per function point
Production rate	15 pages inspected per 2-hour session
Schedule months	2-hour packets with no more than 2 per day
Rate of creep or change	None
Defect potential	1.25 design defects per function point
Defect removal	65% average removal efficiency (peak is 95%)
Delivered defects	Design defects−65% = 0.44 defects per function point
High-severity defects	10% of delivered defects
Bad fix probability	3% of design inspection fixes may yield new errors

Since the purpose of design inspections is finding and fixing errors, the number and severity level of design problems exert a major influence on the timing and costs of the inspection process.

On average, software designs and specifications contain about 1.25 errors or defects per function point, which for a project of 1000 function points can amount to about 1250 design bugs. Of these about 15 percent, or almost 200, will be serious.

Design inspections average about 65 percent defect-removal efficiency overall, but against serious design defects the efficiency of formal design inspections tops 95 percent. Therefore, after a series of formal design inspections on this 1000–function point example, only about 10 serious design issues may remain under best-case conditions.

By contrast, most forms of testing are less than 30 percent efficient in finding bugs, and are even less efficient in finding design defects. If design errors stay in the design, there is a strong chance that testing will not find them at all, because test cases are constructed using the design specifications as the basis. The efficiency of testing in finding design errors is less than 10 percent, which is a very low value indeed.

(Recall that for many years no test cases were constructed that could find the two-digit year-2000 problem, because the two-digit form of date representation originated as a requirement and then passed into design, so testing had a 0 percent efficiency against this problem.)

Inspections are fairly expensive and time-consuming activities. Having from 3 to 6 participants moving through a specification at a rate of less than 10 pages per hour amounts to only about 1.25 pages per staff hour. If the specification being reviewed is large, say 500 pages, then the total costs can amount to 400 staff hours.

Surprisingly, formal inspections have proven both to benefit overall project costs and to shorten project schedules. Indeed, the inventor of the inspection process, Michael Fagan, received an IBM outstanding contribution award for determining that inspections shorten schedules as well as improve quality when applied to major systems software projects.

Assume you have a software project of 1000 function points in size and that the specifications are 500 pages in size. Now assume that preparation and inspection of these specifications requires 500 staff hours, but finds 250 defects, of which 50 are serious. The testing for this project will probably take about 500 staff hours, too.

Now assume that the same 1000–function point project is developed without using design inspections. The 250 design defects—including the 50 serious defects—are not discovered before development, and they find their way into the code. Under this second scenario, when testing occurs it will probably take 2000 staff hours, because serious design flaws are difficult to eliminate during the testing stage.

Thus, the 500 staff hours invested in formal design inspections trigger a savings of 1500 staff hours during testing, and shorten the overall project schedule for delivery. These claims are solidly based on empirical observations.

There is a simple experiment which anyone can perform to validate the schedule and cost assumptions associated with formal design and code inspections:

1. Record the effort, schedule, costs, and number of bug reports for a trial application, such as a 100–function point enhancement that uses both inspections and testing.

2. Record the effort, schedule, costs, and number of bug reports for a similar trial application that does not use inspections, but uses only testing.

Although results will vary, the inspection trials will usually end up with about 15 percent shorter schedules, 20 percent less effort, and perhaps 200 percent more bugs eliminated prior to release of the application. The front end of the inspection trials will take longer and cost more, but when testing begins it won't even be a contest: The inspected portions will usually exit testing in between one-third and one-fourth of the elapsed time, and with less than one-third of the effort devoted to bug repairs, as the uninspected portions.

Although formal design and code inspections originated more than 25 years ago, they still are the top-ranked methodologies in terms of defect-removal efficiency. Further, inspections have a synergistic relationship with other forms of defect removal, such as testing, and also are quite successful as defect-prevention methods.

Recent work on software inspections by Tom Gilb and his colleagues continues to support the early finding that the human mind remains the tool of choice for finding and eliminating complex problems that originate in requirements, design, and other noncode deliverables. Indeed, for finding the deeper problems in source code, formal code inspections still outrank testing in defect-removal efficiency.

The most effective usage of formal inspections among SPR's clients occurs among large corporations that produce systems software, such as computer manufacturers, telecommunication system manufacturers, aerospace equipment manufacturers, and the like. These companies have learned that if software is going to control complex physical devices it has to have state-of-the-art quality levels, and only inspections can achieve the necessary quality.

Most forms of testing are less than 30 percent efficient in finding errors or bugs. The measured defect-removal efficiency of both formal design inspections and formal code inspections is sometimes more than 60 percent efficient, or twice as efficient as most forms of testing.

Tom Gilb, one of the more prominent authors dealing with inspections, reports that some inspection efficiencies have been recorded that are as high as 88 percent. So far as can be determined, this level of efficiency would be a world record that is never even approached by testing, with the possible exception of high-volume Beta testing involving more than 10,000 simultaneous Beta test sites.

A combination of formal inspections, formal testing by test specialists, and a formal (and active) quality-assurance group are the methods which are most often associated with projects achieving a cumulative defect-removal efficiency higher than 99 percent.

Formal inspections are manual activities in which three to eight colleagues go over design specifications page by page, using a formal protocol. In order to term this activity an *inspection* certain criteria must be met, including but not limited to the following:

- There must be adequate preparation time before each session.
- Records must be kept of the defects discovered.
- Defect data should not be used for appraisals or punitive purposes.

The original concept of inspections was based on actual meetings with live participants. The advent of effective online communications and tools for supporting remote inspections, such as the Honeywell Bull system, now means that inspections can be performed electronically, which saves on travel costs for teams that are geographically dispersed.

Any software deliverable can be subject to a formal inspection, and the following deliverables have now developed enough empirical data to indicate that the inspection process is generally beneficial:

- Architecture inspections
- Requirements inspections
- Design inspections
- Database design inspections
- Code inspections
- Test plan inspections
- Test case inspections
- User documentation inspections

For every software artifact where formal inspections are used, they range from just under 50 percent to more than 80 percent in defect-removal efficiency and have an average efficiency level of roughly 60 percent. Overall, this is the best defect-removal efficiency level of any known form of error elimination.

Further, thanks to the flexibility of the human mind and its ability to handle inductive logic as well as deductive logic, inspections are also the most versatile form of defect removal and can be applied to essentially any software artifact. Indeed, inspections have even been applied recursively to themselves, in order to fine-tune the inspection process and eliminate bottlenecks and obstacles.

It is sometimes asked why everyone doesn't use inspections if they are so good. The answer to this question reveals a basic weakness of the software industry. Inspections have been in the public domain for more than 25 years. Therefore, except for a few training companies, no company tries to *sell* inspections, while there are many vendors selling testing tools. If you want to use inspections, you have to seek them out and adopt them.

Most software development organizations don't actually do research or collect data on effective tools and technologies. They make their technology decisions, to a large degree, by listening to tool and methodology vendors and adopting those represented by the most persuasive sales personnel. Since there is comparatively little money to be made in selling inspections, sales personnel tend to concentrate on things like testing tools where the commissions are greater.

It is even easier if the sales personnel make the tool or method sound like a "silver bullet" that will give miraculous results immediately upon deployment with little or no training, preparation, or additional effort. Since inspections are not sold by tool vendors and do require training and effort they are not a glamorous technology. Hence, many software organizations don't even know about inspections and have no idea of their versatility and effectiveness.

The companies that are most likely to use inspections are those that for historical or business reasons have some kind of research capability that looks for *best practices* and tries to adopt them.

It is a telling point that all of the top-gun quality software houses, and even industries, in the United States tend to utilize pretest inspections. For example, formal inspections are very common among computer manufacturers, telecommunication systems manufacturers, aerospace equipment manufacturers, defense systems manufacturers, medical instrument manufacturers, and systems software and operating systems developers. All of these need high-quality software to market their main products, and inspections top the list of effective defect-removal methods.

One of the most effective ways of illustrating the effectiveness of formal inspections is to produce graphs that connect the points where software defects are *discovered* with the points in software development where the defects *originate*.

Whenever there is an acute angle in the line connecting a defect's discovery and origin points, there is a serious problem with software quality control, because the gap between making an error and finding it can amount to many months.

The goal of defect removal is to have the angle connecting defect origins and discoveries approach 90 degrees. Although a 90-degree angle is unlikely, formal inspections can at least bring the angle up from perhaps 30 degrees to more than 60 degrees (see Figs. 20.1 and 20.2).

As can easily be seen in Fig. 20.1, software projects that do not utilize formal inspections enter a *zone of chaos* during the test cycle. This is because deep problems with requirements and specifications suddenly emerge that require extensive and expensive repair and rework.

Note in Fig. 20.2 how the lines connecting the discovery points of defects with their origins have obtuse angles. Even more important, note how defects that originate within a phase tend to be eliminated during that phase, and do not pass on to downstream activities.

Normal Defect Origin/Discovery Gaps

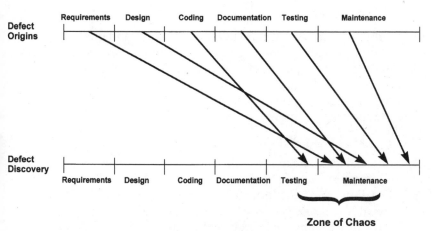

Figure 20.1   Defect origins and discovery points without usage of formal inspections.

Defect Origins/Discovery With Inspections

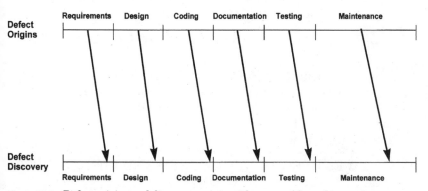

Figure 20.2   Defect origins and discovery points with usage of formal inspections.

There are enough users of software inspections and reviews that they have formed a nonprofit organization called the Software Inspection and Review Organization (SIRO). The SIRO mailing address follows:

Software Inspection and Review Organization (SIRO)
P.O. Box 61015
Sunnyvale, CA 94088-1015

Some of the adjustment factors for dealing with software design inspections include the following set:

PROJECT GOALS   _____

1 Find the standard estimate of schedule, staff, and quality.
2 Find the shortest development schedule with extra staff.
3 Find the lowest effort with reduced staff.
4 Find the highest quality with normal staff.
5 Find the highest quality with shortest schedule.
6 Find the highest quality with least effort.

PROBLEM COMPLEXITY   _____

1 Simple algorithms and simple calculations.
2 Majority are simple algorithms and calculations.
3 Algorithms and calculations are of average complexity.
4 Some difficult or complex calculations.
5 Many difficult and complex calculations.

DATA COMPLEXITY   _____

1 Simple data, few variables, and little complexity.
2 Several data elements, but simple data relationships.
3 Multiple files, switches, and data interactions.
4 Complex data elements and complex data interactions.
5 Very complex data elements and data interactions.

DEVELOPMENT PERSONNEL APPLICATION EXPERIENCE

       _____

1 All are experts in the type of program being developed.
2 Majority are experts, but some are new hires or novices.
3 Even mixture of experts, new hires, and novices.
4 Majority are new hires or novices, with few experts.
5 All personnel are new to this kind of program.

DEVELOPMENT PERSONNEL ANALYSIS AND DESIGN EXPERI-
ENCE   _____

1 All are experts in analysis and design methods.
2 Majority are experts in analysis and design methods.
3 Even mixture of experts, new hires, and novices.
4 Majority are new hires or novices in analysis and design.
5 All personnel are inexperienced in analysis and design.

PRETEST DEFECT-REMOVAL EXPERIENCE   _____

1 All personnel are experienced in reviews/inspections.
2 Most personnel are experienced in reviews/inspections.

3 Even mixture of experienced and inexperienced personnel.
4 Most personnel are inexperienced in reviews/inspections.
5 All personnel are inexperienced in reviews/inspections.

USER PERSONNEL EXPERIENCE WITH SOFTWARE PROJECTS

1 User experience with software is not a key factor.
2 All or a majority of users have software experience.
3 Even mixture of experts and inexperienced users.
4 Majority of users have no prior software experience.
5 All personnel have no prior software experience.

USER PERSONNEL EXPERIENCE WITH APPLICATION TYPE

1 User expertise is not a major factor for the project.
2 All or a strong majority of users are experts.
3 Even mixture of experts, new hires, and novices.
4 Majority are new hires and novices, with few experts.
5 All personnel are new to this kind of program.

USER INVOLVEMENT DURING REQUIREMENTS

1 User involvement is not a major factor for this project.
2 Users are heavily involved during requirements.
3 Users are somewhat involved during requirements.
4 Users are seldom involved during requirements.
5 Users are not involved during requirements.

USER INVOLVEMENT DURING DESIGN REVIEWS

1 User involvement is not a major factor for the project.
2 Users are heavily involved during design reviews.
3 Users are somewhat involved during design reviews.
4 Users are seldom involved during design reviews.
5 Users are not involved during design reviews.

Both in real life and in software cost estimating, the combination of having quality as a key project goal, keeping complexity low, and having experienced users and experienced team members pays off in lower costs, quicker schedules, and higher quality than result through the opposite situations.

Formal design and code inspections are fairly major discriminators between best-in-class organizations and the rest of the software industry. The really good groups tend to use inspections because nothing else can find so many bugs or errors, nor find so many deep and subtle problems, as the human mind.

References

Dunn, Robert, and Richard Ullman: *Quality Assurance for Computer Software,* McGraw-Hill, New York, ISBN 0-07-018312-0, 1982.

Fagan, M. E.: "Design and Code Inspections to Reduce Errors in Program Development," *IBM Systems Journal,* **12**(3):219–248 (1976).

Friedman, Daniel P., and Gerald M. Weinberg: *Handbook of Walkthroughs, Inspections, and Technical Reviews,* Dorset House Press, New York, ISBN 0-932633-19-6, 1990.

Gilb, Tom, and D. Graham: *Software Inspections,* Addison-Wesley, Reading, Mass., 1993.

Jones, Capers: *Assessment and Control of Software Risks,* Prentice Hall, Englewood Cliffs, N.J., ISBN 0-13-741406-4, 1994.

———: *Patterns of Software System Failure and Success,* International Thomson Computer Press, Boston, Mass., ISBN 1-850-32804-8, 1995.

———: *Software Quality—Analysis and Guidelines for Success,* International Thomson Computer Press, Boston, ISBN 1-85032-867-6, 1997.

Putnam, Lawrence H.: *Measures for Excellence—Reliable Software on Time, Within Budget,* Yourdon Press/Prentice Hall, Englewood Cliffs, N.J., ISBN 0-13-567694-0, 1992.

———, and Ware Myers: *Industrial Strength Software—Effective Management Using Measurement,* IEEE Computer Society Press, Washington D.C., ISBN 0-8186-7532-2, 1997.

Rubin, Howard: *Software Benchmark Studies for 1997,* Howard Rubin Associates, Pound Ridge, N.Y., 1997.

Estimating Programming or Coding

For small to medium software projects, estimating the coding effort is the oldest and most important single aspect of cost estimation. Surprisingly for such a critical activity, there is a shortage of solid empirical data on this key task. There is no shortage of estimating tools, however. At least 75 commercial estimating tools can handle estimates for coding, and when private estimation tools and rules of thumb are considered, the total number of code estimating approaches no doubt tops 250.

There are at least 500 programming languages in use as this book is being written, and each language has at least two books in print, although some popular languages, such as Visual Basic, C, and COBOL, have more than 25 books in print. The total number of books in print that deal with programming in various languages tops 1000 titles, and several new books appear every month.

However, books that contain quantitative information on programming productivity are few in number. Some of the works that do quantify programming productivity include Barry Boehm's *Software Engineering Economics* (Boehm 1981), Tom DeMarco and Tim Lister's *Peopleware* (DeMarco and Lister 1987), Larry Putnam and Ware Myer's *Industrial Strength Software* (Putnam and Myers 1997), Howard Rubin's annual benchmark studies (Rubin 1997), and the author's own books (Jones 1981, 1986, 1996). Watts Humphrey's *Personal Software Process* (Humphrey 1997) also provides extensive quantification of software programming performance.

What is more surprising than the large number of books is the fact that brand-new programming languages continue to appear at frequent intervals. The author and his colleagues at Software Productivity Research monitor the appearance of new programming languages so they can be added to SPR's master list of programming languages. At least one new programming language, or a new dialect, has appeared every month for the past 10 years, and some months more than one new language shows up.

The frequent appearance of new programming languages presents a continuous challenge to the developers of software-estimating tools, because when a new language first appears there is usually no available data on the use of the language, so evaluating its impact in an estimating context is quite difficult.

Even though there are hundreds of programming languages, millions of programmers, and millions of software applications, only a few controlled studies have been performed. Also, many of the benchmarking comparisons do not reach the level of specific activities, such as coding, but include the whole universe of software activities, such as requirements, design, coding, testing, and so forth.

When controlled studies of programming are performed, they usually reveal that programmers can code at more or less the same rates in almost every language they are familiar with, but they vary widely in individual capabilities. However, most controlled studies are based on small and simple examples that can be completed in a matter of hours at most.

There are annual contests of programming speed where various contestants utilize different languages to code the same trial application. These contests are interesting, but the trial examples are not necessarily representative of how a language will perform in real-life situations.

In real-life situations where programmers are working on very large applications that may have creeping requirements, and where they need to interact with many other programmers who are all working on the same system, production rates are much lower than for small projects or projects where one person can handle the entire programming assignment.

The nominal default values for estimating coding or programming include those shown in Table 21.1.

Although the set of default values given in Table 21.1 are useful, the range of programming performance is very wide and can range to more than 100 percent greater, or more than 75 percent worse, than the starting default values.

From SPR's analysis and benchmarks at the level of specific activities, the major factors that influence coding rates are the 12 listed in Table 21.2, in descending order of overall significance.

TABLE 21.1   Nominal Default Values for Programming or Coding

Activity sequence	Fifth
Performed by	Development staff
Predecessor activities	Prototypes, design, and specification
Overlap	75% with design and specification
Concurrent activities	Design and unit testing
Successor activities	Function testing; integration testing
Reuse	15% from prior or similar projects
Assignment scope	175 function points
Assignment scope	17,500 logical source code statements
Production rate	25 function points per staff month
Production rate	5.28 work hours per function point
Production rate	2,500 source code statements per month
Production rate	20 source code statements per work hour
Schedule months	Application code size divided by production rate
Rate of creep or change	Identical to requirements (about 2% per month)
Defect potential	1.75 coding defects per function point
Defect potential	17.5 coding bugs per KLOC
Defect removal	90% average removal efficiency
Delivered defects	0.175 coding defects per function point
Delivered defects	0.175 defects per KLOC
High severity defects	15% of delivered defects
Bad fix probability	7% of coding defect fixes may yield new errors

TABLE 21.2   Twelve Factors That Influence Programming Productivity

1. The availability of reusable code
2. The experience of the programming team
3. The number of bugs or errors introduced
4. The amount of unpaid overtime applied
5. The rate at which requirements change or creep during coding
6. The structure or complexity of the application
7. The number of unplanned workday interruptions
8. The size of the application
9. The size and noise level of the programming office space
10. The features of the programming languages used
11. The power of the programming tools available
12. Schedule pressure applied to the team

Adding to the difficulty of estimating programming performance, the ranking of factors that influence programming in a positive or beneficial direction is not exactly the same as the ranking of factors that influence programming a negative or harmful direction.

Tables 21.3 and 21.4 illustrate the ranges of *maximum* impact in both positive and negative directions. The first ranking is sorted in descending order of the factors that can influence programming productivity in a positive direction, with the availability of reusable code now moving above team experience in terms of maximum positive value. (In Dr. Barry Boehm's previous study of influential factors, reported in his 1981 book *Software Engineering Economics,* team experience was the dominant factor. However, software reuse was not a well-known technology in 1981.)

By contrast, Table 21.4 gives the same factors, but ranks them in terms of the maximum negative impacts that can degrade software productivity, with bugs and errors topping the list, followed fairly closely by the impact of creeping user requirements.

In any real-life software project, the positive and negative factors will be present simultaneously, and because the overall impact in both positive and negative directions is roughly equivalent, the net result often approximates average values for programming productivity.

However, for projects where either positive factors or negative factors are dominant, the net results can be either much better than average values or much worse than average values, depending upon which sets of factors predominate.

The fact that both positive and negative factors may be present in unequal amounts explains why it is necessary to be totally honest when using software cost estimating tools. If you are not truthful and indicate to the estimating tool that your team is more experienced or better equipped than they really are, then the estimating tool will generate a much better than average cost estimate but your team may not be better than average in real life.

It is obvious that to achieve really good programming results, enterprises should strive to maximize the positive influential factors and minimize the negative influential factors.

As might be expected, experienced programmers can outperform novices by several hundred percent. However, even very experienced programmers have to deal with changing requirements, schedule pressures, and the fact that bugs or errors are very easy to make but often are hard to eliminate.

Table 21.5 summarizes an overall picture of the coding activity from 1 source code statement through major systems of 100 million source code statements in order to illustrate some of the trends associated with increasing application sizes.

TABLE 21.3   Maximum Impacts of 12 Programming Factors
(Ranked in terms of maximum positive impact)

Factor	Maximum negative impact, %	Maximum positive impact, %
Reusable code	−50	300
Team experience	−115	150
Bugs or errors	−175	100
Unpaid overtime	−30	75
Requirements creep	−125	50
Unplanned interruptions	−100	40
Code complexity	−65	35
Size of the application	−50	35
Programming office space	−55	25
Programming tools	−40	30
Programming languages	−30	25
Schedule pressure	−50	20
Total	−885	885

TABLE 21.4   Maximum Impacts of 12 Programming Factors
(Ranked in terms of maximum negative impact)

Factor	Maximum negative impact, %	Maximum positive impact, %
Bugs or errors	−175	100
Requirements creep	−125	50
Team experience	−115	150
Unplanned interruptions	−100	40
Code complexity	−65	35
Programming office space	−55	25
Reusable code	−50	300
Size of the application	−50	35
Schedule pressure	−50	20
Programming tools	−40	30
Unpaid overtime	−30	75
Programming language(s)	−30	25
Total	−885	885

TABLE 21.5   General Programming Productivity and Defect Rates
(Size data expressed in logical source code statements)

Size, LOC	A scope, LOC	P rate, LOC	Staff	Effort months	Schedule months	Coding defects	Defect removal	Delivered defects
1	1	2,500	1	0.0004	0.0004	0	99	0
10	10	2,500	1	0.0040	0.0040	0	99	0
100	100	2,500	1	0.0400	0.0400	1	99	0
1,000	1,000	2,250	1	0.4444	0.4444	10	98	0
10,000	10,000	2,000	1	5.0000	5.0000	125	96	5
100,000	20,000	1,750	5	57.1429	11.4286	1,500	95	75
1,000,000	25,000	1,500	40	666.6667	16.6667	17,500	94	1,050
10,000,000	30,000	1,200	333	8,333.3333	25.0000	200,000	92	16,000
100,000,000	35,000	1,000	2,857	100,000.0000	35.0000	2,500,000	90	250,000

Recall that the term *assignment scope* (A scope) refers to the amount of work assigned to one person.

The term *production rate* (P rate) refers to the amount of work that one person can do in a standard time period, such as a work month.

Below about 15,000 source code statements, the entire programming task is usually assigned to one person. The table assumes that the programmer will work full-time, but below about 1000 source code statements programmers often work part-time on any single project, because they are dividing their time among several small projects.

Above 15,000 source code statements, the coding activity usually involves multiple programmers, although SPR's data contains examples of projects of up to 75,000 source code statements carried out by only 1 programmer. When multiple programmers are involved, problems begin to occur with the interfaces between the work of separate programmers.

For the larger application sizes in excess of 100,000 source code statements, a number of factors tend to come into play simultaneously. First, because these large systems are often complicated and involve fairly large teams, defect rates begin to escalate (as do creeping requirements).

When defect rates go up, the amount of time that programmers spend debugging must also increase, which, in turn, means that coding productivity must decline as more and more time goes to finding and fixing bugs and, in particular, to interface problems. Not only do defect levels rise, but it becomes harder to remove defects, so removal efficiency suffers. Also, programmers must devote a higher percentage of their time to meetings with other programmers and to making revisions in response to changing requirements.

Because of client and executive demands for fairly short coding schedules, organizations tend to raise the numbers of programmers assigned to a project, which, in turn, increases the complexity and defect levels associated with interfaces.

However, for really large systems above 1 million source code statements, a new problem exists: Keeping the programming assignment scope low (<15,000 source code statements) is not usually possible because literally thousands of programmers would be needed on the application. Therefore, at the high end of the size spectrum, the programming assignment scopes begin to stretch out because of the fact that most organizations do not employ enough programmers to have any other choice!

Even if the enterprise had unlimited resources and could assign 10,000 programmers to a large system, that would not necessarily lead to satisfactory results. Such large teams would probably have to devote half of the workday to meetings and communication, and perhaps another quarter to finding and fixing bugs or dealing with changing requirements.

As can be seen, the needs of really large systems tend to be conflicting, and it is hard to reach an optimal point. Wealthy corporations, such as Microsoft, can approach optimization because of their ability to attract and keep only top-gun programming personnel. This allows Microsoft to have very large assignment scopes (sometimes in excess of 50,000 source code statements) and, hence, keep team sizes within reasonable bounds. However, for applications the size of Windows 95 and Windows NT (in the range of 11 million source code statements) even Microsoft has trouble with schedules and with quality levels.

Coding is the only software development activity for which the older lines-of-code metric can be used without undue error and distortion. Table 21.5 uses *logical source code statements* as the basis of the productivity data. This form of the LOC metric is more stable than the use of *physical lines of code* because of the distressing tendency of physical code counts to include blank lines, comments, and dead code.

The same information can also be expressed in terms of function points, with the caveat that each language will have a more or less unique ratio of source code statements to function points. For example, COBOL averages about 106.7 logical source code statements per function point, using the procedure and data divisions as the base. Table 21.6 shows the same information, only using function points.

Although the first three columns are different when using function points, the remaining columns of Tables 21.5 and 21.6 are identical. This should not be unexpected. For example, the costs and effort of building a home will be the same whether the area is measured in square feet or square meters. Changing the metric between square

TABLE 21.6   General Programming Productivity and Defect Rates
(Size data expressed in function points for COBOL applications)

Size, FP	A scope, FP	P rate, FP	Staff	Effort months	Schedule months	Coding defects	Defect removal, %	Delivered defects
0.01	0.01	23.36	1	0.0004	0.0004	0	99	0
0.09	0.09	23.36	1	0.0040	0.0040	0	99	0
0.93	0.93	23.36	1	0.0400	0.0400	0	99	0
9.35	9.35	21.03	1	0.4444	0.4444	0	98	0
93.46	93.46	18.69	1	5.0000	5.0000	1	96	0
934.58	186.92	16.36	5	57.1429	11.4286	14	95	1
9,345.79	233.64	14.02	40	666.6667	16.6667	164	94	10
93,457.94	280.37	11.21	333	8,333.3333	25.0000	1,869	92	150
934,579.44	327.10	9.35	2,857	100,000.0000	35.0000	23,364	90	2,336

feet and square meters does not change the actual cost of construction in the slightest.

Let us consider the implications of the 12 factors on estimating the work of coding individually, and then in groups or patterns that occur frequently.

The Impact of Reusability on Programming

Informal and personal reuse of source code have been part of the programming occupation since it began. In recent years, the topic of reusability has been elevated to a formal discipline. Some enterprises have established internal libraries of reusable source code. In addition, there is a growing business of marketing reusable code for some programming languages, with Visual Basic, JAVA, Netron CAP, and various object-oriented languages, such as Smalltalk and Objective C, leading the set of languages where reusable routines can be acquired from commercial vendors.

The most recent trend in software reuse is to acquire reusable assets for applications written in JAVA from the Internet and the World Wide Web. Table 21.7, illustrates both *private* and *commercial* reuse for a sampling of common programming languages.

The column labeled "Private reuse" refers to several different forms of software reuse, including personal reuse by individual programmers and shared reuse within the same company, where no fees or charges are levied.

The column labeled "Commercial reuse" also refers to several different forms of software reuse, including purchasing reusable materials

TABLE 21.7   Software Reuse by Language

(Percentage)

Language	Private reuse	Commercial reuse	Total reuse
Visual Basic	30.00	50.00	80.00
JAVA	40.00	30.00	70.00
Netron CAP	30.00	40.00	70.00
Objective C	25.00	30.00	55.00
Smalltalk	30.00	25.00	55.00
Eiffel	25.00	25.00	50.00
Forte	25.00	25.00	50.00
Ada 83	20.00	25.00	45.00
Ada 95	20.00	25.00	45.00
ABAP/4	20.00	25.00	45.00
C++	30.00	15.00	45.00
Macro assembly	20.00	20.00	40.00
COBOL	30.00	10.00	40.00
FORTRAN	15.00	20.00	35.00
C	20.00	10.00	30.00
Quick Basic	15.00	15.00	30.00
Pascal	20.00	5.00	25.00
RPG	20.00	5.00	25.00
SQL	20.00	1.00	21.00
CMS2	15.00	5.00	20.00
Jovial	15.00	5.00	20.00
Algol	15.00	5.00	20.00
Modula II	15.00	1.00	16.00
Basic assembly	5.00	10.00	15.00
PL/I	10.00	5.00	15.00
CHILL	12.50	0.10	12.60
CORAL	12.50	0.10	12.60
Average	20.56	16.01	36.56

from commercial vendors or downloading them from the World Wide Web in the form of shareware or freeware.

Note that the column labeled "Total reuse" indicates the *maximum* amount of an application that could be constructed from reusable materials. This does not imply averages or indicate day-to-day reuse in ordinary applications.

Furthermore, in order for code reuse to be beneficial, the reused code needs to be certified as being approximately zero-defect level. It is hazardous in the extreme to attempt to reuse uncertified material, which may contain serious bugs or even viruses. Either of these situations would damage the application and degrade productivity to unacceptable levels.

The availability of high-quality reusable code modules is now the major positive factor that can influence software coding productivity, ranking even above team experience. However, attempts to reuse code that is buggy and filled with errors can exert a significant impact that degrades or reduces productivity. Reuse is only effective for high-quality deliverables, and is hazardous and uneconomical in the presence of excessive defect levels.

The Impact of Experience on Programming

The word *experience* is multifaceted and can apply to several dimensions. The best results occur when the programmers are experienced in the following topics:

- The application type
- The programming language
- The programming tools or environment

Programmers who, for example, are working on a familiar kind of application in a language they know well are very likely to make few mistakes, and are also likely to have reusable materials available.

Conversely, programmers working on novel kinds of applications, using a programming language with which they have limited experience, and using new tools tend to make quite a few mistakes, which will degrade their overall performance.

The Impact of Bugs or Errors on Programming

Computer programming is an exacting discipline which is much more difficult than writing text. To make an analogy with text, the only form of writing that needs as much precision as computer programming is the writing of medical prescriptions by a physician. In both computer programming and prescriptions, errors involving only a single word can, at least potentially, be fatal.

If it were not for the enormous numbers of bugs or errors that might occur, writing a computer program would be a much easier occupation and productivity levels would be at least twice as high as they actually are.

Designers of programming languages have not always been successful in developing language syntax and notations that can minimize the natural human tendency to make errors. In general, languages with regular syntax, minimal use of complex symbols, and built-in features for dealing with memory utilization have lower levels of bugs than do more arcane languages. Also, the built-in debugging facilities of the compilers, interpreters, and supporting environments can also affect the bug totals.

Table 21.8 illustrates the ranges of coding bugs typically encountered

TABLE 21.8   Programming Bug Patterns by Language
(Coding and syntax bugs only)

Language	Bugs or errors per KLOC	Bugs or errors per FP
Ada 95	9.00	0.50
Ada 83	9.50	0.67
Netron CAP	10.00	0.19
Eiffel	10.00	0.21
Forte	10.00	0.18
Visual Basic	10.50	0.21
Objective C	11.00	0.19
Smalltalk	11.00	0.14
Modula II	12.00	0.84
JAVA	12.50	0.50
ABAP/4	13.00	0.21
Pascal	13.00	1.18
SQL	13.50	0.18
COBOL	14.00	1.50
RPG	14.50	0.54
CMS2	15.00	1.58
Jovial	15.00	1.59
C++	15.50	0.82
FORTRAN	16.00	1.68
Algol	16.00	1.71
PL/I	16.00	1.30
Quick Basic	17.00	1.11
CHILL	17.50	1.87
CORAL	19.50	2.09
C	20.00	2.50
Macro assembly	23.50	5.01
Basic assembly	29.00	9.28
Average	14.57	1.40

in a sample of programming languages, using both *defects per 1000 lines of code* (KLOC) and *defects per function point* (FP) as the metrics.

Individual programmers' knowledge of the language, experience, schedule pressures, and other factors can cause variations of more than 3 to 1 about these average values for each language shown.

The high bug levels for some of the languages, such as C and assembly language, explains why programmers may spend more time and effort on debugging than on actually coding. Bug removal is a major component of software costs, and the bugs that are not removed are a major component of downstream maintenance costs after the release of the software to clients and users.

Overall, the effort and costs required to remove bugs constitute the major cost driver of the programming occupation. There can be no serious or significant productivity gains for software projects without reducing the numbers of bugs that must be removed or maximizing the speed with which bugs are removed.

The Impact of Unpaid Overtime on Programming

The software occupation is very labor intensive and, hence, is extraordinarily sensitive to work habits and the use or absence of overtime, and particularly of unpaid overtime. In the United States, the great majority of software technical workers, including programmers of various kinds, are termed *exempt,* which means they are classed as salaried employees who are legally exempt from receiving paid overtime if they work late or on weekends. The opposite term is *nonexempt,* used by the Bureau of Labor Statistics to classify hourly employees who must receive overtime pay for all work over and above their normal shifts.

Long hours with massive doses of unpaid overtime is more or less a normal cultural phenomenon in the software industry. If you drive by major software companies, such as Microsoft, at night or on weekends you will find most of the lights on, many cars in the parking lot, and more or less continuous activity every day of the week.

The impact of unpaid overtime is important and adds quite a bit of complexity to the tasks of estimation and software measurement. The main impact of unpaid overtime is that it decouples the *cost* of coding from the *effort* devoted to coding.

Table 21.9 presents two different scenarios, with one scenario showing programming effort using only 80 percent of the available monthly work hours, while the other scenario assumes unpaid overtime, and, hence, utilizes 110 percent of the nominally available monthly work hours.

TABLE 21.9   Effects of Unpaid Overtime on Software Costs and Schedules

Activity	Work habits		Difference	Percentage
	Project 1, normal	Project 2, intense		
Size, FP	1,000	1,000	0	0.00
Size, LOC	100,000	100,000	0	0.00
LOC per FP	100	100	0	0.00
Reuse, %	0.00	0.00	0	0.00
A scope, FP	250	250	0	0.00
Nominal P rate, FP	25	25	0	0.00
Availability, %	80.00	110.00	30.00	37.50
Hours per month	128.00	176.00	48.00	37.50
Salary per month	$5,000.00	$5,000.00	$0.00	0.00
Programming staff	4.00	4.00	0.00	0.00
Effort months	50.00	36.36	−13.64	−27.27
Schedule months	15.63	8.26	−7.36	−47.11
Cost	$250,000	$181,818	−$68,182	−27.27
Cost per FP	$250.00	$181.82	−$68.18	−27.27
Work hours per FP	6.40	6.40	0.00	0.00
Virtual P rate, FP	20.00	27.50	7.50	37.50
Cost per LOC	$2.50	$1.82	−$0.68	−27.27
LOC per month	2000	2750	750	37.50

As can be seen, although the actual work hours are the same in both columns, the costs for the application and the apparent productivity expressed in monthly form clearly favors the *intense* column with unpaid overtime.

In the Project 1 column, the "leisurely" rate of 128 hours per month times 50 calendar months totals 6400 work hours.

For the Project 2 column, the intense rate of 176 hours per month times 36.36 calendar months also totals 6400 work hours.

There is no difference in the absolute number of work hours needed between the two versions, but there is a very significant difference in the costs and schedules, because much of the work consists of unpaid overtime in the *intense* example.

Because programmers, for the most part, are treated as salaried professionals who are paid on a monthly rather than an hourly basis, the impact of unpaid overtime creates a major split between productivity measured using *hours of effort* and productivity measured using *costs*.

Unpaid overtime also introduces anomalies in apparent monthly productivity, because projects will require fewer months if unpaid overtime is significant. For example, assume that a 50–function point, 5000–code statement programming project requires 320 hours of programming time.

Assuming standard 8-hour workdays, the project would normally require 2 calendar months. Assuming 2 calendar months, the productivity for this project would be 25 function points per month, or 2500 lines of code per month. Expressed in hourly form, the project would proceed at a rate of 6.4 work hours per function point or 15.6 LOC per work hour. Assuming that the programmer is paid $5,000 per month, the total cost amounts to $10,000. Hence, the project has a cost of $200 per function point or $0.50 per line of code.

Now assume that the programmer who does the project works Saturdays and Sundays plus evening overtime, and finishes the project in 1 calendar month even though it still requires 320 hours of programming.

Under this alternate scenario with 50 percent unpaid overtime, the apparent monthly productivity has doubled to 5000 lines of code or 50 function points per month. However, because the project still takes 320 hours, the actual effort is still 6.4 work hours per function point and 15.6 LOC per work hour.

The cost structure has changed dramatically: Now the project only costs $5000 because the overtime is not paid for, so the apparent cost of the project has dropped to $100 per function point and only $0.25 per LOC.

As can be seen, the presence of massive quantities of unpaid overtime exerts a very tricky impact on productivity studies and also needs to be carefully included in software cost estimating assumptions. Most software cost estimating tools provide default values for paid and unpaid overtime assumptions, and also allow users both to override these defaults and to specify such factors as overtime premium payments if they exist.

The Impact of Creeping Requirements on Programming

One of the chronic problems of the software industry is the fact that programming requirements are seldom stable, and change during the development cycle. Indeed, the monthly rate of change after the requirements are first identified runs from 1 percent to more than 3 percent per month during the subsequent design and coding stages.

The major impact of creeping requirements on the task of programming is that making late additions to software tends to exert very negative impacts in terms of the following:

- Damaging the control-flow structure of the application
- Raising the cyclomatic and essential complexity of the applications
- Raising the number of coding defects
- Reducing the defect-removal efficiency
- Damaging long-range maintenance

The overall impact of creeping requirements has both a near-term and a long-term effect. In the near term, it makes it difficult to predict when the project will be done, and in the long term creeping requirements tend to degrade quality and elevate maintenance costs.

Incidentally, the rate at which requirements creep can be measured directly by calculating the function point total of the application at the end of requirements, and then keeping track of the change in function point volumes for every new feature that the clients demand. This use of function points is now showing up in outsourcing contracts, where costs are expressed in terms of cost per function point.

In contracts, there is often a sliding scale so that the original set of function points might be constructed for a fixed cost, such as $500 per function point. But new requirements added later would have elevated costs, such as $750 per function point for requirements added more than 6 months later.

The Impact of Code Structure and Complexity on Programming

It has been known for more than 30 years that the structure of a software application exerts a major impact on every important software result, including the following:

- Defect levels
- Defect-removal efficiency
- Productivity
- Schedules
- Maintenance
- Reliability

In spite of the fact that well-structured applications are beneficial and poorly structured applications are harmful, structural deficiencies are endemic in the software world. An exact statistical distribution of structural problems has not been published, but among SPR's clients complex structures with hazardous control-flow patterns occurs in more than 50 percent of larger applications of 10,000 source code statements and above.

The reasons for this unfortunate situation can be traced to several interrelated factors:

- Excessive schedule pressure
- Misguided attempts to improve execution speed
- Misguided attempts to conserve space
- Misguided attempts by programmers to do clever things
- Lack of training in structured programming

Software code complexity can be measured directly using a number of commercial or even shareware and freeware tools. The two most common metrics for source code structure are *cyclomatic complexity* and *essential complexity*. Both measure the numbers of branches and the control flow through source code.

In general, programming productivity declines as complexity goes up. Since cyclomatic and essential complexity are measured in integer values, optimum programming productivity tends to occur when cyclomatic and essential complexity levels are close to 1, and in any case stay below 10, at the module level.

Conversely, high levels of cyclomatic and essential complexity, with values greater than 20, are often associated with excessive defect rates and reduced productivity.

There are some anomalies with this general rule, however. Sometimes applications with high levels of cyclomatic and essential complexity have higher productivity rates than similar applications with low complexity levels. When this situation occurs, it is usually because the low-complexity application has been assigned to novices, while the high-complexity application has been assigned to top-gun experts with a great deal of experience in similar applications.

The Impact of Unplanned Interruptions on Programming

Computer programming is a very labor intensive occupation; hence, it is best to allow programming personnel to work with few interruptions, and especially with very few unplanned interruptions.

One of the most frequent and damaging forms of interruption occurs in situations where programmers are performing both development and maintenance tasks at the same time. Often maintenance is driven by the unexpected discovery and reporting of bugs, and sometimes the bugs are very severe and need immediate repairs.

In this kind of situation, development work must be suspended while the programmer attempts to repair the bugs. Since development work is often under schedule pressure, the programmers are anxious to get back to it and may be careless when fixing bugs, hence raising the possibility of a *bad fix,* or a new bug resulting from attempts to fix a prior bug.

Obviously, it is very difficult to estimate development for a programming team that is time-slicing between maintenance and development work, where the maintenance portion is subject to random unplanned bug reports.

The mutual interference of development programming and maintenance programming is significant enough that most top software companies divide the tasks in two and establish full-time maintenance departments. By separating maintenance from development, the performance of both sides will improve, and estimating is a great deal easier.

Also see the section on the impact of office space on programming, because having programmers share offices can lead to very disruptive unplanned interruptions.

The Impact of Application Size on Programming

The amount of code that is normally assigned to one programmer is called the *assignment scope.* Typical ranges of programming assignments on large projects run from about 10,000 statements up to about 50,000 statements.

The determining factors for programming assignment scopes include the skill levels of the programmers and the schedule pressure for completing the project. In theory it would be possible to assign 1 programmer the coding of a 100,000 statement application, but it might take more than 3 calendar years to complete the code.

It would be more common to divide the 100,000 statement application up among 4 or 5 programmers in order to reduce the elapsed time. For example, 4 programmers might complete the project in less than 15 calendar months, while 5 programmers could finish up in perhaps 12 calendar months.

However, as the number of programmers increases the number of interfaces between their components or modules also increases.

Complex interfaces mean more bugs and more time spent on meetings and communication in order to deal with the transfer of information across the interfaces. These interfaces are notoriously troublesome, so defect levels will also increase, and, hence, productivity and quality will decline.

The Impact of Office Space and Ergonomics on Programming

One very significant factor that has a surprisingly strong influence on programming productivity is that of the size, noise level, and ergonomic layout of the programmers' office space. This topic is often ignored and is underreported in the software literature, although there are a few truly excellent studies on programming office environments.

In the mid-1970s when software was becoming a major industry, the IBM corporation built a number of new programming laboratories. One of these labs, the Santa Teresa lab located in the foothills of the coast range in San Jose, California, was intended to be an IBM showpiece for software excellence. This was a major software location, which was originally planned for about 2000 software professionals.

The architect selected to design this lab was Dr. Gerald McCue, the Dean of Architecture at Harvard University (McCue 1978). Dr. McCue and the IBM team working with him interviewed several hundred software developers about what they regarded as an optimal office arrangement, and then the Santa Teresa programming laboratory was constructed in response to their expressed requirements.

The IBM Santa Teresa programming laboratory won a number of architectural awards and featured many interesting innovations, such as using the excess heat from the computer rooms for heating the office space. However, the most notable feature of the Santa Teresa programming laboratory was the fact that every programmer was able to have a full private office that was 10 feet by 10 feet in size, or 100 square feet overall.

The rationale for giving all programmers private offices is based on the typical work patterns of the programming occupation. For at least 75 percent of a typical business day, programmers need to concentrate on programming; hence, interruptions and noise should be minimized or eliminated.

The other 25 percent of the day, programmers need to communicate and coordinate with their peers if they are working on sizable projects that have other programmers involved. In order to deal with this situation, the Santa Teresa office complex featured small conference rooms for every department, and a scattering of larger conference rooms as well.

The overall impact of the Santa Teresa office complex was surprisingly positive. The same IBM programmers who had been working in shared cubicles at the adjacent San Jose and Palo Alto programming centers achieved productivity gains of about 11 percent after the first year of occupancy of Santa Teresa. This was not a case of a *Hawthorn complex,* or measurements themselves artificially introducing higher productivity rates. The IBM productivity measurement system had been in existence for some years, and was the same at Santa Teresa as everywhere else.

Another surprising effect of the Santa Teresa office complex was on morale. The annual opinion surveys carried out throughout IBM noted that the morale levels at the Santa Teresa office complex were the highest of any of IBM's 26 programming centers.

A more recent study of the impact of office environments on software productivity was published by Tom DeMarco and Tim Lister in their well-known book *Peopleware* (DeMarco and Lister 1987). Their study consisted of programming war games, in which more than 300 programmers took part. The programmers each wrote the same trial application in their own offices, using their own computers and tools, and using any programming language which they preferred.

After the data was collected, it was discovered that the size and the noise level of the programmer's office space actually seemed to have a stronger influence than almost any other variable, including the programming language used.

The programmers in the high quartile had more than 80 square feet of noise-free private office space, while those in the low quartile had less than about 44 square feet of rather noisy office space, such as open offices or cubicles with 2 to 3 programmers in the same space.

However, programmers' office space is not universally a factor in every country. For example, the impact of crowded office space is quite significant in the United States and Europe, but appears not to be a factor in Japan, where office space is quite expensive.

The Impact of Tools on Programming

Thirty years ago, when the author was a practicing programmer using assembly language, the only kinds of programming tools that were readily available were the assemblers themselves. Today, as this book is being written, programming tools are extremely sophisticated and growing more sophisticated each day. A full suite of programming support tools circa 1998 supports most of the software life cycle, and includes the following features:

- Assemblers
- Compilers
- Interpreters
- Software design tools
- Interface design tools

- Database design tools
- Reusability-support tools
- Reverse-engineering tools
- Reengineering tools
- Code restructuring tools
- Change management tools
- Code editors
- Standards-checking tools
- Complexity-analysis tools
- Bounds checkers
- Execution simulation tools
- Record/playback tools
- Debugging tools
- Defect-tracking tools
- Inspection-support tools
- Testing-support tools
- Groupware/communication support tools
- Viral protection tools
- Year-2000 search engines

Many of these individual tools are also marketed as integrated suites under the generic name of *computer aided software engineering* (CASE). While specific tool vendors vary widely in features, costs, and usefulness, the overall impact of programming-support tools is positive. Compared to programming in the 1970s, the sets of programming-support tools in the 1990s can greatly facilitate such key activities as design, debugging, and enabling software reuse.

The Impact of Programming Languages on Programming

It is something of a mystery to understand why the programming industry has managed to create more than 500 different programming languages and dialects of programming languages, but there are more than 500 languages in the master table of programming languages SPR uses with its commercial software cost estimating tools. (See the companion book *Applied Software Measurement* for the full list [Jones 1996a], or refer to SPR's Website for the master list: http://www.spr.com.)

Choosing a programming language is more of an art than a science, and many languages' supporters almost resemble members of a cult. However, when considering the various kinds of software that are programmed, certain patterns of language use emerge.

For information systems, programming languages that can deal with large volumes of data and have query facilities for databases are most common. Some of the languages widely used for information systems are the following:

- ABAP/4
- Algol
- +
- COBOL
- Eiffel
- Forte
- FORTRAN
- Macro assembly
- Magic
- Netron CAP
- Objective C
- PL/I
- RPG
- Smalltalk
- SQL
- Visual Basic

For systems software that controls physical devices, languages that can control hardware interrupts and that can generate very efficient and high-performance object code are preferred. Some of the systems software languages are the following:

- Ada 83
- Ada 95
- Basic assembly
- C
- +
- CHILL
- CORAL

- Objective C
- Macro assembly
- Modula II

For commercial software, languages that support maintenance and that can deal with adding new code over time are preferred. Some of the languages used for commercial software include the following:

- C
- +
- Objective C
- Pascal
- PL/I
- Smalltalk
- Visual Basic

For military software, languages designed for military purposes and endorsed by the Department of Defense and the military services are preferred. Some of the military software languages are the following:

- Ada 83
- Ada 95
- Assembly
- C
- +
- CMS2
- Jovial

For end-user applications, languages that are easy to use, support reuse, and have very powerful sets of programming tools and debugging features are preferred, even if the performance or memory utilization of the applications may not be optimal. Some of the languages used for end-user software include the following:

- Eiffel
- Pascal
- Quick Basic
- Realizer
- Smalltalk
- Visual Basic

However, these preferences for programming languages are not rigorous, and many programming languages can be used for multiple purposes.

The Impact of Schedule Pressure on Programming

The most common problem in the software industry for large systems is that of intense but artificial schedule pressure applied to the programmers by their managers, by senior executives in their companies, or by their clients.

Unfortunately, intense schedule pressure leads to carelessness, which in turn drives up the chances of making errors and introducing bugs. The overall impact of intense schedule pressure is not what is desired, but instead tends to lengthen schedules because the software does not work well enough to be released.

Look carefully at the assignment scopes and production rates shown in the tables in this chapter. If you know the size of a software application, and set schedules that are much shorter than those shown in the tables, you will have a very small chance of achieving the schedules and a very large chance of running late and over budget, because the schedule pressure you apply will cause haste and carelessness and will drive up the bug or error probability to dangerous levels.

References

Boehm, Barry Dr.: *Software Engineering Economics,* Prentice Hall, Englewood Cliffs, N.J., 1981.

DeMarco, Tom: *Controlling Software Projects,* Yourdon Press, New York, ISBN 0-917072-32-4, 1982.

———, and Timothy Lister: *Peopleware,* Dorset House Press, New York, ISBN 0-932633-05-6, 1987.

Humphrey, Watts: *Personal Software Process,* Addison-Wesley/Longman, Reading, Mass., 1997.

Jones, Capers: *Programming Productivity,* McGraw-Hill, New York, ISBN 0-07-032811-0, 1986.

———: *Assessment and Control of Software Risks,* Prentice Hall, Englewood Cliffs, N.J., ISBN 0-13-741406-4, 1994.

———: *Patterns of Software System Failure and Success,* International Thomson Computer Press, Boston, Mass., ISBN 1-850-32804-8, 1995.

———: *Applied Software Measurement,* 2d ed., McGraw-Hill, New York, ISBN 0-07-032826-9, 1996a.

———: *Table of Programming Languages and Levels* (8 Versions from 1985 through July 1996), Software Productivity Research, Burlington, Mass., 1996b.

———: *The Year 2000 Software Problem—Quantifying the Costs and Assessing the Consequences,* Addison-Wesley/Longman, Reading, Mass., ISBN 0-201-30964-3, 1998.

McCue, Gerald: "The IBM Santa Teresa Laboratory—Architectural Design for Program Development," *IBM Systems Journal,* **17**(1):4–25 (1978). Reprinted in Capers Jones

Programming Productivity—Issues for the Eighties, 2d ed., IEEE Computer Society Press, Los Alamitos, Calif., Catalog no. 681, ISBN 0-8186-0681-9.

Putnam, Lawrence H.: *Measures for Excellence—Reliable Software on Time, Within Budget,* Yourdon Press/Prentice Hall, Englewood Cliffs, N.J., ISBN 0-13-567694-0, 1992.

———, and Ware Myers: *Industrial Strength Software—Effective Management Using Measurement,* IEEE Computer Society Press, Washington D.C., ISBN 0-8186-7532-2, 1997.

Roetzheim, William H., and Reyna A. Beasley: *Best Practices in Software Cost and Schedule Estimation,* Prentice Hall PTR, Upper Saddle River, N.J., 1998.

Rubin, Howard: *Software Benchmark Studies for 1997* Howard Rubin Associates, Pound Ridge, N.Y., 1997.

Symons, Charles R., *Software Sizing and Estimating—Mk II FPA (Function Point Analysis),* John Wiley & Sons, Chichester, U.K., ISBN 0 471-92985-9, 1991.

Yourdon, Ed: *Death March—The Complete Software Developer's Guide to Surviving Mission Impossible Projects,* Prentice Hall PTR, Upper Saddle River, N.J., ISBN 0-13-748310-4, 1997.

Estimating Code Inspections

The topic of formal code inspections has a continuous stream of empirical data that runs back to the early 1970s. Formal code inspections were originally developed at the IBM Kingston programming laboratory by Michael Fagan (Fagan 1976) and his colleagues, and have since spread throughout the programming world.

(It is interesting that Michael Fagan, the inventor of inspections, received an IBM outstanding contribution award for the discovery that design and code inspections benefit software quality, schedules, and costs simultaneously.)

Other researchers, such as Tom Gilb (Gilb and Graham 1993), Dr. Gerald Weinberg (Friedman and Weinberg 1990), and the author of this book, have followed the use of inspections in recent years, and the method is still the top-ranked method for achieving high levels of overall defect-removal efficiency. Formal code inspections are about twice as efficient as any known form of testing in finding deep and obscure programming bugs, and are the only known method to top 80 percent in defect-removal efficiency.

However, formal code inspections are fairly expensive and time-consuming, so they are most widely utilized on software projects where operational reliability and safety are mandatory, such as the following:

1. Mainframe operating systems

2. Telephone switching systems

3. Aircraft flight control software

4. Medical instrument software

5. Weapons systems software

It is an interesting observation, with solid empirical data to back it up, that large and complex systems (>1000 function points or >100,000 source code statements) that utilize formal code inspections will achieve shorter schedules and lower development and maintenance costs than similar software projects that use only testing for defect removal. Indeed, the use of formal inspections has represented a *best practice* for complex systems software for more than 25 years.

The reason for this phenomenon is based on the fact that for complex software applications the schedule, effort, and costs devoted to finding and fixing bugs take longer and are more expensive than any other known cost factors.

Formal inspections eliminate so many troublesome errors early that when testing does occur, very few defects are encountered; hence, testing costs and schedules are only a fraction of those experienced when testing is the first and only form of defect removal. Thus, the return on investment (ROI) from formal inspections can top $15 for every $1 spent, which ranks as one of the top ROIs of any software technology.

Formal code inspections overlap several similar approaches, and except among specialists the terms *inspection, structured walkthrough,* and *code review* are often used almost interchangeably. Following are the major differences among these variations.

Formal code inspections are characterized by the following attributes:

- Training is given to novices before they participate in their first inspection.

- The inspection team is comprised of a moderator, a recorder, one or more inspectors, and the person whose work product is being inspected.

- Schedule and timing protocols are carefully adhered to for preparation time, the inspection sessions themselves, and follow-up activities.

- Accurate data is kept on the number of defects found, hours of effort devoted to preparation, and the size of the work product inspected.

- Standard metrics are calculated from the data collected during inspections, such as defect-removal efficiency, work hours per function point, work hours per KLOC, and work hours per defect.

The less formal methods of structured walkthroughs and code reviews differ from the formal code inspection method in the following key attributes:

- Training is seldom provided for novices before they participate.

- The usage of a moderator and recorder seldom occurs.

- Little or no data is recorded on defect rates, hours expended, costs, or other quantifiable aspects of the review or walkthrough.

As a result, it is actually harder to estimate the less formal methods, such as code walkthroughs, than it is to estimate formal code inspections. The reason is that formal code inspections generate accurate quantitative data as a standard output, while the less formal methods usually have very little data available on either defects, removal efficiency, schedules, effort, or costs.

However, there is just enough data to indicate that the less formal methods are not as efficient and effective as formal code inspections, although they are still better than many forms of testing.

Formal code inspections will average about 65 percent in defect-removal efficiency, and the best results can top 85 percent.

Less formal structured walkthroughs average about 45 percent in defect-removal efficiency, and the best results can top about 70 percent.

However, since most forms of testing are less than 30 percent efficient in finding bugs, it can be seen that either formal code inspections or informal code walkthroughs can add value to defect-removal operations.

Another common variant on the inspection method is that of doing partial inspections on less than 100 percent of the code in an application. This variant makes estimating tricky, because there is no fixed ratio of code that will be inspected. Some of the variants that SPR's clients have utilized include the following:

- Inspecting only the code that deals with the most complex and difficult algorithms (usually less than 10 percent of the total volume of code).

- Inspecting only modules that are suspected of being error prone due to the volumes of incoming defect reports (usually less than 5 percent of the total volume of code).

- Time-box inspections (such as setting aside a fixed period such as 1 month) for inspections, and doing as much as possible during the assigned time box (often less than 50 percent of the total volume of code).

However, for really important applications which will affect human life or safety (i.e., medical instrument software, weapons systems, nuclear control systems, aircraft flight control, etc.) anything less than 100 percent inspection of the entire application is hazardous and should be avoided.

Another aspect of inspections that makes estimation tricky is the fact that the inspection sessions are intermittent activities which must be slotted into other kinds of work. Using the formal protocols of the inspection process, inspection sessions are limited to a maximum of two hours each, and no more than two such sessions can be held in any given business day.

These protocols mean that for large systems, the inspection sessions can be strung out for several months. Further, because other kinds of work must be done and travel might occur, and because reinspections may be needed, the actual schedules for the inspection sessions are unpredictable using simple algorithms and rules of thumb.

Using a sophisticated scheduling tool, such as Microsoft Project, Timeline, Artemis, and the like, what usually occurs is that inspections are slotted into other activities over a several-month period. A common practice is to run inspections in the morning, and leave the afternoons for other kinds of work.

However, one of the other kinds of work is preparing for the next inspection. Although preparation goes faster than the inspection sessions themselves, the preparation for the next code inspection session can easily amount to one hour per inspector prior to each planned inspection session.

Although the programmer whose work is being inspected may not have as much preparation work as the inspectors, after the inspection he or she may have to fix quite a few defects which the inspection churns up.

Yet another aspect of inspections that adds complexity to the estimation task is the fact that with more and more experience, the participants in formal code inspection benefit in two distinct ways:

1. Programmers who participate in inspections have reduced bug counts in their own work.

2. The inspectors and participants become significantly more efficient in preparation time and also in the time needed for the inspection sessions.

Table 22.1 illustrates these simultaneous improvements for a scenario that assumes that six different software projects will be inspected over time by more or less the same set of programmers. As can be seen, by the time the sixth project is reached, the team is quite a bit better than when it started with its first inspection.

As can be observed, inspections are beneficial in terms of both their defect-prevention aspects and their defect-removal aspects. Indeed, one of the most significant benefits of formal design and code inspections is that they raise the defect-removal efficiency of testing.

TABLE 22.1   Improvement in Code Inspection Performance with Practice
(Time in hours)

Number of projects	Size, in LOC	Defects found	Prep time	Session time	Repair time	Total time
1	1000	20	10.0	12.0	60.0	82.0
2	1000	17	9.0	10.0	55.0	74.0
3	1000	15	7.0	8.0	50.0	65.0
4	1000	12	5.0	7.0	40.0	52.0
5	1000	10	4.0	5.0	30.0	39.0
6	1000	7	3.0	3.0	20.0	26.0
Average	1000	14	6.3	7.5	42.5	56.3

Some of the major problems of achieving high-efficiency testing are that the specifications are often incomplete, the code often does not match the specifications, and the poor and convoluted structure of the code makes testing of every path difficult. Formal design and code inspections will minimize these problems by providing test personnel with more complete and accurate specifications and by eliminating many of the problem areas of the code itself.

A simple rule of thumb is that every hour spent on formal code inspections will probably save close to three hours in subsequent testing and downstream defect removal operations.

Estimating both design and code inspections can be tricky, because both forms of inspection have wide ranges of possible variance, such as the following:

- Preparation time is highly variable.

- The number of participants in any session can range from three to eight.

- Personal factors (flu, vacations, etc.) can cancel or delay inspections.

- Inspections are intermittent events limited to two-hour sessions.

- Inspections have to be slotted into other kinds of work activities.

The nominal default values for code inspections are shown in Table 22.2, although these values should be replaced by local data as quickly as possible. Indeed, inspections lend themselves to template construction because local conditions can vary so widely.

When inspections become a normal part of software development processes in large corporations, there may be several, or even dozens, of inspections going on concurrently on any given business day. For

TABLE 22.2   Nominal Default Values for Code Inspections

Activity sequence	Sixth
Activity performed by	Development personnel; quality assurance; testers
Predecessor activities	Coding
Overlap	50% with coding
Concurrent activities	Both coding and unit testing
Successor activities	Unit testing, regression testing, and function testing
Initial size	2 function points per inspection session
Initial size	250 code statements per inspection session
Assignment scope	2 function points per team member per session
Assignment scope	250 source code statements per team member per session
Production rate	2 function points per hour (0.5 per team member)
Production rate	250 source statements per hour (50 per team member)
Schedule months	2-hour packets, with no more than 2 per day
Rate of creep or change	1%
Defect potential	1.5 code defects present per function point
Defect potential	15 code defects present per 1000 source code statements
Defect removal	65% average removal efficiency
Delivered defects	Code defects −65% or roughly 0.5 per function point
High-severity defects	12% of delivered defects
Bad fix probability	5% of code inspection fixes may yield new errors

some large systems, there may even be dozens of inspections for different components of the same system taking place simultaneously.

This phenomenon raises some practical issues that need to be dealt with:

- Possible conflicts in scheduling inspection conference rooms
- Possible conflicts in scheduling inspection participants

Often, large companies that use inspection have an inspection coordinator, who may be part of the quality-assurance organization. The inspection coordinator handles the conference room arrangements and also the scheduling of participants. For scheduling individual participants, some kind of calendar management tool is usually used.

Although the inspection process originated as a group activity in which all members of the inspection team met face to face, software networking technologies are now powerful enough that some inspections are being handled remotely. There is even commercial software available that allows every participant to interact, to chat with the others, and to mark up the listings and associated documentation.

These online inspections are still evolving, but the preliminary data indicates that they are slightly more efficient than face-to-face inspections. Obviously, with online inspections there is no travel to remote buildings, and another less obvious advantage also tends to occur.

In face-to-face inspection sessions, sometimes as much as 15 to 20 minutes out of each 2-hour session may be diverted into such unrelated topics as sports, the weather, politics, or whatever. With online inspections idle chat tends to be abbreviated, and, hence, the work at hand goes quicker. The usual result is that the inspection sessions themselves are shorter, and the online variants seldom run much more than 60 minutes, as opposed to the 2-hour slots assigned to face-to-face inspections.

Alternatively, the production rates for the online inspection sessions are often faster and some can top 400 source code statements per hour—and with experienced personnel who make few defects to slow down progress, inspections have been clocked at more than 750 source code statements per hour.

Given the power and effectiveness of formal inspections, it is initially surprising that they are not universally adopted and used on every critical software project. The reason why formal inspections are noted only among best-in-class organizations is that the average and lagging organizations simply do not know what works and what doesn't.

In other words, both the project managers and the programming personnel in lagging companies that lack formal measurements of quality, formal process improvement programs, and the other attributes of successful software production do not know enough about the effectiveness of inspections to see how large an ROI they offer.

Consider the fact that lagging and average companies collect no historical data of their own and seldom review the data collected by other companies. As a result, lagging and average enterprises are not in a position to make rational choices about effective software technologies. Instead, they usually follow whatever current cult is in vogue, whether or not the results are beneficial. They also fall prey to pitches of various tool and methodology vendors, with or without any substantial evidence that what is being sold will be effective.

Leading companies, on the other hand, do measure such factors as defect-removal efficiency, schedules, costs, and other critical factors. Leading companies also tend to be more familiar with the external data and the software engineering literature. Therefore, leading enterprises are aware that design and code inspections have a major place in software engineering because they benefit quality, schedules, and costs simultaneously.

Another and surprising reason why inspections are not more widely used is the fact that the method is in the public domain, so none of the testing-tool companies can generate any significant revenues from the inspection technology. Thus, the testing-tool companies tend to ignore inspections as though they did not even exist, although if the testing companies really understood software quality they would include inspection support as part of their offerings.

Judging from visits to at least a dozen public and private conferences by testing-tool and quality-assurance companies, inspections are sometimes discussed by speakers but almost never show up in vendor's showcases or at quality tool fairs. This is unfortunate, because inspections are a powerful adjunct to testing and, indeed, can raise the defect-removal efficiency level of downstream testing by perhaps 15 percent as compared to the results from similar projects that do only testing.

From a software-estimating standpoint, the usage of formal inspections needs to be included in the estimate, of course. Even more significant, the usage of formal design and code inspections will have a significant impact on downstream activities that also need to be included in the estimate. For example, the usage of formal inspections will probably have the following downstream effects:

1. At least 65 percent of latent errors will be eliminated via inspections, so testing will be quicker and cheaper. The timeline for completing testing will be about 25 percent shorter than for similar projects that do not use inspections.

2. The inspections will clean up the specifications and, hence, will allow better test cases to be constructed, so the defect-removal efficiency levels of testing will be about 10 to 12 percent higher than for similar projects that do not use inspections.

3. The combined defect-removal efficiency levels of the inspections coupled with better testing will reduce maintenance costs by more than 50 percent compared to similar projects that don't use inspections.

For additional information on the economics of inspections, refer to the studies of Robert Dunn and Richard Ullman on software quality within ITT (Dunn and Ullman 1982), or to Larry Putnam's work on using measurements for industrial-strength software (Putnam and Myers 1997). Howard Rubin's annual surveys of software practices often contain information on inspections, among other software technologies (Rubin 1997). The author's own books quantify the accumulated industrial data from SPR's clients (Jones 1994, 1995, 1997).

References

Dunn, Robert, and Richard Ullman: *Quality Assurance for Computer Software,* McGraw-Hill, New York, ISBN 0-07-018312-0, 1982.

Fagan, M. E., "Design and Code Inspections to Reduce Errors in Program Development," *IBM Systems Journal,* **12**(3):219–248 (1976).

Friedman, Daniel P., and Gerald M. Weinberg: *Handbook of Walkthroughs, Inspections, and Technical Reviews,* Dorset House Press, New York, ISBN 0-932633-19-6, 1990.

Gilb, Tom, and D. Graham: *Software Inspections,* Addison-Wesley, Reading, Mass., 1993.

Jones, Capers: *Assessment and Control of Software Risks,* Prentice-Hall, Englewood Cliffs, N.J., ISBN 0-13-741406-4, 1994.

———: *Patterns of Software System Failure and Success,* International Thomson Computer Press, Boston, ISBN 1-850-32804-8, 1995.

———: *Software Quality—Analysis and Guidelines for Success,* International Thomson Computer Press, Boston, ISBN 1-85032-867-6, 1997.

Putnam, Lawrence H.: *Measures for Excellence—Reliable Software on Time, Within Budget,* Yourdon Press/Prentice Hall, Englewood Cliffs, N.J., ISBN 0-13-567694-0, 1992.

———, and Ware Myers: *Industrial Strength Software—Effective Management Using Measurement,* IEEE Computer Society Press, Washington, D.C., ISBN 0-8186-7532-2, 1997.

Rubin, Howard: *Software Benchmark Studies for 1997,* Howard Rubin Associates, Pound Ridge, N.Y., 1997.

Estimating Software Configuration Control and Change Management

Software projects change as rapidly as any product ever conceived by the human mind. Therefore, one of the major challenges of the software industry has been to manage change as efficiently as possible.

Estimating the work of change management is also important, not only because change management itself can be expensive, but because the rate of change of various software deliverables is a major factor in the accuracy of overall software cost and schedule estimation.

Every software project changes during development. But the rates of change vary widely from project to project, as do the set of artifacts that are created for the project. In general, estimating change management requires separate estimates for the following variable items:

1. The set of artifacts (requirements, specifications, code, documents, tests, bugs, etc.)

2. The rates of change of each artifact

3. The way proposed changes are evaluated and accepted or rejected

4. The presence or absence of a formal change-control board

5. The way changes to various artifacts are stored and recorded

6. The presence or absence of configuration audits

7. The tools available for building and controlling versions of the application

8. The frequency with which new versions are built

Estimating change management is also a fairly difficult task, because of several unique characteristics of this activity:

- Not every software project uses formal change management methods.
- Not every software project has a change-control board.
- For projects that have change-control boards, their sizes and memberships vary.
- For projects that have change-control boards, their meetings are intermittent.
- Not every project uses configuration-control automation.
- The automated configuration-control tools vary widely in capabilities.

For example, military projects of almost any size usually include formal change management approaches because they are required by such military standards as DoD 2167A and DoD 973. Military configuration management starts early, during the requirements phase. Once started, change control is continuous and includes intermittent audits of configuration status.

Civilian projects are less likely to utilize formal change management unless the corporation is certified using the ISO 9000–9004 standards or is climbing the SEI capability maturity model above level 2, where change management becomes a standard activity. Civilian configuration control typically starts later than military configuration control, and may support fewer artifacts. Indeed, some civilian projects use only rudimentary configuration control for the source code, and no formal methods at all for specifications, user documents, or other artifacts.

However, civilian systems and embedded software typically uses more thorough configuration control than does information systems software, and often follows formal change management standards, such as IEEE Standard 1042-1987 on software configuration management.

Thus, estimating the nature of change management activity requires a knowledge of the nature of the enterprise, the nature of the project, the size of the application in question, and the forms of change management methods to be utilized.

There is a fairly extensive literature on software change management in both its civilian and military forms. For example, Tim Mikkelsen and Suzanne Pherigo of Hewlett-Packard (Mikkelsen and Pherigo 1997) have published an interesting primer entitled *Practical Software Configuration Management*. There are also a number of older books on software configuration control, such as H. R. Berlack's *Software Configuration Management* (Berlack 1992).

In addition to standalone books on software configuration control, the topic is also covered in chapters on general software engineering and management principles in such books as Fred Brooks's classic *The Mythical Man-Month* (Brooks 1974) and Roger Pressman's *Software Engineering—A Practitioner's Approach* (Pressman 1982).

The nominal default values for estimating the activity of software change management or configuration control are shown in Table 23.1.

Once change management and configuration control begin for an application, some aspects of change management are daily events, such as updating records in response to repaired bugs.

Other aspects of change management are intermittent. For example, the change management board may meet at weekly, biweekly, or monthly intervals. The duration of each meeting can run from less than one hour to more than one day.

From time to time on large systems, there may be a configuration audit. Such audits are required for military software and are formal milestones. For civilian projects, configuration audits are not as common and are not as formal when they occur. Variable factors, such as the presence or absence of configuration audits, make estimating change control rather tricky.

In general, large systems of more than 5000 function points in size

TABLE 23.1 Nominal Default Values for Change Management and Configuration Control

Activity sequence	Seventh
Activity performed by	Change-control specialists; developers; auditors; clients
Predecessor activities	Requirements, design, coding, and inspections
Overlap	25% with design; then continuous
Concurrent activities	Multiple: design, coding, testing, and documentation
Successor activities	Release of the project to clients
Assignment scope	1000 function points per change team member
Production rate	1500 function points per staff month
Schedule months	Continuous once begun through release
Rate of creep or change	Varies with artifact
Defect potential	0.2 defects per function point due to change errors
Defect removal	75% average removal efficiency
Delivered defects	0.2 defects -75% or roughly 0.05 per function point
High-severity defects	10% of delivered defects due to change
Bad fix probability	3% of change-control modifications may yield new errors

will utilize very formal change management methods; will have change-control boards; and will have an extensive suite of change management tools that can handle changes to requirements, specifications, code, defects, user documents, and other artifacts.

Software projects between 1000 and 5000 function points may utilize formal change management methods, but often deploy only subsets of the methods used on larger systems. Among SPR's clients, a significant portion use change management automation only for source code, and handle changes to requirements and specifications in a manual fashion. For projects toward the low end of this spectrum, change-control boards are rare rather than the norm.

At the low end, for small projects of only a few hundred function points or less, formal change control tends to concentrate on source code and is handled by the developers themselves. Formal change-control boards essentially never are used, unless the project is an enhancement to a much larger system.

For very small projects of less than 100 function points with a one-person development team, change control is never formal. Unless change management features are part of the development tool suite, there is seldom any automation utilized.

The overall challenge of software change management was poorly met for many years. The primary change management tools for source code were standalone file-based version control systems that supported only code only.

Change management for text specification and planning documents, cost estimates, test libraries, graphics and illustrations, and the inventories of bugs reported against software projects were all performed using only rudimentary standalone tools that often did not communicate or coordinate across domains. Indeed, some projects utilized only source code change-control tools, and handled changes of all other artifacts in an informal, manual fashion.

In recent years, since about 1990, it has been recognized that source code is not the only deliverable that changes. In fact, for many projects source code is not even the major item that changes. For large software projects, there are many more words created than source code and the words change more rapidly! There are also large volumes of bug reports, which need constant surveillance and monitoring during software development and maintenance.

Therefore, modern change management tools, or *configuration-control* tools as they are commonly called, must be capable of dealing with every kind of software deliverable and artifact, as follows:

- Changing requirements
- Changing project plans

- Changing project cost estimates
- Changing contracts
- Changing design
- Changing source code
- Changing user documents
- Changing illustrations and graphics
- Changing test materials
- Changing volumes of bug reports

Ideally, the change management tools can use hypertext capabilities to handle cross-references between deliverables so that when something changes, the corresponding places in related material can be highlighted or even modified semiautomatically.

Another recent development in the software world is the newfound ability to understand the economics of changes. For many years, software costs were normalized using *lines of code* (LOC) as the primary metric. This metric was useless for dealing with the costs of producing text materials, graphics, test cases and all other noncode software artifacts. Therefore, both the development and the modification costs of noncode material were essentially invisible to the software world.

The function point metric can be applied to plans, estimates, specifications, test materials, source code, and all software deliverables. The function point metric has helped enormously in understanding the costs and economic consequences of changes to every software artifact.

In order to discuss the rate at which software deliverables change, it is necessary to know at least approximately how big they are under normal conditions. The function point metric has given the software industry a useful way of normalizing various deliverable items, so that volumes of materials can be discussed using a stable size dimension.

The function point metric is also beginning to be used to assign fairly accurate cost and value amounts to changes. Outsource vendors, for example, are beginning to include *cost per function point* on sliding scales in contracts, so that new features added late in development have higher charges than function points derived during the actual requirements phase.

Table 23.2 shows the nominal sizes and rates of monthly change associated with a generic average systems software project of 1000 function points in size. This project can be assumed to use the C programming language.

The typical calendar time for developing a systems software appli-

TABLE 23.2 Average Deliverable Sizes and Rates of Change for a 1000–Function Point System Software Application

Deliverable	Size per FP	Basic size	Monthly change rate, %
Requirements	0.3 pages	300 pages	2
Plans/estimates	0.2 pages	200 pages	10
External design	0.5 pages	500 pages	5
Logical design	0.7 pages	700 pages	4
Source code	125.0 LOC	125,000 LOC	7
Test cases	5.0 test cases	5,000 cases	10
User manuals	0.4 pages	400 pages	5
Defects (bug reports)	5.0 bugs	5,000 reports	15

TABLE 23.3 Volume of Text and Words Produced for a Generic 1000–Function Point System Software Project

Deliverable	Basic size, pages	English words	English words per FP
Requirements	300	120,000	120
Plans/estimates	100	40,000	40
External design	500	200,000	200
Internal design	700	245,000	245
User manuals	400	160,000	160
Bug reports	5000	1,350,000	1350
Total	7000	2,115,000	2115

cation of 1000 function points would be about 18 months from the start of requirements to the initial delivery to the first customer.

The overall effort to produce this project would total about 200 person months. The productivity rate can be seen to be 5 function points per month. Assuming an average burdened salary rate of $8000 per month, the total cost would be $16 million and the cost per function point would be $1600.

Because such noncode materials as text and graphics actually comprise the bulk of software deliverables, it is of interest to include some information on the approximate volumes of these two items.

Table 23.3 shows the approximate volumes of the major paper deliverables associated with software. There are, of course, many more ephemeral documents produced, such as letters, memos, presentations, progress reports, and the like. (A total of more than 50 kinds

TABLE 23.4 Volume of Graphic Illustrations Produced for a Generic 1000–Function Point System Software Project

Deliverable	Basic size, pages	Graphics	Graphics per FP
Requirements	300	100	0.10
Plans/estimates	100	50	0.05
External design	500	50	0.05
Logical design	700	200	0.50
User manuals	600	300	0.30
Total	2200	700	1.00

of paper document can be produced for large software projects.) However, these ephemeral documents may not come under configuration control, while the basic specifications, contracts, plans, estimates, and user documents often do.

Because the volume of source code in this example is 125,000 logical statements, it can be seen that more than 184 words are created for every source code statement. (Had this been a military project, the total would have been more than 400 English words per source code statement.)

Both the large volume of information associated with bug reports and the significance of this topic imply a need for very strong defect-tracking capabilities in configuration-control tool suites.

Graphics and illustrations vary widely and are more difficult to quantify. Even so, the volume of graphical material in support of software is too large to ignore and is becoming larger very rapidly as better graphics production tools become widespread. Table 23.4 shows the approximate volumes of graphical materials that might be produced for this sample application.

Even as this is being written, graphics and illustrations tend to remain somewhat troublesome for configuration-control purposes. In the future, when dynamic or animated models and simulations become common for software, and when multimedia approaches are used for software representation, change control will become both more difficult and more important.

Changes in User Requirements

Requirements changes, or creeping requirements, are the most important topic for change management, because they cause updates of all downstream deliverables. Requirements changes become progressively more troublesome after the nominal completion of the requirements phase, as discussed earlier in this book.

During the subsequent design phase, the average rate of requirements change may exceed 3 percent per month for many software projects. This burst of rapid requirements changes may last as long as a year for large systems, but would occur only for about three months on this sample project. The burst of new requirements slows down to about 1 percent per month during coding, and eventually stops by the time testing commences. (Requirements changes don't really stop, of course, but the requirements tend to get pushed downstream into follow-on releases.)

For systems software, such as this example, and for commercial software, changes may be due to market needs or competitive products. The average rate is about 2 percent per month from the end of initial requirements until start of testing. But if a competitor suddenly announces a new product, monthly change rates can top 15 percent!

For internal software, requirements changes are driven by user needs and average about 1 percent per month from the start of design until well into coding. For military software, the average is about 2 percent per month.

Military software requirements call for very strict *requirements traceability*. This means that all downstream deliverables need to identify which requirements they include to a very granular level. This implies, ideally, that software requirements would be the base for hypertext linkages to other downstream software artifacts.

Software outsourcers and contractors can now derive the function point totals of software during the requirements phase, and this is leading to a newfound ability to quantify the subsequent downstream costs of changing requirements.

Because the *cost per function point* is now being used to price software features, tools such as Function Point Workbench that can assign function point totals to various features of an application are starting to become important business tools. Currently these are standalone tools, but it is obvious that direct linkages will be needed so that changes in requirements or design can automatically trigger new size and cost estimates.

For example, assume that this project is performed as a contract development effort rather than as an internal project. The contract might include phrasing or concepts similar to the following:

- Development costs for requirements derived during months 1 to 3 or the requirements phase of the project = $1500 per function point.

- Development costs for new requirements added during months 4 to 6 = $1750 per function point.

- Costs for requirements deleted during months 4 to 6 = $150 per function point.

- Development costs for new requirements added during months 6 to 12 = $2250 per function point.

- Costs for requirements deleted during months 6 to 12 = $500 per function point.

- Development costs for new requirements added during months 12 to 18 = $5000 per function point.

- Costs for requirements deleted during months 12 to 18 = $1000 per function point.

The usage of cost per function point as a contractual metric means that clients, accountants, project managers, contract officers, attorneys, and others now have a much better understanding of software economics than was possible during the primitive lines-of-code era. It is also significant that the Internal Revenue Service is now exploring cost per function point as a way of determining the taxable value of software.

Changes in Specifications and Design

Since the design and specifications for a software project are in response to fundamental user requirements, most of the design changes after the initial creation of the design can be attributed to changes in the user requirements.

However, a significant number of design modifications are due to suggested improvements by the development team members themselves, or to factors which only come to light during the detailed design phase. For example, if a software application has very stringent performance targets it may be necessary to revise the design in order to squeeze extra speed out of the system.

However, a study performed by the author on IBM systems software noted that the design and development team introduced a number of changes for what appeared to be insufficient justification. Some changes were made because of personal preferences by the design personnel, or for somewhat nebulous reasons, such as "Someone might need this feature and it was easy to put it in."

On the whole, large systems benefit from the costs of having a formal change-control board with representatives from the client community, the development community, the quality-assurance community, and the testing community.

A multiskilled change-control board with a broad outlook can save time and money by eliminating unnecessary changes and ensuring that when changes do occur, all affected organizations are brought up to speed.

Changes Due to Bugs or Defect Reports

Software development and maintenance are intellectually difficult tasks during which a large number of bugs or defects will be created (and hopefully found and eliminated). Defect removal is the most expensive cost component of software, and the volume of information associated with software defects or bugs is the largest of any software artifact.

Because there are so many bugs in software, so much information about bugs, and the costs of bug removal is such a major component of overall software costs, it is mandatory that configuration control tools have powerful defect tracking and reporting capabilities.

Bugs are not just found in source code, of course. Table 23.5 shows approximate U.S. national averages for software defects and the percentages of defect removed prior to the initial deployment.

A simple rule of thumb can lead to useful approximations of software defects or bugs. Take the size of the application in function points and raise the size to the 1.25 power. That will yield a rough approximation of the total number of bugs that may be faced during development. For enhancement projects, the size is that of the enhancement rather than the base size of the application.

Assuming that the hypothetical project discussed here is an average project, there would be about 1000 errors found in requirements, 1250 in design, 1750 in the source code, and 600 in the user manuals. Another 400 bugs would be secondary errors or bad fixes introduced when a bug repair itself contains a new error. A total of about 5000 bugs would have to be found and eliminated in this average project.

TABLE 23.5   U.S. Averages for Software Defects and Defect-Removal Efficiency

(Data expressed in defects per function point)

Defect origins	Defect potentials	Removal efficiency, %	Delivered defects
Requirements	1.00	77	0.23
Design	1.25	85	0.19
Coding	1.75	95	0.09
Documentation	0.60	80	0.12
Bad fixes	0.40	70	0.12
Total	5.00	85	0.75

Because of the costs and importance of quality control, it can be seen that defect tracking is a vital component of software change management. Defect tracking spans the entire life cycle of a software project. Defect tracking starts during requirements and proceeds all the way through the development cycle and out into the maintenance cycle for as long as the product is used—20 years or more in some cases.

Summary and Conclusions

Change management is one of the most important aspects of successful software development. Recognition of this fact is leading to an interesting new subindustry of companies that build integrated change management tools that can handle far more than just source code revisions.

Part of the impetus for the development of this subindustry is the impact of function point metrics, which allow quantifying the costs of change with a precision that was impossible for many years.

Costs of changes are now beginning to appear in development and maintenance contracts for software, and this, in turn, is leading to a new business understanding of the economics of changing software.

There is still a long way to go before software changes are fully explored and understood, but the rate of progress is now very rapid and even accelerating.

References

Arthur, Jay: *Software Evolution,* John Wiley & Sons, New York, 1988.

Berlack, H. R.: "Configuration Management," in John Marciniak, (ed.), *Encyclopedia of Software Engineering,* vol. 1, John Wiley & Sons, New York, 1994, pp. 180–206.

———: *Software Configuration Management,* John Wiley & Sons, New York, 1992.

Brooks, Fred: *The Mythical Man-Month,* Addison-Wesley, Reading, Mass., 1974, rev. 1995.

IEEE Standard 828-1990: Software Configuration Management, IEEE Standards Department, Piscataway, N.J., 1990.

Mikkelsen, Tim, and Suzanne Pherigo: *Practical Software Configuration Management,* Prentice Hall PTR, Upper Saddle River, N.J., 1997.

MIL STD 973: Configuration Management, Department of Defense, Naval Publications Center, Philadelphia, Pa., 1992.

MIL STD 2167A: Defense System Software Development and Data Item Descriptions, Department of Defense, Naval Publications Center, Philadelphia, Pa., 1988.

Jones, Capers: *Assessment and Control of Software Risks,* Prentice Hall, Englewood Cliffs, N.J., ISBN 0-13-741406-4, 1994.

———: *Patterns of Software System Failure and Success,* International Thomson Computer Press, Boston, ISBN 1-850-32804-8, 1995.

———: *Software Quality—Analysis and Guidelines for Success,* International Thomson Computer Press, Boston, ISBN 1-85032-867-6, 1997.

Pressman, Roger: *Software Engineering—A Practitioner's Approach,* McGraw-Hill, New York, 1982.

Putnam, Lawrence H.: *Measures for Excellence—Reliable Software on Time, Within*

Budget, Yourdon Press/Prentice Hall, Englewood Cliffs, N.J., ISBN 0-13-567694-0, 1992.

————, and Ware Myers: *Industrial Strength Software—Effective Management Using Measurement,* IEEE Computer Society Press, Washington D.C., ISBN 0-8186-7532-2, 1997.

Rubin, Howard: *Software Benchmark Studies for 1997,* Howard Rubin Associates, Pound Ridge, N.Y., 1997.

Estimating Software Testing

From an estimating standpoint, estimating testing effort, testing schedules, and testing costs are rather complex topics because of the many different forms of testing that might be performed, and the fact that the numbers of discrete test stages for applications can run from a single perfunctory form of testing up to a high of about 16 formal test operations.

The literature on testing is quite large, and in total probably exceeds 200 books and thousands of journal articles. However, it appears that most of the testing literature is comprised of various how-to-do-it books. Books and articles that quantify testing in terms of number of test cases needed, defect-removal efficiency, test coverage analysis, or missed defects are remarkably scarce.

Some of the well-known authors who cover testing-related topics include Boris Beizer (Beizer 1995); William Perry (Perry 1995), and Daniel Mosley (Mosley 1993). Testing is also covered within more general kinds of software books, such as Barry Boehm's *Software Engineering Economics* (Boehm 1981) and Roger Pressman's *Software Engineering—A Practitioner's Approach* (Pressman 1982).

Many of the author's own books cover testing, with two overlapping the current book: *Software Quality—Analysis and Guidelines for Success* (Jones 1997b) deals with all aspects of software quality control including testing, while *The Year 2000 Software Problem* (Jones 1998) deals with testing in a year-2000 context.

Table 24.1 provides some nominal default values for estimating testing activities, although these defaults need to be adjusted and applied to each specific form of testing, as will be discussed later in this chapter.

TABLE 24.1   Nominal Default Values for Testing

Activity sequence	Eighth
Activity performed by	Developers; test specialists; quality assurance; clients
Predecessor activities	Coding and code inspections
Overlap	25% with coding
Concurrent activities	Coding, quality assurance, change control, and documentation
Successor activities	Release of the project to clients
Assignment scope	500 function points per test specialist
Production rate	250 function points per staff month
Schedule months	Varies with number of defects found and test stage
Rate of creep or change	5% per month
Defect potential	0.3 defects per function point in test cases themselves
Defect removal	75% average removal efficiency against defective test cases
Delivered defects	0.3 defects −75% or roughly 0.1 per function point
High-severity defects	5% of test-case defects
Bad fix probability	5% of test-case changes may yield new errors

It is obvious from Table 24.1 that testing can vary significantly in who performs it, and even more significantly in the number of kinds of tests that are likely to be performed. Let us consider the implications of these test estimating complexities.

The exact definition of what *testing* means is quite ambiguous. In this book and the author's previous books on software quality (Jones 1997b) and the year-2000 problem (Jones 1998) the basic definition of testing is:

> The dynamic execution of software and the comparison of the results of that execution against a set of known, predetermined criteria. Determining the validity of a specific application output in response to a specific application input is termed a *test case*.

Under this definition of testing, static defect-removal methods, such as formal design and code inspections, are not viewed as *testing*. However, under a broader definition of *defect removal*, both inspections and testing would be considered as complementary activities. Formal inspections actually have higher levels of defect-removal efficiency than almost any form of testing.

It may also be significant to define what *software* means in a testing context. The term *software* can mean any of the following:

- An individual instruction (about .001 function points).
- A small subroutine of perhaps 10 instructions in length (about .01 function points).

- A module of perhaps 100 instructions in length (about 1 function point).

- A complete program of perhaps 1000 instructions in length (10 function points).

- A component of a system of perhaps 10,000 instructions in length (100 function points).

- An entire software system that can range from 100,000 statements (1000 function points) to more than 10 million instructions in length (100,000 function points).

Any one of these software groupings can be tested, and often tested many times, in the course of software development activities.

Also significant in a testing context is the term *execution*. As used here, the term *execution* means running the software on a computer with or without any form of instrumentation or test-control software being present.

The phrase *predetermined criteria* means that what the software is supposed to do is known prior to its execution, so that what the software actually does can be compared against the anticipated results to judge whether or not the software is behaving correctly.

The term *test case* means recording a known set of conditions so that the response of the application to a specific input combination is evaluated to determine that the outputs are valid and fall within predetermined, acceptable ranges.

There are dozens of possible forms of testing, but they can be aggregated into three forms of testing that can be defined as the following broad categories:

1. General testing of applications for validity of outputs in response to inputs

2. Specialized testing for specific kinds of problems, such as performance or capacity

3. Testing that involves the users or clients themselves to evaluate ease of use

The general forms of testing are concerned with almost any kind of software and seek to eliminate common kinds of bugs, such as branching errors, looping errors, incorrect outputs, and the like.

The specialized forms of testing are more narrow in focus and seek specific kinds of errors, such as problems that only occur under full load, or problems that might slow down performance.

The forms of testing involving users are aimed primarily at usability problems and at ensuring that all requirements have, in fact, been implemented.

Not every form of testing is used on every software project, and some forms of testing are used on only 1 project out of every 25 or so. The distribution in Table 24.2 shows the frequency with which various test forms have been noted among SPR's clients for projects of 500 function points or larger.

It is interesting to note that the only form of testing that is truly universal is testing of individual subroutines. Unit testing of entire modules is almost universal, although a few projects have not utilized this method (such as those using the clean-room method). Testing of the entire application upon completion is also very common, although here, too, not every project has done so.

For the other and more specialized forms of testing, such as performance testing or security testing, only a minority of projects among SPR's clients perform such testing. Sometimes the specialized forms

TABLE 24.2   Distribution of Testing Methods for Large Software Projects

Testing stage	Projects utilizing test stage, %
General Testing	
Subroutine testing	100
Unit testing	99
System testing of full application	95
New function testing	90
Regression testing	70
Integration testing	50
Specialized Testing	
Viral protection testing	45
Stress or capacity testing	35
Performance testing	30
Security testing	15
Platform testing	5
Year-2000 testing	5
Independent testing	3
User Testing	
Customer-acceptance testing	35
Field (beta) testing	30
Usability testing	20
Lab testing	1
Clean-room statistical testing	1

of testing are not needed, but sometimes they are needed and are skipped over due to schedule pressure or poor decision making by project managers.

General Forms of Software Testing

The general forms of software testing occur for almost every kind of software: systems software, commercial software, military software, information systems, or anything else.

While the general forms of software testing are common and well understood, not all companies use the same vocabulary to describe them. The following brief definitions explain the general meanings of the general forms of testing discussed here.

Subroutine testing. This is the lowest-level form of testing noted among SPR's clients. Recall that a *subroutine* is a small collection of code that may constitute less than 10 statements, or perhaps one-tenth of a function point.

Subroutine testing is performed almost spontaneously by developers, and is very informal. Essentially, this form of testing consists of executing a just-completed subroutine to see if it compiles properly and performs as expected. Subroutine testing is a key line of defense against errors in algorithms in spite of its being informal and under-reported in the testing literature.

Subroutine testing is too informal to be included in test plans and because it is done by developers themselves, there is usually no data kept on either effort or efficiency in terms of numbers of bugs found. However, since subroutine testing is done immediately after the code is written, it is a key first-line defense against coding defects.

Unit testing. This is the lowest-level form of testing normally discussed in the testing literature. Unit testing is the execution of a complete module or small program that will normally range from perhaps 100 to 1000 source code statements, or roughly from 1 to 10 function points.

Although unit testing may often be performed informally, it is also the stage at which actual test planning and test-case construction begins. Unit testing is usually performed by the programmers who write the module and, hence, seldom includes data on defect levels or removal efficiency. (Note that for testing under clean-room concepts, unit testing is *not* performed by the developers, so data on defect removal may be recorded in this situation.)

Even in the normal situation of unit testing being performed by developers, enough companies have used volunteers who record the defects found during unit testing to have at least an idea of how efficient this form of testing is. Unit testing is also often plagued by bad test cases, which themselves contain errors. Unit testing is the lowest-level form of testing provided for by software-estimating tools.

New function testing.   This is often teamed with regression testing, and both forms are commonly found when existing applications are being updated or modified. As the name implies, new function testing is aimed at validating new features that are being added to a software package.

For entirely new projects, as opposed to enhancements, this form of testing is also known as *component testing* because it tests the combined work of multiple programmers whose programs in aggregate may comprise a component of a larger system.

New function testing is often performed by testing specialists because it covers the work of a number of programmers. For example, typical size ranges of major new functions added to existing software packages can exceed 10,000 source code statements or 100 function points.

New function testing is normally supported by formal test plans and planned test cases, and is performed on software that is under full configuration control. Also, defect reporting for new function testing is both common and reasonably accurate.

New function testing is a key line of defense against errors in intermodule interfaces and the movement of data from place to place through an application. New function testing is also intended to verify that the new or added features work correctly.

Regression testing.   This is the opposite of new function testing. The word *regression* means to slip back, and in the context of testing regression means accidentally damaging an existing feature as an unintended by-product of adding a new feature. Regression testing also checks to ensure that prior known bugs have not inadvertently stayed in the software after they should have been removed.

After a few years of software evolution, regression testing becomes one of the most extensive forms of testing because the library of available test cases from prior releases tends to grow continuously. Also, regression testing involves the entire base code of the application, which for major systems can exceed 10 million lines of code or 100,000 function points.

Regression testing can be performed by developers, professional test personnel, or software quality assurance personnel. Regardless of who performs regression testing, the application is usually under full configuration control.

Regression test libraries, though often extensive, are sometimes troublesome and have both redundant test cases and test cases which themselves contain errors.

Regression testing is a key line of defense against the year-2000 software problem, because it is one of the test stages used to find bad fixes, or secondary defects accidentally injected as a by-product of fixing prior defects—such as new errors introduced while fixing the year-2000 problem.

Integration testing. As the name implies, this is testing on a number of modules or programs that have come together to comprise an integrated software package. Since integration testing may cover the work of dozens, or even hundreds, of programmers, it also deals with rather large numbers of test cases.

Integration testing often occurs in waves as new builds of an evolving application are created. Microsoft, for example, performs daily integration of developing software projects and, hence, also performs daily integration testing. Other companies may have longer intervals between builds, such as weekly or even monthly builds.

Applications undergoing integration testing are usually under formal configuration control. Integration testing normally makes use of formal test plans, planned suites of test cases, and formal defect-reporting procedures. Integration testing can be performed by developers themselves, by professional test personnel, or by software quality assurance personnel, but professional test or QA personnel are usually more efficient and effective than developers.

System testing of full application. This is usually the last form of internal testing before customers get involved with field testing (beta testing). For large systems, a formal system test can take many months and can involve large teams of test personnel. Also, the entire set of development programmers may be needed in order to fix bugs that are found during this critical test stage.

System testing demands formal configuration control and also deserves formal defect-tracking support. System testing can be performed by developers, professional test personnel, or quality-assurance personnel.

For software that controls physical devices (such as telephone switching systems) the phrase *system test* may include concurrent testing of hardware components. In this case, other engineering and quality-assurance specialists may also be involved, such as electrical or aeronautical engineers dealing with the hardware. Microcode may also be part of system testing. For complex hybrid products, system testing is a key event.

System testing may sometimes overlap a specialized form of testing termed *lab testing,* where special laboratories are used to house complex new hardware and software products that will be tested by prospective clients under controlled conditions.

Specialized Forms of Software Testing

These specialized forms of software testing occur with less frequency than the general forms. The specialized forms of testing are most common for systems software, military software, commercial software, contract software, and software with unusually tight criteria for things like high performance or ease of use.

Stress or capacity testing.   This is a specialized form of testing aimed at judging the ability of an application to function when nearing the boundaries of its capabilities in terms of the volume of information used. For example, capacity testing of the word processor used to create this book (Microsoft Word for Windows Version 7) might entail tests against individual large documents of perhaps 200 to 300 pages to judge the upper limits that can be handled before MS Word becomes cumbersome or storage is exceeded.

It might also entail dealing with even larger documents, say 2000 pages, segmented into master documents and various sections. For a database application, capacity testing might entail loading the database with 10,000, 100,000, or 1 million records to judge how it operates when fully populated with information.

Capacity testing is often performed by testing specialists rather than by developers. Capacity testing may either be a separate test stage, or be performed as a subset of integration or system testing. Usually it cannot be performed earlier, since the full application is necessary.

Performance testing.   This is a specialized form of testing aimed at judging whether or not an application can meet the performance goals set for it. For many applications performance is only a minor issue, but for some kinds of applications it is critical. For example, weapons systems, aircraft flight control systems, fuel injection systems, access methods, and telephone switching systems must meet stringent performance goals or the devices the software is controlling may not work.

Performance testing is also important for information systems that need to process large volumes of information rapidly, such as credit card authorizations, airline reservations, and bank ATM transactions.

Performance testing is often performed by professional testers and sometimes is supported by performance or tuning specialists. Some aspects of performance testing can be done at the unit-test level, but the bulk of performance testing is associated with integration and system testing because interfaces within the full product affect performance.

Note that in addition to performance testing, software systems with high performance needs that run on mainframe computers are often *instrumented* by using either hardware or software performance monitoring equipment. Some of these performance monitors can analyze the source code and find areas that may slow down processing, which can then be streamlined or modified.

However, some forms of software with real-time, high-speed requirements are not suitable for performance-monitoring equipment. For example, the onboard flight control software package of a cruise missile has high performance requirements but needs to achieve those requirements prior to deployment.

Viral protection testing.   This is rapidly moving from a specialized form of testing to a general one, although it still has been noted on less than half of SPR's client's projects. The introduction of software viruses by malicious hackers has been a very interesting sociological phenomena in the software world. Viruses number in the thousands, and more are being created daily.

Virus protection has now become a minor but growing subindustry of the software domain. Virus testing is a white-box form of testing. Although commercial virus protection software can be run by anybody, major commercial developers of software also use special proprietary tools to ensure that master copies of software packages do not contain viruses.

Security testing.   This is most common and most sophisticated for military software, followed by software that deals with very confidential information, such as bank records, medical records, tax records, and the like.

The organizations most likely to utilize security testing include the military services, the National Security Agency (NSA), the Central Intelligence Agency (CIA), the Federal Bureau of Investigation (FBI), and other organizations that utilize computers and software for highly sensitive purposes.

Security testing is usually performed by highly trained specialists. Indeed, some military projects use *penetration teams* that attempt to break the security of applications by various covert means, including but not limited to hacking, theft, bribery, and even picking locks or breaking into buildings.

It has been noted that one of the easiest ways to break into secure systems involves finding disgruntled employees, so security testing may have psychological and sociological manifestations.

Platform testing. This is a specialized form of testing found among companies whose software operates on different hardware platforms under different operating systems. Many commercial software vendors market the same applications for Windows 95, Windows NT, OS/2, UNIX, and sometimes for other platforms as well.

While the features and functions of the application may be identical on every platform, the mechanics of getting the software to work on various platforms requires separate versions and separate test stages for each platform. Platform testing is usually a white-box form of testing.

Another aspect of platform testing is ensuring that the software package correctly interfaces with any other software packages that might be related to it. For example, when testing software cost estimating tools, this stage of testing would verify that data can be passed both ways between the estimating tool and various project management tools. For example, suppose cost-estimating tools, such as CHECKPOINT or KnowledgePlan, are intended to share data with Microsoft Project under Windows 95. This is the stage where the interfaces between the two would be verified.

Platform testing is also termed *compatibility testing* by some companies. Regardless of the nomenclature used, the essential purpose remains the same: to ensure software that operates on multiple hardware platforms, under multiple operating systems, and interfaces with multiple tools can handle all varieties of interconnection.

Year-2000 testing. This the most recent form of specialized testing noted among SPR's clients. The first companies among the clients to begin serious attempts to find and fix the year-2000 problem only started in 1994, although perhaps some companies may have started earlier. The year-2000 problem concerns using only two digits for dates, such as 96 for 1996. Many applications will fail when 1999 becomes 2000 because the 00 will disrupt calculations.

As this book is being written, no fewer than 150 commercial tools for seeking out year-2000 hits have entered the commercial market, and several hundred consulting and outsourcing companies have begun year-2000 services.

Independent testing. This is very common for military software, because it was required by Department of Defense standards. It can also be done for commercial software, and indeed there are several commercial testing companies that do testing on a fee basis. However, independent testing is very rare for management information systems, civilian systems software projects, and outsourced or contracted software. Independent testing, as the name implies, is performed by a separate company or at least a separate organization from the one that built the application. Both white-box and black-box forms of independent testing are noted.

A special form of independent testing may occur from time to time as part of litigation when a client charges that a contractor did not achieve acceptable levels of quality. The plaintiff, defendant, or both may commission a third party to test the software.

Another form of independent testing is found among some commercial software vendors who market software developed by subcontractors or other commercial vendors. The primary marketing company usually tests the subcontracted software to ensure that it meets the company's quality criteria.

Forms of Testing Involving Users or Clients

For many software projects, the clients or users are active participants at various stages along the way, including but not limited to requirements gathering, prototyping, inspections, and several forms of testing. The testing stages where users participate are generally the following.

Usability testing. This is a specialized form of testing sometimes performed in usability laboratories. Usability testing involves actual clients who utilize the software under controlled and sometimes instrumented conditions so that their actions can be observed. Usability testing is common for commercial software produced by large companies, such as IBM and Microsoft. Usability testing can occur with any kind of software, however. Usability testing usually occurs at about the same time as system testing. Sometimes usability testing and beta testing are concurrent, but it is more common for usability testing to precede beta testing.

Field (beta) testing. This is a common testing technique for commercial software. *Beta* is the second letter in the Greek alphabet. Its use in testing stems from a testing sequence used by hardware engineers that included alpha, beta, and gamma testing. For software, alpha testing more or less dropped out of the lexicon circa 1980, and gamma testing was almost never part of the software test cycle. Thus, beta is the only one left for software, and is used to mean an external test involving customers.

Microsoft has become famous by conducting the most massive

external beta tests in software history, with more than 10,000 customers participating. High-volume beta testing with thousands of customers is very efficient in terms of defect-removal efficiency levels and can exceed 85 percent removal efficiency if there are more than 1000 beta-test participants. However, if beta-test participation comprises less than a dozen clients, removal efficiency is usually around 35 to 50 percent.

Beta testing usually occurs after system testing, although some companies start external beta tests before system testing is finished (to the dismay of their customers). External beta testing and internal usability testing may occur concurrently. However, beta testing may involve special agreements with clients to avoid the risk of lawsuits should the software manifest serious problems.

Lab testing.   This is a special form of testing found primarily with hybrid products that consist of complex physical devices that are controlled by software, such as telephone switching systems, weapons systems, and medical instruments. It is obvious that conventional field testing or beta testing of something like a PBX switch, a cruise missile, or a CAT scanner is infeasible due to the need for possible structural modifications to buildings, special electrical wiring, and heating and cooling requirements, to say nothing of zoning permits and authorization by various boards and controlling bodies.

Therefore, the companies that build such devices often have laboratories where clients can test out both the hardware and the software prior to having the equipment installed on their own premises.

Customer-acceptance testing.   This is commonly found for contract software and often is found for management information systems, software, and military software. The only form of software where acceptance testing is rare or does not occur is high-volume commercial shrink-wrapped software. Even here, some vendors and retail stores provide a money-back guarantee, which permits a form of acceptance testing. How the customers go about acceptance testing varies considerably. Customer-acceptance testing is not usually part of software cost estimates, since the work is not done by the software vendors but rather by the clients. However, the time in the schedule is still shown, and the effort for fixing client-reported bugs is shown.

Clean-room statistical testing.   This is found only in the context of clean-room development methods. The clean-room approach is unusual in that the developers do not perform unit testing, and the test cases themselves are based on statistical assertions of usage patterns. Clean-room testing is inextricably joined with formal specification methods and proofs of correctness. Clean-room testing is always performed by testing specialists or quality assurance personnel rather than the developers themselves, because under the clean-room concept developers do no testing.

Number of Testing Stages

Looking at the data from another vantage point, if each specific kind of testing is deemed a *testing stage,* it is interesting to see how many discrete testing stages occur for software projects (see Table 24.3). The overall range of testing stages among SPR's clients and their software projects runs from a low of 1 to a high of 16 out of the total number of testing stages of 18 discussed here.

As can be seen from the distribution of results, the majority of software projects in the United States (70 percent) use 6 or fewer discrete testing stages, and the most common pattern of testing observed includes the following:

TABLE 24.3   Approximate Distribution of Testing Stages for U.S. Software Projects

Number of testing stages	Projects utilizing test stages, %
1	2
2	8
3	12
4	14
5	16
6	18
7	5
8	5
9	7
10	5
11	3
12	1
13	1
14	1
15	1
16	1
17	0
18	0
Total	100

- Subroutine testing
- Unit testing
- New function testing
- Regression testing
- Integration testing
- System testing

These 6 forms of testing are very common on applications of 1000 function points or larger. These six also happen to be generalized forms of testing that deal with broad categories of errors and issues.

Below 1000 function points, and especially below 100 function points, sometimes only 3 testing stages are found, assuming the project in question is new and not an enhancement:

- Subroutine testing
- Unit testing
- New function testing

The other forms of testing that are less common are more specialized, such as performance testing or capacity testing, and deal with a narrow band of problems which not every application is concerned with.

Testing Pattern Variations by Industry and Type of Software

There are, of course, very significant variations between industries and between various kinds of software in terms of typical testing patterns utilized, as follows.

End-user software. This the sparsest in terms of testing, and the usual pattern includes only two test stages: subroutine testing and unit testing. Of course, end-user software is almost all less than 100 function points in size.

Management information systems (MIS). MIS software projects use from three up to perhaps eight forms of testing. A typical MIS testing-stage pattern would include subroutine testing, unit testing, new function testing, regression testing, system testing, and user-acceptance testing. MIS testing is usually performed by the developers themselves, so that testing by professional test personnel or by quality-assurance personnel is a rarity in this domain.

Outsource software. Vendors doing information systems are similar to their clients in terms of testing patterns. MIS outsource vendors use typical MIS patterns; systems software vendors use typical systems software patterns; and military outsource vendors use typical military test patterns. This means that the overall range of outsource testing can run from as few as 3 kinds of testing up to a high of 16 kinds of testing. Usually the outsource vendors utilize at least one more stage of testing than their clients. (See the section on "Outsource Estimation" in Chap. 10 for additional information.)

Commercial software. Commercial software developed by major vendors, such as Microsoft, IBM, and Computer Associates, will typically use a 12-stage testing series: (1) subroutine testing, (2) unit testing, (3) new function testing, (4) regression testing, (5) performance testing, (6) stress testing, (7) integration testing, (8) usability testing, (9) platform testing, (10) system testing, (11) viral testing, and (12) field testing, which is often called *external* or *beta* testing.

However, small software vendors who develop small applications of less than 1000 function points may only use 6 testing stages: (1) subroutine testing, (2) unit testing, (3) new function testing, (4) regression testing, (5) system testing, and (6) beta testing.

Major software vendors, such as Microsoft and IBM, utilize large departments of professional testers who take over after unit testing and perform the major testing work at the higher levels, such as integration testing, system testing, and such specialized testing as performance testing or stress testing.

Systems software. This is often extensively tested and may use as many as 14 different testing stages. A typical testing pattern for a software system in the 10,000–function point range would include subroutine testing, unit testing, new function testing, regression testing, performance testing, stress/capacity testing, integration testing, usability testing, system testing, viral testing, security testing, year-2000 testing, and lab testing and/or field testing, which is often called *external* or *beta* testing.

The larger systems software companies such as AT&T, Siemens-Nixdorf, IBM, and the like, typically utilize professional testing personnel after unit testing. Also, the systems software domain typically has the largest and best-equipped software quality assurance groups and the only quality-assurance research labs.

Some of the large systems software organizations may have three different kinds of quality-related laboratories:

1. Quality research labs

2. Usability labs

3. Hardware and software product testing labs

Indeed, the larger systems software groups are among the few kinds of organizations that actually perform research on software quality, in the classical definition of *research* as formal experiments using trial and error methods to develop improved tools and practices.

Military software. This uses the most extensive suite of test stages, and large weapons or logistics systems may include 16 discrete testing stages: (1) subroutine testing; (2) unit testing; (3) new function testing; (4) regression testing; (5) performance testing; (6) stress testing; (7) integration testing; (8) independent testing; (9) usability testing; (10) lab testing; (11) system testing; (12) viral testing; (13) security testing; (14) year-2000 testing; (15) field testing, which is often called *external* or *beta* testing; and (16) customer-acceptance testing.

Only military projects routinely utilize *independent testing*, or testing by a separate company external to the developing or contracting organization. Military projects often utilize the services of professional testing personnel and also quality-assurance personnel.

However, there are several companies that perform independent testing for commercial software organizations. Often, smaller software companies that lack full in-house testing capabilities will utilize such external testing organizations.

Testing Pattern Variations by Size of Application

Another interesting way of looking at the distribution of testing stages is to look at the ranges and numbers of test stages associated with the various sizes of software applications, as shown in Table 24.4.

TABLE 24.4   Ranges of Test Stages Associated with the Size of Software Applications

Application size, FP	Number of test stages performed		
	Minimum	Average	Maximum
1	0	3	4
10	1	4	5
100	2	5	8
1,000	3	9	11
10,000	4	10	13
100,000	6	12	16

TABLE 24.5   **Average Number of Tests Observed by Application Size and Class of Software**

(Application size in function points)

Class of software	1	10	100	1,000	10,000	100,000	Average
End-user	1	2	2				1.67
MIS	2	3	4	6	7	8	5.00
Outsource	2	3	5	7	8	9	5.67
Commercial	3	4	6	9	11	12	7.50
Systems	3	4	7	11	12	14	8.50
Military	4	5	8	11	13	16	9.50
Average	2.50	3.50	5.33	8.80	10.20	11.80	7.02

As can be seen, the larger applications tend to utilize a much more extensive set of testing stages than do the smaller applications, which is not unexpected.

It is interesting to consolidate testing variations by industry and testing variations by size of application. The following table shows the typical number of test stages observed for six size plateaus and six software classes (see Table 24.5.

There are wide variations in testing patterns, so this table has a significant margin of error. However, the data is interesting and explains why the commercial, systems, and military software domains often have higher reliability levels than others.

This table also illustrates that there is no single pattern of testing that is universally appropriate for all sizes of software and all classes of software. The optimal pattern of defect-removal and testing stages must be matched to the nature of the application.

Testing Stages Noted in Lawsuits Alleging Poor Quality

It is an interesting observation that for outsourced, military, and systems software that ends up in court for litigation which involves assertions of unacceptable or inadequate quality, the number of testing stages is much smaller, while formal design and code inspections are not utilized at all.

Table 24.6 shows the typical patterns of defect-removal activities for software projects larger than 1000 function points in size where the developing organization was sued by the client for producing software of inadequate quality.

The table simply compares the pattern of defect-removal operations observed for reliable software packages with high quality levels to the

TABLE 24.6   Defect Removal and Testing Stages Noted During Litigation for Poor Quality

Stages	Reliable software	Software in litigation
Formal design inspections	Used	Not used
Formal code inspections	Used	Not used
Subroutine testing	Used	Used
Unit testing	Used	Used
New function testing	Used	Rushed or omitted
Regression testing	Used	Rushed or omitted
Integration testing	Used	Used
System testing	Used	Rushed or omitted
Performance testing	Used	Rushed or omitted
Capacity testing	Used	Rushed or omitted

pattern noted during lawsuits where poor quality and low reliability were at issue. The phrase *rushed or omitted* indicates that the vendor departed from best standard practices by eliminating a stage of defect removal or by rushing it in order to meet an arbitrary finish date or commitment to the client.

It is interesting that during the depositions and testimony of litigation, the vendor often countercharges that the shortcuts were made at the direct request of the client. Sometimes the vendor asserts that the client ordered the shortcuts even in the face of warnings that the results might be hazardous.

As can be seen, software developed under contractual obligations is at some peril if quality control and testing approaches are not carefully performed. See the section on "Outsource Estimation" in Chap. 10 for additional information.

Using Function Points to Estimate Test-Case Volumes

Function points and the related feature point metrics are starting to provide some preliminary but interesting insights into test-case volumes. This is not unexpected, because the fundamental parameters of both function points and feature points all represent topics that need test coverage, as follows:

- Inputs
- Outputs
- Inquires

- Logical files
- Interfaces
- Algorithms (feature points only)

Since function points and feature points can both be derived during the requirements and early design stages, this approach offers a method of predicting test-case numbers fairly early. The method is still somewhat experimental, but the approach is leading to interesting results and its usage is expanding.

Table 24.7 shows preliminary data on the number of test cases that have been noted among SPR's clients, using *test cases per function point* as the normalizing metric. This table has a high margin of error, but as with any other set of preliminary data points, it is better to publish the results in the hope of future refinements and corrections than to wait until the data is truly complete.

The usage of function point metrics also provides some rough rules of thumb for predicting the overall volumes of test cases that are likely to be created for software projects.

TABLE 24.7   Ranges of Test Cases per Function Point

Testing stage	Minimum	Average	Maximum
Clean-room testing	0.60	1.00	3.00
Regression testing	0.40	0.60	1.30
Unit testing	0.20	0.45	1.20
New function testing	0.25	0.40	0.90
Integration testing	0.20	0.40	0.75
Subroutine testing	0.20	0.30	0.40
Independent testing	0.00	0.30	0.55
System testing	0.15	0.25	0.60
Viral testing	0.00	0.20	0.40
Performance testing	0.00	0.20	0.40
Acceptance testing	0.00	0.20	0.60
Lab testing	0.00	0.20	0.50
Field (beta) testing	0.00	0.20	1.00
Usability testing	0.00	0.20	0.40
Platform testing	0.00	0.15	0.30
Stress testing	0.00	0.15	0.30
Security testing	0.00	0.15	0.35
Year-2000 testing	0.00	0.15	0.30
Total	2.00	5.50	13.25

- Raising the function point total of the application to the 1.2 power will give an approximation of the minimum number of test cases.

- Raising the function point total to the 1.3 power gives an approximation of the average number of test cases.

- Raising the function point total to the 1.4 power gives an approximation of the maximum number of test cases.

These rules of thumb are based on observations of software projects whose sizes range between about 100 and 100,000 function points. Rules of thumb are not accurate enough for serious business purposes, such as contracts, but are useful in providing estimating sanity checks. See the section on "Function Point Sizing Rules of Thumb" in Chap. 11 for additional rules of thumb involving these versatile metrics.

Because of combinatorial complexity, it is usually impossible to write and run enough test cases to fully exercise a software project larger than about 100 function points in size. The number of permutations of inputs, outputs, and control-flow paths quickly becomes astronomical.

For really large systems that approach 100,000 function points in size, the total number of test cases needed to fully test every condition can be regarded, for practical purposes, as infinite. Also, the amount of computing time needed to run such a test suite would also be an infinite number, or at least a number so large that there are not enough computers in any single company to approach the capacity needed.

Therefore, the volumes of test cases shown here are based on empirical observations and the numbers assume standard reduction techniques, such as testing boundary conditions rather than all intermediate values and compressing related topics into equivalency classes.

Using Function Points to Estimate the Numbers of Test Personnel

One of the newest but most interesting uses of function point metrics in a testing context is for predicting the probable number of test personnel that might be needed for each test stage, and then for the overall product.

Table 24.8 has a high margin of error, but the potential value of using function points for test-staffing prediction is high enough to make publication of preliminary data useful.

This table is a bit misleading. While the average test stage might have a ratio of about 1500 function points for every tester, the range

TABLE 24.8   **Ranges in Number of Function Points per Software Tester**

Testing stage	Minimum	Average	Maximum
Subroutine testing	0.1	1.0	3.0
Unit testing	1.0	3.0	12.0
New function testing	100.0	350.0	1500.0
Clean-room testing	100.0	350.0	1000.0
Performance testing	150.0	400.0	1000.0
Integration testing	150.0	700.0	2500.0
Acceptance testing	250.0	750.0	1500.0
Regression testing	500.0	1500.0	7500.0
Platform testing	350.0	1500.0	5000.0
Security testing	200.0	1500.0	3500.0
Field (beta) testing	250.0	1500.0	5000.0
Usability testing	150.0	2000.0	4500.0
Lab testing	750.0	2500.0	4000.0
Viral testing	250.0	2500.0	5000.0
System testing	750.0	2500.0	5000.0
Independent testing	500.0	2500.0	8500.0
Capacity testing	400.0	3000.0	7500.0
Year-2000 testing	250.0	3500.0	9000.0
Average	283.4	1503.0	4000.8

is very broad. Also, the table does not show the ratio of testers to software for testing performed in parallel.

For example, if a common four-stage combination of test stages where professional testers or quality-assurance personnel handle the testing is done in parallel rather than sequentially, the ratio for the entire combination is in the range of 1 testing staff member for about every 250 function points for the following test stages:

- New function testing
- Regression testing
- Integration testing
- System testing

For some of the test stages, such as subroutine testing and unit testing, the normal practice is for the testing to be performed by developers. In this case, the data simply indicates the *average* sizes of subroutines and standalone programs.

Testing and Defect-Removal Efficiency Levels

Most forms of testing, such as unit testing by individual program-mers, are less than 30 percent efficient in finding bugs. That is, less than one bug out of three will be detected during the test period. Sometimes a whole string of test steps (unit testing, function testing, integration testing, and system testing) will find less than 50 percent of the bugs in a software product. By itself, testing alone has never been sufficient to ensure really high quality levels.

Consider also the major categories of defects that affect software:

1. Errors of omission
2. Errors of commission
3. Errors of clarity or ambiguity
4. Errors of speed
5. Errors of capacity

Table 24.9 shows the approximate defect-removal efficiency level of

TABLE 24.9   Average Defect-Removal Efficiency Levels of Software Test Stages Against Five Defect Types

(Percentage of defects removed)

Testing stage	Omission	Commission	Clarity	Speed	Capacity	Average
Beta testing	40	40	35	40	35	38
Lab testing	25	35	30	50	50	38
System testing	20	30	30	50	50	36
Clean-room testing	35	40	35	25	40	35
Usability testing	55	50	60	10	0	35
Acceptance testing	30	35	35	35	30	33
Independent testing	20	30	30	35	40	31
Stress testing	0	40	0	25	80	29
New function testing	30	30	30	20	20	26
Integration testing	20	35	20	25	25	25
Unit testing	10	60	10	20	20	24
Platform testing	20	70	0	30	0	24
Regression testing	10	45	20	20	20	23
Performance testing	0	10	0	75	30	23
Subroutine testing	10	50	0	20	15	19
Virus testing	0	80	0	0	0	16
Security testing	50	30	0	0	0	16
Year-2000 testing	0	80	0	0	0	16
Average	21	44	19	27	25	27

the common forms of testing against these five error categories (with a very large margin of error).

This data is derived in part from measurements by SPR's clients, and in part from discussion with software testing and quality-assurance personnel in a number of companies. The data is based on anecdotes rather than real statistical results because none of SPR's clients actually record this kind of information. However, the overall picture the data gives of testing is interesting and clarifies testing's main strengths and weaknesses.

This table is ranked in descending order of overall efficiency against all forms of defects and, hence, is slightly misleading. Some of the specialized forms of testing, such as year-2000 testing or viral protection testing, are highly efficient but against only one narrow class of problem.

The most obvious conclusion from this table is that testing is much more effective in finding errors of *commission,* or things that are done wrong, than it is in finding errors of *omission,* or things that are left out by accident.

Note that there are wide ranges of observed defect-removal efficiency over and above the approximate averages shown here. Any given form of testing can achieve defect-removal efficiency levels that are perhaps 15 percent higher than these averages, or about 10 percent lower. However, no known form of testing has yet exceeded 90 percent in defect-removal efficiency, so a series of inspections plus a multistage series of tests is needed to achieve really high levels of defect-removal efficiency, such as 99.9999%.

Although testing is often the only form of defect removal utilized for software, the performance of testing is greatly enhanced by the use of formal design and code inspections, both of which tend to elevate testing efficiency levels in addition to finding defects themselves.

Using Function Points to Estimate Testing Effort and Costs

Another use of the function point metric in a testing context is to estimate and later measure testing effort and costs. A full and formal evaluation of testing requires analysis of three discrete activities:

1. Test preparation

2. Test execution

3. Defect repair

Test preparation involves creating test cases, validating them, and putting them into a test library.

Test execution involves running the test cases against the software and recording the results. Note that testing is an iterative process, and the same test cases can be run several times if needed, or even more.

Defect repair concerns fixing any bugs that are found via testing, validating the fix, and then rerunning the test cases that found the bugs to ensure that the bugs have been repaired and that no bad fixes have inadvertently been introduced.

With a total of 18 different kinds of testing to consider, the actual prediction of testing effort is too complex for simplistic rules of thumb. Several commercial estimating tools, such as CHECKPOINT, COCOMO II, KnowledgePlan, PRICE-S, SEER, and SLIM, can predict testing costs for each test stage and then aggregate overall testing effort and expenses for any kind or size of software project. These same tools and others within this class can also predict testing defect-removal efficiency levels.

There are too many variables involved for a static representation in a published table or graph to be really accurate. Therefore, for the purposes of this book, a major simplifying assumption will be used. The assumption is that the proportion of total software effort devoted to testing correlates exactly with the number of test stages that are utilized. This assumption has a few exceptions, but seems to work well enough to have practical value.

The percentages shown in Table 24.10 for testing are based on the total development budget for the software project in question.

The same table also shows the approximate defect-removal efficiency correlated with number of test stages for coding defects. Here, too, as the number of test stages grows larger, defect-removal efficiency levels increase. The essential message is that if you want to approach zero-defect levels, be prepared to perform quite a few testing stages.

This simplified approach is not accurate enough for serious project planning or for contracts, but it shows overall trends well enough to make the economic picture understandable.

This table also explains why large systems have higher testing costs than small applications, and why systems and military software have higher testing costs than information systems: More testing stages are utilized.

Note, however, that the table does not show the whole picture (which is why commercial estimating tools are recommended). For example, if formal pretesting design and code inspections are also utilized, they alone can approach 80 percent in defect-removal efficiency and also raise the efficiency of testing.

Thus, projects that utilize formal inspections plus testing can top 99 percent in cumulative defect-removal efficiency with fewer stages than shown here, since this table illustrates only testing. See Chap.

**TABLE 24.10   Number of Testing Stages, Testing Effort, and
Defect-Removal Efficiency**

Number of testing stages	Effort devoted to testing, %	Cumulative defect removal efficiency, %
1	10	50
2	15	60
3	20	70
4	25	75
5	30	80
6*	33*	85*
7	36	87
8	39	90
9	42	92
10	45	94
11	48	96
12	52	98
13	55	99
14	58	99.9
15	61	99.99
16	64	99.999
17	67	99.9999
18	70	99.99999

*Six test stages, 33 costs, and 85 percent removal efficiency are approximate U.S. averages for software projects = >1000 function points in size.

20, "Estimating Design Inspections" and Chap. 22, "Estimating Code Inspections" for additional information.

There is no shortage of historical data which indicates that formal inspections continue to be one of the most powerful software defect removal operations since the software industry began.

Testing by Developers or by Professional Test Personnel

One of the major questions concerning software testing is who should do it. The possible answers to this question include:

1. The developers themselves

2. Professional test personnel

3. Professional quality-assurance personnel

4. Some combination of the three

Note that several forms of testing, such as external beta testing and customer-acceptance testing, are performed by clients themselves or by consultants that the clients hire to do the work.

There is no definitive answer to this question, but some empirical observations may be helpful.

- The defect-removal efficiency of almost all forms of testing is higher when performed by test personnel or by quality-assurance personnel rather than by the developers themselves. The only exceptions are subroutine and unit tests.

- For usability problems, testing by clients themselves outranks all other forms of testing.

- The defect-removal efficiency of specialized kinds of testing, such as year-2000 testing or viral protection testing, is highest when performed by professional test personnel rather than by the developers themselves.

Table 24.11 shows the author's observations of who typically performs various test stages from among SPR's client organizations. Note that

TABLE 24.11 Observations on Performance of Test Stages by Occupation Group
(Percentage of testing performed)

Testing stage	Developers	Testers	QA personnel	Clients
Subroutine testing	100	0	0	0
Unit testing	90	10	0	0
New function testing	50	30	20	0
Integration testing	50	30	20	0
Viral testing	50	30	20	0
System testing	40	40	20	0
Regression testing	30	50	20	0
Performance testing	30	60	10	0
Platform testing	30	50	20	0
Stress testing	30	50	20	0
Security testing	30	40	30	0
Year-2000 testing	20	50	30	0
Usability testing	10	10	30	50
Acceptance testing	0	0	0	100
Lab testing	0	0	0	100
Field (beta) testing	0	0	0	100
Clean-room testing	0	50	40	10
Independent testing	0	60	40	0
Average	31	31	18	20

since SPR's clients include quite a few systems software, military software, and commercial software vendors there probably is a bias in the data. The systems, commercial, and military software domains are much more likely to utilize the services of professional testing and quality-assurance (QA) personnel than are the MIS and outsource domains.

The table is sorted in descending order of the development column. Note that this order illustrates that the early testing is most often performed by development personnel, but the later stages of testing are most often performed by testing or quality-assurance specialists.

As can be seen from this table, among SPR's clients testing by developers and testing by professional test personnel are equal in frequency, followed by testing involving software quality assurance personnel, and, finally, testing by customers or their designated testers.

Testing by development personnel is much more common for the smaller forms of testing, such as subroutine and unit testing. For the larger forms (i.e., system testing) and for the specialized forms (i.e., performance testing, year-2000 testing, etc.), testing by professional test personnel or by quality-assurance personnel become more common.

Testing should be part of a synergistic and integrated suite of defect-prevention and defect-removal operations that may include prototyping, quality-assurance reviews, pretest inspections, formal test planning, multistage testing, and measurement of defect levels and severities.

For those who have no empirical data on quality, the low average defect-removal efficiency levels of most forms of testing will be something of a surprise. However, it is because each testing step is less than 100 percent efficient that multiple test stages are necessary in the first place.

Testing is an important technology for software. For many years, progress in testing primarily occurred within the laboratories of major corporations who built systems software. However, in recent years a new subindustry has appeared of commercial testing tool and testing-support companies. This new subindustry is gradually improving software test capabilities as the commercial vendors of testing tools and methodologies compete within a fast-growing market for test-support products and services.

Factors That Affect Testing Performance

The key factors that affect testing from the point of view of estimating test schedules, costs, and efficiency levels include the following:

1. The number of bugs or defects in the application being testing
2. The number of test stages selected for the application

3. The structure of the application, measured with cyclomatic and essential complexity

4. The test-tool suite available to the testing personnel

5. The training and experience of the testing personnel

6. Whether or not precursor code inspections were utilized

7. The amount of time allotted to testing in project schedules

Unfortunately, these seven factors tend to be independent variables and each of them can vary significantly. It is interesting to bracket the possible outcomes by means of *best-case, expected-case,* and *worst-case* scenarios for a generic application of 1000 function points or 100,000 procedural source code statements.

The *best-case* scenario would comprise a combination of experienced test personnel with very sophisticated test tools performing a sequence of at least eight test stages on software that is well structured and low in defects.

The forms of testing used in the best-case scenario would include (at a minimum) subroutine testing, unit testing, new function testing, regression testing, integration testing, system testing, performance testing, and external testing. Note that with the best-case scenario, there is a high probability that formal inspections would also have been utilized.

The *expected-case* scenario would include moderately experienced personnel using a few test tools, such as record/playback tools and test execution monitors, performing half a dozen test stages on fairly well structured code that contains a moderate quantity of defects. The forms of testing used would include subroutine testing, unit testing, new function testing, regression testing, system testing, and external testing.

The *worst-case* scenario would consist of inexperienced test personnel with few test tools, attempting to test a very buggy, poorly structured application under tremendous schedule pressure.

However, under the worst-case scenario it is likely that only five kinds of testing might be performed: subroutine testing, unit testing, new function testing, system testing, and external testing.

References

Beizer, Boris: *Software Testing Techniques,* Van Nostrand Reinhold, New York, 1988.
———: *Black Box Testing,* IEEE Computer Society Press, Los Alamitos, Calif., 1995.
Boehm, Barry: *Software Engineering Economics,* Prentice Hall, Englewood Cliffs, N.J., 1981.
Brown, Norm (ed.): *The Program Manager's Guide to Software Acquisition Best Practices,* Version 1.0, U.S. Department of Defense, Washington, D.C., July 1995.
DeMarco, Tom: *Controlling Software Projects,* Yourdon Press, New York, ISBN 0-917072-32-4, 1982.
Department of the Air Force: *Guidelines for Successful Acquisition and Management of*

Software Intensive Systems, vols. 1 and 2, Software Technology Support Center, Hill Air Force Base, Utah, 1994.

Dreger, Brian: *Function Point Analysis,* Prentice Hall, Englewood Cliffs, N.J., ISBN 0-13-332321-8, 1989.

Grady, Robert B.: *Practical Software Metrics for Project Management and Process Improvement,* Prentice Hall, Englewood Cliffs, N.J., ISBN 0-13-720384-5, 1992.

———, and Deborah L. Caswell: *Software Metrics: Establishing a Company-Wide Program,* Prentice Hall, Englewood Cliffs, N.J., ISBN 0-13-821844-7, 1987.

Hutchinson, Marnie L.: *Software Testing Methods and Metrics,* McGraw-Hill, New York, ISBN 0-07-912929-3, 1997.

Jones, Capers: *New Directions in Software Management,* Information Systems Management Group, ISBN 1-56909-009-2, 1993.

———: *Assessment and Control of Software Risks,* Prentice Hall, Englewood Cliffs, N.J., ISBN 0-13-741406-4, 1994.

———: *Patterns of Software System Failure and Success,* International Thomson Computer Press, Boston, ISBN 1-850-32804-8, 1995.

———: *Applied Software Measurement,* 2d ed., McGraw-Hill, New York, ISBN 0-07-032826-9, 1996a.

———: *Table of Programming Languages and Levels* (8 Versions from 1985 through July 1996), Software Productivity Research, Burlington, Mass., 1996.

———: *The Economics of Object-Oriented Software,* Software Productivity Research, Burlington, Mass., April 1997a.

———: *Software Quality—Analysis and Guidelines for Success,* International Thomson Computer Press, Boston, Mass., ISBN 1-85032-876-6, 1997b.

———: *The Year 2000 Software Problem—Quantifying the Costs and Assessing the Consequences,* Addison-Wesley, Reading, Mass., ISBN 0-201-30964-5, 1998.

Howard, Alan (ed.): *Software Testing Tools,* Applied Computer Research (ACR), Phoenix, Ariz., 1997.

Kaner, C., J. Faulk, and H. Q. Nguyen: *Testing Computer Software,* International Thomson Computer Press, Boston, Mass., 1997.

Linegaard, G.: *Usability Testing and System Evaluation,* International Thomson Computer Press, Boston, Mass., 1997.

Love, Tom: *Object Lessons,* SIGS Books, New York, ISBN 0-9627477 3-4, 1993.

Marciniak, John J. (ed.): *Encyclopedia of Software Engineering,* vols. 1 and 2, John Wiley & Sons, New York, ISBN 0-471-54002, 1994.

McCabe, Thomas J.: "A Complexity Measure," *IEEE Transactions on Software Engineering,* December 1976, pp. 308–320.

Mosley, Daniel J.: *The Handbook of MIS Application Software Testing,* Yourdon Press/Prentice Hall, Englewood Cliffs, N.J., ISBN 0-13-907007-9, 1993.

Perry, William: *Effective Methods for Software Testing,* IEEE Computer Society Press, Los Alamitos, Calif., 1995.

Pressman, Roger: *Software Engineering—A Practitioner's Approach,* McGraw-Hill, New York, 1982.

Putnam, Lawrence H.: *Measures for Excellence—Reliable Software on Time, Within Budget,* Yourdon Press/Prentice Hall, Englewood Cliffs, N.J., ISBN 0-13-567694-0, 1992.

———, and Ware Myers: *Industrial Strength Software—Effective Management Using Measurement,* IEEE Press, Los Alamitos, Calif., ISBN 0-8186-7532-2, 1997.

Rethinking the Software Process, CD-ROM, Miller Freeman, Lawrence, Kans., 1996. (This CD-ROM is a book collection jointly produced by the book publisher, Prentice Hall, and the journal publisher, Miller Freeman. It contains the full text and illustrations of five Prentice Hall books: Capers Jones, *Assessment and Control of Software Risks;* Tom DeMarco, *Controlling Software Projects;* Brian Dreger, *Function Point Analysis;* Larry Putnam and Ware Myers, *Measures for Excellence;* and Mark Lorenz and Jeff Kidd, *Object-Oriented Software Metrics.*)

Symons, Charles R.: *Software Sizing and Estimating—Mk II FPA (Function Point Analysis),* John Wiley & Sons, Chichester, U.K., ISBN 0 471-92985-9, 1991.

25

Estimating User and Project Documentation

The software industry has developed three characteristics which are visibly distinct from almost every other industry:

1. Software is the most labor intensive of any U.S. industry in terms of the amount of human effort required to create a product.

2. Software, being abstract, has become a document-intensive industry and tends to create a larger volume of text and graphics-based documents than almost any other industry.

3. Learning to use software applications often requires more training and more tutorial information than any other consumer product.

The second and third of these attributes explain a significant proportion of the first attribute. Software is labor intensive not only because of the source code itself, but because of the enormous number of paper documents that are created to define and explain the source code.

As discussed several times elsewhere in this book, the five major cost drivers for software projects in rank order of total effort are the following:

1. Finding and fixing bugs

2. Producing paper documents

3. Meetings and communications

4. Coding

5. Project management

Indeed, for some kinds of software, such as large military applications, the sequence of cost drivers 1 and 2 are reversed, and *paperwork* is the topmost cost element. Some of SPR's military clients have produced as many as 400 English words for every Ada source code statement. The cost of these words is more than twice that of the code itself.

Curiously, although the production of paper documents is one of the most expensive and time-consuming activities in the history of software, the literature on this topic is almost nonexistent. The most probable reason why such a major topic has little or no quantification is due to the historical use of lines-of-code (LOC) metrics. This unfortunate metric cannot be used for estimating or measuring paper documents; hence, to most software engineering authors, paperwork has been essentially invisible.

Indeed, the primary books that discuss estimation and measurement of software documentation are those written by function point users, such as Charles Symons's *Software Sizing and Estimating* (Symons 1991) or the author's own *Applied Software Measurement* (Jones 1996).

There is, of course, an extensive how-to-do-it literature that covers scores of individual documents, including requirements, various forms of specifications, planning documents, user manuals, and a number of others. However, the books that discuss specific kinds of documents are often silent on document costs, schedules, staffing, and even on such basic factors as the size of the documents correlated with the size of the software projects themselves.

From an estimating standpoint, only a handful of commercial software-estimating tools include predictive capabilities for software paper documents. Some of the estimating tools that can estimate paper documents include SPQR/20 (1985), CHECKPOINT (1989), and KnowledgePlan (1997). It is no coincidence that the designer of these tools (Capers Jones) was formerly the manager of a software documentation department within IBM.

Other estimating tools, such as COCOMO, COCOMO II, SLIM, and the like, can also estimate some forms of software documentation, such as specification sets, but may not support user manuals, training materials, or some forms of planning documents.

In general, software document production is underreported in the software literature and undersupported in both project management and estimating tools. Even configuration-control tools do not always support the major documents and often concentrate on source code rather than on specifications and user documents.

The nominal default values for estimating software documentation are shown in Table 25.1, although there are very large ranges for every factor:

Software documentation has never lent itself to being estimated or

TABLE 25.1   Nominal Default Values for Documentation Estimates

Activity sequence	Ninth
Performed by	Technical writers; developers; clients
Predecessor activities	Design, coding, and partial testing
Overlap	50% with coding
Concurrent activities	Coding and testing
Successor activities	System testing; beta, or field testing
Initial requirements size	0.50 U.S. text pages per function point
Graphics volumes	0.02 illustrations per function point
Reuse	15% from prior or similar projects
Assignment scope	1500 function points per technical staff member
Production rate	125 function points per staff month
Production rate	1.06 work hours per function point
Schedule months	Function points raised to the 0.15 power
Rate of creep or change	2.0% per month
Defect potential	0.6 documentation defects per function point
Defect removal	75% via editing and document inspections
Delivered defects	0.15 document defects per function point
High-severity defects	10% of delivered document defects
Bad fix probability	5% of document fixes may yield new errors

measured using lines-of-code metrics but does have a number of traditional rules of thumb based on text pages or on ratios to other activities. For example, as long ago as 1965 the IBM corporation used rules of thumb for estimating software user manuals that included the following:

- The effort for user manuals comprises about 10% of coding effort for assembly language applications.

- One technical writer can support the work of 10 programmers, if they are coding in low-level languages such as assembly language.

- Technical writers can produce final text at an average rate of one page per working day.

The problem with rules of thumb based on ratios of programming effort is that with 500 or so programming languages in existence, the rules are too erratic to be useful. It is hardly a good estimating practice to assume that if 1 technical writer can support the work of 10 programmers using assembly language, then this ratio would also apply to Visual Basic, C++, Smalltalk, or any of the more powerful modern programming languages.

However, in modern software cost estimating tools, documentation estimates based on function point metrics are now the norm, although some estimating tools support the older methods as well.

Software documentation is rapidly being transformed under the impact of modern graphics-production tools, the World Wide Web, and the more or less unlimited storage capacity of CD-ROM and equivalent optical devices.

Documentation for software during the 1970s and 1980s was primarily textual, with only such rudimentary graphics as flowcharts and simple structure diagrams. Today, in the late 1990s, much of the software documentation is available online, is highly graphical and perhaps even animated, and the sizes of normal text-based user manuals are smaller today than 10 years ago.

Before continuing with a discussion of estimating documentation costs, it is appropriate to illustrate the many kinds of documents associated with software products, to make clear why software paperwork in all its manifestations is a key software cost element.

Table 25.2 illustrates typical sizes for nine general kinds of documents associated with software projects: (1) planning documents, (2) financial documents, (3) project-control documents, (4) technical documents, (5) legal documents, (6) marketing documents, (7) user documents, (8) support documents, and (9) quality-control documents.

The table also shows the ranges for management information system (MIS) software, systems software, military projects software, and commercial software packages. Both the numbers of documents produced and their average sizes vary significantly by class of application, and also by size of application.

With an average of 69 kinds of documents produced for large software applications, it should come as no surprise to see why the sum of all documents under the heading of *paperwork* is the most expensive software cost element for military software projects and the second most expensive software cost element for civilian software projects.

However, because document sizes and costs cannot be easily measured using the lines-of-code metric, the cost implications of software paperwork remained invisible until the advent of function point metrics, which suddenly revealed that paperwork costs are far larger than coding costs for major software systems.

Software document estimation is normally carried out in the following sequence:

1. Determine the specific set of documents to be produced for the application.

2. Determine the size of each document to be produced.

TABLE 25.2   Universe of Software Project Document Types
(Size in pages per function point)

Document type	MIS	Systems	Military	Commercial	Average
Planning documents					
Marketing plans				0.020	0.020
Project staffing plans	0.010	0.010	0.010	0.010	0.010
Building and integration plans	0.012	0.020	0.030	0.020	0.021
Distribution and support plans				0.017	0.017
Documentation plans		0.020	0.020	0.020	0.020
Design review plans		0.010	0.010	0.010	0.010
Code inspection plans		0.015	0.015	0.015	0.015
Unit test plans		0.010	0.015	0.010	0.012
Function test plans	0.010	0.012	0.015	0.010	0.012
Regression test plans		0.010	0.010	0.010	0.010
Integration test plans		0.010	0.015	0.012	0.012
Performance test plans		0.012	0.017	0.012	0.014
Component test plans		0.010	0.015	0.010	0.012
System test plans	0.010	0.012	0.020	0.012	0.014
Independent test plans			0.020		0.020
Field (beta) test plans		0.010	0.010	0.012	0.011
Lab test plans		0.010	0.150		0.080
Usability test plans		0.010	0.200	0.012	0.074
Maintenance and support plans	0.010	0.012	0.250	0.020	0.073
Nationalization plans				0.010	0.010
Year-2000 containment plans	0.020	0.025	0.030	0.015	0.023
Subtotal	0.072	0.218	0.852	0.257	0.350
Financial documents					
Market forecasts				0.010	0.010
Cost estimates	0.010	0.015	0.020	0.010	0.014
Department budgets	0.001	0.001	0.001	0.001	0.001
Capital expenditure requests	0.001	0.001	0.001	0.001	0.001
Travel authorization requests	0.001	0.001	0.002	0.001	0.001
Maintenance cost estimates	0.010	0.020	0.025	0.015	0.018
Year-2000 repair cost estimates	0.010	0.015	0.015	0.010	0.013
Subtotal	0.033	0.053	0.064	0.048	0.050
Control documents					
Budget variance reports	0.010	0.010	0.010	0.010	0.010
Computer utilization reports	0.015	0.020	0.020		0.018
Milestone tracking reports	0.010	0.010	0.015	0.015	0.013
Design inspection reports	0.010	0.025	0.030	0.015	0.020
Code inspection reports	0.010	0.015	0.017	0.010	0.013
Quality-assurance status reports	0.010	0.020	0.025	0.015	0.018

TABLE 25.2   Universe of Software Project Document Types (*Continued*)
(Size in pages per function point)

Document type	MIS	Systems	Military	Commercial	Average
Control documents					
Test status reports	0.020	0.035	0.045	0.035	0.034
Build status reports	0.010	0.025	0.030	0.030	0.024
Phase review reports		0.010	0.030		0.020
Independent verification and validation reports			0.025		0.025
Audit reports	0.010	0.010	0.020		0.013
Project postmortem reports		0.015	0.017		0.016
Year-2000 status reports	0.025	0.045	0.050	0.025	0.036
Subtotal	0.130	0.240	0.334	0.155	0.215
Technical documents					
Requirements specifications	0.150	0.450	0.800	0.200	0.400
Initial functional specifications	0.250	0.550	0.700	0.250	0.438
Final functional specifications	0.600	1.200	2.000	0.550	1.088
Logic specifications	0.500	1.150	1.600	0.600	0.963
System structure specifications	0.100	0.400	0.800	0.100	0.350
Database specifications	0.375	0.250	0.900	0.150	0.419
Data dictionaries	0.030	0.020	0.030	0.020	0.025
Design change requests	0.250	0.400	0.700	0.300	0.413
Configuration-control status	0.010	0.025	0.030	0.030	0.024
Invention/patent disclosures		0.010		0.010	0.010
Subtotal	2.265	4.455	7.560	2.210	4.123
Legal documents					
Trademark search reports				0.010	0.010
Patent applications		0.001	0.001	0.001	0.001
Copyright registrations		0.001	0.001	0.001	0.001
Outsource contracts	0.500	0.500		0.500	0.500
Package acquisition contracts	0.015	0.015	0.100	0.015	0.036
Custom software contracts	0.020	0.020	0.030	0.020	0.023
Employment agreements	0.001	0.001	0.001	0.001	0.001
Noncompetition agreements	0.001	0.001	0.001	0.001	0.001
Year-2000 compliance disclosures	0.010	0.010	0.010	0.010	0.010
Litigation materials	4.000	4.000	4.000	4.000	4.000
Subtotal	4.547	4.549	4.144	4.559	4.450
Marketing Documentation					
Marketing brochures				0.001	0.001
World Wide Web materials				0.010	0.010
Advertisements				0.001	0.001
Television ad copy				0.001	0.001

TABLE 25.2   **Universe of Software Project Document Types** (*Continued*)
(Size in pages per function point)

Document type	MIS	Systems	Military	Commercial	Average
Marketing Documentation					
Sales manual updates		0.001		0.001	0.001
Customer satisfaction surveys	0.010	0.010		0.010	0.010
Competitive analysis reports		0.003	0.004	0.002	0.003
Subtotal	0.010	0.014	0.004	0.026	0.014
User documentation					
Quick-start users guide				0.010	
Full users guides	0.200	0.400	0.800	0.300	0.425
Feature users guides	0.100	0.200	0.500	0.300	0.275
HELP text	0.010	0.100	0.150	0.200	0.115
README files				0.010	0.010
Training course materials	0.100	0.150	0.400	0.150	0.200
Instructors guides	0.010	0.050	0.060	0.040	0.040
Reference manuals	0.600	1.000	1.700	0.700	1.000
Glossaries		0.200	0.350	0.150	0.233
CD-ROM information				1.000	1.000
Subtotal	1.020	2.100	3.960	2.860	2.485
Support documentation					
Operators guides	0.100	0.150	0.220		0.157
Programmers guides	0.100	0.200	0.300	0.250	0.213
Systems programmers guides		0.250	0.650	0.330	0.410
Maintenance guides	0.250	0.350	0.600	0.250	0.363
Message and code guides		0.150	0.150		0.150
Subtotal	0.450	1.100	1.920	0.830	1.075
Quality-control documentation					
Design inspection defect reports	0.500	0.750	0.900	0.650	0.700
Code inspection defect reports	0.300	1.200	1.000	0.800	0.825
Test defect reports	1.650	1.500	1.650	1.500	1.575
Customer defect reports	0.500	0.400	0.500	1.900	0.825
Usability survey reports		0.020		0.150	0.085
Subtotal	2.950	3.870	4.050	5.000	3.968
Total pages per function point	11.477	16.599	22.888	15.945	16.727
Document types produced	52	74	71	79	69

3. Determine the effort to create each basic document.

4. Determine the rate at which each document may change due to new requirements.

5. Determine the defect potential of each document.

6. Determine the additional effort to accommodate changing requirements.

7. Determine the additional effort to repair documentation defects.

8. Determine the mechanical costs of document production and distribution.

In many cases, documentation can be even more extensive than what is shown here, because for international commercial software, many of the technical, user, and marketing document types may be produced in multiple natural languages, so documents may concurrently exist in any or all of the following languages:

- English
- Japanese
- Korean
- Chinese
- German
- French
- Italian
- Spanish
- Portuguese
- Dutch
- Norwegian
- Swedish
- Finnish
- Polish
- Russian

Obviously, when estimating overall documentation costs it is necessary to include the costs of nationalization, or translation into various national languages.

References

Jones, Capers: *Patterns of Software System Failure and Success,* International Thomson Computer Press, Boston, ISBN 1-850-32804-8, 1995.

————: *Applied Software Measurement,* 2d ed., McGraw-Hill, New York, ISBN 0-07-032826-9, 1996.

————: *Software Quality—Analysis and Guidelines for Success,* International Thomson Computer Press, Boston, ISBN 1-85032-867-6, 1997.

Mikkelsen, Tim, and Suzanne Pherigo: *Practical Software Configuration Management,* Prentice Hall PTR, Upper Saddle River, N.J., 1997.

MIL STD 2167A: Defense System Software Development and Data Item Descriptions, Department of Defense, Naval Publications Center, Philadelphia, Pa., 1988.

Pressman, Roger: *Software Engineering—A Practitioner's Approach,* McGraw-Hill, New York, 1982.

Putnam, Lawrence H.: *Measures for Excellence—Reliable Software on Time, Within Budget,* Yourdon Press/Prentice Hall, Englewood Cliffs, N.J., ISBN 0-13-567694-0, 1992.

————, and Ware Myers: *Industrial Strength Software—Effective Management Using Measurement,* IEEE Computer Society Press, Washington D.C., ISBN 0-8186-7532-2, 1997.

Rubin, Howard: *Software Benchmark Studies for 1997,* Howard Rubin Associates, Pound Ridge, N.Y., 1997.

Symons, Charles R.: *Software Sizing and Estimating—Mk II FPA (Function Point Analysis),* John Wiley & Sons, Chichester, U.K., ISBN 0 471-92985-9, 1991.

26

Estimating Software Project Management

Estimating the work of software project managers is surprisingly complicated, and is supported by very little in the way of solid empirical data. In fact, even the roles and responsibilities of project managers can vary from company to company, and from project to project within the same company.

The literature on software project management is extensive, but slanted heavily toward how-to-do-it books. Books that contain quantitative data on the costs of project management or even on such rudimentary topics as the ranges on software project spans of control are quite rare.

Some of the books that do deal with software project management include Fred Brooks's *Mythical Man-Month* (Brooks 1974), Barry Boehm's *Software Engineering Economics,* (Boehm 1981), and several of the author's own books, such as *New Directions in Software Management* (Jones 1993) and *Patterns of Software Systems Failure and Success* (Jones 1995). Lois Zells comes at software project management from the viewpoint of the tools utilized in Managing Software Projects (Zells 1990).

Although not a book about estimating management, Watts Humphrey's book *Managing Technical People* (Humphrey 1997) provides valuable insights. The cognitive psychologist Dr. Bill Curtis succeeded Watts as head of the SEI's assessment research group, and has also contributed to the management literature in the form of the SEI's people capability model (Curtis et al. 1995).

The nominal default values for software project management are easy to state (see Table 26.1), but these values are not very useful

TABLE 26.1   Nominal Project Management Default Estimating Values

Activity sequence	Continuous: Initial and final activity of software projects
Performed by	Project managers, supervisors, or client representatives
Predecessor activities	None
Overlap	100% with requirements
Concurrent activities	All other development activities
Successor activities	Maintenance
Assignment scope	1600 function points per manager
Span of control	8 employees per manager
Production rate	100 function points per staff month
Production rate	1.32 work hours per function point
Schedule months	Concurrent with overall project schedule
Defect potential	1.0 management defects per function point
Defect removal	75% via requirements inspections
Delivered defects	0.25 requirements defects per function point
High-severity defects	30% of delivered requirements defects
Bad fix probability	10% of requirements fixes may yield new errors

because the range of project management functions is extremely broad. Also, the span of control or number of staff reporting to a project manager can range from a low of 1 to a high of more than 30 technical staff members.

The activity of software project management has not traditionally been estimated or measured using lines-of-code metrics. The standard way of dealing with project management, which is used for many kinds of projects and not just software, centers around the *span-of-control* concept.

The management span of control refers to the number of technical employees who report to a specific project manager. The concept has been studied and explored for various industries for more than a century. The nominal average for the number of employees reporting to a manager in the United States is about eight employees per manager.

However, for software projects among SPR's clients the observed ratios of employees to managers has run from 1 to 1 to as high as 30 to 1.

Software project managers have personnel responsibilities as well as project management responsibilities. Most project managers are also responsible for appraisals and personnel counseling, for hiring, and for other aspects of human resource management, such as approving education and training requests.

In addition, software project managers have departmental roles for budgets, arranging for office space, approving travel requisitions, ordering supplies, and so forth. The generic rules of thumb for software project managers among SPR's clients resemble the following:

- One project manager for every eight technical staff members.

- One full-time project manager for every 1600 function points.

- One project manager for roughly every 160,000 source code statements.

- Project management starts before requirements and runs after the project ends.

- Project management work = 35 percent of available management time.

- Personnel work = 30 percent of available management time.

- Meetings with other managers or clients = 22 percent of available management time.

- Departmental work = 8 percent of available management time.

- Miscellaneous work = 5 percent of available management time.

To understand why these nominal default values fluctuate very widely, it is necessary to understand the real-life situations that often affect the work of software project managers. The main variable factors that can influence software project managers' jobs, and hence also influence cost estimates, include the following:

- The roles assigned to (or assumed by) the project manager for activities such as sizing, cost estimating, quality estimating, departmental budgeting, personnel hiring and appraisals, space allocation, milestone tracking, cost tracking, quality tracking, measurement, and the like.

- Whether the project manager is a *pure* manager, or also contributes to the project in a technical way. For example, some software project managers may also serve as *chief programmers* and, hence, perform technical work as well as managerial work.

- The nature of the project, and whether it is a *pure* software project or a hybrid project that also involves engineered components, manufactured components, microcode, or some other kinds of work besides software development.

- External pressures applied to the project, and hence to the project manager, from clients or senior management, in terms of schedule pressure, cost-containment pressure, or some other forms of pressure that occur less often, such as the need to achieve very high performance levels.

- The suite of project management tools available and utilized by the project manager, including cost-estimating tools, project-scheduling tools, methodology management tools or process management tools, quality-estimation tools, tracking tools, and the like.

- The number of other managers involved on the project simultaneously, and whether large projects are organized in a hierarchical or matrix fashion. Surprisingly, software productivity for entire projects tends to correlate very strongly, and inversely, with the number of managers engaged. Large software projects with many managers have a very strong probability of running late, exceeding budgets, being canceled, or even all three at once.

- Time-splitting among multiple projects, which can occur when a project manager is simultaneously responsible for several small projects, rather than one discrete project or one component of a really large system.

- The span of control, or the number of technical workers assigned to any given manager.

- The number of different kinds of software occupations among the workers assigned to a given manager.

- The presence or absence of a *project office* for larger projects, and the division of work between individual project managers and the project office.

- The experience level of the project manager in terms of having managed projects similar to the current project.

- The set of quality-control activities that the project manager establishes for the project.

Let us consider the implications of all of these project management factors in turn.

The Roles of Software Project Management

The responsibilities and roles of a software project manager can be divided into three distinct components:

1. The role of personnel management
2. The role of departmental management
3. The role of specific project management

Personnel management may not always be delegated to a project manager under the matrix method of organization, although it is a normal responsibility under the hierarchical method of organization.

When present, the personnel role includes but is not limited to the following:

1. Interviewing candidates
2. Creating job offers and benefits packages, within human resources guidelines
3. Performing personnel appraisals
4. Approving training or education requests
5. Issuing awards, if indicated
6. Disciplinary matters, if needed
7. Terminations and layoffs, if necessary
8. Participation in various human resources programs
9. Receiving guidance based on morale surveys

The personnel aspects of the project manager's job are important, and personnel-related issues can often occupy 25 to 40 percent of a manager's daily time. In some situations, such as when there are "open door" issues or some kind of serious morale problems present, personnel-related work can top 60 percent of a manager's daily time.

From an estimating point of view, not all of the manager's personnel activities are related to a specific project. Therefore, it is important to know whether the manager's personnel work is to be charged to a specific project, or is general in nature and should be classed as overhead work.

The departmental management role includes but is not limited to the following:

1. Participating in annual or semiannual budget creation exercises
2. Dealing with facilities management on space and office issues
3. Approving travel plans
4. Requesting or approving requisitions for computers and equipment
5. Participating in special studies, such as SEI or SPR assessments, ISO audits, or business process reengineering (BPR) reviews

In larger corporations, the creation of annual departmental budgets is often one of the most expensive "products" that the company builds. Every project manager can devote from two weeks to more than a month each year to budget preparation, budget review meetings, and budget revision work.

The budgeting process is usually a departmental exercise; hence, the work may affect many different software projects, although for very large software systems an entire budget may be devoted to only a single project. However, it is more common for a typical department of eight technical staff members and a manager to have dozens of projects in the course of a single calendar year, and some projects that surface toward the end of the year may not even be visible at the time the annual budgets are first being planned.

Because project managers are often department managers too, the overhead work of managing a department can amount to about 1 month out of 12, or perhaps 8 percent of a project manager's annual effort. Here, too, the departmental work can be much larger, but is seldom smaller.

The project management role, which is the primary focus of this chapter, generally includes 12 key activities that are specifically associated with the project management function:

1. Coordinating with clients on the project

2. Coordinating with higher management on project resources and status

3. Coordinating with other managers on large projects

4. Technology and tool selection for the project

5. Sizing, or predicting the volumes of deliverables to be created

6. Cost estimating, or predicting the probable total expenses for the project

7. Schedule estimating, or predicting the nominal end date for the project

8. Quality estimating, or predicting the probable numbers of bugs or defects

9. Milestone estimating, or predicting the dates of key events

10. Tracking, or monitoring progress against key milestones

11. Progress reporting, or creating monthly (or weekly) status reports

12. Measurement, or collecting and normalizing data about the project

It is the set of key activities associated with actually estimating, planning, and tracking projects that is the heart of the project manager's role. These are the activities that can spell success for projects when they are done well, or failure for projects if they are done poorly or contain significant errors.

Estimating, tracking, and reporting are interleaved activities that can occur almost continuously during the development cycles of software projects. The work of these key tasks will vary significantly based on whether manual methods or automated methods are utilized. If manual methods are used, estimating and planning can absorb about 35 percent of a project manager's time on major projects. If automated estimating and planning tools are used, estimating and planning can drop well below 10 percent.

Project Managers Who Are Also Technical Contributors

Because one of the most common origins for software project managers is a promotion from programmer to project manager, it is not surprising that many project managers also perform technical work, too. In fact, it is extremely common in the software industry for project managers to continue to serve as chief programmers on the projects that they manage.

Obviously, for estimating the work of project managers, it is necessary to separate the managerial tasks from the technical tasks. When project managers are also technical contributors, the task of estimating both the managerial component and the technical component becomes complex.

Many managers who wear two hats and also do technical work tend to have very intense work ethics and put in a lot of overtime. Usually technical work dominates and absorbs about 60 percent of the manager's time, while the usual managerial work absorbs about 40 percent. However, we're dealing with work weeks that often include 20 hours or more of unpaid overtime.

The reason that software project managers often do technical work is because many of them were promoted into management from programming or software engineering work. There is a school of thought which asserts that the personality attributes of good programmers are so different from the personality attributes of good managers that a career progression from software engineer to software manager may not be effective. Although there may be some truth to this hypothesis, there is no other source of software management that has been proven to be more effective than the available pool of programming talent.

Project Management for Hybrid Projects Involving Hardware and Software

Many complex systems include hardware, software, and microcode at the same time. When hybrid projects are being developed, the project management tasks for estimating, schedule planning, and other activities grow more complicated and more time-consuming.

Obviously, the final estimate and plan for hybrid projects must integrate the software and hardware components.

Also, from the point of view of cost tracking and cost management, it is more complicated to keep track of software costs versus hardware costs when both are going on simultaneously.

The distribution of management time between hardware and software components of hybrid systems is seldom a 50/50 split. Obviously, the proportions will vary with the magnitude of software work versus the magnitude of engineering work. However, there are also variations with a sociological origin. For example, if the project manager has an electrical or mechanical engineering background, then less time might be spent on software than if the project manager has a computer science or software engineering background.

However, because software is usually the component that has the greatest chance of running late and exceeding budgets, project managers from all backgrounds will need to concentrate their energies on the software component if problems begin to accumulate.

Project Management and External Schedule Pressures

One of the more difficult aspects of being a project manager is that of being subject to external pressures from both clients and senior executives. The most common pressure applied to project managers is that of schedule pressure, but other topics may also be under external pressures, such as costs or (less frequently) quality.

The best defense for dealing with external pressure is accurate historical data derived from similar projects. For example, suppose you are a project manager responsible for a project of 1000 function points or 100,000 source code statements. You have a team of 5, and a planned 18-month development schedule based on team capabilities. It would not be surprising for either the clients or senior management (or both) to try to force the project schedule to be cut back to 12 months.

If you have no empirical data from similar projects, it is hard to defend your plans against this kind of external pressure. But if you know that based on a sample of 50 similar projects, 0 percent have been completed in 12 months, 50 percent have been completed in 18 months, 40 percent have run longer than 18 months, and 10 percent have been completed in 15 to 18 months, then you have a solid basis for defending your plan, and it is not likely to be overturned in an arbitrary manner.

The primary value of mounting a rational defense against irrational schedule pressure from outside is because project managers who succumb to these external pressures often see their projects fail or suffer severe cost and schedule overruns. Unfortunately, if the project manager has no empirical data from similar projects, and is not using any of the automated estimating tools with a built-in knowledge base, then succumbing to external schedule pressures is hard to avoid.

Many major software disasters occur because clients or executives with little or no knowledge about the realities of software estimating and software schedules force impossible delivery dates on helpless project managers, whose own knowledge of estimating and scheduling is not sufficient or not credible enough to keep the project on a realistic schedule.

Project Management Tools

The phrase *project management* has been artificially narrowed by vendors so that many people think the phrase describes only a limited set of tools which can produce Gantt charts and PERT diagrams, perform critical path analysis, and handle the mechanics of scheduling and cost accumulation.

However, there are a number of specialized software project management tools that are aimed specifically at software projects and can augment the somewhat limited software abilities of the traditional project management tools, such as Microsoft Project, Timeline, Primavera, Artemis, and the like. (The traditional project management tools have no built-in software knowledge base and cannot deal with many important software topics, such as sizing, creeping requirements, and quality estimating.)

Among the specialized tools aimed specifically at software project managers can be found specialized software cost estimating tools and specialized methodology or process management tools.

These tools contain extensive built-in knowledge bases derived from hundreds or thousands of software projects, and can handle such specialized topics as predicting the number of bugs or defects, estimating the rate of creeping user requirements, or automatically changing the estimate in response to different technologies, such as making an adjustment if the programming language switches from C to C++. These specialized software management tools can interface with traditional project management tools, and together the results can be very useful.

The best-in-class software organizations have a suite of very powerful and effective project management tools, of which traditional project management or scheduling tools are only one component, as can be seen from Table 26.2, ranked in descending order of average tool size.

As can be seen, the successful projects have more than an order of magnitude more project management tools available than do the set

TABLE 26.2   Project Management Tool Capacities on Failing, Average, and
Successful Software Projects

Project management tools	Failing	Average	Successful
Statistical analysis			3,000
Project schedule planning	1,000	1,250	2,500
Project cost estimating			2,500
Methodology (process) management		750	2,500
Assessment support			2,000
Resource tracking	300	750	1,500
Project measurement			1,250
Function point analysis		250	750
Backfiring support			750
Benchmark support			500
Total	1,300	3,500	17,250

of failing projects. In fact, the two most significant differences
between failing projects and successful ones are the suites of available tools for project management and for quality control. In both project management and quality-control tools, the leaders outrank the
laggards by about an order of magnitude in terms of tool deployment.

(Interestingly, the suites of software development tools do not show
any major differences between successful, average, and failing projects. All three tend to use between 30,000 and 50,000 function points
of software design and development tools.)

The use of function point metrics for evaluating tool suites is one of
the newer uses of function point metrics, but one which is already
producing very interesting results.

Note that the tools shown here are those directly associated with
software project management roles. In addition to these tools, project
managers may have another 10,000 function points of human-
resource tools and about 5000 function points of departmental tools
for such things as budgets, capital expenditures, travel cost reporting,
and the like.

Project Management on Large Systems
with Many Managers

Really large systems in the 100,000–function point range may have
more than 500 technical staff members and 50 or more project managers. These large systems are very difficult to manage, and a considerable amount of project management effort is devoted to meetings
and coordination with other managers.

Indeed, assuming that the system is large enough to have 10 project managers engaged, about 30 percent of monthly project management time will be spent in meetings with other managers. These coordination meetings can absorb even more than 38 percent of managerial effort, because these large systems usually have multiple layers of management so that the planning meetings may involve first-line managers to whom the technical staff reports, second-line managers to whom the first-line managers report, and perhaps even third-line and fourth-line managers on really large systems. (Above the third line, management titles usually change to something like *director* or even *vice president.*)

It is an interesting phenomenon that software productivity, like any other human activity, declines as the number of workers simultaneously engaged grows larger. However, for software projects the rate at which software productivity declines is directly proportional to the number of managers that are concurrently engaged in the overall system.

This phenomenon explains some otherwise curious results, such as the fact that software projects organized in a *matrix* fashion often have lower productivity than the same size project organized in a *hierarchical* fashion. The matrix style of organization deploys more managers for any given project size than does the hierarchical style, and that alone may be sufficient to explain the reduced productivity levels.

In the matrix organization, the set of project management roles may not include personnel functions. Often, under a matrix organization there are permanent department or *career managers* to whom employees report for appraisal and salary review purposes, and project managers to whom the employees report temporarily for the duration of the project.

The matrix organization more or less resembles a *task force* in the military sense. Under the task force concept military units are aggregated together for a specific mission, and then return to their usual locations when the mission is over. For example, during World War II ships from the American Fifth Fleet and the Seventh Fleet were combined for several months for a specific campaign, and then reverted to their normal commands afterwards.

Under the matrix organization personnel from a number of departments are aggregated together for a specific project, and when the project is over they return to their normal organizations for reassignment.

Under the matrix organization, as previously noted, technical employees usually report simultaneously to two managers:

1. Their departmental managers, for personnel and salary matters

2. The project manager, for technical matters

Under a hierarchical organization, on the other hand, the personnel on larger projects are organized in a pyramidal fashion like a traditional military organization, with the overall project director at the top and all subordinate units reporting upward in a standard chain of command.

For example, suppose you are concerned with a software project that is 10,000 function points or 1 million lines of code in size. If this project is organized in a hierarchical fashion, there might be 50 programmers and 6 project managers involved.

If it is organized in a matrix fashion, there might still be 50 programmers, but now the management complement is up to 10. There is a good chance that the productivity of the matrix version might be about 10 to 15 percent below the productivity of the hierarchical version.

Part of the reduction can be attributed to the four additional managers, but another portion of the reduction is because matrix management tends to add a certain level of confusion to projects which is absent in the hierarchical fashion.

Not all matrix projects fail or even are below the hierarchical style in net results, because many other factors are at play. However, from considering the results of 100 matrix projects and comparing them to 100 hierarchical projects, the matrix projects often lag the hierarchical ones.

Time-Splitting, or Managing Several Projects Simultaneously

In addition to having multiple managers on large systems, it is also common to have multiple small projects assigned to a given project manager. The reason for this is because department sizes are often constant within a company and average about 8 employees per manager, but project sizes can range from a low of less than 1 function point to more than 100,000 function points.

Suppose your company has a traditional department structure with one manager for every eight technical staff members. Now suppose your company is interested in building 2 small projects which are each 800 function points in size and will require about 4 programmers.

Since department sizes are more or less fixed but project sizes are not, it would be typical to see both of these projects assigned to the same department and, hence, both have the same project manager.

This is merely a simple example. Suppose your company wants to do 8 simultaneous projects, each of which is 200 function points in size. Under this second scenario, the same project manager would be responsible for all eight projects concurrently.

Although small projects do not require as much technical effort as large systems, there is a certain amount of irreducible overhead associated with projects in many companies. For example, each project may need its own cost estimate, its own monthly report, its own status meetings, and the like.

This means that project managers supporting multiple projects concurrently will have a much different time distribution than project managers supporting only one project. More time must be devoted to administrative matters and, sometimes, to additional meetings with clients.

This means that time devoted to personnel matters may be reduced, or managerial overtime may go up. In any case, estimating project management time when the manager is supporting multiple, independent projects is a tricky situation.

In companies that do not separate new development work from maintenance work, it is very common for a department that is doing development work in the form of an enhancement to an existing application to also be responsible for bug repairs on prior releases.

Because each incoming bug can be viewed as a kind of microproject, it is very common to have both technical personnel and project managers dealing with new development and maintenance simultaneously. This situation makes project cost estimating very complex, because the maintenance work interferes with the development work, and, hence, development will become erratic and hard to predict.

The Span of Control, or Number of Staff Members per Manager

If every manager had the same number of technical employees reporting in, then estimating project management work would be a great deal easier than it is. The span of control, or number of technical workers reporting to a manager, averages about 8 employees, but the range runs from a low of 1 to a high of about 30.

The span-of-control concept originated more than 100 years ago in some of the pioneering work on army units after the close of the U.S. Civil War. The original purpose was to discover how fast troop units of various sizes could move from one place to another. It was quickly discovered that small units of less than 20 (squads, platoons) could get started and cover ground more quickly than larger units, such as companies, regiments, and brigades.

This research was soon applied to business situations, and led to the development of the span-of-control concept. For many kinds of office work, including software, the average value is roughly eight employees per manager.

Although a ratio of eight employees per manager is widely accepted, it may not be optimal for software projects. There is a great deal of debate about small teams of 3 to 5 being able to outperform normal departments of 8 to 10. However, the literature on small teams tends to overlook the fact that the software projects which the small teams are concerned with are often much smaller than the projects assigned to larger groups. In other words, the apparent benefits of small teams may be at least partly due to the volume of work, rather than to the team size itself.

The author's own research has centered around really large systems in the 10,000 to 100,000 function point size range being constructed in large corporations, such as IBM and ITT. In the larger size ranges, what appears to be the optimal team size is a ratio of about a dozen technical workers reporting to a single project manager.

Although managers often state that large teams are hard to manage and keep track of, a careful analysis of how managers spend their time indicates that managers often spend more time with other managers than with their own employees.

The reason that larger teams appear to be more effective than smaller teams is not very flattering to software managers: Larger teams mean that less-capable managers can be removed from management and return to technical work, where their skills may be better utilized. Hence, larger teams give companies the ability to be more selective in choosing their managers, while also giving their managers better tools and support.

Larger teams and fewer managers also means less time spent in meetings with other managers, and less difficulty coordinating complex projects.

Other advantages of larger teams are that the amount of work that can be assigned to a given team goes up, and every student of management knows that cross-department coordination is much more difficult than coordination within a department. A department or team of a dozen technical workers and a manager can be assigned projects as large as 3000 function points or more than 300,000 source code statements. Conversely, a smaller team of 5 programmers and a manager can usually only handle about 1000 function points or 100,000 source code statements.

Managing Multiple Occupation Groups

As the software industry grows and expands, it is following the path of other industries and is developing a considerable number of specialists. One of the challenges of modern software project management is to select the optimum set of specialists for any given project.

Another challenge is to develop organization structures that can place specialists so that their many diverse talents can best be utilized.

In 1995 AT&T commissioned SPR to perform a research study on the numbers and kinds of specialists utilized in large corporations and government groups. Some of the participants in this study included AT&T itself, IBM, Texas Instruments, and the U.S. Air Force.

Table 26.3 shows the overall occupation group percentages noted among SPR's clients in the study, with some occupations, such as year-2000 specialists, added since the original 1995 study, based on more recent assessment and benchmarking studies in 1996 and 1997.

Although there is some ambiguity in the available data, the presence of specialist occupation groups appears to be beneficial for software development and maintenance work.

TABLE 26.3   Overall Distribution of Software Occupations in Large Corporations

Occupation groups	Percent
Maintenance programming	20.0
Development programming	18.0
Project managers	11.5
Testing specialists	10.5
Systems analysts	9.0
Year-2000 specialists	6.0
Technical writing specialists	4.0
Administration specialists	3.5
Quality-assurance specialists	3.0
Customer-support specialists	2.5
Database administration specialists	2.0
Cost-estimating specialists	1.5
Measurement specialists	1.5
Network specialists	1.5
Configuration-control specialists	1.0
Function point counting specialists	1.0
Web master specialists	1.0
Systems-support specialists	1.0
Process improvement specialists	1.0
Architecture specialists	0.5
Total	100.0

The corporations that use specialists for key activities, such as testing and maintenance, usually outperform similar organizations that use generalists by 15 to 20 percent in terms of both quality and productivity levels.

The presence or absence of specialists is severely skewed based upon the overall size of the total software population in the company or enterprise. Small companies with less than about 100 total software personnel usually make use of generalists who perform development programming, maintenance programming, testing, quality duties, and sometimes even technical writing.

As the overall software population grows larger, more and more kinds of specialist occupations are noted, as in Table 26.4

Although other factors may be involved, the use of specialists rather than generalists is strongly indicated as a possible explanation for an otherwise curious phenomenon. When software productivity rates are normalized based on the size of the software populations, the very large corporations with more than 10,000 software employees (i.e., Andersen, AT&T, EDS, IBM, etc.) have higher productivity rates than midsize organizations with 100 to 1000 total software personnel.

Very small corporations with fewer than 100 total software personnel have the highest productivity rates and don't use specialists very much at all. However, small companies only build small applications where generalists and specialists are roughly equivalent in performance.

Within midsized corporations, some rather large software applications in excess of 10,000 function points may be attempted. If the development personnel are generalists and are attempting every aspect of large systems construction (i.e., design, coding, quality control, testing, etc.), these various roles tend to be conflicting and slow down progress.

In particular, if the same people are simultaneously attempting to do new development and maintenance of earlier versions, the maintenance work will interfere with development work and make both activities inefficient and hard to estimate.

TABLE 24.4   Number of Specialist Occupations and Total Software Employment

Total software population	Number of specialist occupations
10	2
100	4
1,000	10
10,000	50

The Presence or Absence of Project Offices for Large Systems

Large software applications in the 100,000–function point size class (equivalent to roughly 10 million source code statements) are often supported by a specialized group of planning, estimating, and tracking specialists organized into what has come to be known as a *project office.*

Software projects in the 100,000–function point class may have 500 or more technical personnel and 50 to 70 managers deployed, so obviously there is a need for some kind of a central coordinating unit for such mammoth undertakings.

The size of the project office itself for a huge application in the 100,000–function point domain is likely to be about 10 personnel, including the project office manager.

For very large projects that have a project office, a number of the tasks that might normally be assigned to the project managers themselves are instead performed by the specialists in the project office: Sizing, function point analysis, cost estimating, measurement, and so forth are often delegated to the project office.

The project managers' work is made easier by the presence of project offices, but they still have considerable responsibilities for coordinating their own teams, tracking progress against milestones, and reporting on any *red flag* items, which are serious technical or logistical problems that might affect the project's outcome.

Experience Levels of Software Project Managers

Experience is a factor in every human activity, and software is no exception. Novice project managers are seldom entrusted with major projects, for very good reasons. The work of software project management is eased considerably with experience on similar projects—especially on similar projects with a successful outcome, rather than similar projects that were failures or disasters.

Quality-Control Methods Selected by Project Managers

Although quality control is listed last in this discussion of project management roles, it is actually one of the most important factors of all. As discussed several times already, a ranked listing of the five major cost drivers for software projects has *finding and fixing bugs* as the most expensive single activity:

1. Finding and fixing bugs

2. Producing paper documents

3. Meetings and communication

4. Coding

5. Project management

In general, projects that run out of control and are terminated or end up in court usually have skimped on quality control, with the result that the projects could not be successfully delivered or deployed.

Consider the recent disaster associated with the luggage-handling system at the Denver airport, which delayed the opening of the airport for approximately 1 year at a cost of roughly $1 million per day.

The two chief problems leading to this disaster were:

1. Bad project management methods

2. Inadequate quality-control methods

It is quite unfortunate that the impact of inadequate quality control is very deceptive and does not manifest itself until so late in the project that it is difficult to recover from the problem.

Usually, projects that are skimping on software quality methods, such as failing to use pretest design and code inspections, formal test methods, and the like, appear to be ahead of schedule and below cost estimates during the requirements, analysis, design, and even coding phases of development.

It is not until testing begins that the magnitude of the disaster starts to be realized. Then, when testing starts, it is painfully revealed that all of the quality shortcuts made earlier have produced an application that does not work and possibly cannot be made to work, without major revisions and repairs.

All of the apparent early schedule and cost savings disappear in a huge frenzy of round-the-clock overtime as developers and managers frantically try to fix enough bugs so that the project stabilizes and can, perhaps, be released.

References

Boehm, Barry: *Software Engineering Economics,* Prentice Hall, Englewood Cliffs, N.J., 1981.

Brooks, Fred: *The Mythical Man Month,* Addison-Wesley, Reading, Mass., 1974, rev. 1995.

Brown, Norm (ed.): *The Program Manager's Guide to Software Acquisition Best Practices,* Version 1.0, U.S. Department of Defense, Washington, D.C., July 1995.

Curtis, Bill, William E. Hefley, and Sally Miller: *People Capability Maturity Model,* Software Engineering Institute, Carnegie Mellon University, Pittsburgh, Pa., 1995.

Humphrey, Watts: *Managing Technical People,* Addison-Wesley/Longman, Reading, Mass., ISBN 0-201-54597-7, 1997.

Jones, Capers: *New Directions in Software Management,* Information Systems Management Group, ISBN 1-56909-009-2, 1993.

———: *Assessment and Control of Software Risks,* Prentice Hall, Englewood Cliffs, N.J., ISBN 0-13-741406-4, 1994.

———: *Applied Software Measurement,* 2d ed., McGraw-Hill, New York, ISBN 0-07-032826-9, 1996.

———: *Patterns of Software System Failure and Success,* International Thomson Computer Press, Boston, ISBN 1-850-32804-8, 1995.

Putnam, Lawrence H., and Ware Myers: *Industrial Strength Software—Effective Management Using Measurement,* IEEE Computer Society Press, Washington, D.C., ISBN 0-8186-7532-2, 1997.

Rubin, Howard: *Software Benchmark Studies for 1997,* Howard Rubin Associates, Pound Ridge, N.Y., 1997.

Thayer, Richard H. (ed.): *Software Engineering and Project Management,* IEEE Press, Los Alamitos, Calif., ISBN 0-8186-075107, 1988.

Umbaugh, Robert E. (ed.): *Handbook of IS Management,* 4th ed., Auerbach Publications, Boston, ISBN 0-7913-2159-2, 1995.

Zells, Lois: *Managing Software Projects,* QED Information Sciences, Wellesley, Mass., ISBN 0-89435-275-X, 1990.

Zvegintzov, Nicholas: *Software Management Technology Reference Guide,* Dorset House Press, New York, ISBN 1-884521-01-0, 1994.

Maintenance and Enhancement Cost Estimating

Estimating software maintenance and estimating software enhancements are technically quite different, but these two postrelease activities are often treated as though they were one and the same. Maintenance and enhancement are alike in that both deal with modifications to existing software. Maintenance and enhancement are different in the sources of funds and the rigor of the development methods.

For a variety of reasons, software maintenance and enhancement estimates are far more complex than estimates of new projects. One reason for this complexity is the fact that the phrase maintenance and enhancement can actually encompass at least 20 discrete activities, each of which has unique attributes in terms of costs, staffing, schedules, and influential factors.

One of the most important aspects of maintenance and enhancement estimation at the end of the twentieth century is that of estimating the modifications brought on by two massive sets of concurrent updates that affect many legacy applications simultaneously: updates to fix the well-known year-2000 problem and updates to financial applications to support the new unified European currency. These two sets of updates comprise the most massive changes to legacy software applications in human history. Each is a major project in its own right, and the occurrence of both updates separated by only one year will probably exceed the software capabilities of the European Union.

Maintenance and Enhancement Estimating

As the twentieth century winds down, more than 50 percent of the global software population is engaged in modifying existing applications rather than writing new applications. Indeed, under the double impact of the European currency conversion work and year-2000 repair work, during the last 6 months of calendar year 1999 it is likely that almost 80 percent of the world's professional software engineering population will be engaged in various maintenance and enhancement activities. This implies that maintenance and enhancement estimating is actually the most critical aspect of software cost estimating.

Surprisingly, for such an important topic as maintenance, less than half of the current software cost estimating tools have special *maintenance* and *enhancement* estimating modes. The reason for this lack will be discussed later in this chapter, but the essence of the situation is that maintenance and enhancement estimation is much more difficult than estimating brand-new software projects.

In this book the word *maintenance* is defined as repairing defects in software applications in order to correct errors. The word *enhancement* is defined as adding new features to software applications.

Although software enhancements and software maintenance in the sense of defect repairs are usually funded in different ways and have quite different sets of activity patterns associated with them, many companies lump these disparate software activities together for budgeting and cost estimates. The author does not recommend this practice, but it is very common.

Consider some of the basic differences between enhancements, or

TABLE 27.1   Key Differences Between Maintenance and Enhancements

Activity	Enhancements (new features)	Maintenance (defect repair)
Funding source	Clients	Absorbed
Requirements	Formal	None
Specifications	Formal	None
Inspections	Formal	None
User documentation	Formal	None
New function testing	Formal	None
Regression testing	Formal	Minimal

adding new features to applications, and maintenance, or defect repairs, as shown in Table 27.1.

Development estimating is a difficult problem, but estimating maintenance and enhancements is even more complex because of the very tricky relationship between the base application that is being modified and the changes being made to accommodate new features or repair defects.

Indeed, maintenance and enhancement estimating is so complex that a number of first-generation estimating tools could not deal with the intricacies and were limited to new project estimates. However, the newer generation of software-estimating tools, such as COCOMO II, SPQR/20, SLIM, CHECKPOINT, and KnowledgePlan, can handle many forms of modification to existing applications as standard features.

The literature on maintenance estimating is very sparse compared to development estimating. Indeed, any kind of literature on software maintenance is sparse compared to the equivalent literature on software development. During the 1970s and 1980s books on development outnumbered books on maintenance by more than 100 to 1, based on the catalogs of such software book publishers as Addison-Wesley, McGraw-Hill, Prentice Hall, International Thomson, John Wiley & Sons, and the like.

A small number of pioneering software engineers recognized that maintenance would eventually become the dominant work of the software community because applications are being created much faster than they are being withdrawn. Girish Parikh and Nicholas Zvegintzov are perhaps the best known of the early maintenance pioneers who started their research in the 1970s and 1980s.

There are now a number of books on maintenance itself, but the literature on maintenance cost estimating is still fairly sparse. Some books with valuable insights into maintenance topics include the

Handbook of Software Maintenance (Parikh 1986), *Software Evolution—The Software Maintenance Challenge* (Arthur 1988), *Practical Software Maintenance* (Pigoski 1997), *Software Maintenance: The Problem and its Solutions* (Martin and McClure 1983), *Managing Systems in Transition* (Sharon 1996), and *Software Maintenance* (Takang and Grubh 1997).

There are also a number of books on maintenance in more specialized forms, such as reengineering (Sharon 1997), and on available tools, such as the annual catalogs published by ACR (Howard 1997) and the discussion by the maintenance pioneer Nicholas Zvegintzov (Zvegintzov 1994).

There are a host of books on year-2000 maintenance issues, and many of these are discussed in the author's own book on the year-2000 problem (Jones 1997). Many of the author's other books deal with issues that are troublesome during maintenance, such as bad fix injection and the low status of maintenance personnel. See also the author's books *Software Quality—Analysis and Guidelines for Success* (Jones 1997), *Patterns of Software Systems Failure and Success* (Jones 1995), *Applied Software Measurement* (Jones 1996), and *Assessment and Control of Software Risks* (Jones 1994).

In terms of maintenance estimation, some of the standard volumes discuss this topic, such as *Software Engineering Economics* (Boehm 1981) and *Industrial Strength Software* (Putnam and Myers 1997). The well-known software researcher Dr. Howard Rubin also publishes useful information on software maintenance topics, often in the context of his large-scale annual reports (Rubin 1997). The British software metrics researcher, Charles Symons also discusses maintenance estimation using Mark II function points (Symons 1991).

Because the general topic of maintenance is so complicated and includes so many different kinds of work, some companies merely lump all forms of maintenance together and use gross metrics, such as the overall percentage of annual software budgets devoted to all forms of maintenance summed together.

This method is crude, but can convey useful information. Organizations that are proactive in using geriatric tools and services can spend less than 30 percent of their annual software budgets on various forms of maintenance, while organizations that have not used any of the geriatric tools and services can top 60 percent of their annual budgets on various forms of maintenance.

This section deals with 21 topics that are often coupled together under the generic term *maintenance* in day-to-day discussions, but which are actually quite different in many important respects (see Table 27.2).

Four of the 21 forms of updates (warranty repairs, year-2000

TABLE 27.2   Major Kinds of Work Performed Under the Generic Term *Maintenance*

---

1. Major enhancements (new features of >20 function points)
2. Minor enhancements (new features of <5 function points)
3. Maintenance (repairing defects for good will)
4. Warranty repairs (repairing defects under formal contract)
5. Customer support (responding to client phone calls or problem reports)
6. Error-prone module removal (eliminating very troublesome code segments)
7. Mandatory changes (required or statutory changes)
8. Complexity analysis (quantifying control flow using complexity metrics)
9. Code restructuring (reducing cyclomatic and essential complexity)
10. Optimization (increasing performance or throughput)
11. Migration (moving software from one platform to another)
12. Conversion (Changing the interface or file structure)
13. Reverse engineering (extracting latent design information from code)
14. Reengineering (transforming legacy applications to client/server form)
15. Dead code removal (removing segments no longer utilized)
16. Dormant application elimination (archiving unused software)
17. Nationalization (modifying software for international use)
18. Year-2000 repairs (date format expansion or masking)
19. Eurocurrency conversion (adding the new unified currency to financial applications)
20. Retirement (withdrawing an application from active service)
21. Field service (sending maintenance members to client locations)

---

repairs, Eurocurrency conversion, and retirement of applications) have legal and business aspects over and above the technical work involving software and, hence, are not completely encompassed by any commercial software-estimating tool or methodology.

For example, year-2000 repairs may involve repairs to databases, test-library repairs, and hardware upgrades over and above software repairs. The software repairs for the year-2000 problem can be predicted by several commercial estimating tools, but the hardware upgrades, database repairs, and test-library repairs are outside the scope of software cost estimating tools. Also, the costs of possible litigation associated with the year-2000 problem are outside the scope of software cost estimating capabilities. Indeed, the costs associated with litigation are highly unpredictable for any kind of lawsuit and especially so for lawsuits where damages are set by juries and can range from zero to many millions of dollars.

The Eurocurrency maintenance costs are primarily software upgrades or enhancements, although mandatory. These updates can be estimated for any given application with acceptable accuracy.

What is tricky about Eurocurrency estimates is the fact that for any large corporation the euro changes and the year 2000 changes are going to occur simultaneously. Also, the change to the euro will affect many database and data mining operations that are used for long-range analysis, since the abrupt introduction of a new currency will degrade the ability to do long-range analysis of stock and commodity prices and other forms of financial analysis.

When an application is nominally retired or withdrawn from service there may be a legal obligation to continue to support users who do not wish to stop using the software package. Several lawsuits have been filed by clients who felt that a vendor's retirement of a software package violated warranty or service agreements. Hence, there may be a need for special kinds of service and support for individual clients even after a package has been withdrawn from general use.

Although the 21 maintenance topics cited in this section are different in many respects, they all have one common feature that makes a group discussion possible: They all involve modifying an existing application rather than starting from scratch with a new application.

The 21 forms of modifying existing applications have different reasons for being carried out, and it often happens that several of them take place concurrently. For example, enhancements and defect repairs are very common in the same release of an evolving application.

There are also common sequences or patterns to these modification activities. For example, reverse engineering often precedes reengineering and the two occur together so often as to almost comprise a linked set.

Nominal Default Values for Maintenance and Enhancement Activities

The nominal default values for estimating these 21 kinds of maintenance are shown in Table 27.3. However, each of the 21 has a very wide range of variability and reacts to a number of different technical factors, and also to the experience levels of the maintenance personnel.

Let us consider some generic default estimating values for these various maintenance tasks using three common metrics: *assignment scopes* (A scopes), *production rates* (P rates) in terms of *function points* (FP) *per staff month* and the similar but reciprocal metric, *work hours per function point*. We will also include *lines of code* (LOC) *per staff month* with the caveat that the results are merely based on an expansion of 100 statements per function point, which is only a generic value and should not be used for serious estimating purposes.

Each of these forms of modification or support activity have wide variations, but these nominal default values at least show the ranges

TABLE 27.3   Default Values for Maintenance Assignment Scopes and Production Rates

Activities	A scopes, FP	P rates, FP per month	P rates, work hours per FP	P rates, LOC per staff month
Customer support	5,000	3,000	0.04	300,000
Code restructuring	5,000	1,000	0.13	100,000
Complexity analysis	5,000	500	0.26	50,000
Reverse engineering	2,500	125	1.06	12,500
Retirement	5,000	100	1.32	10,000
Field service	10,000	100	1.32	10,000
Dead code removal	750	35	3.77	3,500
Enhancements (minor)	75	25	5.28	2,500
Reengineering	500	25	5.28	2,500
Maintenance (defect repairs)	750	25	5.28	2,500
Warranty repairs	750	20	6.60	2,000
Migration to new platform	300	18	7.33	1,800
Enhancements (major)	125	15	8.80	1,500
Nationalization	250	15	8.80	1,500
Conversion to new interface	300	15	8.80	1,500
Mandatory changes	750	15	8.80	1,500
Performance optimization	750	15	8.80	1,500
Year-2000 repair	2,000	15	8.80	1,500
Eurocurrency conversion	1,500	15	8.80	1,500
Error-prone module removal	300	12	11.00	1,200
Average	2,080	255	5.51	25,450

of possible outcomes for all of the major activities associated with support of existing applications.

None of these values are sufficiently rigorous by themselves for formal cost estimates, but are sufficient to illustrate some of the typical trends in various kinds of maintenance work. Obviously adjustments for team experience, complexity of the application, programming languages, and many other local factors are needed as well. Let us consider the nature of these 21 kinds of modifications to existing software.

Major Enhancements

Major enhancements are concerned with adding or changing features in existing software in response to explicit user requests. Because the new features meet new user requirements, the funding for enhancements is usually derived from user organizations, or at any rate there will be new charges for the augmented version.

There is no fixed size for differentiating *major* and *minor* enhancements. The author suggests that the term *minor enhancement* be restricted to application updates that can be done in a calendar week or less, which would imply a size of no more than about 5 function points or 500 source code statements. This size is sufficient for adding a new report or a new screen element.

For the phrase *major enhancement,* a size of 20 function points or larger (roughly 2000 source code statements) approximates the amount of code that can be added to an application in a month. At this size and larger, significant updates, such as those dealing with changes in tax law or adding a new feature to a system, are often found.

Major enhancements to very large systems, such as IBM's MVS operating system or Microsoft Windows NT, can top 1000 function points or 100,000 source code statements. Of course, both of these large systems are now in the vicinity of 100,000 function points or 10 million source code statements.

Between updates that are definitely minor and those that are definitely major is an ambiguous zone that can be defined either way based on specific circumstances.

(The annual rate of enhancements to existing applications averages a net increase in the function point totals of the applications of about 7 percent per year, although there are, of course, wide variations.)

Major enhancements are usually formal in terms of development methods and use the same kinds of rigor as new projects—that is, formal specifications, design reviews, test plans, quality-assurance involvement, technical writers, formal cost estimates, milestone tracking, and so forth.

From an estimating standpoint, the main difference between estimating a new project and estimating a major enhancement is the fact that the current version of the application needs to be included in the estimate. Some activities, such as gathering requirements, are aimed primarily at the new features to be added. But for many key software activities, such as design, coding, integration, and testing, both the new features and the existing application must be dealt with as a linked system.

For many financial applications the addition of Eurocurrency support is significant enough to classify as a major enhancement, because the updates will top 100 function points per application. This size range is likely to be noted for banking systems, stock market trading systems, and retailing systems.

However, for applications where currency rates are not pivotal to the calculations and algorithms but merely are used for historical purposes, the euro work might comprise a minor enhancement because only a few function points might be required. An example here would be a cost-estimating tool such as SPR's own KnowledgePlan estimating tool, where euro support is being added to the other currencies already supported in the currency conversion routine.

Minor Enhancements

Minor enhancements are those which add some small improvement from the user's point of view, such as improving an interface or adding a new report. Most minor enhancements among the author's clients are less than 5 function points in size, or less than about 500 source code statements.

Minor enhancements are difficult to estimate and measure using function point metrics, because they are below the size range of about 50 function points where function point accuracy starts to decay due to the lower limits of the weighting factors. However, the use of *backfiring,* or creating function points from source code statements, can work down to even a fraction of a function point.

Minor enhancements are often small enough that they are not explicitly budgeted or charged back to users, which makes accumulating empirical data difficult. Indeed, some very minor enhancements can be accomplished in less than a day, have no formal specifications, cost estimates, budgets, or even any written record that the enhancement occurred at all!

The development methodologies for minor enhancements are seldom rigorous. Minor enhancements may lack formal specifications, may not have written test plans, and may not even utilize formal inspections or reviews by quality-assurance personnel.

The combination of informal practices and the difficulty of calibrating function point metrics for very small projects makes estimating minor enhancements a troublesome zone. Indeed, this is one of the rare domains where manual estimates by experienced project managers can exceed automated estimates in terms of accuracy.

It is an interesting phenomenon that the productivity rates for minor enhancements are often lower than for major enhancements. The reason for this unexpected situation is one of the complicating factors associated with enhancement estimating: the impact of the base application.

Let us assume that you are planning to add 5 function points or 500 source code statements to an existing application of 1000 function points or 100,000 source code statements in size. At this low end, it is obvious that the requirements for the new feature are likely to be easy to understand and the design and coding tasks will probably be fairly simple, too.

What is troublesome for small enhancements, and degrades productivity substantially, is the fact that the connection between the new feature and the existing application may be complicated and require small but significant modifications to a number of attachment points within the parent application.

These multiple attachment points, in turn, require extensive recompilation of the entire application and, of course, very extensive regression testing to ensure that the changes have not degraded or shut down existing capabilities.

Compared to a small standalone application of the same size (5 function points or 500 source code statements) the basic tasks of gathering requirements and coding the main features are roughly equivalent in effort and costs. However, the work of testing the application will probably cost at least five times more for the enhancement than for the standalone application. Indeed, for changes to large and poorly structured applications, sometimes the testing costs can be 100 times more expensive for enhancements than for an equivalent amount of new development work.

The complex interactions between the enhancement itself and the size, structure, and state of decay of the parent application are factors that make enhancement estimating very tricky. Adding to the complexity of enhancement estimation are the usual problems of dealing with large software projects. There will probably be latent bugs or defects that will arise unexpectedly, and the specifications for the existing application may be out of date.

Also, as the years go by, the accumulated changes begin to degrade the structure of the original application and make adding any new feature progressively more troublesome as time goes by. For example, adding a 5–function point addition to a poorly structured 15-year-old system can be twice as costly as making the same update to a well-structured 1-year-old system.

Maintenance (Defect Repairs)

One of the reasons why the author makes a sharp distinction between maintenance in the sense of defect repairs and enhancements in the sense of adding new features is due to a court order associated with a 1970s antitrust suit involving IBM. The judge ordered IBM to provide maintenance information to a direct competitor, but did not define what the word *maintenance* meant in the context of the order. As a result, IBM's attorneys suggested that the primary definition of the word *maintenance* was that of defect repair, and that the term *enhancement* should be used for adding new features.

Maintenance, or normal defect repairs, is aimed at keeping software in operational condition after a crash or bug report. The costs for maintenance are usually absorbed by the software group that built the application, or covered under an explicit warranty agreement.

Software defect repairs are endemic because U.S. averages for defect-removal efficiency prior to release of software are only about 85 percent. For the first year or two after the release of a software package, repairing defects reported by users is a significant expense for both internal and commercial software packages.

Maintenance in the sense of defect repairs is seldom measured using normal function point calculations, because the majority of maintenance defects are less than 25 source code statements in size, or perhaps one-quarter of a function point. There are no counting rules for fractional function points, so the only way of enumerating the function point totals of small updates is by means of *backfiring,* or direct conversion from source code statements.

The most common way of estimating and measuring the productivity of maintenance in the sense of defect repairs is to evaluate the number of defect repairs made per month. U.S. norms are about 8 bug or defect repairs per month. Of course, in some months fewer than eight bugs will be reported, so this metric is not very reliable.

There is also a substantial range in terms of monthly defect repair rates. Some maintenance organizations staffed by experienced maintenance personnel and fully supported by change-control tools, defect-tracking tools, and the like can achieve average rates of 16 to 20 bugs repaired per month.

On the other hand, novice maintenance personnel or those who are splitting their time between defect repairs and new development tasks can drop below six bugs repaired per month.

The *cost per defect* metric is also used for maintenance repairs, and here, too, there are severe problems with accuracy of the results. The main problem lies in situations where maintenance personnel are charging time to a project's maintenance budget but no defects have been reported.

In practice, the cost per defect metric tends to be cheaper for applications that are very buggy than for applications that are approaching zero-defect status. For example, one month there may be no defects reported, but the project has a maintenance programmer standing by whose time is being charged to the project's maintenance budget.

The overall impact of cost per defect is to penalize high-quality applications and make low-quality applications look better than they really are.

Estimating maintenance in the sense of defect repairs is a rather tricky problem. Usually, maintenance estimates are broken down into discrete categories based on the severity level of the reported defects, as shown in Table 27.4, using the four-point severity scale developed by the IBM corporation in the 1960s.

TABLE 27.4   Nominal Response Time or Turnaround for Defect Repairs by
Severity Level

Severity level	Meaning	Turnaround time from report to initial repair	Percent reported
Severity 1	Application does not run	24 hours	1
Severity 2	Major function disabled	48 hours	12
Severity 3	Minor function disabled	30 days	52
Severity 4	Cosmetic error	120 days	35

For high-severity defects in the Severity 1 category, maintenance is
often performed on an emergency basis. Indeed, some maintenance
personnel have beepers and home computers and are often roused in
the middle of the night when Severity 1 bugs are reported. Once such
a bug is reported, it is not uncommon for the repair activity to proceed around the clock until the problem is fixed or, at least, a temporary work-around is developed.

Defect repair estimating has some other complicating factors
besides severity levels which must be considered: Abeyant defects,
invalid defects, bad fix injection, and duplicate defects all add to the
complexity of software maintenance estimation.

Incidentally, there are some *maintenance factories* used by outsource vendors that are extremely efficient and highly productive.
Some of these are staffed on a 24-hour basis and use very capable
staff members and full suites of complexity analyzers and mainte-
nance-support tools.

When estimating the performance of specialized groups such as
this, it is obvious that *industry norms* should not be used, because a
normal maintenance group works only part time, may also be
assigned to development work, and seldom has a full maintenance
tool suite available.

The difference between a fully equipped group of maintenance specialists and normal casual maintenance can be several hundred percent in productivity, and more than 50 percent in quality and bad fix
injection levels.

Some of the factors that affect maintenance estimates include the
following.

Abeyant defects.   For about 10 percent of incoming defect reports by
clients, the software maintenance team cannot make the same problem occur. In other words, the client's version of the software may be
dead on the floor, but the same version operating under similar or
identical conditions at the maintenance repair center works just fine.

These troublesome bugs or defects are usually based on some
unique combination of events, or on a specific combination of applica-

tions being run simultaneously on the client's system. Obviously, if the maintenance team can't make a bug occur, they will have trouble fixing it. These troublesome defects were termed *abeyant* by IBM when they were first noted there in the 1960s.

The costs for finding and repairing abeyant defects may be as much as an order of magnitude more expensive than normal defects of any given severity level, and the time required may also be stretched out significantly. Sometimes it is necessary to send field service personnel to the client's location and find out what the problem is on the client's own system. At the very least, quite a bit of additional diagnostic work will be needed.

Invalid defects. For about 15 percent of incoming defect reports by clients, the error is not actually caused by the software application against which it has been reported. Sometimes the client simply makes a mistake, sometimes the error is really a hardware problem, and sometimes the error is caused by some other software application and misdiagnosed.

Whatever the reason for the invalid defect reports, they still must be dealt with by the maintenance group and the client must be given a prompt and courteous reply. For commercial software packages with hundreds or thousands of users, at least 15 percent of the time spent by customer-support personnel and 10 percent of the time spent by maintenance programmers is wrapped up with invalid defect reports.

The reason that so much energy is devoted to invalid defect reports is that until substantial diagnostic work is performed, it may not be immediately obvious that the defect report is invalid. Unless the problem is completely obvious or has occurred before, both customer-support personnel and maintenance programmers can spend quite a bit of time processing invalid defect reports before they are discovered to be errors in something other than the application against which they were initially reported.

Bad fix injection. Any time a software defect is repaired, there is a finite probability that the repair itself may contain a new defect. The general term for these derivative errors or bugs is *bad fix,* and they are surprisingly common. The observed range of bad fix injection runs from less than 1 percent of repaired defects to more than 20 percent. The approximate U.S. average, based on long-range data from such major software corporations as IBM, is that about 7 percent of all defect repairs may trigger a new defect.

The factors which affect the probability of bad fixes being injected into software applications include the structure of the application, the experience of the development team, and the schedule pressure under which the repairs are being made. Other factors include the use or lack of use of repair inspections and the thoroughness with which the application is tested.

Bad fixes are very likely to occur when poorly structured legacy applications are being fixed under severe schedule pressure by developers who are inexperienced with the application. Bad fixes are less likely to occur when the application is well structured, and when the repairs are made carefully without undue haste. However, bad fixes are endemic within the software industry and have been a chronic problem for more than 50 years at relatively constant rates.

From an estimating standpoint, bad fixes need to be included because the secondary bad fix defects are at least as expensive as the primary defects, and the practical impact of bad fixes is to add roughly an unplanned 10 percent or so to both testing and maintenance costs.

Incidentally, both the year-2000 repair work and the Eurocurrency updates have bad fix rates in the 5 to 10 percent range. When companies assign two separate change teams to make both modifications on identical schedules, expect the overall bad fix injection rate to approach or exceed 15 percent. This topic is underreported in the year-2000 literature and has been blissfully ignored by the Eurocurrency political leaders.

Duplicate defects.   For any software package with multiple users, it is very likely that more than one user will find and report the same problem. A few years ago an article appeared in several newspapers about a bug in the install procedure of the WordPerfect word-processing application. This bug was found and reported by more than 10,000 clients on the same day, which temporarily saturated the telephone lines leading into the WordPerfect maintenance facilities.

From an estimating standpoint, duplicate defect reports only need to be fixed once, of course. However, a substantial amount of customer-support time is devoted to dealing with these duplicates. For companies like Corel, Computer Associates, IBM, or Microsoft, about 10 percent of customer-support time will go to dealing with multiple complaints about the same defect. In fact, it is duplicate defect reports that cause most of the delays and hold time when trying to contact the customer-support groups of commercial software vendors.

Warranty Repairs

Warranty repairs are technically similar to normal maintenance defect repairs, but differ in a business or legal sense due to the fact that clients who report the defects are covered by an explicit warranty. For business and tax reasons, it may be desirable to record warranty repairs as a separate category. Warranty repairs are primarily of concern to software vendors and to clients with maintenance contracts.

Repairs made under warranty are often assigned severity codes, with values ranging from 1 (total failure of the application) to 4 or 5 (minor cosmetic errors). Software vendors repair high-severity defects much more rapidly than low-severity defects. Usually, repairs on Severity 1 or catastrophic defects are made in less than 24 hours, while repairs for low-severity defects may not occur until the next planned release of the software package.

Commercial software vendors usually have separate groups responsible for defect repairs, rather than turning over this work to the development teams. If the same team handles both new features and defect repairs, it is difficult to keep accurate records of work and very difficult to estimate new development, because maintenance tends to occur at random intervals and intrude on the work of new development.

On the whole, software warranties have been sparse since the software industry began. It would be beneficial to both clients and the software industry if more robust warranties were provided with commercial software, and also were included as part of custom development contracts.

The onrushing year-2000 problem is focusing legal attention on the topic of warranty repairs, and lawsuits are already starting to be filed by indignant clients for software applications which have failed to achieve year-2000 compliance. Some vendors may well be facing bankruptcy and perhaps even criminal charges if they dawdle on achieving year-2000 compliance.

Customer Support

Customer support refers to the personnel and activities in direct contact with users of software applications. Much of the work of customer support is interrupt-driven and is initiated by the customers themselves when they have problems or need to have questions answered.

For commercial software the bulk of customer-support work is driven by telephone contacts, although faxes, e-mail, and such online information services such as CompuServe, America Online, and similar utilities have many forums sponsored by software and computing companies.

For in-house customer support within specific companies, the work can also include face-to-face meetings between clients and customer-support personnel.

Customer-support estimates are based in part on the anticipated number of bugs in applications, but a more significant estimating variable is the number of users or clients. As a rough rule of thumb, assuming phone contact as the primary channel, 1 customer support specialist can handle the monthly calls from roughly 150 clients, assuming software of average quality with no major Severity-1 defects at the time of release.

For e-mail and electronic contacts with clients the ratios are much larger, and 1 customer support person can sometimes handle queries from as many as 1000 clients or users. An added benefit of the online customer support forums is that other customers may step in with suggestions or helpful advice. For example, Microsoft monitors the responses of clients on its forums and will sometimes invite customers who provide useful insights to speak at Microsoft conferences or events.

For in-house customer support with some face-to-face meetings, the typical ratio would be 1 customer support person for about every 75 to 100 users of a software application.

A variety of tools and automation are available for customer-support use. Contact-logging software and defect-tracking software are two common examples. The customer-support function is a key activity in the commercial software world, and provides very useful information not only for quality-control purposes, but also surprisingly helpful suggestions about desirable new features and functions.

The role of customer support is one of interfacing between the clients and the defect-repair teams. The customer-support personnel usually do not fix the problems themselves. For new problems, the customer-support role is to record the symptoms and route the problem to the correct repair group.

However, the same problems tend to occur over and over. Therefore, after a problem has been fixed, customer-support personnel are often able to guide clients through work-arounds or temporary repairs.

Customer-support groups can also gather very useful information about customer usage patterns and requests for new or missing features. Customer-support organizations should be viewed as an integral part of the software domain, and their advice and counsel should be included in the planning for new releases and even for new products.

Error-Prone Module Removal

Error-prone module removal projects have been part of the systems software domain for more than 30 years. Research at IBM in the 1960s discovered that software bugs in large systems are seldom randomly distributed. Instead, they tend to clump in a small number of very buggy portions, termed *error-prone modules*.

As an example, in the 1970s IBM's large database product, the Information Management System (IMS), contained 425 modules.

About 300 of these modules never received a customer-reported bug. But 31 modules out of 425 received more than 2000 customer bug reports each year in all, or roughly 60 percent of the total bug reports against the entire product.

Some error-prone modules are on record that have received as many as 5 bugs or defects per function point (or 50 bugs per KLOC) per year after release to customers. Error-prone modules may never stabilize because the bad fix injection rate can approach 100 percent, which means that each attempt to repair a bug may introduce a new bug.

Other companies besides IBM soon performed similar research, and it was discovered that error-prone modules were very common among large systems and applications above about 5000 function points or 500,000 source code statements in size. Error-prone modules are so common and so expensive to maintain that every sophisticated software organization should eliminate them completely.

Error-prone modules are the most expensive artifacts in the software domain, and their cumulative costs can be higher than those of normal modules by almost 500 percent. The reason is that the costs of defect repairs exceed the original development costs in less than a year, and continue to grow indefinitely until the error-prone module is totally eliminated.

Extensive research has been performed as to why these modules exist in the first place, and the four most common reasons are:

1. Excessive schedule pressure

2. Poorly trained programmers who lack knowledge of structured techniques

3. Failure to utilize code inspections

4. Failure to track defects well enough to realize that error prone modules were present

Of these four, the use of code inspections can essentially immunize against error-prone modules, and this explains in part why formal inspections are used by all best-in-class organizations, which also have zero error-prone modules in their production software.

Any organization that builds large software projects in excess of 1000 function points or 100,000 source code statements should do periodic surveys of the error-prone module status of all deployed software applications. Error-prone modules are a fully treatable and controllable problem, so only companies that are careless in quality control have them today.

Incidentally, since the bad fix injection rate of repairs to error-prone modules approaches 100 percent, they should definitely be removed prior to commencing year-2000 repairs.

Mandatory Changes

Mandatory changes are modifications to software made in response to changes in law or policy. For example, a change in tax rates or a change in health-care benefits will require modifications to many software packages. The source of funds for mandatory changes is ambiguous and can vary from case to case.

The most notable recent example of a mandatory change is the onrushing conversion work for the unified European currency, or *euro,* that will commence in 1999 and run on through at least 2002. Many applications in Western Europe are being updated to accommodate the euro even as this is being written, as are some U.S. applications.

Incidentally, the politicians of Western Europe apparently failed to realize that the much more serious year-2000 problem would be occurring at the same time. The folly of politicians who don't understand technical issues is likely to create a recession because Western Europe hardly has enough software personnel to do either one of these massive updates, and certainly can't do both on the same timeline.

It is a source of dispute between companies and government agencies that government regulations can require extensive and expensive updates to software, without providing any funding or financial relief. Making matters worse, governments may demand that the changes be made on impossibly short deadlines. Indeed, some mandatory changes are even retroactive!

Mandatory changes are one of the more troubling forms of software maintenance because the costs are often high, the schedule pressure is intense, and there may be severe penalties for noncompliance. The onrushing year-2000 problem is going to make the situation much worse than it is today, but most government agencies have not considered the implications of year-2000 problems.

The unwise decision of the European community to attempt to roll out a common European currency in January 1999 without realizing that year-2000 repairs would be peaking at the same time was one of the worst combinations of mandatory changes in software history, or indeed in human history. More than likely, year-2000 repairs will slip out to around 2002, while it will be surprising if the currency-conversion work can be completed prior to 2005.

Complexity Analysis

Complexity analysis is not usually an independent project with its own budget. Usually complexity analysis is a preliminary stage prior to some other form of maintenance work, such as the following:

1. Code restructuring

2. Error-prone module removal

3. Year-2000 repairs

4. Eurocurrency conversion

5. Migration to another platform

6. Conversion to another form

Complexity analysis cannot easily be done using manual methods. A variety of commercial complexity-analysis tools, some smaller shareware tools, and even a few freeware tools are available that can examine source code in a number of languages, graph control flow, and calculate one or more quantitative indicators of complexity levels, such as cyclomatic complexity or essential complexity.

Unfortunately, of the 24 kinds of complexity known to affect software projects, only cyclomatic and essential complexity have fully automated tools available. As a result, many of the other kinds of complexity that can impact software projects (combinatorial complexity, computational complexity, fan complexity, topologic complexity, syntactic complexity, semantic complexity, etc.) are seldom used for software projects, and almost never are used for source code complexity analysis.

It would be highly valuable to apply some of the semantic complexity models to software requirements and specifications, such as using the FOG index to calculate the reading difficulty of the text documents. Unfortunately, none of the major complexity vendors have yet started to deal with complexity of the noncode portions of software applications.

The phrase *cyclomatic complexity* is derived from graph theory. The concept is basically a measure of the control flow and branching structure of software applications. Cyclomatic complexity is derived from a flowchart or graph of the application's control flow, using the formula edges − nodes + 2. An application which has no branches at all but consists entirely of one straight-through coding sequence has a cyclomatic complexity of 1. In this simple case, *start* and *end* are the two nodes. The control flow is a straight line or *edge* connecting the two nodes.

Applying the formula of edges − nodes + 2 yields the following sequence. There is 1 edge or line and 2 nodes, so the first part of the formula subtracts the 2 nodes from the single line, yielding a value of −1. The second part of the formula adds a constant of + 2, and the final result is a cyclomatic complexity of 1.

Essential complexity uses similar logic, but involves more complex analysis to eliminate duplication of the same patterns in the graph.

In practice, software applications that are low in cyclomatic and essential complexity (with values <5) are easier to maintain than applications that are high in cyclomatic and essential complexity (say, values >20). The correlation between complexity and maintenance difficulty is not perfect, but it is fairly strong.

On the whole, the impact of software complexity is not well covered in the software literature. Indeed, only cyclomatic and essential complexity have any significant citations in a software context, and the pioneering report by Tom McCabe (McCabe 1976) is one of the few examples of actual research into software complexity issues.

Code Restructuring

Code restructuring projects are very common for COBOL, because a number of excellent commercial restructuring tools have been on the market for more than 10 years. The pioneering restructuring tools entered the market circa 1985, and include Recoder, Structured Retrofit, and Superstructure. Code restructuring tools are also available for C, FORTRAN, and PL/I, but the market for these tools is clearly aimed at COBOL because that language is dominant for business applications.

Code restructuring is usually done by an automated tool, and has the effect of lowering both cyclomatic and essential complexity levels. This, in turn, eases maintenance. The restructuring tools also create fresh flowcharts and maintenance documentation. The tools may also allow changes to names and modernization in other fashions. Usually, restructuring is benign in that it does not degrade performance or introduce errors. However, some restructured applications do contain about 10 percent more code than they did previously.

Although the method of operation of code restructuring tools varies from vendor to vendor, a common pattern is that these tools first evaluate the cyclomatic and essential complexity of the applications and produce a structure chart of the current situation. Then, using graph theory, the tools simplify the structure chart and eliminate harmful branching patterns. The actual source code is then taken apart and the application is reconstructed using the simplified graph as the basis.

Code restructuring is most commonly used for aging legacy software that has some long-range strategic value and can't be replaced for several more years. Code restructuring is also showing up as a precursor to year-2000 repair efforts, because it is faster and easier to find things in well-structured software than in highly complex software.

Code restructuring would also be a useful precursor to the software updates being made in response to the European Union unified currency.

Performance Optimization

Optimization projects are normally performed for applications and systems with very high transaction rates, such as credit card processing or real-time applications.

Optimization is concerned with minimizing delays in transactions by looking for approaches that slow things down. Sometimes for really old legacy software, optimization can include obvious steps, such as switching from tape files to disks. However, optimization is also concerned with control flow, loops, calls, caching, and everything else known to affect the speed with which applications perform.

It is interesting that optimization is such a rare commodity that large companies employ performance specialists to do the work. There are also commercial performance-monitoring tools in both hardware and software variants that are used to monitor execution speeds and help identify sections that may need tuning for performance purposes.

It should be noted that fixing the year-2000 problem and adding the Eurocurrency conversion routines to software applications are each likely to degrade performance by 10 percent or more. The fact that both changes are going to occur at almost the same time in a number of aging legacy applications is a very ominous situation. Performance degradation in excess of 20 percent is probable. This means that a number of important applications are going to require extensive retuning in order to get back some of lost performance. Indeed, retuning alone may not be sufficient, so migrating the application to larger, faster computers will probably occur for such critical applications as credit card processing, automatic teller machines, gasoline pump activation, and many others—yet another year-2000 cost element.

There are a number of vendors who build special performance-monitoring tools and software packages, usually aimed at high-transaction mainframe applications. Examples of applications where performance is critical include credit card processing, gasoline pump credit wand processing, and, of course, software that controls automatic teller machines.

Migration Across Platforms

Migration projects are those associated with moving an application from one platform to another. Examples of migration include porting an application from DOS to Windows 95, from UNIX to Windows NT, or from an Intel processor to a DEC Alpha processor.

Migration projects can be made for a variety of reasons, such as user requests, a desire to open up new markets, or to preserve important applications that were written for processors or operating systems now being withdrawn from service.

Funding for migration projects varies from case to case, although a majority of migration projects for internal software are paid for by the user group. For commercial software, migration is usually performed in order to expand markets or reach new ones.

Migration can be either very easy or very difficult depending upon the status of the original software. If the software is written in languages such as COBOL, with extensive tools available for renovation, and if the specifications have been kept up, migration can proceed at rates in excess of 50 function points per staff month.

If the software is written in obscure languages, and if the specifications are missing or obsolete, migration might proceed at a rate of less than 5 function points per staff month—if, indeed, it can be successfully completed at all.

Conversion to New Architectures

Conversion projects are those that change the interface and file structure of applications, such as switching from flat files to relational databases, or switching from a monolithic mainframe application to a client/server application.

Because conversion projects often add features or facilities that benefit users, the users are often motivated to fund these projects.

Conversion projects are often much more troublesome than anticipated because maintenance practices have historically been lax and unprofessional. For many aging legacy applications that are targets for conversion, the specifications are out of date or missing; the original designers have retired or changed jobs; and in some cases, even the source code is missing or is no longer compilable.

Conversion projects can be done using manual methods, or be supported by reverse-engineering and reengineering tools. Also, before the conversion gets under way, the application may be given a thorough complexity analysis and possibly be restructured using a commercial code restructuring tool. All of these situations can be estimated, but add complexity to the estimation process.

Reverse Engineering

Reverse-engineering projects are usually concerned with aging legacy applications where the original specifications are missing or incomplete, but where the application has strategic value and cannot be simply replaced. By means of reverse-engineering tools, some of the missing design information can be extracted from the source code itself. Reverse engineering is usually a prelude to reengineering, and may often be performed in conjunction with complexity analysis, code restructuring, or both.

The need for reverse engineering is because the specifications for many aging software applications no longer exist or are in such bad shape that the essential design information is no longer up to date or complete. Reverse engineering via automated tools is the most common approach. Reverse engineering is normally a precursor stage for applications that are slated to be reengineered, or converted into modern client/server forms.

Note that another form of reverse engineering is sometimes used: Some companies reverse-engineer competitive software packages in an attempt to extract possible trade secrets or proprietary algorithms. This form of reverse engineering is very likely to end up in court, and a number of lawsuits for theft of intellectual property have occurred in recent years in which reverse engineering of trade-secret material was one of the claims by the plaintiff.

Reengineering

Reengineering projects are most often concerned with migrating aging legacy software into a more modern client/server form with a graphical user interface (GUI). These projects are highly variable, based upon the programming languages and platforms involved. Straightforward reengineering involving COBOL applications can be done in a highly automated fashion, which can reduce human programming effort by 70 percent or more compared to manual conversions.

Funding for reengineering projects varies, but often comes from the user or client budget as a (hopefully) cheaper alternative to building an entirely new application.

Restructuring

Restructuring of software applications involves reducing the complexity of the control flow, as commonly measured using cyclomatic or essential complexity metrics. For common languages, such as COBOL and C, automated restructuring tools are available which can reduce complexity with little or no human involvement.

However, there are more than 500 programming languages in use, and automated restructuring tools are available only for about a dozen of these languages. For languages where restructuring automation is not available, the work effort is so enormous that manual restructuring is seldom attempted.

Restructuring has turned out to be a very effective technology in the COBOL world, where many aging legacy applications are given a new lease on life. Restructuring is also a valuable precursor to major updates, and should be performed prior to commencing significant changes, such as year-2000 repairs or Eurocurrency conversion.

Dead Code Removal

Dead code removal projects are fairly uncommon, but are starting to occur in the context of year-2000 repairs. It usually happens that when programmers make repairs to software, they do not physically remove the old code but merely change the structure so that the old code can no longer be reached and, hence, is never executed. The rationale for this is because the new modifications may not work, so it is safer to leave the old code untouched in case the new changes fail or have to be backed out.

Over time, as many changes are made to aging legacy applications, the volume of dead code can approximate 30 percent in some cases. It is not difficult to identify dead code, because many commercial complexity-analysis tools that trace application control flows produce maps that highlight dead code segments.

Until recently, the only major harm from dead code was that it made maintenance by novice programmers more difficult because they would not immediately be aware of which code was dead and which was still active.

However, in a year-2000 context dead code is turning out to be an expensive problem. The billing algorithms for many year-2000 service companies are based on counts of total physical lines of code in the application. If an application of 10,000 physical lines contains 3000 lines of dead code, then the year-2000 repair vendor will probably charge at a rate of between $1 and $2 per line for the dead code as well as for the active portion of the application. Thus, the cost implications of dead code can grow to a substantial amount of money; hence, dead code removal is becoming a frequent precursor step for year-2000 repairs.

Dormant Application Removal

Dormant application removal projects are also a by-product of the year-2000 problem. A large-scale study of 8 IBM data centers found that almost 50 percent of the software applications in the portfolio had not been run for several years, and probably would never be run again. Some of these were systems developed for previous hardware, or prior versions of applications that had undergone major revisions. Some were also packages that were no longer utilized.

Before the year-2000 problem there was no overwhelming reason to remove these dormant applications, but since year-2000 repairs are running between $1 and $2 per physical line of code when contractors are used, it is obvious that dormant applications need to be removed from the suite of active software packages which need year-2000 repairs.

Nationalization

The term *nationalization* concerns the need to translate screens, text, and sometimes comments and programming information into other natural languages so software projects can be successfully marketed abroad. English is the most widely used language in the software world, but many commercial software products also have versions available in French, Italian, Japanese, Korean, Portuguese, Russian, Spanish, or many other languages for countries where a significant number of possible clients may not be able to use technical English.

When nationalization occurs, it is a significant expense element. The overall costs of translating materials into other languages runs from 5 percent of original development to more than 25 percent, based on the availability of translation tools and bilingual personnel for the target languages.

Nationalization is tricky for estimation purposes because the levels of nationalization can run from surface changes of key user manuals and HELP screens through full-bore renovation of the entire application.

Year-2000 Repairs

Year-2000 repairs are a special and expensive form of modification concerned with expanding date fields from two-digit format to four-digit format; that is, converting *97* into *1997*. This is a special case because of the fact that the year-2000 problem permeates software production libraries and, hence, requires simultaneous modification to hundreds, or even thousands, of applications in many companies, all of which have to be completed before the end of 1999.

Funding for year-2000 repairs is a complicated topic, because the costs are huge and were not included in normal annual budgets. Many companies have established special year-2000 repair budgets outside the scope of normal maintenance expenses. In the United States, the accounting practice for year-2000 repairs requires that all costs be charged to the current year, rather than being amortized over multiple years. This is a severe hit on annual profits.

There are a wide variety of year-2000 repair strategies, each with different implications. The original concept was to expand the date fields from two to four digits, but in many cases this is not feasible. Alternative year-2000 repair strategies include compression, encapsulation or date shifting, windowing (both fixed and sliding), bridging, data duplexing, and object-code date interception. For a more extensive discussion of year-2000 repair strategies, refer to the author's book, *The Year 2000 Software Problem—Quantifying the Costs and Assessing the Consequences* (Jones 1998). One of the tables from that book can illustrate the very large range of costs associated with year-

TABLE 27.5   Provisional Rankings of Potential Year-2000 Cost Elements
(Percentages and costs are relative to in-house date field expansions)

Expense category	Percent	Cost per LOC	Cost per FP
Litigation			
Year-2000 deaths or injuries	10,000	$50.00	$5,000.00
Year-2000 damages	5,000	25.00	2,500.00
Shareholder	2,500	12.50	1,250.00
Professional malpractice	750	3.75	375.00
Tax errors	600	3.00	300.00
Post-2000 recovery costs	325	1.95	195.00
Database date field expansion (outsourced)	300	1.35	135.00
Post-2000 damages (missed year-2000 hits)	275	1.65	165.00
Database date field expansion (in-house)	250	1.13	112.50
Software date field expansion (outsourced)	250	1.25	125.00
Date field compression	120	0.60	60.00
Software date field expansion (in-house)	**100**	**0.50**	**50.00**
Software date field expansion (off-shore)	90	0.45	45.00
Bridging (database applications)	65	0.33	32.50
Data duplexing (batch applications)	40	0.20	20.00
Encapsulation (date shifting)	35	0.18	17.50
Regression test library repairs (outsourced)	35	0.18	17.50
Year-2000 regression testing	35	0.18	17.50
Windowing (sliding)	30	0.15	15.00
Year-2000 performance restoration	25	0.13	12.50
Year-2000 insurance	25	0.13	12.50
Windowing (fixed)	20	0.10	10.00
Regression test library repairs (in-house)	20	0.10	10.00
Year-2000 date searching (manual)	20	0.10	10.00
Triage of applications	10	0.05	5.00
Year-2000 date searching (automated)	5	0.03	2.50
Year-2000 awareness briefings	2	0.01	1.00

2000 repair work. Table 27.5 shows the ranges of year-2000 costs, using *in-house date field expansion* as the basis of comparison.

Because each of these disparate year-2000 repair strategies has its own profile of activities and its own cost estimating algorithms, the topic of estimating year-2000 repairs is tricky indeed. Most companies are pursuing a hybrid strategy with windowing, bridging, and encapsulation now exceeding true date field repairs in terms of the way applications are being dealt with.

For database repairs, true date field expansion is very complicated, so alternatives such as windowing and data duplexing are now the norm.

The effect of these temporary masking alternatives is to give companies breathing room, because it is quite unlikely that many companies or government agencies could actually accomplish true date field removal prior to the end of the century.

The long-range impact of masking is that year-2000 repair will continue well into the next century. Indeed, some year-2000 repairs will probably still be going on in 2027, which is when the encapsulation algorithms reach the end of their effectiveness.

A significant percentage of companies have not yet started their year-2000 repairs, and we have only about one full year remaining until the end of the century. This means that there is no longer enough calendar time remaining to expand the date fields in every legacy application, and certainly not time to expand database fields, since that work is even tougher than fixing software applications.

One potential approach for speeding up year-2000 work is *substitution,* or replacing noncompliant applications with compliant ones.

A second strategy is *masking,* or tricking the application by external date manipulation. A number of temporary masking techniques have been developed that are less expensive and somewhat quicker than true date field expansions. These masking methods are not perfect and may not be suited for every application. Some forms of masking may slow down the performance of applications. Also, there might be subtle or indirect dates that are not intercepted by the more common masking strategies.

In general, the masking approaches are temporary solutions that simply push the year-2000 problem out into the next century in the hope that many applications will be replaced before the masking solutions stop working. Because there are a number of alternative substitution and masking strategies, it is interesting to consider their pros and cons.

Replacement via compliant packages.   The most obvious substitution strategy is to replace a noncompliant application with a newer commercial package that is already year-2000 compliant. This strategy works only for applications that have commercial equivalents, so it is obviously no help for proprietary or highly customized software.

Replacement via custom development.   In situations where aging legacy software is due for replacement, it may be possible to accelerate the development of new applications that are year-2000 compliant. The main problem with this strategy is that there is no longer time to build large systems.

A simple rule of thumb based on function point metrics indicates the maximum size of applications which can be built between now and the end of the century. Raise the size of the planned application in function points to the 0.4 power and the result will be the approximate number of calendar months from requirements to delivery. Since as of the time of writing there are about 24 months until the end of the century, applications larger than about 2500 function points can't be completed (this is roughly equivalent to 250,000 COBOL statements). Note that every month this maximum size is declining.

Termination of the application.   Although this alternative is unpalatable, it is probably going to occur fairly often. The noncompliant software application will be shut down, and whatever it was doing will have to be done manually for an indefinite period until it can be repaired or replaced.

This strategy may require hiring a significant number of clerical or administrative employees, or using temporary contractors. Obviously, this solution will be expensive and will degrade a number of services that are now automated but which might have to be done manually.

Windowing.   This is a technology for dealing with dates in databases and software applications that does not require date field expansion. The windowing method establishes a 100-year (or some other fixed interval) time period, such as 1915 to 2014, and uses program logic to deal with all dates within that period.

Using the windowing method, two-digit dates are assigned to the appropriate century. For example, assuming that your window runs from 1915 to 2014, dates below the midpoint of the window, such as 03 or 10, are assigned to the twenty-first century as 2003 or 2010, while dates above the midpoint such as 97 or 98, are assigned to the twentieth century as 1997 and 1998. Windows can either be fixed or sliding. However, windowing exacts a performance penalty and assumes that everyone using the data or the application knows about the existence of the windowing routines.

Compression.   It is obviously possible to use some form of encoding within the allotted two-digit date space to represent any conceivable date. By using a binary or hexadecimal representation rather than a decimal representation, the available two-digit date field can handle dates over almost any period.

However, this method would require knowledge of the specific compression technique used by all applications accessing the data. There will also be performance reductions, but not as severe as windowing.

Encapsulation. This method, interestingly, is the one that Bill Gates, the chairman of Microsoft, recommended in response to a query from the floor at his CEO summit meeting in the Spring of 1997.

The encapsulation method simply shifts all dates downward by 28 years, so that the year 2000 would be represented as 1972. The rationale for using 28 years is that a 28-year shift will bring the days of the week (i.e., Monday, Tuesday, Wednesday, etc.) and the calendar dates (i.e., October 6, 7, 8, etc.) into correct synchronization.

The encapsulation method has the advantages of being fairly easy to do and not needing much in the way of extensive testing. However, here, too, there is a performance penalty. Also, some dates are subtle and are calculated by indirect means. It is not clear if encapsulation will be 100% effective.

Bridging. This is a hybrid method used for database applications where the software itself is converted from two-digit to four-digit form; but the underlying database is not, due to the excessive difficulties associated with database date field expansion. A fixed or sliding window or encapsulation are used with the database itself. Here, too, a performance penalty is exacted.

Data duplexing. This is a specialized method for dealing with database year-2000 problems, without changing the date fields of all of the applications that reference the data. Two versions of a database are created, with one version containing the original two-digit date fields, and the second or "cloned" version containing the same information, but with the date fields expanded to four-digit form.

Software applications whose date fields use four digits can run against the four-digit database, while software applications still using the older two-digit date fields can run against the two-digit database.

Obviously, data duplexing requires a lot of work in keeping both versions of the database synchronized. Data duplexing is a rather complex and expensive strategy, but actually expanding the date fields in databases is one of the most troublesome and expensive aspects of the year-2000 problem.

Object-code date interception. As this book is being written, experimental methods for intercepting dates in executable object code are being researched. These methods do not yet have commercial tools, and may not even work on every platform, but the current research looks very promising.

In particular, object-code year-2000 interception may provide a way of dealing with a very knotty and difficult problem: how to make year-2000 repairs in the aging legacy applications where the source code is missing or uncompilable, but the software is still being executed.

The technology of masking is still in rapid evolution and holds some potential advantages. Masking may perhaps be effective for at least some applications written in proprietary or obscure programming languages where there are no effective year-2000 search engines nor any trained programmers available.

All of the masking approaches should be viewed as temporary methods, because they do not cure the underlying problem of using only two digits for dates. However, if applications are gradually phased out over the next 10 to 15 year period and are replaced by compliant applications, then masking may be an acceptable solution for software that does not have stringent performance needs.

Table 27.6 shows the approximate number of calendar months required to implement a selection of year-2000 repair strategies. The table has a significant margin of error, but one point cannot be overemphasized: Time is running out for the year-2000 problem, and a significant number of companies and applications will not be repaired in time.

Table 27.6 is based on the results of fairly large corporations that own at least 100,000 function points in their portfolios and employ several hundred software personnel. In other words, the table is based on the time needed to fix at least 100 software applications and about the same number of databases.

This table assumes that a company will be doing year-2000 repairs with its own personnel. It is possible to bring in contractors or outsource vendors, and these specialists may be able to do the work somewhat faster.

TABLE 27.6   Approximate Calendar Months to Implement Year-2000 Strategies

Year-2000 strategy	Calendar months to implement
Database date field expansions	40
Software application date field expansions	36
Data duplexing	36
Redevelopment of applications >2500 function points	30
Redevelopment of applications <2500 function points	22
Compression	21
Bridging	20
Windowing	18
Encapsulation	14
Replacement via commercial packages	13
Substitution of manual methods	12
Object-code interception (if possible)	6
Average	22

There are also a number of year-2000 tools available that can find the year-2000 problem and assist in repairing it for common languages, such as COBOL.

Although there are hundreds of tools and vendors aimed at the huge COBOL market and quite a few aimed at the C and FORTRAN markets, there are many other languages without a single commercial year-2000 search engine or any year-2000 service providers available.

For example, software written in CHILL, CORAL 66, or in such proprietary languages as ESPL/I (Electronic Switching PL/I) have essentially zero tools and zero year-2000 service providers as this report is being written, other than the in-house tools and staff at the companies that use these languages. The technologies of substitution and masking may open up at least a possibility of year-2000 protection for obscure languages.

However, the substitution and masking strategies are not perfect and have some drawbacks, such as performance loss. There is no easy and universal strategy that can solve the year-2000 problem without quite a bit of effort and quite a bit of time.

Eurocurrency Conversion

In what must be one of the most hazardous public policy decisions in history, the European Community has scheduled the completion of conversion to a unified currency for the beginning of calendar year 1999, without any apparent concern for the fact that the year-2000 problem will be in direct competition for scarce software resources.

Of course, it would be exciting to start the twenty-first century with a new currency, so you can see why the European Union wanted to make the currency change before this century ends. Unfortunately, the glamour of a standard currency blinded Europe's political leaders to the painful fact that Europe does not have enough software personnel to do both currency conversion and year 2000 repairs at the same time. In fact, it is uncertain if Europe could do either one of these massive software changes by itself, let alone trying to do both together on almost identical schedules.

The main result of the tight conversion schedule set by the European Union is that the Western European countries have been devoting most of their available surplus software resources to the currency conversion problem, and did not expend adequate or even minimal resources on the year-2000 problem. A much wiser policy would have been to defer the European currency conversion until after the year 2000 problem, and not plan for full conversion until about 2003 at the earliest, or perhaps even 2005, which should be after the bulk of the year-2000 problem is behind us.

The European currency conversion impact on software applications is as large as the impact of the year-2000 problem in many industries, and in two industries, banking and retailing, will probably be even more expensive. However, the Eurocurrency situation only affects software dealing with finance, and is not a major factor in weapons systems, telephone switching, aircraft flight control, and some of the other areas where the year-2000 problem may cause safety hazards.

Further, the impact of failing to achieve the European currency conversion target date will only result in financial and political problems, even if they are severe ones. Failing to achieve year-2000 conversion, on the other hand, can result in much more serious problems involving possible disruption of air traffic, shutdown of power and telecommunication facilities, and potential injuries or death due to the failure of medical instruments, airline navigation equipment, or railroad-control devices.

From a software estimating standpoint, the most probable result of the unwise policy of scheduling the European currency conversion to overlap the year-2000 problem will be the following:

In 1998, the Western European countries will realize the far more serious hazards associated with the year-2000 problem and will begin emergency repairs. Because software resources are limited in Europe, as they are in the United States, some of the resources for year-2000 repairs will probably be diverted from the currency conversion projects.

There are not enough software resources available in Western Europe to complete both the year-2000 repairs and the currency conversion work on parallel schedules. The dilution of effort between these two enormous problems will probably result in the following disturbing phenomena:

1. Western Europe will not achieve year-2000 compliance for even 65 percent of the applications that need year-2000 repairs. Emergency year-2000 work will dominate Western European software projects during 1999 and 2000, and probably well into 2001.

2. Since the most convenient pools of surplus software personnel reside in Eastern Europe, the Eastern European countries of Russia, the Ukraine, the Czech Republic, and others will probably end up with very significant outsource contracts, and will grow to become major software powers, while Western Europe may face losses and reductions in software staffing after the two crises have passed.

Essentially, the U.S. software organizations have been ignoring the Eurocurrency issue and concentrating on the year 2000, while their counterparts in Western Europe have been ignoring the year-2000 problem and concentrating on the Eurocurrency conversion.

Although the future is hard to envision, one possible result of the year-2000 problem, the leap-year problem, and the currency conversion problem is that the software industries in South America, the Pacific Rim, and Eastern Europe will receive a major jolt of new business in the form of outsource contracts to either handle the three software problems themselves or perform software work that Western Europe and the United States are unable to perform because they have devoted all available resources to the three problems.

Once the developing geographic regions achieve a major presence in world software markets, it is unwise to assume that they will lose their market shares after the crises are past. The most likely conclusion from the combination of the year-2000 problem, leap year, and the Eurocurrency conversion issue will be that the current software powers—that is, the United States and Western Europe—will lose software market shares, while Eastern Europe, South America, and the Pacific Rim will gain software market shares.

Table 27.7 shows a rough comparison of year-2000 and Eurocurrency work for the 15 countries in the European Union. The Eurocurrency effort is merely set at 90 percent of the year-2000 effort,

TABLE 27.7   Comparison of European Currency Conversion and Year-2000 Effort

Nation	Software staffs	Portfolio size, FP	Year-2000 effort, months	Currency effort, months	Total effort: European Union
Germany	550,000	440,000,000	2,612,500	2,351,250	4,963,750
United Kingdom	390,000	312,000,000	1,852,500	1,667,250	3,519,750
France	385,000	308,000,000	1,828,750	1,645,875	3,474,625
Italy	375,000	290,625,000	1,725,586	1,553,027	3,278,613
Spain	235,000	170,375,000	1,011,602	910,442	1,922,044
Netherlands	100,000	77,500,000	460,158	414,142	874,300
Belgium	65,000	50,375,000	299,102	269,192	568,294
Portugal	65,000	45,500,000	270,156	243,140	513,296
Greece	60,000	45,000,000	249,600	224,640	474,240
Sweden	60,000	45,000,000	267,188	240,469	507,657
Austria	51,000	39,525,000	237,150	213,435	450,585
Denmark	34,000	27,200,000	159,800	143,820	303,620
Finland	32,000	24,800,000	147,200	132,480	279,680
Ireland	24,000	19,200,000	111,600	100,440	212,040
Luxembourg	3,000	2,325,000	13,710	12,339	26,049
Total	2,429,000	1,897,425,000	11,246,602	10,121,942	21,368,544
Costs			$94,471,456,800	$85,024,311,120	$179,495,767,920

on the grounds that fewer applications will be affected. This table is from the author's book, *The Year 2000 Software Problem* (Jones 1997).

If this table is close to reality, then roughly eight months of programming effort on the part of every software professional in the European Union may be devoted to year-2000 or Eurocurrency work over the next two and a half years.

The inescapable conclusion must be that the European Union will fall far behind other geographic regions in terms of the ability to build new applications and become a major software vendor in world markets.

It is quite unfortunate that the European Union is moving into a very hazardous first decade of the next century. The timing of the Eurocurrency conversion could hardly have been worse, and illustrates the basic human problem of *tunnel vision,* or failing to understand how one topic connects to other topics.

Retirement or Withdrawal of Applications

Software retirement is also a special case, and involves withdrawing a software package from active service. For commercial software, many users are reluctant to give up applications or move to newer versions, so it may be necessary to provide continued support for packages long past the nominal end of their useful lives. Failure to provide such support has sometimes led to litigation if the software in question was covered by warranty or maintenance agreement.

The year-2000 problem is likely to accelerate application retirements for several reasons: (1) for some aging legacy applications the source code is missing or is no longer compilable; (2) some vendors of commercial software are limiting year-2000 compliance to new releases, so older releases must be retired; (3) in the United States, the Financial Accounting Standards Board (FASB) accounting rules require that year-2000 repairs be expensed in the year where they were accrued, while new development can be amortized across multiple years; hence, it may be financially advantageous to replace applications rather than repair them.

Field Service

Field service at customer locations is a special form of support offered primarily to major customers of large mainframe applications. As the name implies, field-service personnel visit the customer location (or may even be assigned there full time) and carry out defect repairs, update installations, and other tasks at the customer location.

In the 1970s and 1980s, field service was a common aspect of mainframe software, and sometimes the costs were bundled in with the lease of the application itself. In the 1990s, field service is becoming rare for a number of reasons. One obvious reason is that there is a shortage of software personnel and costs are rising, so software and computer companies are trying to minimize or eliminate field-service expenses. Also, the availability of the internet, e-mail, and other direct computer-to-computer linkages means that remote maintenance is now technically possible.

Field service is still available, and many personal computer manufacturers offer on-site service. (Indeed, the computer used to write this book had its hard drive replaced under a field-service contract.)

Combinations and Concurrent Maintenance Operations

Although 21 discrete forms of maintenance have been discussed separately, it is very common for a number of them to take place simultaneously. This adds complexity to maintenance estimating. For example, some of the common mixtures of maintenance work can include any or all of the following sets:

Set 1: Normal maintenance operations
1. Maintenance (defect repairs)
2. Enhancement (major or minor)

Set 2: Restructuring preceding in-house year-2000 repairs
1. Complexity analysis
2. Restructuring
3. Year-2000 repairs
4. Enhancement (major or minor)

Set 3: Restructuring for quality improvement
1. Complexity analysis
2. Restructuring
3. Error-prone module removal
4. Maintenance (defect repairs)
5. Enhancement (major)

Set 4: Eurocurrency conversion work
1. Complexity analysis
2. Reengineering
3. Restructuring
4. Initial Eurocurrency updates
5. Reoptimization to restore lost performance
6. Secondary bad fix repairs

Set 5: Major commercial year-2000 repair preparations
1. Complexity analysis
2. Reengineering
3. Restructuring
4. Year-2000 repairs
5. Reoptimization to restore lost performance
6. Secondary bad fix repairs

Set 4 (Eurocurrency) and Set 5 (year-2000 repairs) are likely to take place simultaneously, but may be done by separate teams or even by separate outsourcers. This is an awkward situation, which will raise the probability of bad fixes and make estimating both activities even more complex than they would be if they were being carried out on separate schedules.

In some companies both the euro work and the year-2000 work may be assigned to the same teams, but even here estimation is difficult. For that matter, doing the work itself will be difficult. The politicians of the European Union could hardly have picked a worse time for the euro in all of human history.

Note that the euro work is technically an *enhancement,* or adding a new feature, while the year-2000 work is technically *maintenance,* or defect repairs. It is not uncommon to have both defect repairs and new features being added to the same application at the same time, although this practice tends to raise the bad fix rate and makes testing difficult.

This same practice of concurrent maintenance and enhancement also raises the complexity of estimation, since the two separate forms of modification tend to interfere with each other, and it adds complexity to change management, configuration control, and other administrative tasks.

Essentially any combination of the 21 separate maintenance activities can occur at the same time for the same software application.

Maintenance estimation when combinations of different kinds of maintenance are occurring is far more difficult and complex than estimating any of the individual forms. For example, in controlled experiments involving the same application before and after complexity analysis and code restructuring, the effort of making the same update was 40 percent lower for the team working on the well-structured low-complexity version than for the team working on the poorly structured high-complexity version.

Estimating tools vary widely in the approaches they utilize for dealing with hybrid forms of maintenance, such as adding new features at the same time that bug repairs are taking place. To illustrate some of the implications, consider the following five types of maintenance in ascending order of complexity.

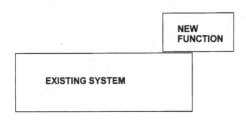

- **Similar to Year 2000 windowing and encapsulation**
- **Possible only with well-structured systems**
- **Productivity close to that of new programs**
- **Productivity = 5 to 15 function points per staff month**

Figure 27.1 Type 1 enhancement (block functions).

Type 1: Additions without internal modification

The first type of maintenance is that of adding new features to an application, without the new features causing any extensive internal changes to the original source code (see Fig. 27.1). This form of addition is uncommon and requires that the original application be designed and developed with expansion in mind. An example of this kind of addition might be adding a dictionary module to a word-processing component. Yet another example could be illustrated by a product developed by the author's company. SPR's KnowledgePlan cost-estimating tool includes support for Microsoft Project, but SPR's tool was originally designed to import and export data from external project management tools.

The productivity rates of Type 1 updates are roughly equivalent to new standalone development, with the exception that testing of both the old and new versions is somewhat more extensive.

Type 2: Additions with internal modifications to the base application

With Type 2 updates, it is necessary to make internal changes to the original application in order to attach the additional features (see Fig. 27.2). Type 2 updates are possible only for applications that were originally designed in a very modular, well-structured manner.

With Type 2 updates, all of the interfaces are concise and are located in one area of the original application. The productivity rate for adding the new features is close to that of new development work, but when the modifications to the existing application are included there is some

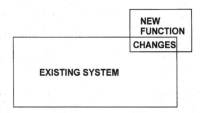

- **Similar to bridging for Year 2000 repairs**
- **Probable only with well-structured systems**
- **Productivity lower than new programs**
- **Productivity = 3 to 10 function points per staff month**

Figure 27.2   Type 2 enhancement (modified blocks).

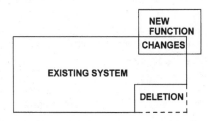

- **Similar to data duplexing for Year 2000 repairs**
- **Probable only with well-structured systems**
- **Productivity lower than new programs**
- **Deletions are hard to measure**
- **Productivity = 2 to 8 function points per staff month**

Figure 27.3   Type 3 enhancements (modification and deletion).

minor reduction due primarily to the need for extensive regression testing to ensure that no accidental damages have occurred.

Type 3: New feature replaces an existing feature

With Type 3 updates, the new feature being added to the software replaces a current feature which is actually being eliminated (see Fig. 27.3). This kind of update may occur with software that handles tax calculation or withholding rates, when there is a change in tax law.

In a year-2000 context, Type 3 modifications are turning out to be a source of deep concern, and especially so for companies that are using year-2000 outsource vendors. The source of the problem is the very common habit by programmers of *not* removing the original code when a new feature is added. The reason for this practice is that until the new feature is fully installed and tested, there is a chance that it might not work and, indeed, may have to be backed out. Therefore, it is simple prudence to leave the prior work alone, in case it has to be used again.

This habit of making updates without removing the former code or modules results in a phenomenon called *dead code*. Dead code consists of source code resident in an application which can no longer be executed, and which probably cannot even be reached via branching or normal operation of the software package.

Because updates for software can occur over many years, dead code can accumulate in substantial volumes—for some applications, as much as 30 percent of the actual volume of source code is dead and is no longer part of the working application.

Normally, dead code causes a reduction in maintenance productivity when new maintenance personnel take over, because they have to learn to avoid it. However, in a year-2000 outsource context the dead code is often quite troublesome for two reasons:

1. The vendor may charge $1 to $2 per line of code for the dead code.
2. Searching the dead code for year-2000 hits slows down repairs to active code.

Both situations are so troublesome that many companies either go through a dead code removal stage before starting year-2000 repairs, or keep the year-2000 repairs in house.

Type 4: New features accompanied by scatter updates

Because well-structured code is something of a rarity in the software world and is found in less than 30 percent of SPR's client's legacy applications, the most common situation for making updates to software is illustrated by the Type 4 category, or *scatter updates* (see Fig. 27.4).

With Type 4 modifications, several new features are being added at the same time. For poorly structured code, the interfaces between the new features and the existing application are not neat or tidy, but instead require extensive changes scattered in almost random patterns throughout the entire base application.

Type 4 modifications are very common and very troublesome. Productivity is much lower than normal development, and the incidence of bad fixes, or new bugs introduced as a by-product of the

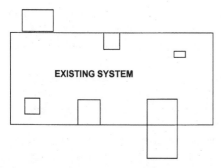

- **Typical of legacy date fields expansion for Year 2000**
- **Typical of old and unstructured systems**
- **Productivity much lower than new programs**
- **"Bad fixes" very common**
- **Productivity = 1 to 5 function points per staff month**

Figure 27.4 Type 4 enhancement (scatter updates).

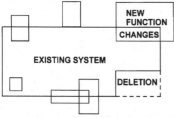

- **Typical of concurrent date repairs and new features for Year 2000**
- **Typical of old and unstructured systems**
- **Productivity much lower than new programs**
- **"Bad fixes" very common**
- **Very difficult to measure accurately**
- **Multiple changes overlap**
- **Productivity = 0.5 to 3 function points per staff month**

Figure 27.5 Type 5 enhancement (hybrid).

updates, can approach unity; that is, a new bug may be added for every change.

Type 5: Scatter updates, deletions, and conflicting repairs

When we arrive at Type 5 updates, we encounter the classic form of maintenance of poorly structured, aging legacy applications (see Fig. 27.5). Here all of the bad problems are occurring at the same time, and in addition, a special kind of problem can occur. When updates are occurring at the same time by different programmers, some of their changes may be in conflict and interfere with each other!

Type 5 updates have a number of both chronic and acute problems associated with them. Obviously, productivity is very low because the original code is quite difficult to work with. Also obviously, bad fix injection rates are very high, which is to say that new bugs will be accidentally introduced with almost every change.

In addition, Type 5 projects are very hard to put under proper configuration control, which means that several programmers may be updating the same modules of the existing application without being aware of each other's work. Only when testing begins will it be noted that some of the changes have interfered with each other, so rework is common and expensive in Type 5 situations.

The problems of Type 4 and Type 5 updates can be alleviated by a number of commercial software tools that provide geriatric services to aging legacy applications:

- Complexity-analysis tools
- Code restructuring tools
- Configuration-control tools
- Defect-tracking tools
- Reverse-engineering tools
- Reengineering tools
- Maintenance workbenches

Not every tool will work for every application or every programming language. Obviously, for common languages, such as COBOL, FORTRAN, and C, there is a large number of tools available. For more uncommon languages, such as CHILL, CORAL, Forth, PL/I, or CMS2, the number of geriatric tools is rather limited.

In conclusion, estimating the various forms of maintenance and enhancement work is among the most difficult problems facing software cost estimating tool developers. It is perhaps appropriate to close the discussion of maintenance estimating by paraphrasing the observation of the eighteenth-century wit, Samuel Johnson, upon seeing a dog that had been trained to walk on its hind legs: "It is not done well, but it is surprising that it can be done at all."

The literature on software maintenance is slowly expanding and rapidly improving. For many years the available books on maintenance topics were outnumbered by books on development topics by perhaps 100 to 1. Thanks to the pioneering work of such maintenance experts as Girish Parikh and Nicholas Zvegintzov in the 1970s the importance of maintenance finally began to achieve mainstream status.

References

Arnold, Robert S.: *Software Reengineering,* IEEE Computer Society Press, Los Alamitos, Calif., ISBN 0-8186-3272-0, 1993.

Arthur, Lowell Jay: *Software Evolution—The Software Maintenance Challenge,* John Wiley & Sons, New York, ISBN 0-471-62871-9, 1988.

Boehm, Barry: *Software Engineering Economics,* Prentice Hall, Englewood Cliffs, N.J., 1981.

Brown, Norm (ed.): *The Program Manager's Guide to Software Acquisition Best Practices,* Version 1.0, U.S. Department of Defense, Washington, D.C., July 1995.

Department of the Air Force, *Guidelines for Successful Acquisition and Management of Software Intensive Systems,* vols. 1 and 2, Software Technology Support Center, Hill Air Force Base, Utah, 1994.

Gallagher, R. S.: *Effective Customer Support,* International Thomson Computer Press, Boston, ISBN 1-85032-209-0, 1997.

Grady, Robert B.: *Practical Software Metrics for Project Management and Process Improvement,* Prentice Hall, Englewood Cliffs, N.J., ISBN 0-13-720384-5, 1992.

———, and Deborah L. Caswell: *Software Metrics: Establishing a Company-Wide Program,* Prentice Hall, Englewood Cliffs, N.J., ISBN 0-13-821844-7, 1987.

Howard, Alan (ed.): *Software Maintenance Tools,* Applied Computer Research (ACR), Phoenix, Ariz., 1997.

Jones, Capers: *Critical Problems in Software Measurement,* Information Systems Management Group, ISBN 1-56909-000-9, 1993a.

———: *New Directions in Software Management,* Information Systems Management Group, ISBN 1-56909-009-2, 1993b.

———: *Software Productivity and Quality Today—The Worldwide Perspective,* Information Systems Management Group, ISBN-156909-001-7, 1993c.

———: *Assessment and Control of Software Risks,* Prentice Hall, Englewood Cliffs, N.J., ISBN 0-13-741406-4, 1994.

———: *Patterns of Software System Failure and Success,* International Thomson Computer Press, Boston, ISBN 1-850-32804-8, 1995.

———: *Applied Software Measurement,* 2d ed., McGraw-Hill, New York, ISBN 0-07-032826-9, 1996.

———: *Software Quality—Analysis and Guidelines for Success,* International Thomson Computer Press, Boston, ISBN 1-85032-876-6, 1997.

———: *The Year 2000 Software Problem—Quantifying the Costs and Assessing the Consequences,* Addison Wesley, Reading, Mass., ISBN 0-201-30964-5, 1998.

Kan, Stephen H.: *Metrics and Models in Software Quality Engineering,* Addison-Wesley, Reading, Mass., ISBN 0-201-63339-6, 1995.

Marciniak, John J. (ed.): *Encyclopedia of Software Engineering,* vols. 1 and 2, John Wiley & Sons, New York, ISBN 0-471-54002, 1994.

McCabe, Thomas J.: "A Complexity Measure," *IEEE Transactions on Software Engineering,* 308–320 (December 1976).

Mertes, Karen R.: *Calibration of the CHECKPOINT Model to the Space and Missile Systems Center (SMC) Software Database (SWDB),* Thesis AFIT/GCA/LAS/96S-11, Air Force Institute of Technology (AFIT), Wright-Patterson AFB, Ohio, September 1996.

Muller, Monika, and Alain Abram (eds.): *Metrics in Software Evolution,* R. Oldenbourg Vertag GmbH, Munich, ISBN 3-486-23589-3, 1995.

Parikh, Girish: *Handbook of Software Maintenance,* John Wiley & Sons, New York, ISBN 0-471-82813-0, 1986.

Pigoski, Thomas M.: *Practical Software Maintenance—Best Practices for Managing Your Software Investment,* IEEE Computer Society Press, Los Alamitos, Calif., ISBN 0-471-17001-1, 1997.

Putnam, Lawrence H.: *Measures for Excellence—Reliable Software on Time, Within Budget,* Yourdon Press/Prentice Hall, Englewood Cliffs, N.J., ISBN 0-13-567694-0, 1992.

———, and Ware Myers: *Industrial Strength Software—Effective Management Using Measurement,* IEEE Press, Los Alamitos, Calif., ISBN 0-8186-7532-2, 1997.

Rethinking the Software Process, CD-ROM, Miller Freeman, Lawrence, Kans., 1996. (This CD-ROM is a book collection jointly produced by the book publisher, Prentice Hall, and the journal publisher, Miller Freeman. It contains the full text and illustrations of five Prentice Hall books: Capers Jones, *Assessment and Control of Software Risks*; Tom DeMarco, *Controlling Software Projects*; Brian Dreger, *Function Point Analysis*; Larry Putnam and Ware Myers, *Measures for Excellence*; and Mark Lorenz and Jeff Kidd, *Object-Oriented Software Metrics.*)

Rubin, Howard: *Software Benchmark Studies for 1997,* Howard Rubin Associates, Pound Ridge, N.Y., 1997.

Sharon, David: *Managing Systems in Transition—A Pragmatic View of Reengineering Methods,* International Thomson Computer Press, Boston, ISBN 1-85032-194-9, 1996.

Shepperd, M.: "A Critique of Cyclomatic Complexity as a Software Metric," *Software Engineering Journal,* **3:**30–36 (1988).

Stukes, Sherry, Jason Deshoretz, Henry Apgar, and Ilona Macias: *Air Force Cost Analysis Agency Software Estimating Model Analysis,* TR-9545/008-2, Contract F04701-95-D-0003, Task 008, Management Consulting & Research, Inc., Thousand Oaks, Calif., September 1996.

Symons, Charles R.: *Software Sizing and Estimating—Mk II FPA (Function Point Analysis),* John Wiley & Sons, Chichester, U.K., ISBN 0 471-92985-9, 1991.

Takang, Armstrong, and Penny Grubh: *Software Maintenance Concepts and Practice,* International Thomson Computer Press, Boston, ISBN 1-85032-192-2, 1997.

Zvegintzov, Nicholas: *Software Management Technology Reference Guide,* Dorset House Press, New York, ISBN 1-884521-0, 1994.

Biographies of Software Estimation Pioneers

In preparing this book an attempt was made to issue invitations for biographical information to all developers of software cost estimating tools who had developed formal estimation methods in the 1970s up through 1985, after which time so many cost-estimating tools entered the market that it was no longer easy to keep track of their developers.

Invitations were issued to Dr. Barry Boehm (COCOMO), Frank Freiman (PRICE-S), Dr. Randall Jensen (SEER), Dr. Howard Rubin (ESTIMACS), and Larry Putnam (SLIM). Because my own first estimation tool was built in 1973, I included myself as well.

Because function point metrics have been so important in software cost estimation, an invitation was also given to Allan Albrecht, the inventor of function point metrics. Due to other business commitments, not all of the estimation pioneers were able to respond.

This appendix contains biographical information from Dr. Barry Boehm, Larry Putnam, and myself. My request for biographical information asked in particular for the original impetus for studying software cost estimating and building software estimation tools. This appendix provides interesting insights into the state of the art of software cost estimation from the point of view of those who built some of the world's first software cost estimating tools.

Barry Boehm's Interest in Software Cost Estimating

My first exposure to software economics came on my first day in the software business, in June 1955 at General Dynamics in San Diego. My supervisor took me on a walking tour through the computer, an ERA 1103 which occupied most of a large room. His most memorable comment was:

> Now listen. We're paying this computer six hundred dollars an hour and we're paying you two dollars an hour and I want you to act accordingly.

This created some good habits for me, such as careful desk checking, test planning, and analyzing before coding. But it also created some bad habits—a preoccupation with saving microseconds, patching object code, and so forth—which were hard to unlearn when the balance of hardware and software costs began to tip the other way.

I joined the Rand Corporation in 1959, and confirmed this changing balance of hardware and software costs in 1971, when Rand lent me to the Air Force to run a study called CCIP-85. This study involved a forecast of Air Force command and control information processing needs into the mid-1980s, an identification of the most critical information processing deficiencies, and a recommended Air Force research and development program to address the deficiencies.

The study's sponsors and I expected that the main deficiencies would be in computer speed and memory, large-screen displays, and so forth. But what we found in visiting Air Force command and control sites was that their biggest operational deficiencies came from shortfalls in the software. And we found that the balance of Air Force hardware–software costs was becoming dominated by the software costs.

This led me to investigate what it was about software production that caused it to cost so much. The main results were presented in a 1973 *Datamation* article, "Software and Its Impact: A Quantitative Assessment." Most of the costs did not involve coding, but analysis and design, testing, and documentation. And much of the work involved repetitive manual tasks which could be largely eliminated by automation. But there was a lot about understanding and reducing software costs that could not be done from a think tank such as Rand, so in 1973 I decided to join TRW as Director of Software Research and Technology.

The first TRW data analysis I was involved in was the "Characteristics of Software Quality" study for NBS in 1973. Its most significant conclusion for TRW was that the bulk of the serious software defects were inserted in the requirements and design phases, but that they weren't being eliminated until testing, when they were much more expensive to fix. This caused us to focus TRW's software technology investments on the front end of the software life cycle, leading to such tools as the Design Assertion Consistency Checker and the Software Requirements Engineering Methodology, now commercialized as RDD-100.

At the time, TRW had a software cost estimation model that had been developed by Ray Wolverton in 1972. It was then a good match to TRW's needs, but as TRW's software business expanded (eventually becoming number 2 in the world to IBM on the Datamation 100 list), top management felt the need for a more general model, and this became my top-priority goal in 1976.

In surveying existing software cost estimation models at the time, I found some very good work being done by Capers Jones, Al Pietrasanta, Joel Aron, and others at IBM; by Larry Putnam in U.S. Army applications; by Frank Freiman and Bob Park with RCA PRICE-S; by Vic La Bolle and others at SDC; by Rachel Black and others at Boeing; and by Doty Associates. In comparing these with TRW project experience and a few early TRW project data points, it appeared that the functional form of the Doty model (cost as an exponential function of size, modified by a set of multiplicative cost drivers) appeared to be the best match, but that it had several problems with stability, definition, and choice of cost drivers.

This led to a group effort at TRW involving 10 experienced software managers and analysts determining the most appropriate initial set of cost drivers, rating scales, and multiplier values for a provisional cost model. This was then calibrated to 20 TRW project data points to produce a model called the *Software Cost Estimating Program* (SCEP). SCEP worked well enough for TRW that it was established as the company standard for use on all proposals and as the basis for software data collection. Its continued use led to a number of upgrades to add new cost drivers, phase and activity distributions, reuse and maintenance effects, and so forth. It also served as the quantitative basis for TRW's investment in productivity enhancing tools, processes, personnel, and management practices in the 1980s, such as the TRW Software Productivity System, rapid prototyping tools, and the Spiral Model.

Concurrently, I was gathering non-TRW data through student term projects in my USC and UCLA courses, and through open sources, such as the NASA Software Engineering Lab via Vic Basili. I tried fitting this data to the TRW SCEP model, but many of the data points did not fit well. In analyzing the patterns among the poorly fitting projects, I found that the differences could be explained fairly well by the concept of a *development mode*. TRW's mode tended to be what became called the *embedded* mode, characterized by tight, ambitious requirements and unprecedented applications. Batch, precedented business and scientific applications with easy-to-relax requirements and schedules fell into a different mode that became called the *organic* mode. By fitting different size-to-cost coefficients and scaling exponents to these modes (and an intermediate mode called *semidetached*), a three-mode model was able to explain the data fairly well (within 20 percent of the actuals, 70 percent of the time).

The resulting model was calibrated to 56 project data points (about half from TRW) in 1978, and produced comparably accurate estimates for another 7 non-TRW project data points collected in 1979. It became the Constructive Cost Model (COCOMO), published in the book *Software Engineering Economics* (Prentice Hall) in 1981.

Since then, over a dozen commercial versions of COCOMO and hundreds of in-house versions of COCOMO have been developed. A number of people have developed significant extensions to cover staffing constraints (Paul Rook, GECOMO), calibration capabilities (Dan Ligett, COSTAR; Bernie Roush, COSTMODL), labor grade distributions (Walker Royce, PCOC), function point sizing (Bob Gordon, BYL), customer costs (Bernie Price and Wolf Goethert, SECOMO), expert system diagnostics and risk advisors (Virginia Day, ESCOMO; Ray Madachy, Expert COCOMO), and numerous tailored versions for defense acquisition (Ray Kile, REVIC) and foreign countries (Ah Miii, TUCOMO, for Tunisia; Yukio Miyazaki and Kuniaki Mori for Fujitsu; and others). Aspects of COCOMO percolated into new models, such as SEER (Randy Jensen and Dan Galorath) and Softcost (Don Reifer).

In 1987 to 1989, Walker Royce and I developed Ada COCOMO, with some revised features and multipliers to cover the effects of using Ada and associated process improvements, such as the Ada Process Model, an extension of the risk-driven Spiral Model. This model capitalized on the ability to create compiler-checkable Ada package specifications to perform much of the software integration prior to developing the code. This and other early architecting and risk-resolution activities shifted more of the cost to the front end, and significantly reduced overall costs. Ada COCOMO also incorporated models for costing incremental development and developing software for subsequent reuse.

In 1989, I early-retired from TRW and worked in Washington, D.C. managing the DARPA Information Science and Technology Office and the DDR&E Software and Computer Technology Office. This enabled me to sponsor such efforts as the SEI Core Metrics program under Anita Carleton, Bob Park, Wolf Goethert, and others, and the Amadeus metrics tool under Rick Selby, but it kept me away from the software cost estimation field until my return to California and the TRW Professorship of Software Engineering at USC in 1992.

By this time, it was clear that many of the assumptions underlying the original COCOMO model were not well matched to the new ways in which software was being developed. Graphical user interface (GUI) builders made sizing parameters, such as delivered source instructions, irrelevant for the GUI portions of the software. Nonsequential process models obscured the definition of a project's beginning and end points, confounding both estimation and data collection. Simple linear models for software adaptation, reuse, and COTS integration did not fit experiential data. Widespread interactive development made such cost drivers as turnaround time irrelevant. Considerable controversy existed over the cost implications of investments in SEI-CMM process maturity.

To address the situation, one of our main projects at the USC Center for Software Engineering is the COCOMO II project. Its goals are to provide a new version of COCOMO better turned to current and likely future software practices, while preserving the open nature of COCOMO's internal algorithms and external interfaces, and preserving those parts of COCOMO which continue to be relevant. The COCOMO II research group includes Chris Abts, Dr. Brad Clark, Sunita Devnani-Chulani, Prof. Ellis Horowitz, Dr. Ray Madachy, Don Reifer, Prof. Bert Steece, and Prof. Rick Selby at UC Irvine. It also includes the 29 industry and government COCOMO II affiliate organizations listed in the acknowledgments, who provide sponsorship, expertise, and data for calibrating the model.

Our first step in scoping COCOMO II was to perform a comparative analysis of the approaches taken by the leading commercial software cost models. The model proprietors were very helpful in providing information, particularly Dan Galorath for SEER, Capers Jones for CHECKPOINT, Don Reifer and Tony Collins for Softcost, and Howard Rubin for Estimacs.

We also performed a forecast of future software development processes, which indicated that cost models would need to address projects using a mix of process models (rapid application development and prototyping, waterfall, incremental, evolutionary, spiral, COTS/reuse-driven, and design-to-cost/schedule). They would have to address more sophisticated forms of reuse, evolution, breakage, and COTS integration. They would have to reflect new technologies, such as GUI builders, object-oriented methods, application generators, and Internet-based distributed development.

Based on the cost model review and technology forecast, we began a series of iterations with the COCOMO II affiliates to converge on a set of functional forms and baseline cost drivers for the model—or, more accurately, for the family of models, as COCOMO II is organized into three stages.

Stage 1 is an *applications composition* model, focused on rapid application development or prototyping with GUI builders, COTS products, and distributed middleware support packages. Its basic sizing parameter is *object points,* a complexity-weighted count of the number of screens developed, reports generated, and third-generation language modules integrated. It is based on recent work done in this area by Rajiv Banker, Robert Kauffman, and Vijaya Kumar.

Stages 2 and 3 of COCOMO II have functional forms similar to the original COCOMO (COCOMO 81). Stage 2 of COCOMO II is an *early design* model, tailored for use in early stages of the life cycle when only partial information is available on the ultimate nature of the software project, product, platform, and personnel.

Stage 3 is a *post-architecture* model, tailored for use once the project has resolved its major risk items and has converged on a thorough and compatible set of plans, requirements, and architecture for the product.

Stage 2 uses function points as its primary size metric, but accommodates the use of source lines of code when appropriate. Stage 3 supports a mixed use of function points for some components and source lines of code for others. Sizing for both stages is adjusted for software breakage during development and for reuse or adaptation of existing software. The model for reuse and adaptation has been changed from a linear to a nonlinear model, based on the results of Selby's and others' data and analyses.

The Stage 3 model has 17 multiplicative cost drivers, most of which are similar to counterparts in COCOMO 81. *Turnaround time* and *modern programming practices* have been dropped, and four cost drivers have been added based on workshops with affiliates. These cover *multisite development, amount of documentation, personnel continuity,* and *development for subsequent reuse.*

The Stage 2 model compresses the 17 Stage 3 cost drivers into 7 aggregate cost drivers; for example, a single *personnel experience* cost driver is used in place of *applications experience, platform experience,* and *language and tool experience.*

Both Stages 2 and 3 replace the COCOMO 81 development modes by a set of five scale factors which adjust the additional costs of scaling up to large projects (diseconomies of scale). Two of these, *precedentedness* and *flexibility,* cover the effects of the COCOMO 81 development modes. Another two, *architecture/risk resolution* and *team cohesion,* are adapted from counterparts in Ada COCOMO. The fifth, *process maturity,* is a test of the hypothesis that increased SEI-CMM process maturity levels reduced costs by reducing the rework involved in immature processes.

Currently, the 1997 release of COCOMO II has been calibrated to 83 affiliate project data points. The overall fit is reasonably good, but the increased variability of current data due to variability of process and product definitions leaves the analysis of some detailed effects currently short of statistical significance.

Recently, however, Brad Clark obtained a statistically significant positive contribution for the COCOMO II cost driver of *SEI-CMM process maturity* on an expanded set of 112 well-defined data points. This result indicates that even after normalizing for the effects of concurrent changes in an organization's environment, use of tools, and reuse of software, a change of 1 CMM maturity level corresponded with a reduction of about 15 to 20 percent in effort. Overall, we are finding that collecting well-defined data points is a much more arduous process than it was for COCOMO 81.

Our USC-CSE Web site (http://sunset.usc.edu) has a pointer to the latest definitions, versions, and experience with COCOMO II.

As is Capers Jones, I am finding that the software cost modeling field needs to keep running to stay current with the rapid pace at which the software field reinvents itself, but that this continuing challenge makes it an increasingly significant and fascinating field in which to work.

Acknowledgments

I would like to acknowledge the support of the COCOMO II program affiliates. The current affiliates are Aerospace Corporation, Air Force Cost Analysis Agency, Allied Signal, Bellcore, Boeing Corporation, Defense Information Systems Agency, Electronic Data Systems Corporation, GDE Systems, Hughes Aircraft Company, Institute for Defense Analysis, Jet Propulsion Laboratory, Litton Data Systems, Lockheed Martin, Lucent Technologies, MCC Inc., Motorola Inc., Network Programs Inc., Northrop Grumman Corporation, Rational Software Corporation, Raytheon, Science Applications International Corporation, Software Engineering Institute (CMU), Software Productivity Consortium, Sun Microsystems Inc., Texas Instruments, TRW Inc., U.S. Air Force Rome Laboratory ,U.S. Army Research Laboratory, and Xerox Corporation.

Capers Jones's Interest in Software Cost Estimating

I entered the software world as a computer programmer in 1965, working for the Public Health Service in Washington, D.C. However, I also had an interest in technical writing and my first job out of college was as an editor of a scientific magazine, so I switched back and forth between programming and technical writing jobs and eventually became a manager of programming publications within IBM.

In 1970 I was working as a publications planner at IBM's San Jose programming laboratory. Some of our manuals were running late, and I became interested in the problem of estimating software technical writing.

After some research, I found that IBM's functional programming specifications were averaging about 8 pages of single-spaced Courier text per 1000 lines of assembly code, which was the only systems software programming language used by IBM at that time. Since the user reference manuals and the functional specifications were roughly the same size, this gave us the ability to do reasonable predictions of the size of IBM's software reference manuals. IBM's technical writers were averaging about 25 pages of text per staff month, so once the probable size of the manuals was known, the writing effort and schedule could be determined with acceptable precision.

In doing the research on estimating technical writing, it became obvious that programming needed more effective estimating methodologies since the programming and testing phases ran late oftener than the technical manuals. My first estimating tool for software was crude, but surprisingly effective circa 1970. Since IBM's functional specifications averaged 8 pages of text per 1000 lines of assembly code, I took a bar of white plastic in the shape of a ruler and marked it with schedule and cost information. By putting the functional specification flat on a table and measuring the thickness with my ruler, we could predict software schedules, effort, and costs with fair precision.

Several changes in software technology negated the value of the cost ruler:

1. As printers became more sophisticated and more flexible, two-sided printing and multiple fonts changed the page volumes.

2. Assembly language was joined by the PL/S programming language for IBM's system software development.

Building software-estimating tools at IBM

By 1973 I had left publications and was working in IBM's quality-assurance research lab in Palo Alto. I suggested that a serious effort be made to study the factors that influenced software quality, productivity, costs, and schedules. IBM's senior managers (Jim Frame, the San Jose and Palo Alto lab director, and Ted Climis, the vice president of the Systems Development Division) were both supportive of this proposal.

(Both Ted Climis and Jim Frame have passed away, but they were great software leaders who served to alert both IBM's corporate management and the industry as a whole that software was becoming a key technology of the future. Many of IBM's software innovations and best practices, and also the state-of-the-art IBM Santa Teresa Programming Laboratory, were due to the vision and energy of these two outstanding executives.)

With the assistance of a colleague, Dave Shough, we began to collect published information on factors that influenced software project outcomes. As it happened, there was a great deal of information starting to become available both from within IBM and from external publications. Dave and I produced a two-volume *Annotated Bibliography of Software Productivity and Quality Information Sources* that contained almost 500 citations and references.

Once started, this research project on software productivity and quality lasted several years. (Indeed, it is still going on.) As more and more data was collected, including examinations of the results of many IBM software projects, the overall patterns that affected software became visible.

It quickly became obvious that software quality had to be part of the software cost estimating equations, because finding and fixing bugs took more time and effort than anything else. It was also obvious that the costs of plans, specifications, and user manuals needed to be included, too, because paperwork sometimes cost more than source code. Finally, it became clear that with many different programming languages coming into use, it was necessary to understand in detail how each programming language affected software project results.

Once the underlying software cost and quality factors had been explored, it seemed possible to build an effective automated estimating tool for software projects. Here, too, IBM software executives Jim Frame and Ted Climis supported the concept and made time and resources available. In 1973, Dr. Charles Turk, who was one of IBM's top APL experts, was able to assist me in developing what was probably IBM's first automated software-estimating tool. The first version was called the *Interactive Productivity and Quality* (IPQ) model.

The first IPQ model handled only IBM's system software and it supported only assembly language, but it was rather sophisticated for the era. For example, IPQ included activity-level cost estimates and full software-quality predictions, and it could estimate the effort associated with the development of specifications and user manuals as well as estimating design, coding, and testing.

In 1974, the IPQ model was redesigned to make it easier to use and to make it support other languages besides assembly language. The full version was renamed *Development Planning System* (DPS). Within IBM, this cost-estimating model was fairly successful, and after a few years it grew to have more than 100 users at more than a dozen IBM systems software labs.

Based on the data we had collected to build DPS, in 1975 I published my first full-length report on software productivity and quality: IBM technical report TR 02.764, *Program Quality and Programmer Productivity*. This report was made available to IBM customers and to the outside world, and was the precursor of my later books and articles on measurement and estimation topics.

There was some discussion about putting the DPS estimating tool on the commercial market, but in the end IBM executives decided that it would be more useful to keep the tool as an internal, proprietary tool because it offered some significant competitive advantages. Dr. Charles Turk and I coauthored an IBM invention disclosure in 1976 on the method we had developed for incorporating quality estimates into software cost estimates.

In retrospect, it is unfortunate that DPS was used only inside IBM. The availability of a commercial software cost estimating tool with integral quality predictions in 1975, backed by IBM's sales and marketing clout, would probably have captured the estimating market, which was only just beginning to appear.

As we began to support multiple programming languages in our estimating tool, Dr. Turk and I were both surprised to discover that the lines-of-code metric did not work well for high-level languages, such as PL/S, PL/I, and APL. In fact, the LOC metric actually moved backwards. The reason was because the effort devoted to paper documents, such as specifications and user manuals, is not related to the volume of source code.

The immediate solution to this problem in 1974 was to convert size into *equivalent assembly statements*. Rather than expressing productivity rates in terms of the true lines of code in the actual language, we expressed productivity in terms of equivalent assembly lines of code. This was a crude and inelegant solution, which was eventually supplanted by using function point metrics.

However, the use of equivalent assembly statements did lead to a useful method for converting source code size between different programming languages. This method, slightly modified and updated, became the basis of the *backfiring* approach for converting lines of code into function points. By 1976, it was possible to convert source code size from any programming language to any other language for about the 50 most common programming languages then in use.

Early in 1978, I published an article in the *IBM Systems Journal*, [**17**(1)], "Measuring Programming Quality and Productivity." This article summarized the problems noted in using lines-of-code metrics and demonstrated that LOC metrics were invalid for high-level languages or cross-language comparisons.

(It is a minor historical footnote that the editor of the *IBM Systems Journal* at the time, George McQuilken, later became my company's first president when I started Software Productivity Research; we commenced operations in 1985.)

However, my article did not offer an elegant solution for solving the LOC problems, only the crude work-around of converting everything into equivalent assembly language. A truly elegant solution to the lines-of-code problem was the invention of function point metrics by Allan Albrecht, who worked for IBM on the East Coast.

In October 1979, IBM had a joint conference on software productivity that was cosponsored by two customer groups: SHARE and GUIDE. The conference was held on October 11 and 12, 1979, in Monterey, California. I was invited to gave a talk on my productivity findings for IBM customers. One of the other invited speakers was Allan Albrecht, of IBM at White Plains, New York..

On October 12, 1979, Allan delivered a talk on function point metrics. This was the first public discussion of function points, and also the first time I had either met Allan or heard of his work. I was tremendously impressed, because Allan's function point metric solved the lines-of-code problem and was much more elegant than merely converting data into equivalent assembly statements.

Software estimating at ITT

In 1978, Jim Frame, who was then the director of IBM's languages and data facilities group headquartered at the new Santa Teresa Programming Center, left IBM and joined the ITT Corporation, where he was named ITT's vice president of programming. Jim was the first to hold that title, and Jim had been hired by Harold Geneen to bring ITT software under control.

ITT, like many other major corporations, was experiencing the trauma of software delays and cost overruns on major applications. Harold Geneen was an astute and capable executive who recognized that a major corporation would need to bring software under control if it was to keep its product development projects on track. It was obvious that special executive skills at the corporate level were going to be required. To this end, Geneen instituted a national search for a top software executive, and Jim Frame of IBM was selected. Jim left IBM in 1978 and moved to ITT headquarters in New York.

Jim began a remarkable series of software programs at ITT, of which the most famous was the creation of the ITT Programming Technology Center in Stratford, Connecticut. This laboratory grew to a peak size of about 150 researchers and managers in 1983, and served as a role model for many other corporate centers of excellence for software.

The accomplishments of the ITT Programming Technology Center were significant, and a number of well-known software experts were employed there. For example, Dr. Ted Biggerstaff headed up the ITT software reusability program; Dr. Bill Curtis, who later led the SEI assessment program, worked there on starting the ITT software metrics program; and Dr. Tom Love and his colleagues in the advanced technology group started the work that would later become the Objective C programming language.

Although not full-time employees, many other software experts passed through the ITT Programming Technology Center to visit the scientists, give presentations, or work on short-term projects: Dr. Barry Boehm, Tom Gilb, James Martin, Larry Putnam, Dr. Howard Rubin, and Dr. Gerald Weinberg come to mind as software industry leaders who visited the ITT research center during its peak in the early 1980s.

(When ITT sold its telecommunications business to the French telecommunication company Alcatel, both the Programming Technology Center and the nearby Telecommunications Technology Center were included in the transaction. Alcatel decided to concentrate on the manufacturing operations and closed down both former ITT research facilities.)

In 1979 I accepted a job under Jim Frame as assistant director of programming at the ITT corporation. At the time ITT was a highly diverse conglomerate that had more than 50 different locations which produced software.

Some of the companies owned by ITT at its peak of maximum diversity included Avis rental cars, Bell telephone manufacturing, Bobbs-Merrill publishing, Burpee seeds, Continental baking, Courier, Hartford insurance, Howard Sams publishing, Morton frozen foods, Qume, Scotts fertilizer, Sheraton hotels, Standard Telefon Lorenz, and Standard Telephone and Cable.

Although IBM and ITT were roughly the same size in terms of employees, the diversity of ITT was extreme. Since ITT was a conglomerate that grew by acquisition, there was no consistency at all in the kinds of software that were being built or in the tools, languages, methods, and approaches used for software development. ITT was also geographically dispersed across much of the world—Europe, South America, North America, and Asia.

The diversity and geographic separation of the ITT software locations got me interested in portable estimating tools. In the late 1970s and early 1980s, modern notebook computers did not exist. However, handheld computers were starting to appear.

The availability of handheld computers with built-in Basic interpreters allowed me to build a series of software-estimating prototypes using the Sharp PC 1500 as the platform (also sold by Radio Shack as the PC-2). These little computers weighed less than a pound, but they had only a single-line display and only 10K of memory.

These limitations meant that my prototype estimating tools could do only one kind of estimate at a time. I built a series of four tools for my handheld computer, called *SIZER/1* through *SIZER/4*. One of these handled sizing of various deliverables, and the others handled estimates for new projects, enhancements, and maintenance, respectively.

The ITT Applied Technology group acquired a dozen or so of the small handheld computers because all of us traveled to visit remote ITT labs on almost a weekly basis. These small computers loaded with our estimating tools left a lot to be desired, but they did give us the ability to perform cost estimates very quickly in a consistent manner.

(In 1980, shortly after I joined ITT and before I had time to build any estimating tools myself, we needed to validate some serious cost estimates for a number of key projects in the United States and Europe. We brought in Larry Putnam and commissioned him to run his SLIM model at several ITT locations.)

For about five years, from 1978 through 1983, ITT was one of the world's top software research establishments. The well-known ITT Programming Technology Center in Stratford, Connecticut had attracted a team of almost 150 software research personnel, including such well-known figures as Dr. Bill Curtis, who later headed up the SEI assessment group; Dr. Tom Love, the developer of Objective C; and Dr. Ted Biggerstaff, who pioneered ITT's research on software reusability.

Formation of Software Productivity Research (SPR)

By 1983, ITT had changed business strategies and no longer planned to compete globally in the telecommunications market. ITT began to sell off portions of its telecommunications business. It was evident that the ITT Programming Technology Center in Connecticut, where I worked, as well as many other ITT business units would soon be sold. As a result, many members of the ITT software research team began to leave.

After a year of consulting at Nolan, Norton & Company in Massachusetts, I formed Software Productivity Research (SPR) in conjunction with a former IBM colleague, George McQuilken. (As mentioned previously, George had been editor of the *IBM Systems Journal* in 1978, when I published my article on the hazards of lines of code.)

In 1984, the software estimating business was still in its infancy. Dr. Barry Boehm had published the algorithms for his constructive cost model (COCOMO) in 1981 in his important book *Software Engineering Economics* (Prentice Hall) but there were not yet any commercial estimating tools using these algorithms.

I had also published my first book in 1981, *Programming Productivity—Issues for the Eighties* (IEEE Computer Society Press). My book included the full text of Allan Albrecht's paper on function point metrics and was the first to make function point information available to a wide audience, although Al's own 1984 report published through IBM extended the usage even more.

There were only three commercial software-estimating tools available in 1984: the PRICE-S, developed by Frank Freiman for what was then RCA; Larry Putnam's SLIM, from Quantitative Software Management (QSM); and Dr. Howard Rubin's ESTIMACS, from the MACS corporation, which was soon to be acquired by Computer Associates.

Because of my background within IBM and ITT as an international consultant dealing with diverse companies doing many different kinds of software in many different countries, I wanted to build an estimating tool that could support any known kind of software, developed in any known programming language or even any combination of multiple programming languages.

Also, since I had to travel all over the world, I wanted to be able to take my estimating tool with me and have it available regardless of the kinds of computer systems my clients were using. Therefore, my first estimating tool after forming SPR was built on and for the Data General/1, which was the first notebook computer aimed at frequent travelers. In fact, the first half dozen computers which we acquired at SPR were various kinds of portables.

My first prototype was called the *Software Productivity, Quality, and Reliability* (SPQR) estimator, and it had 10 adjustment parameters. Using the combination of its name and number of adjustments, I called it *SPQR/10.*

It was obvious that function point metrics were much better than lines of code for sizing and estimating specifications, user manuals, and various paper deliverables. However, the standard IBM function point of 1984 was rather complicated and was not easy to automate. (Curiously, IBM itself never developed any automated tool for counting function points in spite of having the world's largest collection of programmers at that time.)

To facilitate the task of automating function point counts and using them for estimation, I developed a simplified version that used only 3 complexity adjustment factors, rather than the 14 factors used for authentic IBM function points. The three factors I selected were:

1. Problem complexity
2 Code complexity
3. Data complexity

It would be meaningless to simplify function point counting if the results differed from the IBM approach in a significant way. Allan Albrecht of IBM kindly tried out my simplification on a sample of projects, as did several of my colleagues and clients from other companies. From roughly 100 trials, the SPR function point and the IBM 1984 function point produced results that differed by an average of 2 percent and had a maximum difference of 9 percent.

The SPQR/10 tool was essentially a prototype to explore the usage of function point metrics for software-estimation purposes. The results were successful enough to bring out a more full-featured commercial estimating tool built on function point logic.

By 1985, SPR's first commercial software-estimating tool was ready to be marketed (thanks to the very hard work of Scott Moody and Richard Ward). This tool was called *SPQR/20* for the use of 20 adjustment parameters.

Some of the estimating factors utilized in SPQR/20 are still relevant in the more recent generation of software-estimating tools:

- Class of the application (internal, external, civilian, military, etc.)
- Type of the application (embedded, systems, MIS, client/server, etc.)
- Size of the application
- Complexity of the application
- Nature of the application (new, enhancement, module, program, or system)
- Team experience in similar applications
- Methodology or development process rigor
- Tool suites available
- Quality-control methods (inspections, testing, or both)
- Office ergonomics
- Programming languages to be used
- Reusable material available

Considering that the year was 1985, SPQR/20 pioneered a number of estimating innovations that have now become more or less standard features of commercial software-estimating tools. Some of these features include the following:

- Domain adjustments for system software, military software, and information systems
- Separate estimating algorithms for new projects, maintenance, and enhancements
- Sizing logic for specifications, source code, and test cases
- Support for both function points and lines-of-code (LOC) metrics
- Support for *backfiring* or conversion from LOC to function points
- Integrated quality and reliability estimating
- Integrated risk analysis
- Phase-level development schedule, cost, and resource estimates
- Maintenance and enhancement estimates for five years after deployment
- A side-by-side mode for examining alternate development scenarios

Although newer estimating tools, such as our CHECKPOINT product and KnowledgePlan have extended the capabilities of estimation far beyond those of SPQR/20, this early tool can still provide useful estimates. In fact, since SPQR/20 is a fairly concise DOS product rather than a Windows product, I keep a copy in my Hewlett-Packard pocket computer. As a world traveler, it is a great convenience to have a software-estimating tool that can operate in a pocket computer that weighs only 11 ounces.

Integration of estimation, measurement, and assessment

In order to do software estimation well, it is necessary to collect a great deal of very detailed information about thousands of software projects. Three general kinds of information are needed:

1. Quantitative information on costs, schedules, quality, and effort

2. Qualitative assessment data about the experience levels of personnel and the effectiveness of various tools and processes

3. Factual data about the specific tools, platforms, operating systems, and programming languages utilized

The software assessment method developed by the Software Engineering Institute (SEI) has achieved a great deal of publicity. As it happens, SPR was incorporated slightly before SEI and began doing assessments slightly earlier, using our own assessment method.

We've been doing assessment and benchmark studies continuously since 1985, and now have data reflecting about 600 companies and more than 7500 projects. However, we gather new data at a rate of about 100 projects each month, so the overall volume of data grows continuously.

Some of the early results of the SPR assessment method were published in 1986 in my book *Programming Productivity* (McGraw-Hill), which came about three years prior to Watts Humphrey's well-known 1989 book *Managing the Software Process* (Addison-Wesley).

Since Watts and I were both at IBM in the 1970s, our assessment methods had a similar origin. We both independently developed five-point evaluation scales for recording the assessment results, although our scales run in opposite directions. The SPR software excellence scale uses 1 to indicate excellence, as follows:

1. Excellent

2. Good

3. Average

4. Below Average

5. Poor

After the SPQR/20 estimating tool, SPR next built the CHECK-POINT multifunction assessment, measurement, and estimation tool, which came out in 1989. (Note that CHECKPOINT is also marketed under the name CHECKMARK in the United Kingdom and in Japan.)

As a pure estimating tool, CHECKPOINT has about an order of magnitude more detail than the previous SPQR/20. In addition to estimating, CHECKPOINT also includes assessment and measurement features so that it can be used to collect and analyze data. The essential features of the CHECKPOINT tool include the following:

- Full software assessment capability covering more than 100 factors
- Full measurement capabilities for resources, costs, schedules, and quality
- Software fact recording for tools, vendors, and programming methodologies
- Full sizing logic for more than 50 kinds of paper-based plans and specifications
- Backfiring support for more than 500 programming languages
- Automatic conversion among function points, feature points, and LOC metrics
- Activity-based microestimating capability for several hundred development tasks
- Support for early estimates before project requirements are firm

- Integral quality, risk, and reliability estimation
- Twenty-year maintenance and enhancement estimating
- Inflation rate adjustments for long-range estimates, such as multi-year maintenance
- Currency conversion for international projects
- Onboard statistical analysis tool for aggregating entire portfolios
- Comparative mode for comparing projects to industry norms or best-in-class data
- Template construction capability for converting historical data into estimating data

Once such a tool is developed, it tends to have a life of its own. We use the CHECKPOINT tool all over the world to collect information for our international assessment and benchmark consulting studies. Our international consulting group is now bringing in new data at a rate that sometimes reaches 150 projects a month from various parts of the world—Canada, the United States, Europe, India, Japan, and South America.

The steady stream of fresh assessment and benchmark data coming into SPR has given me the opportunity to publish a number of books on software and management topics that are based on large-scale empirical findings: *Applied Software Measurement* (McGraw-Hill, 1991; revised 1996) published U.S. national averages for software productivity and quality; *Assessment and Control of Software Risks* (Prentice Hall, 1994) discussed 65 common risk factors that SPR assessments had turned up; *Patterns of Software Systems Failure and Success* (International Thomson Computer Press, 1995) studied very successful software projects at one end and total failures at the other.

More recently, my books *Software Quality—Analysis and Guidelines for Success* (International Thomson Computer Press, 1997) and *The Year 2000 Software Problem* (Addison-Wesley/Longman, 1998) have applied out historical data to some interesting newer problems, such as client/server quality and the costs of achieving year-2000 compliance.

In 1997, SPR brought out our new KnowledgePlan estimating tool. This tool was built as a native application for Windows 95 and Windows NT and includes a standard bidirectional interface to Microsoft Project.

One of the design goals of our new KnowledgePlan tool is to start the integration of software cost estimating with other forms of project management tools, such as methodology management tools, project management tools, and the like. Interfacing software cost estimating tools with other key software project management tools is starting to become a new wave of the industry.

Using the analogy of office suites, it is obvious that the era of standalone estimation and project management tools will eventually be succeeded by a new era of integrated project management suites which will include full sizing logic, cost estimation, quality estimation, detailed schedule prediction and control, risk analysis, value analysis, budget support, and many other features.

It is also obvious that macroestimating only to the level of phases or complete projects is inadequate for serious business purposes, such as contracts and litigation support. Therefore KnowledgePlan, like CHECKPOINT, includes the ability to drop down to detailed task-level estimation for hundreds of discrete development tasks at a micro level.

However, since task-level estimates are of considerable length and detail (sometimes more than 150 pages of output), KnowledgePlan and CHECKPONT also have the ability to express estimating results to any level of detail specified by the user—task level, activity level, phase level, or project level.

For early or preliminary estimates, using project- or phase-level estimates that show only high-level schedule, cost, and resource data may be sufficient. However, for contracts, tax litigation, or more serious business purposes, the estimates can be expanded down to microlevel task estimation.

Our KnowledgePlan cost-estimating tool uses an estimation engine derived from the previous CHECKPOINT model, but it uses a totally new user interface and much more powerful project scheduling capabilities due to the direct relationship with project management tools.

KnowledgePlan also uses a commercial database rather than a proprietary database, which facilitates the creation of templates and makes portfolio analysis of hundreds of projects quite a bit easier.

Since one of the major problems of software cost estimation is the need to generate fairly accurate estimates before project requirements are fully defined, we always include very extensive support for handling early estimates using incomplete information. To this end, we include a number of early sizing and estimating approaches.

One new form of sizing in KnowledgePlan which was not in our prior estimating tools is *sizing by analogy*. That is, users can search or scroll through similar software projects stored in the database and select one or more projects that resemble the project to be estimated. The size, resources, and costs of the new work can then be derived by analogy with the size and other information from the historical projects that resemble the new work.

We at SPR and all of our competitors have to keep our tools and knowledge bases updated very frequently. This explains the phenomenon that many vendors of estimating tools are also prominent in the assessment and benchmark consulting arena.

Software technologies are changing rapidly as well, so we have to stay at the forefront of new technical developments. For example, in 1998 JAVA is a hot technology, data warehousing is hot, and the costs of the Looming year-2000 and Eurocurrency problems are attracting a great deal of attention and need to be handled by estimating tools.

These are just examples—dozens of new concepts and tools come out every year and need to be evaluated for estimating purposes. Other examples include the ISO 9000–9004 standards, the five levels of the SEI capability maturity model, the new DoD 498 standard, the impact of the Internet and Lotus notes on distributed development, the impact of SAP, and many others. Since we try to stay current with programming languages, new languages and dialects have been occurring at a rate of more than one a month for the past five years.

I've spent much of my professional working life either collecting data or analyzing data in order to develop estimating algorithms. It is fascinating work, and I think none of us in the software-estimating business regard our work as being beyond just getting started. Every day new data is arriving, and there are new technologies to explore and evaluate. I can't imagine a more interesting kind of work.

Larry Putnam's Interest in Software Cost Estimating

Early interest

I first became interested in computers while I was a young officer in the army doing graduate studies in physics at the Naval Postgraduate School during the period 1959 to 1961.

In one of my physics courses I needed to do some very detailed, tedious calculations, which required precision out to 12 decimal places. The only tools to do that kind of work at the time were big, clumsy, desktop mechanical calculators. For one graded exercise I had to go into the local town and hire one of these machines over the weekend to be able to do the necessary calculations. This was back in slide-rule days; it was just impossible to get more than about 2 to 3 decimal places of precision. So that made computers very appealing to me when they first appeared on the scene.

1961 to 1964: Army Nuclear Weapons Program Office

Following graduate school I was assigned to the army's Special Weapons Development Division in the Combat Development Command at Fort Bliss, Texas. One of my jobs there was supervising the preparation of the army's nuclear weapons selection tables. This involved a great deal of calculation of tables pertaining to the effects of nuclear weapons. These tables were used to pick the right weapon for a particular tactical operation. The army would have to redo these tables every time its inventory of weapons changed. Consequently we were continually turning out new tables, which were several hundred pages in length.

We were doing this work on a small computer about the size of a refrigerator, manufactured by the Bendix Corporation. It was a model G15 computer and had about the power that a programmable calculator has today. This machine was programmed in assembly language. Later I had an opportunity to program the machine in a higher-order language, ALGOL. These were simple engineering programs of perhaps 50-odd lines of code, very small programs indeed.

In 1966, while an instructor in nuclear weapons effects at the Defense Atomic Support Agency (now called the Defense Nuclear Agency) in Albuquerque, New Mexico, I needed to do some blast calculations to support some of the teaching that I was doing. We were located immediately adjacent to the Sandia Laboratories, which was the principle Atomic Energy Commission contractor responsible for the arming, fusing, and firing components that went into our nuclear weapons.

The national nuclear program has always been a big user of computers in its research and development work. It was always on the forefront of computing technology and bought the biggest and best that was available from the computer industry. Just at the time I needed to do these calculations, Sandia Labs had just received the largest available scientific computer from UNIVAC, a Model 1108. It was installed next door to our facilities. At first the Sandia people had far more computing capacity in that machine than they needed for their own work. So they advertised that their machine would be available for use by other people on the base for their own scientific calculations. They even offered to teach people to program the machine in FORTRAN.

I signed up for the course. In about 15 to 20 sessions, I learned enough about FORTRAN programming that they would grant me access to their machine.

At that time, one had to prepare a deck of IBM punch cards and submit the job the day before; the computer operators would put the job into the run stream for the computer that night. In the course of learning how to program in FORTRAN, I never did learn the procedure to punch up the job-control cards to initiate the actual execution of the FORTRAN program. So I found I had some unplanned lessons to learn when I got kicked off the machine about 10 times before I could finally generate the right sequence of job-control cards for my FORTRAN program.

I also quickly got acquainted with debugging programs because even when my job was initiated, I'd get kicked off because of syntax errors in the programs I had written. It turned out to be a quite lengthy period of time before I finally got a successful program to compile, run, and generate the data that I was interested in.

The really significant thing that came out of this was that I got a very pretty certificate of completion for the FORTRAN programming course. Naturally, I wanted this to reflect favorably in my army records, so I mailed it off to my personnel file kept at the Pentagon. Thought no more about it for a number of years.

Computer duty in the army

In 1972, after completing a tour in Vietnam and another two years commanding troops at Fort Knox, Kentucky, it came time for me to do some duty in the Pentagon. The army personnel organization did not have any jobs in the nuclear business at the time, but here's where my FORTRAN programming certificate came into play. In reviewing my records the personnel people decided, based on my computer programming experience, that I was eminently qualified to take charge of the army's automatic data processing budget. I was going to deal with the budgetary process for the army's procurement of computers and funding of software development programs.

I didn't know anything about software other than the little, bitty FORTRAN, ALGOL, and Basic programs I had written. At that time the army was spending close to $100 million a year to automate the business functions that it was performing—its payroll, its inventory management, its real property management on bases around the world, its mobilization plans, its force deployment plans, its command and control structure, and virtually everything that had anything to do with business and logistic operations in the army. This had been automated on the first large-scale computers that came along. Most of this initial work had been done in assembly language. At the time I arrived, it was just being done over in higher-order languages, principally COBOL. We were in the midst of trying to get about 50 to 70 large-scale systems completed and out doing their jobs in the active army. All of this amounted to about $100 million of expense annually. Hardware was another couple hundred million.

In the midst of all this, I began to hear those ominous words about overruns and slippages. We were having a significant number of those occur with these large army programs, which were running from 50,000 to 400,000 lines of COBOL code.

I really became aware of problems with software the first time I went to the budget table with the people from the Office of the Secretary of Defense. We were going through the justification of our

ADP program. The software aspects of this budget were only a third of the total budget, and yet it was occupying almost all the time in the hearing. We were looking at the next fiscal year and the five following fiscal years after that. In the case of the army's Standard Installation Division Personnel System (SIDPERS), we were looking at a system that had become operational the year before. When it first became operational, its personnel complement was up to 118 people; the next year we projected it to fall to about 116; then we were saying we needed 90 people for each of the next 5 years.

The budget analyst from the Office of the Secretary of Defense, rightly enough, asked, "What are the people going to do? The system became operational a year ago. How many bases is it deployed to? Once it's out there, what are you going to use these ninety people for? Isn't it finished?"

Well, there was a big silence in the room. I was new, first time on the job. I didn't know the answer to this. So I looked to my left then to my right—to those long-term army civilian employees that had come into the Pentagon with the first computer and were the acknowledged experts. They were strangely quiet as well. Nobody on the army side of the table knew what the real reason was for those 90 people. The very lame answer that finally dribbled out was "Maintenance." So all the dialogue and conversation came to a halt, a big silence. Finally, the analyst from OSD said, "Look, this is a ten-million-dollar item. Unless I can get some satisfactory answers on this, I guess I will have to delete it out. Why don't we adjourn the meeting, [it was almost 4 in the afternoon] reconvene at nine o'clock in the morning and perhaps by then you can call a few people that know more about it and we can come up with a satisfactory answer. See you in the morning."

So we scurried off, called the Army Computer Systems Command. We waited by the phone for several hours into the evening. Finally, we got a response back that was lame, inadequate. Upshot: Nobody in the army really knew what the 90 people were going to do for the next 5 years, except "maintenance."

So, the next day by 9:15 A.M. we had lost $10 million from the army's ADP budget.

The following day, while walking down the halls of the Pentagon away from the budget meeting, my boss, a major general from the Corps of Engineers, said, "You know Larry, this business of trying to plan the resources and the schedule for software projects is a very mystifying business to me. All my experience in the Corps of Engineers has been that we always, even early on in a project—the big dams, the waterways projects—we always had some feel for the physical resources required—how many dump trucks, how many cubic yards of concrete, how many shovels, how many people we needed to do the job. For these sorts of things we could make some crude estimate, based on a little bit of previous data. Yet any time I try to get similar types of answers on computer programs, things having to do with software, I immediately get a dialogue on the internal architecture of the computer itself, the bits and bytes. Never anything about how long is it going to take, how much it is going to cost, how many people I am going to need, how good is it going to be when I deliver it. We need to have a way to address these kinds of things at our level here at the Department of the Army so we can come to grips with this business of planning and managing software development."

So, that was really the motivation that got me thinking about how software systems behave and how we might be able to effectively model that with a few parameters that would be useful—to get the answers that senior managers wanted.

Within a couple weeks of this budget disaster, by pure luck I happened to stumble across a small paperback book in the Pentagon bookstore. It had a chapter on managing research and development projects by Peter Norden of IBM. Peter showed a series of curves, which I will later identify as Rayleigh curves. These curves traced out the time history of the application of people to a particular project. It showed the buildup, the peaking, and the tailoff of the staffing levels required to get a research and development project through that process and into production. Norden pointed out that some of these projects were for software projects, some were hardware related, and some were composites of both. The thing that was striking about the function was that it had just two parameters. One parameter was the area under the curve, which was proportional to the effort (and cost), applied, and the other one was the time parameter, which related to the schedule (see Fig. A.1).

I found that I could take these Rayleigh curves and easily adapt them to the budgetary data that I had on the army software projects. That data was collected by fiscal years. We had the data on the number of person years applied for each of the fiscal years throughout the history of any project in our budget. So, I went ahead and quickly plotted up all the software systems that we had in inventory and under development. I was able to determine what the Rayleigh parameters were in terms of the effort and the schedule, and once knowing that, I could make projections out to the end of the curve, which was essentially to the end of the budgeting cycle. Within a month, I was able to get about 50 large army development projects under control and was able to do credible budget forecasts for those projects—at least 5 years into the future.

The next time the budget hearings came around, a year later, we were in the downsizing phase at the end of the Vietnam war—budget

**Staff,
No. of People**

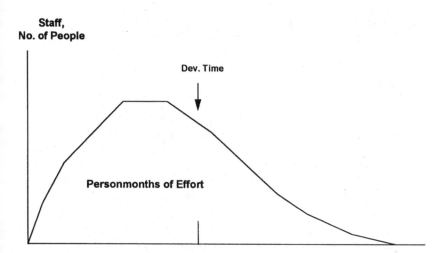

Figure A.1   A typical Rayleigh staffing curve.

cuts were endemic; we were asked to cut the application of effort on a number of existing systems. The turnaround was short; we had to respond to what impact this would have within a 24-hour period.

Now, having the Rayleigh curve and understanding that methodology, I was able, with a pocket calculator programmed with the Norden Rayleigh function, to quickly make estimates of what would happen if we reduced the projections for several of the projects. It was easy to show that the aggregate of these cuts would wipe out the capability to start any new software projects in the army for the next three years.

The result of that budget hearing—we did not lose any money.

Naturally, the next important question that arose was "How do I use these Rayleigh equations to generate an estimate for a new project? It's nice to be able to pick up those that are already under way, but is there some way I can find out the time and effort for a new project so I can build one of these budgeting and staffing profiles for getting the work done?"

I looked into that. Right away the notion arose that somehow we had to be able to relate the size of the Rayleigh curve—its associated time and effort—with the amount of function that had to be created. How did people building software for the army—in its own in-house organizations like the Army Computer Systems Command, and their contractors—how did those people think about the functionality that they were creating?

I found out that they thought about the lines of code they had to write, they talked a lot about the number of files they were creating, the number of reports they were generating, the number of screens that they had to bring up—those types of entities that were clearly related to the amount of functionality that had to be created. Clearly, these functional entities had to be related to the schedule and effort to get the job done.

I spent the next year and a half to two years of my army time, about a third to half my daily schedule, doing analyses of data. The first set of data I worked with came from the Army Computer Systems Command. It was 15 to 20 systems. I attempted to do some mathematical curve fitting, relating the size of those systems in lines of code, in files, in reports, and in screens to the known development schedules and the associated person months of effort.

The first approach was to use simple regression analysis of functionality, of lines of code, as the independent variable and then person months of effort as the dependent variable. I did the same thing with schedules.

Next I did some multiple regression analysis where I related effort to combinations of lines of code, files, reports, and screens. The statistical parameters that came out showed they might be useful for predicting, but they were not extraordinarily good fits. Certainly, more work and investigation was needed before drawing any conclusions.

By this time, 1975 to 1976, I had been in contact with other investigators working in this area. Judy Clapp from the Mitre Corporation had done some studies on 10 to 15 scientific and engineering systems that were being done for the Electronics Systems Division of the Air Force Systems Command at Hanscom Air Force Base. Felix and Walston at IBM Federal Systems Division had published a paper in the *IBM Systems Journal* and had amassed a database of about 75 projects that gave a good feel for a range of different parameters related to software. All of this information was very useful in trying to establish relationships between lines of code, pages of documentation, time, effort, and staffing.

In trying to do this analytical work I had to go back about 20 years to my academic training at the Naval Postgraduate School to refresh my memory on how to do the statistical analyses, how to do work with data, and how to come up with some logical inferences and conclusions as a result of that. There was a lot of relearning to build up skills that had become very rusty in the course of not using those techniques for many years.

Software equation

One of the very promising experiments was trying to do some multiple regression analysis relating the size of the systems in lines of code to the schedule and the person months of effort applied. I did these curve fits first with the army data, then with the Electronics Systems Division data followed by the IBM data. I was lucky in that I got some very nice fits in about 20 of the army data systems. Concurrent with these curve fits, I also did some theoretical work on integrating Rayleigh curves and tried to establish the parameters of integration from a little bit of the historic data from the army and IBM. I found there was good consistency in being able to generate the key parameters for the Rayleigh equation—the work effort (area under the curve) and the schedule parameter. These different, independent approaches at getting a parameter-estimating equation were both leading me in the same direction and producing similar results.

What ultimately fell out of this is what I now call the *quantitative software management* (QSM) software equation. It related the amount of function that had to be created to the time and effort required to do it. It looked like this:

Quantity of function = constant × effort × schedule

In the curve-fitting process, I found that there were exponents associated with both the time and effort parameters and that there was also a constant that got generated in the process. I thought a lot about what the physical meaning of this constant was. Somehow it seemed to be related to the efficiency of the development organization, or the technology which it was applying to its software development practices. The first name I used to describe this empirically determined constant was *technology factor.* I used that term in the first early papers I wrote on this subject, published by the IEEE Computer Society in the 1976 to 1977 time frame. I have continued to use that parameter to represent the efficiency of the software development organization. I have, over the years, renamed it several times—first a *technology factor,* then a *technology constant,* then a *productivity constant.* Our most recent name for this is the *process productivity parameter,* which I think is probably the most descriptive term to use in describing what its real relationship is to the software development process.

This was the genesis of the software equation that we still use today. It has proven to be a very good measurement and estimating tool for QSM and me over the past 20 years.

This software equation was a macro model that linked the amount of function to be created to the management parameters of schedule and effort required to produce it. The empirically determined factor represented the productive capability of the organization doing the work. This also suggested that this was a very good way to easily tune an estimating process, because if you knew the size, time, and effort of your completed historic projects, you could easily calculate what that process productivity parameter was. Then you could use that calculated parameter in making an estimate for a new project. So long as the environment, tools, methods, practices, and skills of the people did not change dramatically from one project to the next, this process of playing back historic data became a very useful, simple, straightforward calibration tool.

Manpower buildup equation

The other key relationship that emerged in these studies was the direct relationship between time and effort. Clearly, these were the parameters of our Rayleigh equation. But was there anything we could learn from the basic data as to what this behavior characteristic was? Again, more curve fitting. I found that there was a distinct relationship between the effort and the development schedule. It turned out that the effort was proportional to the schedule cubed. This was also something that had been noted and discovered earlier by Felix and Walston and several other investigators who had done research in software cost estimating.

This finding was especially important because it now gave me the basis for making estimates. I had two equations and two unknowns. The first was the software equation involving size, time, effort, and the process productivity parameter. The second equation (which I now call the *manpower buildup relationship*) linked effort with the third power of the development time.

This latter equation required some parametric determinations. We found a parameter family that seemed to relate to the staffing style of the organization. Those organizations that tended to use large teams of people built up their staffing rapidly. This produced a high value of the ratio of effort divided by development time cubed. Those organizations that worked in small teams took a longer period of time to complete their development. This was typical of engineering companies that tended to solve a sequential set of problems one step at a time. For such companies I saw that the relationship of their effort divided by development time cubed produced a much smaller number for the buildup parameter. This was telling us is that there were different staffing styles that organizations adopted. The parameter of effort divided by development time cubed was really a measure of the manpower acceleration being applied to a software project.

It became evident in studying these different types of organizations that those organizations that used large teams of people seemed to finish their projects a little bit faster than those that used the small teams and took a little bit longer to complete their work, all other things being equal. This suggested there was some sort of trade-off going on between team size and how long it took to get the work done.

The other significant idea that I started working on during this period in the army was the notion of the Rayleigh curve being a good process control vehicle for projects while they were under way. The idea was to take real data as it was happening on a project and then update and adaptively forecast the right Rayleigh curve to project onward from wherever the project was at the time. This would let you dynamically predict cost, schedule, and defects to completion of the project.

I did some early curve-fitting investigations but ran into some problems and snags that prevented this idea from being fully realized at that point. Nevertheless, there was enough work and enough positive results to suggest that this had considerable promise and should be pursued. One other consideration that was evident at the time was that not many people were interested in dynamic control. Most organizations were having so much trouble trying to come up with the initial forecast that the idea of learning about how to control an ongoing project was not high on their priority lists. This suggested that trying to reach good solutions in dynamic measurement and control was premature.

Duty with the Army Computer System Command

After my tour of duty in the Office of the Chief of Staff and with the Office of the Assistant Secretary of the Army, Financial Management in the Pentagon, I was transferred to the Army Computer Systems Command at Fort Belvoir, where I continued to work on the software-estimating problem and on some useful ways in which the Army could apply these techniques. I wrote several papers during this time which were presented at forums sponsored by the IEEE Computer Society. There appeared to be a growing interest in software estimation.

These papers produced contacts with other people in this area, such as Lazlo Belady of IBM and Manny Lehman of City College in London. Manny suggested the idea of doing a conference of interested parties to discuss the progress that was being made. I was able to get the Army Computer Systems Command to sponsor such a meeting, which was held in the Spring of 1976 at the Airlie House in Virginia. Fifty to sixty participants from government and industry came together and presented their latest thoughts and observations relating to software estimating. Peter Norden was able to come and present his latest thoughts, as well as John Gaffney, Ray Wolverton, and other notables in the field.

During most of this period, I continued to do small-scale modeling experiments using programmable calculators from Hewlett-Packard. I found this was preferable to time-sharing services and using the large-scale computers available from the army because it was so easy to conceptualize things on paper and immediately write a small program to implement it and see what the behavior pattern was. Moreover, I was not at the mercy of programmers and waiting for them to write the programs that were needed. I could do that myself, take the machine home and continue my work into the evening without interruption. I found this a very efficient way to build and test algorithms. When the algorithms worked on the HP calculator, they could immediately be implemented bug-free in FORTRAN or Basic on a medium to large machine for a more comprehensive analysis.

During the 1976 to 1977 time frame, the Department of the Army decided to take the early work I had done on determining parameters for the Rayleigh curve and put those ideas out for broad distribution throughout the army. They did this in the form of a Department of the Army pamphlet. These parameter estimators were based on the number of files, number of reports, and number of screens to determine the effort and the time parameter for the Rayleigh equation. This happened about the time that I was doing most of the development and testing work on the software equation, but it wasn't ready for full-scale implementation and use at that time. The army decided to proceed ahead with its information pamphlet using the earlier work.

During the first half of 1977, I did considerable development work on the implementation of the software equation involving the linking together of the effort and time parameters of the Rayleigh equation and relating those two management parameters with the amount of functionality that had to be delivered. I did extensive work with a family of parameter values for the technology factor, later called the process productivity parameter. I also tried to learn over what range of software application types this factor pertained to. We had some reasonable data for the army's business systems, some reasonable values for some of the Air Force Command and Control and Radar Control projects from Hanscom Air Force Base, and some engineering applications from the IBM FSD suite of data. Much of my research time during 1977 was devoted to validating and testing reasonableness ranges for parameters that seemed to describe these different application environments.

GE days

At the end of August 1977, I retired from active duty in the army and shortly afterwards went to work with the Space Division of General Electric Company in its Arlington, Virginia office. I was with GE a little less than a year but continued to develop the model, applying it to estimates that were used by GE in some software development activities related to the space program. I also spent a considerable amount of time working on estimates related to large-scale manufacturing software that was being built in support of the GE Aircraft Engine Division in Evendale, Ohio.

One important aspect of the software equation arose during this period when I established contact with Professor Victor Basili at the University of Maryland. He was doing work with the NASA Goddard Space Flight Center and was one of the principles in their software engineering laboratory. In my conversations with Professor Basili, I found that they had collected a substantial body of data related to scientific data reduction systems for satellites being launched and controlled by NASA. Most of this software was being written in FORTRAN; the size regime was significantly smaller than the systems I had been working with in the army, notably in the range of 15,000 to 80,000 FORTRAN lines of code. I observed that the Rayleigh staffing profiles were quite different than I had seen in the army. Most of the army Rayleigh curves reached their peak staffing at about the time the software was ready to ship. The NASA Goddard software reached its peak staffing intensity considerably before the software ship time. By then the staffing profile had come down, and the number of people was at a relatively low level at the time the software went into operational service. This suggested that the Rayleigh model was more complex than I had originally thought and would require an additional parameter that would control where the peak of the Rayleigh curve occurred as a function of how big the software product was.

So I spent some time providing an additional parameter in the software equation to control this peaking, and tried to interpret what the physical meaning of that parameter was. Ultimately, I came to call it a *complexity factor*. It seemed to kick in when the size of the system was in the neighborhood of 15,000 to 18,000 lines of code. Most of the change in the Rayleigh shape occurred between 18,000 and 70,000 lines of code. Beyond that size, I found that the behavior of the Rayleigh shape seemed very much the same as that I had observed in the army. That is, it reached its peak staffing at about the time the software product was ready to be put into operational service.

During the time I was at GE I met Ann Fitzsimmons, who was a FORTRAN programmer working there. She was very helpful in building some early prototype models of the Rayleigh equation, the software equation, and simple prototype estimating models. Ann became interested in pursuing an opportunity to turn these ideas into a commercial product. She suggested that we leave GE, organize a company, and try to build a commercial estimating tool. This was based on her observation that there was considerable interest in such a product, because we had been getting a number of inquiries and phone calls, both from within GE and externally from other companies that we had met through conferences or through papers that she and I had written individually and which had been published in the technical and trade press.

So while I was mulling over these suggestions from Ann, I was developing a business plan and looking at how I might raise money to form up a company and start a business from the ideas we had come up with for estimating tools. Ann precipitated the whole thing by announcing that she had quit GE and was ready to go to work full-time building this system. It took me about two more weeks to make up my mind, resign, and start the process of getting Quantitative Software Management, Inc. under way.

Noisy data

My army and General Electric experience pointed out rather clearly that there was a great deal of noise in the data we were collecting. In particular, organizations were unable to report the time more accurately than a whole month. Sometimes the effort would be rounded off to the nearest 5 or 10 person months. This suggested that as I considered the notion of creating commercial products, this problem would have to be researched and addressed. I would have to learn how to deal with this uncertainty and be able to reflect it in the answers and in the risk buffering that would need to be done.

QSM days

The first version of SLIM® was built on a DEC System 20 time-sharing machine belonging to American Management Systems. It was written in FORTRAN by Ann Fitzsimmons and was about 8000 lines of code. It was designed to be as simple as possible to use and to require a minimal amount of user-supplied input information.

The notion of being able to specifically tune the model to the development organization was very much on my mind at this time. So, what we did was include a history (calibration) function in which the user could collect a little historic data—as simple as the number of new or modified lines of code, the development time, and the person months of development effort that had gone into producing a completed project. This could then be put into the software equation, and a process productivity parameter could be determined from it.

We also decided that we would use the concept of a *productivity index,* a simple series of integer numbers from 1 to 18, as a surrogate for the engineering family of numbers called *technology factors.* This was designed to make it easy to use and simple for managers to understand. Once the user had a productivity index from 3, 4, 5, or more previous projects and was tuned to the right environment, then all the user had to supply was the SLOC size estimate in the form of a range—the smallest, the largest, the best guess. The user could either do this for a whole system, or break it up into a number of subsystems and SLIM would roll up the individual subsystems for itself.

The earliest version of SLIM generated a minimum-time solution. This was the fastest possible solution. It would also be the most expensive. Uncertainty was present; therefore, it was important to do a Monte Carlo simulation where the uncertainty that existed with respect to the size and the productivity index could be factored into the simulation and mapped through to the outputs of development time, peak staffing, development effort, and cost. These uncertainties in the form of standard deviations could then be applied in a risk sense so that if someone needed a 95 percent cost biased number to quote to a prospective customer, that could be easily obtained. SLIM provided this in the form of risk tables. Similar capability was provided for schedule and staffing profiles.

The software equation provided a solution in the form of time-effort pairs. There was a range of different staffing profiles possible. If one took a little longer time, a smaller staff could be used; this let the effort go down. Since the relationship between time and effort varied as the fourth power of schedule, a small change in time produced a big change in effort. This appeared to be exploitable by management, so within SLIM we built a range of what-if functions that had a great deal of power in being able to use the concept of management constraints and trade-off. For example, let's say the minimum-time solution turned out to be 21 months and 388 person months of effort and built up to a peak staffing of 29 people. But we might find out that only 15 people were going to be available to work on this project. The implication here is that it will take a little bit longer time and quite a bit less effort if a solution could be found for a peak staff of 15 people.

We provided a trade-off function that allowed the user to directly input a peak staff of 15 people and the output produced the appropriate time-effort pair associated with that staffing profile (250 person months, 25.7 months).

A whole range of such trade-off scenarios was presented—design to schedule, design to cost, design to peak staffing, design to a certain level of risk on schedule, and so forth. All of these were very simple trade-off relationships in a time-sharing environment. A user picked the appropriate one from the menu and was then prompted for the appropriate inputs; the computer immediately calculated the solution and brought it up on the screen or printed it out on the terminal.

With this version of SLIM all of the output was in tabular form. There was no graphics capability. There were no remote output devices that could handle data quickly enough to make high-quality graphics a feasible capability. This was because at the time we had 300-baud terminals that were very slow in graphics mode. Similarly, plotters were very slow at these data-communication rates.

We started building the first version of SLIM in September 1978. We had a working prototype version by December 1978 and were able to provide beta versions for prospective customers by January 1979. The system ran well on the DEC System 20. It was accessible from anywhere in the country through Telenet, and the reliability of the system was quite high. The time to solve a problem using this system was typically 30 to 45 minutes to get every answer that one could think of.

A family of implementation functions was provided as output. Once the user made a decision for the schedule, effort, and peak staffing that was desired for the solution, then the complete staffing profile month by month, including the high-level functional front end, and the main software build, and the maintenance work, could be provided throughout the entire life cycle. The person months of effort could be given in this same tabular form. If you wanted the cost for just a single fiscal year, you could get that cost. If you wanted the cost over the whole life cycle, that was possible. If you wanted just the development effort for the main software construction phase, that was possible as well. It was a very flexible tool. Anything that you wanted as a function of elapsed calendar time, month by month, could be obtained.

HP-85 version of SLIM

We used the DEC System 20 for about 2 years. About that time the new HP-85, a typewriter-size, desktop machine with built-in Basic language, became available. This appeared to be an ideal piece of hardware for us to use to build a portable version of SLIM. Going from FORTRAN to Basic was not a problem. The chief advantage one had with the HP-85 desktop computer was that it had built-in graphics. It had a small-format, built-in printer as well, which had the capability of turning graphics output on its side and printing out a very acceptable, readable graph of all of the functions that were important in the SLIM environment.

About 1980 or 1981, we came across a body of data from the Rome Air Development Center that had defect information, which led us to construct a reliability model that was tied in with the schedule, effort, and size of the software product. This gave us a capability to make a reliability-prediction model that would estimate the defects that should occur in development. Defect prediction was useful from as early as the start of systems integration testing out to the time the product was delivered to the customer, and even out into the operations and maintenance phase after that. The reliability model seemed to be very Raleigh-like, so we built it as a time-based Raleigh defect model.

We discovered that the defects were very closely correlated with the productivity index, such that if an organization was very efficient (a high productivity index) then it also had a correspondingly small number of defects. The other interesting observation was that if you used a large team of people (a high staffing buildup profile) then you also got a correspondingly large increase in the number of defects. We built the model in such a way that the projected number of defects would scale corresponding to these parameters—the staffing profile and the productivity index. We included the reliability model in our first HP-85 version of SLIM.

The HP-85 was very easy to use, very easy to write code for, and easy to make code modifications for. The quality of the output was not ideally suited to business users' needs. The 32-character format for the tables was not standard; but soon HP came out with the HP-86 and 87 series of computers, which had the same processor and the same Basic language but had the capability to provide full-page, 80-character output and a large-scale graphic capability driven out to pen plotters. Soon, very high quality output was available from these companion pieces to the HP desktop line. We also found that these desktop machines got around people's concerns about storing their proprietary data on a time-sharing machine where they worried about their competitors gaining access to their data.

The reliability function gave good results from the outset and has been an excellent predictor of what one might expect in the way of defects month by month while development is going on. It gives a good indication of when the product is going to be good enough to put into operational service.

I felt this was a very important function because it got development organizations away from the strong tendency to deliver a product early before sufficient defects had been removed. When this happened the product did not work well or did not run long enough to do its job. In most cases this was because the product had not been sufficiently debugged and tested to guarantee good levels of performance and reliability. With the reliability function we now had the capability to measure this while development was going on, letting people control defect elimination far better than they had been able to do previously.

Linear program

I also developed the notion of being able to apply a linear program to the software-estimation model. The idea was that we had the software equation and we had an array of different constraints. We could use the constraints in the same way people did in a linear program to bound a feasible region. From this we got a minimum-time solution which was also the most costly and had the lowest reliability. At the other end of the spectrum, we got a minimum-cost solution which took the longest time and had the highest reliability. In between these two solutions were all other feasible solutions. One might choose to adopt one of these in-between solutions because of other concerns.

So *linear programming* became an extraordinarily powerful tool to identify this feasible region and then pick and choose other possible solutions within this range, depending upon the priority of management constraints. It was important to be able to tie management constraints into the normal operating routine in solving estimating problems. A picture of the linear program in the two management dimensions is shown in Fig. A.2.

The HP-85 capability with graphics also led us into the notion of looking at the historic data in a graphical format. We found that we had a fairly substantial database of completed projects by that time, maybe 500 to 600 systems. When we put those all into the history mode of SLIM we found that a nice pattern emerged. We identified the spectrum of person months of effort as a function of system size that had gone into all the historic projects; we did the same thing for

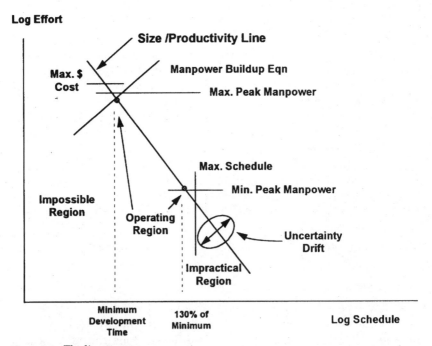

Figure A.2 The linear program concept.

the number of people working on projects, and for the development schedule. These graphs were very informative in outlining what the feasible region was. We also put statistically generated trend lines on a log-log scale through these data points. We could take away the historic data points, leave the trendlines in place, and then take a small set of data—3, 4, or 5 projects from a specific organization—and plot them against the trendlines. From this we could see how that organization behaved with respect to the industry average. For example, if a particular organization was taking longer than the industry average, and was costing more, then we found that its productivity index was significantly lower than the industry average. This lets us say, "We see that this particular developer is not as efficient—it takes longer, it costs more, and it generates more defects."

This graphical technique gave us a quick way to compare development organizations with each other and with the broader context of the whole industry represented by the trendlines of our large database. This concept became the basis for our next product, the *Productivity Analysis Database System* (PADS).

PADS®—Productivity Analysis
Database System

We started work on PADS about 1982. We introduced it into operational service in 1984. It was a desktop-based system, initially done on the IBM PC under DOS, and it utilized the graphics capability that was provided by the IBM PC family.

PADS provided the capability to keep track of an organization's productivity over time by computing the productivity index (PI) after each new project was completed and being able to associate that PI with the environment, the tools, the skills, and the management capabilities of the organization being used at that point in time. So, beyond being able to say this is the productivity of XYZ Corporation, PADS would let you say these are the environmental influences that probably had a large impact on *why* XYZ Corporation is where it is now.

With PADS it was possible to study the introduction of new technology, new products, and new management practices and see if those produced an impact on the productivity index. For example, we studied a number of developers when they went from developing in batch mode in COBOL to an online interactive development environment. The immediate impact was to boost the productivity index by 2 to 3 integer values—a very significant reduction in the management parameters. For example, 3 productivity indices would bring down development time by about 26 percent and cut the development effort by a factor of 59 percent.

PADS provided the capability for long-term studies of software behavior. It became a repository for an organizations' software metrics data. It had an excellent capability to do economic analysis—to see the high-payoff investments and practices.

SIZE PLANNER

By 1984 to 1985, we found that we were getting a considerable number of questions related to sizing. People were happy with the results they were getting from SLIM on schedule, effort, cost, and implementation plans, but they still had trouble coming up with the estimates of size that needed to be fed into SLIM as input.

In my consulting experience I had come across a number of ways of approaching this. I decided it would be good for us to develop a sizing model and include it with the SLIM estimating package for people who felt they needed it. But a large number of our customers had no problem with sizing. So, there was no need to get them to buy it when they had no need for it. That guided us into making it a separate product. We would sell it to just those people who felt they needed some supplemental help in coming to grips with the sizing input to SLIM.

We built an independent, DOS-based product for the IBM PC, which we called *SIZE PLANNER*. It was a fairly small utility program designed to come up with combined estimates from a number of different approaches.

For example, a user could make estimates in function points, lines of code, programs, and subsystems. Or, very early in the process, the user could use fuzzy logic sizing based on historical data in QSM's database. SIZE PLANNER could even handle reused code, some of which was modified, some of which was unmodified. SIZE PLANNER would convert this all into an equivalent line-of-code estimate in the form of a *low,* a *high,* and a *most likely* that were suitable for input into SLIM. It was introduced for sale in 1987.

SIZE PLANNER did a good job. I used it quite frequently in consulting. A good number of our customers who felt that they wanted a cross-check for their size estimates, or did not feel comfortable with their existing methods, adopted it and found they got excellent results. Essentially, SIZE PLANNER was a front end for SLIM or for other estimating tools.

SLIM-Control®

By 1986, there was considerable interest in being able to control ongoing projects. Many organizations would start a development and then find they couldn't stay up with the original plan formulated, or that they couldn't get the people as fast as they anticipated. After the first

30 percent of the project they would sense that they were falling behind but didn't have any idea how much. They didn't know when the project was really going to be completed. If they could get all the people they wanted, could they throw more people on it and catch up? These were the problems that we wanted to be able to address with a new product that we named *SLIM-Control*.

The concept was to use statistical process-control ideas from the manufacturing area of expertise and tie it together with the notion of adaptive forecasting. This would let us feed in the actual data coming from the project, compare it with the plan, and then generate a new plan that would realistically project when the project was going to get there, what the staffing should be, what the cost would be to that new end point, and what the reliability would be, as well. All of this would be consistent with the underlying SLIM model.

SLIM-Control was difficult to do. It was hard to get the algorithms to work well together. It was also difficult to model the impact of playing what-if games. For example, if I am halfway through a project and I know I am falling behind with a predicted slippage of 2.5 months, what would happen if I added an additional 15 people to the project? How much of the lost time could I make up?

These were the issues we were trying to model. Since everything was happening dynamically month by month, the algorithms had to be responsive to where you were along the timeline. The model had to have different sensitivities at different points in time, because things that were done earlier in the process would have far more impact. Adding 15 people after all the code was written wouldn't help much; there is not a great deal one could do to influence the project and play catch-up at that point in time.

So, it was not a simple process to model. It took us about three years to complete the development of SLIM-Control. When it did get out into our user community, we found it was well liked, did an excellent job of prediction, and filled an important void in the ability to deal with software development projects once they were under way. It suggested intelligent things to do that could be quantitatively determined from what had happened so far. SLIM-Control was released in 1989. This was the last completely new product introduced within the QSM family of tools to date.

Windows products

By the early part of the 1990s, we saw some new trends that suggested major changes to our product line. Most important were the advent of the Windows operating system, higher resolution screens, and much faster processors. Suddenly the opportunity to make very major improvements to the user interface and provide higher-quality color graphics output became possible. That became our next goal—to take our product line and convert it over to the Windows environment and make the user interface much more intuitive and natural for the user.

All this meant that the users now had the opportunity to solve problems the way they wanted to approach them, not in the serial, sequential fashion that we had forced them to do with the old DOS products. With the DOS products, users had to think the way the developer did. They did not always do that naturally. It presented a frustrating dilemma at times. Windows, VGA resolution, and the high speed of the new processors provided the ability to get much more information on the screen. With a mouse, users could attack problems in any way they liked, their own way. They could solve problems in ways that made the most sense to them. That was the driving motivation for how we redid our products in the Windows environment.

With the Windows version of SLIM, we were able to innovate by providing new ways for analysts to look at their solutions and compare them with the industry trendlines taken from PADS. Users could even superimpose their own data on the industry trendlines. This could be useful when a marketing manager proposed an impossibly short schedule. When this solution was generated with SLIM (perhaps requiring a productivity index that was 4 or 5 values higher than the organization had ever done before), it could be shown graphically, and the probability of this solution could be seen right on the screen. The very short schedule would be very much out of line with anything the organization had been able to do before. So, with the graphical view it would become immediately obvious that this was not a good solution. It was not likely to happen.

Similarly, we were able to put in a graphical consistency check for schedule, effort, staffing, and defects. This let the analyst and the analyst's boss look at the solutions and see if they were consistent with what other people were doing, as well as with their own historic data.

In addition to this there was considerable interest in doing sensitivity profiling in the form of what-ifs. The question might come up, "What if this product were to grow by an additional 25,000 lines of code? What would that do to our schedule? What would that do to the cost and the effort?" We were able to put in a sensitivity capability to look at these issues graphically and see what the incremental differences were. We could do that in terms of size, productivity index, or staffing. All of this provided a very quick capability to explore what-if situations that might be posed by management.

The other major Windows innovation was putting dynamic risk gauges on the problem-solving screen. If one wanted to play what-if on the schedule, one could grab a handle on the staffing diagram and make it longer or shorter. In the lower left-hand corner of the screen we were able to display a probability scale for each of the key management parameters—schedule, effort, maximum peak staff, minimum peak staff, and mean time to defect. As one changed the plan with respect to schedule and its effect on staffing and effort, one could instantly see which way the risk gauges moved. So, if I happened to have a 24-month constraint on schedule and I stretched the schedule out, I would see my probability gauge for schedule go down. This gave us a capability to keep the different risks balanced—being able to see it visually all at one time gave a much better appreciation of the interaction of these different management impacts.

Summary

I have been involved in software estimating for 20 years. Much has occurred in the field over that time. I have found it exciting to try to understand the software development process and how to model that. Thinking back, I believe looking at it as a time-based, parameter-driven macromodel has been a good approach that has been close enough to reality to produce excellent results with enough flexibility to adapt to the new development paradigms that have arisen. I am confident that it will continue to do so for a reasonable time into the future.

I have found that the software estimating and control problem is a lot more complicated than I originally thought it would be. But that has kept it challenging and interesting.

Moreover, it has been gratifying to have worked with major corporations and government organizations in the United States and abroad—to have tackled some of their tough problems in software planning and management, to have been able to contribute to solving their problems, and to have had a positive impact on their business. This has made all the hard work worthwhile.

Publications

Publications that I have written or have been coauthor of include the first book done for the IEEE Computer Society, *Software Cost Estimating and Life Cycle Control: Getting the Management Numbers,* published in 1980. This was done with Ware Myers, who has been my writing sidekick since that time. This book was an assembly of my key thoughts on software estimating at that particular time, along with a collection of germinal papers on software estimating done either by myself or by other authors.

The next book that I coauthored with Ware Myers was *Measures for Excellence: Reliable Software on Time, Within Budget,* published by

Prentice Hall in 1992. This was a complete statement of my entire philosophy of estimating control and measurement as I understood it at that time, 1990 to 1991. It also included some capability to implement the QSM techniques by manual methods, with a calculator. Also shown was an extensive collection of computer-generated output from SLIM and SLIM-Control as an illustration of the way in which we had implemented the key functions in our commercial tools.

Another more recent publication is a management-oriented book published in 1996 by the IEEE Computer Society, *Executive Briefing: Controlling Software Development,* again by Ware Myers and myself. It's a 12-chapter book focused at senior management. The objective was to present the key ideas with a minimum of mathematics and diagrams, with just the key management concepts to get across the idea that it is possible to control software projects—that there are a few simple things you need to know about how software projects behave. These concepts are simple and work with all the traditional, straightforward, well-understood management practices.

The most recent book I have written with Ware Myers is *Industrial Strength Software: Effective Management Using Measurement,* published by IEEE Computer Society in 1997. This book is more broadly based and spends more time on measuring process improvement and discussing what organizations should be doing in this area to make process improvement happen at a faster rate than what happens randomly.

In addition to these books I have written a large number of papers, by myself or jointly with others, related to specific topics in software estimating. Copies of these are available from:

Quantitative Software Management
2000 Corporate Ridge—Suite 900
McLean, VA 22102.

Software Cost Estimating Vendors and Associations

As software cost estimation grows in numbers of vendors and numbers of clients, this growth has been mirrored by a need to associate with those who share an interest in software cost estimating. Several nonprofit associations have been formed which center around software cost estimation, or which include software cost estimation as a major subgroup of the overall membership.

This contact list of software cost estimating vendors is known to be incomplete, because new cost-estimating tools have been entering the market at approximate monthly intervals since about 1995.

Also, a wave of mergers and acquisitions has been sweeping through the project management tool domain, so estimating vendors that started as independent companies often have become divisions of companies with other kinds of project management tools.

Software Cost Estimating Associations

International Function Point Users Group (IFPUG)
IFPUG Executive Office
Blendonview Office Park
5008-28 Pine Creek Drive
Westerville, OH 43081-4899
Phone: (614) 895-7130
Fax: (614) 895-3466
Web: http://www.IFPUG.org

IFPUG is a nonprofit organization for users of function point metrics. Because function point metrics are now widely used for software cost estimating and are supported by almost all commercial software estimating tools, IFPUG's conferences and tool fairs usually have at least half a dozen software estimating companies displaying their wares.

Membership in the IFPUG organization has been going up at about 50 percent per year for the last 4 or 5 years in a row. Affiliated function point users groups can be found in many other countries, including Australia, Canada, France, Italy, Japan, the Netherlands, and Scandinavia.

Responsibility for determining the rules for counting function points transferred from IBM to IFPUG circa 1986, so all function point users should have copies of the latest version of the IFPUG counting practices manual, which is currently as close to a standard for function points as exists. However, the ISO is working with IFPUG and the British Mark II users group and other interested parties to create an ISO standard on functional size measurement.

IFPUG currently offers and administers examinations for those interested in becoming certified function point counters. For consultants interested in counting function points with accuracy, it is important to successfully complete one of these certification exams. The consistency of counts by certified counters was studied by Dr. Chris Kemerer of MIT and found to vary by only about 9 percent at a national level, which is about as small a variance as any known business metric and is much smaller than the variations in counting lines of code.

International Society of Parametric Analysts (ISPA)
P.O. Box 6402
Town & Country Branch
Chesterfield, MO 63006-6402
Phone: (314) 527-2955
Fax: (314) 246-8358
E-mail: clydeperry@aol.com
Web: http://mijuno.LARC.NASA.gov/dfc/societies/ispa.html

ISPA is a nonprofit association with perhaps 1000 members throughout the world. ISPA's membership consists primarily of individuals and organizations that build parametric models, including software cost estimating tools but also economic models and hardware cost estimating models.

ISPA features large and well-attended annual conferences and also publishes a newsletter. ISPA is an interesting organization since it aims to be a focal point for those who build estimation tools, rather than for those who merely utilize them.

Society of Cost Estimating and Analysis (SCEA)
101 South Whiting Street, Suite 201
Alexandria, VA 22304
Phone: (703) 751-8069
Fax: (703) 461-7328

This is a nonprofit cost-estimating society located in the greater Washington, D.C. area. SCEA is a nonprofit association with a heavy emphasis on military and defense estimation. Software estimation is not the only kind of cost estimation supported by SCEA but is obviously an important subgroup within this organization.

Software Estimating and Engineering Group (SEE)
Bedag Informatik
3012 Bern
Switzerland
Phone: + 41 31 633 22 22
Web: http://www.csse.swin.edu.au/see
E-mail: see@casse.swin.edu.au

This is a new international software-estimating organization formed by Dr. Simon Moser of Swinburne University in Australia, who will soon be moving to Switzerland. Membership is open to all who share a common interest in software cost estimating. The organization is new, and was formed in the summer of 1997. Currently, as of autumn 1997 there are 24 member companies and individuals. Dr. Moser states that the SEE organization should be contacted at the Swiss address listed here.

Software Cost Estimating Vendors

This list of software cost estimating vendors includes companies that market standalone software cost estimating tools, and also vendors that offer software cost estimating functions as part of larger, integrated project management tool suites.

Some software cost estimating tools are in the public domain because they were produced by government or military groups. Usually the public domain software cost estimating tools utilize the *constructive cost model* (COCOMO) algorithms published by Dr. Barry Boehm in *Software Engineering Economics* (Prentice Hall, 1981). The commercial software-estimation tools utilize proprietary algorithms which are treated as trade secrets.

An annual catalog of software cost estimating tools is edited by Alan Howard and published by Applied Computer Research, Inc. (ACR) of Phoenix, Arizona. This catalog is part of a larger family of catalogs of all forms of software management and development tools. Cost-estimating tools may be found in the ACR *Directory of Software Metrics and Project Management Tools.*

Because of the volatility of the estimating-tool market, this list is known to be incomplete. New vendors are appearing at approximately monthly intervals, while existing vendors are often pursuing mergers and acquisitions.

Because the author is also a vendor of cost-estimating tools, it would be a conflict of interest to evaluate the capabilities of competitive tools. For those interested in such evaluations, the U.S. military services produce interesting comparative studies of software cost estimating tools.

For an example of an interesting comparison of seven software cost estimating tools (CHECKPOINT, PRICE-S, REVIC, SASET, SEER, SOFTCOST, and SLIM), refer to the September 1996 technical report TR-9545/008-2 by Sherry Stukes et al: *Air Force Cost Analysis Agency Software Estimating Model Analysis.* This report was prepared under contract F04701-95-D-003, Task 008 and is available from Management Consulting & Research in Thousand Oaks, California.

A somewhat more extensive but older (1993) comparison of more than 20 software cost estimating tools was produced by the Air Force's well-known Software Technology Support Center—Dean Barrow et al.: *Software Estimating Technology Report,* March 1993, Software Technology Support Center, Hill Air Force Base, Utah. This report covers COCOMO and half a dozen COCOMO clones, plus models built using such proprietary algorithms as SLIM, SPQR/20, CHECKPOINT, PRICE-S, and about a dozen others.

The most massive of the military software cost estimating comparisons, although somewhat specialized, was an interesting study in which seven software cost estimating tools were given the same case study and asked to produce full cost estimates. The projects being estimated were reengineering projects for converting legacy applications into more modern forms.

The estimating tools selected for this study were CHECKPOINT, COCOMO, PRICE-S, SEER SEM, SLIM, SOFTCOST, and REVIC. The final report was produced for the Department of Defense: *Technical Report—Software Reengineering Assessment Handbook,* Report JLC-HDBK-SRAH, March 1995.

The handbook is stated to be "available for use by all departments and agencies of the Department of Defense." The contact point cited is:

Robert E. Johnson
HQDA ODISC4, SAIS-ADW
Pentagon, Room 1C676
Washington DC 20310-0107
Phone: (703) 697-4393
E-mail: robert.johnson@pentagon1dms2.army.mil

Obviously, these military studies view software cost estimation from the vantage point of how well they can serve military software needs, but they still provide useful surveys of features, strengths, and weaknesses.

AFMS/FMCI
Wright-Patterson AFB, OH 45433
Phone: (513) 336-2359

Wright-Patterson Air Force Base is the home of the well-known Air Force Institute of Technology, which both teaches and studies software cost estimation tools. The COCOMOID software cost estimation tool is derived from the published algorithms of Dr. Barry Boehm's original COCOMO model.

Air Force Cost Analysis Agency (AFCAA/FMP)
111 Jefferson Davis Highway, Suite 403
Arlington, VA 22202
Phone: (703) 692-0006
Fax: (703) 692-0001

The U.S. military services produce significant volumes of software and also build the largest and most complex software projects ever constructed. As a result, the military services are key users of software cost estimating tools, and make some of these tools available to other service organizations.

The Air Force Cost Analysis Agency supplies two estimating tools derived from the well-known COCOMO algorithms published by Dr. Barry Boehm, SASET and REVIC. SASET stands for *Software Architecture Sizing and Estimating*. SASET was originally developed by the Naval Center for Cost Analysis under a contract with Martin Marietta. REVIC stands for *revised COCOMO* and refers to some military extensions added for Department of Defense (DoD) standards and the Ada programming language.

AGS Management Systems, Inc.
1012 W. Ninth Avenue
King of Prussia, PA
Phone: (610) 265-1550, (800) 220-2741
Fax: (610) 265-1230

AGS Management systems markets the integrated FirstCase® development and project management tool. This tool supports function point metrics and includes software cost estimating capabilities. This tool is aimed primarily at management information systems projects. The AGS tool suite is an example of software cost estimation as part of a suite of other technical and management tool capabilities.

Applied Business Technology Corp. (ABT)
361 Broadway
New York, NY 10013
Phone: (212) 219-8945
Fax: (212) 219-3597

ABT has long marketed a well-known project management tool called the Project Management Workbench (PMW). In addition ABT has brought out a methodology-based software cost estimation tool called Bridge Modeler, as part of its Total Project Management Suite. Bridge Modeler supports function point metrics and includes macrobased software cost estimation in support of several development methodologies. Bridge Modeler is aimed primarily at management information systems projects.

Andersen Consulting
69 West Washington Street
Chicago, IL 60602
Phone: (312) 580-0069
Fax: (312) 507-2548
Web: http://www.Andersen.com

The Andersen Method/1® process management tool includes a variety of software project management functions, including software cost estimating. The cost-estimation portion of the Andersen tool suite is not a general-purpose software cost estimating tool, but rather is optimized for software projects using other Andersen methodologies and tools. This form of specialized estimation within a specific environment is quite common, and at least half a dozen methodology vendors have similar capabilities.

D. F. Benn & Associates
6723 Rolling Vista
Dallas, TX 75248

Dr. Douglas Benn is the developer of a software cost estimating tool called ValPro. Based on testimony in an IRS tax case, the ValPro model appears to derive in some measure from Larry Putnam's SLIM estimating tool and methodology. The ValPro model is often used in Internal Revenue Service (IRS) tax cases, although the IRS is beginning to utilize function point–based tools, such as CHECK-POINT.

Charismatek
Pam Morris, Total Metrics Pty. Ltd.
44 Guenivere Parade
Glen Waverly, Victoria
Australia 3150
Phone: 613 9 803-1522
Fax: 613 9 803-2932
E-mail: 100351.3330@compuserve.com

Charismatek is an Australian company specializing in function point tools, such as the Function Point Workbench (FPW), which is widely distributed in other countries. The Function Point Workbench is not a full software cost estimating tool, but does assist in enumerating costs based on function points. The tool includes full function point sizing capabilities and a repository of projects that have been sized. The Function Point Workbench is often used in addition to other forms of software cost estimation, such as CHECKPOINT or KnowledgePlan.

Computer Associates International Inc. (CA)
One Computer Associates Plaza
Islandia, NY 11788
Phone: (516) 342-5224, (800) 225-5224
Fax: (516) 342-5329

Computer Associates is a software conglomerate which grew by acquisition. One of the companies acquired was the MACS corporation, which had been licensed to sell a software cost estimating tool, ESTIMACS, designed by the well-known metrics researcher Dr. Howard Rubin. ESTIMACS is a macroestimation tool aimed primarily at management information systems. ESTIMACS supports function point metrics, although the first release of ESTIMACS predates the major revision of function point counting rules in 1984.

Computer Associates brought out several related tools which share data with ESTIMACS. These include FPXpert (a function point counting and repository tool) and PLANMACS, which is a project scheduling or project management tools.

Computer Economics, Inc.
4560 Admiralty Way, Suite 109
Marina Del Rey, CA 90292-5424
Phone: (310) 827-7300
Fax: (310) 632-0694

Computer Economics markets a software cost estimating tool named SYSTEM-4. This is a phase-based software cost estimating model using proprietary algorithms developed by the vendor.

COSMIC
The University of Georgia
382 E. Broad Street
Athens, GA 30602-4272
Phone: (404) 542-3265
Fax: (404) 542-4807

This company offers two software cost estimating tools, COSTMODL and SOFTCOST. The COSTMODL tool is based on Dr. Barry Boehm's well-known COCOMO algorithms and is a macroestimating tool aimed at systems and defense software, but used for information systems, too. SOFTCOST has a more detailed work-breakdown structure and includes schedule planning and critical path analysis. SOFT-COST is aimed at systems and defense software but can also be used on information systems.

Decisioneering, Inc.
1724 Conestoga Street
Boulder, CO 80301
Phone: (303) 292-2291
Fax: (303) 292-9352

This vendor markets a modified form of Dr. Barry Boehm's COCOMO estimating equations under the name Crystal Ball COCOMO (CB COCOMO). CB COCOMO adds risk-analysis features, and also logic for showing best-case, expected-case, and worst-case results.

DDB Software
1935 Salt Myrtle Lane
Orange Park, FL 32073
Phone: (904) 278-9092
Fax: (904) 215-0444

The DDB company in conjunction with the David Consulting group have assembled a suite of software management tools built around function point metrics. The cost-estimating portion of this suite is called PREDICTOR.

Development Support Center, Inc.
1625 Lindhurst Drive, Suite 100
Elm Grove, WI 53122
Phone: (414) 789-9190
Fax: (414) 243-9130

The Development Support Center is one of several consulting organizations whose work centers around function point analysis. This company is headed by the well-known function point consultant Bill Huffschmidt and offers a function point sizing and repository tool called Function Point System (FPSSII).

Digital Equipment Corporation (DEC)
110 Spitbrook Avenue
Nashua, NH 03082
Phone: (603) 881-1894
Fax: (603) 881-2790

Like other computer manufacturers, DEC employs thousands of software personnel and builds hundreds of software products. DEC offers two software tools with some estimating capabilities, DECplan and VAX Software Project Manager. These tools are more concerned with systems software than with other kinds, but are advertised as general-purpose project-planning tools. The VAX Software Project Manager tool integrates a software cost estimating module derived from Dr. Barry Boehm's well-known COCOMO algorithms. DEC has been changing its business models fairly often in the wake of its up-and-down earnings history, so its product lines and specific tools may vary.

East Tennessee State Universty
E-mail: henry@etsu.east-tenn-st.edu

A number of universities have put together experimental software cost estimating tools. These university-based tools are usually based on the published COCOMO algorithms taken from Dr. Barry Boehm's book *Software Engineering Economics*. East Tennessee State University has built a freeware estimating tool called COSMOS which is based upon the COCOMO model, but adds function point support for sizing and a Windows-based front end.

Ernst and Young
787 Seventh Avenue
New York, NY 10019
Phone: (212) 773-3000

The Ernst and Young NAVIGATOR® tool suite includes software cost estimating abilities. The cost-estimating portion is not a general-purpose software cost estimating tool, but rather is optimized for software projects built in and using other NAVIGATOR capabilities. This form of specialized software cost estimating is very common, and such features are offered by most methodology management tool vendors.

Galorath Associates, Inc.
SEER Technologies Division
P.O. Box 90579
Los Angeles, CA 90009
Phone: (310) 670-3404

The SEER family of software cost models supports a variety of military standards and, hence, are well-known for military software cost estimating. They can also be used for civilian projects, although their main emphasis is supporting various military projects which adhere to DoD standards 2167A, 1703, 498, and the like. A knowledge base of completed military software projects is included as well as estimating capabilities.

GEC-Marconi Software Systems
1861 Wiehle Avenue, Suite 300
Reston, VA 22090-5200
Phone: (703) 736-3500

This is the U.S. subsidiary of a well-known British company. It offers two software cost related tools, GECOMO Plus and Size Plus. GECOMO is a software cost estimating tool based on Dr. Barry Boehm's well-known COCOMO algorithms, but modified to include function point support and feature point support. Size Plus is an auxiliary tool which aids in determining the sizes of software applications based on their requirements and specifications.

ICONIX Software Engineering, Inc.
2800 28th Street, Suite 320
Santa Monica, CA 90405
Phone: (310) 458-0092
Fax: (310) 396-3454

Iconix offers a software cost estimating tool derived from Dr. Barry Boehm's well-known COCOMO algorithms. This tool is called CoCoPro, and since it is derived from COCOMO is aimed at systems and defense software, although it can be used for information systems applications.

IIT Research Institute
201 Mill Street
Rome, NY 13440
Phone: (315) 336-2359

The IIT Research Institute offers the SWAN software cost estimating tool, which seems to be yet another tool derived from Dr. Barry Boehm's COCOMO algorithms.

Information Engineering Systems Corporation
201 North Union Street, 5th floor
Arlington, VA 22314
Phone: (703) 739-2242
Fax: (703) 739-0074

A significant number of CASE tool vendors who support the Information Engineering (IE) paradigm also include software cost estimation and project management functions. This company's product is IE-Advantage, which includes a cost-estimation feature for predicting the outcomes of IE projects using the other tool capabilities.

James Martin & Company
3050 Chain Bridge Road, Suite 600
Fairfax, VA 22030-2834
Phone: (703) 352-0900

Named after the well-known software consultant James Martin, this company offers both consulting and tools. In the software cost estimating domain, it offers FastPROJECT™, which integrates schedule planning and cost estimating. The outputs from this tool can be interfaced to a companion methodology management tool called FastPACE™.

Kapur International, Inc.
108 One Annabel Lane
San Ramon, CA 94583
Phone: (510) 275-8000
Fax: (510) 275-8115

This company was founded by the well-known management consultant and lecturer, Gopal Kapur. It offers a software management tool suite called ProjectBASE®. This tool integrates macro-level software cost estimating and software schedule planning, and can interface with a variety of other project management tools, such as Microsoft Project, Timeline, Super Project, and the Project Manager's Workbench (PMW). The Kapur tool is aimed primarily at management information systems.

Koch Productivity Consulting (KPC)
814 Pecan Circle
Bel Air, MD 21014-2651
Phone: (410) 838-8721
Fax: (410) 265-0889

This company offers a tool called Adaptive Estimating Model (AEM). The AEM tool supports function point metrics and is aimed primarily at management information systems. However as the word *adaptive* implies, the tool can be used for other kinds of software. The AEM tool also includes tracking capabilities and various report capabilities.

KnowledgeWare, Inc.
3340 Peachtree Road
Atlanta, GA
Phone: (404) 231-8575, (800) 338-4130
Fax: (404) 364-0883

KnowledgeWare is known primarily as an integrated CASE tool company. Its main CASE tool is the Application Development Workbench® (ADW), which, like many CASE tools, includes project management and software cost estimating functions. Usually the cost-estimating features are restricted to estimating projects built using the other CASE components. KnowledgeWare's tools and estimating methods are centered around Information Engineering (IE), which is equivalent to saying that the estimates are aimed at management information systems, rather than military or systems software applications. In addition to the ADW, KnowledgeWare also markets the ForeSight™ methodology management tool. Here too, methodology management tools often support software cost estimating functions.

LBMS
1800 West Loop South, 6th floor
Houston, TX 77027-3210
Phone: (713) 625-9300

Learmonth and Burchart (LBMS) specializes in software methodology management. Its well-known Process Engineer tool includes basic software cost estimating, and LBMS has recently decided to extend its software cost estimating range by becoming a distributor for the Software Productivity Research (SPR) KnowledgePLAN software cost and schedule estimating tool. KnowledgePLAN also includes quality and risk predictions, as well as integral sizing logic based on either analogy with other projects in its database, function point metrics, or source code metrics.

Note that LBMS was acquired by Platinum Technology and the LBMS tools will now be joined to the Platinum Continuum tool suite.

Lucas Management Systems
10530 Rosehaven Street, #600
Fairfax, VA 22030-2840
Phone: (703) 222-1111
Fax: (703) 222-8203

This company was formerly the management systems division of Lucas Industries, a large British conglomerate. Over the past five years the division has moved through a series of acquisitions, and is now owned by Gores, which is a software conglomerate with a variety of project management offerings. The flagship product of Lucas is Artemis™, which is a mainframe project management tool with some estimating capabilities, although scheduling is its primary focus. The Windows version is Artemis Prestige™; there are other modules, too, for dealing with reports; and also Artemis 7000™ for client/server applications and other topics.

Lyndon B. Johnson Space Center
National Aeronautics and Space Administration
Mail Code: P14/Roush
Houston, TX 77058-3696

The National Aeronautics and Space Administration (NASA) is fairly sophisticated in its software development and project management disciplines. NASA has developed its own software cost estimating tool, called NASA Cost Modeler, which is available to government agencies and military services.

MarCon & Associates, Inc.
11520 North Central Expressway, Suite 210
Dallas, TX 75243
Phone: (800) 477-8725
Fax: (214) 343-3971

MarCon & Associates offers a mainframe project management tool called TRAK which also has software cost estimating capabilities. TRAK is aimed at management information systems, and its cost estimates are aimed at being keyed to specific client requests so they can serve for cost allocations among multiple users.

Marotz, Inc.
13518 Jamul Drive
Jamul, CA 91935-1635
Phone: (619) 669-3100
Fax: (619) 669-6914
Web: http://www.Martotz.com
E-mail: sales@marotz.com

Marotz markets CostXpert, which is a Windows-based cost-estimating and project-planning tool. This is based on Dr. Barry Boehm's COCOMO model but has added function point metrics, GUI metrics, and object metrics, and can perform both top-down and bottom-up estimation. The tool also creates a project plan using user-defined or standard methodologies. Outputs include cost and schedule estimates, work-breakdown structures, labor-loading diagrams, risk profiles, staffing profiles, and definitions of deliverables.

Martin Marietta
PRICE Systems
300 Route 38
Moorestown, NJ 08057-3270
Phone: (800) 437-7432

Martin Marietta is the vendor of the PRICE-S software cost estimating tool. This was one of the first commercial software estimating tools in the world, introduced in the early 1970s by the former RCA company. The original designer of PRICE-S was the estimating pioneer Frank Freiman, and Bob Park, now of the Software Engineering Institute (SEI), was also part of the original PRICE-S team. It should be noted that PRICE-S is only one of a family of estimating models developed by RCA, with PRICE-H being the hardware cost estimating model. It is interesting that hardware and software cost estimates were joined together in the 1970s, but grew into two very different domains in the 1980s and 1990s.

Milt Bryce & Associates
777 Alderman Road
Palm Harbor, FL 34683
Phone: (813) 786-4567

Milt Bryce & Associates are pioneers in software methodology management, and their integrated PRIDE tool suite was first released in the mid 1970s. The company itself was created in 1971, and has a large clientele in both the United States and Japan. The PRIDE tool suite has an integrated software cost estimating tool, which is one of the class of specialized tools that, in this case, estimate projects using other PRIDE components.

Monterege Design, Inc.
P.O. Box 1222
Dartmouth, NS
Canada B2Y 4B9
Phone: (902) 466-0246
Fax: (902) 464-1134

Monterege Design is a Canadian company, and is one of only a few Canadian companies offering commercial software cost estimating tools. Its tool is called REKON.

National Information Systems, Inc.
4040 Moorpark Avenue, Suite 200
San Jose, CA 95117-1852
Phone: (800) 441-5758
Fax: (408) 985-7100

This company offers a multipurpose project management tool called ACCENT Graphic VUE which includes software cost estimating capabilities, although scheduling is its main purpose. As the name of the company implies, this tool is aimed at management information systems. The tool has the ability to consolidate the costs for multiple projects, which is a useful ability for accumulating the costs of various components of large systems.

Nichols & Company, Inc.
12555 West Jefferson Boulevard, Suite 202
Los Angeles, CA 90066-7000
Phone: (310) 670-6400
Fax: (310) 670-6409

Nichols & Company offers an integrated project planning and cost estimating tool called the ORO Project Management System. This tool supports various Department of Defense (DoD) standards and is aimed at the very detailed kinds of plans and estimates which U.S. military standards demand. However, the tool can also be used for other kinds of software, such as systems software or management information systems. The tool integrates planning, estimating, tracking, and cost reporting.

Object Oriented Pty. Ltd.
Level 11, 75 Miller Street
North Sydney, NSW
Australia
Web: http://www.oopi.com.au

Object Oriented Pty. Ltd. is an Australian company which includes both tools and consulting. Its estimation capability is called Process MeNtOr and it supports estimation for OO projects and C++.

PLATINUM Technology, Inc.
1815 South Meyers Road
Oakbrook Terrace, IL 60181
Phone: (708) 620-5000, (800) 890-7258
Fax: (800) 442-4230
Web: http://www.Platinum.com

PLATINUM technology markets a variety of software development, project management, and change-control tools. In the cost-estimating and project management domain, it offers the PLATINUM Process Continuum. This tool includes the ability to construct software cost estimates and schedule plans. Since it is a fairly new tool, it includes template support for the five levels of the Software Engineering Institute (SEI) capability maturity model (CMM). The management component is termed Advisor.

Note that PLATINUM has just acquired LBMS, so the LBMS Process Engineer tools will now be joined to the PLATINUM tools.

POC-IT Management Services, Inc.
900 South La Cienega Boulevard, 4th floor
Inglewood, CA 90301-4440
Phone: (310) 393-4552
Fax: (310) 451-2888

The POC-IT organization builds and sells the MicroMan II software cost estimating tool, which also includes staffing and schedule planning functions. The MicroMan II is aimed at management information systems. It supports the linking of multiple projects.

Productivity Solutions, Inc.
2352 Main Street
Concord, MA 01742-3814

Productivity Solutions markets the Ultra PLANNER® schedule and cost-estimating tool. This is not a pure software-estimating tool, but the vendor states that half of the clients use the tool for software-estimating purposes and the tool has built-in features for software estimating.

Project Software & Development, Inc.
20 University Road
Cambridge, MA 02138
Phone: (617) 661-1444
Fax: (617) 661-1642

This company markets the PROJECT/2 schedule and cost-estimating tool. Here too, the tool is not a pure software-estimation tool but the tool is often utilized for software projects. This tool supports activity-based costing and also allows multiple components of large systems to be linked and aggregated using *parent/child* logic, under which the system is the parent and the individual components are the children, which is a useful feature for large applications.

Quantitative Software Management, Inc.
2000 Corporate Ridge, Suite 900
McLean, VA 22102
Phone: (703) 790-0055
Fax: (703) 749-3795

Quantitative Software Management (QSM) was founded by the well-known estimating expert, Larry Putnam. QSM offers a suite of software project management tools, with the Software Life Cycle Management tool (SLIM®) as its flagship software-estimating tool.

This tool is supported and surrounded by other tools, such as the Productivity Analysis Database System (PADS), and SLIM-Control for tracking ongoing projects.

The SLIM estimating tool originated as a tool for estimating military software applications, and was one of the first commercial software cost estimating tools on the market, appearing circa 1979. In recent years the capabilities of the SLIM estimating tool have been broadened so that it now supports systems software, information systems, and commercial software, as well as military software. The SLIM tool supports lines-of-code metrics, but has added function point support and backfiring, or direct conversion between LOC and function point metrics.

The QSM tools have popularized the concept of Rayleigh curves, which is a family of curves that can describe staffing buildups for software projects. An interesting feature of the Rayleigh curve concept is that when the schedule dimension is shortened, the resource dimension can rise alarmingly. This phenomenon is widely cited, and is often discussed in the software management literature.

Q/P Management Group, Inc.
10 Bow Street
Stoneham, MA 02180
Phone: (781) 438-2692
Fax: (781) 438-5549
Web: www.QPMG.com

The Q/P Management Group was founded by the well-known function point consultant Scott Goldfarb. It is the main U.S. distributor for a set of software project management and cost-estimating tools developed by Union Pacific Technologies, a subsidiary of the Union Pacific Railroad. The three tools marketed all support function point metrics for both estimation and measurement purposes, and are aimed at management information system. The tools are PQMPlus Manager™, PQMPlus Analyst™, and PQMPlus Planner™.

Reifer Consultants, Inc.
P.O. Box 4046
Torrance, CA 90510
Phone: (310) 373-8728
Fax: (310) 375-9845
Web: http://www.Reifer.com
E-mail: dreifer@sprintmail.com

Don Reifer is a well-known software management consultant who has developed several software sizing and cost estimation models and methods over the past decade. He is currently working with Dr. Barry

Boehm at the University of Southern California as a member of the COCOMO II project team. He also teaches and lectures on software cost estimating, software reuse, and other software management topics.

SES Software Engineering Service GmbH
Rosenheimer Landstrasse 37
D-85521 Ottobrun
Germany

This is a software project management and cost-estimating company located in Germany. Its software cost estimating tool is SOFT-CALC. This estimating tool has a basic engine derived from Dr. Barry Boehm's COCOMO software cost estimating algorithms, but it also includes function point support for sizing, and a few other specialized metrics, such as object points and data points. This tool also includes quality estimating.

SHL System House
50 O'Conner Street, Suite 501
Ottowa, Ontario K1P 6L2
Canada
Phone: (613) 236-1428
Fax: (613) 563-1428

SHL System House is best known as a methodology management company, and is a major Canadian consulting and software services company. Most such companies offer at least rudimentary estimating capabilities, but SHL is attempting to break new ground by building a software cost estimating tool using the basic engine of the well-known interactive game, SIM City.

Software Productivity Centre, Inc.
460—1122 Mainland Street
Vancouver, BC V6B 5L1
Canada
Phone: (604) 662-8181
Fax: (604) 689-0140
E-mail: tools@spc.com

The Software Productivity Centre is a Canadian nonprofit organization whose activities include training, consulting, conferences, and software management tools which include software cost estimation capabilities. Its overall tool suite consists of a variety of templates and is called Essential Set. This tool suite includes a software-estimation feature. It also offers a separate metrics tool, called Metricate.

Software Productivity Research, Inc.
1 New England Executive Park
Burlington, MA 01803-5005
Phone: (781) 273-0140
Fax: (781) 273-5176
Web: www.SPR.com
E-mail: Capers@SPR.com

Software Productivity Research (SPR) was founded by the author, Capers Jones, in 1984. SPR has developed three commercial software cost estimating tools and has also built customized proprietary cost-estimating tools under contract for specific clients. The SPR commercial software cost estimating tools are the Software Productivity and Quality estimating tool (SPQR/20™), 1985; CHECKPOINT®, 1989 (marketed under the name CHECKMARK® in Japan and the United Kingdom); and KnowledgePLAN™, 1997. The latter tool includes a native bidirectional interface with Microsoft Project™ and generic interfaces with other project-scheduling tools.

The SPR software cost estimating tools include sizing logic, sizing by analogy, support for both function points and lines-of-code metrics, include risk analysis, and support both quality and reliability estimation. The SPR tools include extensive assessment and benchmarking capabilities, and allow any given project to be compared to industry averages or best-in-class results from the integral knowledge bases.

The SPR tools support activity-based costing down to the level of several hundred tasks, and can also estimate postdeployment maintenance and enhancements for up to a maximum of 20 years. The SPR tools support multiple software classes, including systems software, commercial software, management information systems, and military software. Estimates for new projects, enhancements, maintenance, and conversion projects are all supported. SPR is also the U.S. distributor for the Australian Function Point Workbench™ (FPW) tool.

Softstar Systems
28 Ponemah Road
Amherst, NH 03031
Phone: (603) 672-0987

This company markets the COSTAR software cost estimating tool. This tool is based on the COCOMO algorithms published by Dr. Barry Boehm, but differs from many COCOMO clones in that the vendor has added function point metric support for sizing purposes.

Spectrum International, Inc.
104 Woodside Drive
McMurray, PA 15317-3244
Phone: (412) 221-8580
Fax: (412) 221-8741

This vendor markets the SPECTRUM/Productivity and SPEC-TRUM/Manager project management tools, which also include software cost estimation capabilities. The SPECTRUM tools support activity-based costing, and also support tracking of ongoing projects. As with many CASE and methodology management tools, the estimating features are not general-purpose estimates, but estimate the results of projects using the other tools that are part of the same suite.

Structured Solutions Inc.
400 Interstate North Parkway, Suite 800
Atlanta, GA 30339
Phone: (770) 618-7900
Fax: (770) 618-7909

Structured Solutions offers a suite of methodology and project management tools, including software cost estimating, under the name MAP-Methodology Platform. MAP/Estimator is the software cost estimating component of this tool suite.

Swinburne University of Technology
Hawthorne Campus
P.O. Box 218
Hawthorne 3122
Victoria, Australia
Phone: 61 3 9214-8180
Fax: 61 3 9819-0823

Swinburne University in Australia is a major research center into software cost estimation, under the guidance of Dr. Simon Moser. Dr. Moser has also started a new software cost estimating association, and is the designer of the SYSTEM METER software cost estimating tool. This estimating tool uses algorithms from Dr. Barry Boehm's COCOMO model, and augments the basic model with some extended sizing features based on a new form of function point analysis which Dr. Moser states is especially suited for object-oriented projects and software-reusability analysis.

System Research Services
570 Taxter Road
Elmsford, NY 10523
Phone: (914) 345-9800
Fax: (914) 345-8161

This vendor markets the Sys/PLANRpc software-estimating tool, which includes both schedule and cost-estimating capabilities. This tool allows multiple projects to be linked together. It also includes value analysis and return on investment calculations for software projects.

System Software Associates, Inc.
500 West Madison
Chicago, IL 60661
Phone: (312) 641-2900
Fax: (312) 641-3737

This vendor offers the project resource manager PRM AS/SET tool, which includes software cost estimating capabilities. The tool also includes measurement capabilities, and allows users to utilize historical data as a method of improving estimating precision.

Texas Instruments, Inc.
13500 North Central Expressway
Dallas, TX 75265-5474
Phone: (214) 995-3773
Fax: (214) 995-4630

Texas Instruments has been a long-time supporter of Information Engineering (IE) and also a long-time supporter of function point metrics. This vendor's Information Engineering Facility (IEF) tool includes a software cost estimating module which uses function point metrics to predict the outcomes of IE projects. This is a specialized software cost estimating tool which is aimed at management information systems that utilize the Texas Instruments IEF product. The IEF was one of the pioneers in the use of function point metrics for software cost estimation. In addition, to minimize the complexity of function point calculations, the IEF includes an automatic function point derivation feature which extracts information from the requirements and design documents that are created using the IEF capabilities.

Union Pacific Technologies
7930 Clayton Road
St. Louis, MO 63117-1368

Union Pacific Technologies, a subsidiary of Union Pacific Railroads, has an active research program underway into software cost estimating. A major result of this program is the PRO QMS software cost estimating tool. PRO QMS includes function point sizing, cost estimating, and schedule estimating. The tool can interface data with many project management and scheduling tools, such as Microsoft Project.

When used with Union Pacific's own methodologies, PRO QMS features activity-based cost estimation. The tool also includes tracking capabilities.

University of Southern California
Los Angeles, CA 90089-0781
Phone: (213) 740-8163
Email: Boehm@sunset.USC.EDU

The University of Southern California is where Dr. Barry Boehm has assumed the position of TRW Professor of Software Engineering. Dr. Boehm is the originator of the Constructive Cost Model (COCOMO). Dr. Boehm and his colleagues at both USC and several commercial and industrial companies have been developing the new COCOMO II cost-estimating model, which is aimed at modern classes of software project that use alternatives to the classic "waterfall" model assumed by the original COCOMO model. The new COCOMO II also adds function point support and a number of extended features for sizing which were not present in the original COCOMO. An extensive set of new projects have been used for calibration and validation.

Work Management Solutions, Inc.
119 Beach Street
Boston, MA 02111-2520
Phone: (617) 482-6677
Fax: (617) 482-6233

This vendor offers the MULTITRAK tool which, as the name implies, is geared at linking estimates and cost accounting for multiple projects. The tool suite handles estimates, tracking, and cost accounting. It features standard interfaces to a number of other project management and scheduling tools, such as Microsoft Project, Project Managers Workbench, Primavera, and the like. This tool is not primarily a software cost estimating tool, but a general-purpose estimation tool which can deal with software projects.

C

Annotated Bibliography of Software Estimation

Boehm, Barry: *Software Engineering Economics,* Prentice Hall, Englewood Cliffs, N.J., 1981, 900 pp. This book has become a classic in the field, and is still selling well even after more than 17 years (Dr. Boehm is reportedly working on a revision, but Prentice Hall does not have any date scheduled for it.) This book discusses the algorithms of the *constructive cost model,* which is now widely known by the acronym COCOMO. This book discusses various aspects of measuring and estimating software projects, and has a large set of references, examples, case studies, and useful additional information.

On the down side, this book was published shortly after the function point metric began its explosive growth through the software industry. Unfortunately, there is no recent information on function points and their role in modern estimating tools. The book also assumes a traditional "waterfall" development model, and it assumes using lines of code (LOC) as the basic normalizing metric. Note that the COCOMO model itself has been updated to COCOMO II, and this new version does support functional metrics and has estimating facilities for client/server applications which do not follow the waterfall approach.

Brooks, Fred: *The Mythical Man Month,* Addison-Wesley, Reading, Mass., 1995, 295 pp. This is the twentieth anniversary edition of a software classic. Fred Brooks was manager of IBM's OS/360 operating system. This was one of the first software systems to exceed 1 million LOC in its first release. It was also the first IBM software system to be significantly late on its announced delivery date. Fred Brooks wrote a thoughtful historical analysis of why the software was late, initially published in 1974. This twentieth anniversary edition adds new material and gives Dr. Brooks a chance to discuss recent changes in software technologies. The fact that Microsoft's Windows 95 product was also late, 20 years after Fred Brooks's first warning, is a sign that many of the problems discussed are still current and highly relevant. This book has been one of the best-sellers in the software world for 20 years.

Conte, S. D., H. E. Dunsmore, and V. Y. Shen: *Software Engineering Metrics and Models,* Benjamin Cummings, Menlo Park, Calif., 1986, 396 pp. This is a fairly solid academic attempt to summarize the state of the art of software metrics and cost estimation circa the mid-1980s. The book does a very good job of dealing with the topics that were popular at that time, such as Halstead's *software-science* metrics, complexity theory, and several manifestations of Dr. Barry Boehm's COCOMO software cost estimating model. However, academia tends to lag the commercial world by about five years, and this book follows that pattern. For example, it contains little or no information on function point metrics, and does not discuss the three best-selling commercial estimating tools of the 1980s—ESTIMACS, SLIM, and SPQR/20. However, as a good survey of metrics and their use, and of the COCOMO model, this is a useful volume.

DeMarco, Tom: *Controlling Software Projects,* Yourdon Press, New York, ISBN 0-917072-32-4, 1982, 284 pp.   This book, together with Barry Boehm's *Software Engineering Economics,* is among the first to deal seriously with the quantitative aspects of software management; that is, measurement, metrics, cost estimating, and tracking. Although the book was first published in 1982, Tom DeMarco's excellent prose style and clear thinking still make the book a useful addition to a manager's bookshelf.

In addition, historians of software metrics will note that DeMarco invented an independent form of function point metric at about the same time as Allan Albrecht and his colleagues within IBM invented the standard function point metric. In a sense, DeMarco and Albrecht are the Darwin and Wallace of the software metrics world, with DeMarco playing the part of Wallace since Albrecht published his metric in 1978 while DeMarco's was not published until 1982 in this book. As with Darwin and Wallace, both DeMarco and Albrecht worked independently and neither was aware of the other's work until both had published their initial results.

————: *Why Does Software Cost So Much?,* Dorset House, New York, ISBN 0-932633-34-X, 1995, 237 pp.   This book is a collection of about two dozen essays by Tom DeMarco and some his colleagues. Both the title and the first essay deal with the costs of software, and as usual with Tom's writings, the discussion is interesting and unusual. Tom makes the point that few other human constructs have made as much change in the world as software, and, hence, the value of the results are probably worth the costs. Tom is a gifted writer, and often clarifies points about software by drawing from other domains. His essay "Mad About Metrics" has an amusing anecdote about a Russian nail factory which went from making small brads to railroad spikes when its performance was judged on the weight of nails produced rather than the number of nails.

————: *The Deadline,* Dorset House, New York, ISBN 0-932633-05-6, 1997, 310 pp. This is an unusual book by the well-known management consultant Tom DeMarco— a book about software schedules and estimation written in the form of a novel. While a novel is a rare teaching aid in the software world, the book follows a long and illustrious chain of similar books, such as Abbot's *Flatland,* which was a novel about geometry, and the fictional stories of the physicist George Gamow, which deal with such topics as quantum mechanics. Tom's new book is both a useful primer of software project management, including estimation, and also an easy book to read. It may begin a new software genre.

————, and Tim Lister: *Peopleware,* Dorset House, New York, ISBN 0-932633-05-6, 1987, 200 pp.   This book has become yet another classic, with very large sales in the software community. This was one of the pioneering books to deal with social and even ergonomic topics that affect the outcomes of software projects. In particular, this book has become famous for its exploration of the impact of office space on software productivity. The research noted that programmers in the high quartile of performance tended to have private offices of more than about 80 square feet in size. Conversely, programmers in the low quartile tended to occupy less than about 45 square feet, or to be crammed into multiperson cubicles or to work in noisy open-office environments.

Department of the Air Force: *Guidelines for Successful Acquisition and Management of Software Intensive Systems,* vols. 1 and 2, Software Technology Support Center, Hill Air Force Base, Utah, 1994.   The U.S. military is by far the world's largest consumer of software, and also the largest producer of custom software. The U.S. military also produces the largest software systems ever created. As a by-product, the U.S. military forces deploy more software cost estimating tools than any other organization. This book does not identify specific authors, but is produced in part by the editorial staff of *Crosstalk* magazine, which is an excellent journal of defense software. Also identified as coordinators and contributors are Major Mike McPherson and Professor Daniel Ferens.

The two volumes of this huge set of guidelines total almost 2000 pages in size. Although the book is obviously aimed at the defense community, there is enough useful information to recommend it to civilian software managers too. This recommendation is an easy one, because the books are distributed without charge! To receive copies, contact the Software Technology Support Center at 7278 Fourth Street, Hill AFB, Utah 84056-5205 or call (801) 775-2054. What makes the volumes useful is the enormous number of references to the software literature and a surprising amount of quantitative data from both the civilian and military software domains.

Dreger, Brian: *Function Point Analysis,* Prentice Hall, Englewood Cliffs, N.J., 1989, 225 pp. This was the first college primer intended to teach function points to those without any prior knowledge of the metric. This book is a very readable introduction to an important topic. It even manages to add a few items of humor to lighten up what might otherwise be a very dry topic. The only caveat about this book is that it was published in 1989, and the rules for counting function points underwent both a minor revision in 1993 and a major revision in 1994. To learn the rudiments of function point counting the book is still useful, but to learn the most current rules and practices, the book is unfortunately out of date. Since 1996, this book has been available in a CD-ROM edition under license to Miller Freeman publishers, together with several other books by Larry Putnam, Capers Jones, and David Card.

Duncan, William R. (ed.): *A Guide to the Project Management Body of Knowledge,* Project Management Institute, Upper Darby, Pa., ISBN 1-880410-12-5, 1996, 176 pp. The Project Management Institute (PMI) is a large nonprofit association that serves the needs of project managers throughout the world, including software project managers. PMI has a number of conferences aimed at project managers, and also publishes a growing library of useful information for project managers, of which this book is a good example.

This book is not limited to software projects, but has extensive sections on software project management. Other topics that are relevant to software as well as other kinds of projects include risk management, value analysis, planning, and cost control.

Garmus, David, and David Herron: *Measuring the Software Process: A Practical Guide to Functional Measurement,* Prentice Hall, Englewood Cliffs, N.J., 1995. Function point metrics are expanding rapidly throughout the world. David Garmus is a member of the counting practices committee of the International Function Point Users Group (IFPUG). David Herron is a former member of the same committee, and the two authors have formed a consulting company specializing in function point metrics. This is a new primer aimed at introducing function point metrics to a wide audience. The book covers the new Version 4.0 counting practices revision and hence is current through 1995 in terms of IFPUG counting rules.

Grady, Robert B.: *Practical Software Metrics for Project Management and Process Improvement,* Prentice Hall, Englewood Cliffs, N.J., ISBN 0-13-720384-5, 1992, 270 pp. Bob Grady has a very clear writing style, and he writes pragmatically about the real-world measurements actually used for software within Hewlett-Packard. This is an excellent book for learning about how real companies go about measurement work. The book is dated, however, in that Grady does not deal with the well-known problems of the lines-of-code metric, such as their tendency to penalize high-level languages. Once you get past the surprise that such a major topic is ignored, the book contains many useful illustrations of measurement practices.

————, and Deborah L. Caswell: *Software Metrics: Establishing a Company-Wide Program,* Prentice Hall, Englewood Cliffs, N.J., ISBN 0-13-821844-7, 1987, 288 pp. Bob Grady and Deborah Caswell work for Hewlett-Packard. It is always interesting to see first-hand case studies of how real companies go about things. This book discusses the sequence and results of establishing HP's corporatewide software measurement program. The book has both good and questionable features. The good parts deal with the social and cultural aspects of establishing profound social programs, such as a corporate software measurement system. The questionable parts are those dealing with metrics themselves. Unfortunately, neither author had enough data when the book was published to understand the serious problems with lines-of-code metrics and the economic advantages of function point metrics. Except for this problem, the book is very readable and is especially good in dealing with the social reactions to measurements within a major corporation.

Gulledge, Thomas R., William P. Hutzler, and Joan S. Lovelace (eds.): *Cost Estimating and Analysis—Balancing Technology and Declining Budgets,* Springer-Verlag, New York, Berlin, 1992, 297 pp. This book is a series of essays on cost-estimating topics, with a number of them being associated with software cost estimating. Perhaps the most useful of the software cost estimating essays is a useful calibration and comparison of several military cost estimating models by Professor Dan Ferens and Gerald Ourada of the Air Force Institute of Technology.

However, even some of the nonsoftware essays are interesting and useful. For example, Alan Goldfarb et al. have a discussion on cost sensitivity analysis which is as relevant to software as to any other kind of estimation.

Humphrey, Watts: *Managing the Software Process,* Addison-Wesley/Longman, Reading, Mass., 1990. Watts Humphrey is a retired IBM software executive who was the first director of the Software Engineering Institute's (SEIs) software assessment program. This book introduced many of the pivotal concepts of the SEI's capability maturity model. The book has become a best-seller, and is now widely quoted throughout the software world. This is the book that started the SEI capability maturity model (CMM) on its explosive growth in popularity. Humphrey's book also touches upon estimation, with emphasis on coding rather than the entire life cycle.

———: *A Discipline for Software Engineering,* Addison-Wesley/Longman, Reading, Mass., 1995, 785 pp. This new book contains Watts's view of how each individual can achieve software excellence. It differs from his previous book in that it is aimed at single practitioners rather than entire corporations. Although the book contains many interesting insights, it discusses estimation primarily in terms of the lines-of-code (LOC) metric. Humphrey discusses measurement and estimation, but his method of using lines of code is purely to programming. Unfortunately, Watts does not deal with the 50 percent or so of ancillary software professionals, such as technical writers, database administrators, or quality-assurance personnel, whose work and contributions cannot be measured using LOC metrics.

———: *Introduction to the Personal Software Process™,* Addison-Wesley/Longman, Reading, Mass., 1997, 278 pp. This new book is a primer about Watts's view of how individual programmers can achieve software excellence. The book includes worksheets and extensive discussions of software estimation, but is aimed primarily at coding programmers where the lines-of-code metric can be used. As usual with Watts's work, the book is clearly written and has much useful advice. As a treatise on estimation, however, the book covers only the code-related portions of the life cycle and does not deal with other kinds of software personnel estimation, such as technical writers, quality-assurance personnel, or project managers. However, the book does stress the important relationship of defects, costs, and schedules and recommends extensive defect prediction and estimation.

Also, for some reason the book does not include discussions of the many commercial estimation tools that are available to ease the task of creating useful software estimates.

Although following the roles that Watts lays out in his Personal Software Process has led to some tangible improvements in software quality and reductions in schedule slippages, the hard work involved is not always palatable to managers or even to programmers, so the effort involved in adhering to Watts's concepts has limited the acceptance of his useful ideas.

Jones, Capers: *Critical Problems in Software Measurement,* Information Systems Management Group, ISBN 1-56909-000-9, 1993, 195 pp. This book discusses some of the practical issues of establishing a large multinational, multiindustry database of software productivity and quality data. The book includes chapters on what kind of data should be recorded, on validating the data, and on ensuring the confidentiality of client organizations that provide the data. This book is somewhat controversial in that it was the first of the author's books to assert that the traditional lines-of-code metric should be considered to be professional malpractice if it continued to be used after 1995 for cross-language analysis or large-scale economic studies. Although lines-of-code metrics can be used for small-scale programming languages using one or a few similar languages, this metric cannot be used for large-scale life-cycle studies involving dissimilar programming languages.

————: *Assessment and Control of Software Risks,* Prentice Hall, Englewood Cliffs, N.J., ISBN 0-13-741406-4, 1994, 711 pp. This book discusses some 65 technical and sociological risk factors associated with software development and maintenance operations. The data has been collected during the course of SPR's software process assessment activities. Among the technical risks are those of inadequate cost estimation, inadequate tools, inadequate methodologies, and inadequate support for quality assurance.

Among the social risks are those of excessive schedule pressure, the low status of the software community within many corporations, and the high risks of litigation. Other risks include the tendency of vendors to make false claims about quality and productivity, and the tendency of software managers and staff to believe those claims without requiring proof. The book was translated into Japanese by Kozo Keikaku Engineering, the company that distributes the author's software cost estimating tools in Japan.

————: *Patterns of Software System Failure and Success,* International Thomson Computer Press, Boston, ISBN 1-850-32804-8, 1995, 292 pp. This book was published in December 1995. The contents are based on large-scale comparative studies of failed projects (i.e., projects that were either terminated prior to completion or had severe cost and schedule overruns or massive quality problems) and successful projects (i.e., projects that achieved new records for high quality, low costs, short schedules, and high customer satisfaction).

On the whole, management problems appear to outweigh technical problems in both successes and failures. For example, failure to estimate costs and schedules well is a frequent attribute of software disasters. Factors discussed include the use of planning and estimating tools; quality-control approaches; experience levels of managers, staff, and clients; and stability of requirements.

This book introduced the usage of function point metrics to measure the management tool suites used on successful and unsuccessful projects. The successful project managers had access to more than 15,000 function points of project management tools, including software cost estimation, software quality estimation, project schedule planning, risk analysis, value analysis, milestone tracking, and methodology management. By contrast, project managers on failing projects usually had less than 3000 function points of management tools available.

————: *Applied Software Measurement,* 2d ed., McGraw-Hill, New York, ISBN 0-07-032826-9, 1996, 618 pp. This book has become a standard reference volume in many companies, and in some university software management curricula as well. The new second edition of this book includes U.S. national averages for software productivity and quality derived from more than 6700 projects, using the function point metric for normalizing the data. It also includes comparative data on productivity from 50 industries, including banking, insurance, telecommunications, computer manufacturers, government, and the like.

A major revision was published in August 1996 that includes substantial new data on about 2000 new software projects, and discusses the emerging results of various new technologies, such as object-oriented approaches, client/server applications, ISO 9000 certification, and the Software Engineering Institute (SEI) approach. The new edition shows data for six subindustries (system software, military software, commercial software, information systems software, contracted and outsourced software, and end-user software). National averages are then derived from the overall results of these six domains.

————: *Software Quality—Analysis and Guidelines for Success,* International Thomson Computer Press, Boston, ISBN 1-85032-876-6, 1997, 492 pp. This book covers 70 topics that influence software quality—inspections, ISO 9000–9004 standards, the SEI CMM, all forms of testing, total quality management (TQM), and many more. This book differs from many other books on software quality in that it shows the actual measured impact of the various methods in terms of defect potentials, defect-removal efficiency levels, costs, and other relevant quantified information. Because of the historical data, the book is a useful source for estimating software defect levels. The contents are based on large-scale studies of many software projects in the U.S., Europe, and the Pacific Rim.

Software project management problems appear to outweigh technical problems in projects with poor quality levels. Other factors discussed include the use of quality-estimating tools; quality measurements; quality-control approaches; experience levels of managers, staff, and clients; and stability of requirements.

————: *The Year 2000 Software Problem—Quantifying the Costs and Assessing the Consequences,* Addison-Wesley/Longman, Reading, Mass., ISBN 0-201-30964-5, 1997, 335 pp.   The year-2000 software problem presents some very challenging problems for software cost estimation. Indeed, a full estimate of every aspect of the year-2000 problem is actually beyond the current state of the art of estimation, since it includes cost elements, such as litigation damages, which for estimating purposes are unpredictable. Also, the year-2000 problem is a complex estimating task for other reasons, too. For one thing, thousands of applications are involved at once. For another, the year-2000 problem is not limited to software but also involves costly repairs to hardware devices, databases, test libraries, and physical equipment, such as fax machines, elevators, weapons systems, and the like.

More than 500 programming languages are involved in the year-2000 problem. For some of these languages, such as Visual Basic, the lines-of-code metric cannot really be used because applications are constructed in part by means of menus, buttons, and other approaches which do not use lines of code at all.

This book does deal with year-2000 cost estimates, and normalizes the results using both function point metrics and lines-of-code metrics. However, for a problem as vast as the year-2000 issue, no single metric is suitable for every component. The book also points out a major gap in both metrics and estimation technology. There are no current metrics or estimating tools that can handle database and data warehouse updates.

Kan, Stephen H.: *Metrics and Models in Software Quality Engineering,* Addison-Wesley, Reading, Mass., ISBN 0-201-63339-6, 1995, 344 pp.   This is a thoughtful overview of a number of metrics in the software quality domain. The book also covers topics of great importance to the software management community, such as the Baldrige Award, the ISO 9000–9004 standards, the Software Engineering Institute (SEI) capability maturity model (CMM), and total quality management (TQM). The chapters and sections are fairly complete, and give context and background information. A full reading of this book will transfer a considerable amount of useful information to the reader, and it covers many topics well enough to give fresh insights. The book illustrates the close ties between accurate measurement and the ability to estimate well.

Marciniak, John J. (ed.): *Encyclopedia of Software Engineering,* vols. 1 and 2, John Wiley & Sons, New York, ISBN 0-471-54002, 1994.   This is a massive compilation of information in two large volumes that total about 1500 pages. Although most of the topics relate to software engineering, there are also many topics of interest to software managers as well. For example, there are topics on software cost estimating, software measurements, function point metrics, and many other subjects that appeal to the software managerial community. As usual with encyclopedias, there are hundreds of articles written by hundreds of authors. The quality of the contributions varies from marginally adequate to truly excellent.

Muller, Monika, and Alain Abram (eds.): *Metrics in Software Evolution,* R. Oldenbourg Vertag GmbH, Munich, ISBN 3-486-23589-3, 1995.   This is an interesting book and also represents an interesting research collaboration between Canada and Germany. The German National Center for Information Technology (GMD) and the Computer Research Institute of Montreal (CRIM) have collected a number of essays by various authors and have assembled them into a significant book on both measurement and the usage of function points in a business and industrial context. What sets this book apart from the usual academic mode of theory without empirical data is the inclusion of a number of case studies from industry, such as one from Volkswagen from the German side and the Trillium project of Bell Canada on the Canadian side. Since metrics research is now a global topic, it is very useful to U.S. software project managers to gain a perspective of how their colleagues in Canada and Europe are using metrics and function points.

Paulk, Mark, and Bill Curtis et al: *The Capability Maturity Model,* Addison-Wesley, Reading, Mass., ISBN 0-201 54664-7, 1995, 441 pp.   The Software Engineering Institute (SEI) was incorporated in 1985, so this book marks its tenth anniversary.

The capability maturity model (CMM) is a way of assessing the "maturity" of software production. The CMM creates a five-level excellence scale:

1 Initial (chaotic and unstructured)
2 Repeatable (beginning to achieve discipline)
3 Defined (capable of successful results in most situations)
4 Managed (very disciplined, with full reusability)
5 Optimizing (state of the art; highly advanced)

This book is a group effort by almost a score of SEI personnel and consultants. It serves as a very good general introduction to the overall concepts of the CMM. Of course, the book does not deal at all with the many gaps and omissions of the CMM. For example, the SEI assessment approach only covers about half of the factors that can influence the outcomes of software projects. The CMM does not collect any quantitative data at all, so there is no easy way to determine if the SEI claims of "higher productivity and quality" associated with CMM levels 3, 4, and 5 are true or merely fanciful assertions.

Perry, William E.: *Handbook of Diagnosing and Solving Computer Problems,* TAB Books, Blue Ridge Summit, Pa., ISBN 0-8306-9233-9, 1989, 255 pp. Bill Perry is the chairman and CEO of the well-known Quality Assurance Institute (QAI) in Orlando, Florida. Bill has dedicated his professional life to advancing software quality, and ranks as one of the top U.S. experts in this area. Bill is both an excellent speaker and a very clear writer. This book discusses a series of real-world problems that software managers are likely to encounter, such as cost overruns, schedule overruns, organizational disputes, and the like. Then the book suggests some possible solutions. Although the book was published in 1989, many of the problems are still current, and the advice is still valid.

Pressman, Roger S.: *A Manager's Guide to Software Engineering,* McGraw-Hill, New York, ISBN 0-07-050820-8, 1993, 528 pp. Roger Pressman is a very good writer, and most of his books are interesting, informative, and even entertaining. This one is no exception. Roger's book is aimed at software managers and executives who might have come into their jobs from a nonsoftware background. He covers many basic topics in an introductory way that is easy to grasp. One could wish for more depth in some of the topics, however. For example, there are more than 50 commercial software cost estimating tools sold in the United States, yet Roger's discussion of estimating seems to assume that manual estimating is the norm. In spite of occasional gaps such as this, there is enough useful information for this book to find a place on many management bookshelves.

Putnam, Lawrence H.: *Measures for Excellence—Reliable Software on Time, Within Budget,* Yourdon Press/Prentice Hall, Englewood Cliffs, N.J., ISBN 0-13-567694-0, 1992, 336 pp. Larry Putnam is the originator of the well-known SLIM software cost estimating tool. He is also a respected management consultant and the chairman of Quantitative Software Management (QSM). This book covers Larry's view of software metrics, with some interesting examples of the Rayleigh curve as it applies to software. Lord Rayleigh, a pioneering British physicist of the early part of the century, derived an interesting curve that approximates the growth patterns of many natural phenomena. Larry Putnam found that Rayleigh curves could also be applied to software projects. The most notable aspect of Rayleigh curves for software is the imbalance between effort and schedules. Attempts to compress schedules tend to drive up the effort to sometimes unmanageable levels.

———, and Ware Myers: *Industrial Strength Software,* IEEE Computer Society Press, Los Alamitos, Calif., ISBN 0-13-8186-7532-2, 1997, 309 pp. Larry Putnam and Ware Myers are both management consultants, authors, and estimating specialists. Larry Putnam is the chairman of Quantitative Software Management (QSM). This book covers the intersection of measurement, estimation, and process improvement. The book contains a wealth of examples and substantial amounts of useful quantitative data. Books such as this illustrate the fact that software cost estimation is built upon a framework of solid measurement practices.

Rethinking the Software Process, CD-ROM, Miller Freeman, Lawrence, Kans., 1996. This CD-ROM is a book collection jointly produced by the book publisher, Prentice

Hall, and the journal publisher, Miller Freeman. It contains the full text and illustrations of five Prentice Hall books: Capers Jones, *Assessment and Control of Software Risks*; Tom DeMarco, *Controlling Software Projects*; Brian Dreger, *Function Point Analysis*; Larry Putnam and Ware Myers, *Measures for Excellence*; Mark Lorenz and Jeff Kidd, *Object-Oriented Software Metrics*. In addition, it contains more than 30 articles from *Software Development* magazine. The advertised price of $59.50 for five complete books and a large set of journal articles is quite attractive. The hardcover versions of the books alone would total almost $200.

Rubin, Howard: *Software Benchmark Studies for 1997*, Howard Rubin Associates, Pound Ridge, N.Y., 1997.   Dr. Howard Rubin publishes an annual survey of software productivity and quality data gathered from around the world. Dr. Rubin is also the developer of the ESTIMACS software cost estimating tool, and illustrates in his own work the close ties between estimation and measurement. The annual versions of the Rubin benchmark studies are very useful for exploring trends from year to year. Here, too, the close ties between measurement and estimation can be seen, because the kinds of data included in this book are what makes estimation possible.

Software Productivity Consortium: *The Software Measurement Guidebook*, International Thomson Computer Press, Boston, ISBN 1-850-32195-7, 1995, 308 pp. This book has a large collection of authors and contributors and, hence, tends to be varied in tone and content from chapter to chapter. The overall sponsor is the Software Productivity Consortium, which originated about 10 years ago as an early attempt to improve the software performance of the military and defense community. Hence, the consortium is located in Herndon, Virginia, in the heart of the U.S. government and military world. It is important to remember the military emphasis of the consortium, because some of the approaches and methods discussed in this book are seldom encountered in the civilian sector. For example, the discussion on software cost estimating mentions only a small sample of tools aimed at military projects, such as COCOMO and SLIM, while totally ignoring 40 or so commercial software-estimating tools used by civilians, such as Bridge, BYL, CHECKPOINT, KnowledgePlan, ProQMS, ESTIMACS, and dozens more.

Symons, Charles R.: *Software Sizing and Estimating—Mk II FPA*, John Wiley & Sons, Chichester, U.K., ISBN 0-471-92985-9, 1991, 200 pp.   Charles Symons is a well-known British management consultant and a partner in the consulting company of Nolan & Norton. Charles was an early pioneer in the usage of function point metrics, but was dissatisfied with some of the results he achieved with the original Albrecht and IBM version. Therefore, Symons developed an alternative form of function point metric, which he termed *Mark II function points*. The Mark II method includes counts of entities and relationships, and differs in other respects as well from the U.S. form of function point. Usage of the Mark II method is concentrated in the United Kingdom, but is found in Canada, Hong Kong, and other countries as well. By interesting coincidence, U.S. function points and British Mark II function points tend to produce results that differ by approximately the same amount as the difference between U.S. gallons and Imperial gallons.

Tufte, Edward R.: *The Visual Display of Quantitative Information*, Graphics Press, Cheshire, Conn., 1983, 197 pp.   This large-format book has become a cult classic. Its purpose is to show how various kinds of technical and quantitative information can be displayed in a fashion that optimizes the human understanding of the results. The book is excellent in all respects, and is a must-read book for all those concerned with software productivity and quality measurements, management reporting, and function point metrics.

Umbaugh, Robert E. (ed.): *Handbook of IS Management*, 4th ed., Auerbach, Boston, ISBN 0-7913-2159-2, 1995, 703 pp.   Auerbach is a well-known company that evaluates software tools and methods. From time to time it publishes compendiums of information on specific topics, and this book is one of them. This is a very large book with 6 major sections, more than 60 articles, and, hence, more than 60 contributors. As usual with multiauthor collections, the quality of the contributions varies from mediocre to excellent. Many of the articles here are interesting and relevant. The most appropriate sections for software managers are those dealing with strategy, managing information technology, managing data, and developing applications.

Some of the authors are very well known. Two of the well-known gurus included are Dr. Rudy Hirschheim, a well-known outsourcing expert, and J. Daniel Couger, whose work on creativity is often quoted.

Wiegers, Karl E: *Creating a Software Engineering Culture,* Dorset House, New York, ISBN 0-932633-33-1, 1996, 358 pp. This is the first book by a promising new author, Karl Wiegers of Eastman Kodak. The book is very well written and also very practical. It discusses the evolution of the software engineering culture within Kodak. Unlike many books on software process improvement, Wiegers's book is based on real empirical observations over a number of years. In a sense, this is a very large case study. Real life does not run smoothly, and Wiegers points out many problems that occurred along the path to improvement, as well as the successes. This book deserves thoughtful reading by any manager or technical worker interested in quality, process improvement, or software sociological issues. The book is not a treatise on software measurement and estimation, but does include useful information about sociological barriers to the adoption of these technologies in real-life situations.

Zells, Lois: *Managing Software Projects,* QED Information Sciences, Wellesley, Mass., ISBN 0-89435-275-X, 485 pp. This book is an attempt to put together a discussion of all of the available software tools for project managers, such as Microsoft Project, Timeline, CHECKPOINT, and the like. The book has a useful premise and was one of the first attempts to show the commercial estimating tools and how they might be used in parallel. Unfortunately, many new tools have emerged since the book was published, but the concept remains valuable and perhaps the author and publisher will bring out a revised edition.

Yourdon, Ed: *Death March,* Prentice Hall, Upper Saddle River, N.J., ISBN 0-13-748310-4, 1997. Ed Yourdon is a well-known author, management consultant, and speaker on software management topics. He is also the editor of *American Programmer* magazine, which comes closest to achieving the literary quality of *Scientific American* of any known software journal.

Yourdon's "death march" refers to projects that are essentially impossible to achieve in terms of their stated schedules and costs, but which companies plunge into anyway.

This book should be required reading for estimating-tool vendors and project management consultants, because it contains a wealth of practical information about why managers continue to march toward certain failure in spite of warnings and advice that the goals are untenable.

In essence, those who set the schedules (executives, senior management, and clients) are too remote and ignorant of real-life schedules to be effective. Basically, schedules are not set by determining the capabilities of the development team, but primarily are set to reflect market needs. The fact that such schedules are technically impossible is usually known to at least some team members, but social and political powers are so strong that they are helpless to correct the situation.

(Incidentally, all of Western Europe is marching toward an enormous death-march project called the *euro*—the unified European currency which is currently scheduled to be phased in from 1999 through 2002.)

Zvegintzov, Nicholas: *Software Management Technology Reference Guide,* Dorset House, New York, ISBN 1-884521-01-0, 1994, 240 pp. Nicholas Zvegintzov has been a pioneer in a number of topics. He was among the first to recognize that software maintenance would grow almost uncontrollably. He was also among the first to realize that software project management is a critical topic, perhaps even more critical than software engineering itself. This book is an attempt to consolidate information on some of the tools and approaches that impact software management. Nicholas is an excellent writer, although sometimes acidic in his side comments. This book contains a considerable amount of useful information for the software management community and some useful discussions of software cost estimating tools.

Index

A scope, 200, 374
Abeyant defects, 605, 606
Abram, Alain, 706
Abts, Chris, 641
ACCENT Graphic VUE, 693
ACR Directory of Software Metrics and Project Management Tools, 682
Activity, 54
Activity-based costing, 38, 386–388
Activity-based estimation:
  advantages, 421
  change management, 521–532
  code inspections, 511–519
  design and specifications, 463–473
  design inspections, 475–486
  documentation, 563–571
  programming/coding, 487–510
  project management, 573–591
  prototyping, 449–462
  requirements, 423–448
  testing, 533–561
Activity-based software cost estimating, 60
Activity pattern adjustment factors, 381–389
Activity patterns, 59
Activity-selection errors, 141–143, 153
Ada COCOMO, 640
Adaptive Estimating Model (AEM), 689, 690
Adjustment factors, 355
  activity pattern adjustment factors, 381–389
  compensation and work pattern adjustment, 357–380
  software technology adjustment factors, 391–420
  topical areas, 357, 358
Advice mode, 38
Advice/tips, 19
ADW, 690
AEM, 689, 690
AFMS/FMCI, 683
AGS Management Systems, Inc., 683

Air Force Cost Analysis Agency (AFCAA/FMP), 683
Air Force Cost Analysis Agency Software Estimating Model Analysis, 22, 682
Albrecht, Allan, 27, 28, 29, 30, 31, 33, 182, 215, 236, 262, 270, 637, 647
Albrecht function point, 270
Algorithmic complexity, 289
Algorithms, 32, 272
Andersen Consulting, 684
Andersen Method/1, 684
Annotated bibliography, 701–709
Annotated Bibliography of Software Productivity and Quality Information Sources, 645
Application Development Workbench (ADW), 690
Application Prototyping, 450
Application size, 101–111
Applied Business Technology Corp. (ABT), 684
Applied Software Measurement, 21, 132, 190, 384, 465, 564, 597, 654, 705
Approximation modes, 38
Aron, Joel, 26, 639
Art of Rapid Prototyping, The, 450
Artemis, 691
Assessment and Control of Software Risks, 123, 424, 597, 654, 705
Assessment support, 38
Assessment support tools, 80
Assignment scope (A scope), 200, 374
Assignment-scope errors, 144, 145, 153
Associations, 679–681
Automated estimate from minimal data, 217–264
  automated sizing approximation methods, 242–257
  nature/scope/class/type of project, 223–231
  producing preliminary cost estimate, 257
  project sizing/code sizing, 234–242
  recording administrative/project information, 218–234

Automated estimate from minimal data, (*Cont.*):
steps in process, 218
work patterns/staff salaries/overhead rates, 231–234
Automated sizing approximation methods, 242–257
creeping user requirements, 250–257
function point ranges, 245, 246
function point reconstruction, 246–248
scope/class type, 243–245
sizing by analogy, 248–250
Automated software-estimating methods, 49, 52–66
Automatic metric conversion, 39
Average cost per function point, 378, 384

Backfiring, 191, 192, 283–287
Backfiring support, 39
Bad fix injection, 606, 607
Bang metric, 29
Barrow, Dean, 48, 66, 91, 156, 378, 682
Basili, Victor, 639, 667
Beasley, Reyna, 20, 111
Before You Leap (BYL), 65
Beizer, Boris, 533
Belady, Lazlo, 665
Benchmark mode, 39
Benn, Douglas, 684
Berlack, H.R., 523
Best-in-class quality organizations, 339
Best Practices in Software Cost and Schedule Estimation, 20
Beta testing, 543, 544
Bibliography, 701–709
Biggerstaff, Ted, 648, 649
Biographies:
Boehm, Barry, 638–643
Jones, Capers, 643–656
Putnam, Larry, 656–678
Black, Rachel, 639
Boar, Bernard, 450
Boehm, Barry, 20, 26, 27, 29, 33, 65, 66, 131, 215, 262, 378, 388, 418, 465, 487, 533, 573, 638–643, 648, 649, 700, 701
Boeing 3D function points, 29
Bogan, Christopher, 388
Briand, Loic, 111, 126
Bridge Modeler, 684
Bridging, 622
Brooks, Fred, 27, 66, 111, 120, 181, 523, 573, 701

Brown, Norm, 21, 91, 111, 388, 418
Budget support tools, 83
Bugs (*see* Errors)
Burden rates, 39, 370–373

Calibration mode, 39
Capability Maturity Model, The, 706
Capacity testing, 540
Carleton, Anita, 640
CASE tools, 506
Caswell, Deborah L., 703
Catalogs, 72
project management tools, 72
software cost estimating tools, 38, 48, 682
CB COCOMO, 686
Change-control boards, 433, 434
Change management, 521–532
bugs/defects, and, 530, 531
creeping requirements, and, 527–529
design changes, 529
economics of changes, 525–527
items to be estimated, 521
literature, 522, 523
nominal default values, 523
tools, 524, 525
unique characteristics, 522
Chaos theory, 291
Charette, Robert, 21, 111, 120
Charismatek, 685
Charts of accounts, 57
CHECKPOINT, 653, 654
Clapp, Judy, 662
Clark, Brad, 641
Clean-room statistical testing, 544, 545
Client/server estimation, 40
Climis, Ted, 644, 645
COCOMO, 29, 640–643, 700
COCOMO II, 29, 641–643, 700
COCOMOID, 683
CoCoPro, 688
Code complexity, 289, 297
Code-counting tools, 87
Code inspections, 511–519
attributes, 512
benefits, 514, 515
downstream effects, 518
inspection coordinator, 516
literature, 518
nominal default values, 515, 516
partial inspections, 513
structured walkthroughs/code reviews, contrasted, 512, 513

Code inspections (*Cont.*):
  time requirements, 514
  where most widely used, 512
  why not widely used, 517, 518
Code restructuring, 613
Code reviews, 512
Code sizing (*see* Source and sizing)
Coding (*see* Programming/coding)
Collins, Tony, 641
Combinations of programming languages, 237
Combinatorial complexity, 289
Commercial software projects, 96, 97
Comparative mode, 40
Compatibility testing, 542
Compensation and overhead, 40
Compensation and work pattern adjust-
    ments, 357–380
  overhead costs/burden rates, 370–373
  overtime, 374, 375
  salaries, 366–370
  work patterns, 373–377
Complexity, 288–300
Complexity adjustments, 40
Complexity analysis, 611–613
Complexity analysis tools, 81, 82
Complexity factor, 667
Component testing, 538
Compression, 621
Computational complexity, 289, 290
Computer aided software engineering
    (CASE), 506
Computer Associates International Inc.,
    685
Computer Economics, Inc., 685
Confidence levels, 40
Configuration control (*see* Change man-
    agement)
Conte, S.D., 701
Contracted projects (*see* Outsourced/con-
    tracted projects)
Controlling Software Projects, 29, 66, 111,
    271, 465, 702
Conversion projects, 40, 615
COSMIC, 686
COSMOS, 687
Cost buckets, 362, 363
Cost drivers, 563
*Cost Estimating and Analysis—Balancing
    Technology and Declining Budgets*, 704
Cost to complete estimates, 40
COSTAR, 697
COSTMODL, 686

CostXpert, 691
Creating a Software Engineering Culture,
    709
Creeping requirements adjustments, 40
Creeping user requirements:
  change management, 527–529
  programming/coding, 500, 501
  sizing, 193–195, 250–257
  software requirements, and, 429
Creeping user requirements errors,
    147–149, 154
Critical path errors, 149, 150, 154
Critical Problems in Software
    Measurement, 704
Crystal Ball COCOMO, 686
Currency conversion, 41
Curtis, Bill, 418, 573, 648, 649, 706
Customer-acceptance testing, 544
Customer support, 41, 608, 609
Cyclomatic complexity, 290, 502, 612

D.F. Benn & Associates, 684
Data complexity, 290, 298
Data duplexing, 622
Data metrics, 159
Davis, Alan, 424
Day, Virginia, 640
DDB Software, 686
Dead code, 632
Dead code removal, 617
Deadline, The, 22, 111, 702
Death March, 21, 111, 120, 419, 709
Decisioneering, Inc., 686
DECplan, 687
Default values, 365
Defect removal efficiency, 337, 338
Defect-tracking measurement tools, 85, 86
DeMarco, Tom, 21, 22, 29, 33, 66, 88, 111,
    120, 263, 270, 378, 388, 418, 465,
    487, 505, 702
DeMarco function point, 270, 271
Depth of inheritance tree (DIT), 323
Design and specifications (*see* Software
    specifications and design)
Design inspections, 475–486
  companies most likely to use inspec-
      tions, 482
  effectiveness, 482, 483
  factors to consider, 484, 485
  literature, 475, 476
  nominal default values, 477, 478
  nonprofit organization, 483

Design inspections, (*Cont.*):
  participants, 476, 477
  time requirements, 479
Development Support Center, Inc., 686
Devnani-Chulani, Sunita, 641
Diagnostic complexity, 290
Digital Equipment Corporation (DEC), 687
Discipline for Software Engineering, A, 704
Disposable prototypes, 452, 453
DIT, 323
Documentation, 563–571
  changing trends, 566
  literature, 564
  nominal default values, 565
  rules of thumb, 565
  steps in process, 566, 570
  tools, 564
  translation costs, 570
  types of, 567–569
Domain adjustments, 41
Dorfman, Merlin, 424
Dormant application removal, 617
DPS, 27, 645, 646
Dreger, Brian, 66, 215, 262, 465, 703
Duncan, William R., 703
Dunn, Robert, 475, 518
Dunsmore, H.E., 701
Duplicate defects, 607

Early estimation and approximation (*see*
    Preliminary estimation methods)
Early warnings, 41
East Tennessee State University, 687
EI, 304, 306
EIF, 304, 309
Encapsulation, 622
Encyclopedia of Software Engineering, 21,
    706
End-user software applications, 96
Enhancement estimates (*see*
    Maintenance/enhancement estimat-
    ing)
Enterprise estimation, 162–164
Enterprise-level Euro-currency estima-
    tion tools, 89, 90
Enterprise-level year-2000 cost-estimat-
    ing tools, 89
Enterprise software planning tools, 88, 89
Entropic complexity, 290, 291
Environment factors, 7
EO, 304, 308
EQ, 304, 308

Equivalent assembly statements, 646
Ernst and Young, 687
Error-prone module removal, 609, 610
Error-prone modules, 400–403
Errors, 129–156
  change management, and, 530, 531
  classes of, 137–152
  historical data collection, and, 129–133
  impact of, 152–156
  programming, and, 496–498
  sizing, 334–342
  software requirements, and, 428, 429
Essential complexity, 291, 502, 612
Essential Set, 696
ESTIMACS, 30, 685
Estimating software costs (*see* Software
    cost estimation)
Estimation on handheld computers, 166,
    167
Eurocurrency conversion, 212, 213,
    624–627
Eurocurrency support, 41
Evolutionary prototypes, 454–456
Executive and client errors, 140, 141, 153
*Executive Briefing: Controlling Software
    Development*, 678
*Exploring Requirements—Quality Before
    Design*, 424
External input (EI) types, 306
External inquiry (EQ) types, 308
External interface (EIF) files, 309
External output (EO) types, 308

Fagan, Michael, 475, 511
Failure/success rates, 113–120
Fan complexity, 291
FastPROJECT, 689
Feature points, 32, 272
Ferens, Daniel, 21, 135, 156
Field (beta) testing, 543, 544
Field service, 627, 628
Financial documents, 567
Fitzsimmons, Ann, 667, 668
Five-point adjustment scale, 406–410
Five-point software excellence scale, 405
Flow complexity, 291
ForeSight, 690
Formal inspections (*see* Code inspections,
    Design inspections)
FPSSII, 687
Frame, Jim, 644, 645, 647, 648
Freiman, Frank, 27, 28, 637, 639, 650, 692

Friedman, Daniel, 475
Full sizing logic, 41
Fully burdened salary rate, 370
Function point adjustment table, 311
Function point analysis, 182
Function Point Analysis, 465, 703
Function point analysis tools, 86, 87
Function point complexity, 291, 292
Function point complexity adjustments,
    310–316
Function point counting worksheet, 310
Function point metrics, 270, 271, 302–317
Function point sizing rules of thumb:
  prior to completion of requirements,
    184–188
  sizing by analogy, 188
  sizing creeping user requirements,
    193–195
  sizing paper deliverables, 192, 193
  sizing software defect potentials, 196,
    197
  sizing software defect-removal efficien-
    cy, 198, 199
  sizing source code volumes, 188–192
  sizing test-case volumes, 195, 196
Function point support, 41
Function Point System (FPSSII), 687
Function point types, 304
Function point variations, 273–280
Function Point Workbench, 685
Function points, 29–32, 182, 270, 271, 272

Gaffney, John, 665
Galorath, Dan, 640, 641
Galorath Associates, Inc., 688
Gantt chart, 62
Garmus, David, 215, 262, 703
Gartner, Gideon, 392
Gates, Bill, 622
Gause, Don, 424
GEC-Marconi Software Systems, 688
GECOMO, 65
GECOMO Plus, 688
Geneen, Harold, 647
Gilb, Tom, 475, 480, 511, 648
Goethert, Wolf, 640
Goldfarb, Scott, 695
Grady, Bob, 21, 215, 262, 703
Graham, D., 475
Graph complexity, 292
Graphical software design representation,
    332

Graphics and visualization, 42
*Guide to the Project Management Body of
    Knowledge, A*, 703
*Guidelines for Successful Acquisition and
    Management of Software Intensive
    Systems*, 702
Gulledge, Thomas R., 21, 704

Halstead, Maurice, 292
Halstead complexity, 292
Halstead software-science metrics, 349
Hamid, Tarik Abdel, 88
*Handbook of Diagnosing and Solving
    Computer Problems*, 21, 707
Handbook of IS Management, 708
Handbook of Software Maintenance, 597
Harmon, Paul, 378
Herron, David, 215, 262, 703
Historical data, 129–133
Horowitz, Ellis, 641
House of quality, 434
Howard, Alan, 22, 38, 48, 91, 682
Huffschmidt, Bill, 687
Human judgment, 360
Humphrey, Watts, 66, 215, 262, 378, 418,
    487, 573, 704
Hutzler, William P., 704

IBM Santa Teresa programming laborato-
    ry, 504, 505
ICONIX Software Engineering, Inc., 688
IE-Advantage, 689
IEF, 699
*IEEE Transactions on Software
    Engineering*, 29
IFPUG, 183, 273, 278, 679, 680
IFPUG function point metrics, 272
IFPUG method of complexity adjustment,
    313
IIT Research Institute, 688
ILF, 304, 309
Import and export of data, 42
Inch pebbles, 85
Independent testing, 542, 543
*Industrial Strength Software: Effective
    Management Using Measurement*,
    465, 487, 597, 678, 707
Inflation rate adjustments, 42
Information complexity, 292
Information Engineering Systems
    Corporation, 689

Initial conditions/default values, 364, 365
Inspections (*see* Code inspections, Design inspections)
Integrated tool suites, 157, 158
Integration testing, 539
Internal logical file (ILF) types, 309
International cost comparison, 377
Internet applications, 42
Internet-enabled estimation benchmarking services, 158
Introduction to the Personal Software Process, 704
Invalid defects, 606
Investment costs, 121–127
IPQ, 27, 645
Isensee, Scott, 450
ISO functional size standard, 287, 288
ISO standards support, 42
ISPA, 680, 681

JAD, 432
James Martin & Company, 689
Jensen, Randall, 27, 28, 637, 640
Johnson, Samuel, 634
Joint application design (JAD), 432
Jones, Capers, 27, 32, 33, 34, 66, 113, 120, 123, 132, 210, 215, 263, 272, 388, 419, 424, 450, 475, 487, 518, 533, 564, 597, 639, 643–656, 704

Kan, Stephen H., 21, 215, 263, 706
Kappelman, Leon, 215
Kapur, Gopal, 689
Kapur International, Inc., 689
Kemerer, Chris, 156, 315, 680
Keys, Jessica, 419
Kile, Ray, 640
KLOC, 322
KnowledgePlan, 654, 655
KnowledgeWare, Inc., 690
Koch Productivity Consulting (KPC), 689
KSLOC, 322
La Bolle, Vic, 639
Lab testing, 540, 544
Lack of cohesion of methods (LCOM), 324
Language levels, 235, 239, 240
Language tables, 235
LBMS, 690
LCOM, 324
Lefkon, Dick, 215
Legal documents, 568

Lehman, Manny, 665
Life-cycle historical data, 17
Ligett, Dan, 640
Linear programming, 671–673
Lines-of-code (LOC) metrics, 29, 137
Lister, Tim, 66, 418, 487, 505, 702
LOC, 321
LOC metrics, 29, 137
LOC rules of thumb, 174–177
Logical complexity, 292
Logical statements, 319, 320
Love, Tom, 215, 378, 419, 648, 649
Lovelace, Joan S., 704
Lucas Management Systems, 690
Lyndon B. Johnson Space Center, 691

Macroestimation tools, 52, 392–397, 404
Madachy, Ray, 640, 641
Maintenance, 400
Maintenance/enhancement estimating, 42, 595–636
    code restructuring, 613
    combinations/concurrent operations, 628
    complexity analysis, 611–613
    conversion, 615
    customer support, 608, 609
    dead code removal, 617
    dormant application removal, 617
    error-prone module removal, 609, 610
    Eurocurrency conversion, 624–627
    field service, 627, 628
    literature, 596, 597
    maintenance (defect repairs), 603–607
    maintenance/enhancement, defined, 595
    major enhancements, 600–602
    mandatory changes, 611
    migration, 614, 615
    minor enhancements, 602, 603
    nationalization, 618
    nominal default values, 599, 600
    performance optimization, 614
    reengineering, 616
    restructuring, 616
    retirement/withdrawal of applications, 627
    reverse engineering, 615, 616
    type 1 enhancements (block functions), 630
    type 2 enhancements (modified blocks), 630, 631
    type 3 enhancements (modification and deletion), 631, 632

Maintenance/enhancement estimating, (*Cont.*):
  type 4 enhancements (scatter updates), 632, 633
  type 5 enhancements (hybrid), 633, 634
  warranty repairs, 607, 608
  year-2000 repairs, 618–624
Management Information System projects (*see* MIS projects)
Management war game tools, 166
Manager's Guide to Software Engineering, A, 707
Managing Software Projects, 709
Managing Systems in Transition, 597
Mandatory changes, 611
Manpower buildup equation, 664
Manual software estimating methods, 49–52
  (*See also* Rules of thumb)
MAP/Estimator, 698
Marciniak, John J., 21, 419, 706
MarCon & Associates, Inc., 691
Mark II function points, 29, 30, 272
Mark II method of complexity adjustment, 313
Marketing documentation, 568, 569
Marotz, Inc., 691
Martin, James, 648, 689
Martin Marietta, 692
Masking, 623
McCabe, Tom, 290, 291, 613
McCue, Gerald, 504
McQuilken, George, 649
Measurement mode, 42
Measures for Excellence—Reliable Software on Time, Within Budget, 20, 707
Measuring the Software Process: A Practical Guide to Functional Measurement, 703
Meeting Deadlines in Hard Real-Time Systems, 111
Mertes, Karen R., 134, 156
Methodology adjustments, 43
Methodology management tools, 75, 76
Metrics and Models in Software Quality Engineering, 21, 706
Metrics errors, 137–139, 153
Metrics in Software Evolution, 706
Metrics support, 43
Micro-function point, 282
Microestimating, 421
  (*See also* Activity-based estimation)
Microestimation tools, 52, 406–418

MicroMan II, 694
Migration projects, 614, 615
Miii, Ah, 640
Mikkelsen, Tim, 522
Milestone tracking tools, 84, 85
Military software projects, 99, 100
  software requirements, 444
  software testing, 548
Milt Bryce & Associates, 692
MIS projects, 93, 94
  software requirements, 441, 442
  software testing, 546
Missing historical data, 129–133
Mixed hardware/software microcode projects, 161, 162
Mixed-language applications, 237, 238
Mixed programming languages, 43
Miyazaki, Yukio, 640
Mnemonic complexity, 292, 293
Monterege Design, Inc., 692
Mori, Kuniaki, 640
Moser, Simon, 681, 698
Mosley, Daniel, 533
Muller, Monika, 706
MULTITRAK, 700
Myers, Ware, 262, 465, 487, 677, 678, 707
Mythical Man Month, The, 27, 66, 111, 181, 523, 573, 701

NASA Cost Modeler, 691
National Information Systems, Inc., 692
Nationalization, 618
Nationalization costs, 43
Natural metrics, 349
NAVIGATOR, 687
New Directions in Software Management, 573
New function testing, 538
Nichols & Company, Inc., 693
NOC, 324
Nominal production rate, 375
Norden, Peter, 660, 665
Number of children (NOC), 324
Object-code date interception, 622
Object-oriented (OO) estimation, 43
Object-oriented (OO) metrics, 323–325, 328
Object Oriented Pty. Ltd., 693
Object point metrics, 323
Occupation group estimation, 43
OLAP, 159
Omissions from cost-tracking systems, 129–133

1 function point (125 C statements), 105
10 function points (1250 C statements), 106
100 function points (12,500 C statements), 106, 107
1,000 function points (125,000 C statements), 107
10,000 function points (1.25 million C statements), 108
100,000 function points (12.5 million C statements), 109, 110
Online analytical processing (OLAP), 159
OO estimation, 43
OO metrics, 323–325, 348
Optimization projects, 614
Organizational complexity, 293
ORO Project Management System, 693
Orr, Ken, 424
Ourada, Gerald, 21
Outsource estimation, 165, 166
Outsourced/contracted projects, 95, 96
    software requirements, 442
    software testing, 547
Overhead, 39
Overhead costs, 370–373
Overtime, 374, 375, 498–500

P rate, 200, 375
Package acquisition estimation, 44
PADS, 673
Paper deliverables:
    rules of thumb, 192, 193
    software sizing, 325–331
    (*See also* Documentation)
Parent/child logic, 44
Parikh, Girish, 596, 635
Park, Bob, 639, 640, 692
Patterns of Software System Failure and Success, 113, 424, 431, 475, 573, 597, 654, 705
Paulk, Mark, 226, 418, 706
Penetration teams, 541
Peopleware, 111, 487, 505, 702
Perceptional complexity, 293
Performance optimization, 614
Performance testing, 540, 541
Perry, William E., 21, 120, 533, 707
Personal Software Process, 487
Phase, 54
Pherigo, Suzanne, 522
Physical lines, 319, 320
Pietrasanta, Al, 639

Pioneers (*see* Biographies)
Planning documents, 567
Platform testing, 542
PLATINUM Process Continuum, 693
PLATINUM Technology, Inc., 693
PMW, 684
POC-IT Management Service, Inc., 694
Portfolio analysis, 44
Portfolio analysis tools, 79
Postrelease activities (*see* Maintenance/enhancement estimating)
Postrelease defect-repair rates, 199
PQMPlus Manager (Analyst/Planner), 695
Practical Software Configuration Management, 522
Practical Software Metrics for Project Management and Process Improvement, 703
PREDICTOR, 686
Preliminary estimation methods:
    automated methods (*see* Automated estimate from minimal data)
    manual estimates (*see* Rules of thumb)
    overview, 171, 172
    when to be used, 262
Pressman, Roger S., 523, 533, 707
Price, Bernie, 640
PRICE-S, 28, 692
PRIDE, 692
PRM AS/SET, 699
PRO QMS, 699
Problem complexity, 293, 294, 297
Process complexity, 294
Process-improvement estimation, 164, 165
Process management, 75, 76
Process MeNtOr, 693
Process productivity parameter, 663
Production rate (P rate), 200, 375
Production-rate errors, 145–147, 154
Productivity constant, 663
Productivity index, 668
Productivity Solutions, Inc., 694
Programming/coding, 487–510
    application size, and, 503
    bugs/errors, and, 496–498
    code structure/complexity, and, 501, 502
    creeping requirements, and, 500, 501
    experience, and, 496
    factors influencing productivity, 489
    general productivity/defect rates, 492–494

Programming/coding (*Cont.*):
  literature, 487
  maximum impacts of programming factors, 491
  nominal default values, 488, 489
  office space/ergonomics, and, 504, 505
  programming languages, and, 506–509
  reusability, and, 494–496
  schedule pressure, and, 509
  tools, and, 505, 506
  unpaid overtime, and, 498–500
  unplanned interruptions, and, 502, 503
Programming language combinations, 237
Programming language support, 44
Programming languages, 237–242, 506–509
Programming Productivity, 653
Programming Productivity—Issues for the Eighties, 650
Project, 53
Project class, 224, 226, 227
Project-control documents, 567, 568
Project goals, 230
Project management, 573–591
  experience, 589
  external schedule pressures, and, 580, 581
  hybrid projects, 579, 580
  large projects, 582–584
  literature, 573
  nominal default values, 573, 574
  optimal team size, 586
  project offices, 589
  quality control, 589, 590
  roles/responsibilities, 576–579
  rules of thumb, 575
  span of control, 585, 586
  specialists, 586–588
  technical work, 579
  time-splitting/multiple small projects, 584, 585
  tools, 581, 582
  variable factors, 575, 576
Project management tools, 581, 582
  application size, and, 101–111
  catalog, 72
  experimental tools, 88–90
  industry segments, and, 93–100
  investment costs/ROI, 121–127
  kinds/types, 73–88
  usage patterns, 100, 101
  (*See also* Software cost-estimating tools)

Project Management Workbench (PMW), 684
Project manager, 53
Project measurement tools, 80, 81
Project milestone tracking tools, 84, 88
Project nature, 224, 225
Project offices, 589
Project-planning tools, 74, 75
Project scope, 224, 225
Project size, 101–111
Project Software & Development, Inc., 694
PROJECT/2, 694
Project type, 224, 227, 228
ProjectBASE, 689
Proprietary languages, 240, 241
Prototyping (*see* Software prototypes)
Putnam, Larry, 20, 26, 27, 29, 33, 34, 126, 131, 215, 262, 378, 388, 418, 465, 476, 487, 518, 639, 648, 650, 656–678, 694, 707

Q/P Management Group, Inc., 695
QFD, 434
QSM software equation, 663
Quality Assurance for Computer Software, 475
Quality control, 403, 404
Quality-control documentation, 569
Quality estimation, 44
Quality-estimating tools, 77, 78
Quality function deployment (QFD), 434
Quantitative Software Management, Inc., 694
Quantitative software management (QSM) software equation, 663
Rapid Prototyping, 450
Rayleigh curves, 45, 660, 661
Reengineering, 616
Reengineering and reverse engineering support, 45
Regression testing, 538, 539
Reifer, Don, 91, 641, 695
Reifer Consultants, Inc., 695
Reilly, John, 450
REKON, 692
Reliability support, 45
Requirements (*see* Software requirements)
Requirements traceability, 528
Response for a class (RFC), 324
Restructuring, 616
Rethinking the Software Process, 707

Return on investment (ROI), 121–127
Reusability, 430, 494–496
Reusability support, 45
Reusable artifacts, 397, 398
Reusable components, 300
Reverse engineering, 615, 616
REVIC, 65, 683
RFC, 324
Risk analysis support, 45
Risk analysis tools, 78, 79
Risk books, 111
Roetzheim, William, 20, 111, 215, 263, 388, 418
ROI calculations, 121–127
Role-playing games, 166
Rook, Paul, 640
Roush, Bernie, 640
Roy, Daniel, 111, 126
Royce, Walker, 640
Rubin, Howard, 20, 30, 33, 34, 88, 131, 215, 263, 378, 388, 418, 465, 476, 487, 518, 597, 637, 648, 650, 708
Rudd, Jim, 450
Rules of thumb, 173–216
    activity-based cost analysis, and, 204–210
    Eurocurrency conversion, 212, 213
    function point metrics, and, 181–184
    function point sizing, 184–199 (See also Function point sizing rules of thumb)
    limitations/weaknesses, 173, 214
    LOC, 174–177
    ratios/percentages, and, 177–181
    schedules/resources/costs, 199–204
    year-2000 repair estimation, 210–212

Salaries, 366–370
SAP estimation, 45
SASET, 683
Scaling errors, 139, 140, 153
Scatter updates, 632, 633
SCEA, 681
SCEP, 639
Schedule estimation, 45
Security testing, 541, 542
SEE, 681
SEER, 688
SEI CMM assumptions, 404, 405
SEI CMM levels, 46
SEI code counting standards, 285, 286, 319
Selby, Rick, 640

Semantic complexity, 294
SES Software Engineering Service GmbH, 696
Shen, V.Y., 701
SHL System House, 696
Shough, Dave, 645
SIC code, 220–222
SIRO, 483
SIZE PLANNER, 674
Size Plus, 688
SIZER/1 through SIZER/4, 649
Sizes of selected software applications, 251, 252, 253, 254
Sizing:
    defined, 269
    general logic, 269, 270
    preliminary methods (see Automated sizing approximation methods)
    rules of thumb (see Function point sizing rules of thumb)
    software deliverables, of (see Software sizing)
    usefulness, 271
Sizing by analogy, 655
Sizing errors, 141, 153
Sizing methods, 46
SLIM, 29, 668–671, 695
SLIM-Control, 674, 675
Society of Cost Estimating and Analysis (SCEA), 681
SOFT-CALC, 696
SOFTCOST, 686
Softstar Systems, 697
Software Benchmark Studies for 1997, 20, 708
Software changes (see Change management)
Software complexity, 288–300
Software Configuration Management, 523
Software Cost Estimating and Life Cycle Control: Getting the Management Numbers, 677
Software cost estimating associations, 679–681
Software cost-estimating tools, 73, 74
    accuracy, 129–156
    catalog, 38, 48, 682
    comparisons, 48
    evaluations, 682
    features, 37–48
    how they work, 4–8
    life-cycle historical data, 17
    logging/average/leading enterprises, 71

Software cost-estimating tools (*Cont.*):
  macroestimation tools, 392–397, 404
  microestimation tools, 406–418
  preliminary estimation tools (*see*
    Automated estimates from minimal
    data)
  underlying technologies, 69
  (*See also* Project management tools)
Software cost estimating vendors,
    681–700
Software cost estimation:
  accidental omissions, 15–17
  activity-based, 60
  adjustment factors (*see* Adjustment fac-
    tors)
  automated methods, 49, 52–66
  errors (*see* Errors)
  exclusions, 362, 363
  future of, 157–170
  human judgement, and, 360
  litigation, and, 4
  manual methods, 49–52, 64
  origins, 25–35
  parameters, knowledge of, 1
  preliminary methods (*see* Preliminary
    estimation methods)
  reference books, 20–22
  special factors/adjustments, 361
  step-by-step breakdown for construct-
    ing estimates, 359
  steps in, process, 8–14
  success/failure rates, 113–120
  tools (*see* Software cost-estimating tools)
  uses, 4
Software defect prediction, 334–342
Software development productivity,
    397–400
Software documentation (*see*
    Documentation)
*Software Engineering—A Practitioner's
    Approach*, 523, 533
Software Engineering Economics, 20, 29,
    66, 378, 388, 465, 487, 490, 533, 573,
    597, 640, 701
Software Engineering Metrics and Models,
    701
Software Estimating and Engineering
    Group (SEE), 681
Software Estimating Technology Report,
    682
Software-estimating templates, 360, 362
Software estimation pioneers (*see*
    Biographies)

*Software Evolution—The Software
    Maintenance Challenge*, 597
Software excellence scale (SES), 405
Software Inspection and Review
    Organization (SIRO), 483
Software Inspections, 475
Software Maintenance, 597
*Software Maintenance: The Problem and
    its Solution*, 597
Software maintenance productivity,
    400–403
*Software Management Technology
    Reference Guide*, 709
Software management tools (*see* Project
    management tools)
Software Measurement Guidebook, The,
    708
*Software Metrics: Establishing a
    Company-Wide Program*, 703
Software Productivity Centre, Inc., 696
Software Productivity Research, Inc.
    (SPR), 649, 697
Software project management (*see* Project
    management)
Software project management informa-
    tion categories, 70
Software prototypes, 449–462
  default values, 456–458
  disposable prototypes, 452, 453
  evolutionary prototypes, 454–456
  factors to consider, 459–461
  literature, 450, 451
  negative adjustment factors, 459
  positive adjustment factors, 459
  time-box prototypes, 453, 454
Software quality, 340
*Software Quality—Analysis and
    Guidelines for Success*, 424, 465, 475,
    533, 597, 654, 705
Software requirements, 423–448
  change-control boards, 433, 434
  combination of factors, 445–448
  commercial software, and, 444
  conflicting requirements, 429
  creeping requirements, 429
  defect prevention, 427
  defect removal, 428
  end-user software, and, 441
  errors/defects, 428, 429
  factors to consider, 439–441
  function points, and, 430–436
  fundamental topics, 436, 437
  JAD, 432

Software requirements (*Cont.*):
  literature, 424
  methodologies, 427
  military software projects, and, 444
  MIS projects, and, 441, 442
  negative adjustment factors, 439
  nominal default values, 424, 425
  outsourced projects, and, 442
  performed by, 426
  positive adjustment factors, 438
  productivity rates, 427
  prototypes, 432, 433
  QFD, 434
  reusability, 430
  sliding scale of costs, 434–436
  supplemental topics, 437, 438
  systems software, and, 442, 443
  tools, 427
  use cases, 433
Software Requirements, 424
Software Requirements Engineering, 424
Software retirement, 627
Software reuse, 397, 398
Software sizing, 265–354
  bugs/defects, 334–342
  database volumes, 344, 345
  desirable improvements, 349, 350
  function point metrics, 270, 271, 302–317
  graphics/illustrations, 331–334
  information normally provided by users, 347
  ISO functional size standard, 287, 288
  most accurate/best method, 351
  multimedia artifacts, 345, 346
  objected-oriented (OO) metrics, 323–325, 348
  paper deliverables, 325–331
  reusable components, and, 300–302
  software complexity analysis, 288–300
  source code sizing, 317–323
  strengths/weaknesses, 347–349
  test cases, 342–344
  uses, 348
Software Sizing and Estimating—Mk II FPA, 20, 465, 708
Software specifications and design, 463–473
  common design methods, 464
  estimating assumptions, 467
  factors to consider, 470–472
  literature, 465
  negative design adjustment factors, 469, 470

Software specifications and design (*Cont.*):
  nominal default values, 466
  positive design adjustment factors, 468, 469
  templates, 465, 466
Software technology adjustment factors, 391–420
  author's five-point adjustment scale, 406–410
  macroestimation tools, 392–397, 404
  microestimating tools, 406–418
  SEI vs. SPR assessment scales, 404, 405
  software development productivity, and, 397–400
  software maintenance productivity, and, 400–403
Software testing, 533–561
  commercial software, and, 547
  defect-removal efficiency levels, 554, 555
  end-user software, and, 546
  factors affecting testing performance, 559, 560
  frequency of use of testing methods, 535–537
  function points, and, 550–553, 555–557
  general forms of testing, 537–540
  integration testing, 539
  lawsuits for poor quality, and, 549, 550
  literature, 534
  military software, and, 548
  MIS software projects, and, 546
  new function testing, 538
  nominal default values, 534
  outsource software, and, 547
  regression testing, 538, 539
  size of software application, and, 548, 549
  software, defined, 534, 535
  specialized forms of testing, 540–543
  subroutine testing, 537
  system testing, 539, 540
  systems software, and, 547, 548
  test-case volumes, 550–552
  test personnel, 552, 553
  testing, defined, 534, 535
  testing effort/costs, 555–557
  testing involving users/clients, 543–545
  unit testing, 537, 538
  who should do it, 557–559
Software war game tools, 88
Source code counting tools, 87

Source code sizing:
  overview, 317–323
  preliminary estimation, 234–242
  problems, 322
  rules of thumb, 188–192
Special cost factors, 46
Special or unique situation errors, 152, 155
Specifications and design (*see* Software specifications and design)
Spectrum International, Inc., 698
SPECTRUM tools, 698
SPQR/10, 650
SPQR/20, 31, 272, 651
SPR, 649, 697
SPR backfire complexity adjustments, 299
SPR code counting rules, 285, 286, 319
SPR feature points, 32, 272
SPR method of complexity adjustment, 313–316
SPR software excellence scale, 405
Staffing build-up errors, 150, 154
Standard industry classification (SIC) code, 220–222
Statistical analysis tools, 75
Steece, Bert, 641
Stevens, Wayne, 466
Stress/capacity testing, 540
Structured Requirements Definition, 424
Structured Solutions Inc., 698
Structured walkthrough, 512, 513
Stukes, Sherry, 22, 48, 91, 682
Subroutine testing, 537
Success/failure rates, 113–120
Support documentation, 569
SWAN, 688
Swinburne University of Technology, 698
Symons, Charles, 20, 29, 66, 215, 263, 272, 388, 418, 465, 564, 597, 708
Syntactic complexity, 294
Sys/PLANRpc, 699
SYSTEM-4, 686
SYSTEM METER, 698
System Research Services, 698
System Software Associates, Inc., 699
System testing, 539, 540
Systems software projects, 97–99
Task, 55
Task-selection errors, 141–143, 153
Technical documents, 568
Technical Report—Software Reengineering Assessment Handbook, 682
Technology adjustment errors, 151, 154, 155

Technology adjustment factors (*see* Software technology adjustment factors)
Technology factor, 663
Template construction, 46
Templates, 6, 7, 360, 362
10 function points (1250 C statements), 106
10,000 function points (1.25 million C statements), 108
Test-case sizing, 342–344
Testing (*see* Software testing)
Texas Instruments, Inc., 699
Thayer, Richard, 91, 424
3D function points, 263
Time-box prototypes, 453, 454
Tips/advice, 19
Tool catalogs, 46
Tools (*see* Project management tools, Software cost-estimating tools)
Topologic complexity, 294
TRAK, 691
Translation costs, 570
Tufte, Edward R., 708
Turk, Charles, 27, 645, 646

Ullman, Richard, 475, 518
Ultra PLANNER, 694
Umbaugh, Robert E., 708
Union Pacific Technologies, 699
Unit testing, 56, 537, 538
University of Southern California, 700
Unpaid overtime, 374, 375, 498–500
Usability testing, 543
Usage patterns, 100, 101
Use cases, 433
User documentation, 569

ValPro, 684
Value analysis, 46
Value analysis tools, 82
Variance-reporting tools, 83
VAX Software Project Manager, 687
Vendors, 681–700
Viral protection testing, 541
Virtual production rate, 375
Visual Display of Quantitative Information, The, 708

Warranty repairs, 607, 608

Weighted methods per class (WMC), 323
Weinberg, Gerald, 424, 475, 511, 648
Whitmire, Scott, 263
Why Does Software Cost So Much?, 702
Wiegers, Karl E., 709
Windowing, 621
Withdrawal of applications, 627
Wizard support, 47
WMC, 323
Wolverton, Ray, 639, 665
Work hours per function point, 375
Work Management Solutions Inc., 700
Work patterns, 373–377
Work unit conversion, 47

Year-2000 analysis tools, 76, 77

Year-2000 repairs, 618–624
Year-2000 software estimation, 47
Year 2000 Software Problem—
    Quantifying the Costs and Assessing
    the Consequences, The, 21, 210, 533,
    627, 654, 706
Year-2000 testing, 542
Yourdon, Ed, 21, 88, 111, 120, 419,
    709

Zells, Lois, 22, 48, 91, 573, 709
Zero-defect estimation, 47
Zone of chaos, 482
Zuse, Horst, 289
Zvegintzov, Nicholas, 22, 48, 91, 596, 597,
    635, 709

ABOUT THE AUTHOR

T. Capers Jones is founder and chairman of Software
Productivity Research, Inc., in Burlington, Massachusetts
(http://www.spr.com), and a true notable in the field of
software engineering. He has more than 25 years of
experience with software cost estimation, having designed
IBM's first software estimating tool in 1973 and subsequently
designing such tools for ITT Corporation and Bell Labs.
Jones personally invented the SPQR/20 and CHECKPOINT
tools, and in 1997 his company released the KnowledgePlan
software estimation tool with direct links to Microsoft
Project. He frequently leads workshops and seminars and is
a featured speaker at industry conferences. Jones is also
the author of the bestselling *Applied Software Measurement*
(McGraw-Hill), now in its Second Edition.